Pre-Calculus

University of Kentucky

Custom Edition

Thomas W. Hungerford | Douglas J. Shaw

CENGAGE
Learning

Australia • Brazil • Japan • Korea • Mexico • Singapore • Spain • United Kingdom • United States

CENGAGE
Learning·

Pre-Calculus
University of Kentucky
Custom Edition

Contemporary Precalculus: A Graphing Approach, 5th Edition
Thomas W. Hungerford | Douglas J. Shaw

© 2009, 2004, 2004, 2000 Cengage Learning. All rights reserved.

Senior Manager, Student Engagement:

Linda deStefano

Janey Moeller

Manager, Student Engagement:

Julie Dierig

Marketing Manager:

Rachael Kloos

Manager, Production Editorial:

Kim Fry

Manager, Intellectual Property Project Manager:

Brian Methe

Senior Manager, Production and Manufacturing:

Donna M. Brown

Manager, Production:

Terri Daley

Cover Photo:

Roger Guffey

For product information and technology assistance, contact us at
Cengage Learning Customer & Sales Support, 1-800-354-9706
For permission to use material from this text or product,
submit all requests online at cengage.com/permissions
Further permissions questions can be emailed to
permissionrequest@cengage.com

This book contains select works from existing Cengage Learning resources and
was produced by Cengage Learning Custom Solutions for collegiate use. As such,
those adopting and/or contributing to this work are responsible for editorial
content accuracy, continuity and completeness.

Compilation © 2014 Cengage Learning

ISBN-13: 978-1-305-30148-1

WCN: 01-100-101

Cengage Learning
5191 Natorp Boulevard
Mason, Ohio 45040
USA

Cengage Learning is a leading provider of customized learning solutions with
office locations around the globe, including Singapore, the United Kingdom,
Australia, Mexico, Brazil, and Japan. Locate your local office at:
international.cengage.com/region.

Cengage Learning products are represented in Canada by Nelson Education, Ltd.
For your lifelong learning solutions, visit www.cengage.com/custom.
Visit our corporate website at www.cengage.com.

Printed in the United States of America

Chapter 1

BASICS

© Neil Rabinowitz/CORBIS

Chapter Outline

Interdependence of Sections

1.1   The Real Number System

Section Objectives

- Identify important types of real numbers.
- Simplify mathematical expressions.
- Represent sets of real numbers with interval notation.
- Graph intervals on a number line.
- Use scientific notation.
- Understand and apply the properties of square roots.
- Understand and apply the properties of absolute value.
- Compute the distance between two points on the number line.

Most of this book deals with the real number system, so it may be helpful to review the types of real numbers.

Name	Definition/Description
Natural numbers	$1, 2, 3, 4, 5, \ldots$ Natural numbers are also called **counting numbers** or **positive integers.**
Integers	$\ldots, -5, -4, -3, -2, -1, 0, 1, 2, 3, 4, 5, \ldots$ The integers consist of the natural numbers, their negatives, and zero.

Continued

2

Name	Definition/Description
Rational numbers	A rational number is a number that can be expressed as a fraction $\frac{r}{s}$, with r and s integers and $s \neq 0$, such as $$\frac{1}{2}, \qquad -9.83 = \frac{-983}{100}, \qquad 47 = \frac{47}{1}, \qquad 8\frac{3}{5} = \frac{43}{5}.$$
	Alternatively, rational numbers are numbers that can be expressed as terminating decimals, such as $.25 = \frac{1}{4}$, or as nonterminating repeating decimals in which a single digit or block of digits eventually repeats forever, such as $$\frac{5}{3} = 1.66666 \cdots \qquad \text{or} \qquad \frac{362}{1665} = .2174174174 \cdots.$$
Irrational numbers	An irrational number is a number that cannot be expressed as a fraction with an integer numerator and denominator, such as the number π, which is used to calculate the area of a circle.*
	Alternatively, irrational numbers are numbers that can be expressed as nonterminating, nonrepeating decimals (no block of digits repeats forever).

More information about decimal expansions of real numbers is given in Special Topics 1.1.A.

The relationships among the types of numbers in the preceding table are summarized in Figure 1–1, in which each set of numbers is contained in the set to its right. So, for example, integers are also rational numbers and real numbers, but not irrational numbers.

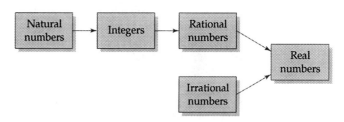

Figure 1–1

 **ARITHMETIC**

To avoid ambiguity when dealing with expressions such as $6 + 3 \times 5$, mathematicians have made the following agreement, which is also followed by your calculator.

Order of Operations

> In an expression without parentheses, multiplication and division are performed first (from left to right). Addition and subtraction are performed last (from left to right).

In light of this convention, there is only one correct way to interpret $6 + 3 \times 5$:

$$6 + 3 \times 5 = 6 + 15 = 21. \qquad \text{[Multiplication first, addition last]}$$

---

*The proof that π is irrational is beyond the scope of this book. In the past you may have used 22/7 or 3.1416 as π and a calculator may display π as 3.141592654. However, these numbers are just *approximations* of π.

On the other hand, if you want to "add $6 + 3$ and then multiply by 5," you must use parentheses:

$$(6 + 3) \cdot 5 = 9 \cdot 5 = 45.$$

This is an illustration of the first of two basic rules for dealing with parentheses.

Rules for Parentheses

1. Do all computations inside the parentheses before doing any computations outside the parentheses.

2. When dealing with parentheses within parentheses, begin with the innermost pair and work outward.

For example,

$$8 + [11 - (6 \times 3)] = 8 + (11 - 18) = 8 + (-7) = 1.$$

Inside parentheses first

We assume that you are familiar with the basic properties of real number arithmetic, particularly the following fact.

Distributive Law

For all real numbers $a, b, c,$

$$a(b + c) = ab + ac \quad \text{and} \quad (b + c)a = ba + ca.$$

The distributive law doesn't usually play a direct role in easy computations, such as $4(3 + 5)$. Most people don't say $4 \cdot 3 + 4 \cdot 5 = 12 + 20 = 32$. Instead, they mentally add the numbers in parentheses and say 4 times 8 is 32. But when symbols are involved, you can't do that, and the distributive law is essential. For example,

$$4(3 + x) = 4 \cdot 3 + 4x = 12 + 4x.$$

THE NUMBER LINE AND ORDER

The real numbers are often represented geometrically as points on a **number line,** as in Figure 1–2. We shall assume that there is exactly one point on the line for every real number (and vice versa) and use phrases such as "the point 3.6" or "a number on the line." This mental identification of real numbers and points on the line is often helpful.

Figure 1–2

The statement $c < d$, which is read "**c is less than d**," and the statement $d > c$ (read "**d is greater than c**") mean exactly the same thing:

c lies to the *left* of d on the number line.

For example, Figure 1–2 shows that $-5.78 < -2.2$ and $4 > \pi$.

The statement $c \le d$, which is read "c **is less than or equal to** d," means

Either c is less than d or c is equal to d.

Only one part of an "either . . . or" statement needs to be true for the entire statement to be true. So the statement $5 \le 10$ is true because $5 < 10$, and the statement $5 \le 5$ is true because $5 = 5$. The statement $d \ge c$ (read "d **is greater than or equal to c**") means exactly the same thing as $c \le d$.

The statement $b < c < d$ means

$$b < c \qquad \text{and simultaneously} \qquad c < d.$$

For example, $3 < x < 7$ means that x is a number that is strictly between 3 and 7 on the number line (greater than 3 and less than 7). Similarly, $b \le c < d$ means

$$b \le c \qquad \text{and simultaneously} \qquad c < d,$$

and so on.

Certain sets of numbers, defined in terms of the order relation, appear frequently enough to merit special notation. Let c and d be real numbers with $c < d$. Then

Interval Notation

> $[c, d]$ denotes the set of all real numbers x such that $c \le x \le d$.
>
> (c, d) denotes the set of all real numbers x such that $c < x < d$.
>
> $[c, d)$ denotes the set of all real numbers x such that $c \le x < d$.
>
> $(c, d]$ denotes the set of all real numbers x such that $c < x \le d$.

All four of these sets are called **intervals** from c to d. The numbers c and d are the **endpoints** of the interval. $[c, d]$ is called the **closed interval** from c to d (both endpoints included and *square* brackets), and (c, d) is called the **open interval** from c to d (neither endpoint included and *round* brackets). Some examples are shown in Figure 1–3.*

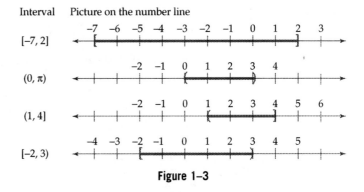

Figure 1–3

---

*In Figures 1–3 and 1–4, a round bracket such as) or (indicates that the endpoint is *not* included, whereas a square bracket such as] or [indicates that the endpoint *is* included.

If b is a real number, then the half-line extending to the right or left of b is also called an **interval.** Depending on whether or not b is included, there are four possibilities.

*Interval
Notation*

> $[b, \infty)$ denotes the set of all real numbers x such that $x \geq b$.
>
> (b, ∞) denotes the set of all real numbers x such that $x > b$.
>
> $(-\infty, b]$ denotes the set of all real numbers x such that $x \leq b$.
>
> $(-\infty, b)$ denotes the set of all real numbers x such that $x < b$.

Some examples are shown in Figure 1–4.

> **NOTE**
>
> The symbol ∞ is read "infinity," and we call the set $[b, \infty)$ "the interval from b to infinity." The symbol ∞ does *not* denote a real number; it is simply part of the notation used to label the first two sets of numbers defined in the previous box. Analogous remarks apply to the symbol $-\infty$, which is read "negative infinity."

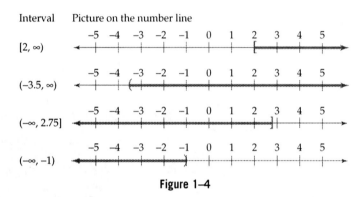

Figure 1–4

In a similar vein, $(-\infty, \infty)$ **denotes the set of all real numbers.**

> **TECHNOLOGY TIP**
>
> To enter a negative number, such as -5, on most calculators, you must use the negation key: $(-)$ 5. If you use the subtraction key on such calculators and enter -5, the display will read
>
> ANS -5
>
> which tells the calculator to subtract 5 from the previous answer.

NEGATIVE NUMBERS AND NEGATIVES OF NUMBERS

The **positive numbers** are those to the right of 0 on the number line, that is,

All numbers c with $c > 0$.

The **negative numbers** are those to the left of 0, that is,

All numbers c with $c < 0$.

The **nonnegative** numbers are the numbers c with $c \geq 0$.

The word "negative" has a second meaning in mathematics. The **negative *of a number*** c is the number $-c$. For example, the negative of 5 is -5, and the negative of -3 is $-(-3) = 3$. Thus the negative of a negative number is a positive number. Zero is its own negative, since $-0 = 0$. In summary,

Negatives

> The negative of the number c is $-c$.
>
> If c is a positive number, then $-c$ is a negative number.
>
> If c is a negative number, then $-c$ is a positive number.

SCIENTIFIC NOTATION

In mid-2006 the U.S. national debt was 8.4 trillion dollars. Since one trillion is 10^{12} (that is, 1 followed by 12 zeros), the national debt is the number

$$8.4 \times 10^{12}.$$

This is an example of *scientific notation*. A positive number is said to be in **scientific notation** when it is written in the form

$$a \times 10^n \qquad \text{where } 1 \le a < 10 \text{ and } n \text{ is an integer.}$$

You should be able to translate between scientific notation and ordinary notation and vice versa.

EXAMPLE 1

Express these numbers in ordinary notation:

(a) 1.55×10^9 　　　　(b) 2.3×10^{-8}

SOLUTION

(a) $1.55 \times 10^9 = 1.55 \times 1,000,000,000 = 1,550,000,000$

You can do this multiplication in your head by using the fact that multiplying by 10^9 is equivalent to moving the decimal point 9 places to the right.

(b) $2.3 \times 10^{-8} = \dfrac{2.3}{10^8} = .000000023*$

This computation can also be done mentally by using the fact that dividing by 10^8 is equivalent to moving the decimal point 8 places to the left. ∎

EXAMPLE 2

Write each of these numbers in scientific notation:

(a) 356 　　　(b) 1,564,000 　　　(c) .072 　　　(d) .00000087

SOLUTION 　In each case, move the decimal point to the left or right to obtain a number between 1 and 10; then write the original number in scientific notation as follows.

(a) Move the decimal point in 356 two places to the left to obtain the number 3.56, which is between 1 and 10. You can get the original number back by multiplying by 100: $356 = 3.56 \times 100$. So the scientific notation form is

$$356 = 3.56 \times 10^2$$

Note that the original decimal point is moved 2 places to the *left* and 10 is raised to the power 2.

(b) $1,564,000 = 1.564 \times 1,000,000 = 1.564 \times 10^6$ [Decimal point is moved 6 places to the *left,* and 10 is raised to the 6th power.]

(c) $.072 = 7.2 \times \dfrac{1}{100} = 7.2 \times 10^{-2}$ [Decimal point is moved 2 places to the *right,* and 10 is raised to -2.]

---

*Negative exponents are explained in the first section of the Algebra Review Appendix.

(d) $.00000087 = 8.7 \times \dfrac{1}{10,000,000} = 8.7 \times 10^{-7}$ [Decimal point is moved 7 places to the *right,* and 10 is raised to the -7.] ∎

Scientific notation is useful for computations with very large or very small numbers.

EXAMPLE 3

$$(.00000002)(4,300,000,000) = (2 \times 10^{-8})(4.3 \times 10^{9})$$
$$= 2(4.3)10^{-8+9} = (8.6)10^{1} = 86. \blacksquare$$

Calculators automatically switch to scientific notation whenever a number is too large or too small to be displayed in the standard way. If you try to enter a number with more digits than the calculator can handle, such as 45,000,000,333,222,111, a typical calculator will approximate it using scientific notation as 4.500000033 E 16, that is, as 45,000,000,330,000,000.

SQUARE ROOTS

A *square root* of a nonnegative real number d is any number whose square is d. For instance both 5 and -5 are square roots of 25 because

$$5^{2} = 25 \qquad \text{and} \qquad (-5)^{2} = 25.$$

The nonnegative square root (in this case, 5) is given a special name and notation.

> If d is a nonnegative real number, the **principal square root** of d is the *nonnegative* number whose square is d. It is denoted $\sqrt{d}$.* Thus,
>
> $$\sqrt{d} \geq 0 \qquad \text{and} \qquad \left(\sqrt{d}\right)^{2} = d.$$

TECHNOLOGY TIP

To compute $\sqrt{7^2 + 51} + 3$ on a calculator, you must use a pair of parentheses:

$$\sqrt{(7^2 + 51)} + 3.$$

Otherwise the calculator will not compute the correct answer, which is:

$$\sqrt{7^2 + 51} + 3 = \sqrt{49 + 51} + 3$$
$$= \sqrt{100} + 3$$
$$= 13.$$

Try it!

For example,

$$\sqrt{25} = 5 \qquad \text{because} \qquad 5 \geq 0 \text{ and } 5^2 = 25.$$

The radical symbol always denotes a nonnegative number. To express the negative square root of 25 in terms of radicals, we write $-5 = -\sqrt{25}$.

Although $-\sqrt{25}$ is a real number, the expression $\sqrt{-25}$ is *not defined* in the real numbers because there is no real number whose square is -25. In fact, since the square of every real number is nonnegative,

No negative number has a square root in the real numbers.

Some square roots can be found (or verified) by hand, such as

$$\sqrt{225} = 15 \qquad \text{and} \qquad \sqrt{1.21} = 1.1.$$

Usually, however, a calculator is needed to obtain rational *approximations* of roots. For instance, we know that $\sqrt{87}$ is between 9 and 10 because $9^2 = 81$ and $10^2 = 100$. A calculator shows that $\sqrt{87} \approx 9.327379.$†

---

*The symbol $\sqrt{}$ is called a **radical.**
†$\approx$ means "approximately equal."

CAUTION

If c and d are positive real numbers, then
$$\sqrt{c + d} \neq \sqrt{c} + \sqrt{d}.$$

For example,
$$\sqrt{9 + 16} = \sqrt{25} = 5,$$

but
$$\sqrt{9} + \sqrt{16} = 3 + 4 = 7.$$

We shall often use the following property of square roots:

$$\sqrt{cd} = \sqrt{c}\sqrt{d} \textbf{ for any nonnegative real numbers } c \textbf{ and } d.$$

For example, $\sqrt{9 \cdot 16} = \sqrt{9}\sqrt{16} = 3 \cdot 4 = 12$. But be careful—*there is no similar property for sums*, as the Caution in the margin demonstrates.

EXAMPLE 4

Suppose you are located h feet above the ground. Because of the curvature of the earth, the maximum distance you can see is approximately d miles, where
$$d = \sqrt{1.5h + (3.587 \times 10^{-8})h^2}.$$

How far can you see from the 500-foot-high Smith Tower in Seattle and from the 1454-foot-high Sears Tower in Chicago?

SOLUTION For the Smith Tower, substitute 500 for h in the formula, and use your calculator:
$$d = \sqrt{1.5(500) + (3.587 \times 10^{-8})500^2} \approx 27.4 \text{ miles.}$$

For the Sears Tower, you can see almost 47 miles because
$$d = \sqrt{1.5(1454) + (3.587 \times 10^{-8})1454^2} \approx 46.7 \text{ miles.}$$ ∎

ABSOLUTE VALUE

On an informal level, most students think of absolute value like this:

The absolute value of a positive number is the number itself.

The absolute value of a negative number is found by "erasing the minus sign."

If $|c|$ denotes the absolute value of c, then, for example, $|5| = 5$ and $|-4| = 4$.

This informal approach is inadequate, however, for finding the absolute value of a number such as $\pi - 6$. It doesn't make sense to "erase the minus sign" here. So we must develop a more precise definition. The statement $|5| = 5$ suggests that the absolute value of a nonnegative number ought to be the number itself. For negative numbers, such as -4, note that $|-4| = 4 = -(-4)$, that is, the absolute value of the negative number -4 is the *negative* of -4. These facts are the basis of the formal definition.

Absolute Value

> The **absolute value** of a real number c is denoted $|c|$ and is defined as follows.
>
> If $c \geq 0$, then $|c| = c$.
>
> If $c < 0$, then $|c| = -c$.

EXAMPLE 5

(a) $|3.5| = 3.5$ and $|-7/2| = -(-7/2) = 7/2$.

(b) To find $|\pi - 6|$, note that $\pi \approx 3.14$, so $\pi - 6 < 0$. Hence, $|\pi - 6|$ is defined to be the *negative* of $\pi - 6$, that is,
$$|\pi - 6| = -(\pi - 6) = -\pi + 6.$$

(c) $|5 - \sqrt{2}| = 5 - \sqrt{2}$ because $5 - \sqrt{2} \geq 0$. ∎

Here are the important facts about absolute value.

Properties of Absolute Value

Property	Description
1. $\lvert c \rvert \ge 0$	The absolute value of a number is nonnegative.
2. If $c \ne 0$, then $\lvert c \rvert > 0$.	The absolute value of a nonzero number is positive.
3. $\lvert c \rvert = \lvert -c \rvert$	A number and its negative have the same absolute value.
4. $\lvert cd \rvert = \lvert c \rvert \cdot \lvert d \rvert$	The absolute value of the product of two numbers is the product of their absolute values.
5. $\left\lvert \dfrac{c}{d} \right\rvert = \dfrac{\lvert c \rvert}{\lvert d \rvert}$ $(d \ne 0)$	The absolute value of the quotient of two numbers is the quotient of their absolute values.

EXAMPLE 6

TECHNOLOGY TIP

To find $\lvert 9 - 3\pi \rvert$ on a calculator, key in

Abs $(9 - 3\pi)$.

The *Abs* key is located in this menu/submenu:

TI: MATH/NUM
Casio: OPTN/NUM
HP-39gs: Keyboard

Here are examples of the last three properties in the box.

3. $\lvert 3 \rvert = 3$ and $\lvert -3 \rvert = 3$, so $\lvert 3 \rvert = \lvert -3 \rvert$.

4. If $c = 6$ and $d = -2$, then

$$\lvert cd \rvert = \lvert 6(-2) \rvert = \lvert -12 \rvert = 12$$

and

$$\lvert c \rvert \cdot \lvert d \rvert = \lvert 6 \rvert \cdot \lvert -2 \rvert = 6 \cdot 2 = 12,$$

so $\lvert cd \rvert = \lvert c \rvert \cdot \lvert d \rvert$.

5. If $c = -5$ and $d = 4$, then

$$\left\lvert \frac{c}{d} \right\rvert = \left\lvert \frac{-5}{4} \right\rvert = \left\lvert -\frac{5}{4} \right\rvert = \frac{5}{4} \quad \text{and} \quad \frac{\lvert c \rvert}{\lvert d \rvert} = \frac{\lvert -5 \rvert}{\lvert 4 \rvert} = \frac{5}{4},$$

so $\left\lvert \dfrac{c}{d} \right\rvert = \dfrac{\lvert c \rvert}{\lvert d \rvert}$.

When c is a positive number, then $\sqrt{c^2} = c$, but when c is negative, this is *false*. For example, if $c = -3$, then

$$\sqrt{c^2} = \sqrt{(-3)^2} = \sqrt{9} = 3 \qquad (not\ -3),$$

so $\sqrt{c^2} \ne c$. In this case, however, $\lvert c \rvert = \lvert -3 \rvert = 3$, so $\sqrt{c^2} = \lvert c \rvert$. The same thing is true for any negative number c. It is also true for positive numbers (since $\lvert c \rvert = c$ when c is positive). In other words,

Square Roots of Squares

For every real number c,

$$\sqrt{c^2} = \lvert c \rvert.$$

When dealing with long expressions inside absolute value bars, do the computations inside first, and then take the absolute value.

EXAMPLE 7

(a) $|5(2 - 4) + 7| = |5(-2) + 7| = |-10 + 7| = |-3| = 3.$

(b) $4 - |3 - 9| = 4 - |-6| = 4 - 6 = -2.$ ∎

CAUTION

When c and d have opposite signs, $|c + d|$ is *not equal* to $|c| + |d|$. For example, when $c = -3$ and $d = 5$, then

$$|c + d| = |-3 + 5| = 2,$$

but

$$|c| + |d| = |-3| + |5| = 3 + 5 = 8.$$

The caution shows that $|c + d| < |c| + |d|$ when $c = -3$ and $d = 5$. In the general case, we have the following fact.

The Triangle Inequality

For any real numbers c and d,

$$|c + d| \le |c| + |d|.$$

DISTANCE ON THE NUMBER LINE

Observe that the distance from -5 to 3 on the number line is 8 units:

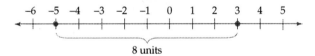

8 units

Figure 1–5

This distance can be expressed in terms of absolute value by noting that

$$|(-5) - 3| = 8.$$

That is, the distance is the *absolute value of the difference* of the two numbers. Furthermore, the order in which you take the difference doesn't matter; $|3 - (-5)|$ is also 8. This reflects the geometric fact that the distance from -5 to 3 is the same as the distance from 3 to -5. The same thing is true in the general case.

Distance on the Number Line

The distance between c and d on the number line is the number

$$|c - d| = |d - c|.$$

EXAMPLE 8

The distance from 4.2 to 9 is $|4.2 - 9| = |-4.8| = 4.8$, and the distance from 6 to $\sqrt{2}$ is $|6 - \sqrt{2}|$. ∎

When $d = 0$, the distance formula shows that $|c - 0| = |c|$. Hence,

Distance to Zero

> $|c|$ is the distance between c and 0 on the number line.

Algebraic problems can sometimes be solved by translating them into equivalent geometric problems. The key is to interpret statements involving absolute value as statements about distance on the number line.

EXAMPLE 9

Solve the equation $|x + 5| = 3$ geometrically.

SOLUTION   We rewrite it as $|x - (-5)| = 3$. In this form it states that

*The distance between x and -5 is 3 units.**

Figure 1–6 shows that -8 and -2 are the only two numbers whose distance to -5 is 3 units:

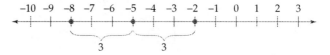

Figure 1–6

Thus $x = -8$ and $x = -2$ are the solutions of $|x + 5| = 3$. ∎

EXAMPLE 10

The solutions of $|x - 1| \geq 2$ are all numbers x such that

The distance between x and 1 is greater than or equal to 2.

Figure 1–7 shows that the numbers 2 or more units away from 1 are the numbers x such that

$$x \leq -1 \qquad \text{or} \qquad x \geq 3.$$

So these numbers are the solutions of the inequality. ∎

Figure 1–7

---

*It's necessary to rewrite the equation first because the distance formula involves the *difference* of two numbers, not their sum.

EXAMPLE 11

The solutions of $|x - 7| < 2.5$ are all numbers x such that

The distance between x and 7 is less than 2.5.

Figure 1–8 shows that the solutions of the inequality, that is, the numbers within 2.5 units of 7, are the numbers x such that $4.5 < x < 9.5$, that is, the interval $(4.5, 9.5)$. ∎

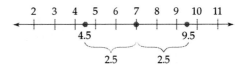

Figure 1–8

EXERCISES 1.1

1. Draw a number line and mark the location of each of these numbers: $0, -7, 8/3, 10, -1, -4.75, 1/2, -5$, and 2.25.

2. Use your calculator to determine which of the following rational numbers is the best approximation of the irrational number π.

$$\frac{22}{7}, \quad \frac{355}{113}, \quad \frac{103{,}993}{33{,}102}, \quad \frac{2{,}508{,}429{,}787}{798{,}458{,}000}.$$

If your calculator says that one of these numbers equals π, it's lying. All you can conclude is that the number agrees with π for as many decimal places as your calculator can handle (usually 12–14).

In Exercises 3–8, b, c, and d are real numbers such that $b < 0$, $c > 0$, and $d < 0$. Determine whether the given number is positive or negative.

3. $-b$

4. $-c$

5. bcd

6. $b - c$

7. $bc - bd$

8. $b^2c - c^2d$

In Exercises 9 and 10, use a calculator and list the given numbers in order from smallest to largest.

9. $\dfrac{189}{37}, \dfrac{4587}{691}, \sqrt{47}, 6.735, \sqrt{27}, \dfrac{2040}{523}$

10. $\dfrac{385}{177}, \sqrt{10}, \dfrac{187}{63}, \pi, \sqrt{\sqrt{85}}, 2.9884$

In Exercises 11–19, express the given statement in symbols.

11. -4 is greater than -8.

12. -17 is less than 6.

13. π is less than 100.

14. x is nonnegative.

15. z is greater than or equal to -4.

16. t is negative.

17. d is not greater than 7.

18. c is at most 3.

19. z is at least -17.

In Exercises 20–24, fill the blank with $<$, $=$, or $>$ so that the resulting statement is true.

20. -6 _____ -2

21. 5 _____ -3

22. $3/4$ _____ $.75$

23. 3.1416 _____ π

24. $1/3$ _____ $.33$

The consumer price index for urban consumers (CPI-U) measures the cost of consumer goods and services such as food, housing, transportation, medical costs, etc. The table shows the yearly percentage increase in the CPI-U over a decade.*

Year	Percentage change
1996	3.0
1997	2.3
1998	1.6
1999	2.2
2000	3.4
2001	2.8
2002	1.6
2003	2.3
2004	2.7
2005	2.5

*U.S. Bureau of Labor Statistics; data for 2005 is for the first half.

In Exercises 25–29, let p denote the yearly percentage increase in the CPI-U. Find the number of years in this period which satisfied the given inequality.

25. $p \geq 2.8$ **26.** $p < 2.6$ **27.** $p > 2.3$

28. $p \leq 3.0$ **29.** $p > 3.4$

In Exercises 30–36, fill the blank so as to produce two equivalent statements. For example, the arithmetic statement "a is negative" is equivalent to the geometric statement "the point a lies to the left of the point 0."

Arithmetic Statement	Geometric Statement
30. $a \geq b$	_____
31. _____	a lies c units to the right of b
32. _____	a lies between b and c
33. $a - b > 0$	_____
34. a is positive	_____
35. _____	a lies to the left of b
36. $a + b < c$ $(b > 0)$	_____

In Exercises 37–42, draw a picture on the number line of the given interval.

37. $(0, 8]$ **38.** $(0, \infty)$ **39.** $[-2, 1]$

40. $(-1, 1)$ **41.** $(-\infty, 0]$ **42.** $[-2, 7)$

In Exercises 43–48, use interval notation to denote the set of all real numbers x that satisfy the given inequality.

43. $5 \leq x \leq 10$ **44.** $-2 \leq x \leq 7$

45. $-3 < x < 14$ **46.** $7 < x < 77$

47. $x \geq -9$ **48.** $x \geq 12$

In Exercises 49–53, express the given numbers (based on 2006 estimates) in scientific notation.

49. Population of the world: 6,506,000,000

50. Population of the United States: 298,400,000

51. Average distance from Earth to Pluto: 5,910,000,000,000 meters

52. Radius of a hydrogen atom: .00000000001 meter

53. Width of a DNA double helix: .000000002 meter

In Exercises 54–57, express the given number in normal decimal notation.

54. Speed of light in a vacuum: 2.9979×10^8 miles per second

55. Average distance from the earth to the sun: 1.50×10^{11} meters

56. Electron charge: 1.602×10^{-27} coulomb

57. Proton mass: 1.6726×10^{-19} kilogram

58. One light-year is the distance light travels in a 365-day year. The speed of light is about 186,282.4 miles per second.

(a) How long is 1 light-year (in miles)? Express your answer in scientific notation.

(b) Light from the North Star takes 680 years to reach the earth. How many miles is the North Star from the earth?

59. The gross federal debt was about 8365 billion dollars in 2006, when the U.S. population was approximately 298.4 million people.

(a) Express the debt and the population in scientific notation.

(b) At that time, what was each person's share of the federal debt?

60. Apple reported that it had sold 28 million iPods through the end of 2005 and that 14 million iPods were sold in the first quarter of 2006. If the rate in the first quarter of 2006 continues through the end of 2008, how many iPods will be sold? Express your answer in scientific notation.

In Exercises 61–68, simplify the expression without using a calculator. Your answer should not have any radicals in it.

61. $\sqrt{2}\sqrt{8}$ **62.** $\sqrt{12}\sqrt{3}$

63. $\sqrt{\dfrac{3}{5}}\sqrt{\dfrac{12}{5}}$ **64.** $\sqrt{\dfrac{1}{2}}\sqrt{\dfrac{1}{6}}\sqrt{\dfrac{1}{12}}$

65. $\sqrt{6} + \sqrt{2}(\sqrt{2} - \sqrt{3})$ **66.** $\sqrt{12}(\sqrt{3} - \sqrt{27})$

67. $\sqrt{u^4}$ (u any real number)   **68.** $\sqrt{3x}\sqrt{75x^3}$ ($x \geq 0$)

In Exercises 69–78, simplify, and write the given number without using absolute values.

69. $|3 - 14|$ **70.** $|(-2)3|$ **71.** $3 - |2 - 5|$

72. $-2 - |-2|$ **73.** $|(-13)^2|$ **74.** $-|-5|^2$

75. $|\pi - \sqrt{2}|$ **76.** $|\sqrt{2} - 2|$ **77.** $|3 - \pi| + 3$

78. $|4 - \sqrt{2}| - 5$

In Exercises 79–84, fill the blank with <, =, or > so that the resulting statement is true.

79. $|-2|$ ____ $|-5|$ **80.** 5 ____ $|-2|$

81. $|3|$ ____ $-|4|$ **82.** $|-3|$ ____ 0

83. -7 ____ $|-1|$ **84.** $-|-4|$ ____ 0

In Exercises 85–92, find the distance between the given numbers.

85. -3 and 4 **86.** 7 and 107

87. -7 and $15/2$ **88.** $-3/4$ and -10

89. π and 3 **90.** π and -3

91. $\sqrt{2}$ and $\sqrt{3}$ **92.** π and $\sqrt{2}$

93. Galileo discovered that the period of a pendulum depends only on the length of the pendulum and the acceleration of gravity. The period T of a pendulum (in seconds) is

$$T = 2\pi\sqrt{\dfrac{l}{g}},$$

where l is the length of the pendulum in feet and $g \approx 32.2$ ft/sec^2 is the acceleration due to gravity. Find the period of a pendulum whose length is 4 feet.

94. Suppose you are k miles (not feet) above the ground. The radius of the earth is approximately 3960 miles. At the point where your line of sight meets the earth, it is perpendicular to the radius of the earth, as shown in the figure.

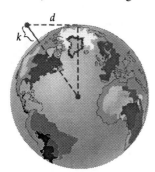

(a) Use the Pythagorean Theorem (see the Geometry Review Appendix) to show that
$$d = \sqrt{(3960 + k)^2 - 3960^2}.$$

(b) Show that the equation in part (a) simplifies to
$$d = \sqrt{7920k + k^2}.$$

(c) If you are h feet above the ground, then you are $h/5280$ miles high (why?). Use this fact and the equation in part (b) to obtain the formula used in Example 4.

95. According to data from the Center for Science in the Public Interest, the healthy weight range for a person depends on the person's height. For example,

Height	Healthy Weight Range (lb)
5 ft 8 in.	143 ± 21
6 ft 0 in.	163 ± 26

Express each of these ranges as an absolute value inequality in which x is the weight of the person.

96. At Statewide Insurance, each department's expenses are reviewed monthly. A department can fail to pass the budget variance test in a category if either (i) the absolute value of the difference between actual expenses and the budget is more than \$500 or (ii) the absolute value of the difference between the actual expenses and the budget is more than 5% of the budgeted amount. Which of the following items fail the budget variance test? Explain your answers.

Item	Budgeted Expense (\$)	Actual Expense (\$)
Wages	220,750	221,239
Overtime	10,500	11,018
Shipping and Postage	530	589

The wind-chill factor, shown in the table, calculates how a given temperature feels to a person's skin when the wind is taken into account. For example, the table shows that a temperature of 20° in a 40 mph wind feels like −1°.*

		Wind (mph)							
	Calm	**5**	**10**	**15**	**20**	**25**	**30**	**35**	**40**
Temperature (°F)	40	36	34	32	30	29	28	28	27
	30	25	21	19	17	16	15	14	13
	20	13	9	6	4	3	1	0	−1
	10	1	−4	−7	−9	−11	−12	−14	−15
	0	−11	−16	−19	−22	−24	−26	−27	−29
	−10	−22	−28	−32	−35	−37	−39	−41	−43
	−20	−34	−41	−45	−48	−51	−53	−55	−57
	−30	−46	−53	−58	−61	−64	−67	−69	−71
	−40	−57	−66	−71	−74	−78	−80	−82	−84

In Exercises 97–99, find the absolute value of the difference of the two given wind-chill factors. For example, the difference between the wind-chill at 30° with a 15 mph wind and one at −10° with a 10 mph wind is $|19-(-28)| = 47°$ or, equivalently, $|-28 - 19| = 47°$.

97. 10° with a 25 mph wind and 20° with a 20 mph wind

98. 30° with a 10 mph wind and 10° with a 30 mph wind

99. −30° with a 5 mph wind and 0° with a 10 mph wind

100. The graph shows the number of Schedule C and C-EZ forms (in millions) that were filed with the IRS over a six-year period.[†]

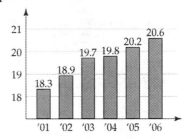

In what years was the following statement true:
$$|x - 19,500,000| \geq 600,000,$$
where x is the number of Schedule C and C-EZ forms in that year?

In Exercises 101–108, write the given expression without using absolute values.

101. $|t^2|$

102. $|-2 - y^2|$

103. $|b - 3|$ if $b \geq 3$

104. $|a - 5|$ if $a < 5$

---

*Table from the Joint Action Group for Temperature Indices, 2001.
[†]Internal Revenue Service. These schedules are for self-employed individuals.

105. $|c - d|$ if $c < d$ **106.** $|c - d|$ if $c \geq d$

107. $|u - v| - |v - u|$ **108.** $\dfrac{|u - v|}{|v - u|}$ if $u \neq v, u \neq 0, v \neq 0$

In Exercises 109 and 110, explain why the given statement is true for any numbers c and d. [Hint: Look at the properties of absolute value on page 10.]

109. $|(c - d)^2| = c^2 - 2cd + d^2$

110. $\sqrt{9c^2 - 18cd + 9d^2} = 3|c - d|$

In Exercises 111–116, express the given geometric statement about numbers on the number line algebraically, using absolute values.

111. The distance from x to 5 is less than 4.

112. x is more than 6 units from c.

113. x is at most 17 units from -4.

114. x is within 3 units of 7.

115. c is closer to 0 than b is.

116. x is closer to 1 than to 4.

In Exercises 117–120, translate the given algebraic statement into a geometric statement about numbers on the number line.

117. $|x - 3| < 2$ **118.** $|x - c| > 6$

119. $|x + 7| \leq 3$ **120.** $|u + v| \geq 2$

121. Match each of the following graphs with the appropriate absolute value equation or inequality.

(a)
    10   24

i. $|x - 17| = 7$

(b)
    10   24

ii. $|x - 17| = -7$

(c)

iii. $|x - 17| \leq 7$

(d)
    10   24

iv. $|x - 17| \geq -7$

(e)

v. $|x - 17| > 7$

122. Explain geometrically why this statement is always false:
$$|c - 1| < 2 \text{ and simultaneously } |c - 12| < 3.$$

In Exercises 123–134, use the geometric approach explained in the text to solve the given equation or inequality.

123. $|x| = 1$ **124.** $|x| = 3/2$

125. $|x - 2| = 1$ **126.** $|x + 3| = 2$

127. $|x + \pi| = 4$ **128.** $\left|x - \frac{3}{2}\right| = 5$

129. $|x| < 7$ **130.** $|x| \geq 5$

131. $|x - 5| < 2$ **132.** $|x - 6| > 2$

133. $|x + 2| \geq 3$ **134.** $|x + 4| \leq 2$

THINKERS

135. Explain why the statement $|a| + |b| + |c| > 0$ is algebraic shorthand for "at least one of the numbers a, b, c, is different from zero."

136. Find an algebraic shorthand version of the statement "none of the numbers a, b, c, is zero."

1.1.A SPECIAL TOPICS Decimal Representation of Real Numbers

Section Objectives
- Convert a repeating decimal to a rational number, and vice versa.
- Distinguish between rational and irrational numbers.

Every rational number can be expressed as a terminating or repeating decimal. For instance, $3/4 = .75$. To express $15/11$ as a decimal, divide the numerator by the denominator:

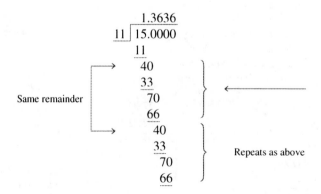

Since the remainder at the first step (namely, 4) occurs again at the third step, it is clear that the division process goes on forever with the two-digit block "36" repeating over and over in the quotient $15/11 = 1.3636363636 \cdots$.

The method used in the preceding example can be used to express any rational number as a decimal. During the division process, some remainder *necessarily repeats*. If the remainder at which this repetition starts is 0, the result is a repeating decimal ending in zeros—that is, a terminating decimal (for instance, $.75000 \cdots = .75$). If the remainder at which the repetition starts is nonzero, then the result is a nonterminating repeating decimal, as in the example above.

Conversely, there is a simple method for converting any repeating decimal into a rational number.

TECHNOLOGY TIP

To convert repeating decimals to fractions on TI, use *Frac* in this menu/submenu:

TI-84+: MATH

TI-86: MATH/MISC

On HP-39gs, select *Fraction* number format in the MODE menu; then enter the decimal.

   On Casio, use the FRAC program in the Program Appendix.

EXAMPLE 1

Write $d = .272727 \cdots$ as a rational number.

SOLUTION   Assuming that the usual rules of arithmetic hold, we see that

$$100d = 27.272727 \cdots \qquad \text{and} \qquad d = .272727 \cdots.$$

Now subtract d from $100d$:

$$
\begin{aligned}
100d &= 27.272727 \cdots \\
-d &= -.272727 \cdots \\
\hline
99d &= 27
\end{aligned}
$$

Dividing both sides of this last equation by 99 shows that $d = 27/99 = 3/11$. ∎

 IRRATIONAL NUMBERS

Many nonterminating decimals are *nonrepeating* (that is, no block of digits repeats forever), such as $.202002000200002 \cdots$ (where after each 2 there is one more zero than before). Although the proof is too long to give here, it is true that every nonterminating and nonrepeating decimal represents an *irrational* real number. Conversely every irrational number can be expressed as a nonterminating and nonrepeating decimal (no proof to be given here).

A typical calculator can hold only the first 10–14 digits of a number in decimal form. Consequently, a calculator can contain the *exact* value only of those rational numbers whose decimal expansion terminates after 10–14 places. It must *approximate* all other real numbers.

Since every real number is either a rational number or an irrational one, the preceding discussion can be summarized as follows.

Decimal Representation

1. Every real number can be expressed as a decimal.

2. Every decimal represents a real number.

3. The terminating decimals and the nonterminating repeating decimals are the rational numbers.

4. The nonterminating, nonrepeating decimals are the irrational numbers.

EXERCISES 1.1.A

In Exercises 1–6, express the given rational number as a repeating decimal.

1. 7/9   **2.** 19/88   **3.** 9/11

4. 2/13   **5.** 22/7   **6.** 1/19 (long)

In Exercises 7–13, express the given repeating decimal as a fraction.

7. .373737 · · ·   **8.** .929292 · · ·

9. 76.63424242 · · · [*Hint:* Consider $10{,}000d - 100d$, where $d = 76.63424242 · · ·$.]

10. 13.513513 · · · [*Hint:* Consider $1000d - d$, where $d = 13.513513 · · ·$.]

11. .135135135 · · · [*Hint:* See Exercise 10.]

12. .33030303 · · ·   **13.** 52.31272727 · · ·

14. If two real numbers have the same decimal expansion through three decimal places, how far apart can they be on the number line?

In Exercises 15–22, state whether a calculator can express the given number exactly.

15. 2/3   **16.** 7/16   **17.** 1/64   **18.** 1/22

19. $3\pi/2$ **20.** $\pi - 3$ **21.** 1/.625   **22.** 1/.16

23. Use the methods in Exercises 7–13 to show that both .74999 · · · and .75000 · · · are decimal expansions of 3/4. [Every terminating decimal can also be expressed as a decimal ending in repeated 9's. It can be proved that these are the only real numbers with more than one decimal expansion.]

Finding remainders with a calculator

24. If you use long division to divide 369 by 7, you obtain:

$$\begin{array}{r} 52 \quad \leftarrow \text{Quotient} \\ 7\,\overline{)\,369} \quad \leftarrow \text{Dividend} \\ \underline{35} \\ 19 \\ \underline{14} \\ 5 \quad \leftarrow \text{Remainder} \end{array}$$

Divisor → 7

If you use a calculator to find 369 ÷ 7, the answer is displayed as 52.71428571. Observe that the integer part of this calculator answer, 52, is the quotient when you do the problem by long division. The usual "checking procedure" for long division shows that

$$7 \cdot 52 + 5 = 369 \quad \text{or, equivalently} \quad 369 - 7 \cdot 52 = 5.$$

Thus, the remainder is

$$\text{Dividend} - (\text{divisor}) \left(\begin{array}{c} \text{integer part of} \\ \text{calculator answer} \end{array} \right).$$

Use this method to find the quotient and remainder in these problems:

(a) 5683 ÷ 9   (b) 1,000,000 ÷ 19

(c) 53,000,000 ÷ 37

In Exercises 25–30, find the decimal expansion of the given rational number. All these expansions are too long to fit in a calculator but can be readily found by using the hint in Exercise 25.

25. 1/17 [*Hint:* The first part of dividing 1 by 17 involves working this division problem: 1,000,000 ÷ 17. The method of Exercise 24 shows that the quotient is 58,823 and the remainder is 9. Thus the decimal expansion of 1/17 begins .058823, and the next block of digits in the expansion will be the quotient in the problem 9,000,000 ÷ 17. The remainder when 9,000,000 is divided by 17 is 13, so the next block of digits in the expansion of 1/17 is the quotient in the problem 13,000,000 ÷ 17. Continue in this way until the decimal expansion repeats.]

26. 3/19   **27.** 1/29   **28.** 3/43   **29.** 283/47

30. 768/59

THINKERS

31. If your calculator has a *Frac* key or program (see the Program Appendix), test its limitations by entering each of the following numbers and then pressing the *Frac* key.

(a) .058823529411   (b) .0588235294117

(c) .058823529411724   (d) .0588235294117985

Which of your answers are correct? [*Hint:* Exercise 25 may be helpful.]

32. (a) Show that there are at least as many irrational numbers (nonrepeating decimals) as there are terminating decimals. [*Hint:* With each terminating decimal associate a nonrepeating decimal.]

(b) Show that there are at least as many irrational numbers as there are repeating decimals. [*Hint:* With each repeating decimal, associate a nonrepeating decimal by inserting longer and longer strings of zeros: for instance, with .11111111 · · · associate the number .101001000100001 · · · .]

1.2   Radicals and Rational Exponents

Section Objectives

- Find exact and approximate roots of real numbers.
- Simplify expressions with rational exponents.
- Interpret radical notation.
- Rationalize numerators and denominators.

A **square root** of a nonnegative number c is a number whose square is c, that is, a solution of $x^2 = c$. For a real number c and a positive integer n, we define the **nth roots** of c as the solutions of the equation $x^n = c$. The graphs on the next page show that this equation may have two, one, or no solutions, depending on whether n is even or odd and whether c is positive or negative.*

$x^n = c$ *n* odd	$x^n = c$ *n* even		
Exactly one solution for any c	$c > 0$ One positive and one negative solution	$c = 0$ One solution $x = 0$	$c < 0$ No solution

Consequently, we have the following definition.

nth Roots

Let c be a real number and n a positive integer. The principal **nth root of c** is denoted by either of the symbols

$$\sqrt[n]{c} \qquad \text{or} \qquad c^{1/n}$$

and is defined to be

The solution of $x^n = c$, when n is odd;

The nonnegative solution of $x^n = c$, when n is even and $c \geq 0$.

As before, principal square roots are denoted $\sqrt{}$ rather than $\sqrt[2]{}$.

---

*The solutions of $x^n = c$ are the x-coordinates of the intersection points of the graph of $y = x^n$ and the horizontal line $y = c$. The graph of $y = x^n$ was discussed on page 165.

EXAMPLE 1

Find the following roots.

(a) $\sqrt[3]{-8}$ (b) $81^{1/4}$ (c) $\sqrt[5]{32}$ (d) $\sqrt{\dfrac{1}{4}}$

SOLUTION

(a) $\sqrt[3]{-8} = (-8)^{1/3} = -2$ because -2 is the solution of $x^3 = -8$.

(b) $81^{1/4} = \sqrt[4]{81} = 3$ because 3 is the positive solution of $x^4 = 81$.

(c) $\sqrt[5]{32} = 32^{1/5} = 2$ because 2 is the solution of $x^5 = 32$.

(d) $\sqrt{\dfrac{1}{4}} = \dfrac{1}{2}$ because $\dfrac{1}{2}$ is the positive solution of $x^2 = \dfrac{1}{4}$. ∎

```
40^.2
          2.091279105
225^(1/11)
          1.636193919
225^.0909
          1.63611336
```

Figure 1–9

EXAMPLE 2

Use a calculator to approximate

(a) $40^{1/5}$ (b) $225^{1/11}$

SOLUTION

(a) Since $1/5 = .2$, you can compute $40^{.2}$, as in Figure 1–9.

(b) $1/11$ is the infinite decimal $.090909\ldots$. In such cases, it is best to leave the exponent in fractional form and use parentheses, as shown in Figure 1–9. If you round off the decimal equivalent of $1/11$, say as $.0909$, you will not get the same answer, as Figure 1–9 shows. ∎

RATIONAL EXPONENTS

The next step is to give a meaning to fractional exponents for any fraction, not just those of the form $1/n$. If possible, they should be defined in such a way that the various exponent rules continue to hold. Consider, for example, how $4^{3/2}$ might be defined. The exponent $3/2$ can be written as either

$$3 \cdot \left(\frac{1}{2}\right) \qquad \text{or} \qquad \left(\frac{1}{2}\right) \cdot 3.$$

If the power of a power property $(c^m)^n = c^{mn}$ is to hold, we might define $4^{3/2}$ as either $(4^3)^{1/2}$ or $(4^{1/2})^3$. The result is the same in both cases:

$$(4^3)^{1/2} = 64^{1/2} = \sqrt{64} = 8 \qquad \text{and} \qquad (4^{1/2})^3 = (\sqrt{4})^3 = 2^3 = 8.$$

It can be proved that the same thing is true in the general case, which leads to this definition.

Rational Exponents

Let c be a positive real number and let t/k be a rational number in lowest terms with positive denominator. Then,

$$c^{t/k} \text{ is defined to be the number } (c^t)^{1/k} = (c^{1/k})^t.$$

Since every terminating decimal is a rational number, expressions such as $13^{3.77}$ now have a meaning, namely, $13^{377/100}$. (Actually, we used this fact earlier when we computed $40^{.2}$ and $225^{.0909}$ in Figure 5–1.)

TECHNOLOGY TIP

TI-89 will produce real number answers to computations like $(-8)^{2/3}$ if you select "Real" in the COMPLEX FORMAT submenu of the MODE menu.

NOTE

The preceding definition is also valid when c is negative, *provided that* the exponent has an odd denominator, such as $(-8)^{2/3}$ (see Exercise 69). Nevertheless, if you try to compute $(-8)^{2/3}$ on your calculator, you may get an error message or a complex number (indicated by an ordered pair or an expression involving i) instead of the correct answer,

$$(-8)^{2/3} = [(-8)^2]^{1/3} = \sqrt[3]{(-8)^2} = \sqrt[3]{64} = 4.$$

If this happens, you can probably get the correct answer by keying in either $[(-8)^2]^{1/3}$ or $[(-8)^{1/3}]^2$, each of which is equal to $(-8)^{2/3}$.

Rational exponents were defined in a way that guaranteed that one of the familiar exponent laws would remain valid. In fact, all exponent laws developed for integer exponents are valid for rational exponents, as summarized here and illustrated in Examples 3 through 5.

Exponent Laws

Let c and d be nonnegative real numbers, and let r and s be any rational numbers. Then

1. $c^r c^s = c^{r+s}$

2. $\dfrac{c^r}{c^s} = c^{r-s}$ $(c \neq 0)$

3. $(c^r)^s = c^{rs}$

4. $(cd)^r = c^r d^r$

5. $\left(\dfrac{c}{d}\right)^r = \dfrac{c^r}{d^r}$ $(d \neq 0)$

6. $c^{-r} = \dfrac{1}{c^r}$ $(c \neq 0)$

CAUTION

The exponent laws deal only with products and quotients. There are no analogous properties for sums. In particular, if both c and d are nonzero, then

$(c + d)^r$ is **not** equal to $c^r + d^r$.

EXAMPLE 3

Compute the product $x^{1/2}(x^{3/4} - x^{3/2})$.

SOLUTION

Distributive law:
$$x^{1/2}(x^{3/4} - x^{3/2}) = x^{1/2}x^{3/4} - x^{1/2}x^{3/2}$$

Multiplication with exponents (law 1):
$$= x^{1/2+3/4} - x^{1/2+3/2}$$

$\dfrac{1}{2} + \dfrac{3}{4} = \dfrac{5}{4}$ and $\dfrac{1}{2} + \dfrac{3}{2} = 2$:
$$= x^{5/4} - x^2. \qquad \blacksquare$$

EXAMPLE 4

Simplify $(8r^{3/4}s^{-3})^{2/3}$, and express it without negative exponents.

SOLUTION

Product to a power (law 4):	$(8r^{3/4}s^{-3})^{2/3} = 8^{2/3}(r^{3/4})^{2/3}(s^{-3})^{2/3}$
Power of a power (law 3):	$= 8^{2/3}r^{(3/4)(2/3)}s^{(-3)(2/3)}$
$\dfrac{3}{4} \cdot \dfrac{2}{3} = \dfrac{1}{2}$ and $(-3)\dfrac{2}{3} = -2$:	$= 8^{2/3}r^{1/2}s^{-2}$
Negative exponents (law 6):	$= \dfrac{8^{2/3}r^{1/2}}{s^2}$
$8^{2/3} = \sqrt[3]{8^2} = \sqrt[3]{64} = 4$:	$= \dfrac{4r^{1/2}}{s^2}$ or $\dfrac{4\sqrt{r}}{s^2}.$ ∎

EXAMPLE 5

Simplify $\dfrac{x^{7/2}y^3}{(xy^{7/4})^2}$ and express it without negative exponents.

SOLUTION

Product to a power (law 4):	$\dfrac{x^{7/2}y^3}{(xy^{7/4})^2} = \dfrac{x^{7/2}y^3}{x^2(y^{7/4})^2}$
$\dfrac{7}{4} \cdot 2 = \dfrac{7}{2}$:	$= \dfrac{x^{7/2}y^3}{x^2 y^{7/2}}$
Division with exponents (law 2):	$= x^{7/2-2}y^{3-7/2}$
$\dfrac{7}{2} - 2 = \dfrac{3}{2}$ and $3 - \dfrac{7}{2} = -\dfrac{1}{2}$:	$= x^{3/2}y^{-1/2}$
Negative exponents (law 6):	$= \dfrac{x^{3/2}}{y^{1/2}}$ ∎

RADICAL NOTATION

As we saw above, there are two notations for nth roots: $\sqrt[n]{c}$ and $c^{1/n}$. Similarly, $c^{t/k}$ can be expressed in terms of radicals.

$$c^{t/k} = (c^t)^{1/k} = \sqrt[k]{c^t} \quad \text{and} \quad c^{t/k} = (c^{1/k})^t = (\sqrt[k]{c})^t.$$

When radical notation is used, the exponent laws have a different form. For instance,

$$(cd)^{1/n} = c^{1/n}d^{1/n} \quad \text{means the same thing as} \quad \sqrt[n]{cd} = \sqrt[n]{c}\,\sqrt[n]{d};$$

$$\left(\dfrac{c}{d}\right)^{1/n} = \dfrac{c^{1/n}}{d^{1/n}} \quad \text{means the same thing as} \quad \sqrt[n]{\dfrac{c}{d}} = \dfrac{\sqrt[n]{c}}{\sqrt[n]{d}}.$$

When simplifying an expression involving radicals, either you can change to rational exponents and proceed as in Examples 3–5, or you can use the exponent laws in their radical notation, as in the next example.

EXAMPLE 6

Simplify each of the following.

(a) $\sqrt{63}$ (b) $\sqrt{12} - \sqrt{75}$ (c) $\sqrt[3]{40k^4}$

SOLUTION

(a) Look for perfect squares.

Factor a perfect square out of 63: $\sqrt{63} = \sqrt{9 \cdot 7}$

Write as a product of roots: $= \sqrt{9}\,\sqrt{7}$

$= 3\,\sqrt{7}$

(b) Look for perfect squares.

Factor perfect squares out of 12 and 75: $\sqrt{12} - \sqrt{75} = \sqrt{4 \cdot 3} - \sqrt{25 \cdot 3}$

Product of roots: $= \sqrt{4}\,\sqrt{3} - \sqrt{25}\,\sqrt{3}$

$= 2\sqrt{3} - 5\sqrt{3} = -3\sqrt{3}.$

(c) Look for perfect cubes. We note that $8k^3 = (2k)^3$ is a perfect cube.

Factor out $8k^3$: $\sqrt[3]{40k^4} = \sqrt[3]{8k^3 \cdot 5k}$

Product of roots: $= \sqrt[3]{8k^3}\,\sqrt[3]{5k}$

$= \sqrt[3]{(2k)^3}\,\sqrt[3]{5k} = 2k\,\sqrt[3]{5k}.$ ∎

EXAMPLE 7

Compute each of the following

(a) $27^{-5/3}$ (b) $2^{3/2}$ (c) $256^{3/4}$ (d) $(-1)^{2/6}$

SOLUTION

(a) $27^{-5/3} = \dfrac{1}{27^{5/3}} = \dfrac{1}{(\sqrt[3]{27})^5} = \dfrac{1}{3^5} = \dfrac{1}{243}$

(b) $2^{3/2} = (\sqrt{2})^3 = 2\sqrt{2}$

(c) $256^{3/4} = (\sqrt[4]{256})^3 = 4^3 = 64$

(d) Recall that, in order to use our definition of rational exponents, the fraction must be in lowest terms. So $(-1)^{2/6} = (-1)^{1/3} = \sqrt[3]{-1} = -1$. Notice that we get an *incorrect* answer if we do not first reduce the fraction, because $\sqrt[6]{(-1)^2} = \sqrt[6]{1} = 1$. ∎

 RATIONALIZING DENOMINATORS AND NUMERATORS

When dealing with fractions in the days before calculators, it was customary to *rationalize the denominators*, that is, write equivalent fractions with no radicals in the denominator, because this made many computations easier. With calculators, of course, there is no computational advantage to rationalizing denominators. Nevertheless, rationalizing denominators or numerators is sometimes needed to simplify expressions and to derive useful formulas. For example, several key calculus formulas can be derived by rationalizing the numerator of a rational expression.

EXAMPLE 8

(a) To rationalize the denominator of $\dfrac{7}{\sqrt{5}}$, multiply it by 1, with 1 written as a suitable radical fraction.

$$\frac{7}{\sqrt{5}} = \frac{7}{\sqrt{5}} \cdot 1 = \frac{7}{\sqrt{5}} \cdot \frac{\sqrt{5}}{\sqrt{5}} = \frac{7\sqrt{5}}{5}.$$

(b) To rationalize the denominator of $\dfrac{2}{3 + \sqrt{6}}$, multiply by 1 written as a radical fraction and use the multiplication pattern $(a + b)(a - b) = a^2 - b^2$.

$$\frac{2}{3 + \sqrt{6}} = \frac{2}{3 + \sqrt{6}} \cdot 1$$

$$= \frac{2}{3 + \sqrt{6}} \cdot \frac{3 - \sqrt{6}}{3 - \sqrt{6}} = \frac{2(3 - \sqrt{6})}{(3 + \sqrt{6})(3 - \sqrt{6})}$$

$$= \frac{6 - 2\sqrt{6}}{3^2 - (\sqrt{6})^2} = \frac{6 - 2\sqrt{6}}{9 - 6} = \frac{6 - 2\sqrt{6}}{3}.$$ ∎

EXAMPLE 9

Assume that $h \neq 0$, and rationalize the numerator of $\dfrac{\sqrt{x + h} - \sqrt{x}}{h}$; that is, write an equivalent fraction with no radicals in the numerator.

SOLUTION   Again, the technique is to multiply the fraction by 1, with 1 written as a suitable radical fraction:

$$\frac{\sqrt{x + h} - \sqrt{x}}{h} = \frac{\sqrt{x + h} - \sqrt{x}}{h} \cdot 1$$

$$= \frac{\sqrt{x + h} - \sqrt{x}}{h} \cdot \frac{\sqrt{x + h} + \sqrt{x}}{\sqrt{x + h} + \sqrt{x}} = \frac{(\sqrt{x + h})^2 - (\sqrt{x})^2}{h(\sqrt{x + h} + \sqrt{x})}$$

$$= \frac{x + h - x}{h(\sqrt{x + h} + \sqrt{x})} = \frac{h}{h(\sqrt{x + h} + \sqrt{x})} = \frac{1}{\sqrt{x + h} + \sqrt{x}}.$$

Notice that in its original form, it is hard to determine what happens to this fraction when h is close to zero. In the final form, we can see that when h gets close to zero, the expression gets close to $1/2\sqrt{x}$. ∎

IRRATIONAL EXPONENTS

An example will illustrate how a^t is defined when t is an irrational number.* To compute $10^{\sqrt{2}}$ we use the infinite decimal expansion $\sqrt{2} \approx 1.414213562 \cdots$ (see Special Topics 1.1.A). Each of

$$1.4, \ 1.41, \ 1.414, \ 1.4142, \ 1.41421, \ldots$$

---

*This example is not a proof but should make the idea plausible. Calculus is required for a rigorous proof.

is a rational number approximation of $\sqrt{2}$, and each is a more accurate approximation than the preceding one. We know how to raise 10 to each of these rational numbers:

$$10^{1.4} = 10^{14/100} \approx 25.1189$$

$$10^{1.41} = 10^{141/1,000} \approx 25.7040$$

$$10^{1.414} = 10^{1,414/10,000} \approx 25.9418$$

$$10^{1.4142} = 10^{14,142/100,000} \approx 25.9537$$

$$10^{1.41421} = 10^{141,421/1,000,000} \approx 25.9543$$

$$10^{1.414213} = 10^{1,414,213/10,000,000} \approx 25.9545$$

It appears that as the exponent r gets closer and closer to $\sqrt{2}$, 10^r gets closer and closer to a real number whose decimal expansion begins 25.954 . . . . We define $10^{\sqrt{2}}$ to be this number.

Similarly, for any $a > 0$,

a^t **is a well-defined *positive* number for each real exponent t.**

We shall also assume this fact.

The exponent laws (page 21) are valid for *all* real exponents.

EXERCISES 1.2

Note: *Unless directed otherwise, assume that all letters represent positive real numbers.*

In Exercises 1–10, simplify the expression. Assume a, b, c, d > 0.

1. $(25k^2)^{3/2}(16k^{1/3})^{3/4}$
2. $(4x^{5/6})(2y^{3/4})(x^{7/6})(3y^{-1/4})$

3. $(c^{2/5}d^{-2/3})(c^6d^3)^{4/3}$
4. $\left(\sqrt[3]{3x^2y}\right)\left(\sqrt[3]{9x^{-1/3}y^{3/5}}\right)^{-2}$

5. $\dfrac{(x^2)^{1/3}(y^2)^{2/3}}{3x^{2/3}y^2}$
6. $\dfrac{(a^{1/2}b^2)^3(a^{1/2}b^0c)}{(ab^2)^2(bc^5)^0}$

7. $\dfrac{(7a)^2(5b)^{3/2}}{(5a)^{3/2}(7b)^4}$
8. $\dfrac{\sqrt{ab}\,\sqrt[3]{ab^4}}{\sqrt{a}\left(\sqrt[3]{b}\right)^4}$

9. $(a^{x^2})^{1/x}$
10. $\dfrac{(b^x)^{x-1}}{b^{-x}}$

In Exercises 11–16, compute and simplify.

11. $x^{1/2}(x^{2/3} - x^{4/3})$
12. $x^{1/2}(3x^{3/2} + 2x^{-1/2})$
13. $(x^{1/2} + y^{1/2})(x^{1/2} - y^{1/2})$
14. $(x^{1/3} + y^{1/2})(2x^{1/3} - y^{3/2})$
15. $(x + y)^{1/2}[(x + y)^{1/2} - (x + y)]$
16. $(x^{1/3} + y^{1/3})(x^{2/3} - x^{1/3}y^{1/3} + y^{2/3})$

In Exercises 17–22, factor the given expression. For example,

$$x - x^{1/2} - 2 = (x^{1/2} - 2)(x^{1/2} + 1).$$

17. $x^{2/3} + x^{1/3} - 6$
18. $x^{2/7} - 2x^{1/7} - 15$
19. $x + 4x^{1/2} + 3$
20. $x^{1/3} + 11x^{1/6} + 24$
21. $x^{4/5} - 81$
22. $x + 3x^{2/3} + 3x^{1/3} + 1$

In Exercises 23–28, write the given expression without using radicals.

23. $\dfrac{1}{\sqrt{x}}$
24. $\sqrt[5]{x^2}$
25. $a\sqrt{a+b}$
26. $\sqrt{\sqrt[3]{a^3b^4}}$
27. $\sqrt[5]{t\sqrt{16t^5}}$
28. $\sqrt{x}(\sqrt[3]{x^2})(\sqrt[4]{x^3})$

In Exercises 29–44, simplify the expression without using a calculator.

29. $\sqrt{80}$
30. $\sqrt{120}$
31. $\sqrt{6}\,\sqrt{12}$
32. $\sqrt[3]{12}\,\sqrt[3]{10}$
33. $\dfrac{-6 + \sqrt{99}}{15}$
34. $\dfrac{18 - \sqrt{126}}{3}$
35. $\sqrt{50} - \sqrt{72}$
36. $\sqrt{150} + \sqrt{24}$
37. $5\sqrt{20} - \sqrt{45} + 2\sqrt{80}$
38. $\sqrt[3]{40} + 2\sqrt[3]{135} - 5\sqrt[3]{320}$

39. $\sqrt{16a^8b^{-2}}$

40. $\sqrt{54m^{-6}n^3}$

41. $\dfrac{\sqrt{c^2d^6}}{\sqrt{4c^3d^{-4}}}$

42. $\dfrac{\sqrt{a^{-10}b^{-12}}}{\sqrt{a^{14}d^{-4}}}$

43. $\dfrac{\sqrt[3]{a^5b^4c^3}}{\sqrt[3]{a^{-1}b^2c^6}}$

44. $\dfrac{\sqrt[5]{16a^4b^2}}{\sqrt[5]{2^{-1}a^{14}b^{-3}}}$

In Exercises 45–52, rationalize the denominator and simplify your answer.

45. $\dfrac{3}{\sqrt{8}}$

46. $\dfrac{2}{\sqrt{6}}$

47. $\dfrac{3}{2+\sqrt{12}}$

48. $\dfrac{1+\sqrt{3}}{5+\sqrt{10}}$

49. $\dfrac{2}{\sqrt{x}+2}$

50. $\dfrac{\sqrt{x}}{\sqrt{x}-\sqrt{c}}$

51. $\dfrac{10}{\sqrt[3]{2}}$

52. $\dfrac{-6}{\sqrt[3]{4}}$

In Exercises 53–56, use the fact that $x^3 + y^3 = (x+y)(x^2 - xy + y^2)$ to rationalize the denominator.

53. $\dfrac{1}{\sqrt[3]{3}+1}$

54. $\dfrac{5}{6-\sqrt[3]{5}}$

55. $\dfrac{1}{\sqrt[3]{4}-\sqrt[3]{2}+1}$

56. $\dfrac{3}{\sqrt[3]{2}+\sqrt[3]{3}}$

In Exercises 57–60, find the difference quotient of the given function. Then rationalize its numerator and simplify.

57. $f(x) = \sqrt{x+1}$

58. $g(x) = 2\sqrt{x+3}$

59. $f(x) = \sqrt{x^2+1}$

60. $g(x) = \sqrt{x^2-x}$

In Exercises 61–64, use the equation $y = 92.8935 \cdot x^{.6669}$ which gives the approximate distance y (in millions of miles) from the sun to a planet that takes x earth years to complete one orbit of the sun. Find the distance from the sun to the planet whose orbit time is given.

61. Mercury (.24 years)

62. Mars (1.88 years)

63. Saturn (29.46 years)

64. Pluto (247.69 years)

Between 1790 and 1860, the population y of the United States (in millions) in year x was given by $y = 3.9572(1.0299^x)$, where $x = 0$ corresponds to 1790. In Exercises 65–68, find the U.S. population in the given year.

65. 1800

66. 1817

67. 1845

68. 1859

69. Here are some of the reasons why restrictions are necessary when defining fractional powers of a negative number.

(a) Explain why the equations $x^2 = -4$, $x^4 = -4$, $x^6 = -4$, etc., have no real solutions. Hence, we cannot define $c^{1/2}$, $c^{1/4}$, $c^{1/6}$ when $c = -4$.

(b) Since $1/3$ is the same as $2/6$, it should be true that $c^{1/3} = c^{2/6}$, that is, that $\sqrt[3]{c} = \sqrt[6]{c^2}$. Show that this is false when $c = -8$.

70. Use a calculator to find $(3141)^{-3141}$. Explain why your answer cannot possibly be the number $(3141)^{-3141}$. Why does your calculator behave the way that it does?

71. (a) Graph $f(x) = x^5$ and explain why this function has an inverse function.

(b) Show algebraically that the inverse function is $g(x) = x^{1/5}$.

(c) Does $f(x) = x^6$ have an inverse function? Why or why not?

72. If n is an odd positive integer, show that $f(x) = x^n$ has an inverse function and find the rule of the inverse function. [*Hint:* Exercise 71 is the case when $n = 5$.]

In Exercises 73–75, use the catalog of basic functions (page 104) and Section 3.4 to describe the graph of the given function.

73. $g(x) = \sqrt{x+3}$

74. $h(x) = \sqrt{x} - 2$

75. $k(x) = \sqrt{x+4} - 4$

76. (a) Suppose r is a solution of the equation $x^n = c$ and s is a solution of $x^n = d$. Verify that rs is a solution of $x^n = cd$.

(b) Explain why part (a) shows that $\sqrt[n]{cd} = \sqrt[n]{c}\,\sqrt[n]{d}$.

77. The output Q of an industry depends on labor L and capital C according to the equation

$$Q = L^{1/4}C^{3/4}.$$

(a) Use a calculator to determine the output for the following resource combinations.

L	C	$Q = L^{1/4}C^{3/4}$
10	7	
20	14	
30	21	
40	28	
60	42	

(b) When you double both labor and capital, what happens to the output? When you triple both labor and capital, what happens to the output?

78. Do Exercise 77 when the equation relating output to resources is $Q = L^{1/4}C^{1/2}$.

79. Do Exercise 77 when the equation relating output to resources is $Q = L^{1/2}C^{3/4}$.

80. In Exercises 77–79, how does the sum of the exponents on L and C affect the increase in output?

1.3 Complex Numbers

Section Objectives

■ Add, subtract and multiply complex numbers.

■ Use the conjugate of the denominator to express complex fractions in standard form.

■ Express the square root of a negative number as an imaginary number.

■ Find all solutions of a quadratic equation in the complex number system.

Using mathematics to solve real-world problems is usually the same, regardless of the application. A situation is modeled mathematically, then the model is worked on using the tools of mathematics (algebra, trigonometry, calculus, differential equations, etc.). Finally, some sort of real world prediction or answer is taken from the result. In many applications (such as those dealing with electrical impedance or sound waves with a fixed frequency), it is necessary to be able to work with square roots in the model, even if negative numbers are involved. Complex numbers were created to deal with this situation.

The first step in constructing the complex numbers is to define a number i with the property that $i^2 = -1$ (or equivalently that $i = \sqrt{-1}$). Many people are bothered when they see this definition, for no real number can produce a negative result when squared. The great mathematician Rene Descartes was one of those people, and he derisively called i an "imaginary number," a name which it retains to this day even though, in many real contexts, i is just as important a number as 5.

The formal construction of the **complex number system** is rather involved, and is presented in Exercise 81. For now, we simply summarize the results.

Properties of the Complex Number System

1. The complex number system contains all real numbers.

2. The complex number system contains a number i such that $i^2 = -1$.

3. Addition, subtraction, multiplication, and division of complex numbers obey the same rules of arithmetic that hold in the real number system, with one exception: The exponent laws hold for *integer* exponents, but not necessarily for fractional ones.

4. Every complex number can be written in the **standard form** $a + bi$, where a and b are real numbers.*

5. Two complex numbers $a + bi$ and $c + di$ are equal exactly when $a = c$ and $b = d$.

The real numbers are the complex numbers of the form $a + 0i$, such as $7 = 7 + 0i$. Following Descartes, complex numbers of the form $0 + bi$ such as $5i$ and $(-1/4)i$ are called **imaginary numbers.** Since the usual laws of arithmetic still hold, it's easy to add, subtract, and multiply complex numbers. As

---

*Hereafter, whenever we write $a + bi$ or $c + di$, it is assumed that a, b, c, d are real numbers and $i^2 = -1$.

the following examples demonstrate, *all symbols can be treated as if they were real numbers, provided that i^2 is replaced by -1.* Unless directed otherwise, express your answers in the standard form $a + bi$.

EXAMPLE 1

(a) $(1 + i) + (3 - 7i) = 1 + i + 3 - 7i$
$$= (1 + 3) + (i - 7i) = 4 - 6i.$$

(b) $(4 + 3i) - (8 - 6i) = 4 + 3i - 8 - (-6i)$
$$= (4 - 8) + (3i + 6i) = -4 + 9i.$$

(c) $4i\left(2 + \dfrac{1}{2}i\right) = 4i \cdot 2 + 4i\left(\dfrac{1}{2}i\right)$
$$= 8i + 4 \cdot \dfrac{1}{2} \cdot i^2$$
$$= 8i + 2i^2$$
$$= 8i + 2(-1)$$
$$= -2 + 8i.$$

(d) $(2 + i)(3 - 4i) = 2 \cdot 3 + 2(-4i) + i \cdot 3 + i(-4i)$
$$= 6 - 8i + 3i - 4i^2$$
$$= 6 - 8i + 3i - 4(-1)$$
$$= (6 + 4) + (-8i + 3i)$$
$$= 10 - 5i. \qquad \blacksquare$$

The familiar multiplication patterns and exponent laws for integer exponents hold in the complex number system.

EXAMPLE 2

(a) $(3 + 2i)(3 - 2i) = 3^2 - (2i)^2$
$$= 9 - 4i^2$$
$$= 9 - 4(-1)$$
$$= 9 + 4 = 13.$$

(b) $(4 + i)^2 = 4^2 + 2 \cdot 4 \cdot i + i^2$
$$= 16 + 8i + (-1)$$
$$= 15 + 8i.$$

(c) To find i^{54}, we first note that $i^4 = i^2 i^2 = (-1)(-1) = 1$ and that
$$54 = 52 + 2 = 4 \cdot 13 + 2.$$

Consequently,
$$i^{54} = i^{52+2} = i^{52}i^2 = i^{4 \cdot 13}i^2 = (i^4)^{13}i^2 = 1^{13}(-1) = -1. \qquad \blacksquare$$

The **conjugate** of the complex number $a + bi$ is the number $a - bi$, and the conjugate of $a - bi$ is $a + bi$. For example, the conjugate of $3 + 4i$ is $3 - 4i$ and the conjugate of $-3i = 0 - 3i$ is $0 + 3i = 3i$. *Every real number is its own conjugate;* for instance, the conjugate of $17 = 17 + 0i$ is $17 - 0i = 17$.

For any complex number $a + bi$, we have

$$(a + bi)(a - bi) = a^2 - (bi)^2 = a^2 - b^2i^2 = a^2 - b^2(-1) = a^2 + b^2.$$

Since a^2 and b^2 are nonnegative real numbers, so is $a^2 + b^2$. Therefore, *the product of a complex number and its conjugate is a nonnegative real number.* This fact enables us to express quotients of complex numbers in standard form.

EXAMPLE 3

To express $\dfrac{3 + 4i}{1 + 2i}$ in the form $a + bi$, *multiply both numerator and denominator by the conjugate of the denominator,* namely, $1 - 2i$:

$$\begin{aligned}
\frac{3 + 4i}{1 + 2i} &= \frac{3 + 4i}{1 + 2i} \cdot \frac{1 - 2i}{1 - 2i} \\
&= \frac{(3 + 4i)(1 - 2i)}{(1 + 2i)(1 - 2i)} \\
&= \frac{3 + 4i - 6i - 8i^2}{1^2 - (2i)^2} \\
&= \frac{3 + 4i - 6i - 8(-1)}{1 - 4i^2} \\
&= \frac{11 - 2i}{1 - 4(-1)} \\
&= \frac{11 - 2i}{5} = \frac{11}{5} - \frac{2}{5}i.
\end{aligned}$$

This is the form $a + bi$ with $a = 11/5$ and $b = -2/5$.   ∎

EXAMPLE 4

Express $\dfrac{1}{1 - i}$ in standard form.

SOLUTION   We note that the conjugate of the denominator is $1 + i$, and therefore

$$\begin{aligned}
\frac{1}{1 - i} &= \frac{1 \cdot (1 + i)}{(1 - i)(1 + i)} \\
&= \frac{1 + i}{1^2 - i^2} \\
&= \frac{1 + i}{1 - (-1)} \\
&= \frac{1 + i}{2} = \frac{1}{2} + \frac{1}{2}i.
\end{aligned}$$

We can check this result by multiplying $\frac{1}{2} + \frac{1}{2}i$ by $1 - i$ to see whether the product is 1 $\left(\text{which it should be if } \frac{1}{2} + \frac{1}{2}i = \frac{1}{1 - i}\right)$:

$$\left(\frac{1}{2} + \frac{1}{2}i\right)(1 - i) = \frac{1}{2} \cdot 1 - \frac{1}{2}i + \frac{1}{2}i \cdot 1 - \frac{1}{2}i^2 = \frac{1}{2} - \frac{1}{2}(-1) = 1. \quad \blacksquare$$

Since $i^2 = -1$, we define $\sqrt{-1}$ to be the complex number i. Similarly, since $(5i)^2 = 5^2i^2 = 25(-1) = -25$, we define $\sqrt{-25}$ to be $5i$. In general,

Square Roots of Negative Numbers

> Let b be a positive real number.
>
> $$\sqrt{-b} \text{ is defined to be } \sqrt{b}\,i$$
>
> because $(\sqrt{b}\,i)^2 = (\sqrt{b})^2i^2 = b(-1) = -b$.

CAUTION

$\sqrt{b}\,i$ is *not* the same as $\sqrt{bi}$. To avoid confusion it may help to write $\sqrt{b}\,i$ as $i\sqrt{b}$.

EXAMPLE 5

Express the following in the form $a + bi$:   (a) $\sqrt{-3}$ (b) $\dfrac{1 - \sqrt{-7}}{3}$

SOLUTION

(a) $\sqrt{-3} = \sqrt{3}\,i = 0 + \sqrt{3}\,i$ or $0 + i\sqrt{3}$.

(b) $\dfrac{1 - \sqrt{-7}}{3} = \dfrac{1 - \sqrt{7}\,i}{3} = \dfrac{1}{3} - \dfrac{\sqrt{7}}{3}i.$ $\blacksquare$

CAUTION

The property $\sqrt{cd} = \sqrt{c}\sqrt{d}$ (or equivalently in exponential notation, $(cd)^{1/2} = c^{1/2}d^{1/2}$), which is valid for positive real numbers, does *not hold* when both c and d are negative.

$$\sqrt{-20}\,\sqrt{-5} = \sqrt{20}\,i \cdot \sqrt{5}\,i = \sqrt{20}\,\sqrt{5} \cdot i^2 = \sqrt{20 \cdot 5}(-1)$$

$$= \sqrt{100}(-1) = -10.$$

But $\sqrt{(-20)(-5)} = \sqrt{100} = 10$, so that

$$\sqrt{(-20)(-5)} \neq \sqrt{-20}\,\sqrt{-5}.$$

To avoid difficulty, *always write square roots of negative numbers in terms of i before doing any simplification.*

TECHNOLOGY TIP

Most calculators that do complex number arithmetic automatically return a complex number when asked for the square root of a negative number. On TI-84+/89, however, the MODE must be set to "rectangular" or "$a + bi$."

EXAMPLE 6

$$(7 - \sqrt{-4})(5 + \sqrt{-9}) = (7 - \sqrt{4}i)(5 + \sqrt{9}i)$$
$$= (7 - 2i)(5 + 3i)$$
$$= 35 + 21i - 10i - 6i^2$$
$$= 35 + 11i - 6(-1) = 41 + 11i. \qquad \blacksquare$$

Since every negative real number has a square root in the complex number system, we can now find complex solutions for equations that have no real solutions. For example, the solutions of $x^2 = -25$ are $x = \pm\sqrt{-25} = \pm5i$. In fact,

Every quadratic equation with real coefficients has solutions in the complex number system.

EXAMPLE 7

To solve the equation $2x^2 + x + 3 = 0$, we apply the quadratic formula.

$$x = \frac{-1 \pm \sqrt{1^2 - 4 \cdot 2 \cdot 3}}{2 \cdot 2} = \frac{-1 \pm \sqrt{-23}}{4}.$$

Since $\sqrt{-23}$ is not a real number, this equation has no real number solutions. But $\sqrt{-23}$ *is* a complex number, namely, $\sqrt{-23} = \sqrt{23}i$. Thus, the equation does have solutions in the complex number system.

$$x = \frac{-1 \pm \sqrt{-23}}{4} = \frac{-1 \pm \sqrt{23}i}{4} = -\frac{1}{4} \pm \frac{\sqrt{23}}{4}i.$$

Note that the two solutions, $-\frac{1}{4} + \frac{\sqrt{23}}{4}i$ and $-\frac{1}{4} - \frac{\sqrt{23}}{4}i$, are conjugates of each other. $\blacksquare$

TECHNOLOGY TIP

The polynomial solvers on TI-86, HP-39gs and Casio produce all real and complex solutions of any polynomial equation that they can solve. See Exercise 105 in Section 1.2 for details.

On TI-89, use cSOLVE in the COMPLEX submenu of the ALGEBRA menu to find all solutions.

EXAMPLE 8

To find *all* solutions of $x^3 = 1$, we rewrite the equation and use the Difference of Cubes pattern (see the Algebra Review Appendix) to factor:

$$x^3 = 1$$
$$x^3 - 1 = 0$$
$$(x - 1)(x^2 + x + 1) = 0$$
$$x - 1 = 0 \qquad \text{or} \qquad x^2 + x + 1 = 0.$$

The solution of the first equation is $x = 1$. The solutions of the second can be obtained from the quadratic formula.

$$x = \frac{-1 \pm \sqrt{1^2 - 4 \cdot 1 \cdot 1}}{2 \cdot 1} = \frac{-1 \pm \sqrt{-3}}{2} = \frac{-1 \pm \sqrt{3}i}{2} = -\frac{1}{2} \pm \frac{\sqrt{3}}{2}i.$$

Therefore, the equation $x^3 = 1$ has one real solution ($x = 1$) and two nonreal complex solutions [$x = -1/2 + (\sqrt{3}/2)i$ and $x = -1/2 - (\sqrt{3}/2)i$]. Each of these solutions is said to be a **cube root of 1** or a **cube root of unity.** Observe that the two nonreal complex cube roots of unity are conjugates of each other.   ∎

The preceding examples illustrate this useful fact (whose proof is discussed in Section 4.8).

Conjugate Solutions

If $a + bi$ is a solution of a polynomial equation with *real* coefficients, then its conjugate $a - bi$ is also a solution of this equation.

EXERCISES 1.3

In Exercises 1–54, perform the indicated operation and write the result in the form $a + bi$.

1. $(2 + 3i) + (6 - i)$

2. $(-3 + 2i) + (8 + 6i)$

3. $(2 - 8i) - (4 + 2i)$

4. $(3 + 5i) + (2 - 5i)$

5. $\dfrac{5}{4} - \left(\dfrac{7}{4} + 2i\right)$

6. $(\sqrt{3} + i) + (\sqrt{5} - 2i)$

7. $\left(\dfrac{\sqrt{2}}{2} + i\right) - \left(\dfrac{\sqrt{3}}{2} - i\right)$

8. $\left(\dfrac{1}{2} + \dfrac{\sqrt{3}i}{2}\right) + \left(\dfrac{3}{4} - \dfrac{5\sqrt{3}i}{2}\right)$

9. $(2 + i)(3 + 5i)$

10. $(2 - i)(5 + 2i)$

11. $(0 - 6i)(5 + 0i)$

12. $(4 + 3i)(4 - 3i)$

13. $(2 - 5i)^2$

14. $(3 + i)(5 - i)i$

15. $(\sqrt{3} + i)(\sqrt{3} - i)$

16. $\left(\dfrac{1}{2} - i\right)\left(\dfrac{1}{4} + 2i\right)$

17. i^{19}

18. i^{26}

19. i^{33}

20. $(-i)^{53}$

21. $(-i)^{107}$

22. $(-i)^{213}$

23. $\dfrac{1}{3 + 2i}$

24. $\dfrac{1}{i}$

25. $\dfrac{4}{3i}$

26. $\dfrac{i}{2 + i}$

27. $\dfrac{3}{4 + 5i}$

28. $\dfrac{2 + 3i}{i}$

29. $\dfrac{1}{i(4 + 5i)}$

30. $\dfrac{1}{(2 - i)(2 + i)}$

31. $\dfrac{2 + 3i}{i(4 + i)}$

32. $\dfrac{2}{(2 + 3i)(4 + i)}$

33. $\dfrac{2 + i}{1 - i} + \dfrac{1}{1 + 2i}$

34. $\dfrac{1}{2 - i} + \dfrac{3 + i}{2 + 3i}$

35. $\dfrac{i}{3 + i} - \dfrac{3 + i}{4 + i}$

36. $6 + \dfrac{2i}{3 + i}$

37. $\sqrt{-36}$

38. $\sqrt{-121}$

39. $\sqrt{-14}$

40. $\sqrt{-800}$

41. $-\sqrt{-16}$

42. $-\sqrt{-12}$

43. $\sqrt{-16} + \sqrt{-49}$

44. $\sqrt{-25} - \sqrt{9}$

45. $\sqrt{-15} - \sqrt{-18}$

46. $\sqrt{-12}\,\sqrt{-3}$

47. $\sqrt{-16}/\sqrt{-36}$

48. $-\sqrt{-64}/\sqrt{-4}$

49. $(\sqrt{-25} + 2)(\sqrt{-49} - 3)$

50. $(5 - \sqrt{-3})(-1 + \sqrt{-9})$

51. $(2 + \sqrt{-5})(1 - \sqrt{-10})$

52. $\sqrt{-3}(3 - \sqrt{-27})$

53. $1/(1 + \sqrt{-5})$

54. $(1 + \sqrt{-4})(3 - \sqrt{-9})$

In Exercises 55–58, find x and y. Remember that

$$a + bi = c + di$$

exactly when a = c and b = d.

55. $3x - 4i = 6 + 2yi$ **56.** $5 + 3yi = 10x + 36i$

57. $3 + 4xi = 2y - 3i$ **58.** $10 = (6 + 8i)(x + yi)$

In Exercises 59–70, solve the equation and express each solution in the form a + bi.

59. $3x^2 - 2x + 5 = 0$ **60.** $5x^2 + 2x + 1 = 0$

61. $x^2 + 5x + 6 = 0$ **62.** $x^2 + 6x + 25 = 0$

63. $2x^2 - x = -4$ **64.** $x^2 + 1 = 4x$

65. $x^2 + 1770.25 = -84x$ **66.** $3x^2 + 4 = -5x$

67. $x^3 - 8 = 0$ **68.** $x^3 + 125 = 0$

69. $x^4 - 1 = 0$ **70.** $x^4 - 81 = 0$

71. Simplify: $i + i^2 + i^3 + \cdots + i^{15}$

72. Simplify: $i - i^2 + i^3 - i^4 + i^5 - \cdots + i^{15}$

THINKERS

73. It is easy to compare two real numbers. For instance, $5 < 8$, $4 = \dfrac{28}{7}$, and $-3 > -10$. It is harder to compare two complex numbers. Is $5 + 12i$ less than, greater than, or equal to $11 + 6i$? On the face of it, this question is not possible to answer. When comparing complex numbers, mathematicians look at their *moduli*, a measure of how "far away" they are from $0 + 0i$, or zero. The modulus of a complex number is defined this way:

$$\text{mod}(a + bi) = \sqrt{a^2 + b^2}$$

 (a) Compute the modulus of the following complex numbers:
  (i) $3 - 4i$
  (ii) $24 + 7i$
  (iii) $8 + 0i$
  (iv) $-8 + 0i$
  (v) $0 + 8i$
 (b) Which is larger, $\text{mod}(5 + 12i)$ or $\text{mod}(11 + 6i)$?

If z = a + bi is a complex number, then its conjugate is usually denoted $\bar{z}$, that is, $\bar{z} = a - bi$. In Exercises 74–78, prove that for any complex numbers z = a + bi and w = c + di:

74. $\overline{z + w} = \bar{z} + \bar{w}$ **75.** $\overline{zw} = \bar{z} \cdot \bar{w}$

76. $\overline{\left(\dfrac{z}{w}\right)} = \dfrac{\bar{z}}{\bar{w}}$ **77.** $\overline{\bar{z}} = z$

78. z is a real number exactly when $\bar{z} = z$.

79. The **real part** of the complex number $a + bi$ is defined to be the real number a. The **imaginary part** of $a + bi$ is defined to the real number b (*not bi*).
 (a) Show that the real part of $z = a + bi$ is $\dfrac{z + \bar{z}}{2}$.
 (b) Show that the imaginary part of $z = a + bi$ is $\dfrac{z - \bar{z}}{2i}$.

80. If $z = a + bi$ (with a, b real numbers, not both $\bar{0}$), express $1/z$ in standard form.

81. Construction of the Complex Numbers. We assume that the real number system is known. To construct a new number system with the desired properties, we must do the following:
 (i) Define a set C (whose elements will be called complex numbers).
 (ii) Ensure that the set C contains the real numbers or at least a copy of them.
 (iii) Define addition and multiplication in the set C in such a way that the usual laws of arithmetic are valid.
 (iv) Show that C has the other properties listed in the box on page 27.
We begin by defining C to be the set of all ordered pairs of real numbers. Thus, $(1, 5)$, $(-6, 0)$, $(4/3, -17)$, and $(\sqrt{2}, 12/5)$ are some of the elements of the set C. More generally, a complex number (= element of C) is any pair (a, b), where a and b are real numbers. By definition, two complex numbers are *equal* exactly when they have the same first and the same second coordinate.

 (a) *Addition in C* is defined by this rule:

$$(a, b) + (c, d) = (a + c, b + d)$$

  For example,

$$(3, 2) + (5, 4) = (3 + 5, 2 + 4) = (8, 6).$$

  Verify that this addition has the following properties. For any complex numbers (a, b), (c, d), (e, f) in C:
  (i) $(a, b) + (c, d) = (c, d) + (a, b)$
  (ii) $[(a, b) + (c, d)] + (e, f) = (a, b) + [(c, d) + (e, f)]$
  (iii) $(a, b) + (0, 0) = (a, b)$
  (iv) $(a, b) + (-a, -b) = (0, 0)$
 (b) *Multiplication in C* is defined by this rule:

$$(a, b)(c, d) = (ac - bd, bc + ad)$$

  For example,

$$(3, 2)(4, 5) = (3 \cdot 4 - 2 \cdot 5, 2 \cdot 4 + 3 \cdot 5)$$
$$= (12 - 10, 8 + 15) = (2, 23).$$

  Verify that this multiplication has the following properties. For any complex numbers (a, b), (c, d), (e, f) in C:
  (i) $(a, b)(c, d) = (c, d)(a, b)$
  (ii) $[(a, b)(c, d)](e, f) = (a, b)[(c, d)(e, f)]$
  (iii) $(a, b)(1, 0) = (a, b)$
  (iv) $(a, b)(0, 0) = (0, 0)$
 (c) Verify that for any two elements of C with second coordinate zero:
  (i) $(a, 0) + (c, 0) = (a + c, 0)$
  (ii) $(a, 0)(c, 0) = (ac, 0)$
  Identify $(t, 0)$ with the real number t. Statements (i) and (ii) show that when addition or multiplication in C is performed on two real numbers (that is, elements of C with second coordinate 0), the result is the usual sum or product of real numbers. Thus, C contains (a copy of) the real number system.

(d) *New Notation.* Since we are identifying the complex number $(a, 0)$ with the real number a, we shall hereafter denote $(a, 0)$ simply by the symbol a. Also, let i denote the complex number $(0, 1)$.

(i) Show that $i^2 = -1$, that is,

$$(0, 1)(0, 1) = (-1, 0).$$

(ii) Show that for any complex number $(0, b)$, $(0, b) = bi$ [that is, $(0, b) = (b, 0)(0, 1)$].

(iii) Show that any complex number (a, b) can be written: $(a, b) = a + bi$, that is,

$$(a, b) = (a, 0) + (b, 0)(0, 1).$$

In this new notation, every complex number is of the form $a + bi$ with a, b real and $i^2 = -1$, and our construction is finished.

1.4   The Coordinate Plane

Section Objectives
- ■ Locate points in the coordinate plane.
- ■ Create a scatter plot and line graph from a data set.
- ■ Determine the distance between two points in the plane.
- ■ Find the midpoint of a line segment.
- ■ Understand the relationship between equations and their graphs.
- ■ Find the intercepts of a graph.
- ■ Find the equation of a circle.
- ■ Identify equations whose graphs are circles.

Just as real numbers are identified with points on the number line, ordered *pairs* of real numbers can be identified with points in the plane. To do this, draw two number lines in the plane, one vertical and one horizontal, as in Figure 1–10. The horizontal line is usually called the **x-axis,** and the vertical line the **y-axis,** but other letters may be used if desired. The point where the axes intersect is the **origin.** The axes divide the plane into four regions, called **quadrants,** that are numbered as in Figure 1–10.

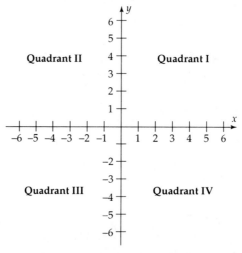

Figure 1–10

If P is a point in the plane, draw vertical and horizontal lines through P to the coordinate axes, as shown in Figure 1–11, on the next page. These lines intersect the x-axis at some number c and the y-axis at d. We say that P has **coordinates** (c, d).

The number c is the **x-coordinate** of P, and d is the **y-coordinate** of P. The plane is said to have a **rectangular** (or **Cartesian**) **coordinate system.**

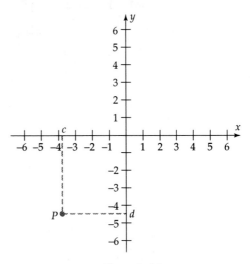

Figure 1–11

You can think of the coordinates of a point as directions for locating it. For instance, to find $(4, -3)$, start at the origin and move 4 units to the right along the x-axis, then move 3 units downward, as shown in Figure 1–12, which also shows other points and their coordinates.

CAUTION

The coordinates of a point are an *ordered* pair. Figure 1–12 shows that the point P with coordinates $(-5, 2)$ is quite different from the point Q with coordinates $(2, -5)$. The same numbers (2 and −5) occur in both cases, but in *different order.*

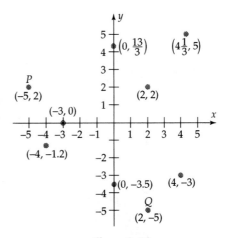

Figure 1–12

EXAMPLE 1

The following table, from the U.S. Department of Education shows the maximum Pell Grant for college students in selected years.

Year	1990	1992	1994	1996	1998	2000	2002	2004
Amount	2300	2400	2300	2470	3000	3300	4000	4050

One way to represent this data graphically is to represent each year's maximum by a point; for instance (1990, 2300) and (2004, 4050). Alternatively, to avoid using large numbers, we can let x be the number of years since 1990, so that $x = 0$ is 1990 and $x = 14$ is 2004. We can also list the dollar amounts in *hundreds*, so the points for 1990 and 2004 are (0, 23) and (14, 40.5). Plotting all the data in this way leads to the **scatter plot** in Figure 1–13. Connecting these data points with line segments produces the **line graph** in Figure 1–14. ∎

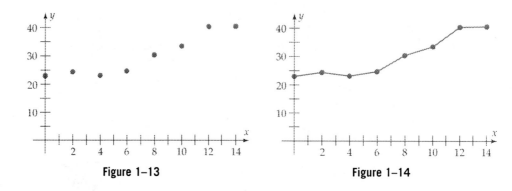

Figure 1–13   Figure 1–14

THE DISTANCE FORMULA

We shall often identify a point with its coordinates and refer, for example, to the point (2, 3). When dealing with several points simultaneously, it is customary to label the coordinates of the first point (x_1, y_1), the second point (x_2, y_2), the third point (x_3, y_3), and so on.* Once the plane is coordinatized, it's easy to compute the distance between any two points:

The Distance Formula

> The distance between points (x_1, y_1) and (x_2, y_2) is
> $$\sqrt{(x_1 - x_2)^2 + (y_1 - y_2)^2}.$$

Before proving the distance formula, we shall see how it is used.

EXAMPLE 2

To find the distance between the points $(-1, -3)$ and $(2, -4)$ in Figure 1–15, substitute $(-1, -3)$ for (x_1, y_1) and $(2, -4)$ for (x_2, y_2) in the distance formula:

Distance formula: $\text{Distance} = \sqrt{(x_1 - x_2)^2 + (y_1 - y_2)^2}$

Substitute: $= \sqrt{(-1 - 2)^2 + (-3 - (-4))^2}$

Simplify: $= \sqrt{(-3)^2 + (-3 + 4)^2}$

                                       $= \sqrt{9 + 1} = \sqrt{10}.$

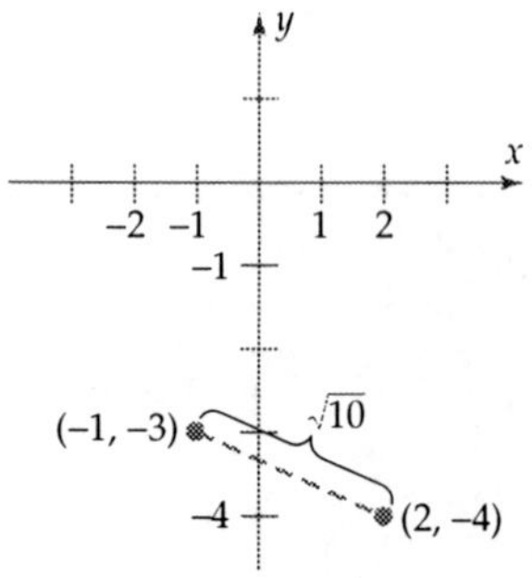

Figure 1–15

---

*"x_1" is read "x-one" or "x-sub-one"; it is a *single symbol* denoting the first coordinate of the first point, just as c denotes the first coordinate of (c, d). Analogous remarks apply to y_1, x_2, and so on.

The order in which the points are used in the distance formula doesn't make a difference. If we substitute $(2, -4)$ for (x_1, y_1) and $(-1, -3)$ for (x_2, y_2), we get the same answer:

$$\sqrt{[2 - (-1)]^2 + [-4 - (-3)]^2} = \sqrt{3^2 + (-1)^2} = \sqrt{10}. \qquad \blacksquare$$

EXAMPLE 3

In a Cubs game at Wrigley Field, a fielder catches the ball near the right-field corner and throws it to second base. The right-field corner is 353 feet from home plate along the right-field foul line. If the fielder is 5 feet from the outfield wall and 5 feet from the foul line, how far must he throw the ball?

SOLUTION   Imagine that the playing field is placed on the coordinate plane, with home plate at the origin and the right-field foul line along the positive x-axis, as shown in Figure 1–16 (not to scale).

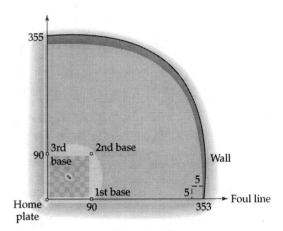

Figure 1–16

Since the four bases form a square whose sides measure 90 ft each, second base has coordinates $(90, 90)$. The fielder is located 5 feet from the wall, so his x-coordinate is $353 - 5 = 348$. His y-coordinate is 5, since he is 5 feet from the foul line. Therefore the distance he throws is the distance from $(348, 5)$ to $(90, 90)$, which can be found as follows.

Distance formula: $\text{Distance} = \sqrt{(x_1 - x_2)^2 + (y_1 - y_2)^2}$

Substitute: $= \sqrt{(348 - 90)^2 + (5 - 90)^2}$

Simplify: $= \sqrt{258^2 + (-85)^2}$

$= \sqrt{73{,}789} \approx 271.6 \text{ feet.}$

Therefore, he must throw about 272 feet. $\blacksquare$

EXAMPLE 4

CAUTION

$\sqrt{a^2 + 4b^2}$ cannot be simplified. In particular, it is *not* equal to $a + 2b$.

To find the distance from (a, b) to $(2a, -b)$, where a and b are fixed real numbers, substitute a for x_1, b for y_1, $2a$ for x_2, and $-b$ for y_2 in the distance formula:

$$\sqrt{(x_1 - x_2)^2 + (y_1 - y_2)^2} = \sqrt{(a - 2a)^2 + (b - (-b))^2}$$
$$= \sqrt{(-a)^2 + (b + b)^2} = \sqrt{a^2 + (2b)^2}$$
$$= \sqrt{a^2 + 4b^2}.$$ ∎

PROOF OF THE DISTANCE FORMULA

Figure 1–17 shows typical points P and Q in the plane. We must find length d of line segment PQ.

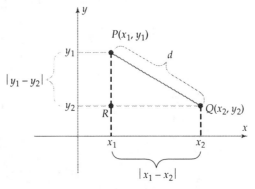

Figure 1–17

As shown in Figure 1–17, the length of RQ is the same as the distance from x_1 to x_2 on the x-axis (number line), namely, $|x_1 - x_2|$. Similarly, the length of PR is the same as the distance from y_1 to y_2 on the y-axis, namely, $|y_1 - y_2|$. According to the Pythagorean Theorem* the length d of PQ is given by

$$(\text{Length } PQ)^2 = (\text{length } RQ)^2 + (\text{length } PR)^2$$
$$d^2 = |x_1 - x_2|^2 + |y_1 - y_2|^2.$$

Since $|c|^2 = |c| \cdot |c| = |c^2| = c^2$ (because $c^2 \geq 0$), this equation becomes

$$d^2 = (x_1 - x_2)^2 + (y_1 - y_2)^2.$$

Since the length d is nonnegative, we must have

$$d = \sqrt{(x_1 - x_2)^2 + (y_1 - y_2)^2}.$$ ∎

The distance formula can be used to prove the following useful fact (see Exercise 96).

The Midpoint Formula

The midpoint of the line segment from (x_1, y_1) to (x_2, y_2) is

$$\left(\frac{x_1 + x_2}{2}, \frac{y_1 + y_2}{2} \right).$$

*See the Geometry Review Appendix.

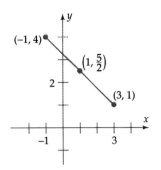

Figure 1–18

EXAMPLE 5

To find the midpoint of the segment joining $(-1, 4)$ and $(3, 1)$, use the formula in the box with $x_1 = -1$, $y_1 = 4$, $x_2 = 3$, and $y_2 = 1$. The midpoint is

$$\left(\frac{x_1 + x_2}{2}, \frac{y_1 + y_2}{2}\right) = \left(\frac{-1 + 3}{2}, \frac{4 + 1}{2}\right) = \left(1, \frac{5}{2}\right)$$

as shown in Figure 1–18. ∎

EXAMPLE 6

The annual revenues of the Dell Computer company were \$31.2 billion in 2002 and \$55.9 billion in 2006.* Assume that revenues are growing approximately linearly and estimate the revenues in 2004.

SOLUTION   Let the point (x, y) denote the revenues y (in billions of dollars) in year x. Then the points $(2002, 31.2)$ and $(2006, 55.9)$ represent the given data. The midpoint of the line segment joining these points is

$$\left(\frac{2002 + 2006}{2}, \frac{31.2 + 55.9}{2}\right) = (2004, 43.55).$$

Since the data is growing linearly, this suggests that 2004 revenues were approximately \$43.55 billion. ∎

GRAPHS

A **graph** is a set of points in the plane. Some graphs are based on data points, such as Figures 1–13 and 1–14. Other graphs arise from equations, as follows. A **solution** of an equation in variables x and y is a pair of numbers such that the substitution of the first number for x and the second for y produces a true statement. For instance, $(3, -2)$ is a solution of $5x + 7y = 1$ because

$$5 \cdot 3 + 7(-2) = 1,$$

and $(-2, 3)$ is *not* a solution because $5(-2) + 7 \cdot 3 \neq 1$. The **graph of an equation** in two variables is the set of points in the plane whose coordinates are solutions of the equation. Thus the graph is a *geometric picture of the solutions*.

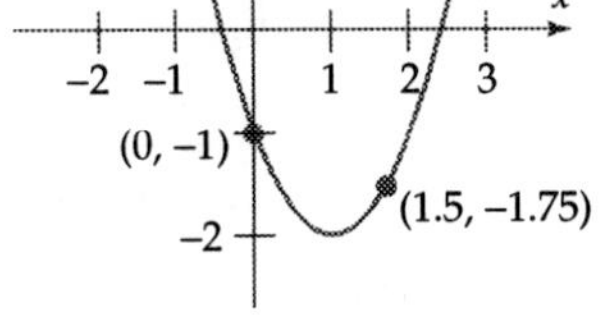

EXAMPLE 7

The graph of $y = x^2 - 2x - 1$ is shown in Figure 1–19. You can readily verify that each of the points whose coordinates are labeled is a solution of the equation. For instance, $(0, -1)$ is a solution because $-1 = 0^2 - 2(0) - 1$. ∎

A graph may intersect the x- or y-axis at one or more points. The x-coordinate of a point where the graph intersects the x-axis is called an ***x*-intercept** of the graph. Similarly, the y-coordinate of a point where the graph intersects the y-axis is called a ***y*-intercept** of the graph. Figure 1–20 shows some examples.

Figure 1–19

---

*Dell, Inc.

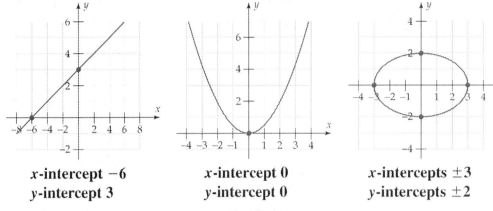

x-intercept −6   x-intercept 0   x-intercepts ±3
y-intercept 3   y-intercept 0   y-intercepts ±2

Figure 1–20

When the x- and y-intercepts cannot easily be read from the graph, they can often be found algebraically.

EXAMPLE 8

Find the x- and y-intercepts of the graph of $y = x^2 - 2x - 1$ in Figure 1–19.

SOLUTION   The points where the graph intersects the x-axis have 0 as their y-coordinate (see Figure 1–19). We can find their x-coordinates by setting $y = 0$ and solving the resulting equation,

$$x^2 - 2x - 1 = 0.$$

By the quadratic formula

$$x = \frac{-(-2) \pm \sqrt{(-2)^2 - 4 \cdot 1 \cdot (-1)}}{2 \cdot 1} = \frac{2 \pm \sqrt{8}}{2} \approx \begin{cases} -.4142 \\ 2.4142. \end{cases}$$

So the x-intercepts are approximately −.4142 and 2.4142.

In this case, you can read the y-intercept from the graph; it is −1. Because points on the y-axis have 0 as their x-coordinate, the y-intercept can be found algebraically by setting $x = 0$ in the equation and solving for y. ∎

The process in Example 8 can be summarized as follows.

x- and y-Intercepts

> To find the x-intercepts of the graph of an equation, set $y = 0$ and solve for x.
>
> To find the y-intercepts, set $x = 0$ and solve for y.

Reading and interpreting information from graphs is an essential skill if you want to succeed in this course and calculus.

EXAMPLE 9

Leslie Lahr takes out a 30-year mortgage on which her monthly payment is $850. One of the graphs in Figure 1–21 shows the portion of each payment that goes to interest and the other shows the portion that goes to paying off the principal.

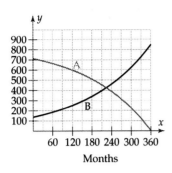

Figure 1–21

(a) Which graph is the interest portion and which is the principal portion?

(b) At the end of ten years (120 months), about how much of each payment goes for interest and how much for the principal?

SOLUTION

(a) The interest portion of the payment is the monthly interest due on the unpaid balance. This balance (and hence, the interest) is large at the beginning but slowly decreases as more payments are made. So the interest graph begins high and ends low—it must be graph A. Consequently, graph B shows the portion of each payment that goes to reducing the principal.

(b) The point (120, 600) on graph A shows that about $600 of the $850 payment was for interest. Hence, $250 was for principal, as the point (120, 250) on graph B indicates.   ∎

CIRCLES

If (c, d) is a point in the plane and r a positive number, then the **circle with center (c, d) and radius r** consists of all points (x, y) that lie r units from (c, d), as shown in Figure 1–22. According to the distance formula, the statement that "the distance from (x, y) to (c, d) is r units" is equivalent to:

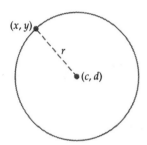

Figure 1–22

$$\sqrt{(x - c)^2 + (y - d)^2} = r$$

Squaring both sides shows that (x, y) satisfies this equation:

$$(x - c)^2 + (y - d)^2 = r^2$$

Reversing the procedure shows that any solution (x, y) of this equation is a point on the circle. Therefore

Circle Equation

The circle with center (c, d) and radius r is the graph of
$$(x - c)^2 + (y - d)^2 = r^2.$$

We say that $(x - c)^2 + (y - d)^2 = r^2$ is the **equation of the circle** with center (c, d) and radius r.

EXAMPLE 10

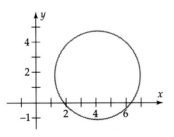

Figure 1–23

Identify the graph of the equation $(x - 4)^2 + (y - 2)^2 = 9$.

SOLUTION   Since $9 = 3^2$, we can write the equation as

$$(x - 4)^2 + (y - 2)^2 = 3^2.$$

Now the equation is of the form shown in the box above, with $c = 4$, $d = 2$ and $r = 3$. So the graph is a circle with center $(4, 2)$ and radius 3, as shown in Figure 1–23.   ∎

EXAMPLE 11

Find the equation of the circle with center $(-3, 2)$ and radius 2 and sketch its graph.

SOLUTION   Here the center is $(c, d) = (-3, 2)$ and the radius is $r = 2$, so the equation of the circle is

$$(x - c)^2 + (y - d)^2 = r^2$$
$$[x - (-3)]^2 + (y - 2)^2 = 2^2$$
$$(x + 3)^2 + (y - 2)^2 = 4.$$

Its graph is shown in Figure 1–24.   ■

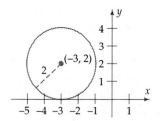

Figure 1–24

EXAMPLE 12

Find the equation of the circle with center $(3, -1)$ that passes through $(2, 4)$.

SOLUTION   We must first find the radius. Since $(2, 4)$ is on the circle, the radius is the distance from $(2, 4)$ to $(3, -1)$ as shown in Figure 1–25, namely,

$$\sqrt{(2 - 3)^2 + (4 - (-1))^2} = \sqrt{1 + 25} = \sqrt{26}.$$

The equation of the circle with center at $(3, -1)$ and radius $\sqrt{26}$ is

$$(x - 3)^2 + (y - (-1))^2 = (\sqrt{26})^2$$
$$(x - 3)^2 + (y + 1)^2 = 26$$
$$x^2 - 6x + 9 + y^2 + 2y + 1 = 26$$
$$x^2 + y^2 - 6x + 2y - 16 = 0.$$ ■

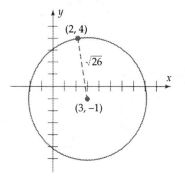

Figure 1–25

The equation of any circle can always be written in the form

$$x^2 + y^2 + Bx + Cy + D = 0$$

for some constants B, C, D, as in Example 12 (where $B = -6$, $C = 2$, $D = -16$). Conversely, the graph of such an equation can always be determined.

EXAMPLE 13

Show that the graph of

$$3x^2 + 3y^2 - 12x - 30y + 45 = 0$$

is a circle and find its center and radius.

SOLUTION   We will be completing the square, which requires that x^2 and y^2 each have coefficient 1. So we begin by dividing both sides of the equation by 3 and regrouping the terms.

$$x^2 + y^2 - 4x - 10y + 15 = 0$$
$$(x^2 - 4x) + (y^2 - 10y) = -15.$$

Next we complete the square in both expressions in parentheses (see page 22). To complete the square in $x^2 - 4x$, we add 4 (the square of half the coefficient of x), and to complete the square in $y^2 - 10y$, we add 25 (why?). To have an equivalent equation, we must add these numbers to *both* sides:

$$(x^2 - 4x + 4) + (y^2 - 10y + 25) = -15 + 4 + 25$$

$$(x - 2)^2 + (y - 5)^2 = 14$$

Since $14 = (\sqrt{14})^2$, this is the equation of the circle with center $(2, 5)$ and radius $\sqrt{14}$. ■

When the center of a circle of radius r is at the origin $(0, 0)$, its equation takes a simpler form.

Circle at the Origin

The circle with center $(0, 0)$ and radius r is the graph of
$$x^2 + y^2 = r^2.$$

Proof   Substitute $c = 0$ and $d = 0$ in the equation for the circle with center (c, d) and radius r.

$$(x - c)^2 + (y - d)^2 = r^2$$

$$(x - 0)^2 + (y - 0)^2 = r^2$$

$$x^2 + y^2 = r^2. \qquad ■$$

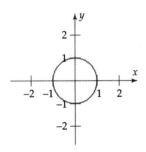

Figure 1–26

EXAMPLE 14

Letting $r = 1$ shows that the graph of $x^2 + y^2 = 1$ is the circle of radius 1 centered at the origin, as shown in Figure 1–26. This circle is called the **unit circle.** ■

EXERCISES 1.4

1. Find the coordinates of points *A–I*.

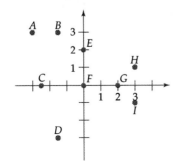

In Exercises 2–5, find the coordinates of the point P.

2. *P* lies 4 units to the left of the *y*-axis and 5 units below the *x*-axis.

3. *P* lies 3 units above the *x*-axis and on the same vertical line as $(-6, 7)$.

4. *P* lies 2 units below the *x*-axis, and its *x*-coordinate is three times its *y*-coordinate.

5. *P* lies 4 units to the right of the *y*-axis, and its *y*-coordinate is half its *x*-coordinate.

In Exercises 6–8, sketch a scatter plot and a line graph of the given data.

6. Tuition and fees at four-year public colleges in the fall of each year are shown in the table (*Source:* The College Board). Let $x = 0$ correspond to 2000.

Year	2000	2001	2002	2003	2004	2005
Tuition and Fees	3487	3725	4081	4694	5127	5491

7. The table shows sales of personal digital video recorders.* Let $x = 0$ correspond to 2000, and measure y in thousands.

Year	Number Sold
2000	257,000
2001	129,000
2002	143,000
2003	214,000
2004	315,000
2005	485,000

8. The maximum yearly contribution to an individual retirement account (IRA) was $3000 in 2003. It changed to $4000 in 2005 and will change to $5000 in 2008. Assuming 3% inflation, however, the picture is somewhat different. The table shows the maximum IRA contribution in fixed 2003 dollars. Let $x = 0$ correspond to 2000.

Year	Maximum Contribution
2003	3000
2004	2910
2005	3764
2006	3651
2007	3541
2008	4294

9. (a) If the first coordinate of a point is greater than 3 and its second coordinate is negative, in what quadrant does it lie?
(b) What is the answer in part (a) if the first coordinate is less than 3?

10. In what quadrant(s) does a point lie if the product of its coordinates is
(a) positive?   (b) negative?

11. (a) Plot the points $(3, 2)$, $(4, -1)$, $(-2, 3)$, and $(-5, -4)$.
(b) Change the sign of the y-coordinate in each of the points in part (a), and plot these new points.

----

*eBrain Market Research

(c) Explain how the points (a, b) and $(a, -b)$ are related graphically. [*Hint:* What are their relative positions with respect to the x-axis?]

12. (a) Plot the points $(5, 3)$, $(4, -2)$, $(-1, 4)$, and $(-3, -5)$.
(b) Change the sign of the x-coordinate in each of the points in part (a), and plot these new points.
(c) Explain how the points (a, b) and $(-a, b)$ are related graphically. [*Hint:* What are their relative positions with respect to the y-axis?]

In Exercises 13–20, find the distance between the two points and the midpoint of the segment joining them.

13. $(-3, 5)$, $(2, -7)$ **14.** $(2, 4)$, $(3, 6)$

15. $(-2, 5)$, $(-1, 2)$ **16.** $(-2, 3)$, $(-3, 2)$

17. $(\sqrt{2}, 1)$, $(\sqrt{3}, 2)$ **18.** $(-1, \sqrt{5})$, $(\sqrt{2}, -\sqrt{3})$

19. (a, b), (b, a) **20.** (s, t), $(0, 0)$

21. Which of the following points is closest to the origin?

$$(4, 4.2), (-3.5, 4.6), (-3, -5), (2, -5.5)$$

22. Which of the following points is closest to $(3, 2)$?

$$(0, 0), (4, 5.3), (-.6, 1.5), (1, -1)$$

23. Find the perimeter of the shaded region in the figure.

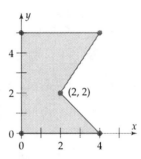

24. What is the perimeter of the triangle with vertices $(1, 1)$, $(5, 4)$, and $(-2, 5)$?

25. Find the area of the shaded region in Exercise 23. [*Hint:* What is the area of the triangle with vertices $(4, 0)$, $(2, 2)$, and $(4, 5)$?]

26. Find the area of the triangle with vertices $(1, 4)$, $(4, 3)$, and $(-2, -5)$. You may assume that there is a right angle at vertex $(1, 4)$.

In Exercises 27–29, show that the three points are the vertices of a right triangle, and state the length of the hypotenuse. [You may assume that a triangle with sides of lengths a, b, c is a right triangle with hypotenuse c provided that $a^2 + b^2 = c^2$.]

27. $(0, 0)$, $(1, 1)$, $(2, -2)$

28. $(3, -2)$, $(0, 4)$, $(-2, 3)$

29. $(1, 4)$, $(5, 2)$, $(3, -2)$

30. Suppose a baseball playing field is placed on the coordinate plane, as in Example 3.

    (a) Find the coordinates of first and third base.

    (b) If the left fielder is at the point (50, 325), how far is he from first base?

    (c) How far is the left fielder in part (b) from the right fielder, who is at the point (280, 20)?

31. A standard football field is 100 yards long and $53\frac{1}{3}$ yards wide. The quarterback, who is standing on the 10-yard line, 20 yards from the left sideline, throws the ball to a receiver who is on the 45-yard line, 5 yards from the right sideline, as shown in the figure.

    (a) How long was the pass? [*Hint:* Place the field in the first quadrant of the coordinate plane, with the left sideline on the *y*-axis and the goal line on the *x*-axis. What are the coordinates of the quarterback and the receiver?]

    (b) A player is standing halfway between the quarterback and the receiver. What are his coordinates?

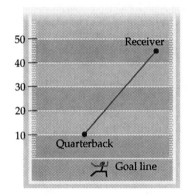

32. How far is the quarterback in Exercise 31 from a player who is on the 50-yard line, halfway between the sidelines?

33. The number of passengers annually on U.S. commercial airlines was 650 million in 2002 and is expected to be 1.05 billion in 2016.*

    (a) Represent this data graphically by two points.

    (b) Find the midpoint of the line segment joining these two points.

    (c) How might this midpoint be interpreted? What assumptions, if any, are needed to make this interpretation?

34. The net revenues of Pepsico were $26,971 million in 2003 and $32,562 million in 2005.† Estimate the net revenue in 2004.

In Exercises 35–40, determine whether the point is on the graph of the given equation.

35. (2, −1); $3x - y - 5 = 0$

36. (2, −1); $x^2 + y^2 - 6x + 8y = -15$

---

37. (6, 2); $3y + x = 12$

38. (1, −2); $3x + y = 12$

39. (1, −4); $(x - 2)^2 + (y + 5)^2 = 4$

40. (1, −1); $\dfrac{x^2}{2} + \dfrac{y^2}{3} = 1$

In Exercises 41–46, find the x- and y-intercepts of the graph of the equation.

41. $x^2 - 6x + y + 5 = 0$

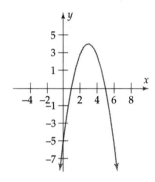

42. $x^2 - 2xy + 3y^2 = 1$

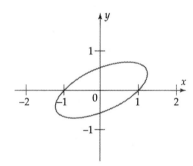

43. $(x - 2)^2 + y^2 = 9$

44. $(x + 1)^2 + (y - 2)^2 = 4$

45. $9x^2 + 24xy + 16y^2 + 90x - 128y = 0$

46. $2x^2 - 4xy + 2y^2 + 3x + 5y = 10$

47. The graph on the next page, which is based on data from the Actuarial Society of South Africa and assumes no changes in current behavior, shows the projected new cases of AIDS in South Africa (in millions) in coming years ($x = 0$ corresponds to 2000).

    (a) Estimate the number of new cases in 2010.

    (b) Estimate the year in which the largest number of new cases will occur. About how many new cases will there be in that year?

    (c) In what years will the number of new cases be below 7,000,000?

---

*Federal Aviation Agency.

†Pepsico annual reports.

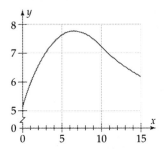

48. The graph shows the total number of alcohol-related car crashes in Ohio at a particular time of the day for the years 1991–2000.* Time is measured in hours after midnight. During what periods is the number of crashes

(a) below 5000?
(b) above 15,000?

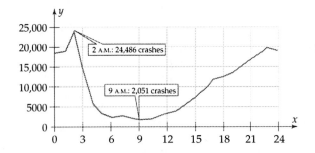

49. Many companies are changing their traditional employee pension plans to so-called cash balance plans. The graph shows pension accrual by age for two hypothetical plans.†

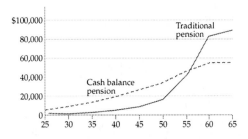

(a) Assuming that you can take your accrued pension benefits in cash when you leave the company before retirement, for what age group is the cash balance plan better?
(b) At what age is the accrued amount the same for either type of pension plan?
(c) If you remain with the company until retirement, how much better off are you with a traditional instead of a cash balance plan?

*The Cleveland *Plain Dealer.*
†Data from Steve J. Kopp and Lawrence W. Sher, *The Pension Forum,* Vol 11, No. 1. Graph from "What if a Pension Shift Hit Lawmakers Too?" by M. W. Walsh, *New York Times,* March 9, 2003. Copyright © 2003 The New York Times Co.

50. In an ongoing consumer confidence survey, respondents are asked two questions: Are jobs plentiful? Are jobs hard to get? The graph shows the percentage of people answering "yes" to each question over the years.*

(a) In what year did the most people feel that jobs were plentiful? In that year, approximately what percentage of people felt that jobs were hard to get?
(b) In what year did the most people feel that jobs were hard to get? In that year approximately what percentage of people felt that jobs were plentiful?
(c) In what years was the percentage of those who thought jobs were plentiful the same as the percentage of those that thought jobs were hard to get?

In Exercises 51–54, determine which of graphs A, B, C best describes the given situation.

51. You have a job that pays a fixed salary for the week. The graph shows your salary.

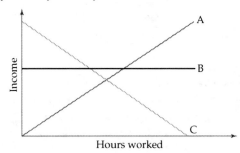

52. You have a job that pays an hourly wage. The graph shows your salary.

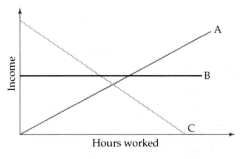

*Data for The Conference Board. Graph from "Tight U.S. Job Market Adds to Jitters Among Consumers." by A. Berenson, *The New York Times,* March 1, 2003. Copyright © 2003 The New York Times Co.

53. You take a ride on a Ferris wheel. The graph shows your distance from the ground.*

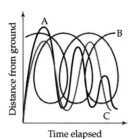

54. Alison's wading pool is filled with a hose by her big sister Emily, and Alison plays in the pool. When they are finished, Emily empties the pool. The graph shows the water level of the pool.

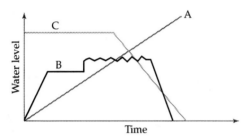

In Exercises 55–58, find the equation of the circle with given center and radius r.

55. $(-3, 4)$; $r = 2$

56. $(-3, -5)$; $r = 3$

57. $(0, 0)$; $r = \sqrt{3}$

58. $(5, -2)$; $r = 1$

In Exercises 59–62, sketch the graph of the equation. Label the x- and y-intercepts.

59. $(x - 5)^2 + (y + 2)^2 = 5$

60. $(x + 6)^2 + y^2 = 4$

61. $(x + 1)^2 + (y - 3)^2 = 9$

62. $(x - 2)^2 + (y - 4)^2 = 1$

In Exercises 63–68, find the center and radius of the circle whose equation is given.

63. $x^2 + y^2 + 8x - 6y - 15 = 0$

64. $15x^2 + 15y^2 = 10$

65. $x^2 + y^2 + 6x - 4y - 15 = 0$

66. $x^2 + y^2 + 10x - 75 = 0$

67. $x^2 + y^2 + 25x + 10y = -12$

68. $3x^2 + 3y^2 + 12x + 12 = 18y$

---

69. Determine whether each point lies inside, or outside, or on the circle

$$(x - 1)^2 + (y - 3)^2 = 4.$$

(a) $(2.2, 4.6)$ (b) $(-.2, 4.7)$ (c) $(-.1, 1.4)$
(d) $(2.6, 4.3)$ (e) $(-.6, 1.8)$

70. Do the circles with the following equations intersect?

$$(x - 3)^2 + (y + 2)^2 = 25 \quad \text{and} \quad (x + 3)^2 + (y - 2)^2 = 4$$

[*Hint:* Consider the radii and the distance between the centers.]

In Exercises 71–78, find the equation of the circle.

71. Center $(3, 3)$; passes through the origin.

72. Center $(-1, -3)$; passes through $(-4, -2)$.

73. Center $(1, 2)$; intersects x-axis at -1 and 3.

74. Center $(3, 1)$; diameter 2.

75. Center $(-5, 4)$; tangent (touching at one point) to the x-axis.

76. Center $(2, -6)$; tangent to the y-axis.

77. Endpoints of a diameter are $(3, 3)$ and $(1, -1)$.

78. Endpoints of a diameter are $(-3, 5)$ and $(7, -5)$.

79. One diagonal of a square has endpoints $(-3, 1)$ and $(2, -4)$. Find the endpoints of the other diagonal.

80. Find the vertices of all possible squares with this property: Two of the vertices are $(2, 1)$ and $(2, 5)$. [*Hint:* There are three such squares.]

81. Do Exercise 80 with (c, d) and (c, k) in place of $(2, 1)$ and $(2, 5)$.

82. Find the three points that divide the line segment from $(-4, 7)$ to $(10, -9)$ into four parts of equal length.

83. Find all points P on the x-axis that are 5 units from $(3, 4)$. [*Hint:* P must have coordinates $(x, 0)$ for some x and the distance from P to $(3, 4)$ is 5.]

84. Find all points on the y-axis that are 8 units from $(-2, 4)$.

85. Find all points with first coordinate 3 that are 6 units from $(-2, -5)$.

86. Find all points with second coordinate -1 that are 4 units from $(2, 3)$.

87. Find a number x such that $(0, 0)$, $(3, 2)$, and $(x, 0)$ are the vertices of an isosceles triangle, neither of whose two equal sides lie on the x-axis.

88. Do Exercise 87 if one of the two equal sides lies on the positive x-axis.

89. Show that the midpoint M of the hypotenuse of a right triangle is equidistant from the vertices of the triangle. [*Hint:* Place the triangle in the first quadrant of the plane, with right angle at the origin so that the situation looks like the figure.]

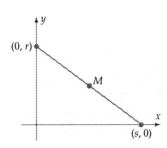

90. Show that the diagonals of a parallelogram bisect each other. [*Hint:* Place the parallelogram in the first quadrant with a vertex at the origin and one side along the x-axis so that the situation looks like the figure.]

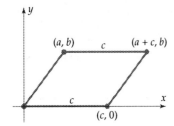

91. Show that the diagonals of a rectangle have the same length. [*Hint:* Place the rectangle in the first quadrant of the plane and label its vertices appropriately, as in Exercises 89–90.]

92. If the diagonals of a parallelogram have the same length, show that the parallelogram is actually a rectangle. [*Hint:* See Exercise 90.]

THINKERS

93. For each nonzero real number k, the graph of $(x - k)^2 + y^2 = k^2$ is a circle. Describe all possible such circles.

94. Suppose every point in the coordinate plane is moved 5 units straight up.

 (a) To what point does each of these points go:$(0, -5)$, $(2, 2)$, $(5, 0)$, $(5, 5)$, $(4, 1)$?
 (b) Which points go to each of the points in part (a)?
 (c) To what point does (a, b) go?
 (d) To what point does $(a, b - 5)$ go?
 (e) What point goes to $(-4a, b)$?
 (f) What points go to themselves?

95. Let (c, d) be any point in the plane with $c \neq 0$. Prove that (c, d) and $(-c, -d)$ lie on the same straight line through the origin, on opposite sides of the origin, the same distance from the origin. [*Hint:* Find the midpoint of the line segment joining (c, d) and $(-c, -d)$.]

96. *Proof of the Midpoint Formula*   Let P and Q be the points (x_1, y_1) and (x_2, y_2), respectively, and let M be the point with coordinates

$$\left(\frac{x_1 + x_2}{2}, \frac{y_1 + y_2}{2} \right).$$

Use the distance formula to compute the following:

 (a) The distance d from P to Q;
 (b) The distance d_1 from M to P;
 (c) The distance d_2 from M to Q.
 (d) Verify that $d_1 = d_2$.
 (e) Show that $d_1 + d_2 = d$. [*Hint:* Verify that $d_1 = \frac{1}{2}d$ and $d_2 = \frac{1}{2}d$.]
 (f) Explain why parts (d) and (e) show that M is the midpoint of PQ.

1.5   Lines

Section Objectives

■ Find the slope of a line.

■ Understand what its slope tells you about a line.

■ Construct and interpret the slope-intercept form of the equation of a line.

■ Identify the equations of horizontal and vertical lines.

■ Use point-slope form of the equation of a line.

■ Recognize the general form of the equation of a line.

■ Understand the relationship between parallel lines and their equations.

■ Understand the relationship between perpendicular lines and their equations.

■ Interpret slope as a rate of change.

When you move from a point P to a point Q on a line,* two numbers are involved, as illustrated in Figure 1–27:

(i) The vertical distance you move (the **change in y,** denoted Δy);

(ii) The horizontal distance you move (the **change in x,** denoted Δx).[†]

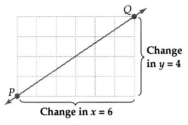

Change in $y = 4$

Change in $x = 6$

$$\frac{\Delta y}{\Delta x} = \frac{\text{Change in } y}{\text{Change in } x} = \frac{4}{6} = \frac{2}{3}$$

(a)

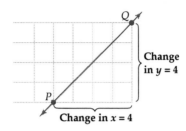

Change in $y = 4$

Change in $x = 4$

$$\frac{\Delta y}{\Delta x} = \frac{\text{Change in } y}{\text{Change in } x} = \frac{4}{4} = 1$$

(b)

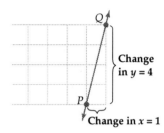

Change in $y = 4$

Change in $x = 1$

$$\frac{\Delta y}{\Delta x} = \frac{\text{Change in } y}{\text{Change in } x} = \frac{4}{1} = 4$$

(c)

Figure 1–27

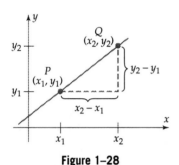

Figure 1–28

The number $\dfrac{\text{change in } y}{\text{change in } x}$ measures the steepness of the line: the steeper the line, the larger the number. In Figure 1–28, the grid allowed us to measure the change in y and the change in x. When the coordinates of P and Q are given, as in Figure 1–29, then:

The change in y is the difference of the y-coordinates of P and Q;

The change in x is the difference of the x-coordinates of P and Q.

Consequently, we have the following definition.

Slope of a Line

If (x_1, y_1) and (x_2, y_2) are points with $x_1 \neq x_2$, then the **slope** of the line through these points is the number

$$\frac{\Delta y}{\Delta x} = \frac{\text{change in } y}{\text{change in } x} = \frac{y_2 - y_1}{x_2 - x_1}.$$

EXAMPLE 1

Find the slope of the line through the two points.

(a) $(0, -1)$ and $(4, 1)$ (b) $(-2, 3)$ and $(2, -1)$

(c) $(1, 1)$ and $(3, 1)$ (d) $(3, -1)$ and $(3, 2)$

SOLUTION

(a) We apply the formula in the preceding box, with $x_1 = 0$, $y_1 = -1$ and $x_2 = 4$, $y_2 = 1$:

$$\text{Slope} = \frac{\Delta y}{\Delta x} = \frac{y_2 - y_1}{x_2 - x_1} = \frac{1 - (-1)}{4 - 0} = \frac{2}{4} = \frac{1}{2}.$$

*In this section, "line" means "straight line" and movement is from left to right.
[†]Δ (pronounced "delta") is the Greek letter D.

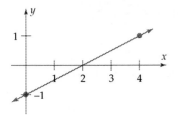

Figure 1–29

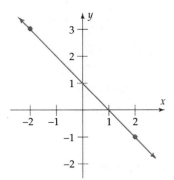

Figure 1–301

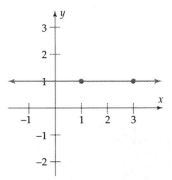

Figure 1–31

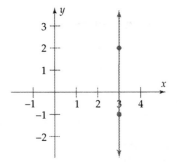

Figure 1–32

The order of the points makes no difference; if you use $(4, 1)$ for (x_1, y_1) and $(0, -1)$ for (x_2, y_2), you obtain the same number:

$$\text{Slope} = \frac{\Delta y}{\Delta x} = \frac{y_2 - y_1}{x_2 - x_1} = \frac{-1 - 1}{0 - 4} = \frac{-2}{-4} = \frac{1}{2}.$$

The slope is positive and the line through the two points rises from left to right, as shown in Figure 1–29.

(b) We have $(x_1, y_1) = (-2, 3)$ and $(x_2, y_2) = (2, -1)$, as shown in Figure 1–30. Hence,

$$\text{Slope} = \frac{\Delta y}{\Delta x} = \frac{y_2 - y_1}{x_2 - x_1} = \frac{-1 - 3}{2 - (-2)} = \frac{-4}{4} = -1.$$

The slope is negative and the line through the points falls from left to right.

(c) The points $(1, 1)$ and $(3, 1)$ lie on a horizontal line, as shown in Figure 1–31, and

$$\text{Slope} = \frac{\Delta y}{\Delta x} = \frac{y_2 - y_1}{x_2 - x_1} = \frac{1 - 1}{3 - 1} = \frac{0}{2} = 0.$$

A similar argument shows that *every horizontal line has slope* 0.

(d) Figure 1–32 shows that the points lie on a vertical line. Applying the slope formula to $(x_1, y_1) = (3, -1)$ and $(x_2, y_2) = (3, 2)$ yields

$$\text{Slope} = \frac{y_2 - y_1}{x_2 - x_1} = \frac{2 - (-1)}{3 - 3} = \frac{3}{0} \text{ not defined!}$$

The same argument works for any vertical line: *the slope of a vertical line is not defined.* ∎

CAUTION

When finding slopes, you must subtract the *y*-coordinates and *x*-coordinates in the same order. With the points $(3, 4)$ and $(1, 8)$, for instance, if you use $8 - 4$ in the numerator, you must use $1 - 3$ in the denominator (*not* $3 - 1$).

EXAMPLE 2

The lines shown in Figure 1–33 on the next page are determined by these points:

L_1: $(-1, -1)$ and $(0, 2)$ L_2: $(0, 2)$ and $(2, 4)$ L_3: $(-6, 2)$ and $(3, 2)$

L_4: $(-3, 5)$ and $(3, -1)$ L_5: $(1, 0)$ and $(2, -2)$.

Their slopes are as follows:

Points	Slopes
$(-1, -1)$ and $(0, 2)$	$L_1: \dfrac{2 - (-1)}{0 - (-1)} = \dfrac{3}{1} = 3$
$(0, 2)$ and $(2, 4)$	$L_2: \dfrac{4 - 2}{2 - 0} = \dfrac{2}{2} = 1$
$(-6, 2)$ and $(3, 2)$	$L_3: \dfrac{2 - 2}{3 - (-6)} = \dfrac{0}{9} = 0$
$(-3, 5)$ and $(3, -1)$	$L_4: \dfrac{-1 - 5}{3 - (-3)} = \dfrac{-6}{6} = -1$
$(1, 0)$ and $(2, -2)$	$L_5: \dfrac{-2 - 0}{2 - 1} = \dfrac{-2}{1} = -2$

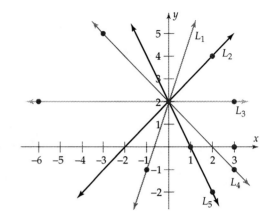

Figure 1–33 ∎

As Examples 1 and 2 illustrate, the slope is a number m that measures how steeply a line rises or falls, as summarized below.

Properties of Slope

There are four possibilities for a line L with slope m.

$m > 0$	$m < 0$	$m = 0$	m is not defined
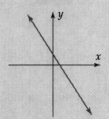	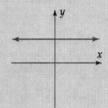		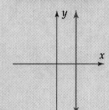
The line rises from left to right.	The line falls from left to right.	The line is horizontal.	The line is vertical.
The larger m is, the more steeply the line rises.	The larger $|m|$ is, the more steeply the line falls.		
[*See Example 1(a) and lines L_1 and L_2 in Example 2.*]	[*See Example 1(b) and lines L_4 and L_5 in Example 2.*]	[*See Example 1(c) and line L_3 in Example 2.*]	[*See Example 1(d)*]

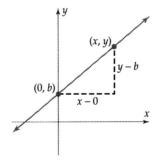

Figure 1–34

SLOPE-INTERCEPT FORM

Let L be a nonvertical line with slope m and y-intercept b. Then $(0, b)$ is a point on L. Let (x, y) be any other point on L. Using the points $(0, b)$ and (x, y) to compute the slope of L (see Figure 1–34), we have

$$\text{Slope of } L = \frac{y - b}{x - 0}.$$

Since the slope of L is m, this equation becomes

$$m = \frac{y - b}{x}$$

Multiply both sides by x: $mx = y - b$

Rearrange terms: $y = mx + b$

Thus the coordinates of any point on L satisfy the equation $y = mx + b$. So we have the following fact.

Slope-Intercept Form

> The line with slope m and y-intercept b is the graph of the equation
>
> $$y = mx + b.$$

EXAMPLE 3

List the slope and y-intercept of the line whose equation is given and describe its graph.

(a) $y = 3x - 5$ (b) $2x + y = 7$

SOLUTION

(a) The equation has the form in the preceding box, with $m = 3$ and $b = -5$, so the line has slope 3 and y-intercept -5. This shows that the line rises from left to right and passes through $(0, -5)$.

(b) First, solve the equation for y: $y = -2x + 7$. Here the slope is $m = -2$ and the y-intercept is $b = 7$. The line falls from left to right and passes through $(0, 7)$. ∎

EXAMPLE 4

Show that the graph of $2y - 5x = 2$ is a straight line. Find its slope, and graph the line.

SOLUTION   We begin by solving the equation for y:

Add $5x$ to both sides: $2y = 5x + 2$

Divide both sides by 2: $y = 2.5x + 1.$

The equation now has the form in the preceding box, with $m = 2.5$ and $b = 1$. Therefore, its graph is the line with slope 2.5 and y-intercept 1.

Since the y-intercept is 1, the point $(0, 1)$ is on the graph. To find another point on the line, choose a value for x, say, $x = 2$, and compute the corresponding value of y:

$$y = 2.5x + 1 = 2.5(2) + 1 = 6.$$

Hence, $(2, 6)$ is on the line. Plotting the line through $(0, 1)$ and $(2, 6)$ produces Figure 1–35. ∎

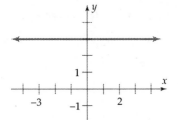

Figure 1–35

EXAMPLE 5

Describe and sketch the graph of the equation $y = 3$.

SOLUTION   We can write $y = 3$ as $y = 0x + 3$. So its graph is a line with slope 0, which means that the line is horizontal, and y-intercept 3, which means that the line crosses the y-axis at 3. This is sufficient information to obtain the graph in Figure 1–36. ∎

Figure 1–36

Example 5 is an illustration of this fact.

Horizontal Lines

The horizontal line with y-intercept b is the graph of the equation

$$y = b.$$

Because slope is not defined for vertical lines, the equations of such lines have a different form from those examined above.

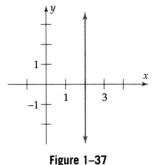

Figure 1–37

EXAMPLE 6

We can easily list some points on the line in Figure 1–37: $(2, 0)$, $(2, 1)$, $(2, -1)$, $(2, -1.5)$, and so on. Every point on this line has first coordinate 2. So every point satisfies $x + 0y = 2$. Hence, the line is the graph of $x = 2$. ■

Example 6 illustrates these facts:

Vertical Lines

The vertical line with x-intercept c is the graph of the equation

$$x = c.$$

The slope of this line is undefined.

POINT-SLOPE FORM

Suppose the line L passes through the point (x_1, y_1) and has slope m. Let (x, y) be any other point on L. Using the points (x_1, y_1) and (x, y) to compute the slope m of L (see Figure 1–38), we have

$$\frac{y - y_1}{x - x_1} = \text{slope of } L$$

$$\frac{y - y_1}{x - x_1} = m$$

Multiply both sides by $x - x_1$: $y - y_1 = m(x - x_1).$

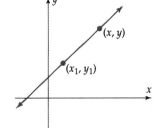

Figure 1–38

Thus, the coordinates of every point on L satisfy the equation

$$y - y_1 = m(x - x_1),$$

and we have this fact:

Point-Slope Form

The line with slope m through the point (x_1, y_1) is the graph of the equation

$$y - y_1 = m(x - x_1).$$

EXAMPLE 7

The tangent line to the graph of $y = 2x^2 - 8$ at the point $(1, -6)$ is shown in Figure 1–39. In calculus, it is shown that this line passes through $(1, -6)$ and has slope 4. Find the equation of the tangent line.

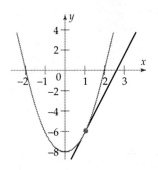

Figure 1–39

SOLUTION   Substitute 4 for m and $(1, -6)$ for (x_1, y_1) in the point-slope equation:

$$y - y_1 = m(x - x_1)$$

$$y - (-6) = 4(x - 1) \qquad \text{[point-slope form]}$$

$$y + 6 = 4x - 4$$

$$y = 4x - 10 \qquad \text{[slope-intercept form]} \qquad \blacksquare$$

EXAMPLE 8

The annual out-of-pocket spending (per person) on doctors and clinical services was approximately \$105 in 1997. According to projections from the Health Care Financing Committee, this cost is expected to rise linearly to \$196 in 2010, as indicated in Figure 1–40.

(a) Find an equation that gives the out-of-pocket cost y in year x.

(b) Use this equation to estimate the out-of-pocket costs in 2006 and 2009.

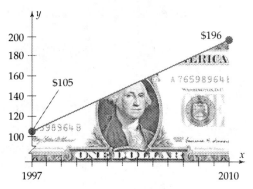

Figure 1–40

SOLUTION

(a) Let $x = 0$ correspond to 1997, so that $x = 13$ corresponds to 2010. Then the given information can be represented by the points $(0, 105)$ and $(13, 196)$. We must find the equation of the line through these points. Its slope is

$$\frac{196 - 105}{13 - 0} = \frac{91}{13} = 7.$$

Now we use the slope 7 and one of the points $(0, 105)$ or $(13, 196)$ to find the equation of the line. It doesn't matter which point, since both lead to the same equation.

$$y - y_1 = m(x - x_1) \qquad\qquad y - y_1 = m(x - x_1)$$

$$y - 105 = 7(x - 0) \qquad\qquad y - 196 = 7(x - 13)$$

$$y = 7x + 105 \qquad\qquad y - 196 = 7x - 91$$

$$y = 7x + 105.$$

(b) Since 2006 corresponds to $x = 9$, the projected out-of-pocket costs in 2006 are

$$y = 7x + 105 = 7 \cdot 9 + 105 = \$168.$$

The costs in 2009 $(x = 12)$ are

$$y = 7x + 105 = 7 \cdot 12 + 105 = \$189. \qquad \blacksquare$$

GENERAL FORM

By rearranging terms, if necessary, the equation of any line can be written in the **general form** $Ax + By = C$ for some constants A, B, and C. For instance,

This equation	can be written as
$y = 4x - 10$	$4x - 1y = 10$
$y - 196 = 7(x - 13)$	$-7x + 1y = 105$
$y = 3$	$0x + 1y = 3$
$x = 2$	$1x + 0y = 2$

In summary:

General Form

> Every line is the graph of an equation of the form
> $$Ax + By = C,$$
> where A and B are not both zero.

EXAMPLE 9

Graph $3x + 2y = 6$.

SOLUTION   From the preceding box, we know that the graph is a line. It is easily graphed by finding its intercepts.

y-intercept	*x*-intercept
Set $x = 0$ and solve for y.	Set $y = 0$ and solve for x.
$3x + 2y = 6$	$3x + 2y = 6$
$3 \cdot 0 + 2y = 6$	$3x + 2 \cdot 0 = 6$
$2y = 6$	$3x = 6$
$y = 3$	$x = 2$

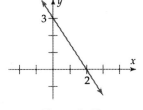

Figure 1–41

The y-intercept is 3 and the x-intercept is 2, which leads to the graph in Figure 1–41. ∎

PARALLEL AND PERPENDICULAR LINES

The slope of a line measures how steeply it rises or falls. Since parallel lines rise or fall equally steeply, the following fact should be plausible (see Exercises 93–94 for a proof).

Parallel Lines

> Two nonvertical lines are parallel exactly when they have the same slope.

EXAMPLE 10

Find the equation of the line L through $(2, -1)$ that is parallel to the line M whose equation is $3x - 2y + 6 = 0$.

SOLUTION   First find the slope of M by rewriting its equation in slope-intercept form:

$$3x - 2y + 6 = 0$$
$$-2y = -3x - 6$$
$$y = \frac{3}{2}x + 3.$$

Therefore M has slope $3/2$. The parallel line L must have the same slope, $3/2$. Since $(2, -1)$ is on L, we can use the point-slope form to find its equation:

$$y - y_1 = m(x - x_1)$$

$$y - (-1) = \frac{3}{2}(x - 2) \qquad \text{[point-slope form]}$$

$$y + 1 = \frac{3}{2}x - 3$$

$$y = \frac{3}{2}x - 4 \qquad \text{[slope-intercept form]} \qquad ■$$

Two lines that meet in a right angle (90° angle) are said to be **perpendicular.** As you might suspect, there is a close relationship between the slopes of two perpendicular lines.

Perpendicular Lines

> Two nonvertical lines, with slopes m_1 and m_2, are perpendicular exactly when the product of their slopes is -1, that is,
>
> $$m_1 m_2 = -1, \quad \text{or equivalently,} \quad m_1 = -\frac{1}{m_2}.$$

A proof of this fact is outlined in Exercise 96.

EXAMPLE 11

In Figure 1–42, the line L through $(0, 2)$ and $(1, 5)$ appears to be perpendicular to the line M through $(-3, -2)$ and $(3, -4)$. Verify algebraically that the lines are perpendicular.

SOLUTION   Compute the slope of the lines:

$$\text{Slope } L = \frac{5 - 2}{1 - 0} = 3 \quad \text{and} \quad \text{slope } M = \frac{-4 - (-2)}{3 - (-3)} = \frac{-2}{6} = -\frac{1}{3}.$$

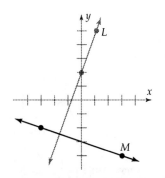

Figure 1–42

Since $3(-1/3) = -1$, the lines L and M are perpendicular.   ■

EXAMPLE 12

Find the equation of the perpendicular bisector of the line segment with endpoints $(-5, -4)$ and $(7, 2)$.

SOLUTION   The perpendicular bisector M goes through the midpoint of the line segment from $(-5, -4)$ and $(7, 2)$. The midpoint formula (page 38) shows that this midpoint is

$$\left(\frac{x_1 + x_2}{2}, \frac{y_1 + y_2}{2}\right) = \left(\frac{-5 + 7}{2}, \frac{-4 + 2}{2}\right) = (1, -1).$$

The line L through $(-5, -4)$ and $(7, 2)$ has slope

$$\frac{y_2 - y_1}{x_2 - x_1} = \frac{2 - (-4)}{7 - (-5)} = \frac{6}{12} = \frac{1}{2}.$$

Since M is perpendicular to L, we have (slope M)(slope L) $= -1$, so that

$$\text{Slope } M = \frac{-1}{\text{slope } L} = \frac{-1}{1/2} = -2.$$

Thus M is the line through $(1, -1)$ with slope -2, and its equation is

$$y - (-1) = -2(x - 1) \qquad \text{[point-slope form]}$$

$$y = -2x + 1. \qquad \text{[slope-intercept form]}$$

RATES OF CHANGE

We have seen that the geometric interpretation of slope is that it measures the *steepness* or direction of a line. The next examples show that slope can also be interpreted as a *rate of change*.

EXAMPLE 13

According to the *Kelley Blue Book,* a Ford Focus ZX5 hatchback that is worth $14,632 today will be worth $10,120 in 3 years (if it is in good condition with average mileage).

(a) Assuming linear depreciation, find the equation that gives the value y of the car in year x.

(b) At what rate is the car depreciating?

(c) What will the car be worth in 6 years?

SOLUTION

(a) Linear depreciation means that the value equation is linear. So the equation is of the form $y = mx + b$ for some constants m and b. Since the car is worth $14,632 now (that is, $y = 14{,}632$ when $x = 0$), we have

$$y = mx + b$$

Let $x = 0$ and $y = 14{,}632$: $14{,}632 = m \cdot 0 + b$

$$b = 14{,}632.$$

So the equation is $y = mx + 14{,}632$. Since the car is worth \$10,120 in 3 years (that is, $y = 10{,}120$ when $x = 3$), we have

$$y = mx + 14{,}632$$

Let $x = 3$ and $y = 10{,}120$:	$10{,}120 = m \cdot 3 + 14{,}632$
Subtract 14,632 from both sides:	$-4512 = 3m$
Divide both sides by 3:	$m = -1504$

Therefore, the value equation is $y = -1504x + 14{,}632$.

(b) Consider this table:

Year x	0	1	2	3	4
$y = -1504x + 14{,}632$	14,632	13,128	11,624	10,120	8616

You can easily verify that the car depreciates (decreases in value) \$1504 each year (that is, each time x changes by 1). In other words, the value changes at the *rate* of -1504 per year. This *rate* is the *slope* of the line $y = -1504x + 14{,}632$.

(c) The value of the car after 6 years ($x = 6$) is given by

$$y = -1504x + 14{,}632$$

Let $x = 6$: $y = -1504(6) + 14{,}632 = 5608.$

The car is worth \$5608 in 6 years. ■

EXAMPLE 14

A factory that makes can openers has fixed costs (for building, fixtures, machinery, etc.) of \$26,000. The variable cost (materials and labor) for making one can opener is \$2.75.

(a) Find the cost equation that gives the total cost y of producing x can openers and sketch its graph.

(b) At what rate does the total cost increase as more can openers are made?

(c) What is the total cost of making 1000 can openers? 20,000? 40,000?

(d) In part (c), what is the average cost per can opener in each case?

SOLUTION

(a) Since each can opener costs \$2.75, the variable cost of making x can openers is $2.75x$. The total cost y of making x can openers is

$$y = \text{variable costs} + \text{fixed costs}$$
$$y = 2.75x + 26{,}000.$$

The graph of this equation is the line in Figure 1–43.

(b) The cost equation shows that y increases by 2.75 each time x increases by 1. That is, total cost is increasing at the rate of \$2.75 per can opener. This rate of change is the slope the cost equation line $y = 2.75x + 26{,}000$.

(c) The cost of making 1000 can openers is

$$y = 2.75x + 26{,}000 = 2.75(1000) + 26{,}000 = \$28{,}750.$$

Similarly, the cost of making 20,000 can openers is

$$y = 2.75(20{,}000) + 26{,}000 = \$81{,}000,$$

and the cost of 40,000 is

$$y = 2.75(40{,}000) + 26{,}000 = \$136{,}000.$$

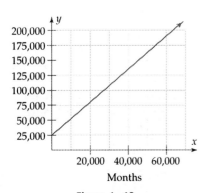

Months

Figure 1–43

(d) The average cost per can opener in each case is the total cost divided by the number of can openers. So the average cost per can opener is as follows.

For 1000: $28,750/1000 = $28.75 per can opener;
For 20,000: $81,000/20,000 = $4.05 per can opener;
For 40,000: $136,000/40,000 = $3.40 per can opener.   ■

Examples 13 and 14 illustrate this fact.

Linear Rate of Change

> The slope m of the line with equation
> $$y = mx + b$$
> is the rate of change of y with respect to x.

EXERCISES 1.5

1. For which of the line segments in the figure is the slope
  (a) largest?   (b) smallest?
  (c) largest in absolute value? (d) closest to zero?

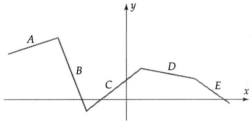

2. The doorsill of a campus building is 5 feet above ground level. To allow wheelchair access, the steps in front of the door are to be replaced by a straight ramp with constant slope $1/12$, as shown in the figure. How long must the ramp be? [The answer is *not* 60 feet.]

In Exercises 3–6, find the slope of the line through the given points.

3. $(1, 2); (3, 7)$

4. $(-1, -2); (2, -1)$

5. $(1/4, 0); (3/4, 2)$

6. $(\sqrt{2}, -1); (2, -9)$

In Exercises 7–10, find a number t such that the line passing through the two given points has slope -2.

7. $(0, t); (9, 4)$

8. $(1, t); (-2, 4)$

9. $(t + 1, 5); (6, -3t + 7)$

10. $(t, t); (5, 9)$

11. Let L be a nonvertical straight line through the origin. L intersects the vertical line through $(1, 0)$ at a point P. Show that the second coordinate of P is the slope of L.

12. On one graph, sketch five line segments, not all meeting at a single point, whose slopes are five different positive numbers. Do this in such a way that the left-hand line has the largest slope, the second line from the left has the next largest slope, and so on.

In Exercises 13–16, match the given equation with the line shown below that most closely resembles its graph.

(a) 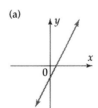   (b)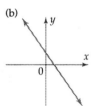

(c) 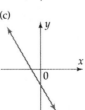   (d)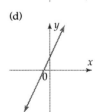

13. $y = 3x + 2$

14. $y = -3x + 2$

15. $y = 3x - 2$

16. $y = -3x - 2$

In Exercises 17–20, find the equation of the line with y-intercept b and slope m.

17. $b = 5, m = 4$

18. $b = -3, m = -7$

19. $b = 1.5, m = -2.3$ **20.** $b = -4.5, m = 2.5$

In Exercises 21–24, find the equation of the line.

21.

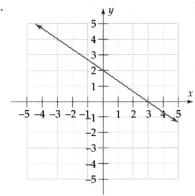

22.

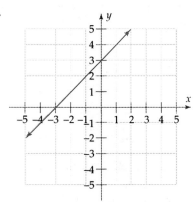

23.

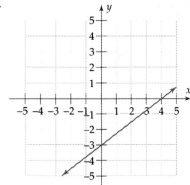

24.

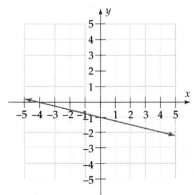

In Exercises 25–28, find the slope and y-intercept of the line whose equation is given.

25. $2x - y + 5 = 0$ **26.** $4x + 3y = 5$

27. $3(x - 2) + y = 7 - 6(y + 4)$

28. $2(y - 3) + (x - 6) = 4(x + 1) - 2$

In Exercises 29–32, find the equation of the line with slope m that passes through the given point.

29. $m = 1; (4, 7)$ **30.** $m = 2; (-2, 1)$

31. $m = -1; (6, 2)$ **32.** $m = 0; (-4, -5)$

In Exercises 33–36, find the equation of the line through the given points.

33. $(0, -5)$ and $(-3, -2)$ **34.** $(4, 3)$ and $(2, -1)$

35. $(6/5, 3/5)$ and $(1/5, 3)$ **36.** $(6, 7)$ and $(6, 15)$

In Exercises 37–42, graph the equation. Label all intercepts.

37. $3x + 5y = 15$ **38.** $2x - 3y = 12$

39. $2y - x = 2$ **40.** $4x + 5y = -10$

41. $3x - 2y = 0$ **42.** $2x + 6y = 0$

In Exercises 43–46, determine whether the line through P and Q is parallel or perpendicular to the line through R and S or neither.

43. $P = (2, 5), Q = (-1, -1)$ and $R = (4, 2), S = (6, 1)$.

44. $P = (0, 3/2), Q = (1, 1)$ and $R = (2, 7), S = (3, 9)$.

45. $P = (-3, 1/3), Q = (1, -1)$ and $R = (2, 0), S = (4, -2/3)$.

46. $P = (3, 3), Q = (-3, -1)$ and $R = (2, -2), S = (4, -5)$.

In Exercises 47–49, determine whether the lines whose equations are given are parallel, perpendicular, or neither.

47. $2x + y - 2 = 0$ and $4x + 2y + 18 = 0$.

48. $3x + y - 3 = 0$ and $6x + 2y + 17 = 0$.

49. $y = 2x + 4$ and $.5x + y = -3$.

50. Do the points $(-4, 6), (-1, 12)$, and $(-7, 0)$ all lie on the same straight line? [*Hint:* Use slopes.]

51. Are $(9, 6), (-1, 2)$, and $(1, -3)$ the vertices of a right triangle? [*Hint:* Use slopes.]

52. Are the points $(-5, -2) (-3, 1), (3, 0)$, and $(5, 3)$ the vertices of a parallelogram?

In Exercises 53–56, find the equation of the perpendicular bisector of the line segment joining the two given points.

53. $(1, 3), (3, 7)$ **54.** $(-3, 6), (7, 2)$

55. $(2, -3), (4, 7)$ **56.** $(-6, 2), (6, -7)$

In Exercises 57–64, find an equation for the line satisfying the given conditions.

57. Through $(-2, 1)$ with slope 3.

58. y-intercept -7 and slope 1.

59. Through $(2, 3)$ and parallel to $3x - 2y = 5$.

60. Through $(1, -2)$ and perpendicular to $y = 2x - 3$.

61. x-intercept 5 and y-intercept -5.

62. Through $(-5, 2)$ and parallel to the line through $(1, 2)$ and $(4, 3)$.

63. Through $(-1, 3)$ and perpendicular to the line through $(0, 1)$ and $(2, 3)$.

64. y-intercept 3 and perpendicular to $2x - y + 6 = 0$.

65. Find a real number k such that $(3, -2)$ is on the line $kx - 2y + 7 = 0$.

66. Find a real number k such that the line $3x - ky + 2 = 0$ has y-intercept -3.

If P is a point on a circle with center C, then the tangent line to the circle at P is the straight line through P that is perpendicular to the radius CP. In Exercises 67–70, find the equation of the tangent line to the circle at the given point.

67. $x^2 + y^2 = 25$ at $(3, 4)$ [*Hint:* Here C is $(0, 0)$ and P is $(3, 4)$; what is the slope of radius CP?]

68. $x^2 + y^2 = 169$ at $(-5, 12)$

69. $(x - 1)^2 + (y - 3)^2 = 5$ at $(2, 5)$

70. $x^2 + y^2 + 6x - 8y + 15 = 0$ at $(-2, 1)$

71. Let A, B, C, D be nonzero real numbers. Show that the lines $Ax + By + C = 0$ and $Ax + By + D = 0$ are parallel.

72. Let L be a line that is neither vertical nor horizontal and that does not pass through the origin. Show that L is the graph of $\dfrac{x}{a} + \dfrac{y}{b} = 1$, where a is the x-intercept and b is the y-intercept of L.

73. Worldwide motor vehicle production was about 60 million in 2000 and about 66 million in 2005.

(a) Let the x-axis denote time and the y-axis the number of vehicles (in millions). Let $x = 0$ correspond to 2000. Fill in the blanks: the given data is represented by the points (___, 60) and (5, ___).

(b) Find the linear equation determined by the two points in part (a).

(c) Use the equation in part (b) to estimate the number of vehicles produced in 2004.

(d) If this model remains accurate, when will vehicle production reach 72 million?

74. Carbon dioxide (CO_2) concentration is measured regularly at the Mauna Loa observatory in Hawaii. The mean annual concentration in parts per million in various years is given in the table.*

Year	Concentration (ppm)
1984	344.4
1989	352.9
1994	358.9
1999	368.3
2004	377.4

*C. D. Keeling and T. P. Whorf, Scripps Institution of Oceanography

(a) Let $x = 0$ correspond to 1980. List the five data points given by the table. Do these points all lie on a single line? How can you tell?

(b) Use the data points from 1984 and 2004 to write a linear equation to model CO_2 concentration over time.

(c) Do part (b), using the data points from 1994 and 2004.

(d) Use the two models to estimate the CO_2 concentration in 1989 and 1999. Do the models overestimate or underestimate the concentration?

(e) What do the two models say about the concentration in 2008? Which model do you think is the more accurate? Why?

75. Suppose you drive along the Ohio Turnpike in an area where the grade of the road is 3% (which means that the line representing the road in the figure has slope .03.)

(a) Find the equation of the line representing the road. [*Hint:* Your trip begins at the origin.]

(b) If you drive on the road for one mile, how many feet higher are you at the end of the mile than you were at the beginning? [*Hint:* Express one mile as 5280 feet. Use the equation from part (a) to express x in terms of y, and then use the Pythagorean Theorem to find y.]

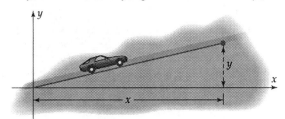

76. The Missouri American Water Company charges residents of St. Louis County $6.15 per month plus $2.0337 per thousand gallons used.*

(a) Find the monthly bill when 3000 gallons of water are used. What is the bill when no water is used?

(b) Write a linear equation that gives the monthly bill y when x thousand gallons are used.

(c) If the monthly bill is $22.42, how much water was used?

77. At sea level, water boils at 212°F. At a height of 1100 feet, water boils at 210°F. The relationship between boiling point and height is linear.

(a) Find an equation that gives the boiling point y of water at a height of x feet.

Find the boiling point of water in each of the following cities (whose altitudes are given).

(b) Cincinnati, OH (550 feet)

(c) Springfield, MO (1300 feet)

(d) Billings, MT (3120 feet)

(e) Flagstaff, AZ (6900 feet)

78. According to the Center of Science in the Public Interest, the maximum healthy weight for a person who is 5 feet 5 inches tall is 150 pounds, and the maximum healthy

*Residential rates for a 5/8 inch meter in March 2006, assuming monthly billing and maximum usage of 16,000 gallons.

weight for someone 6 feet 3 inches tall is 200 pounds. The relationship between weight and height here is linear.

(a) Find a linear equation that gives the maximum healthy weight y for a person whose height is x inches over 4 feet 10 inches. (Thus $x = 0$ corresponds to 4 feet 10 inches, $x = 2$ to 5 feet, etc.)

(b) What is the maximum healthy weight for a person whose height is 5 feet? 6 feet?

(c) How tall is a person who is at a maximum healthy weight of 220 pounds?

79. The number of unmarried couples in the United States who live together was 3.2 million in 1990 and grew in a linear fashion to 5.5 million in 2000.*

(a) Let $x = 0$ correspond to 1990. Write a linear equation expressing the number y of unmarried couples living together (in millions) in year x.

(b) Assuming the equation remains accurate, estimate the number of unmarried couples living together in 2010.

(c) When will the number of unmarried couples living together reach 10,100,000?

80. The percentage of people 25 years old and older who have a Bachelor's degree or higher was about 25.6 in 2000 and 27.7 in 2004.*

(a) Find a linear equation that gives the percentage of people 25 and over who have a Bachelor's degree or higher in terms of time t, where t is the number of years since 2000. Assume that this equations remains valid in the future.

(b) What will the percentage be in 2010?

(c) When will 34% of those 25 and over have a Bachelor's degree or higher?

81. At the Factory in Example 14, the cost of producing x can openers is given by $y = 2.75x + 26,000$.

(a) Write an equation that gives the average cost per can opener when x can openers are produced.

(b) How many can openers should be made to have an average cost of $3 per can opener?

82. Suppose the cost of making x TV sets is given by $y = 145x + 120,000$.

(a) Write an equation that gives the average cost per set when x sets are made.

(b) How many sets should be made in order to have an average cost per set of $175?

83. The profit p (in thousands of dollars) on x thousand units of a specialty item is $p = .6x - 14.5$. The cost c of manufacturing x thousand items is given by $c = .8x + 14.5$.

(a) Find an equation that gives the revenue r from selling x thousand items.

(b) How many items must be sold for the company to break even (i.e., for revenue to equal cost)?

84. A publisher has fixed costs of $110,000 for a mathematics text. The variable costs are $50 per book. The book sells for $72. Find equations that give

(a) The cost c of making x books

(b) The revenue r from selling x books

(c) The profit p from selling x books

(d) What is the publisher's break-even point (see Exercise 83(b))?

Use the graph and the following information for Exercises 85–86. Rocky is an "independent" ticket dealer who markets choice tickets for Los Angeles Lakers home games. (California currently has no laws against ticket scalping.) Each graph shows how many tickets will be demanded by buyers at a particular price. For instance, when the Lakers play the Chicago Bulls, the graph shows that at a price of $160, no tickets are demanded. As the price (y-coordinate) gets lower, the number of tickets demanded (x-coordinate) increases.

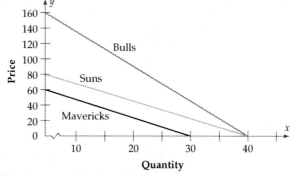

85. Write a linear equation that relates the quantity x of tickets demanded at price y when the Lakers play the

(a) Dallas Mavericks   (b) Phoenix Suns

(c) Chicago Bulls

[*Hint:* In each case, use the x- and y-intercepts to determine its slope.]

86. Use the equations from Exercise 85 to find the number of tickets Rocky would sell at a price of $40 for a game against the

(a) Mavericks   (b) Bulls

87. The Fahrenheit and Celsius scales for measuring temperatures are linearly related. They are calibrated using the freezing and boiling points of water at sea level.

Temperature Scale	Fahrenheit Scale	Celsius Scale
Water Freezes	32°	0°
Water Boils	212°	100°

(a) Use the data in the table to write a formula that relates the Fahrenheit temperature F to the Celsius temperature C. Your answer should be in the form $F = mC + b$.

(b) Solve the equation in part (a) for C to find a formula that relates the Celsius temperature to the Fahrenheit temperature.

(c) When is the temperature in degrees Fahrenheit the same as the temperature in degrees Celsius?

88. (a) If the temperature changes 1° Fahrenheit, how many degrees does the Celsius temperature change? [*Hint:* See Exercise 87.]

(b) What happens to the Fahrenheit temperature when the Celsius temperature changes 1°?

(c) How are your answers in parts (a) and (b) related to the formulas in Exercises 87?

89. A 75-gallon water tank is being emptied. The graph shows the amount of water in the tank after x minutes.

(a) At what rate is the tank emptying during the first 2 minutes? During the next 3 minutes? During the last minute?

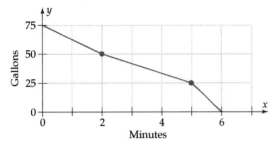

(b) Suppose the tank is emptied at a constant rate of 10 gallons per minute. Draw the graph that shows the amount of water after x minutes. What is the equation of the graph?

90. The poverty level income for a family of four was $13,359 in 1990. Because of inflation and other factors, the poverty level rose approximately linearly to $19,307 in 2004.*

(a) At what rate is the poverty level increasing?

(b) Estimate the poverty level in 2000 and 2009.

91. A Honda Civic LX sedan is worth $15,350 now and will be worth $9910 in four years.

(a) Assuming linear depreciation, find the equation that gives the value y of the car in year x.

(b) At what rate is the car depreciating?

(c) Estimate the value of the car six years from now.

92. A house in Shaker Heights, Ohio was bought for $160,000 in 1980. It increased in value in an approximately linear fashion and sold for $359,750 in 1997.

(a) At what rate did the house appreciate (increase in value) during this period?

(b) If this appreciation rate remained accurate what would the house be worth in 2010?

THINKERS

93. Show that two nonvertical lines with the same slope are parallel. [*Hint:* The equations of distinct lines with the same slope must be of the form $y = mx + b$ and $y = mx + c$ with $b \neq c$ (why?). If (x_1, y_1) were a point on both lines, its coordinates would satisfy both equations. Show that this leads to a contradiction, and conclude that the lines have no point in common.]

94. Prove that nonvertical parallel lines L and M have the same slope, as follows. Suppose M lies above L, and choose two points (x_1, y_1) and (x_2, y_2) on L.

(a) Let P be the point on M with first coordinate x_1. Let b denote the vertical distance from P to (x_1, y_1). Show that the second coordinate of P is $y_1 + b$.

(b) Let Q be the point on M with first coordinate x_2. Use the fact that L and M are parallel to show that the second coordinate of Q is $y_2 + b$.

(c) Compute the slope of L using (x_1, y_1) and (x_2, y_2). Compute the slope of M using the points P and Q. Verify that the two slopes are the same.

95. Show that the diagonals of a square are perpendicular. [*Hint:* Place the square in the first quadrant of the plane, with one vertex at the origin and sides on the positive axes. Label the coordinates of the vertices appropriately.]

96. This exercise provides a proof of the statement about slopes of perpendicular lines in the box on page 56. First, assume that L and M are nonvertical perpendicular lines that both pass through the origin. L and M intersect the vertical line $x = 1$ at the points $(1, k)$ and $(1, m)$, respectively, as shown in the figure.

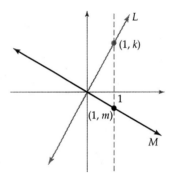

(a) Use $(0, 0)$ and $(1, k)$ to show that L has slope k. Use $(0, 0)$ and $(1, m)$ to show that M has slope m.

(b) Use the distance formula to compute the length of each side of the right triangle with vertices $(0, 0)$, $(1, k)$, and $(1, m)$.

(c) Use part (b) and the Pythagorean Theorem to find an equation involving k, m, and various constants. Show that this equation simplifies to $km = -1$. This proves half of the statement.

(d) To prove the other half, assume that $km = -1$, and show that L and M are perpendicular as follows. You may assume that a triangle whose sides a, b, c satisfy $a^2 + b^2 = c^2$ is a right triangle with hypotenuse c. Use this fact, and do the computation in part (b) in reverse (starting with $km = -1$) to show that the triangle with vertices $(0, 0)$, $(1, k)$, and $(1, m)$ is a right triangle, so that L and M are perpendicular.

(e) Finally, to prove the general case when L and M do not intersect at the origin, let L_1 be a line through the origin that is parallel to L, and let M_1 be a line through the origin that is parallel to M. Then L and L_1 have the same slope, and M and M_1 have the same slope (why?). Use this fact and parts (a)–(d) to prove that L is perpendicular to M exactly when $km = -1$.

1.6   Polar Coordinates

Section Objectives
- Convert from rectangular to polar coordinates and vice versa.
- Graph polar coordinate equations.

In the past, we used a rectangular coordinate system in the plane, based on two perpendicular coordinate axes. Now we introduce another coordinate system for the plane, based on angles.

Choose a point O in the plane (called the **origin** or **pole**) and a half-line extending from O (called the **polar axis**). As shown in Figure 1–44, a point P is given **polar coordinates** (r, θ), where

r = Distance from P to O

θ = Angle with polar axis as initial side and OP as terminal side.

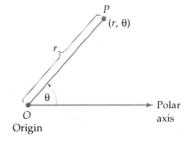

Figure 1–44

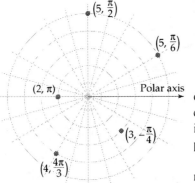

Figure 1–45

We shall usually measure the angle θ in radians; it may be either positive or negative, depending on whether it is generated by a clockwise or counterclockwise rotation. Some typical points are shown in Figure 1–45, which also illustrates the "circular grid" that a polar coordinate system imposes on the plane.

The polar coordinates of a point P are *not* unique. The angle θ may be replaced by any angle that has the same terminal side as θ, such as $\theta \pm 2\pi$. For instance, the coordinates $(2, \pi/3)$, $(2, 7\pi/3)$, and $(2, -5\pi/3)$ all represent the same point, as shown in Figure 1–46.

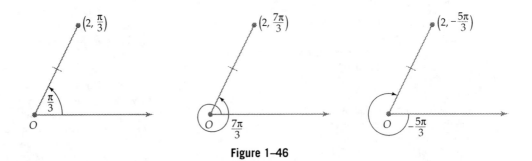

Figure 1–46

We shall consider the coordinates of the origin to be $(0, \theta)$, where θ is *any* angle.

Negative values for the first coordinate will be allowed according to this convention: For each positive r, the point $(-r, \theta)$ lies on the straight line containing the terminal side of θ, at distance r from the origin, on the *opposite* side of the origin from the point (r, θ), as shown in Figure 1–47 on the next page.

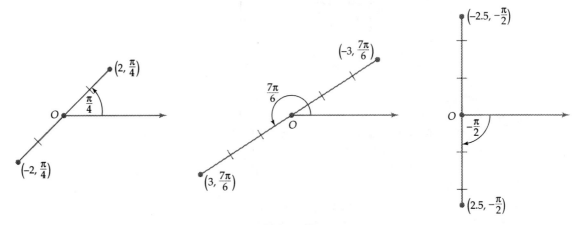

Figure 1–47

It is sometimes convenient to use both a rectangular and a polar coordinate system in the plane, with the polar axis coinciding with the positive x-axis. Then the y-axis is the polar line $\theta = \pi/2$. Suppose P has rectangular coordinates (x, y) and polar coordinates (r, θ), with $r > 0$, as in Figure 10–48.

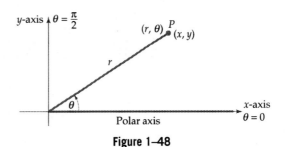

Figure 1–48

Since r is the distance from (x, y) to $(0, 0)$, the distance formula shows that $r = \sqrt{x^2 + y^2}$, and hence, $r^2 = x^2 + y^2$. The point-in-the-plane description of the trigonometric functions shows that

$$\cos \theta = \frac{x}{r}, \qquad \sin \theta = \frac{y}{r}, \qquad \tan \theta = \frac{y}{x}.$$

Solving the first two equations for x and y, we obtain the relationship between polar and rectangular coordinates.*

Coordinate Conversion Formulas

If a point has polar coordinates (r, θ), then its rectangular coordinates (x, y) are

$$x = r \cos \theta \qquad \text{and} \qquad y = r \sin \theta.$$

If a point has rectangular coordinates (x, y), with $x \neq 0$, then its polar coordinates (r, θ) satisfy

$$r^2 = x^2 + y^2 \qquad \text{and} \qquad \tan \theta = \frac{y}{x}.$$

*The conclusions in the next box are also true when $r < 0$ (Exercise 86).

TECHNOLOGY TIP

Keys to convert from rectangular to polar coordinates, or vice versa, are in this menu/submenu:

TI-84+:   ANGLE

TI-86:   VECTOR/OPS

TI-89:   MATH/ANGLE

Casio: OPTN/ANGLE

Conversion programs for HP-39gs are in the Program Appendix.

EXAMPLE 1

Convert each of the following points in polar coordinates to rectangular coordinates.

(a) $(2, \pi/6)$ (b) $(3, 4)$

SOLUTION

(a) Apply the first set of equations in the box with $r = 2$ and $\theta = \pi/6$.

$$x = 2 \cos \frac{\pi}{6} = 2 \cdot \frac{\sqrt{3}}{2} = \sqrt{3} \quad \text{and} \quad y = 2 \sin \frac{\pi}{6} = 2 \cdot \frac{1}{2} = 1$$

So the rectangular coordinates are $(\sqrt{3}, 1)$.

(b) The point with polar coordinates $(3, 4)$ has $r = 3$ and $\theta = 4$ radians. Therefore, its rectangular coordinates are

$$(r \cos \theta, r \sin \theta) = (3 \cos 4, 3 \sin 4) \approx (-1.9609, -2.2704).$$ ■

EXAMPLE 2

Find the polar coordinates of the point with rectangular coordinates $(2, -2)$.

SOLUTION
The second set of equations in the box, with $x = 2$, $y = -2$, shows that

$$r = \sqrt{2^2 + (-2)^2} = \sqrt{8} = 2\sqrt{2} \quad \text{and} \quad \tan \theta = -2/2 = -1.$$

We must find an angle θ whose terminal side passes through $(2, -2)$ and whose tangent is -1. Figure 1–49 shows that two of the many possibilities are

$$\theta = -\frac{\pi}{4} \quad \text{and} \quad \theta = \frac{7\pi}{4}.$$

So one pair of polar coordinates is $\left(2\sqrt{2}, -\frac{\pi}{4}\right)$, and another is $\left(2\sqrt{2}, \frac{7\pi}{4}\right)$. ■

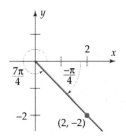

Figure 1–49

Rectangular to polar conversion is relatively easy when special angles are involved, as in Example 2. In other cases technology may be necessary.

EXAMPLE 3

Find the polar coordinates of the points whose rectangular coordinates are

(a) $(3, 5)$ (b) $(-2, 4)$

SOLUTION

(a) Applying the second set of equations in the box, with $x = 3$, $y = 5$, we have

$$r = \sqrt{3^2 + 5^2} = \sqrt{34} \quad \text{and} \quad \tan \theta = 5/3.$$

The TAN^{-1} key on a calculator shows that $\theta \approx 1.0304$ radians is an angle between 0 and $\pi/2$ with tangent $5/3$. Since $(3, 5)$ is in the first quadrant, one pair of (approximate) polar coordinates is $(\sqrt{34}, 1.0304)$.

(b) In this case,

$$r = \sqrt{(-2)^2 + 4^2} = \sqrt{20} = 2\sqrt{5} \quad \text{and} \quad \tan \theta = \frac{4}{-2} = -2.$$

Using the TAN^{-1} key, we find that $\theta \approx -1.1071$ is an angle between $-\pi/2$ and 0 with tangent -2. However, we want an angle between $\pi/2$ and π because $(-2, 4)$ is in the second quadrant. Since tangent has period π,

$$\tan(-1.1071 + \pi) = \tan(-1.1071) = -2.$$

Thus, $-1.1071 + \pi \approx 2.0344$ is an angle between $\pi/2$ and π whose tangent is -2. Therefore, one pair of polar coordinates is $(2\sqrt{5}, 2.0344)$. ∎

The technique used in Example 3 may be summarized as follows.

Rectangular to
Polar Conversion

If the rectangular coordinates of a point are (x, y), let $r = \sqrt{x^2 + y^2}$. If (x, y) lies in the first or fourth quadrant, then its polar coordinates are

$$\left(r, \tan^{-1} \frac{y}{x} \right).$$

If (x, y) lies in the second or third quadrant, then its polar coordinates are

$$\left(r, \tan^{-1}\left(\frac{y}{x}\right) + \pi \right).$$

EQUATION CONVERSION

When an equation in rectangular coordinates is given, it can be converted to polar coordinates by making the substitutions $x = r \cos \theta$ and $y = r \cos \theta$. Converting a polar equation to rectangular coordinates, however, is a bit trickier.

EXAMPLE 4

Find an equivalent rectangular equation for the given polar equation, and use it to identify the shape of the graph.

(a) $r = 4 \cos \theta$ (b) $r = \dfrac{1}{1 - \sin \theta}$

SOLUTION

(a) Rewrite the equation $r = 4 \cos \theta$ as follows.

Multiply both sides by r:	$r^2 = 4r \cos \theta$
Substitute $r^2 = x^2 + y^2$ and $r \cos \theta = x$:	$x^2 + y^2 = 4x$
	$x^2 - 4x + y^2 = 0$
Add 4 to both sides:	$(x^2 - 4x + 4) + y^2 = 4$
Factor:	$(x - 2)^2 + y^2 = 2^2$

As we saw in Section 1.1, the graph of this equation is the circle with center $(2, 0)$ and radius 2.

(b) Begin by eliminating fractions.

$$r = \frac{1}{1 - \sin\theta}$$

$$r(1 - \sin\theta) = 1$$

$$r - r\sin\theta = 1$$

Substitute $r = \sqrt{x^2 + y^2}$ and $y = r\sin\theta$: $\sqrt{x^2 + y^2} - y = 1$

Rearrange terms: $\sqrt{x^2 + y^2} = y + 1$

Square both sides: $x^2 + y^2 = (y + 1)^2$

Simplify: $x^2 + y^2 = y^2 + 2y + 1$

$$x^2 = 2y + 1$$

$$y = \frac{1}{2}(x^2 - 1)$$

As we saw in Section 4.1, the graph is an upward-opening parabola. ■

POLAR GRAPHS

The graphs of a few polar coordinate equations can be easily determined from the appropriate definitions.

EXAMPLE 5

Graph the equations

(a) $r = 3$*   (b) $\theta = \pi/6$.*

SOLUTION

(a) The graph consists of all points (r, θ) with first coordinate 3, that is, all points whose distance from the origin is 3. So the graph is a circle with center O and radius 3, as shown in Figure 1–50.

(b) The graph consists of all points $(r, \pi/6)$. If $r \geq 0$, then $(r, \pi/6)$ lies on the terminal side of an angle of $\pi/6$ radians, whose initial side is the polar axis. If $r < 0$, then $(r, \pi/6)$ lies on the extension of this terminal side across the origin. So the graph is the straight line in Figure 1–51. ■

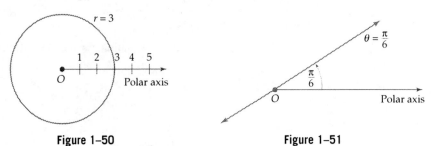

Figure 1–50   Figure 1–51

*Every equation is understood to involve two variables, but one may have coefficient 0, as is the case here: $r = 3 + 0 \cdot \theta$ and $\theta = 0 \cdot r + \pi/6$. This is analogous to equations such as $y = 5$ and $x = 2$ in rectangular coordinates.

Some polar graphs can be sketched by hand by using basic facts about trigonometric functions.

EXAMPLE 6

Graph $r = 1 + \sin \theta$.

SOLUTION   Remember the behavior of $\sin \theta$ between 0 and 2π:

As θ increases from 0 to $\pi/2$, $\sin \theta$ increases from 0 to 1. So $r = 1 + \sin \theta$ increases from 1 to 2.

As θ increases from $\pi/2$ to π, $\sin \theta$ decreases from 1 to 0. So $r = 1 + \sin \theta$ decreases from 2 to 1.

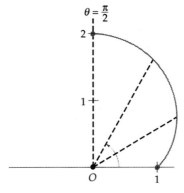

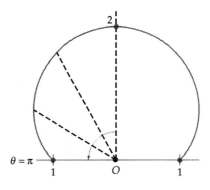

As θ increases from π to $3\pi/2$, $\sin \theta$ decreases from 0 to −1. So $r = 1 + \sin \theta$ decreases from 1 to 0.

As θ increases from $3\pi/2$ to 2π, $\sin \theta$ increases from −1 to 0. So $r = 1 + \sin \theta$ increases from 0 to 1.

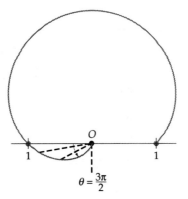

Figure 1–52

As θ takes values larger than 2π, $\sin \theta$ repeats the same pattern, and hence, so does $r = 1 + \sin \theta$. The same is true for negative values of θ. The full graph (called a **cardioid**) is at the lower right in Figure 1–52.

The easiest way to graph polar equation $r = f(\theta)$ is to use a calculator in polar graphing mode. A second way is to use parametric graphing mode, with the coordinate converison formulas as a parameterization.

$$x = r \cos \theta = f(\theta) \cos \theta,$$

$$y = r \sin \theta = f(\theta) \sin \theta.$$

EXAMPLE 7

Graph $r = 2 + 4 \cos \theta$.

SOLUTION   ***Polar Method:***   Put your calculator in polar graphing mode and enter $r = 2 + 4 \cos \theta$ in the function memory. Set the viewing window by entering minimum and maximum values for x, y, and θ. Since cosine has period 2π, a complete graph can be obtained by taking $0 \le \theta \le 2\pi$. You must also set the θ step (or θ pitch), which determines how many values of θ the calculator uses to plot the graph. With an appropriate θ step, the graph should look like Figure 1–53.

Parametric Method: Put your calculator in parametric graphing mode. The parametric equations for $r = 2 + 4 \cos \theta$ are as follows (using t as the variable instead of θ with $0 \le t \le 2\pi$):

$$x = r \cos t = (2 + 4 \cos t) \cos t = 2 \cos t + 4 \cos^2 t$$

$$y = r \sin t = (2 + 4 \cos t) \sin t = 2 \sin t + 4 \sin t \cos t.$$

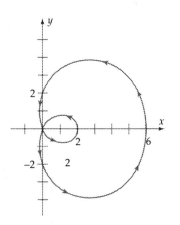

Figure 1–53

They also produce the graph in Figure 10–88.   ∎

EXAMPLE 8

The graph of $r = \sin 2\theta$ in Figure 1–54 can be obtained either by graphing directly in polar mode or by using parametric mode and the equations

$$x = r \cos t = \sin 2t \cos t \quad \text{and} \quad y = r \sin t = \sin 2t \sin t \quad (0 \le t \le 2\pi). \quad ∎$$

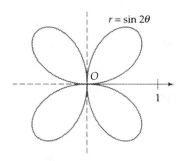

$r = \sin 2\theta$

Figure 1–54

Here is a summary of commonly encountered polar graphs (in each case, a and b are constants).

Equation	Name of Graph	Shape of Graph*
$r = a\theta\ (\theta \geq 0)$ $r = a\theta\ (\theta \leq 0)$	Archimedean spiral	 $r = a\theta\ (\theta \geq 0)$ $\qquad$ $r = a\theta\ (\theta \leq 0)$
$r = a(1 \pm \sin\theta)$ $r = a(1 \pm \cos\theta)$	cardioid	 $r = a(1 + \cos\theta)$ $\qquad$ $r = a(1 - \sin\theta)$
$r = a \sin n\theta$ $r = a \cos n\theta$ $(n \geq 2)$	rose (There are n petals when n is odd and $2n$ petals when n is even.)	 $r = a \cos n\theta$ $\qquad$ $r = a \sin n\theta$

*Depending on the plus or minus sign and whether sine or cosine is involved, the basic shape of a specific graph may differ from those shown by a rotation, reversal, or horizontal or vertical shift.

Equation	Name of Graph	Shape of Graph		
$r = a \sin \theta$ $r = a \cos \theta$	circle	$r = a \cos \theta$	$r = a \sin \theta$	
$r^2 = \pm a^2 \sin 2\theta$ $r^2 = \pm a^2 \cos 2\theta$	lemniscate	$r^2 = a^2 \sin 2\theta$	$r^2 = a^2 \cos 2\theta$	
$r = a \pm b \sin \theta$ $r = a \pm b \cos \theta$ $(a, b > 0; a \neq b)$	limaçon	$a < b$ $r = a + b \cos \theta$	$b < a < 2b$ $r = a + b \sin \theta$	$a \geq 2b$ $r = a - b \sin \theta$

EXERCISES 1.6

1. What are the polar coordinates of the points P, Q, R, S, T, U, V in the figure?

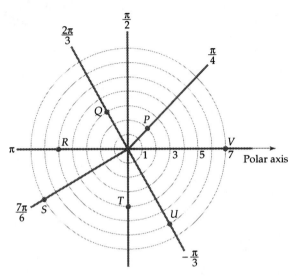

In Exercises 2–6, plot the point whose polar coordinates are given.

2. $(1, \pi/4)$ **3.** $(2, -3\pi/4)$ **4.** $(-2, 2\pi/3)$

5. $(-3, -5\pi/3)$ **6.** $(3, \pi/6)$

In Exercises 7–12, list four other pairs of polar coordinates for the given point, each with a different combination of signs (that is, $r > 0$, $\theta > 0$; $r > 0$, $\theta < 0$; $r < 0$, $\theta > 0$; $r < 0$, $\theta < 0$).

7. $(3, \pi/3)$ **8.** $(-5, \pi)$ **9.** $(2, -2\pi/3)$

10. $(-1, -\pi/6)$ **11.** $(\sqrt{3}, 3\pi/4)$ **12.** $(-3, 7\pi/6)$

In Exercises 13–20, convert the polar coordinates to rectangular coordinates.

13. $(3, \pi/3)$ **14.** $(-2, \pi/4)$ **15.** $(-1, 5\pi/6)$

16. $(2, 0)$ **17.** $(1.5, 5)$ **18.** $(2.2, -2.2)$

19. $(-4, -\pi/7)$ **20.** $(-1, 1)$

In Exercises 21–34, convert the rectangular coordinates to polar coordinates.

21. $(3\sqrt{3}, -3)$ **22.** $(2\sqrt{3}, 2)$ **23.** $(1, 1)$

24. $(\sqrt{2}, -\sqrt{2})$ **25.** $(3, 3\sqrt{3})$ **26.** $(-\sqrt{2}, \sqrt{6})$

27. $(2, 4)$ **28.** $(3, -2)$ **29.** $(-5, 2.5)$

30. $(-6.2, -3)$ **31.** $(0, -2)$ **32.** $(.5, 3.5)$

33. $(-2, 4)$ **34.** $(\sqrt{5}, \sqrt{10})$

In Exercises 35–40, find a polar equation that is equivalent to the given rectangular equation.

35. $x^2 + y^2 = 25$ **36.** $4xy = 1$ **37.** $x = 12$

38. $y = 4$ **39.** $y = 2x + 1$ **40.** $y = x - 2$

In Exercises 41–52, find a rectangular equation that is equivalent to the given polar equation.

41. $r = 3$ [*Hint:* Square both sides, then substitute.]

42. $r = 5$

43. $\theta = \pi/6$ {*Hint:* Take the tangent of both sides, then substitute.]

44. $\theta = -\pi/4$

45. $r = \sec \theta$ [*Hint:* Express the right side in terms of cosine.]

46. $r = \csc \theta$ **47.** $r^2 = \tan \theta$ **48.** $r^2 = \sin \theta$

49. $r = 2 \sin \theta$ **50.** $r = 3 \cos \theta$

51. $r = \dfrac{4}{1 + \sin \theta}$ **52.** $r = \dfrac{6}{1 - \cos \theta}$

In Exercises 53–58, sketch the graph of the equation without using a calculator.

53. $r = 4$ **54.** $r = -1$ **55.** $\theta = -\pi/3$

56. $\theta = 5\pi/6$ **57.** $\theta = 1$ **58.** $\theta = -4$

In Exercises 59–82, sketch the graph of the equation.

59. $r = \theta$ $(\theta \le 0)$ **60.** $r = 3\theta$ $(\theta \ge 0)$

61. $r = 1 - \sin \theta$ **62.** $r = 3 - 3 \cos \theta$

63. $r = -2 \cos \theta$ **64.** $r = -6 \sin \theta$

65. $r = \cos 2\theta$ **66.** $r = \cos 3\theta$

67. $r = \sin 3\theta$ **68.** $r = \sin 4\theta$

69. $r^2 = 4 \cos 2\theta$ **70.** $r^2 = \sin 2\theta$

71. $r = 2 + 4 \cos \theta$ **72.** $r = 1 + 2 \cos \theta$

73. $r = \sin \theta + \cos \theta$ **74.** $r = 4 \cos \theta + 4 \sin \theta$

75. $r = \sin (\theta/2)$ **76.** $r = 4 \tan \theta$

77. $r = \sin \theta \tan \theta$ (cissoid)

78. $r = 4 + 2 \sec \theta$ (conchoid)

79. $r = e^\theta$ (logarithmic spiral)

80. $r^2 = 1/\theta$ **81.** $r = 1/\theta$ $(\theta > 0)$ **82.** $r^2 = \theta$

83. (a) Find a complete graph of $r = 1 - 2 \sin 3\theta$.
(b) Predict what the graph of $r = 1 - 2 \sin 4\theta$ will look like. Then check your prediction with a calculator.
(c) Predict what the graph of $r = 1 - 2 \sin 5\theta$ will look like. Then check your prediction with a calculator.

84. (a) Find a complete graph of $r = 1 - 3 \sin 2\theta$.
(b) Predict what the graph of $r = 1 - 3 \sin 3\theta$ will look like. Then check your prediction with a calculator.
(c) Predict what the graph of $r = 1 - 3 \sin 4\theta$ will look like. Then check your prediction with a calculator.

85. If a, b are nonzero constants, show that the graph of $r = a \sin \theta + b \cos \theta$ is a circle. [*Hint:* Multiply both sides by r and convert to rectangular coordinates.]

86. Prove that the coordinate conversion formulas are valid when $r < 0$. [*Hint:* If P has coordinates (x, y) and (r, θ), with $r < 0$, verify that the point Q with rectangular coordinates $(-x, -y)$ has polar coordinates $(-r, \theta)$. Since $r < 0$, $-r$ is positive and the conversion formulas proved in the text apply to Q. For instance, $-x = -r \cos \theta$, which implies that $x = r \cos \theta$.]

87. *Distance Formula for Polar Coordinates:* Prove that the distance from (r, θ) to (s, β) is

$$\sqrt{r^2 + s^2 - 2rs \cos(\theta - \beta)}$$

[*Hint:* If $r > 0$, $s > 0$, and $\theta > \beta$, then the triangle with vertices (r, θ), (s, β), $(0, 0)$ has an angle of $\theta - \beta$, whose sides have lengths r and s. Use the Law of Cosines.]

88. Explain why the following symmetry tests for the graphs of polar equations are valid.

(a) If replacing θ by $-\theta$ produces an equivalent equation, then the graph is symmetric with respect to the line $\theta = 0$ (the x-axis).

(b) If replacing θ by $\pi - \theta$ produces an equivalent equation, then the graph is symmetric with respect to the line $\theta = \pi/2$ (the y-axis).

(c) If replacing r by $-r$ produces an equivalent equation, then the graph is symmetric with respect to the origin.

Chapter 2

FUNCTIONS AND GRAPHS

© Bob Perzel/Mira.com/drr.net

Chapter Outline

Interdependence of Sections

2.1 Functions

Section Objectives

■ Understand the definition of a function.
■ Recognize functions in various formats: table, graph, verbal description.
■ Define a function using an equation or a graph.
■ Create a table of inputs and outputs.

While it is possible to think of functions as completely abstract mathematical objects, it is usually simpler to picture a function as a description of how one quantity determines another.

EXAMPLE 1

The amount of state income tax Louisiana residents pay depends on their income. The way that the income determines the tax is given by the following tax law.*

Income		Tax
At Least	But Less Than	
0	$12,500	2.1%
$12,500	$25,000	$262.50 + 3.45% of amount over $12,500
$25,000		$693.75 + 4.8% of amount over $25,000

*2006 rates for a single person with one exemption and no deductions; actual tax amount may vary slightly from this formula when tax tables are used.

So if a single person's income were \$30,000 the income tax would be 693.75 + .048(5,000) = \$933.75. ∎

EXAMPLE 2

The graph in Figure 2–1 shows the temperatures in Cleveland, Ohio, on April 11, 2001, as recorded by the U.S. Weather Bureau at Hopkins Airport. The graph indicates the temperature that corresponds to each given time. For example, at 8 A.M. on April 11, 2001, the temperature was 47°F. ∎

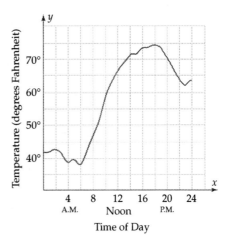

Figure 2–1

EXAMPLE 3

Suppose a rock is dropped straight down from a high place. Physics tells us that the distance traveled by the rock in t seconds is $16t^2$ feet. Therefore, after 5 seconds the rock has fallen $16(5^2) = 400$ feet. ∎

These examples share several common features. Each involves two sets of numbers, which we can think of as inputs and outputs. In each case, there is a rule by which each input determines an output, as summarized here.

	Set of Inputs	**Set of Outputs**	**Rule**
Example 1	All incomes	All tax amounts	The tax law
Example 2	Hours since midnight	Temperatures during the day	Time/temperature graph
Example 3	Seconds elapsed after dropping the rock	Distance rock travels	Distance = $16t^2$

Each of these examples may be mentally represented by an idealized calculator that has a single operation key: A number is entered [*input*], the rule key is pushed [*rule*], and an answer is displayed [*output*]. The formal definition of function incorporates these common features (input/rule/output), with a slight change in terminology.

Functions

> A **function** consists of
>
> A set of inputs (called the **domain**);
>
> A **rule** by which each input determines exactly one output;
>
> A set of outputs (called the **range**).

Think about the phrase "exactly one output." In Example 2, for each time of day, there is exactly one temperature. But it is quite possible to have the same temperature (output) occur at different times (inputs). In general,

For each input, the rule of a function determines exactly one output. But different inputs may produce the same output.

Although real-world situations, such as Examples 1–3, are the motivation for functions, much of the emphasis in mathematics courses is on the functions themselves, independent of possible interpretations in specific situations, as illustrated in the following examples.

EXAMPLE 4

The graph in Figure 2–2 defines a function whose rule is as follows:

For input x, the output is the unique number y such that (x, y) is on the graph.

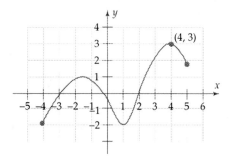

Figure 2–2

Input 4, for example, produces output 3 because (4, 3) is on the graph. Similarly, $(-3, 0)$ is on the graph, which means that input -3 produces output 0. Since the first coordinates of all points on the graph (the inputs) lie between -4 and 5, the domain of this function is the interval $[-4, 5]$. The range is the interval $[-2, 3]$ because all the second coordinates of points on the graph (the outputs) lie between -2 and 3. ■

EXAMPLE 5

Could either of the following be the table of values of a function?

(a)

Input	−4	−2	0	2	4
Output	21	7	1	3	7

(b)

Input	3	2	1	3	5
Output	4	0	2	6	9

SOLUTION
(a) Two different inputs (−2 and 4) produce the same output, but that's okay because each input produces exactly one output. So this table could represent a function.
(b) The input 3 produces two different outputs (4 and 6), so this table cannot possibly represent a function. ■

EXAMPLE 6

Using the procedure of Example 4, does this graph define a function?

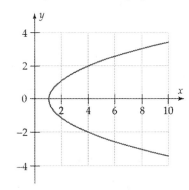

Figure 2–3

SOLUTION   No, because the input 4, for example, produces two outputs 2 and −2. (Both (4, 2) and (4, −2) are on the graph.) ■

EXAMPLE 7

The **greatest integer function** is the function whose domain is the set of all real numbers, whose range is the set of integers, and whose rule is:

For each input x, the output is the largest integer that is less than or equal to x. We denote the output by $[\![x]\!]$. For example:

$$[\![5]\!] = 5 \quad [\![4.124]\!] = 4 \quad \left[\!\left[\frac{5}{3}\right]\!\right] = 1 \quad [\![\pi]\!] = 3$$

$$[\![-3]\!] = -3 \quad [\![-1.5]\!] = -2 \quad [\![-0.01]\!] = -1 \quad [\![-\pi]\!] = -4 \quad ■$$

TECHNOLOGY TIP

The greatest integer function is denoted INT or FLOOR on TI and HP-39gs, and INTG on Casio. It is in this menu/submenu:

TI: MATH/NUM

HP-39gs: MATH/REAL

Casio: OPTN/NUM

FUNCTIONS DEFINED BY EQUATIONS AND GRAPHS

Equations in two variables are *not* the same things as functions. However, many equations can be used to define functions.

EXAMPLE 8

The equation $4x - 2y^3 + 5 = 0$ can be solved uniquely for y:

$$2y^3 = 4x + 5$$

$$y^3 = 2x + \frac{5}{2}$$

$$y = \sqrt[3]{2x + \frac{5}{2}}.$$

If a number is substituted for x in this equation, then exactly one value of y is produced. In other words, for every real number x there exists exactly one y such that the equation $4x - 2y^3 + 5 = 0$ is true.

So we can define a function whose domain is the set of all real numbers and whose rule is

The input x produces the output $\sqrt[3]{2x + 5/2}$.

In this situation, we say that the equation defines **y as a function of x.**

The original equation can also be solved for x:

$$4x = 2y^3 - 5$$

$$x = \frac{2y^3 - 5}{4}.$$

Now if a number is substituted for y, exactly one value of x is produced. So we can think of y as the input and the corresponding x as the output and say that the equation defines **x as a function of y.** ■

EXAMPLE 9

Does the equation $x^2 - y + 1 = 0$ define y as a function of x, or x as a function of y, or both?

SOLUTION   Solving for y, we have

$$x^2 + 1 = y$$

$$y = x^2 + 1.$$

This equation defines y as a function of x, since each value of x produces exactly one value of y.

Solving for x, we obtain

$$x^2 = y - 1$$

$$x = \pm\sqrt{y - 1}.$$

This equation does *not* define x as a function of y because, for example, the input $y = 5$ produces two outputs: $x = \pm 2$. ■

EXAMPLE 10

A group of students drives from Cleveland to Seattle, a distance of 2350 miles, at an average speed of 52 mph.

(a) Express their distance from Cleveland as a function of time.

(b) Express their distance from Seattle as a function of time.

SOLUTION

(a) Let t denote the time traveled in hours after leaving Cleveland, and let D be the distance from Cleveland at time t. Then the equation that expresses D as a function of t is

$$D = \text{Distance traveled in } t \text{ hours at 52 mph} = 52t.$$

(b) At time t, the car has traveled $52t$ miles of the 2350-mile journey, so the distance K remaining to Seattle is given by $K = 2350 - 52t$. This equation expresses K as a function of t. ∎

Graphing calculators are designed to deal with equations that define y as a function of x. Calculators can evaluate such functions (that is, produce the outputs from various inputs). One method is illustrated in the next example.

EXAMPLE 11

The equation $y = x^3 - 2x + 3$ defines y as a function of x. Use the table feature of a calculator to find the outputs for each of the following inputs:

(a) $-4, -3, -2, -1, 0, 1, 2, 3, 4$　　(b) $-5, -11, 8, 7.2, -.44$

SOLUTION

(a) To use the table feature, we first enter $y = x^3 - 2x + 3$ in the equation memory, say, as y_1. Then we call up the setup screen (see the Technology Tip in the margin and Figure 2–4) and enter the *starting number* (-4), the *increment* (the amount the input changes for each subsequent entry, which is 1 here), and the *table type* (AUTO, which means the calculator will compute all the outputs at once).* Then press TABLE to obtain the table in Figure 2–5. To find values that don't appear on the screen in Figure 2–5, use the up and down arrow keys to scroll through the table.

(b) With an apparently random list of inputs, as here, we change the table type to ASK (or USER or BUILD YOUR OWN).† Then key in each value of x, and hit ENTER. This produces the table one line at a time, as in Figure 2–6. ∎

TECHNOLOGY TIP

To find the table setup screen, look for TBLSET (or RANG or NUM SETUP) on the keyboard or in the TABLE menu.

　　The increment is called ΔTBL on TI (and PITCH or NUMSTEP on others).

　　The table type is called INDPNT on TI, and NUMTYPE on HP-39gs.

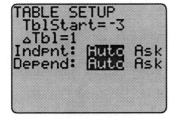

Figure 2–4

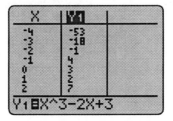

Figure 2–5

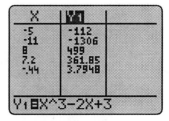

Figure 2–6

CALCULATOR EXPLORATION

Construct a table of values for the function in Example 11 that shows the outputs for these inputs: 2, 2.4, 2.8, 3.2, 3.6, and 4. What is the increment here?

EXAMPLE 12

The revenues y of MTV in year x can be approximated by the equation

$$y = .257x^3 + 11.6x^2 + 4.5x + 177.5 \qquad (0 \le x \le 14),$$

---

*There is no table type selection on Casio, but you must enter a maximum value for x.
†Casio users should see Exercise 51.

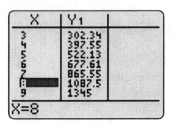

Figure 2–7

where $x = 0$ corresponds to 1987 and y is in millions of dollars.* So the revenue y is a function of the year x. In what year did revenues first exceed one billion dollars?

SOLUTION   Since y is in millions, one billion dollars corresponds to $y = 1000$. Make a table of values for the function (Figure 2–7). It shows that the revenue was approximately \$865,550,000 in 1994 ($x = 7$) and \$1,087,500,000 in 1995 ($x = 8$). ∎

---

*Based on data from MTV Networks.

EXERCISES 2.1

In Exercises 1–4, determine whether or not the given table could possibly be a table of values of a function. Give reasons for your answer.

1.

Input	1	0	3	1	−5
Output	2	3	−2.5	2	14

2.

Input	−5	3	0	−3	5
Output	0	3	0	5	−3

3.

Input	−5	1	3	−5	7
Output	0	2	4	6	8

4.

Input	1	−1	2	−2	3
Output	1	−2	±5	−6	8

Exercises 5–10 deal with the greatest integer function of Example 7, which is given by the equation $y = [\![x]\!]$. Compute the following values of the function:

5. $[\![6.75]\!]$ **6.** $[\![.75]\!]$

7. $[\![-4/3]\!]$ **8.** $[\![5/3]\!]$

9. $[\![-16.0001]\!]$

10. Does the equation $y = [\![x]\!]$ define x as a function of y? Give reasons for your answer.

In Exercises 11–18, determine whether the equation defines y as a function of x or defines x as a function of y.

11. $y = 3x^2 - 12$ **12.** $y = 2x^4 + 3x^2 - 2$

13. $y^2 = 4x + 1$ **14.** $5x - 4y^4 + 64 = 0$

15. $3x + 2y = 12$ **16.** $y - 4x^3 - 14 = 0$

17. $x^2 + y^2 = 9$ **18.** $x^2 + 2xy + y^2 = 0$

In Exercises 19–22, each equation defines y as a function of x. Create a table that shows the values of the function for the given values of x.

19. $y = x^2 + x - 4$; $x = -2, -1.5, -1, \ldots, 3, 3.5, 4$.

20. $y = \sqrt{4 - x^2}$; $x = -2, -1.2, -.4, .4, 1.2, 2$

21. $y = |x^2 - 5|$; $x = -8, -6, \ldots, 8, 10, 12$

22. $y = x^{10} - 100x$ $x = -1, 0, 1, 2, 3, 4$

23. Consider the Louisiana Tax law in Example 1. Find the output (tax amount) that is produced by each of the following inputs (incomes):

\$400	\$1509	\$25000
\$20,000	\$12,500	\$55,342

24. One proposed tax code looks like this:

Income		Tax
At Least	**But Less Than**	
0	\$12,500	0
\$12,500	\$100,000	5% of amount over \$12,500
\$100,000		\$5,000 + 10% of amount over \$100,000

Find four different numbers in the domain of this function that produce the same output (number in the range).

25. Explain why your answer in Exercise 24 does *not* contradict the definition of a function (in the box on page 78).

26. Is it possible to do Exercise 24 if all four numbers in the domain are required to be greater than 12,500? Why or why not?

27. The amount of postage required to mail a first-class letter is determined by its weight. In this situation, is weight a function of postage? Or vice versa? Or both?

28. Chinese philosopher Laotze (600 BC) said, "the farther one travels, the less one knows." Let x be the distance one travels, and y be the amount one knows. If Laotze is right, is y a function of x? Is x a function of y? Why or Why not?

29. Could the following statement ever be the rule of a function?

> For input x, the output is the number whose square is x.

Why or why not? If there is a function with this rule, what is its domain and range?

30. (a) Use the following chart to make two tables of values (one for an average man and one for an average woman) in which the inputs are the number of drinks per hour and the outputs are the corresponding blood alcohol contents.*

Blood alcohol content
A look at the number of drinks consumed and blood alcohol content in one hour under optimum conditions:

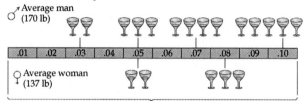

1 hour

(b) Does each of these tables define a function? If so, what are the domain and range of each function? [Remember that you can have part of a drink.]

31. The prime rate is the rate that large banks charge their best corporate customers for loans. The graph shows how the prime rate charged by a particular bank has varied in recent years.[†] Answer the following questions by reading the graph as best you can.

(a) What was prime rate in January, 2000? In January 2001? In mid-2005?
(b) In what time period was the prime rate below 5%?
(c) On the basis of the data provided by this graph, can the prime rate be considered a function of time? Can time be considered a function of the prime rate?

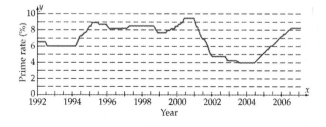

32. Find an equation that expresses the area A of a circle as a function of its

(a) radius r (b) diameter d

33. Find an equation that expresses the area of a square as a function of its

(a) side x (b) diagonal d

34. A box with a square base of side x is four times higher than it is wide. Express the volume V of the box as a function of x.

35. The surface area of a cylindrical can of radius r and height h is $2\pi r^2 + 2\pi rh$. If the can is twice as high as the diameter of its top, express its surface area S as a function of r.

36. Suppose you drop a rock from the top of a 400-foot-high building. Express the distance D from the rock to the ground as a function of time t. What is the range of this function? [*Hint:* See Example 3.]

37. A bicycle factory has weekly fixed costs of $26,000. In addition, the material and labor costs for each bicycle are $125. Express the total weekly cost C as a function of the number x of bicycles that are made.

38. The table below shows the percentage of single-parent families in various years.*

Year	1960	1970	1980	1990	2000	2003
Percent	12.8	13.2	17.5	20.8	23.2	27.5

(a) The equation

$$y = (2.4542 \times 10^{-6})x^5 - (2.2459 \times 10^{-4})x^4 + (.0065232)x^3 - (.055795)x^2 + .14568x + 12.8$$

in which $x = 0$ corresponds to 1960, defines y as a function of x. Make a table of values that includes the x-values corresponding to the years in the Census Bureau table.
(b) How do the values of y in your table compare with the percentages in the Census Bureau table? Does this equation seem to provide a reasonable model of the Census Bureau data?
(c) Use the equation to estimate the percentage of single-parent families in 1995 and 2005.
(d) Assuming that this model remains reasonably accurate, in what year will 50% of families be single-parent families?

39. The table shows the amount spent on student scholarships (in millions of dollars) by Oberlin College in recent years. [1995 indicates the school year 1995–96, and so on.]

Year	1995	1996	1997	1998	1999	2000	2001
Scholarships	19.8	22.0	25.7	27.5	28.7	31.1	34.3

---

*National Highway Traffic Safety Administration. Art by AP/Amy Kranz.
[†]Federal Reserve Board.

*U.S. Census Bureau.

(a) Use linear regression to find an equation that expresses the amount of scholarships y as a function of the year x, with $x = 0$ corresponding to 1995.

(b) Assuming that the function in part (a) remains accurate, estimate the amount spent on scholarships in 2004.

Use the following figures for Exercises 40–45. Each of the graphs in the figure defines a function, as in Example 4.

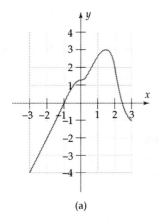

(a)

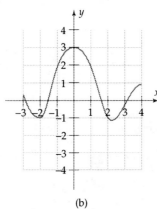

(b)

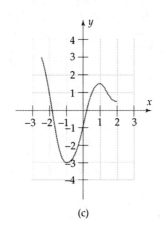

(c)

40. State the domain and range of the function defined by graph (a).

41. State the output (number in the range) that the function of Exercise 40 produces from the following inputs (numbers in the domain): $-2, -1, 0, 1$.

42. State the domain and range of the function defined by graph (b).

43. State the output (number in the range) that the function of Exercise 42 produces from the following inputs (numbers in the domain): $-2, 0, 1, 2.5, -1.5$.

44. State the domain and range of the function defined by graph (c).

45. State the output (number in the range) that the function of Exercise 44 produces from the following inputs (numbers in the domain): $-2, -1, 0, 1/2, 1$.

46. Explain why none of the graphs in the figure below defines a function according to the procedure in Example 6. What goes wrong?

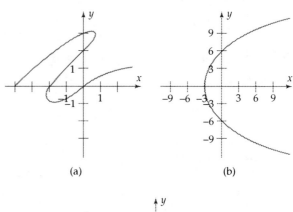

(a)   (b)

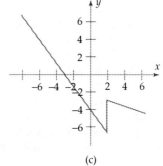

(c)

THINKERS

47. Consider the function whose rule uses a calculator as follows: "Press COS, and then press LN; then enter a number in the domain, and press ENTER."* Experiment with this function, then answer the following questions. You may not be able to prove your answers—just make the best estimate you can based on the evidence from your experiments.

---

*You don't need to know what these keys mean to do this exercise.

(a) What is the largest set of real numbers that could be used for the domain of this function? [If applying the rule to a number produces an error message or a complex number, that number cannot be in the domain.]

(b) Using the domain in part (a), what is the range of this function?

48. Do Exercise 47 for the function whose rule is "Press 10^x, and then press TAN; then enter a number in the domain, and press ENTER."

49. The *integer part* function has the set of all real numbers (written as decimals) as its domain. The rule is "For each input number, the output is the part of the number to the left of the decimal point." For instance, the input 37.986 produces the output 37, and the input -1.5 produces the output -1. On most calculators, the integer part function is denoted "iPart." On calculators that use "Intg" or "Floor" for the greatest integer function, the integer part function is denoted by "INT."

(a) For each nonnegative real number input, explain why both the integer part function and the greatest integer function [Example 7] produce the same output.

(b) For which negative numbers do the two functions produce the same output?

(c) For which negative numbers do the two functions produce different outputs?

50. It is possible to write every even natural number uniquely as the product of two natural numbers, one odd and one a power of two. For example:

$$46 = 23 \times 2 \qquad 36 = 9 \times 2^2 \qquad 8 = 1 \times 2^3.$$

Consider the function whose input is the set of even integers and whose output is the odd number you get in the above process. So if the input is 36, the output is 9. If the input is 46, the output is 23.

(a) Write a table of values for inputs 2, 4, 6, 8, 10, 12 and 14.

(b) Find five different inputs that give an output of 3.

51. Example 11(b) showed how we create a table of values for a function when you get to choose all the values of the inputs. The technique presented does not work for Casio calculators. This exercise is designed for users of Casio calculators.

- Enter an equation such as $y = x^3 - 2x + 3$ in the equation memory. This can be done by selecting TABLE in the MAIN menu.

- Return to the MAIN menu and select LIST. Enter the numbers at which you want to evaluate the function as List 1.

- Return to the MAIN menu and select TABLE. Then press SET-UP [that is, 2nd MENU] and select LIST as the Variable; on the LIST menu, choose List 1. Press EXIT and then press TABL to produce the table.

- Use the up/down arrow key to scroll through the table. If you change an entry in the X column, the corresponding y_1 value will automatically change.

(a) Use this technique to duplicate the table in Example 11(b).

(b) Change the number -11 to 10, and confirm that you've obtained $10^3 - 2(10) + 3$.

2.2 Functional Notation

Section Objectives
- ■ Use functional notation.
- ■ Compute the difference quotient of a function.
- ■ Identify common mistakes made with functional notation.
- ■ Determine the domain of a function.
- ■ Use a piecewise-defined function.

Functional notation is a convenient shorthand language that facilitates the analysis of mathematical problems involving functions. It arises from real-life situations, such as the following.

EXAMPLE 1

In Section 3.1, we saw that the 2006 Louisiana state income tax rates (for a single person with one exemption and no deductions) were as follows:

Income		Tax
At Least	**But Less Than**	
0	$12,500	2.1%
$12,500	$25,000	$262.50 + 3.45% of amount over $12,500
$25,000		$693.75 + 4.8% of amount over $25,000

Let I denote income, and write $T(I)$ (read "T of I") to denote the amount of tax on income I. In this shorthand language, $T(7500)$ denotes "the tax on an income of $7500." The sentence "The tax on an income of $7500 is $157.50" is abbreviated as $T(7500) = 157.5$. Similarly, $T(25,000) = 693.75$ says that the tax on an income of $25,000 is $693.75. There is nothing that forces us to use the letters T and I here:

> **Any choice of letters will do, provided that we make clear what is meant by these letters.** ∎

EXAMPLE 2

Recall that a falling rock travels $16t^2$ feet after t seconds. Let $d(t)$ stand for the phrase "the distance the rock has traveled after t seconds." Then the sentence "The distance the rock has traveled after t seconds is $16t^2$ feet" can be abbreviated as $d(t) = 16t^2$. For instance,

$$d(1) = 16 \cdot 1^2 = 16$$

means "the distance the rock has traveled after 1 second is 16 feet," and

$$d(4) = 16 \cdot 4^2 = 256$$

means "the distance the rock has traveled after 4 seconds is 256 feet." ∎

CAUTION

The parentheses in $d(t)$ do *not* denote multiplication as in the algebraic equation $3(a + b) = 3a + 3b$. The entire symbol $d(t)$ is part of a *shorthand language*. In particular

$d(1 + 4)$ is *not* equal to $d(1) + d(4)$.

We saw above that $d(1) = 16$ and $d(4) = 256$, so $d(1) + d(4) = 16 + 256 = 272$. But $d(1 + 4)$ is "the distance traveled after $1 + 4$ seconds," that is, the distance after 5 seconds, namely, $16 \cdot 5^2 = 400$. In general,

Functional notation is a convenient shorthand for phrases and sentences in the English language. It is *not* the same as ordinary algebraic notation.

Functional notation is easily adapted to mathematical settings, in which the particulars of time, distance, etc., are not mentioned. Suppose a function is given. Denote the function by f and let x denote a number in the domain. Then

> $f(x)$ **denotes the output produced by input x.**

For example, $f(6)$ is the output produced by the input 6. The sentence

"y is the output produced by input x according to the rule of the function f"

is abbreviated

$$y = f(x),$$

which is read "y equals f of x." The output $f(x)$ is sometimes called the **value** of the function f at x.

In actual practice, functions are seldom presented in the style of domain, rule, range, as they have been here. Usually, you will be given a phrase such as "the function $f(x) = \sqrt{x^2 + 1}$." This should be understood as a set of directions:

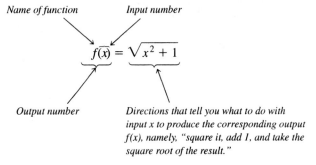

Name of function   Input number

$$\underbrace{f(x)}_{\text{Output number}} = \underbrace{\sqrt{x^2 + 1}}$$

Output number

Directions that tell you what to do with input x to produce the corresponding output $f(x)$, namely, "square it, add 1, and take the square root of the result."

For example, to find $f(3)$, the output of the function f for input 3, simply replace x by 3 in the formula:

$$f(x) = \sqrt{x^2 + 1}$$
$$f(3) = \sqrt{3^2 + 1} = \sqrt{10}.$$

Similarly, replacing x by -5 and 0 shows that

$$f(-5) = \sqrt{(-5)^2 + 1} = \sqrt{26} \quad \text{and} \quad f(0) = \sqrt{0^2 + 1} = 1.$$

EXAMPLE 3

The expression

$$h(x) = \frac{x^2 + 5}{x - 1}$$

defines the function h whose rule is

For input x, the output is the number $\dfrac{x^2 + 5}{x - 1}$.

Find each of the following:

$$h(\sqrt{3}), \qquad h(-2), \qquad h(-a), \qquad h(r^2 + 3), \qquad h(\sqrt{c + 2}).$$

SOLUTION   To find $h(\sqrt{3})$ and $h(-2)$, replace x by $\sqrt{3}$ and -2, respectively, in the rule of h:

$$h(\sqrt{3}) = \frac{(\sqrt{3})^2 + 5}{\sqrt{3} - 1} = \frac{8}{\sqrt{3} - 1} \quad \text{and} \quad h(-2) = \frac{(-2)^2 + 5}{-2 - 1} = -3.$$

The value of the function h at any quantity, such as $-a, r^2 + 3$, etc., can be found by using the same procedure: *Replace x in the formula for $h(x)$ by that quantity:*

$$h(-a) = \frac{(-a)^2 + 5}{-a - 1} = \frac{a^2 + 5}{-a - 1}$$

$$h(r^2 + 3) = \frac{(r^2 + 3)^2 + 5}{(r^2 + 3) - 1} = \frac{r^4 + 6r^2 + 9 + 5}{r^2 + 2} = \frac{r^4 + 6r^2 + 14}{r^2 + 2}$$

$$h(\sqrt{c + 2}) = \frac{(\sqrt{c + 2})^2 + 5}{\sqrt{c + 2} - 1} = \frac{c + 2 + 5}{\sqrt{c + 2} - 1} = \frac{c + 7}{\sqrt{c + 2} - 1}. \qquad \blacksquare$$

TECHNOLOGY TIP

One way to evaluate a function $f(x)$ is to enter its rule as an equation $y = f(x)$ in the equation memory and use TABLE or (on TI-86) EVAL; see Example 11 in Section 3.1.

When functional notation is used in expressions such as $f(-x)$ or $f(x + h)$, the same basic rule applies: Replace x in the formula by the *entire* expression in parentheses.

EXAMPLE 4

If $f(x) = x^2 + x - 2$, then

$$f(-3) = (-3)^2 + (-3) - 2 = 4$$

$$-f(3) = -(3^2 + 3 - 2) = -10$$

$$f(-x) = (-x)^2 + (-x) - 2 = x^2 - x - 2.$$

Note that for this function, $f(-x)$ is *not* the same as $-f(x)$, because $-f(x)$ is the negative of the number $f(x)$, that is,

$$-f(x) = -(x^2 + x - 2) = -x^2 - x + 2. \qquad ■$$

EXAMPLE 5

If $f(x) = x^2 - x + 2$ and $h \neq 0$, find

(a) $f(x + h)$ (b) $f(x + h) - f(x)$ (c) $\dfrac{f(x + h) - f(x)}{h}$.

SOLUTION

(a) Replace x by $x + h$ in the rule of the function:

$$f(x + h) = (x + h)^2 - (x + h) + 2$$

$$= x^2 + 2xh + h^2 - x - h + 2.$$

(b) By part (a),

$$f(x + h) - f(x) = [(x + h)^2 - (x + h) + 2] - [x^2 - x + 2]$$

$$= [x^2 + 2xh + h^2 - x - h + 2] - [x^2 - x + 2]$$

$$= x^2 + 2xh + h^2 - x - h + 2 - x^2 + x - 2$$

$$= 2xh + h^2 - h.$$

(c) By part (b), we have

$$\frac{f(x + h) - f(x)}{h} = \frac{2xh + h^2 - h}{h}$$

$$= \frac{h(2x + h - 1)}{h}$$

$$= 2x + h - 1. \qquad ■$$

If f is a function, then the quantity $\dfrac{f(x + h) - f(x)}{h}$, as in Example 5(c), is called the **difference quotient** of f. Difference quotients, whose significance is explained in Section 3.6, play an important role in calculus.

EXAMPLE 6

Compute and simplify the difference quotient for the function $f(x) = x^3 + 2x$.

SOLUTION

$$\frac{f(x + h) - f(x)}{h} = \frac{\overbrace{[(x + h)^3 + 2(x + h)]}^{f(x + h)} - \overbrace{[x^3 + 2x]}^{f(x)}}{h}$$

$$= \frac{[x^3 + 3x^2h + 3xh^2 + h^3 + 2x + 2h] - [x^3 + 2x]}{h}$$

$$= \frac{x^3 + 3x^2h + 3xh^2 + h^3 + 2x + 2h - x^3 - 2x}{h}$$

$$= \frac{3x^2h + 3xh^2 + h^3 + 2h}{h}$$

$$= \frac{h(3x^2 + 3xh + h^2 + 2)}{h}$$

$$= 3x^2 + 3xh + h^2 + 2. \quad\blacksquare$$

As the preceding examples illustrate, functional notation is a specialized shorthand language. Treating it as ordinary algebraic notation may lead to mistakes.

EXAMPLE 7

> **CAUTION**
>
> It is common to make mistakes with functional notation.
> Remember that, in general:
>
> $f(a + b) \neq f(a) + f(b)$
>
> $f(a - b) \neq f(a) - f(b)$
>
> $f(ab) \neq f(a)f(b)$
>
> $f(ab) \neq af(b)$
>
> $f(ab) \neq f(a)b$

Many students make untrue assumptions when working with functional notation. Here are examples of three of the items listed in the Caution box.

If $f(x) = x^2$, then

$$f(3 + 2) = f(5) = 5^2 = 25.$$

But

$$f(3) + f(2) = 3^2 + 2^2 = 9 + 4 = 13.$$

So $f(3 + 2) \neq f(3) + f(2)$.

If $f(x) = x + 7$, then

$$f(3 \cdot 4) = f(12) = 12 + 7 = 19.$$

But

$$f(3)f(4) = (3 + 7)(4 + 7) = 10 \cdot 11 = 110.$$

So $f(3 \cdot 4) \neq f(3)f(4)$.

If $f(x) = x^2 + 1$, then

$$f(2 \cdot 3) = (2 \cdot 3)^2 + 1 = 36 + 1 = 37.$$

But

$$f(2) \cdot 3 = (2^2 + 1)3 = 5 \cdot 3 = 15.$$

So $f(2 \cdot 3) \neq f(2) \cdot 3$. $\quad\blacksquare$

DOMAINS

When the rule of a function is given by a formula, as in Examples 3–7, its domain (set of inputs) is determined by the following convention.

Domain Convention

> Unless specific information to the contrary is given, the domain of a function f includes every real number (input) for which the rule of the function produces a real number as output.

Thus, the domain of a polynomial function such as $f(x) = x^3 - 4x + 1$ is the set of all real numbers, since $f(x)$ is defined for every value of x. In cases in which applying the rule of a function leads to division by zero or to the square root of a negative number, however, the domain may not consist of all real numbers, as illustrated in the next example.

EXAMPLE 8

Find the domain of the function given by

(a) $k(x) = \dfrac{x^2 + 5}{x - 1}$ (b) $f(u) = \sqrt{u + 2}$

SOLUTION

(a) When $x = 1$, the denominator of $\dfrac{x^2 + 5}{x - 1}$ is 0, and the fraction is not defined.

When $x \neq 1$, however, the denominator is nonzero and the fraction *is* defined. Therefore, the domain of the function k consists of all real numbers *except* 1.

(b) Since negative numbers do not have real square roots, $\sqrt{u + 2}$ is a real number only when $u + 2 \geq 0$, that is, when $u \geq -2$. Therefore, the domain of f consists of all real numbers greater than or equal to -2, that is, the interval $[-2, \infty)$. ∎

EXAMPLE 9

A **piecewise-defined** function is one whose rule includes several formulas, such as

$$f(x) = \begin{cases} 2x + 3 & \text{if } x < 4 \\ x^2 - 1 & \text{if } 4 \leq x \leq 10. \end{cases}$$

Find each of the following.

(a) $f(-5)$ (b) $f(8)$ (c) $f(k)$ (d) The domain of f.

SOLUTION

(a) Since $-5 < 4$, the first part of the rule applies:

$$f(-5) = 2(-5) + 3 = -7.$$

(b) Since 8 is between 4 and 10, the second part of the rule applies:

$$f(8) = 8^2 - 1 = 63.$$

(c) We cannot find $f(k)$ unless we know whether $k < 4$ or $4 \le k \le 10$.

(d) The rule of f gives no directions when $x > 10$, so the domain of f consists of all real numbers x with $x \le 10$, that is, $(-\infty, 10]$. ■

EXAMPLE 10

Use Example 1 to write the rule of the piecewise-defined function T that gives the Louisiana state income tax $T(x)$ on an income of x dollars.

SOLUTION   By translating the information in the table in Example 1 into functional notation, we obtain

$$T(x) = \begin{cases} .021x & \text{if } 0 \le x < 12{,}500 \\ 262.50 + .0345(x - 12{,}500) & \text{if } 12{,}500 \le x < 25{,}000 \\ 693.75 + .048(x - 25{,}000) & \text{if } x \ge 25{,}000. \end{cases}$$ ■

 ## APPLICATIONS

The domain convention does not always apply when dealing with applications. Consider, for example, the distance function for falling objects, $d(t) = 16t^2$ (see Example 2). Since t represents time, only nonnegative values of t make sense here, even though the rule of the function is defined for all values of t.

> **A real-life situation may lead to a function whose domain is smaller than the one dictated by the domain convention.**

EXAMPLE 11

A glassware factory has fixed expenses (mortgage, taxes, machinery, etc.) of $12,000 per week. It costs 80 cents to make one cup (labor, materials, shipping). A cup sells for $1.95. At most 18,000 cups can be manufactured and sold each week.

(a) Express the weekly revenue as a function of the number x of cups made.

(b) Express the weekly costs as a function of x.

(c) Find the domain and the rule of the weekly profit function.

SOLUTION

(a) If $R(x)$ is the weekly revenue from selling x cups, then

$$R(x) = (\text{price per cup}) \times (\text{number sold})$$

$$R(x) = 1.95x.$$

(b) If $C(x)$ is the weekly cost of manufacturing x cups, then

$$C(x) = (\text{cost per cup}) \times (\text{number sold}) + (\text{fixed expenses})$$

$$C(x) = .80x + 12{,}000.$$

(c) If $P(x)$ is the weekly profit from selling x cups, then

$$P(x) = \text{Revenue} - \text{Cost}$$
$$P(x) = R(x) - C(x)$$
$$P(x) = 1.95x - (.80x + 12{,}000) = 1.95x - .80x - 12{,}000$$
$$P(x) = 1.15x - 12{,}000.$$

Although this rule is defined for all real numbers x, the domain of the function P consists of the possible number of cups that can be made each week. Since you can make only whole cups and the maximum production is 18,000, the domain of P consists of all integers from 0 to 18,000. ■

EXAMPLE 12

Let P be the profit function in Example 11.

(a) What is the profit from selling 5000 cups? From 14,000 cups?

(b) What is the break-even point?

SOLUTION

(a) We evaluate the function $P(x) = 1.15x - 12{,}000$ at the required values of x:

$$P(5000) = 1.15(5000) - 12{,}000 = -\$6250$$

$$P(14{,}000) = 1.15(14{,}000) - 12{,}000 = \$4100.$$

Thus, sales of 5000 cups produce a loss of $6250, while sales of 14,000 produce a profit of $4100.

(b) The break-even point occurs when revenue equals costs (that is, when profit is 0). So we set $P(x) = 0$ and solve for x:

$$1.15x - 12{,}000 = 0$$

$$1.15x = 12{,}000$$

$$x = \frac{12{,}000}{1.15} \approx 10{,}434.78.$$

Thus, the break-even point occurs between 10,434 and 10,435 cups. There is a slight loss from selling 10,434 cups and a slight profit from selling 10,435. ■

EXERCISES 2.2

In Exercises 1 and 2, find the indicated values of the function by hand and by using the table feature of a calculator (or the EVAL key on TI-85/86). If your answers do not agree with each other or with those at the back of the book, you are either making algebraic mistakes or incorrectly entering the function in the equation memory.

1. $f(x) = \dfrac{x-3}{x^2+4}$

    (a) $f(-1)$ (b) $f(0)$ (c) $f(1)$ (d) $f(2)$ (e) $f(3)$

2. $g(x) = \sqrt{x+4} - 2$

    (a) $g(-2)$ (b) $g(0)$ (c) $g(4)$ (d) $g(5)$ (e) $g(12)$

Exercises 3–24 refer to these three functions:

$$f(x) = \sqrt{x+3} - x + 1$$

$$g(t) = t^2 - 1$$

$$h(x) = x^2 + \frac{1}{x} + 2.$$

In each case, find the indicated value of the function.

3. $f(0)$ 4. $f(1)$

5. $f(\sqrt{2})$ **6.** $f(\sqrt{2} - 1)$

7. $f(-2)$ 8. $f(-3/2)$

9. $h(-4)$ 10. $h(3/2)$

11. $h(\pi + 1)$ 12. $h(m)$

13. $h(a + k)$ 14. $f(a)$

15. $h(-x)$ 16. $h(2 - x)$

17. $h(x - 3)$ 18. $g(3)$

19. $g(s + 1)$ **20.** $g(1 - r)$

21. $g(-t)$ 22. $g(t + h)$

23. $f(g(3))$ 24. $f(g(t))$

In Exercises 25–34, assume $h \neq 0$. Compute and simplify the difference quotient

$$\frac{f(x + h) - f(x)}{h}$$

25. $f(x) = x + 1$ 26. $f(x) = -10x$

27. $f(x) = 3x + 7$ 28. $f(x) = x^2$

29. $f(x) = x - x^2$ 30. $f(x) = x^3$

31. $f(x) = \sqrt{x}$ **32.** $f(x) = 1/x$

33. $f(x) = x^2 + 3$ 34. $f(x) = 3$

35. In each part, compute $f(a)$, $f(b)$, and $f(a + b)$, and determine whether the statement "$f(a + b) = f(a) + f(b)$" is true or false for the given function.

   (a) $f(x) = x^2$ (b) $f(x) = 3x$ (c) $f(x) = 5$

36. In each part, compute $g(a)$, $g(b)$, and $g(ab)$, and determine whether the satement "$g(ab) = g(a) \cdot g(b)$" is true or false for the given function.

   (a) $g(x) = x^3$ (b) $g(x) = 5x$ (c) $g(x) = -2$

37. If $f(x) = x^3 + cx^2 + 4x - 1$ for some constant c and $f(1) = 2$, find c. [*Hint:* Use the rule of f to compute $f(1)$.]

38. If $f(x) = \dfrac{dx - 5}{x - 3}$ and $f(4) = 3$, find d.

39. The rule of the function f is given by the graph, as in Example 4 of Section 3.1. Find

   (a) The domain of f

   (b) The range of f

   (c) $f(-3)$

   (d) $f(-1)$

   (e) $f(1)$

   (f) $f(2)$

40. The rule of the function g is given by the graph. Find

   (a) The domain of g

   (b) The range of g

   (c) $g(-3)$

   (d) $g(-1)$

   (e) $g(1)$

   (f) $g(4)$

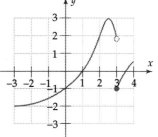

41. Let $f(x) = \begin{cases} -x & \text{if } x < 2 \\ x & \text{if } x \geq 0 \end{cases}$

This function is identical to a function you already know. What is that function?

42. Let $f(x) = \begin{cases} 1/x & \text{if } x \neq 0 \\ 2 & \text{if } x = 0 \end{cases}$

Find the domain of f.

43. If $f(x) = \begin{cases} x^2 + 2x & \text{if } x < 2 \\ 3x - 5 & \text{if } 2 \leq x \leq 20 \end{cases}$ find

   (a) The domain of f

   (b) $f(-3)$ (c) $f(-1)$ (d) $f(2)$ (e) $f(7/3)$

44. If $g(x) = \begin{cases} 2x - 3 & \text{if } x < -1 \\ |x| - 5 & \text{if } -1 \leq x \leq 2 \\ x^2 & \text{if } x > 2 \end{cases}$ find

   (a) The domain of g

   (b) $g(-2.5)$ (c) $g(-1)$ (d) $g(2)$ (e) $g(4)$

In Exercises 45–58, determine the domain of the function according to the usual convention.

45. $f(x) = x^2$ 46. $g(x) = \dfrac{1}{x^2} + 2$

47. $h(t) = |t| - 1$ 48. $k(u) = \sqrt{u}$

49. $k(x) = |x| + \sqrt{x} - 1$ **50.** $h(x) = \sqrt{(x + 1)^2}$

51. $g(u) = \dfrac{|u|}{u}$ 52. $h(x) = \dfrac{\sqrt{x - 1}}{x^2 - 1}$

53. $g(y) = [\![-y]\!]$ 54. $f(t) = \sqrt{-t}$

55. $g(u) = \dfrac{u^2 + 1}{u^2 - u - 6}$ 56. $f(t) = \sqrt{4 - t^2}$

57. $f(x) = -\sqrt{9 - (x - 9)^2}$

58. $f(x) = \sqrt{-x} + \dfrac{2}{x + 1}$

59. Give an example of two different functions f and g that have all of the following properties:

$$f(-1) = 1 = g(-1) \quad \text{and} \quad f(0) = 0 = g(0)$$
$$\text{and} \quad f(1) = 1 = g(1).$$

60. Give an example of a function g with the property that $g(x) = g(-x)$ for every real number x.

61. Give an example of a function g with the property that $g(-x) = -g(x)$ for every real number x.

In Exercises 62–65, find the values of x for which $f(x) = g(x)$.

62. $f(x) = 2x^2 + 4x - 4$; $g(x) = x^2 + 12x + 6$

63. $f(x) = 2x^2 + 13x - 14$; $g(x) = 8x - 2$

64. $f(x) = 3x^2 - x + 5$; $g(x) = x^2 - 2x + 26$

65. $f(x) = 2x^2 - x + 1$; $g(x) = x^2 - 4x + 4$

In Exercises 66–68, the rule of a function f is given. Write an algebraic formula for $f(x)$.

66. Triple the input, subtract 8, and take the square root of the result.

67. Square the input, multiply by 3, and subtract the result from 8.

68. Cube the input, add 6, and divide the result by 5.

69. A potato chip factory has a daily overhead from salaries and building costs of $1800. The cost of ingredients and packaging to produce a pound of potato chips is 50¢. A pound of potato chips sells for $1.20. Show that the factory's daily profit is a function of the number of pounds of potato chips sold, and find the rule of this function. (Assume that the factory sells all the potato chips it produces each day.)

70. Jack and Jill are salespersons in the suit department of a clothing store. Jack is paid $200 per week plus $5 for each suit he sells, whereas Jill is paid $10 for every suit she sells.

(a) Let $f(x)$ denote Jack's weekly income, and let $g(x)$ denote Jill's weekly income from selling x suits. Find the rules of the functions f and g.

(b) Use algebra or a table to find $f(20)$ and $g(20)$, $f(35)$ and $g(35)$, $f(50)$ and $g(50)$.

(c) If Jack sells 50 suits a week, how many must Jill sell to have the same income as Jack?

71. A person who needs crutches can determine the correct length as follows: a 50-inch-tall person needs a 38-inch-long crutch. For each additional inch in the person's height, add .72 inch to the crutch length.

(a) If a person is y inches taller than 50 inches, write an expression for the proper crutch length.

(b) Write the rule of a function f such that $f(x)$ is the proper crutch length (in inches) for a person who is x inches tall. [*Hint:* Replace y in your answer to part (a) with an expression in x. How are x and y related?]

72. The table shows the 2006 federal income tax rates for a single person.

Taxable Income		Tax
Over	**But Not Over**	
0	$7,300	10% of income
$7,300	$29,700	$730.00 + 15% of amount over $7,300
$29,700	$71,950	$4090.00 + 25% of amount over $29,700
$71,950	$150,150	$14,652.50 + 28% of amount over $71,950
$150,150	$326,450	$36,548.50 + 33% of amount over $150,150
$326,450		$94,727.50 + 35% of amount over $326,450

(a) Write the rule of a piecewise-defined function T such that $T(x)$ is the tax due on a taxable income of x dollars.

(b) Find $T(24,000)$, $T(35,000)$, and $T(200,000)$.

73. Suppose a car travels at a constant rate of 55 mph for 2 hours and travels at 45 mph thereafter. Show that distance traveled is a function of time, and find the rule of the function.

74. A man walks for 45 minutes at a rate of 3 mph, then jogs for 75 minutes at a rate of 5 mph, then sits and rests for 30 minutes, and finally walks for $1\frac{1}{2}$ hours. Find the rule of the function that expresses his distance traveled as a function of time. [*Caution:* Don't mix up the units of time; use either minutes or hours, not both.]

75. Suppose that the width and height of the box in the figure are equal and that the sum of the length and the girth is 108 (the maximum size allowed by the post office).

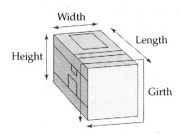

(a) Express the length y as a function of the width x. [*Hint:* Use the girth.]

(b) Express the volume V of the box as a function of the width x. [*Hint:* Find a formula for the volume and use part (a).]

76. A rectangular region of 6000 square feet is to be fenced in on three sides with fencing costing $3.75 per foot and on the fourth side with fencing costing $2.00 per foot. Express the cost of the fence as a function of the length x of the fourth side.

77. A box with a square base measuring $t \times t$ ft is to be made of three kinds of wood. The cost of the wood for the base is 85¢ per square foot; the wood for the sides costs 50¢ per square foot, and the wood for the top $1.15 per square foot. The volume of the box is to be 10 cubic feet. Express the total cost of the box as a function of the length t.

78. Average tuition and fees in private four-year colleges in recent years were as follows.*

Year	Tuition and Fees	Year	Tuition and Fees
1995	$12,432	1999	$15,380
1996	$12,823	2000	$16,332
1997	$13,664	2001	$17,727
1998	$14,709	2002	$18,723

(a) Use linear regression to find the rule of a function f that gives the approximate average tuition in year x, where $x = 0$ corresponds to 1990.

*The College Board.

(b) Find $f(6)$, $f(8)$, and $f(10)$. How do they compare with the actual figures?
(c) Use f to estimate tuition and fees in 2011.

79. The number of U.S. commercial radio stations whose primary format is top 40 hits has been increasing in recent years, as shown in the table.*

Year	Number of Stations
1998	379
1999	401
2001	468
2002	474
2003	491
2004	497
2005	502

(a) Use linear regression to find the rule of a function g that gives the number of top-40 stations in year x, where $x = 0$ corresponds to 1990.
(b) Find $g(8)$ and $g(11)$. How do they compare with the actual figures?
(c) Data for the year 2000 is missing. Estimate the number of stations in 2000.
(d) Assuming that this function remains accurate, estimate the number of stations in 2011.

*World Almanac and Book of Facts 2006.

2.3 Graphs of Functions

Section Objectives

- Recognize the general shape and behavior of graphs of basic functions.
- Graph step functions and piecewise-defined functions.
- Find local maxima and minima.
- Determine intervals on which a function is increasing or decreasing.
- Use the vertical line test to identify the graph of a function.
- Interpret information presented in a graph.

The graph of a function f is the graph of the equation $y = f(x)$. Hence

The graph of the function f consists of the points $(x, f(x))$ for every number x in the domain of f.

When the rule of a function is given by an algebraic formula, the graph is easily obtained with technology. However, machine-generated graphs can sometimes be

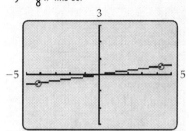
incomplete or misleading. So the emphasis here is on using your algebraic knowledge *before* reaching for a calculator. Doing so will often tell you that a calculator is inappropriate or help you to interpret screen images when a calculator is used.

Some functions appear so frequently that you should memorize the shapes of their graphs, which are easily obtained by hand-graphing or by using technology. Regardless of how you first find these graphs, you should be able to reproduce them without looking them up or resorting to technology. These basic graphs are summarized in the **catalog of functions** at the end of this section. A title on an example (such as "linear function" in Example 1) indicates a function that is in the catalog.

EXAMPLE 1

Linear Functions   The graph of a function of the form

$$f(x) = mx + b \qquad \text{(with } m \text{ and } b \text{ constants)}$$

is the graph of the equation $y = mx + b$. As we saw in Section 1.4, the graph is a straight line with slope m and y-intercept b that can easily be obtained by hand. Some typical linear functions are graphed in Figure 2–8 (several of them have special names). ∎

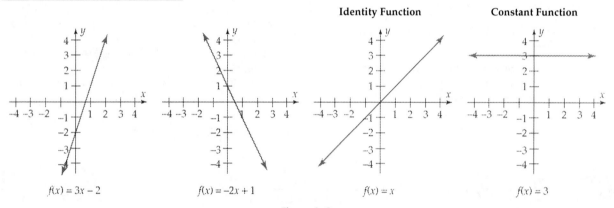

$f(x) = 3x - 2$ $f(x) = -2x + 1$ $f(x) = x$ $f(x) = 3$

Figure 2–8

EXAMPLE 2

Square and Cube Functions   Figure 2–9 shows the graphs of $f(x) = x^2$ and $g(x) = x^3$. They can be obtained by plotting points (as was done for f in Example 1 of Section 2.1) or by using technology. ∎

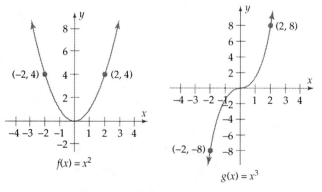

$f(x) = x^2$ $g(x) = x^3$

Figure 2–9

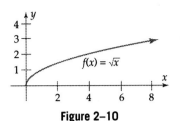

Figure 2–10

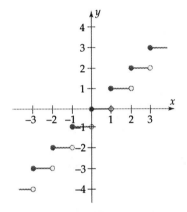

Figure 2–11

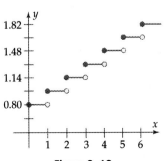

Figure 2–12

EXAMPLE 3

Square Root Function   The graph of $f(x) = \sqrt{x}$ in Figure 2–10 is easily found. Why does it lie entirely in the first quadrant?   ∎

◐ STEP FUNCTIONS

The greatest integer function $f(x) = [\![x]\!]$ was introduced in Example 7 of Section 3.1. It can easily be graphed by hand, as in the next example.

EXAMPLE 4

Greatest Integer Function   We graph $f(x) = [\![x]\!]$ by considering the values of the function between each two consecutive integers. For instance,

x	$-2 \le x < -1$	$-1 \le x < 0$	$0 \le x < 1$	$1 \le x < 2$	$2 \le x < 3$
$[\![x]\!]$	-2	-1	0	1	2

Thus, between $x = -2$ and $x = -1$, the value of $f(x) = [\![x]\!]$ is always -2, so the graph there is a horizontal line segment, all of whose points have second coordinate -2. The rest of the graph is obtained similarly (Figure 2–11). An open circle in Figure 2–11 indicates that the endpoint of the segment is *not* on the graph, whereas a closed circle indicates that the endpoint is on the graph.   ∎

A function whose graph consists of horizontal line segments, such as Figure 2–11, is called a **step function.** Graphing step functions with reasonable accuracy on a calculator requires some care. Even then, some features of the graph might not be shown.

GRAPHING EXPLORATION

Graph the greatest integer function $f(x) = [\![x]\!]$ on your calculator (see the Technology Tip on page 79). Does your graph look like Figure 2–11, or does it include vertical segments? Now change the graphing mode of your calculator to "dot" rather than "connected", and graph again. How does this graph compare with Figure 2–11? Can you tell from the graph which endpoints are included and which are excluded?

EXAMPLE 5

As of this writing, United States postage rates for large envelopes are 80 cents for the first ounce (or fraction thereof) plus 17 cents for each additional ounce or fraction thereof. Verify that the postage $P(x)$ for a letter weighing x ounces is given by $P(x) = .80 - .17[\![1 - x]\!]$. For instance, the postage for a 2.5 ounce large envelope is

$$P(2.5) = .80 - .17[\![1 - 2.5]\!] = .80 - .17(-2) = 1.14$$

Although the rule of P makes sense for all real numbers, the domain of the function consists of positive numbers (why?). The graph of P is in Figure 2–12.   ∎

PIECEWISE-DEFINED FUNCTIONS

Piecewise-defined functions were introduced in Example 9 of Section 3.2. Graphing them correctly requires some care.

EXAMPLE 6

The graph of the piecewise-defined function

$$f(x) = \begin{cases} x^2 & \text{if } x \leq 1 \\ x + 2 & \text{if } 1 < x \leq 4 \end{cases}$$

is made up of *parts* of two graphs, corresponding to the different parts of the rule of the function:

$x \leq 1$ For these values of x, the graph of f coincides with the graph of $y = x^2$, which was sketched in Figure 2–9.

$1 < x \leq 4$ For these values of x, the graph of f coincides with the graph of $y = x + 2$, which is a straight line.

Therefore, we must graph

$$y = x^2 \quad \text{when } x \leq 1 \qquad \text{and} \qquad y = x + 2 \quad \text{when } 1 < x \leq 4.$$

Combining these partial graphs produces the graph of f in Figure 2–13. ■

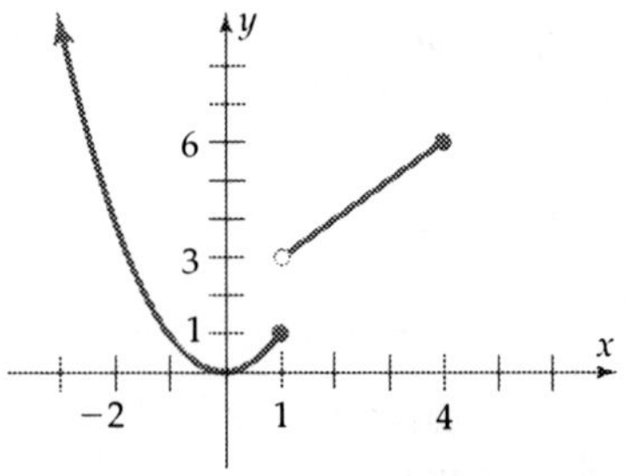

Figure 2–13

Piecewise-defined functions can be graphed on a calculator, provided that you use the correct syntax. Once again, however, the screen does not show which endpoints are included or excluded from the graph.

TECHNOLOGY TIP

Inequality symbols can be found in the following menu/submenu:

TI-84+/86: TEST

TI-89: MATH/TEST

HP-39gs: MATH/TESTS

GRAPHING EXPLORATION

Use the Technology Tip in the margin and the directions here to graph the function f of Example 6 on a calculator. On TI-84+/86 and HP-39gs, graph these two equations on the same screen:

$$y_1 = \frac{x^2}{(x \leq 1)}$$

$$y_2 = \frac{(x + 2)}{(x > 1)(x \leq 4)}.$$

On TI-89, graph the following equations on the same screen (the symbol | is on the keyboard; "and" is in the TESTS submenu of the MATH menu):

$$y_1 = x^2 | x \leq 1$$

$$y_2 = x + 2 | x > 1 \quad \text{and} \quad x \leq 4.$$

To graph f on Casio, with the viewing window of Figure 3–13, graph these equations on the same screen (including commas and square brackets):

$$y_1 = x^2, [-6, 1]$$

$$y_2 = x + 2, [1, 4].$$

How does your graph compare with Figure 3–13?

EXAMPLE 7

Absolute Value Function   The absolute value function $f(x) = |x|$ is also a piecewise-defined function, since by definition,

$$|x| = \begin{cases} x & \text{if } x \geq 0 \\ -x & \text{if } x < 0. \end{cases}$$

Its graph can be obtained by drawing the part of the line $y = x$ to the right of the origin and the part of the line $y = -x$ to the left of the origin (Figure 2–14) or by graphing $y = \text{ABS } x$ on a calculator (Figure 2–15). ■

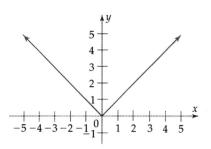

Figure 2–14

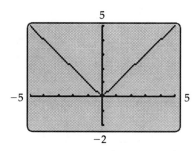

Figure 2–15

LOCAL MAXIMA AND MINIMA

The graph of a function may include some peaks and valleys (Figure 2–16). A peak is not necessarily the highest point on the graph, but it is the highest point in its neighborhood. Similarly, a valley is the lowest point in the neighborhood but not necessarily the lowest point on the graph.

    More formally, we say that a function f has a **local maximum** at $x = c$ if the graph of f has a peak at the point $(c, f(c))$. This means that all nearby points $(x, f(x))$ have smaller y-coordinates, that is,

$$f(x) \leq f(c) \quad \text{for all } x \text{ near } c.$$

Similarly, a function has a **local minimum** at $x = d$ provided that

$$f(x) \geq f(d) \quad \text{for all } x \text{ near } d.$$

In other words, the graph of f has a valley at $(d, f(d))$ because all nearby points $(x, f(x))$ have larger y-coordinates.

    Calculus is usually needed to find the exact location of local maxima and minima (the plural forms of maximum and minimum). However, they can be accurately approximated by the maximum finder or minimum finder of a calculator.

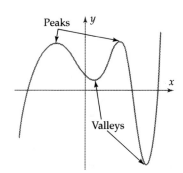

Figure 2–16

EXAMPLE 8

The graph of $f(x) = x^3 - 1.8x^2 + x + 1$ in Figure 2–17 on the next page does not appear to have any local maxima or minima. However, if you use the trace feature to move along the flat segment to the right of the y-axis, you find that the y-coordinates increase, then decrease, then increase (try it!). To see what's really going on, we change viewing windows (Figure 2–18) and see that the function actually has a

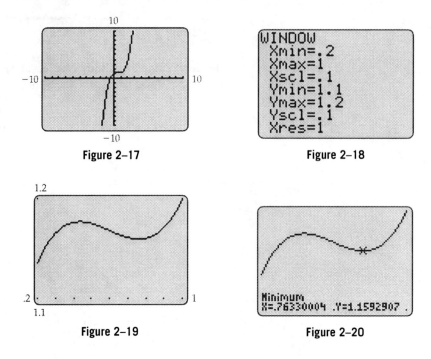

Figure 2–17

Figure 2–18

Figure 2–19

Figure 2–20

local maximum and a local minimum (Figure 2–19). The calculator's minimum finder shows that the local minimum occurs when $x \approx .7633$ (Figure 2–20). ■

GRAPHING EXPLORATION

Graph the function in Example 8 in the viewing window of Figure 2–18. Use the maximum finder to approximate the location of the local maximum.

EXAMPLE 9

A box with no top is to be made from a 44×28 inch sheet of cardboard by cutting squares of equal size from each corner and folding up the flaps, as shown in Figure 2–21.

What size square maximizes the volume of the box?

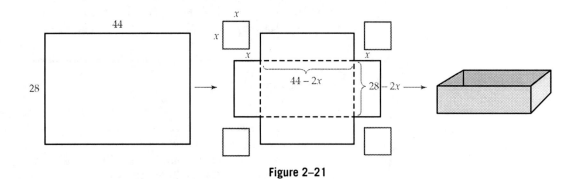

Figure 2–21

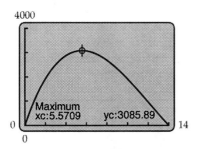

Figure 2–22

SOLUTION The situation here is similar to the one in Example 10 of Section 2.3. As that example shows, the function that gives the volume of the box is

$$V(x) = \text{Length} \times \text{Width} \times \text{Height}$$
$$= (44 - 2x)(28 - 2x)x$$
$$= 4x^3 - 144x^2 + 1232x.$$

We graph the function and use the maximum finder to determine that the local maximum occurs when the squares are approximately 5.57 inches on a side (Figure 2–22). ■

INCREASING AND DECREASING FUNCTIONS

A function is said to be **increasing on an interval** if its graph always rises as you move from left to right over the interval. It is **decreasing on an interval** if its graph always falls as you move from left to right over the interval. A function is said to be **constant on an interval** if its graph is horizontal over the interval.

EXAMPLE 10

Figure 2–23 suggests that $f(x) = |x| + |x - 2|$ is decreasing on the interval $(-\infty, 0)$, increasing on $(2, \infty)$, and constant on $[0, 2]$. You can confirm that the function is actually constant between 0 and 2 by using the trace feature to move along the graph there (the y-coordinates remain the same, as they should on a horizontal segment). For an algebraic proof that f is constant on $[0, 2]$, see Exercise 25. ■

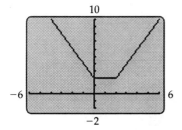

Figure 2–23

CAUTION

A horizontal segment on a calculator graph does not always mean that the function is constant there. There may be **hidden behavior,** as was the case in Example 8. When in doubt, either change the viewing window, or use the trace feature to see if the y-coordinates remain constant as you move along the "horizontal" segment.

EXAMPLE 11

On what (approximate) intervals is the function $g(x) = .5x^3 - 3x$ increasing or decreasing?

SOLUTION The (complete) graph of g in Figure 2–24 shows that g has a local maximum at P and a local minimum at Q. The maximum and minimum finders show that the approximate coordinates of P and Q are

$$P = (-1.4142, 2.8284) \qquad \text{and} \qquad Q = (1.4142, -2.8284).$$

Therefore, f is increasing on $(-\infty, -1.4142)$ and $(1.4142, \infty)$. It is decreasing on $(-1.4142, 1.4142)$. ■

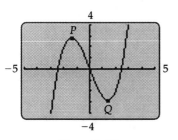

Figure 2–24

GRAPH READING

Until now, we have concentrated on translating statements into functional notation and functional notation into graphs. It is just as important, however, to be able
to translate graphical information into equivalent statements in English or functional notation.

EXAMPLE 12

The entire graph of a function f is shown in Figure 2–25. Find the domain and
range of f.

SOLUTION   The graph of f consists of all points of the form $(x, f(x))$. Thus, the
first coordinates of points on the graph are the inputs (numbers in the domain
of f) and the second coordinates are the outputs (the numbers in the range of f).
Figure 2–25 shows that the first coordinates of points on the graph all satisfy
$-1 \leq x \leq 1$, so these numbers are the domain of f. Similarly, the range of f consists of all numbers y such that $0 \leq y \leq \pi$, because these are the second coordinates of points on the graph.   ∎

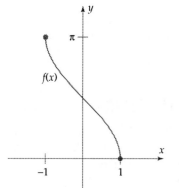

Figure 2–25

EXAMPLE 13

The consumer confidence level reflects people's feelings about their employment
opportunities and income prospects. Let $C(t)$ be the consumer confidence level at
time t (with $t = 0$ corresponding to 1970) and consider the graph of the function
C in Figure 2–26.*

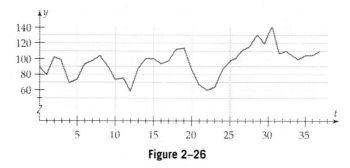

Figure 2–26

(a) How did the consumer confidence level vary in the 1980s?

(b) What was the lowest level of consumer confidence during the 1990s?

(c) When was the biggest drop in consumer confidence in the 2000s?

(d) During what time periods was the confidence level above 110?

(e) What is the range of C?

SOLUTION

(a) The 1980s correspond to the interval $10 \leq t \leq 20$, so we consider the part of
the graph that lies between the vertical lines $t = 10$ and $t = 20$. The second
coordinates of these points range from approximately 60 to 115. So the

*The consumer confidence level is scaled to be 100 in 1985.

consumer confidence level varied from a low of 60 to a high of 115 during the 1980s.

(b) The 1990s correspond to the interval $20 \leq t \leq 30$. Figure 2–26 shows that the graph has local minimums at $t = 22$ and $t = 29$. The lowest of these three points is the one at $t = 22$. Hence, the lowest level of consumer confidence in the 1990s occurred at the beginning of 1992.

(c) The 2000s correspond to the interval $30 \leq t \leq 37$. Figure 2–26 shows the fastest drop occurred between 2001 and 2002.

(d) We must find the values of t for which the graph lies above the horizontal line through 110. Figure 2–26 shows that this occurs approximately when $17.5 \leq t \leq 19.5$ and when $26.5 \leq t \leq 31.5$. Thus, the confidence level was above 110 from the middle of 1987 to the middle of 1989 and from the middle of 1996 to the middle of 2001.

(e) The range of C will be all numbers y such that (t, y) appears on the graph. Examining the graph gives an approximate range of $60 \leq y \leq 140$. ■

THE VERTICAL LINE TEST

The following fact distinguishes graphs of functions from other graphs.

Vertical Line Test

The graph of a function $y = f(x)$ has this property:

No vertical line intersects the graph more than once.

Conversely, any graph with this property is the graph of a function.

To see why this is true, consider Figure 2–27, in which the graph intersects the vertical line at two points. If this were the graph of a function f, then we would have $f(3) = 2$ [because (3, 2) is on the graph] *and* $f(3) = -1$ [because $(3, -1)$ is on the graph]. This means that the input 3 produces two different outputs, which is impossible for a function. Therefore, Figure 2–27 is not the graph of a function. A similar argument works in the general case.

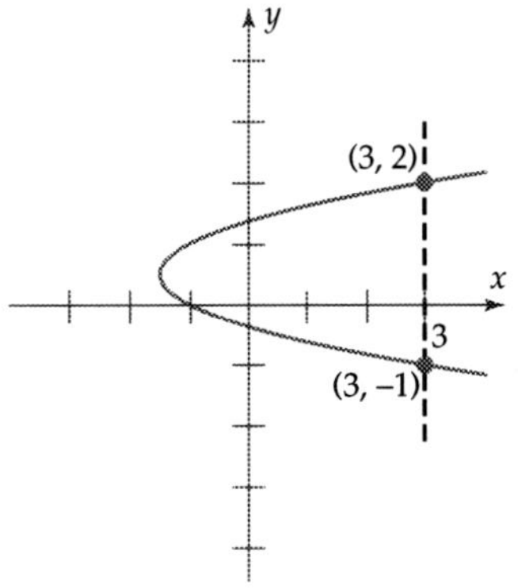

Care must be used when applying the Vertical Line test to a calculator graph. For example, if we graph $g(x) = 4 - |x^{10} - 2|$ in the standard viewing window, it looks like it fails the vertical line test near $x = 1$, among other places (Figure 2–28). But if we use the window with $1 \leq x \leq 1.25$, $5 \leq y \leq 5$ we see that $g(x)$ does pass the vertical line test at $x = 1$ (Figure 2–29).

Figure 2–27

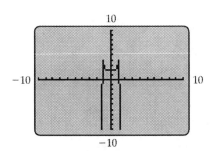

Figure 2–28

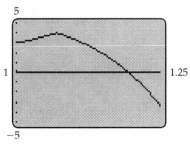

Figure 2–29

CATALOG OF BASIC FUNCTIONS

As was noted at the beginning of this section, there are a number of functions whose graphs you should know by heart. The ones in this section are listed below; others will be added as we go along. The entire catalog appears on the inside front cover of this book.

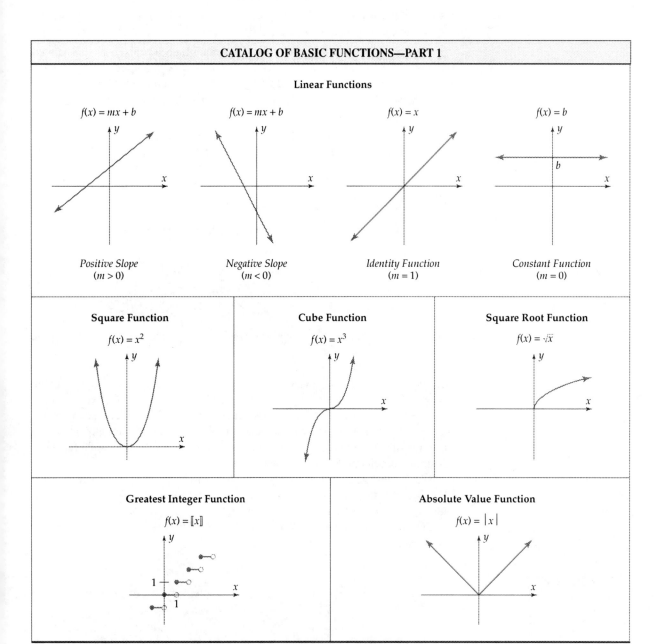

CATALOG OF BASIC FUNCTIONS—PART 1

Linear Functions

$f(x) = mx + b$ — Positive Slope ($m > 0$)

$f(x) = mx + b$ — Negative Slope ($m < 0$)

$f(x) = x$ — Identity Function ($m = 1$)

$f(x) = b$ — Constant Function ($m = 0$)

Square Function
$f(x) = x^2$

Cube Function
$f(x) = x^3$

Square Root Function
$f(x) = \sqrt{x}$

Greatest Integer Function
$f(x) = [\![x]\!]$

Absolute Value Function
$f(x) = |x|$

EXERCISES 2.3

In Exercises 1–4, state whether or not the graph is the graph of a function. If it is, find f (3).

1.

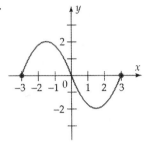

2.

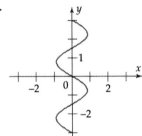

3.

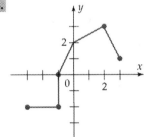

4.

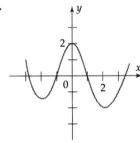

In Exercises 5–11, sketch the graph of the function, being sure to indicate which endpoints are included and which ones are excluded.

5. $f(x) = 2[\![x]\!]$ **6.** $f(x) = -[\![x]\!]$

7. $g(x) = [\![-x]\!]$ [This is *not* the same function as in Exercise 6.]

8. $f(x) = \begin{cases} x^2 & \text{if } x \geq -1 \\ 2x + 3 & \text{if } x < -1 \end{cases}$

9. $k(u) = \begin{cases} -2u - 2 & \text{if } u < -3 \\ u - [\![u]\!] & \text{if } -3 \leq u \leq 1 \\ 2u^2 & \text{if } u > 1 \end{cases}$

10. As of this writing, U.S. postage rates for large envelopes are 80 cents for the first ounce (or fraction thereof) plus 17 cents for each additional ounce or fraction thereof (see Example 5). Assume that each large envelope carries one 80 cent stamp and as many 17 cent stamps as necessary. Then the *number* of stamps required for a large envelope is a function of the weight of the envelope in ounces. Call this function the *postage stamp function.*

    (a) Describe the rule of the postage stamp function algebraically.

    (b) Sketch the graph of the postage stamp function.

11. A common mistake is to graph the function f in Example 6 by graphing both $y = x^2$ and $y = x + 2$ on the same screen (with no restrictions on x). Explain why this graph could not possibly be the graph of a function.

Exercises 12–21 deal with the graph of g shown in the figure.

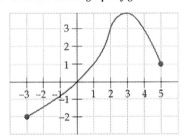

12. Is g a function? Why or why not?

13. What is the domain of g?

14. What is the range of g?

15. Find the approximate intervals where g is increasing.

16. Find the approximate intervals where g is decreasing.

17. If $t = 2$, then $g(t + 1.5) = ?$

18. If $t = 2$, then $g(t) + g(1.5) = ?$

19. If $t = 2$, then $g(t) + 1.5 = ?$

20. For what values of x is $g(x) < 0$?

21. For what values of a is $g(a) = 1$?

In Exercises 22–24, (a) Use the fact that the absolute value function is piecewise-defined (see Example 7) to write the rule of the given function as a piecewise-defined function whose rule does not include any absolute value bars. (b) Graph the function.

22. $g(x) = |x| - 4$ **23.** $h(x) = |x|/2 - 2$

24. $g(x) = |x + 3|$

25. Show that the function $f(x) = |x| + |x - 2|$ is constant on the interval $[0, 2]$. [*Hint:* Use the definition of absolute value (see Example 7) to compute $f(x)$ when $0 \leq x \leq 2$.]

In Exercises 26–31, find the approximate location of all local maxima and minima of the function.

26. $f(x) = x^3 - x$

27. $g(t) = -\sqrt{16 - t^2}$

28. $h(x) = \dfrac{x}{x^2 + 1}$

29. $k(x) = x^3 - 3x + 1$

30. $l(x) = \dfrac{1}{1 + x^2}$

31. $m(x) = x^3$

In Exercises 32–35, find the approximate intervals on which the function is increasing, those on which it is decreasing, and those on which it is constant.

32. $f(x) = |x - 1| - |x + 1|$

33. $f(x) = -x^3 - 8x^2 + 8x + 5$

34. $f(x) = \sqrt{x}$

35. $f(x) = \dfrac{1}{x}$

36. Let $F(x) =$ the U.S. federal debt in year x, and let $p(x) =$ the federal debt as a percent of the gross domestic product in year x. The graphs of these functions appear below.* Explain why the graph of F is increasing from 1996–2001, while the graph of p is decreasing during that period.

Gross Federal Debt

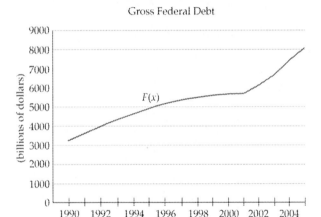

Federal Debt as a Percent of Gross Domestic Product

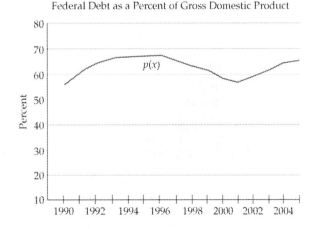

*Graphs prepared by U.S. Census Bureau, based on data from the U.S. Office of Management and Budget.

37. Find the dimensions of the rectangle with perimeter 100 inches and largest possible area, as follows.

(a) Use the figure to write an equation in x and z that expresses the fact that the perimeter of the rectangle is 100.

(b) The area A of the rectangle is given by $A = xz$ (why?). Write an equation that expresses A as a function of x. [*Hint:* Solve the equation in part (a) for z, and substitute the result in the area equation.]

(c) Graph the function in part (b), and find the value of x that produces the largest possible value of A. What is z in this case?

38. Find the dimensions of the rectangle with area 240 square inches and smallest possible perimeter, as follows.

(a) Using the figure for Exercise 37, write an equation for the perimeter P of the rectangle in terms of x and z.

(b) Write an equation in x and z that expresses the fact that the area of the rectangle is 240.

(c) Write an equation that expresses P as a function of x. [*Hint:* Solve the equation in part (b) for z, and substitute the result in the equation of part (a).]

(d) Graph the function in part (c), and find the value of x that produces the smallest possible value of P. What is z in this case?

39. Find the dimensions of a box with a square base that has a volume of 867 cubic inches and the smallest possible surface area, as follows.

(a) Write an equation for the surface area S of the box in terms of x and h. [Be sure to include all four sides, the top, and the bottom of the box.]

(b) Write an equation in x and h that expresses the fact that the volume of the box is 867.

(c) Write an equation that expresses S as a function of x. [*Hint:* Solve the equation in part (b) for h, and substitute the result in the equation of part (a).]

(d) Graph the function in part (c), and find the value of x that produces the smallest possible value of S. What is h in this case?

40. Find the radius r and height h of a cylindrical can with a surface area of 60 square inches and the largest possible volume, as follows.

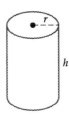

(a) Write an equation for the volume V of the can in terms of r and h.
(b) Write an equation in r and h that expresses the fact that the surface area of the can is 60. [*Hint:* Think of cutting the top and bottom off the can; then cut the side of the can lengthwise and roll it out flat; it's now a rectangle. The surface area is the area of the top and bottom plus the area of this rectangle. The length of the rectangle is the same as the circumference of the original can (why?).]
(c) Write an equation that expresses V as a function of r. [*Hint:* Solve the equation in part (b) for h, and substitute the result in the equation of part (a).]
(d) Graph the function in part (c), and find the value of r that produces the largest possible value of V. What is h in this case?

41. Match each of the functions (a)–(e) with the graph that best fits the situation.

(a) The phases of the moon as a function of time;
(b) The demand for a product as a function of its price;
(c) The height of a ball thrown from the top of a building as a function of time;
(d) The distance a woman runs at constant speed as a function of time;
(e) The temperature of an oven turned on and set to 350° as a function of time.

In Exercises 42 and 43, sketch a plausible graph of the given function. Label the axes and specify a reasonable domain and range.

42. The distance from the top of your head to the ground as you jump on a trampoline as a function of time.

43. The temperature of an oven that is turned on, set to 350°, and 45 minutes later turned off as a function of time.

44. A plane flies from Austin, Texas, to Cleveland, Ohio, a distance of 1200 miles. Let f be the function whose rule is $f(t)$ = distance (in miles) from Austin at time t hours. Draw a plausible graph of f under the given circumstances. [There are many possible correct answers for each part.]

(a) The flight is nonstop and takes less than 4 hours.
(b) Bad weather forces the plane to land in Dallas (about 200 miles from Austin), remain overnight (for 8 hours), and continue the next day.
(c) The flight is nonstop, but owing to heavy traffic, the plane must fly in a holding pattern over Cincinnati (about 200 miles from Cleveland) for an hour before going on to Cleveland.

In Exercises 45–46, the graph of a function f is shown. Find and label the given points on the graph.

45. (a) $(k, f(k))$
(b) $(-k, f(-k))$
(c) $(k, -f(k))$

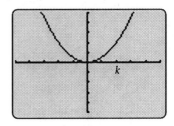

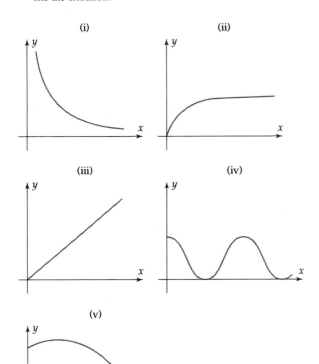

46. (a) $(k, f(k))$
(b) $(k, .5f(k))$
(c) $(.5k, f(.5k))$
(d) $(2k, f(2k))$

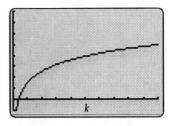

47. The graph of the function *f*, whose rule is $f(x)$ = average interest rate on a 30-year fixed-rate mortgage in year *x*, is shown in the figure.* Use it to answer these questions (reasonable approximations are OK).

(a) Compute $f(1977)$, $f(1982)$ and $f(2000)$

(b) In what year between 1990 and 2006 were rates the lowest? The highest?

(c) During what three-year period were rates changing the fastest? How do you determine this from the graph?

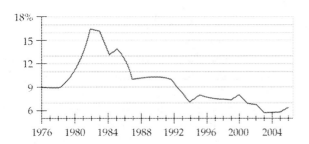

48. The annual percentage changes in various consumer price indexes (CPIs) are shown in the figure.† Use it to answer the following questions. In each case, explain how you got your answer from the graph.

(a) Did the CPI for medical care increase or decrease from 1990 to 1996?

(b) During what time intervals was the CPI for fuel oil increasing?

(c) If the CPI for fuel oil stood at 91 at the beginning of 1999, approximately what was it at the beginning of 2000?

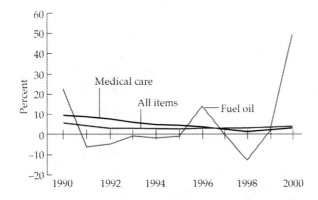

49. The Cleveland temperature graph from Example 2 of Section 3.1, is reproduced below. Let $T(x)$ denote the temperature at time *x* hours after midnight.

Determine whether the following statements are true or false.

(a) $T(4 \cdot 3) = T(4) \cdot T(3)$

(b) $T(4 \cdot 3) = 4 \cdot T(3)$

(c) $T(4 + 14) = T(4) + T(14)$

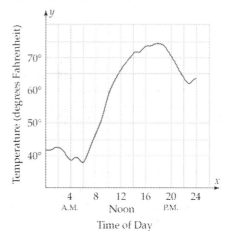

Time of Day

50. Draw the graph of a function *f* that satisfies the following four conditions:

(i) domain $f = [-2, 4]$

(ii) range $f = [-5, 6]$

(iii) $f(-1) = f(3)$

(iv) $f\left(\dfrac{1}{2}\right) = 0$

51. Sketch the graph of a function *f* that satisfies these five conditions:

(i) $f(-1) = 2$

(ii) $f(x) \geq 2$ when *x* is in the interval $\left(-1, \frac{1}{2}\right)$

(iii) $f(x)$ starts decreasing when $x = 1$

(iv) $f(3) = 3 = f(0)$

(v) $f(x)$ starts increasing when $x = 5$

[*Note:* The function whose graph you sketch need not be given by an algebraic formula.]

52. Wireless telephone services are growing rapidly. The table shows the industry's revenue (in billions of dollars) over a five-year period.*

Year	Revenue
1999	40.018
2000	52.966
2002	76.508
2003	87.624
2004	100.600

---

*Federal Home Mortgage Corporation.
†Graph prepared by U.S. Census Bureau, based on data from the Bureau of Labor Statistics.

New York Times 2006 Almanac.

(a) Make a scatter plot of the data, with $x = 0$ corresponding to 1999.

(b) Use linear regression to find a function that models this data. Assume that the model remains accurate.

(c) Use the model to estimate the revenue in 2001.

(d) When will revenue reach $170 billion?

53. The percentage of adults in the United States who smoke has been decreasing, as shown in the table.*

Year	Percent Who Smoke
1965	42.5
1974	37.0
1980	33.3
1987	29.2
1994	25.4
2000	22.9
2005	20.9

(a) Make a scatter plot of the data, with $x = 0$ corresponding to 1965.

(b) Use linear regression to find a function that models this data.

(c) Use the model to estimate the percentage of smokers in 1991 and 2013. [For comparison purposes, the actual figure for 1991 is 25.8%.]

(d) If this model remains accurate, when will less than 15% of adults smoke?

(e) According to this model, will smoking even disappear entirely? If so, when?

In Exercises 54 and 55, sketch the graph of the equation.

54. $|x| + |y| = 1$ **55.** $|y| = x^2$

THINKERS

56. Assume that on Sunday you read a long book containing a lot of factual material. Assume that by Monday you only remember 2/3 of the material. On Tuesday you remember 2/3 of what you remembered on Monday. On Wednesday

---

*Centers for Disease Control and Prevention.

you remember 2/3 of what you remembered on Tuesday, and so on. Let $f(t)$ be the percent of the material you remember t days after Sunday. (So $f(0) = 100$, and $f(1) = 66\frac{2}{3}$). Sketch $f(t)$ from $t = 0$ to $t = 12$.

57. For each m, let $f(m)$ be the largest real solution to this equation: $x^2 - 4x + m = 0$.

(a) Find the domain of f

(b) Find the range of f

(c) Sketch a graph of f

58. Let $f(x) = \begin{cases} x^2 & \text{if } x \text{ is an integer} \\ x & \text{if } x \text{ is not an integer} \end{cases}$

Sketch f.

59. A jogger begins her daily run from her home. The graph shows her distance from home at time t minutes. The graph shows, for example, that she ran at a slow but steady pace for 10 minutes, then increased her pace for 5 minutes, all the time moving farther from home. Describe the rest of her run.

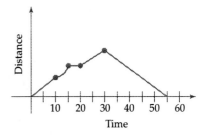

60. The graph shows the speed (in mph) at which a driver is going at time t minutes. Describe his journey.

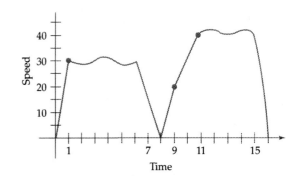

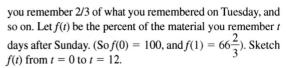

2.4 Parametric Graphing

Section Objectives   ■ Obtain graphs of parametric equations.
■ Graph equations that define x as a function of y.

As we have seen, functional notation is an excellent way to describe certain kinds of relationships and curves. It is less helpful, however, when describing curves that fail the vertical line test. For example, Figure 2–30 shows a curve (called a *Lissajous Figure*) that is important in electrical engineering, yet would be troublesome to describe in functional notation.

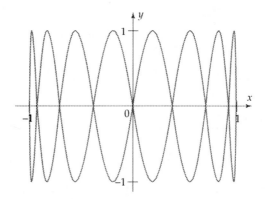

Figure 2–30

When we describe a curve by $y = f(x)$, we are thinking of the curve as the set of points satisfying that equation—the set of all the points where the y coordinate is equal to the value of the function f at the x coordinate. Now we take a different approach. We picture a point moving on the plane, and let the curve be the path the point has taken. The equations that describe the coordinates of this point at a given time t are called **parametric equations,** and the variable t is called the **parameter.**

EXAMPLE 1

Let $x = \dfrac{1}{2}t + 1$ and $y = t^2$.

(a) Make a table of values of x and y for $t = -3, -2, -1, 0, 1, 2,$ and 3.

(b) Plot the points in the table.

(c) Connect the points to find the curve traced out by this set of parametric equations.

SOLUTION

(a)

t	-3	-2	-1	0	1	2	3
$x = \dfrac{1}{2}t + 1$	$-.5$	0	$.5$	1	1.5	2	2.5
$y = t^2$	9	4	1	0	1	4	9
The point (x, y)	$(-.5, 9)$	$(0, 4)$	$(.5, 1)$	$(1, 0)$	$(1.5, 1)$	$(2, 4)$	$(2.5, 9)$

(b) We plot the points from the final row of the table to obtain Figure 2–31.

(c) We may plot a few more points to see the shape of the curve before we connect them all. The resultant curve is shown in Figure 2–32.

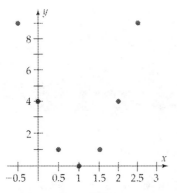

Figure 2–31

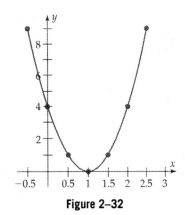

Figure 2–32

EXAMPLE 2

Use a calculator to graph the parametric equations

$$x = t^3 - t \quad y = 4 - t^2$$

in the window $-7 \leq x \leq 7$, $-2 \leq y \leq 5$.

SOLUTION   We change to parametric graphing mode, as suggested in the Technology Tip, and enter the equations (Figure 2–33). Setting up the viewing window requires some additional steps (first three lines of Figure 2–34). We don't know a suitable t-range, so we choose $-10 \leq t \leq 10$. The t-step (called t-pitch on Casio) determines how much t changes after a point is plotted; we set it at .15*. Both the t-range and t-step can be adjusted later if necessary.

TECHNOLOGY TIP

To change to parametric graphing mode, select PAR(AMETRIC) in the following menu/submenu:

   TI: MODE

   Casio: GRAPH/TYPE

   HP-39gs: APLET

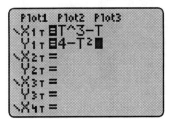

Figure 2–33

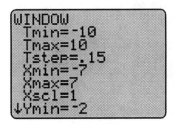

Figure 2–34   **Figure 2–35**

Finally, we obtain the graph in Figure 2–36.

EXAMPLE 3

Graph the curve given by

$$x = t^2 - t - 1 \quad \text{and} \quad y = t^3 - 4t - 6 \quad (-2 \leq t \leq 3).$$

SOLUTION   Using the standard viewing window, we obtain the graph in Figure 2–37 on the next page. Note that the graph crosses over itself at one point and that it does not extend forever to the left and right but has endpoints.

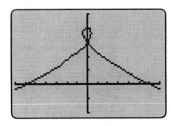

Figure 2–36

---

*If the t-step is much smaller than .15, the graph may take a long time to plot. If it is too large, the graph may look like a series of connected line segments rather than a smooth curve.

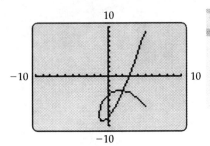

Figure 2–37

As we have seen, when given y as a function of x, we can graph it using the standard mode on our calculator. When we have x as a function of y, we can graph the curve using parametric equations.

EXAMPLE 4

Graph $x = y^3 - 3y^2 - 4y + 7$

SOLUTION   Let t be any real number. If $y = t$, then $x = t^3 - 3t^2 - 4t + 7$. So the graph of $x = y^3 - 3y^2 - 4y + 7$ is the same as the graph of the parametric equations

$$x = t^3 - 3t^2 - 4t + 7 \quad y = t$$

As before, we change to parametric mode, enter the equations, set up the viewing window, and graph (Figures 2–38, 2–39). ■

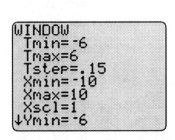

Figure 2–38

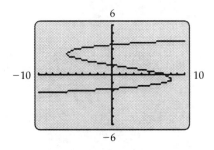

Figure 2–39

Any function of the form $y = f(x)$ can be expressed in terms of parametric equations and graphed that way. For instance, to graph $f(x) = x^2 + 1$, let $x = t$ and $y = f(x) = t^2 + 1$. Parametric graphing will be used hereafter whenever it is convenient and will be studied more thoroughly in Section 10.5.

EXERCISES 2.4

In Exercises 1–6, find a viewing window that shows a complete graph of the curve determined by the parametric equations.

1. $x = 3t^2 - 5$ and $y = t^2$ $(-4 \leq t \leq 4)$

2. The Zorro curve: $x = .1t^3 - .2t^2 - 2t + 4$ and $y = 1 - t$ $(-5 \leq t \leq 6)$

3. $x = t^2 - 3t + 2$ and $y = 8 - t^3$ $(-4 \leq t \leq 4)$

4. $x = t^2 - 6t$ and $y = \sqrt{t + 7}$ $(-5 \leq t \leq 9)$

5. $x = 1 - t^2$ and $y = t^3 - t - 1$ $(-4 \leq t \leq 4)$

6. $x = t^2 - t - 1$ and $y = 1 - t - t^2$

In Exercises 7–12, use parametric graphing. Find a viewing window that shows a complete graph of the equation.

7. $x = y^3 + 5y^2 - 4y - 5$ 8. $\sqrt[3]{y^2 - y - 1} - x + 2 = 0$

9. $xy^2 + xy + x = y^3 - 2y^2 + 4$
   [*Hint:* First solve for x.]

10. $2y = xy^2 + 180x$ **11.** $x - \sqrt{y} + y^2 + 8 = 0$

12. $y^2 - x - \sqrt{y + 5} + 4 = 0$

THINKERS

13. Graph the curve given by

$$x = (t^2 - 1)(t^2 - 4)(t + 5) + t + 3$$

$$y = (t^2 - 1)(t^2 - 4)(t^3 + 4) + t - 1$$

$$(-2.5 \le t \le 2.5)$$

How many times does this curve cross itself?

14. Use parametric equations to describe a curve that crosses itself more times than the curve in Exercise 13. [Many correct answers are possible.]

2.5   Graphs and Transformations

Section Objectives
- ■ Recognize the basic geometric transformations of a graph.
- ■ Explore the relationship between algebraic changes in the rule of a function and geometric transformations of its graph.

If we know the rule of a function, then we can obtain new, related functions by carefully modifying the rule. In this section, we will explore how certain algebraic changes to a function's rule affect its graph. The same format will be used for each kind of change.

First: You will assemble some evidence by doing a graphing exploration on your calculator.

Second: We will draw some general conclusions from the evidence you obtained.

Third: We may discuss how these conclusions can be proved.

GRAPHING EXPLORATION

Consider the functions

$$f(x) = x^2 \qquad g(x) = x^2 + 5 \qquad h(x) = x^2 - 7$$

Graph f in the standard window and look at the graph, then graph g and see how the 5 changed the basic graph. Then graph h and notice the change the -7 made. Now answer these questions:

   Do the graphs of g and h look very similar to the graph of f in *shape*?

   How do their vertical positions differ?

   Where would you predict that the graph of $k(x) = x^2 - 9$ is located relative to the graph $f(x) = x^2$, and what is its shape?

Confirm your prediction by graphing k on the same screen as f, g, and h.

The results of this Exploration should make the following statements plausible.

Vertical Shifts

Let f be a function and c a positive constant.

The graph of $g(x) = f(x) + c$ is the graph of f shifted c units upward.

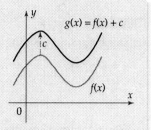

The graph of $h(x) = f(x) - c$ is the graph of f shifted c units downward.

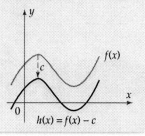

To see why these statements are true, suppose $f(x) = x^2$ and $g(x) = x^2 + 5$. For any given value of x, consider the points

$P = (x, x^2)$ on the graph of f and $Q = (x, x^2 + 5)$ on the graph of g.

The x-coordinates show that P and Q lie in the same vertical line. The y-coordinates show that Q lies 5 units directly above P. Thus, the graph of $g(x) = f(x) + 5$ is just the graph of f shifted 5 units upward.

EXAMPLE 1

A calculator was used to obtain a graph of $f(x) = .04x^3 - x - 3$ in Figure 2–40. The graph of

$$h(x) = f(x) - 4 = (.04x^3 - x - 3) - 4$$

is the graph of f shifted 4 units downward, as shown in Figure 2–41.

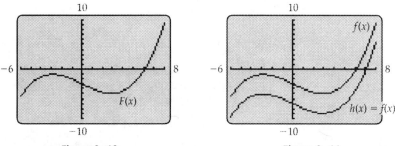

Figure 2–40   **Figure 2–41**

Although it may appear that the graph of h is closer to the graph of f at the right edge of Figure 2–41 than in the center, this is an optical illusion. The *vertical* distance between the graphs is always 4 units.

GRAPHING EXPLORATION

Use the trace feature of your calculator as follows to confirm that the vertical distance is always 4:*

Move the cursor to any point on the graph of f, and note its coordinates.

Use the down arrow to drop the cursor to the graph of h, and note the coordinates of the cursor in its new position.

The x-coordinates will be the same in both cases, and the new y-coordinate will be 4 less than the original y-coordinate.

■

HORIZONTAL SHIFTS

GRAPHING EXPLORATION

Consider the functions

$$f(x) = 2x^3 \qquad g(x) = 2(x + 6)^3 \qquad h(x) = 2(x - 8)^3$$

Graph f in the standard window and look at the graph, then graph g and see how the 6 changed the basic graph. Then graph h and notice the change the -8 made. Now answer these questions:

Do the graphs of g and h look very similar to the graph of f in *shape*?

How do their horizontal positions differ?

Where would you predict that the graph of $k(x) = 2(x + 2)^3$ is located relative to the graph of $f(x) = 2x^3$, and what is its shape?

Confirm your prediction by graphing k on the same screen as f, g, and h.

The results of this Exploration should make the following statements plausible.

Horizontal Shifts

Let f be a function and c a positive constant.

The graph of $g(x) = f(x + c)$ is the graph of f shifted horizontally c units to the left.

The graph of $h(x) = f(x - c)$ is the graph of f shifted horizontally c units to the right.

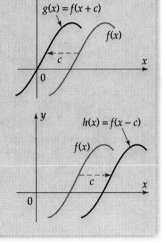

---

*The trace cursor can be moved vertically from graph to graph by using the up and down arrows.

To see why the first statement is true, suppose $g(x) = f(x + 4)$. Then the value of g at x is the same as the value of f at $x + 4$, which is 4 units to the right of x on the horizontal axis. So the graph of f is the graph of g shifted 4 units to the *right*, which means that the graph of g is the graph of f shifted 4 units to the *left*. An analogous argument works for the second statement in the box.

EXAMPLE 2

In some cases, shifting the graph of a function f horizontally may produce a graph that overlaps the graph of f. For instance, a graph of $f(x) = x^2 - 7$ is shown in red in Figure 2–42. The graph of

$$g(x) = f(x + 5) = (x + 5)^2 - 7$$

is the graph of f shifted 5 units to the left, and the graph of

$$h(x) = f(x - 4) = (x - 4)^2 - 7$$

is the graph of f shifted 4 units to the right, as shown in Figure 2–42.   ∎

TECHNOLOGY TIP

If the function f of Example 2 is entered as $y_1 = x^2 - 7$, then the functions g and h can be entered as $y_2 = y_1(x + 5)$ and $y_3 = y_1(x - 4)$ on calculators other than TI-86 and Casio.

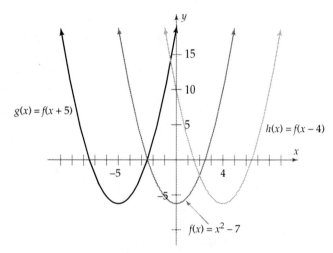

Figure 2–42

EXPANSIONS AND CONTRACTIONS

TECHNOLOGY TIP

On most calculators, you can graph both functions in the Exploration at the same time by keying in

$$y = \{1, 3\}(x^2 - 4).$$

GRAPHING EXPLORATION

In the viewing window with $-5 \le x \le 5$ and $-15 \le y \le 15$, graph these functions on the same screen:

$$f(x) = x^2 - 4 \qquad g(x) = 3f(x) = 3(x^2 - 4).$$

The table of values in Figure 2–43 shows that the y-coordinates on the graph of $Y_2 = g(x)$ are always 3 times the y-coordinates of the corresponding points on the graph of $Y_1 = f(x)$. To translate this into visual terms, imagine that the graph of f is nailed to the x-axis at its intercepts (± 2). The graph of g is then obtained by

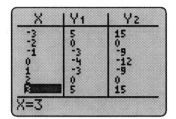

Figure 2–43

"stretching" the graph of f away from the x-axis (with the nails holding the x-intercepts in place) by a factor of 3, as shown in Figure 2–44.

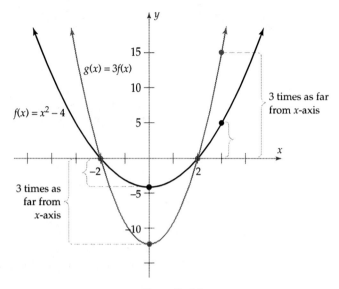

Figure 2–44

GRAPHING EXPLORATION

In the viewing window with $-4 \le x \le 4$ and $-5 \le y \le 12$, graph these functions on the same screen:

$$f(x) = x^2 - 4 \qquad h(x) = \frac{1}{4}(x^2 - 4).$$

Your screen should suggest that the graph of h is the graph of f "shrunk" vertically toward the x-axis by a factor of 1/4.

Analogous facts are true in the general case.

Expansions and Contractions

If $c > 1$, then the graph of $g(x) = cf(x)$ is the graph of f stretched vertically away from the x-axis by a factor of c.

If $0 < c < 1$, then the graph of $h(x) = cf(x)$ is the graph of f shrunk vertically toward the x-axis by a factor of c.

REFLECTIONS

In the standard viewing window, graph these functions on the same screen.

$$f(x) = .04x^3 - x \qquad g(x) = -f(x) = -(.04x^3 - x).$$

By moving your trace cursor from graph to graph, verify that for every point on the graph of f, there is a point on the graph of g with the same first coordinate that is on the opposite side of the x-axis, the same distance from the x-axis.

This Exploration shows that the graph of g is the mirror image (reflection) of the graph of f, with the x-axis being the mirror. The same thing is true in the general case.

Reflections

Let f be a function. The graph of $g(x) = -f(x)$ is the graph of f reflected in the x-axis.

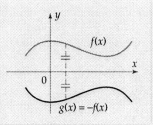

EXAMPLE 3

If $f(x) = x^2 - 3$, then the graph of

$$g(x) = -f(x) = -(x^2 - 3)$$

is the reflection of the graph of f in the x-axis, as shown in Figure 2–45.   ∎

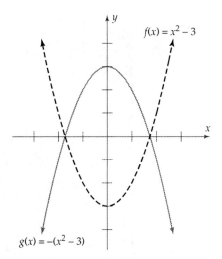

Figure 2–45

We now examine a different kind of reflection.

GRAPHING EXPLORATION

In the standard viewing window, graph these functions on the same screen:

$$f(x) = \sqrt{5x + 10} \quad \text{and} \quad h(x) = f(-x) = \sqrt{5(-x) + 10}.$$

Think carefully: How are the two graphs related to the y-axis? Now graph these two functions on the same screen:

$$f(x) = x^2 + 3x - 3$$

$$h(x) = f(-x) = (-x)^2 + 3(-x) - 3 = x^2 - 3x - 3.$$

Are the graphs of f and h related in the same way as the first pair?

This Exploration shows that the graph of h in each case is the mirror image (reflection) of the graph of f, with the y-axis as the mirror. The same thing is true in the general case.

Reflections

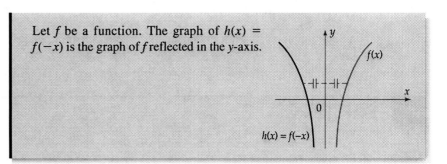

Let f be a function. The graph of $h(x) = f(-x)$ is the graph of f reflected in the y-axis.

To see why this is true, let a be any number. Then

$$(a, f(a)) \text{ is on the graph of } f \quad \text{and} \quad (-a, h(-a)) \text{ is on the graph of } h.$$

However, $h(-a) = f(-(-a)) = f(a)$, so the two points are

$$(a, f(a)) \text{ on the graph of } f \quad \text{and} \quad (-a, f(a)) \text{ on the graph of } h.$$

These points lie on opposite sides of the y-axis, the same distance from the axis, because their first coordinates are negatives of each other. The points are on the same horizontal line because their second coordinates are the same. Thus, every point on the graph of f has a mirror-image point on the graph of h, the y-axis being the mirror.

Other algebraic operations and their graphical effects are considered in Exercises 48–61.

◗ COMBINING TRANSFORMATIONS

The transformations described above may be used in sequence to analyze the graphs of functions whose rules are algebraically complicated.

EXAMPLE 4

To understand the graph of $g(x) = 2(x - 3)^2 - 1$, note that the rule of g may be obtained from the rule of $f(x) = x^2$ in three steps:

$$f(x) = x^2 \xrightarrow{\text{Step 1}} (x - 3)^2 \xrightarrow{\text{Step 2}} 2(x - 3)^2 \xrightarrow{\text{Step 3}} 2(x - 3)^2 - 1 = g(x).$$

Step 1 shifts the graph of f horizontally 3 units to the right; step 2 stretches the resulting graph away from the x-axis by a factor of 2; step 3 shifts this graph 1 unit downward, thus producing the graph of g in Figure 2–46. ∎

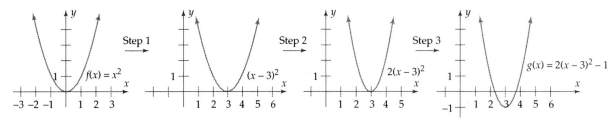

Figure 2–46

EXERCISES 2.5

In Exercises 1–8, use the catalog of functions at the end of Section 3.3 and information from this section to match each function with its graph, which is one of A–L.

A.

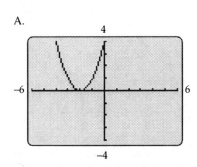

B.

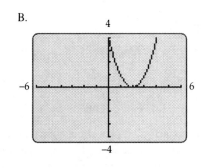

C.

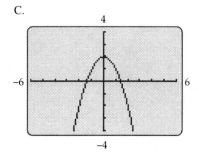

D.

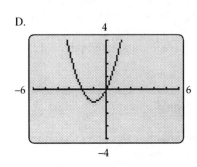

E.

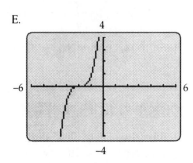

F.

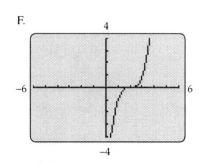

G.

H.
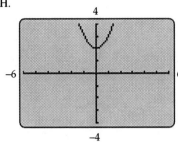

I.
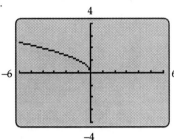

J.
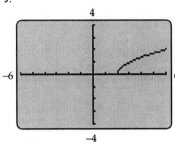

K.
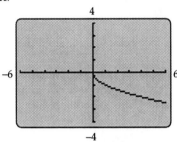

L.
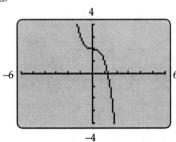

1. $f(x) = x^2 + 2$ **2.** $f(x) = \sqrt{x - 2}$

3. $g(x) = (x - 2)^3$ **4.** $g(x) = (x - 2)^2$

5. $f(x) = -\sqrt{x}$ **6.** $f(x) = (x + 1)^2 - 1$

7. $g(x) = -x^2 + 2$ **8.** $g(x) = -x^3 + 2$

9. The figure shows the graphs of $f(x) - 2$, $2f(x)$, and $f(x + 1)$. Sketch a graph of the function f.

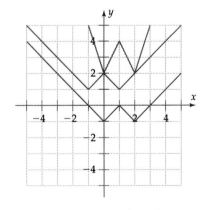

10. Fill in the entries in the following table

x	$f(x)$	$g(x) = f(x) + 2$	$h(x) = \frac{1}{2}f(x)$	$i(x) = 3f(x) - 2$
-1	$-1/2$			
0	1			
1	2			
2	6			
3	8			

11. Fill in the entries in the following table. If it is impossible to fill in an entry, put an X in it.

t	$f(t)$	$g(t) = f(t) - 3$	$h(t) = 4f(-t)$	$i(t) = f(t - 1) - 2$
-2	3			
-1	6			
0	8			
1	0			
2	5			

In Exercises 12–15, use the graph of $y = |x|$ and information from this section (but not a calculator) to sketch the graph of the function.

12. $f(x) = |x - 2|$ **13.** $g(x) = |x| - 2$

14. $g(x) = -|x|$ **15.** $f(x) = |x + 2| - 2$

In Exercises 16–19, find a single viewing window that shows complete graphs of the functions f, g, and h.

16. $f(x) = .25x^3 - 9x + 5$; $g(x) = f(x) + 15$;
$h(x) = f(x) - 20$

17. $f(x) = \sqrt{x^2 - 9} - 5$; $g(x) = 3f(x)$;
$h(x) = .5f(x)$

18. $f(x) = |x^2 - 5|$; $g(x) = f(x + 8)$;
$h(x) = f(x - 6)$

19. $f(x) = .125x^3 - .25x^2 - 1.5x + 5$;
$g(x) = f(x) - 5$; $h(x) = 5 - f(x)$

In Exercises 20 and 21, find complete graphs of the functions f and g in the same viewing window.

20. $f(x) = \dfrac{4 - 5x^2}{x^2 + 1}$; $g(x) = -f(x)$

21. $f(x) = x^4 - 4x^3 + 2x^2 + 3$; $g(x) = f(-x)$

In Exercises 22–25, describe a sequence of transformations that will transform the graph of the function f into the graph of the function g.

22. $f(x) = x^2 + x$; $g(x) = (x - 3)^2 + (x - 3) + 2$

23. $f(x) = x^2 + 5$; $g(x) = (x + 2)^2 + 10$

24. $f(x) = \sqrt{x^3 + 5}$; $g(x) = -\dfrac{1}{2}\sqrt{x^3 + 5} - 6$

25. $f(x) = \sqrt{x^4 + x^2 + 1}$; $g(x) = 10 - \sqrt{4x^4 + 4x^2 + 4}$

In Exercises 26–29, write the rule of a function g whose graph can be obtained from the graph of the function f by performing the transformations in the order given.

26. $f(x) = x^2 + 2$; shift the graph horizontally 5 units to the left and then vertically upward 4 units.

27. $f(x) = x^2 - x + 1$; reflect the graph in the *x*-axis, then shift it vertically upward 3 units.

28. $f(x) = \sqrt{x}$; shift the graph horizontally 6 units to the right, stretch it away from the *x*-axis by a factor of 2, and shift it vertically downward 3 units.

29. $f(x) = \sqrt{-x}$; shift the graph horizontally 3 units to the left, then reflect it in the *x*-axis, and shrink it toward the *x*-axis by a factor of $1/2$.

30. Let $f(x) = x^2 + 3x$, and let $g(x) = f(x) + 2$.

   (a) Write the rule of $g(x)$.
   (b) Find the difference quotients of $f(x)$ and $g(x)$. How are they related?

31. Let $f(x) = x^2 + 5$, and let $g(x) = f(x - 1)$.

   (a) Write the rule of $g(x)$ and simplify.
   (b) Find the difference quotients of $f(x)$ and $g(x)$.
   (c) Let $d(x)$ denote the difference quotient of $f(x)$. Show that the difference quotient of $g(x)$ is $d(x - 1)$.

In Exercises 32–35, use the graph of the function f in the figure to sketch the graph of the function g.

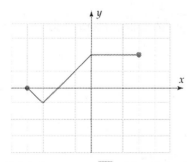

32. $g(x) = f(x) + 3$

33. $g(x) = f(x) - 1$

34. $g(x) = 3f(x)$

35. $g(x) = .25f(x)$

In Exercises 36–39, use the graph of the function f in the figure to sketch the graph of the function h.

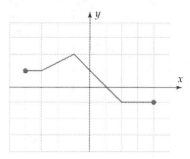

36. $h(x) = -f(x)$

37. $h(x) = -4f(x)$

38. $h(x) = f(-x)$

39. $h(x) = f(-x) + 2$

In Exercises 40–45, use the graph of the function f in the figure to sketch the graph of the function g.

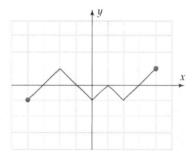

40. $g(x) = f(x + 3)$

41. $g(x) = f(x - 2)$

42. $g(x) = f(x - 2) + 3$

43. $g(x) = f(x + 1) - 3$

44. $g(x) = 2 - f(x)$

45. $g(x) = f(-x) + 2$

46. Graph $f(x) = -|x - 3| - |x - 17| + 20$ in the window with $0 \le x \le 20$ and $-2 \le y \le 12$. Think of the *x*-axis as a table and the graph as a side view of a fast-food carton placed upside down on the table (the flat part of the graph is the bottom of the carton). Find the rule of a function *g* whose graph (in this viewing window) looks like another fast-food carton, which has been placed right side up on top of the first one.

47. A factory has a linear cost function $c(x) = ax + b$, where *b* represents fixed costs and *a* represents the variable costs (labor and materials) of making one item, both in thousands of dollars.

   (a) If property taxes (part of the fixed costs) are increased by \$35,000 per year, what effect does this have on the graph of the cost function?
   (b) If variable costs increase by 12 cents per item, what effect does this have on the graph of the cost function?

In Exercises 48–50, assume $f(x) = (.2x)^6 - 4$. Use the standard viewing window to graph the functions f and g on the same screen.

48. $g(x) = f(2x)$ **49.** $g(x) = f(3x)$ **50.** $g(x) = f(4x)$

51. On the basis of the results of Exercises 48–50, describe the transformation that transforms the graph of a function $f(x)$

into the graph of the function $f(cx)$, where c is a constant with $c > 1$. [*Hint:* How are the two graphs related to the y-axis? Stretch your mind.]

In Exercises 52–55, assume $f(x) = x^2 - 3$. Use the standard viewing window to graph the functions f and g on the same screen.

52. $g(x) = f\left(\dfrac{1}{2}x\right)$

53. $g(x) = f\left(\dfrac{1}{3}x\right)$

54. $g(x) = f\left(\dfrac{1}{4}x\right)$

55. $g(x) = f\left(\dfrac{1}{10}x\right)$

56. On the basis of the results of Exercises 52–55, describe the transformation that transforms the graph of a function $f(x)$ into the graph of the function $f(cx)$, where c is a constant with $0 < c < 1$. [*Hint:* How are the two graphs related to the y-axis?]

In Exercises 57–60, use the standard viewing window to graph the function f and the function $g(x) = f(|x|)$ on the same screen.

57. $f(x) = x - 4$

58. $f(x) = x^3 - 3$

59. $f(x) = .5(x - 4)^2 - 9$

60. $f(x) = x^3 - 2x$

61. On the basis of the results of Exercises 57–60, describe the relationship between the graph of a function $f(x)$ and the graph of the function $f(|x|)$.

In Exercises 62–65, use the standard viewing window to graph the function f and the function $g(x) = |f(x)|$ on the same screen. Exercise 66 may be helpful for interpreting the results.

62. $f(x) = .5x^2 - 5$

63. $f(x) = x^3 - 4x^2 + x + 3$

64. $f(x) = x + 3$

65. $f(x) = x^3 - 2x$

66. (a) Let f be a function, and let g be the function defined by $g(x) = |f(x)|$. Use the definition of absolute value (page 9) to explain why the following statement is true:

$$g(x) = \begin{cases} f(x) & \text{if } f(x) \geq 0 \\ -f(x) & \text{if } f(x) < 0 \end{cases}$$

(b) Use part (a) and your knowledge of transformations to explain why the graph of g consists of those parts of the graph of f that lie above the x-axis together with the reflection in the x-axis of those parts of the graph of f that lie below the x-axis.

67. Because of a calculator's small screen size, it is not always easy (or even possible!) to find a viewing window that displays what its user desires.

(a) Graph $f(x) = x^2 - x - 6$ in the standard viewing window. Let $h(x) = f(x - 1000)$. What should $h(x)$ look like?

(b) Find an appropriate viewing window for the graph of $h(x)$.

(c) Try to find a viewing window that clearly displays both the graph of f and the graph of h. What makes this problem difficult?

(d) Let $g(x) = 1000 f(x)$. What should $g(x)$ look like?

(e) Find an appropriate viewing window for the graph of $g(x)$. Can you find a viewing window that clearly displays both the graph of f and the graph of g?

2.6   Operations on Functions

Section Objectives

- ■ Find the sum, difference, product, and quotient of two functions.
- ■ Compose functions to create a new function.
- ■ Write a function as the composite of two or more functions.

We now examine ways in which two or more given functions can be used to create new functions. If f and g are functions, then their **sum** is the function h defined by the rule

$$h(x) = f(x) + g(x).$$

For example, if $f(x) = 3x^2 + x$ and $g(x) = 4x - 2$, then

$$\begin{aligned} h(x) &= f(x) + g(x) \\ &= (3x^2 + x) + (4x - 2) \\ &= 3x^2 + 5x - 2. \end{aligned}$$

Instead of using a different letter h for the sum function, we shall usually denote it by $f + g$. Thus, the sum $f + g$ is defined by the rule

$$(f + g)(x) = f(x) + g(x).$$

This rule is *not* just a formal manipulation of symbols. If x is a number, then so are $f(x)$ and $g(x)$. The plus sign in $f(x) + g(x)$ is addition of *numbers,* and the result is a number. But the plus sign in $f + g$ is addition of *functions,* and the result is a new function.

The **difference** $f - g$ is the function defined by the rule

$$(f - g)(x) = f(x) - g(x).$$

The domain of the sum and difference functions is the set of all real numbers that are in both the domain of f and the domain of g.

EXAMPLE 1

If $f(x) = \sqrt{9 - x^2}$ and $g(x) = \sqrt{x - 2}$, find the rules of the functions $f + g$ and $f - g$ and their domains.

SOLUTION   We have

$$(f + g)(x) = f(x) + g(x) = \sqrt{9 - x^2} + \sqrt{x - 2};$$
$$(f - g)(x) = f(x) - g(x) = \sqrt{9 - x^2} - \sqrt{x - 2}.$$

The domain of f consists of all x such that $9 - x^2 \geq 0$ (so that the square root will be defined), that is, all x with $-3 \leq x \leq 3$. Similarly, the domain of g consists of all x such that $x \geq 2$. The domain of $f + g$ and $f - g$ consists of all real numbers in both the domain of f and the domain of g, namely, all x such that $2 \leq x \leq 3$. ∎

TECHNOLOGY TIP

If you have two functions entered in the equation memory as y_1 and y_2, you can graph their sum by entering $y_1 + y_2$ as y_3 in the equation memory and graphing y_3. Differences, products, and quotients are graphed similarly. To find the correct keys for y_1 and y_2, see the Tip on page 153.

The **product** and **quotient** of functions f and g are the functions defined by the rules

$$(fg)(x) = f(x)g(x) \qquad \text{and} \qquad \left(\frac{f}{g}\right)(x) = \frac{f(x)}{g(x)}.$$

The domain of fg consists of all real numbers in both the domain of f and the domain of g. The domain of f/g consists of all real numbers x in both the domain of f and the domain of g such that $g(x) \neq 0$.

EXAMPLE 2

If $f(x) = \sqrt{3x}$ and $g(x) = x^2 - 1$, find the rules of the functions fg and f/g and their domains.

SOLUTION   The rules are

$$(fg)(x) = f(x)g(x)$$
$$= \sqrt{3x}\,(x^2 - 1)$$
$$= (\sqrt{3x})\,x^2 - \sqrt{3x}$$

$$\left(\frac{f}{g}\right)(x) = \frac{f(x)}{g(x)}$$
$$= \frac{\sqrt{3x}}{x^2 - 1}$$

The domain of fg consists of all numbers x in both the domain of f (all nonnegative real numbers) and the domain of g (all real numbers), that is, all $x \geq 0$. The domain of f/g consists of all these x for which $g(x) \neq 0$, that is, all nonnegative real numbers *except* $x = 1$. ∎

If c is a real number and f is a function, then the product of f and the constant function $g(x) = c$ is usually denoted cf. For example, if the function

$$f(x) = x^3 - x + 2,$$

and $c = 5$, then $5f$ is the function given by

$$(5f)(x) = 5 \cdot f(x)$$
$$= 5(x^3 - x + 2)$$
$$= 5x^3 - 5x + 10$$

COMPOSITION OF FUNCTIONS

Another way of combining functions is illustrated by the function $h(x) = \sqrt{x^3}$. To compute $h(4)$, for example, you first find $4^3 = 64$ and then take the square root $\sqrt{64} = 8$. So the rule of h may be rephrased as follows:

First apply the function $f(x) = x^3$,

Then apply the function $g(t) = \sqrt{t}$ to the result.

The same idea can be expressed in functional notation like this:

$$x \xrightarrow{\text{first apply } f} f(x) \xrightarrow{\text{then apply } g \text{ to the result}} g(f(x)).$$
$$x \qquad\qquad x^3 \qquad\qquad \sqrt{x^3}$$

apply h

So the rule of h may be written as $h(x) = g(f(x))$, where $f(x) = x^3$ and $g(t) = \sqrt{t}$. We can think of h as being made up of two simpler functions f and g, or we can think of f and g being "composed" to create the function h. Both viewpoints are useful.

EXAMPLE 3

Suppose $f(x) = 4x^2 + 1$ and $g(t) = \dfrac{1}{t+2}$. Define a new function h whose rule is "first apply f; then apply g to the result." In functional notation,

$$x \xrightarrow{\text{first apply } f} f(x) \xrightarrow{\text{then apply } g \text{ to the result}} g(f(x)).$$

So the rule of the function h is $h(x) = g(f(x))$. Evaluating $g(f(x))$ means that whenever t appears in the formula for $g(t)$, we must replace it by $f(x) = 4x^2 + 1$:

$$h(x) = g(f(x)) = \frac{1}{f(x) + 2}$$

$$= \frac{1}{(4x^2 + 1) + 2}$$

$$= \frac{1}{4x^2 + 3}$$ ∎

The function h in Example 3 is an illustration of the following definition.

Composite Functions

Let f and g be functions. The **composite function** of f and g defined as follows.

For input x, the output is $g(f(x))$.

This composite function is denoted $g \circ f$.

The symbol "$g \circ f$" is read "g circle f" or "f followed by g." (Note the order carefully; the functions are applied *right* to *left*.) So the rule of the composite function is

$$f)(x) = g(f(x)).$$

EXAMPLE 4

If $f(x) = 2x + 5$ and $g(t) = 3t^2 + 2t + 4$, then find

$$(f \circ g)(2), \qquad (g \circ f)(-1), \qquad (g \circ f)(5), \qquad (g \circ f)(x).$$

SOLUTION

$$(f \circ g)(2) = f(g(2)) \qquad\qquad \text{Similarly,} \qquad (g \circ f)(-1) = g(f(-1))$$
$$= f(3 \cdot 2^2 + 2 \cdot 2 + 4) \qquad\qquad\qquad\qquad = g(2(-1) + 5)$$
$$= f(20) \qquad\qquad\qquad\qquad\qquad\qquad = g(3)$$
$$= 2 \cdot 20 + 5 \qquad\qquad\qquad\qquad\qquad = 3 \cdot 3^2 + 2 \cdot 3 + 4$$
$$= 45. \qquad\qquad\qquad\qquad\qquad\qquad = 37.$$

The value of a composite function can also be computed like this:

$$(g \circ f)(5) = g(f(5)) = 3(f(5)^2) + 2(f(5)) + 4 = 3(15^2) + 2(15) + 4 = 709.$$

and

$$(g \circ f)(x) = g(f(x)) = 3(2x + 5)^2 + 2(2x + 5) + 4 = 12x^2 + 64x + 89.$$ ∎

The domain of $g \circ f$ is determined by this convention.

Domain of
$$g \circ f$$

> The domain of the composite function $g \circ f$ is the set of all real numbers x such that x is in the domain of f and $f(x)$ is in the domain of g.

EXAMPLE 5

Find the rule and domain of $g \circ f$, when $f(x) = \sqrt{x}$ and $g(t) = t^2 - 5$.

SOLUTION

$$(g \circ f)(x) = g(f(x)) = (f(x))^2 - 5 = (\sqrt{x})^2 - 5 = x - 5.$$

Although $x - 5$ is defined for every real number x, the domain of $g \circ f$ is *not* the set of all real numbers. The domain of g is the set of all real numbers, but the function $f(x) = \sqrt{x}$ is defined only when $x \geq 0$. So the domain of $g \circ f$ is the set of nonnegative real numbers, that is, the interval $[0, \infty)$. ∎

EXAMPLE 6

Write the function $h(x) = \sqrt{3x^2 + 1}$ in two different ways as the composite of two functions.

TECHNOLOGY TIP

Evaluating composite functions is easy on calculators other than TI-86 and most Casio calculators. If the functions are entered in the equation memory as $y_1 = g(x)$ and $y_2 = h(x)$ (with f in place of y on HP-39gs), then keying in $y_2(y_1(5))$ ENTER produces the number $h(g(5))$.

On TI-86 and most Casio calculators, this syntax does *not* produce $h(g(5))$; it produces

$$h(x) \cdot g(x) \cdot 5$$

for whatever number is stored in the x-memory.

SOLUTION   Let $f(x) = 3x^2 + 1$ and $g(x) = \sqrt{x}$.* Then

$$(g \circ f)(x) = g(f(x)) = g(3x^2 + 1) = \sqrt{3x^2 + 1} = h(x).$$

Similarly, h is also the composite $j \circ k$, where $j(x) = \sqrt{x + 1}$ and $k(x) = 3x^2$:

$$(j \circ k)(x) = j(k(x)) = j(3x^2) = \sqrt{3x^2 + 1} = h(x).$$ ∎

EXAMPLE 7

If $k(x) = (x^2 - 2x + \sqrt{x})^3$, then k is $g \circ f$, where $f(x) = x^2 - 2x + \sqrt{x}$ and $g(x) = x^3$ because

$$(g \circ f)(x) = g(f(x)) = g(x^2 - 2x + \sqrt{x}) = (x^2 - 2x + \sqrt{x})^3 = k(x).$$ ∎

By using the function operations above, a complicated function may be considered as being built up from simple parts.

---

*Now that you have the idea of composite functions, we'll use the same letter for the variable in both functions.

EXAMPLE 8

The function

$$f(x) = \sqrt{\frac{3x^2 - 4x + 5}{x^3 + 1}}$$

may be considered as the composite $f = g \circ h$, where

$$h(x) = \frac{3x^2 - 4x + 5}{x^3 + 1} \qquad \text{and} \qquad g(x) = \sqrt{x},$$

since

$$(g \circ h)(x) = g(h(x)) = g\!\left(\frac{3x^2 - 4x + 5}{x^3 + 1}\right) = \sqrt{\frac{3x^2 - 4x + 5}{x^3 + 1}} = f(x).$$

The function

$$h(x) = \frac{3x^2 - 4x + 5}{x^3 + 1}$$

is the quotient $\dfrac{p}{q}$, where

$$p(x) = 3x^2 - 4x + 5 \qquad \text{and} \qquad q(x) = x^3 + 1.$$

The function $p(x) = 3x^2 - 4x + 5$ may be written $p = k - s + r$, where

$$k(x) = 3x^2, \qquad s(x) = 4x, \qquad r(x) = 5.$$

The function k, in turn, can be considered as the product $3I^2$, where I is the *identity function* [whose rule is $I(x) = x$]:

$$(3I^2)(x) = 3(I^2(x)) = 3(I(x)I(x)) = 3 \cdot x \cdot x = 3x^2 = k(x).$$

Similarly, $s(x) = (4I)(x) = 4I(x) = 4x$. The function $q(x) = x^3 + 1$ may be "decomposed" in the same way.

Thus, the complicated function f is just the result of performing suitable operations on the identity function I and various constant functions. ∎

As you may have noticed, there are two possible ways to form a composite function from two given functions. If f and g are functions, we can consider either

$$(g \circ f)(x) = g(f(x)), \qquad \text{[the composite of } f \text{ and } g]$$
$$(f \circ g)(x) = f(g(x)). \qquad \text{[the composite of } g \text{ and } f]$$

The *order is important*, as we shall now see:

$g \circ f$ **and** $f \circ g$ **usually are** *not* **the same function.**

EXAMPLE 9

If $f(x) = x^2$ and $g(x) = x + 3$, then

$$
\begin{aligned}
(f \circ g)(x) &= f(g(x)) \\
&= f(x + 3) \\
&= (x + 3)^2 \\
&= x^2 + 6x + 9.
\end{aligned}
\qquad
\begin{aligned}
(g \circ f)(x) &= g(f(x)) \\
&= g(x^2) \\
&= x^2 + 3,
\end{aligned}
$$

Obviously, $g \circ f \neq f \circ g$, since, for example, they have different values at $x = 0$. ∎

CAUTION

Don't confuse the product function fg with the composite function $f \circ g$ (g followed by f). For instance, if $f(x) = 2x^2$ and $g(x) = x - 3$, then the product fg is given by

$$(fg)(x) = f(x)g(x) = 2x^2(x - 3) = 2x^3 - 6x^2.$$

It is *not* the same as the composite $f \circ g$ because

$$(f \circ g)(x) = f(g(x)) = f(x - 3) = 2(x - 3)^2 = 2x^2 - 12x + 18.$$

APPLICATIONS

Compositions of functions arise in applications involving several functional relationships simultaneously. In such cases, one quantity may have to be expressed as a function of another.

EXAMPLE 10

A circular puddle of liquid is evaporating and slowly shrinking in size. After t minutes, the radius r of the puddle measures $\dfrac{18}{2t + 3}$ inches; in other words, the radius is a function of time. The area A of the puddle is given by $A = \pi r^2$, that is, area is a function of the radius r. We can express the area as a function of time by substituting $r = \dfrac{18}{2t + 3}$ in the area equation:

$$A = \pi r^2 = \pi\left(\frac{18}{2t + 3}\right)^2.$$

This amounts to forming the composite function $f \circ g$, where $f(r) = \pi r^2$ and $g(t) = \dfrac{18}{2t + 3}$:

$$(f \circ g)(t) = f(g(t)) = f\left(\frac{18}{2t + 3}\right) = \pi\left(\frac{18}{2t + 3}\right)^2.$$

When area is expressed as a function of time, it is easy to compute the area of the puddle at any time. For instance, after 12 minutes, the area of the puddle is

$$A = \pi\left(\frac{18}{2t + 3}\right)^2 = \pi\left(\frac{18}{2 \cdot 12 + 3}\right)^2 = \frac{4\pi}{9} \approx 1.396 \text{ square inches.} \quad ∎$$

EXAMPLE 11

At noon, a car leaves Podunk on a straight road, heading south at 45 mph, and a plane 3 miles above the ground passes over Podunk heading east at 350 mph.

(a) Express the distance r traveled by the car and the distance s traveled by the plane as functions of time.

(b) Express the distance d between the plane and the car in terms of r and s.

(c) Express d as a function of time.

(d) How far apart were the plane and the car at 1:30 P.M.?

SOLUTION

(a) Traveling at 45 mph for t hours, the car will go a distance of $45t$ miles. Hence, the equation $r = 45t$ expresses the distance r as a function of the time t. Similarly, the equation $s = 350t$ expresses the distance s as a function of the time t.

(b) To express the distance d as a function of r and s, consider Figure 2–47.

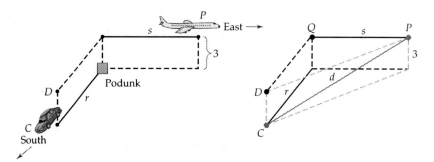

Figure 2–47

Right triangle PQD and the Pythagorean Theorem show that $(PD)^2 = r^2 + s^2$; hence, $PD = \sqrt{r^2 + s^2}$. Applying the Pythagorean Theorem to right triangle PDC, we have

$$d^2 = 3^2 + (PD)^2$$
$$d^2 = 3^2 + (\sqrt{r^2 + s^2})^2$$
$$d^2 = 9 + r^2 + s^2$$
$$d = \sqrt{9 + r^2 + s^2}.$$

(c) The preceding equation expresses d in terms of r and s. By substituting $r = 45t$ and $s = 350t$ in this equation, we can express d as a function of the time t:

$$d = \sqrt{9 + r^2 + s^2}$$
$$d = \sqrt{9 + (45t)^2 + (350t)^2}$$
$$d = \sqrt{9 + 2025t^2 + 122{,}500t^2} = \sqrt{9 + 124{,}525t^2}.$$

(d) At 1:30 P.M., we have $t = 1.5$ (since noon is $t = 0$). At this time,

$$d = \sqrt{9 + 124{,}525t^2} = \sqrt{9 + 124{,}525(1.5)^2} = \sqrt{280{,}190.25}$$
$$\approx 529.33 \text{ miles.}$$

EXERCISES 2.6

In Exercises 1–4, find $(f + g)(x)$, $(f - g)(x)$, *and* $(g - f)(x)$.

1. $f(x) = -3x + 2$, $g(x) = x^3$
2. $f(x) = x^2 + 2$, $g(x) = x^2 - 4x - 2$
3. $f(x) = 1/x$, $g(x) = x^2 + 2x - 5$
4. $f(x) = \sqrt{x}$, $g(x) = x^2 + 1 + \sqrt{x}$

In Exercises 5–8, find $(fg)(x)$, $(f/g)(x)$, *and* $(g/f)(x)$.

5. $f(x) = -3x + 2$, $g(x) = x^3$
6. $f(x) = 4x^2 + x^4$, $g(x) = \sqrt{x^2 + 4}$
7. $f(x) = x + 5$, $g(x) = x - 5$
8. $f(x) = \sqrt{x^2 - 1}$, $g(x) = \sqrt{x - 1}$

In Exercises 9–12, find the domains of fg *and* f/g.

9. $f(x) = x^2 + 1$, $g(x) = 1/x$
10. $f(x) = x^2 + 2$, $g(x) = \dfrac{1}{x^2 + 2}$
11. $f(x) = \sqrt{4 - x^2}$, $g(x) = \sqrt{3x + 4}$
12. $f(x) = 3x^2 + x^4 + 2$, $g(x) = 4x - 3$

In Exercises 13–16, find the indicated values, where

$$g(t) = t^2 - t \text{ and } f(x) = 1 + x.$$

13. $g(f(0))$
14. $(f \circ g)(3)$
15. $g(f(2) + 3)$
16. $f(2g(1))$

In Exercises 17–20, find $(g \circ f)(3)$, $(f \circ g)(1)$, *and* $(f \circ f)(0)$.

17. $f(x) = 3x - 2$, $g(x) = x^2$
18. $f(x) = |x + 2|$, $g(x) = -x^2$
19. $f(x) = x$, $g(x) = -3$
20. $f(x) = x^2 - 1$, $g(x) = \sqrt{x}$

In Exercises 21–24, find the rule of the function $f \circ g$, *the domain of* $f \circ g$, *the rule of* $g \circ f$, *and the domain of* $g \circ f$.

21. $f(x) = -3x + 2$, $g(x) = x^3$
22. $f(x) = 1/x$, $g(x) = \sqrt{x}$
23. $f(x) = \dfrac{1}{2x + 1}$, $g(x) = x^2 - 1$
24. $f(x) = (x - 3)^2$, $g(x) = \sqrt{x} + 3$

In Exercises 25–28, find the rules of the functions ff *and* $f \circ f$.

25. $f(x) = x^3$ 26. $f(x) = (x - 1)^2$
27. $f(x) = 1/x$ 28. $f(x) = \dfrac{1}{x - 1}$

In Exercises 29–32, verify that $(f \circ g)(x) = x$ *and* $(g \circ f)(x) = x$ *for every* x.

29. $f(x) = 9x + 8$, $g(x) = \dfrac{x - 8}{9}$
30. $f(x) = \sqrt[3]{x - 1}$, $g(x) = x^3 + 1$
31. $f(x) = \sqrt[3]{x} + 2$, $g(x) = (x - 2)^3$
32. $f(x) = 2x^3 - 5$, $g(x) = \sqrt[3]{\dfrac{x + 5}{2}}$

Exercises 33 and 34 refer to the function f whose graph is shown in the figure.

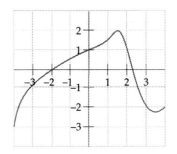

33. Let g be the composite function $f \circ f$. Use the graph of f to fill in the following table (approximate where necessary).

x	$f(x)$	$g(x) = f(f(x))$
-4		
-3		
-2	0	1
-1		
0		
1		
2		
3		
4		

34. Use the information obtained in Exercise 33 to sketch the graph of the function g.

In Exercises 35–38, fill the blanks in the given table. In each case the values of the functions f and g are given by these tables:

x	$f(x)$
1	3
2	5
3	1
4	2
5	3

t	$g(t)$
1	5
2	4
3	4
4	3
5	2

35.

x	$(g \circ f)(x)$
1	4
2	
3	5
4	
5	

36.

t	$(f \circ g)(t)$
1	
2	2
3	
4	
5	

37.

x	$(f \circ f)(x)$
1	
2	
3	3
4	
5	

38.

t	$(g \circ g)(t)$
1	
2	
3	
4	4
5	

In Exercises 39–42, write the given function as the composite of two functions, neither of which is the identity function, as in Examples 6 and 7. (There may be more than one way to do this.)

39. $f(x) = \sqrt[3]{x^2 + 2}$

40. $g(x) = \sqrt{x + 3} - \sqrt[3]{x + 3}$

41. $h(x) = (7x^3 - 10x + 17)^7$

42. $f(x) = \dfrac{1}{3x^2 + 5x - 7}$

43. If $f(x) = x + 1$ and $g(t) = t^2$, then

$$(g \circ f)(x) = g(f(x)) = g(x + 1) = (x + 1)^2$$
$$= x^2 + 2x + 1$$

Find two other functions $h(x)$ and $k(t)$ such that $(k \circ h)(x) = x^2 + 2x + 1$.

44. If f is any function and I is the identity function, what are $f \circ I$ and $I \circ f$?

In Exercises 45–48, determine whether the functions $f \circ g$ and $g \circ f$ are defined. If a composite is defined, find its domain.

45. $f(x) = x^3$, $g(x) = \sqrt{x}$

46. $f(x) = x^2 + 1$, $g(x) = \sqrt{x}$

47. $f(x) = \sqrt{x + 10}$, $g(x) = 5x$

48. $f(x) = -x^2$, $g(x) = \sqrt{x}$

49. (a) If $f(x) = 2x^3 + 5x - 1$, find $f(x^2)$.
  (b) If $f(x) = 2x^3 + 5x - 1$, find $(f(x))^2$.
  (c) Are the answers in parts (a) and (b) the same? What can you conclude about $f(x^2)$ and $(f(x))^2$?

50. Give two examples of functions f such that

$$f\left(\frac{1}{x}\right) \neq \frac{1}{f(x)}.$$

In Exercises 51 and 52, graph both $f \circ g$ and $g \circ f$ on the same screen. Use the graphs to determine whether $f \circ g$ is the same function as $g \circ f$.

51. $f(x) = x^5 - x^3 - x$; $g(x) = x - 2$

52. $f(x) = x^3 + x$; $g(x) = \sqrt[3]{x - 1}$

In Exercises 53–56, find $g \circ f$, and find the difference quotient of the function $g \circ f$.

53. $f(x) = x + 3$; $g(x) = x^2 + 1$

54. $f(x) = 2x$; $g(x) = 8x$

55. $f(x) = x + 1$; $g(x) = \dfrac{2}{x - 1}$

56. $f(x) = x^3$; $g(x) = x + 2$

57. (a) What is the area of the puddle in Example 10 after one day? After a week? After a month?
  (b) Does the puddle ever totally evaporate? Is this realistic? Under what circumstances might this area function be an accurate model of reality?

58. In a laboratory culture, the number $N(d)$ of bacteria (in thousands) at temperature d degrees Celsius is given by the function

$$N(d) = \frac{-90}{d + 1} + 20 \quad (4 \leq d \leq 32).$$

The temperature $D(t)$ at time t hours is given by the function $D(t) = 2t + 4 \quad (0 \leq t \leq 14)$.

  (a) What does the composite function $N \circ D$ represent?
  (b) How many bacteria are in the culture after 4 hours? After 10 hours?

59. A certain fungus grows in a circular shape. Its diameter after t weeks is $6 - \dfrac{50}{t^2 + 10}$ inches.

  (a) Express the area covered by the fungus as a function of time.
  (b) What is the area covered by the fungus when $t = 0$? What area does it cover at the end of 8 weeks?
  (c) When is its area 25 square inches?

60. Tom left point P at 6 A.M. walking south at 4 mph. Anne left point P at 8 A.M. walking west at 3.2 mph.

  (a) Express the distance between Tom and Anne as a function of the time t elapsed since 6 A.M.
  (b) How far apart are Tom and Anne at noon?
  (c) At what time are they 35 miles apart?

61. As a weather balloon is inflated, its radius increases at the rate of 4 centimeters per second. Express the volume of the balloon as a function of time and determine the volume of the balloon after 4 seconds. [*Hint:* The volume of a sphere of radius r is $4\pi r^3 / 3$.]

62. Express the surface area of the weather balloon in Exercise 61 as a function of time. [*Hint:* The surface area of a sphere of radius r is $4\pi r^2$.]

63. Charlie, who is 6 feet tall, walks away from a streetlight that is 15 feet high at a rate of 5 feet per second, as shown in the figure on the next page. Express the length s of Charlie's shadow as a function of time. [*Hint:* First use similar triangles to express *s* as a function of the distance *d* from the streetlight to Charlie.]

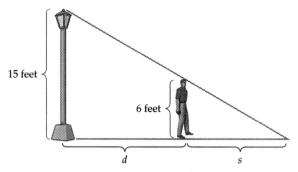

15 feet

6 feet

d

s

64. A water-filled balloon is dropped from a window 120 feet above the ground. Its height above the ground after *t* seconds is $120 - 16t^2$ feet. Laura is standing on the ground 40 feet from the point where the balloon will hit the ground, as shown in the figure.

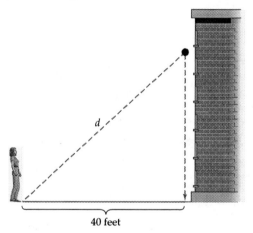

d

40 feet

(a) Express the distance *d* between Laura and the balloon as a function of time.
(b) When is the balloon exactly 90 feet from Laura?

THINKER

65. Find a function *f* (other than the identity function) such that $(f \circ f \circ f)(x) = x$ for every *x* in the domain of *f*. [Several correct answers are possible.]

66. If *f* is an increasing function, does $f \circ f$ have to be increasing? Why or why not?

67. Let $f(x) = x^2 - .2$
  (a) Using a calculator, compute $f(0)$, $(f \circ f)(0)$, $(f \circ f \circ f)(0)$, ... etc. What happens as you keep going?
  (b) Does the same thing happen if you look at $f(1)$, $(f \circ f)(1)$, $(f \circ f \circ f)(1)$, ... ?
  (c) Repeat parts (a) and (b) using $f(x) = x^2 - .9$.
  (d) Repeat parts (a) and (b) using $f(x) = x^2 - 1.3$.

[*Hint:* You may be able to save yourself some keystrokes using the ANS and ENTRY keys on your calculator.]

2.7   Rates of Change

Section Objectives

■ Determine the average rate of change of a function on an interval.

■ Understand average rate of change as applied to real-life situations.

■ Interpret average rate of change graphically.

■ Use the difference quotient to find the average rate of change over very small intervals.

■ Approximate the instantaneous rate of change of a function at a point.

Rates of change play a central role in the analysis of many real-world situations. To understand the basic ideas involved in rates of change, we take another look at the falling rock from Sections 3.1 and 3.2. We saw that when the rock is dropped from a high place, then the distance it travels (ignoring wind resistance) is given by the function

$$d(t) = 16t^2$$

with distance $d(t)$ measured in feet and time t in seconds. The following table shows the distance the rock has fallen at various times:

Time t	0	1	2	3	3.5	4	4.5	5
Distance $d(t)$	0	16	64	144	196	256	324	400

To find the distance the rock falls from time $t = 1$ to $t = 3$, we note that at the end of three seconds, the rock has fallen $d(3) = 144$ feet, whereas it had fallen only $d(1) = 16$ feet at the end of one second. So during this time interval, the rock traveled

$$d(3) - d(1) = 144 - 16 = 128 \text{ feet.}$$

The distance traveled by the rock during other time intervals can be found similarly:

Time Interval	Distance Traveled
$t = 1$ to $t = 4$	$d(4) - d(1) = 256 - 16 = 240$
$t = 2$ to $t = 3.5$	$d(3.5) - d(2) = 196 - 64 = 132$
$t = 2$ to $t = 4.5$	$d(4.5) - d(2) = 324 - 64 = 260$

The same procedure works in general:

The distance traveled from time $t = a$ to time $t = b$ is $d(b) - d(a)$ feet.

In the preceding chart, the length of each time interval can be computed by taking the difference between the two times. For example, from $t = 1$ to $t = 4$ is a time interval of length $4 - 1 = 3$ seconds. Similarly, the interval from $t = 2$ to $t = 3.5$ is of length $3.5 - 2 = 1.5$ seconds, and in general,

The time interval from $t = a$ to $t = b$ is an interval of $b - a$ seconds.

Since Distance = Average speed × Time,

$$\text{Average speed} = \frac{\text{Distance traveled}}{\text{Time interval}}.$$

Hence, the average speed over the time interval from $t = a$ to $t = b$ is

$$\text{Average speed} = \frac{\text{Distance traveled}}{\text{Time interval}} = \frac{d(b) - d(a)}{b - a}.$$

For example, to find the average speed from $t = 1$ to $t = 4$, apply the preceding formula with $a = 1$ and $b = 4$:

$$\text{Average speed} = \frac{d(4) - d(1)}{4 - 1} = \frac{256 - 16}{4 - 1} = \frac{240}{3} = 80 \text{ ft per second.}$$

Similarly, the average speed from $t = 2$ to $t = 4.5$ is

$$\frac{d(4.5) - d(2)}{4.5 - 2} = \frac{324 - 64}{4.5 - 2} = \frac{260}{2.5} = 104 \text{ ft per second.}$$

The units in which average speed is measured here (feet per second) indicate the number of units of distance traveled during each unit of time, that is, the *rate of change* of distance (feet) with respect to time (seconds). The preceding discussion can be summarized by saying that the average speed (rate of change of distance with respect to time) as time changes from $t = a$ to $t = b$ is given by

$$\text{Average speed} = \text{Average rate of change}$$

$$= \frac{\text{Change in distance}}{\text{Change in time}} = \frac{d(b) - d(a)}{b - a}.$$

Although speed is the most familiar example, rates of change play a role in many other situations as well, as illustrated in Examples 1–3 below. Consequently, we define the average rate of change of any function as follows.

Average Rate of Change

Let f be a function. The **average rate of change of $f(x)$** with respect to x as x changes from a to b is the number

$$\frac{\text{Change in } f(x)}{\text{Change in } x} = \frac{f(b) - f(a)}{b - a}.$$

EXAMPLE 1

Heidi started a big driving trip at 3 P.M. The odometer reading on her car said 103,846. She finished her trip at 9 P.M., and now the odometer read 104,176. What was her average speed during the trip?

SOLUTION

Her average speed was $\dfrac{\text{Distance traveled}}{\text{Time interval}}$. Her distance traveled was $104,176 - 103,846$ miles. Her time interval was $9 - 3$ hours. So her average speed was

$$\frac{104,176 - 103,846}{9 - 3} = \frac{330 \text{ miles}}{6 \text{ hours}} = 55 \text{ miles per hour.} \qquad \blacksquare$$

EXAMPLE 2

A large heavy-duty balloon is being filled with water. Its approximate volume (in gallons) is given by

$$V(x) = \frac{x^3}{55},$$

where x is the radius of the balloon (in inches). Find the average rate of change of the volume of the balloon as the radius increases from 5 to 10 inches.

SOLUTION

$$\frac{\text{Change in volume}}{\text{Change in radius}} = \frac{V(10) - V(5)}{10 - 5} \approx \frac{18.18 - 2.27}{10 - 5} = \frac{15.91}{5}$$

$$= 3.182 \text{ gallons per inch.} \quad \blacksquare$$

EXAMPLE 3

According to the *Encyclopedia Britannica* almanac, these are the estimated number of cell phone users in the United States, from 1993 to 2004.

Year	1993	1994	1995	1996	1997	1998
Millions of subscribers	16.009	24.134	33.786	44.043	55.312	69.209

Year	1999	2000	2001	2002	2003	2004
Millions of subscribers	86.047	109.478	128.375	140.767	158.722	182.140

Let $f(t)$ be the number of cell phone users in year t. Find the average rate of change in cell-phone use during the following time periods:

(a) 1993–1998   (b) 2002–2004

SOLUTION

(a) Average rate of change $= \dfrac{f(1998) - f(1993)}{1998 - 1993}$

$$= \frac{69,209,000 - 16,009,000}{1998 - 1993}$$

$$= \frac{53,200,000}{5} = 10,640,000 \text{ users/year.}$$

(b) Average rate of change $= \dfrac{f(2004) - f(2002)}{2004 - 2002}$

$$= \frac{182,140,000 - 140,767,000}{2004 - 2002}$$

$$= \frac{41,373,000}{2}$$

$$= 20,686,500 \text{ users/year.} \quad \blacksquare$$

EXAMPLE 4

Figure 2–48 is the graph of the temperature function f during a particular day; $f(x)$ is the temperature at x hours after midnight. What is the average rate of change of the temperature (a) from 4 A.M. to noon? (b) from 3 P.M. to 8 P.M.?

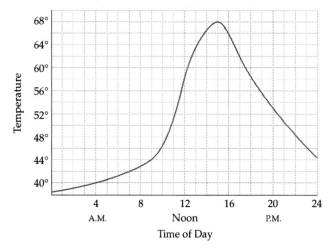

Figure 2–48

SOLUTION

(a) The graph shows that the temperature at 4 A.M. is $f(4) = 40°$ and the temperature at noon is $f(12) = 58°$. The average rate of change of temperature is

$$\frac{\text{Change in temperature}}{\text{Change in time}} = \frac{f(12) - f(4)}{12 - 4} = \frac{58 - 40}{12 - 4} = \frac{18}{8}$$

$$= 2.25° \text{ per hour.}$$

The rate of change is positive because the temperature is increasing at an average rate of 2.25° per hour.

(b) Now 3 P.M. corresponds to $x = 15$ and 8 P.M. to $x = 20$. The graph shows that $f(15) = 68°$ and $f(20) = 53°$. Hence, the average rate of change of temperature is

$$\frac{\text{Change in temperature}}{\text{Change in time}} = \frac{f(20) - f(15)}{20 - 15} = \frac{53 - 68}{20 - 15} = \frac{-15}{5}$$

$$= -3° \text{ per hour.}$$

The rate of change is negative because the temperature is decreasing at an average rate of 3° per hour. ∎

GEOMETRIC INTERPRETATION OF AVERAGE RATE OF CHANGE

If P and Q are points on the graph of a function f, then the straight line determined by P and Q is called a **secant line**. Figure 2–49 shows the secant line joining the points $(4, 40)$ and $(12, 58)$ on the graph of the temperature function f of Example 4.

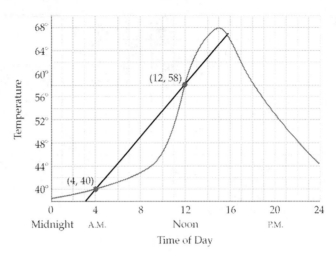

Figure 2–49

Using the points (4, 40) and (12, 58), we see that the slope of this secant line is

$$\frac{58 - 40}{12 - 4} = \frac{18}{8} = 2.25.$$

To say that (4, 40) and (12, 58) are on the graph of f means that $f(4) = 40$ and $f(12) = 58$. Thus,

$$\text{Slope of secant line} = 2.25 = \frac{58 - 40}{12 - 4} = \frac{f(12) - f(4)}{12 - 4}$$

$$= \text{Average rate of change as } x \text{ goes from 4 to 12.}$$

The same thing happens in the general case.

Secant Lines and Average Rates of Change

If f is a function, then the average rate of change of $f(x)$ with respect to x as x changes from $x = a$ to $x = b$ is the slope of the secant line joining the points $(a, f(a))$ and $(b, f(b))$ on the graph of f.

EXAMPLE 5

Assume we have 20 liters of oxygen gas in a thick, unmoving container. The pressure exerted on the walls of the container is a function of the temperature in the room:

$$p(T) = .00411T + 1.1213$$

where T is in degrees Celsius and $p(T)$ is in atmospheres. So at zero degrees Celsius (the temperature at which water freezes) the pressure is 1.1213 atmospheres, and at 100 degrees Celsius (the temperature at which water boils) the pressure is 1.5323 atmospheres.

At what average rate does the pressure change as the temperature increases?

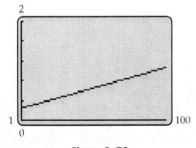

Figure 2–50

SOLUTION   The graph of $p(T) = .00411T + 1.1213$ is a straight line (Figure 2–50). So the secant line joining any two points on the graph is just the graph itself, the line $y = .00411T + 1.1213$. As we saw in Section 1.4, the slope of this line is .00411. Therefore, the average rate of change of the pressure function between any two values of T is .00411. In other words, at any temperature, the pressure will increase at a rate of .00411 atmospheres per degree.   ■

The argument used in Example 5 works for any function whose graph is a straight line and leads to this conclusion.

Rates of Change of Linear Functions

> The average rate of change of a linear function $f(x) = mx + b$, as x changes from one value to another, is the slope m of the line.

THE DIFFERENCE QUOTIENT

Average rates of change are often computed for very small intervals. For instance, we might compute the rate from 4 to 4.01 or from 4 to 4.001. Since $4.01 = 4 + .01$ and $4.001 = 4 + .001$, we are doing essentially the same thing in both cases: computing the rate of change over the interval from 4 to $4 + h$ for some small nonzero quantity h. Furthermore, it's often possible to use a single calculation to determine the average rate for all possible values of h.

EXAMPLE 6

Consider the falling rock with which this section began. The distance the rock has traveled at time t is given by $d(t) = 16t^2$, and its average speed (rate of change) from $t = 4$ to $t = 4 + h$ is

$$\text{Average speed} = \frac{d(4 + h) - d(4)}{(4 + h) - 4} = \frac{16(4 + h)^2 - 16 \cdot 4^2}{h}$$

$$= \frac{16(16 + 8h + h^2) - 256}{h} = \frac{256 + 128h + 16h^2 - 256}{h}$$

$$= \frac{128h + 16h^2}{h} = \frac{h(128 + 16h)}{h} = 128 + 16h.$$

Thus, we can quickly compute the average speed over the interval from 4 to $4 + h$ seconds for any value of h by using the formula

$$\text{Average speed} = 128 + 16h.$$

For example, the average speed from 4 seconds to 4.001 seconds (here $h = .001$) is

$$128 + 16h = 128 + 16(.001) = 128 + .016 = 128.016 \text{ feet per second.}\quad ■$$

Similar calculations can be done with any number in place of 4. In each such case, we are dealing with an interval from x to $x + h$ for some number x. As in Example 6, a single computation can often be used for all possible x and h.

EXAMPLE 7

The average speed of the falling rock of Example 6 from time x to time $x + h$ is:*

$$\text{Average speed} = \frac{d(x + h) - d(x)}{(x + h) - x} = \frac{16(x + h)^2 - 16x^2}{h}$$

$$= \frac{16(x^2 + 2xh + h^2) - 16x^2}{h} = \frac{16x^2 + 32xh + 16h^2 - 16x^2}{h}$$

$$= \frac{32xh + 16h^2}{h} = \frac{h(32x + 16h)}{h} = 32x + 16h.$$

When $x = 4$, then this result states that the average speed from 4 to $4 + h$ is $32(4) + 16h = 128 + 16h$, which is exactly what we found in Example 4. To find the average speed from 3 to 3.1 seconds, apply the formula

$$\text{Average speed} = 32x + 16h$$

with $x = 3$ and $h = .1$:

$$\text{Average speed} = 32 \cdot 3 + 16(.1) = 96 + 1.6 = 97.6 \text{ feet per second.} \quad \blacksquare$$

More generally, we can compute the average rate of change of any function f over the interval from x to $x + h$ just as we did in Example 7: Apply the definition of average rate of change in the box on page 135 with x in place of a and $x + h$ in place of b:

$$\textbf{Average rate of change} = \frac{f(b) - f(a)}{b - a} = \frac{f(x + h) - f(x)}{(x + h) - x}$$

$$= \frac{f(x + h) - f(x)}{h}.$$

This last quantity is just the difference quotient of f (see page 88). Therefore,

Difference Quotients and Rates of Change

> If f is a function, then the average rate of change of f over the interval from x to $x + h$ is given by the difference quotient
>
> $$\frac{f(x + h) - f(x)}{h}.$$

EXAMPLE 8

Find the difference quotient of $V(x) = x^3/55$, and use it to find the average rate of change of V as x changes from 8 to 8.01.

---

*Note that this calculation is the same as in Example 6 except that 4 has been replaced by x.

SOLUTION   Use the definition of the difference quotient and algebra:

$$\frac{V(x+h)-V(x)}{h}=\frac{\overset{V(x+h)}{\overbrace{\frac{(x+h)^3}{55}}}-\overset{V(x)}{\overbrace{\frac{x^3}{55}}}}{h}=\frac{\frac{1}{55}[(x+h)^3-x^3]}{h}$$

$$=\frac{1}{55}\cdot\frac{(x+h)^3-x^3}{h}=\frac{1}{55}\cdot\frac{x^3+3x^2h+3xh^2+h^3-x^3}{h}$$

$$=\frac{1}{55}\cdot\frac{3x^2h+3xh^2+h^3}{h}=\frac{1}{55}\cdot\frac{h(3x^2+3xh+h^2)}{h}$$

$$=\frac{3x^2+3xh+h^2}{55}.$$

When x changes from 8 to $8.01 = 8 + .01$, we have $x = 8$ and $h = .01$. So the average rate of change is

$$\frac{3x^2+3xh+h^2}{55}=\frac{3\cdot8^2+3\cdot8(.01)+(.01)^2}{55}\approx3.495.\qquad\blacksquare$$

If you've been reading carefully, you might be thinking that this process makes something simple (computing the average rate of change of a function from $x = 8$ to $x = 8.01$) into something difficult (FIRST computing the average rate of change from x to $x + h$, using some messy algebra, and then letting $x = 8$ and $h = .01$). If all we wanted to do was compute one such rate, you would be right. We usually use this technique when we want to look at the same function for many values of h, as we will in the next example. We basically are doing an ugly calculation one time to make a series of future calculations simpler.

 INSTANTANEOUS RATE OF CHANGE

Rates of change are a major theme in calculus—not just the average rate of change discussed above, but also the *instantaneous rate of change* of a function (that is, its rate of change at a particular instant). Even without calculus, however, we can obtain quite accurate approximations of instantaneous rates of change by using average rates appropriately.

EXAMPLE 9

A rock is dropped from a high place. What is its speed exactly 3 seconds after it is dropped?

SOLUTION   The distance the rock has fallen at time t is given by the function $d(t) = 16t^2$. The exact speed at $t = 3$ can be approximated by finding the average speed over very small time intervals, say, 3 to 3.01 or even shorter intervals. Over a very short time span, such as a hundredth of a second, the rock cannot change speed very much, so these average speeds should be a reasonable approximation of its speed at the instant $t = 3$. Example 7 shows that the average speed is given by the difference quotient $32x + 16h$. When $x = 3$, the difference quotient is $32 \cdot 3 + 16h = 96 + 16h$, and we have the following:

Change in Time 3 to 3 + h	h	Average Speed [Difference Quotient at $x = 3$] $96 + 16h$
3 to 3.1	.1	$96 + 16(.1) = 97.6$ ft per second
3 to 3.01	.01	$96 + 16(.01) = 96.16$ ft per second
3 to 3.005	.005	$96 + 16(.005) = 96.08$ ft per second
3 to 3.00001	.00001	$96 + 16(.00001) = 96.00016$ ft per second

The table suggests that the exact speed of the rock at the instant $t = 3$ seconds is very close to 96 feet per second. ∎

EXAMPLE 10

A balloon is being filled with water in such a way that when its radius is x inches, then its volume is $V(x) = x^3/55$ gallons. In Example 2, we saw that the average rate of change of the volume as the radius increases from 5 inches to 10 inches is 3.182 gallons per inch. What is the rate of change at the instant when the radius is 7 inches?

SOLUTION   The average rate of change when the radius goes from x to $x + h$ inches is given by the difference quotient of $V(x)$, which was found in Example 8:

$$\frac{V(x + h) - V(x)}{h} = \frac{3x^2 + 3xh + h^2}{55}.$$

Therefore, when $x = 7$, the difference quotient is

$$\frac{3 \cdot 7^2 + 3 \cdot 7 \cdot h + h^2}{55} = \frac{147 + 21h + h^2}{55},$$

and we have these average rates of change over small intervals near 7:

Change in Radius 7 to 7 + h	h	Average Rate of Change of Volume [Difference Quotient at $x = 7$] $\dfrac{147 + 21h + h^2}{55}$
7 to 7.01	.01	2.6765 gallons per inch
7 to 7.001	.001	2.6731 gallons per inch
7 to 7.0001	.0001	2.6728 gallons per inch
7 to 7.00001	.00001	2.6727 gallons per inch

The chart suggests that at the instant the radius is 7 inches, the volume is changing at a rate of approximately 2.673 gallons per inch. ∎

EXERCISES 2.7

1. A car moves along a straight test track. The distance traveled by the car at various times is shown in this table:

Time (seconds)	0	5	10	15	20	25	30
Distance (feet)	0	20	140	400	680	1400	1800

Find the average speed of the car over the interval from

(a) 0 to 10 seconds   (b) 10 to 20 seconds
(c) 20 to 30 seconds   (d) 15 to 30 seconds

2. Find the average rate of change of the volume of the balloon in Example 2 as the radius increases from

(a) 2 to 5 inches   (b) 4 to 8 inches

3. Use the function of Example 3 to find the average rate of change in cell-phone use from

(a) 1994–1996   (b) 1999–2004

4. The graph shows the total amount spent on advertising (in millions of dollars) in the United States, as estimated by a leading advertising publication.* Find the average rate of change in advertising expenditures over the following time periods:

(a) 1950–1970   (b) 1970–1980
(c) 1980–2000   (d) 1950–2000
(e) During which of these periods were expenditures increasing at the fastest rate?

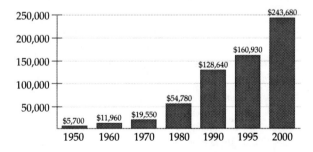

5. The following table shows the total projected elementary and secondary school enrollment (in thousands) for selected years.[†] Find the average rate of change of enrollment from

(a) 1980 to 1985   (b) 1985 to 1995
(c) 1995 to 2005   (d) 2005 to 2014
(e) During which of these periods was enrollment increasing at the fastest rate? At the slowest rate?

Year	Enrollment
1980	40,877
1985	39,422
1990	41,217
1995	44,840
2000	47,204
2005	48,375
2010	48,842
2014	49,993

6. The graph shows the minimum wage (in constant 2000 dollars), with $x = 0$ corresponding to 1950.* Find the average rate of change in the minimum wage from

(a) 1950 to 1976   (b) 1976 to 1995
(c) 1995 to 2000   (d) 1976 to 2000

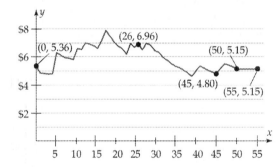

7. The table shows the total number of shares traded (in billions) on the New York Stock Exchange in selected years.[†]

Year	1995	1997	1999	2001	2003	2005
Volume	87.2	133.3	203.9	307.5	352.4	403.8

Find the average rate of change in share volume from
(a) 1995 to 1999   (b) 1999 to 2001
(c) 2001 to 2005   (d) 1995 to 2005
(e) During which of these periods did share volume increase at the fastest rate?

8. The graph in the figure[‡] shows the popularity of the name Frances since the 1880s, when records started to be kept. The y-axis shows the usage of "Frances" per million babies. The name increased in popularity until the 1910s, and then its popularity decreased. Estimate the average rate of change of popularity (in usage per million per year) over the interval:

(a) 1880 to 1890   (b) 1880 to 1930
(c) 1930 to 1950   (d) 1950 to 1990

---

*Advertising Age.
[†]U.S. National Center for Education Statistics.

*U.S. Employment Standards Administration.
[†]NYSE Factbook.
[‡]Baby Name Wizard.

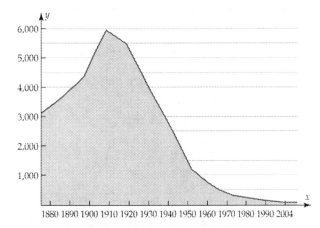

1880 1890 1900 1910 1920 1930 1940 1950 1960 1970 1980 1990 2004

9. The Pennyfarthing Bicycle Company has found that its sales are related to the amount of advertising it does in trade magazines. The graph in the figure shows the sales (in thousands of dollars) as a function of the amount of advertising (in number of magazine ad pages). Find the average rate of change of sales when the number of ad pages increases from

(a) 10 to 20   (b) 20 to 60
(c) 60 to 100   (d) 0 to 100
(e) Is it worthwhile to buy more than 70 pages of ads, if the cost of a one-page ad is $2000? If the cost is $5000? If the cost is $8000?

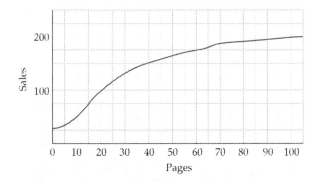

Pages

10. When blood flows through an artery (which can be thought of as a cylindrical tube) its velocity is greatest at the center of the artery. Because of friction along the walls of the tube, the blood's velocity decreases as the distance r from the center of the artery increases, finally becoming 0 at the wall of the artery. The velocity (in centimeters per second) is given by the function $v = 18{,}500(.000065 - r^2)$, where r is measured in centimeters. Find the average rate of change of the velocity as the distance from the center changes from

(a) $r = .001$ to $r = .002$ (b) $r = .002$ to $r = .003$
(c) $r = 0$ to $r = .005$

In Exercises 11–17, find the average rate of change of the function f over the given interval.

11. $f(x) = 3 + x^3$ from $x = 0$ to $x = 2$

12. $f(x) = .25x^4 - x^2 - 2x + 4$ from $x = -1$ to $x = 4$

13. $f(x) = x^3 - 3x^2 - 8x + 6$ from $x = -1$ to $x = 3$

14. $f(x) = -\sqrt{x^4 - x^3 + 2x^2 - x + 4}$ from $x = 0$ to $x = 3$

15. $f(x) = \sqrt{x^3 + 2x^2 - 6x + 5}$ from $x = 1$ to $x = 1.01$

16. $f(x) = \sqrt{x^3 + 2x^2 - 6x + 5}$ from $x = 1$ to $x = 1.00001$

17. $f(x) = \dfrac{x^2 - 3}{2x - 4}$ from $x = 3$ to $x = 8$

In Exercises 18–25, compute and simplify the difference quotient of the function.

18. $f(x) = x + 5$ **19.** $f(x) = 7x + 2$

20. $f(x) = x^2 + 3$ **21.** $f(x) = x^2 + 3x - 1$

22. $f(t) = 160{,}000 - 8000t + t^2$

23. $V(x) = x^3$

24. $A(r) = \pi r^2$ **25.** $V(p) = 5/p$

26. Water is draining from a large tank. After t minutes, there are $160{,}000 - 8000t + t^2$ gallons of water in the tank.

(a) Use the results of Exercise 22 to find the average rate at which the water runs out in the interval from 10 to 10.1 minutes.
(b) Do the same for the interval from 10 to 10.01 minutes.
(c) Estimate the rate at which the water runs out after exactly 10 minutes.

27. Use the results of Exercise 23 to find the average rate of change of the volume of a cube whose side has length x as x changes from

(a) 4 to 4.1   (b) 4 to 4.01   (c) 4 to 4.001
(d) Estimate the rate of change of the volume at the instant when $x = 4$.

28. Use the results of Exercise 24 to find the average rate of change of the area of a circle of radius r as r changes from

(a) 4 to 4.5   (b) 4 to 4.2   (c) 4 to 4.1
(d) Estimate the rate of change at the instant when $r = 4$.
(e) How is your answer in part (d) related to the circumference of a circle of radius 4?

29. Under certain conditions, the volume V of a quantity of air is related to the pressure p (which is measured in kilopascals) by the equation $V = 5/p$. Use the results of Exercise 25 to estimate the rate at which the volume is changing at the instant when the pressure is 50 kilopascals.

30. Two cars race on a straight track, beginning from a dead stop. The distance (in feet) each car has covered at each time during the first 16 seconds is shown in the figure.

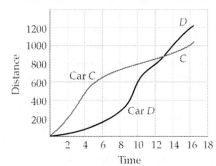

(a) What is the average speed of each car during this 16-second interval?

(b) Find an interval beginning at $t = 4$ during which the average speed of car D was approximately the same as the average speed of car C from $t = 2$ to $t = 10$.

(c) Use secant lines and slopes to justify the statement "car D traveled at a higher average speed than car C from $t = 4$ to $t = 10$."

31. The figure shows the profits earned by Soupy Soy Sauce during the last quarters of three consecutive years.

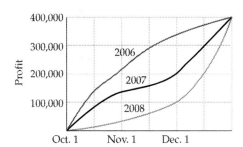

(a) Explain why the average rate of change of profits from October 1 to December 31 was the same in all three years.

(b) During what month in what year was the average rate of change of profits the greatest?

32. The graph in the figure shows the chipmunk population in a certain wilderness area. The population increases as the chipmunks reproduce but then decreases sharply as predators move into the area.

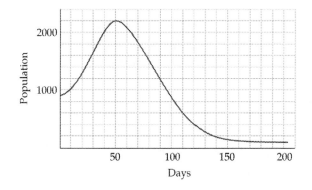

(a) During what approximate time period, beginning on day 0, is the average growth rate of the chipmunk population positive?

(b) During what approximate time period, beginning on day 0, is the average growth rate of the chipmunk population 0?

(c) What is the average growth rate of the chipmunk population from day 50 to day 100? What does this number mean?

(d) What is the average growth rate from day 45 to day 50? From day 50 to day 55? What is the approximate average growth rate from day 49 to day 51?

33. The following is a graph of the price of a share of stock in the International House of Pancakes from June of 2001 through June of 2006

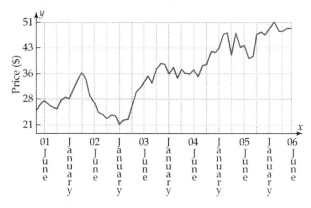

(a) What was the average rate of change of IHOP stock (in dollars per year) between September of 2001 and March of 2002?

(b) What was the average rate of change of IHOP stock between March of 2002 and January of 2003?

(c) What was the average rate of change of IHOP stock between June of 2001 and June of 2006?

34. Lucy has a viral flu. How bad she feels depends primarily on how fast her temperature is rising at that time. The figure shows her temperature during the first day of the flu.

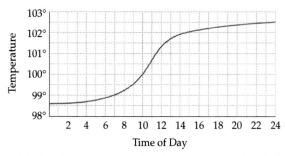

(a) At what average rate does her temperature rise during the entire day?

(b) During what two-hour period during the day does she feel worst?

(c) Find two time intervals, one in the morning and one in the afternoon, during which she feels about the same (that is, during which her temperature is rising at the same average rate).

35. The table shows the average weekly earnings (including overtime) of production workers and nonsupervisory employees in industry (excluding agriculture) in selected years.*

Year	1980	1985	1990	1995	2000	2005
Weekly Earnings	$191	$257	$319	$369	$454	$538

*U.S. Bureau of Labor Statistics.

(a) Use linear regression to find a function that models this data, with $x = 0$ corresponding to 1980.

(b) According to your function, what is the average rate of change in earnings over any time period between 1980 and 2005?

(c) Use the data in the table to find the average rate of change in earnings from 1980 to 1990 and from 2000–2005. How do these rates compare with the ones given by the model?

(d) If the model remains accurate, when will average weekly earnings reach $600?

36. The estimated number of 15- to 24-year-old people worldwide (in millions) who are living with HIV/AIDS in selected years is given in the table.*

Year	2001	2003	2005	2007	2009
15- to 24-year-olds with HIV/AIDS	12	14.5	17	19	20.5

(a) Use linear regression to find a function that models this data, with $x = 0$ corresponding to 2000.

(b) According to your function, what is the average rate of change in this HIV/AIDS population over any time period between 2001 and 2009?

(c) Use the data in the table to find the average rate of change in this HIV/AIDS population from 2001 to 2009. How does this rate compare with the one given by the model?

(d) If the model remains accurate, when will the number of people in this age group with HIV/AIDS reach 25 million?

---

*Kaiser Family Foundation, UNICEF, U.S. Census Bureau.

2.8   Inverse Functions*

Section Objectives

- ■ Determine graphically if a function is one-to-one.
- ■ Find inverse functions algebraically.
-   Explore the properties of inverse functions.
- ■ Graph inverse functions.

Consider the functions f and h given by these tables:

f-input	−2	−1	0	1	2
f-output	−3	−2	1	4	5

h-input	1	2	3	4	5
h-output	−1	3	0	3	2

With the function h, two different inputs (2 and 4) produce the same output 3. With the function f, however, different inputs always produce different outputs. Functions with this property have a special name. A function f is said to be **one-to-one** if distinct inputs always produce distinct outputs, that is,

$$\text{if } a \neq b, \text{ then } f(a) \neq f(b)$$

In graphical terms, this means that two points on the graph, $(a, f(a))$ and $(b, f(b))$, that have different x-coordinates [$a \neq b$] must also have different y-coordinates [$f(a) \neq f(b)$]. Consequently, these points cannot lie on the same horizontal line because all points on a horizontal line have the same y-coordinate. Therefore, we have this geometric test to determine whether a function is one-to-one.

---

*This section is used only in Section 5.3, Special Topics 5.3.A, and Section 7.4. It may be postponed until then.

The Horizontal Line Test

If a function f is one-to-one, then it has this property:

No horizontal line intersects the graph of f more than once.

Conversely, if the graph of a function has this property, then the function is one-to-one.

EXAMPLE 1

Which of the following functions are one-to-one?

(a) $f(x) = 7x^5 + 3x^4 - 2x^3 + 2x + 1$

(b) $g(x) = x^3 - 3x - 1$

(c) $h(x) = 1 - .2x^3$

SOLUTION   Complete graphs of each function are shown in Figure 2–51.

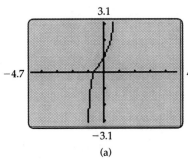

(a)

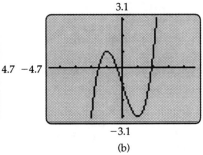

(b)

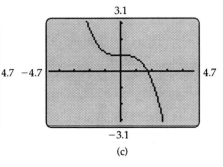

(c)

Figure 3–51

(a) The graph of f in Figure 2–54(a) passes the horizontal line test, since no horizontal line intersects the graph more than once. Hence, f is one-to-one.

(b) The graph of g in Figure 2–52(b) obviously fails the horizontal line test because many horizontal lines (including the x-axis) intersect the graph more than once. Therefore, g is not one-to-one.

(c) The graph of h in Figure 2–51(c) appears to contain a horizontal line segment. So h appears to fail the Horizontal Line Test because the horizontal line through $(0, 1)$ seems to intersect the graph infinitely many times. But appearances are deceiving.

TECHNOLOGY TIP

Although a horizontal segment may appear on a calculator screen when the graph is actually rising or falling, there is another possibility. The graph may have a tiny wiggle (less than the height of a pixel) and thus fail the horizontal line test:

You can usually detect such a wiggle by zooming in to magnify that portion of the graph or by using the trace feature to see whether the y-coordinates increase and then decrease (or vice versa) along the "horizontal" segment.

GRAPHING EXPLORATION

Graph $h(x) = 1 - .2x^3$ and use the trace feature to move from left to right along the "horizontal" segment. Do the y-coordinates stay the same, or do they decrease?

The Exploration shows that the graph is actually falling from left to right, so that each horizontal line intersects it only once. (It appears to have a horizontal segment because the amount the graph falls there is less than the height of a pixel on the screen.) Therefore, h is a one-to-one function. ∎

The function f in Example 1 is an **increasing function** (its graph is always rising from left to right), and the function h is a **decreasing function** (its graph is always falling from left to right). Every increasing or decreasing function is necessarily one-to-one because its graph can never touch the same horizontal line twice (it would have to change from rising to falling, or vice versa, to do so).

 ## INVERSE FUNCTIONS

We begin with a simple example that illustrates the basic idea of an inverse function. Consider the one-to-one function f introduced at the beginning of this section.

f-input	-2	-1	0	1	2
f-output	-3	-2	1	4	5

Now define a new function g by the following table (which simply *switches* the rows in the f table).

g-input	-3	-2	1	4	5
g-output	-2	-1	0	1	2

Note that the inputs of f are the outputs of g and the outputs of f are the inputs of g. In other words,

$$\text{Domain of } f = \text{Range of } g \qquad \text{and} \qquad \text{Range of } f = \text{Domain of } g.$$

The rule of g *reverses* the action of f by taking each output of f back to the input it came from. For instance,

$$g(4) = 1 \qquad \text{and} \qquad f(1) = 4$$

$$g(-3) = -2 \qquad \text{and} \qquad f(-2) = -3$$

and in general,

$$g(y) = x \qquad \text{exactly when} \qquad f(x) = y.$$

We say that g is the *inverse function* of f.

The preceding construction works for any one-to-one function f. Each output of f comes from exactly one input (because different inputs produce different outputs). Consequently, we can define a new function g that reverses the action of f by sending each output back to the unique input it came from. For instance, if $f(7) = 11$, then $g(11) = 7$. Thus, the outputs of f become the inputs of g, and we have this definition.

Inverse Functions

Let f be a one-to-one function. Then the **inverse function** of f is the function g whose rule is

$$g(y) = x \qquad \text{exactly when} \qquad f(x) = y.$$

The domain of g is the range of f and the range of g is the domain of f.

EXAMPLE 2

The graph of $f(x) = 3x - 2$ is a straight line that certainly passes the Horizontal Line Test, so f is one-to-one and has an inverse function g. From the definition of g we know that

$$g(y) = x \qquad \text{exactly when} \qquad f(x) = y$$

that is,

$$g(y) = x \qquad \text{exactly when} \qquad 3x - 2 = y.$$

To find the rule of g, we need only solve this last equation for x:

$$3x - 2 = y$$

Add 2 to both sides: $\qquad 3x = y + 2$

Divide both sides by 3: $\qquad x = \dfrac{y + 2}{3}$

Since $g(y) = x$, we see that the rule of g is $g(y) = \dfrac{y + 2}{3}$. ∎

Recall that the letter used for the variable of a function doesn't matter. For instance, $h(x) = x^2$ and $h(t) = t^2$ and $h(u) = u^2$ all describe the same function, whose rule is "square the input." When dealing with inverse functions, it is customary to use the same variable for both f and its inverse g. Consequently, the inverse function in Example 2 would normally be written as

$$g(x) = \dfrac{x + 2}{3}.$$

We can summarize this procedure as follows.

Finding Inverse Functions Algebraically

To find the inverse function of a one-to-one function f:

1. Solve the equation $f(x) = y$ for x.

2. The solution is an expression in y, which is the rule of the inverse function g, that is, $x = g(y)$.

3. Rewrite the rule of $x = g(y)$ by interchanging x and y.

EXAMPLE 3

Use your calculator to verify that the function $f(x) = x^3 + 5$ passes the Horizontal Line Test and hence is one-to-one. Its inverse can be found by solving for x in the equation $x^3 + 5 = y$:

Subtract 5 from both sides: $\qquad x^3 = y - 5$

Take cube roots on both sides: $\qquad x = \sqrt[3]{y - 5}.$

Therefore, $g(y) = \sqrt[3]{y - 5}$ is the inverse function of f. Interchanging x and y, we write this rule as $g(x) = \sqrt[3]{x - 5}$. ∎

EXAMPLE 4

The function $f(x) = \sqrt{x - 3}$ is one-to-one, as you can verify with your calculator. Find its inverse.

SOLUTION   We solve the equation:

$$y = \sqrt{x - 3}$$

Square both sides: $y^2 = x - 3$

Add 3 to both sides: $x = y^2 + 3.$

Although this last equation is defined for all real numbers y, the original equation $y = \sqrt{x - 3}$ has $y \geq 0$ (since square roots are nonnegative). In other words, the range of the function f (the possible values of y) consists of all nonnegative real numbers. Consequently, the domain of the inverse function g is the set of all nonnegative real numbers, and its rule is

$$g(y) = y^2 + 3 \quad (y \geq 0).$$

Once again, it's customary to use the same variable to describe both f and its inverse function, so we write the rule of g as $g(x) = x^2 + 3$ $(x \geq 0)$. ∎

EXAMPLE 5

In Example 2 of Section 3.6, we considered a water balloon whose volume (in gallons) was $V(x) = x^3/55$, where x was the radius of the balloon (in inches). This function is one-to-one because as the radius changes, so does the volume. Therefore, $V(x)$ has an inverse function. Its rule can be found by solving $V = x^3/55$ for x:

Multiply both sides by 55: $55V = x^3$

Take cube roots of both sides: $x = \sqrt[3]{55V}.$

Since the original function had radius x as input and volume V as output, the inverse function has volume as input and radius as output. In other words, the inverse function allows us to compute the radius of our balloon for any given volume. For instance, a balloon with a volume of 24 gallons has radius $x = \sqrt[3]{55 \cdot 24} = \sqrt[3]{1320} \approx 10.97$ inches. ∎

EXAMPLE 6

A rule of thumb to figure out how long it would take an investment to double is the *Rule of* 72: If i is the interest rate on the investment, then the approximate doubling time is $72/i$. If the rate is 10% per year, for example, then it will take approximately $72/10 = 7.2$ years for the investment to double. (This rule of thumb is good for interest rates below 20%.)

(a) Let f be the "doubling function" whose rule is $f(i) = 72/i$. Find the rule of the inverse function g and explain what it represents.

(b) What interest rate is needed to double your investment in 5 years?

SOLUTION

(a) We solve the equation $y = f(i)$ for i:

$$y = \frac{72}{i}$$

$$iy = 72$$

$$i = \frac{72}{y}.$$

So the rule of the inverse function is $g(y) = 72/y$.* The function g gives the interest rate needed to double your money in y years.

(b) Using the inverse function, we see that $g(5) = 72/5 = 14.4$. We need an interest rate of 14.4% to double our money in 5 years. ∎

THE ROUND-TRIP PROPERTIES

The inverse function g of a function f was designed to send each output of f back to the input it came from. Consequently, if you first apply f and then apply g to the result, you obtain the number you started with, as illustrated in the next example.

EXAMPLE 7

As we saw in Example 2, the inverse function of $f(x) = 3x - 2$ is

$$g(x) = \frac{x + 2}{3}.$$

If we start with a number c and apply f, we obtain $f(c) = 3c - 2$. If we now apply g to this result, we obtain

$$g(f(c)) = g(3c - 2) = \frac{(3c - 2) + 2}{3} = c.$$

So we are back where we started. Similarly, if we first apply g and then apply f to a number, we end up where we started:

$$f(g(c)) = f\left(\frac{c + 2}{3}\right) = 3\left(\frac{c + 2}{3}\right) - 2 = c.$$

The function $f(x) = x^3 + 5$ of Example 3 and its inverse function

$$g(x) = \sqrt[3]{x - 5}$$

also have these "round-trip" properties. If you apply one function and then the other, you wind up at the number you started with:

$$g(f(x)) = g(x^3 + 5) = \sqrt[3]{(x^3 + 5) - 5} = \sqrt[3]{x^3} = x$$

and

$$f(g(x)) = f(\sqrt[3]{x - 5}) = (\sqrt[3]{x - 5})^3 + 5 = (x - 5) + 5 = x. \quad ∎$$

---

*Since the name of the variable doesn't matter, the rule can be written as $g(i) = 72/i$. Hence, the doubling function $f(i) = 72/i$ is its own inverse. This happens occasionally.

Not only do a function and its inverse have the round-trip properties illustrated in Example 7, but somewhat more is true.

Round-Trip Theorem

A one-to-one function f and its inverse function g have these properties:

$$g(f(x)) = x \quad \text{for every } x \text{ in the domain of } f;$$

$$f(g(x)) = x \quad \text{for every } x \text{ in the domain of } g.$$

Conversely, if f and g are functions having these properties, then f is one-to-one and its inverse is g.

Proof   By the definition of inverse function,

$$g(d) = c \qquad \text{exactly when} \qquad f(c) = d.$$

Consequently, for any c in the domain of f.

$$g(f(c)) = g(d) \quad (\text{because } f(c) = d)$$
$$= c \quad (\text{because } g(d) = c).$$

A similar argument shows that $f(g(d)) = d$ for any d in the domain of g. The last statement in the Theorem is proved in Exercise 50.   ■

EXAMPLE 8

Let

$$f(x) = \frac{5}{2x - 4} \qquad \text{and} \qquad g(x) = \frac{4x + 5}{2x}.$$

Show the following:

(a) For every x in the domain of f (that is, all $x \neq 2$), $g(f(x)) = x$.
(b) For every x in the domain of g (all $x \neq 0$), $f(g(x)) = x$.

SOLUTION

(a) $g(f(x)) = g\left(\dfrac{5}{2x - 4}\right)$

$$= \frac{4\left(\dfrac{5}{2x - 4}\right) + 5}{2\left(\dfrac{5}{2x - 4}\right)}$$

$$= \frac{\dfrac{20 + 5(2x - 4)}{2x - 4}}{\dfrac{10}{2x - 4}}$$

$$= \frac{20 + 5(2x - 4)}{10}$$

$$= \frac{20 + 10x - 20}{10} = x.$$

(b) $f(g(x)) = f\left(\dfrac{4x + 5}{2x}\right)$

$$= \frac{5}{2\left(\dfrac{4x + 5}{2x}\right) - 4}$$

$$= \frac{5}{\dfrac{4x + 5}{x} - 4}$$

$$= \frac{5}{\dfrac{4x + 5 - 4x}{x}}$$

$$= \frac{5}{\dfrac{5}{x}} = x.$$

By the Round-Trip Theorem, f is a one-to-one function with inverse g.   ■

GRAPHS OF INVERSE FUNCTIONS

Finding the rule of the inverse function g of a one-to-one function f by solving the equation $y = f(x)$ for x, as in the preceding examples, is not always possible (some equations are hard to solve). But even if you don't know the rule of g, you can always find its graph, as shown below.

Suppose f is a one-to-one function and g is its inverse function. Then by the definition of inverse function:

$$f(a) = b \qquad \text{exactly when} \qquad g(b) = a.$$

But $f(a) = b$ means that (a, b) is on the graph of f and $g(b) = a$ means that (b, a) is on the graph of g. Therefore,

Inverse Function Graphs

> If f is a one-to-one function and g is its inverse function, then
>
> (a, b) is on the graph of f exactly when (b, a) is on the graph of g.

Therefore, the graph of the inverse function g can be obtained by reversing the coordinates of each point on the graph of f. There are two practical ways of doing this, each of which is illustrated below.

EXAMPLE 9

Verify that $f(x) = .7x^5 + .3x^4 - .2x^3 + 2x + .5$ has an inverse function g. Use parametric graphing to graph both f and g. *

SOLUTION   First, we graph f in parametric mode by letting

$$x = t \qquad \text{and} \qquad y = f(t) = .7t^5 + .3t^4 - .2t^3 + 2t + .5.$$

The complete graph in Figure 2–52 shows that f is one-to-one (why?) and hence has an inverse function g. According to the preceding box, the graph of g can be obtained by taking each point on the graph of f and reversing its coordinates. Thus, g can be graphed parametrically by letting

$$x = f(t) = .7t^5 + .3t^4 - .2t^3 + 2t + .5 \qquad \text{and} \qquad y = t.$$

Figure 2–53 shows the graphs of g and f on the same screen.   ∎

TECHNOLOGY TIP

The inverse function of y_1 can be graphed directly by using this menu/command:

TI: DRAW/DRAWINV y_1

Casio: SKETCH/INV

[DRAW is a submenu of the GRAPH menu on TI-86/89.]

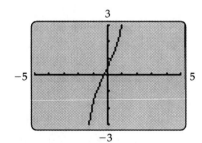

Figure 2–52

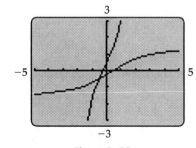

Figure 2–53

---

*Parametric graphing is explained in Special Topics 3.3.A.

The second method of graphing inverse functions by reversing coordinates depends on this geometric fact, which is proved in Exercise 49:

> The line $y = x$ is the perpendicular bisector of
> the line segment from (a, b) to (b, a),

as shown in Figure 2–54 when $a = 7$, $b = 2$.

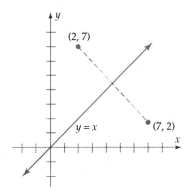

Figure 2–54

Thus (a, b) and (b, a) lie on opposite sides of $y = x$, the same distance from it: They are mirror images of each other, with the line $y = x$ being the mirror.* Consequently, the graph of the inverse function g is the mirror image of the graph of f. In formal terms,

***Inverse Function
Graphs***

> If g is the inverse function of f, then the graph of g is the reflection of the graph of f in the line $y = x$.

GRAPHING EXPLORATION

Illustrate this fact by graphing the line $y = x$, the function

$$f(x) = x^3 + 5$$

of Example 3, and its inverse $g(x) = \sqrt[3]{x - 5}$ on the same screen (use a square viewing window so that the mirror effect won't be distorted).

NOTE

In many texts, the inverse function of a function f is denoted f^{-1}. In this notation, for instance, the inverse of the function $f(x) = x^3 + 5$ in Example 3 would be written as $f^{-1}(x) = \sqrt[3]{x - 5}$. Similarly, the reversal properties of inverse functions become

$$f^{-1}(f(x)) = x \text{ for every } x \text{ in the domain of } f; \text{ and}$$
$$f(f^{-1}(x)) = x \text{ for every } x \text{ in the domain of } f^{-1}.$$

In this context, f^{-1} does *not* mean $1/f$ (see Exercise 45).

---

*In technical terms, (a, b) and (b, a) are **symmetric with respect to the line** $y = x$.

EXERCISES 2.8

In Exercises 1–8, use a calculator and the Horizontal Line Test to determine whether or not the function f is one-to-one.

1. $f(x) = x^4 - 4x^2 + 3$

2. $f(x) = x^4 - 4x + 3$

3. $f(x) = x^3 + x - 5$

4. $f(x) = \begin{cases} x - 3 & \text{if } x \le 3 \\ 2x - 6 & \text{if } x > 3 \end{cases}$

5. $f(x) = x^5 + 2x^4 - x^2 + 4x - 5$

6. $f(x) = x^3 - 4x^2 + x - 10$

7. $f(x) = .1x^3 - .1x^2 - .005x + 1$

8. $f(x) = .1x^3 + .005x + 1$

In Exercises 9–22, use algebra to find the inverse of the given one-to-one function.

9. $f(x) = -x$

10. $f(x) = -x + 1$

11. $f(x) = 5x - 4$

12. $f(x) = -3x + 5$

13. $f(x) = 5 - 2x^3$

14. $f(x) = (x^5 + 1)^3$

15. $f(x) = \sqrt{4x - 7}$

16. $f(x) = 5 + \sqrt{3x - 2}$

17. $f(x) = 1/x$

18. $f(x) = 1/\sqrt{x}$

19. $f(x) = \dfrac{1}{2x + 1}$

20. $f(x) = \dfrac{x}{x + 1}$

21. $f(x) = \dfrac{x^3 - 1}{x^3 + 5}$

22. $f(x) = \sqrt[5]{\dfrac{3x - 1}{x - 2}}$

In Exercises 23–28, use the Round-Trip Theorem on page 152 to show that g is the inverse of f.

23. $f(x) = x + 1$, $\quad g(x) = x - 1$

24. $f(x) = 2x - 6$, $\quad g(x) = \dfrac{x}{2} + 3$

25. $f(x) = \dfrac{1}{x + 1}$, $\quad g(x) = \dfrac{1 - x}{x}$

26. $f(x) = \dfrac{-3}{2x + 5}$, $\quad g(x) = \dfrac{-3 - 5x}{2x}$

27. $f(x) = x^5$, $\quad g(x) = \sqrt[5]{x}$

28. $f(x) = x^3 - 1$, $\quad g(x) = \sqrt[3]{x + 1}$

29. Show that the inverse function of the function f whose rule is $f(x) = \dfrac{2x + 1}{3x - 2}$ is f itself.

30. List three different functions (other than the ones in Example 6 and Exercise 29), each of which is its own inverse. [Many correct answers are possible.]

31. Let $f(t)$ be the population of rabbits on Christy's property t years after she received 10 of them as a gift.

t	$f(t)$
0	10
1	23
2	48
3	64
4	70
5	71

Compute the following, including units, or write "not enough information to tell." f^{-1} denotes the inverse function of f.

(a) $f(2)$ (b) $f^{-1}(48)$

(c) $f^{-1}(71)$ (d) $3 \cdot f^{-1}(70)$

(e) $f^{-1}(2 \cdot 48)$ (f) $f(70)$

(g) $f^{-1}(4)$

In Exercises 32 and 33, the graph of a function f is given. Sketch the graph of the inverse function of f. [Reflect carefully.]

32.

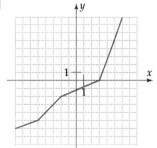

33.

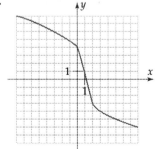

In Exercises 34–39, each given function has an inverse function. Sketch the graph of the inverse function.

34. $f(x) = \sqrt{x + 3}$

35. $f(x) = \sqrt{3x - 2}$

36. $f(x) = .3x^5 + 2$

37. $f(x) = \sqrt[3]{x + 3}$

38. $f(x) = \sqrt[5]{x^3 + x - 2}$

39. $f(x) = \begin{cases} x^2 - 1 & \text{if } x \le 0 \\ -.5x - 1 & \text{if } x > 0 \end{cases}$

In Exercises 40–42, none of the functions has an inverse. State at least one way of restricting the domain of the function (that is, find a function with the same rule and a smaller domain) so that the restricted function has an inverse. Then find the rule of the inverse function.

Example: $f(x) = x^2$ has no inverse. But the function h with domain all $x \ge 0$ and rule $h(x) = x^2$ is increasing (its graph is the right half of the graph of f—see Figure 2–2 on page 78)— and therefore has an inverse.

40. $f(x) = |x|$

41. $f(x) = -x^2$

42. $f(x) = \sqrt{4 - x^2}$

43. $f(x) = \dfrac{1}{x^2 + 1}$

44. $f(x) = 3(x + 5)^2 + 2$

45. (a) Using the f^{-1} notation for inverse functions, find $f^{-1}(x)$ when $f(x) = 3x + 2$.
(b) Find $f^{-1}(1)$ and $1/f(1)$. Conclude that f^{-1} is not the same function as $1/f$.

46. Let C be the temperature in degrees Celsius. Then the temperature in degrees Fahrenheit is given by $f(C) = \frac{9}{5}C + 32$. Let g be the function that converts degrees Fahrenheit to degrees Celsius. Show that g is the inverse function of f and find the rule of g.

THINKERS

47. Let m and b be constants with $m \ne 0$. Show that the function $f(x) = mx + b$ has an inverse function g and find the rule of g.

48. Prove that the function $h(x) = 1 - .2x^3$ of Example 1(c) is one-to-one by showing that it satisfies the definition:

$$\text{If } a \ne b, \text{ then } h(a) \ne h(b).$$

[*Hint:* Use the rule of h to show that when $h(a) = h(b)$, then $a = b$. If this is the case, then it is impossible to have $h(a) = h(b)$ when $a \ne b$.]

49. Show that the points $P = (a, b)$ and $Q = (b, a)$ are symmetric with respect to the line $y = x$ as follows.
(a) Find the slope of the line through P and Q.
(b) Use slopes to show that the line through P and Q is perpendicular to $y = x$.
(c) Let R be the point where the line $y = x$ intersects line segment PQ. Since R is on $y = x$, it has coordinates (c, c) for some number c, as shown in the figure. Use the distance formula to show that segment PR has the same length as segment RQ. Conclude that the line $y = x$ is the perpendicular bisector of segment PQ. Therefore, P and Q are symmetric with respect to the line $y = x$.

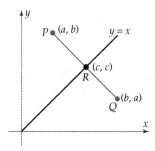

50. Suppose that functions f and g have these round-trip properties:
(1) $g(f(x)) = x$ for every x in the domain of f.
(2) $f(g(y)) = y$ for every y in the domain of g.

To complete the proof of the Round-Trip Theorem, we must show that g is the inverse function of f. Do this as follows.

(a) Prove that f is one-to-one by showing that

$$\text{if } \quad a \ne b, \quad \text{then} \quad f(a) \ne f(b).$$

[*Hint:* If $f(a) = f(b)$, apply g to both sides and use (1) to show that $a = b$. Consequently, if $a \ne b$, it is impossible to have $f(a) = f(b)$.]
(b) If $g(y) = x$, show that $f(x) = y$. [*Hint:* Use (2).]
(c) If $f(x) = y$, show that $g(y) = x$. [*Hint:* Use (1).]

Parts (b) and (c) prove that

$$g(y) = x \qquad \text{exactly when} \qquad f(x) = y.$$

Hence, g is the inverse function of f (see page 219).

51. Prove that every function f that has an inverse function g is one-to-one. [*Hint:* The proof of the Round-Trip Theorem on page 223 shows that f and g have the round-trip properties; use Exercise 50(a).]

52. True or false: If a function has an inverse, then its inverse has an inverse. Justify your answer.

53. True or false: If a one-to-one function is increasing, then its inverse is increasing. Justify your answer.

2.9 Polynomial Functions

Section Objectives

■ Recognize the algebraic forms of a polynomial.
■ Use the Division Algorithm.
■ Apply the Remainder Theorem.
■ Apply the Factor Theorem.
■ Find the rule of a polynomial with given degree and roots.
■ Determine the maximum possible number of roots a polynomial may have.

Informally, a **polynomial** is an algebraic expression such as

$$x^3 - 6x^2 + \tfrac{1}{2} \quad \text{or} \quad x^{15} + x^{10} + 7 \quad \text{or} \quad x - 6.7 \quad \text{or} \quad 12.$$

Formally, a **polynomial in x** is an algebraic expression that can be written in the form

$$a_n x^n + a_{n-1} x^{n-1} + \cdots + a_3 x^3 + a_2 x^2 + a_1 x + a_0,$$

where n is a nonnegative integer, x is a variable,* and each of $a_0, a_1, \ldots, a_n$ is a constant, called a **coefficient.** The coefficient a_0 is called the **constant term.** A polynomial that consists only of a constant term, such as 12, is called a **constant polynomial.** The **zero polynomial** is the constant polynomial 0.

The *exponent* of the highest power of x that appears with *nonzero* coefficient is the **degree** of the polynomial, and the nonzero coefficient of this highest power of x is the **leading coefficient.** For example,

Polynomial	Degree	Leading Coefficient	Constant Term
$6x^7 + 4x^3 + 5x^2 - 7x + 10$	7	6	10
x^3	3	1	0
12 (think of this as $12x^0$)	0	12	12
$0x^9 + 2x^6 + 3x^7 + x^8 - 2x - 4$	8	1	-4

The degree of the zero polynomial is *not defined* since no exponent of x occurs with nonzero coefficient.

EXAMPLE 1

Which of the following are polynomials?

(a) $x^2 - x^3 + 2x - x^4$
(b) $3x^4 - 2x^2 - \dfrac{1}{x} + 3$
(c) $(x^2 + 5)(3x^2 - 2)$
(d) $x^2 + 3x + 5^x$
(e) $x^2 + 3x + \pi^3$
(f) $x + x^{3/2} + 1$

---

*Any letter may be used as the variable in a polynomial.

SOLUTION

(a) $x^2 - x^3 + 2x - x^4$ is a polynomial. The order in which we write the terms doesn't change whether or not an expression is a polynomial.

(b) $3x^4 - 2x^2 - \dfrac{1}{x} + 3$ is not a polynomial. The term $-\dfrac{1}{x}$ cannot be written in the form ax^n for any positive integer n.

(c) $(x^2 + 5)(3x^2 - 2)$ is a polynomial. Its expanded form is $3x^4 + 13x^2 - 10$.

(d) $x^2 + 3x + 5^x$ is not a polynomial. The exponents in a polynomial cannot be variables.

(e) $x^2 + 3x + \pi^3$ is a polynomial. π^3 is just a constant.

(f) $x + x^{3/2} + 1$ is not a polynomial. The exponents of x must be whole numbers, and 3/2 is not a whole number.   ∎

A **polynomial function** is a function whose rule is given by a polynomial, such as $f(x) = x^5 + 3x^2 - 2$. First-degree polynomial functions, such as $g(x) = 3x - 4$, are called **linear functions,** and, as we saw in Section 4.1, second-degree polynomial functions are called **quadratic functions.**

POLYNOMIAL ARITHMETIC

You should be familiar with addition, subtraction, and multiplication of polynomials, which are presented in the Algebra Review Appendix. Long division of polynomials is quite similar to long division of numbers, as we now see.

EXAMPLE 2

Divide $8x^3 + 2x^2 + 1$ by $2x^2 - x$.

SOLUTION   We set up the division in the same way that is used for numbers.

$$\text{Divisor} \rightarrow \quad 2x^2 - x\,\overline{\smash{\big)}\,8x^3 + 2x^2 + 1} \quad \leftarrow \text{Dividend}$$

Begin by dividing the first term of the divisor $(2x^2)$ into the first term of the dividend $(8x^3)$ and putting the result $\left(\text{namely, } \dfrac{8x^3}{2x^2} = 4x\right)$ on the top line, as shown below. Then multiply $4x$ times the entire divisor, put the result on the third line, and subtract

$$
\begin{array}{r}
4x \qquad\qquad\quad \leftarrow \text{Partial Quotient} \\
2x^2 - x\,\overline{\smash{\big)}\,8x^3 + 2x^2 + 1} \\
\underline{8x^3 - 4x^2} \qquad\quad \leftarrow 4x(2x^2 - x) \\
6x^2 + 1 \qquad\quad \leftarrow \text{Subtraction*}
\end{array}
$$

Now divide the first term of the divisor $(2x^2)$ into $6x^2$ and put the result $\left(\dfrac{6x^2}{2x^2} = 3\right)$ on the top line, as shown below. Then multiply 3 times the entire divisor, put the result on the fifth line, and subtract

---

*If this subtraction is confusing, write it out horizontally and watch the signs:

$$(8x^3 + 2x^2 + 1) - (8x^3 - 4x^2) = 8x^3 + 2x^2 + 1 - 8x^3 + 4x^2 = 6x^2 + 1.$$

$$
\begin{array}{r}
4x + 3 \quad\quad\quad \leftarrow \text{Quotient} \\
2x^2 - x \overline{\smash{\big)}\, 8x^3 + 2x^2 \quad\quad + 1} \\
\underline{8x^3 - 4x^2} \quad\quad\quad\quad \leftarrow 4x(2x^2 - x) \\
6x^2 \quad + 1 \quad \leftarrow \text{Subtraction} \\
\underline{6x^2 - 3x} \quad\quad\quad \leftarrow 3(2x^2 - x) \\
\text{Remainder} \rightarrow 3x + 1 \quad \leftarrow \text{Subtraction}
\end{array}
$$

The division process stops when the remainder is 0 or has smaller degree than the divisor, which is the case here. ∎

We review the process of checking a long division problem by computing 4509/31:

$$
\begin{array}{r}
145 \\
31 \overline{\smash{\big)}\, 4509} \\
\underline{31} \\
140 \\
\underline{124} \\
169 \\
\underline{155} \\
14
\end{array}
\qquad
\begin{array}{ll}
\text{Check:} & 145 \quad \leftarrow \text{Quotient} \\
& \underline{\times\, 31} \quad \leftarrow \text{Divisor} \\
& 4495 \\
& \underline{+\, 14} \quad \leftarrow \text{Remainder} \\
& 4509 \quad \leftarrow \text{Dividend}
\end{array}
$$

We can summarize this process in one line:

$$\text{Divisor} \cdot \text{Quotient} + \text{Remainder} = \text{Dividend}.$$

The same thing works for division of polynomials, as you can see by examining the division problem from Example 2.

$$
\begin{array}{ccc}
\text{Divisor} \cdot \text{Quotient} & + & \text{Remainder} \\
\end{array}
$$
$$(2x^2 - x) \cdot (4x + 3) + (3x + 1) = (8x^3 + 2x^2 - 3x) + (3x + 1)$$
$$= 8x^3 + 2x^2 + 1$$
$$\text{Dividend}$$

This fact is so important that it is given a special name and a formal statement.

The Division Algorithm

If a polynomial $f(x)$ is divided by a nonzero polynomial $h(x)$, then there is a quotient polynomial $q(x)$ and a remainder polynomial $r(x)$ such that

$$\text{Dividend} = \text{Divisor} \cdot \text{Quotient} + \text{Remainder}$$

$$f(x) = h(x)\, q(x) + r(x),$$

where either $r(x) = 0$ or $r(x)$ has degree less than the degree of the divisor $h(x)$.

EXAMPLE 3

Show that $2x^2 + 1$ is a factor of $6x^3 - 4x^2 + 3x - 2$.

SOLUTION   We divide $6x^3 - 4x^2 + 3x - 2$ by $2x^2 + 1$ and find that the remainder is 0.

$$
\begin{array}{r}
3x - 2 \\
2x^2 + 1 \overline{\smash{\big)}\ 6x^3 - 4x^2 + 3x - 2} \\
\underline{6x^3 \qquad\quad + 3x} \\
-4x^2 \qquad\ - 2 \\
\underline{-4x^2 \qquad\ - 2} \\
0.
\end{array}
$$

Since the remainder is 0, the Division Algorithm tells us that

$$\text{Dividend} = \text{Divisor} \cdot \text{Quotient} + \text{Remainder}$$

$$6x^3 - 4x^2 + 3x - 2 = (2x^2 + 1)(3x - 2) + 0$$

$$= (2x^2 + 1)(3x - 2).$$

Therefore, $2x^2 + 1$ is a factor of $6x^3 - 4x^2 + 3x - 2$, and the other factor is the quotient $3x - 2$. ∎

Example 3 illustrates this fact.

Remainders and Factors

> The remainder in polynomial division is 0 exactly when the divisor is a factor of the dividend. In this case, the quotient is the other factor.

REMAINDERS AND ROOTS

When a polynomial $f(x)$ is divided by a first-degree polynomial, such as $x - 3$ or $x + 5$, the remainder is a constant (because constants are the only polynomials of degree less than 1). This remainder has an interesting connection with the values of the polynomial function $f(x)$.

EXAMPLE 4

Let $f(x) = x^3 - 2x^2 - 4x + 5$.

(a) Find the quotient and remainder when $f(x)$ is divided by $x - 3$.

(b) Find $f(3)$.

SOLUTION

(a) Using long division, we have

$$
\begin{array}{r}
x^2 + x - 1 \\
x - 3 \overline{\smash{\big)}\ x^3 - 2x^2 - 4x + 5} \\
\underline{x^3 - 3x^2} \\
x^2 - 4x + 5 \\
\underline{x^2 - 3x} \\
-x + 5 \\
\underline{-x + 3} \\
2.
\end{array}
$$

Therefore, the quotient is $x^2 + x - 1$, and the remainder is 2.

(b) Using the Division Algorithm, we can write the dividend
$$f(x) = x^3 - 2x^2 - 4x + 5 \text{ as}$$

$$\text{Dividend} = \text{Divisor} \cdot \text{Quotient} + \text{Remainder}$$

$$f(x) = (x - 3)(x^2 + x - 1) + 2.$$

Hence,

$$f(3) = (3 - 3)(3^2 + 3 - 1) + 2 = 0 + 2 = 2.$$

Note that the number $f(3)$ is the same as the remainder when $f(x)$ is divided by $x - 3$. ■

The argument used in Example 4 to show that $f(3)$ is the remainder when $f(x)$ is divided by $x - 3$ also works in the general case and proves this fact.

Remainder Theorem

> If a polynomial $f(x)$ is divided by $x - c$, then the remainder is the number $f(c)$.

EXAMPLE 5

To find the remainder when $f(x) = x^{79} + 3x^{24} + 5$ is divided by $x - 1$, we apply the Remainder Theorem with $c = 1$. The remainder is

$$f(1) = 1^{79} + 3 \cdot 1^{24} + 5 = 1 + 3 + 5 = 9.$$ ■

EXAMPLE 6

To find the remainder when $f(x) = 3x^4 - 8x^2 + 11x + 1$ is divided by $x + 2$, we must apply the Remainder Theorem *carefully*. The divisor in the theorem is $x - c$, not $x + c$. So we rewrite $x + 2$ as $x - (-2)$ and apply the theorem with $c = -2$. The remainder is

$$f(-2) = 3(-2)^4 - 8(-2)^2 + 11(-2) + 1 = 48 - 32 - 22 + 1 = -5.$$ ■

If $f(x)$ is a polynomial, then a solution of the equation $f(x) = 0$ is called a **root** or **zero** of $f(x)$. Thus, a number c is a root of $f(x)$ if $f(c) = 0$. A root that is a real number is called a **real root.** For example, 4 is a real root of the polynomial $f(x) = 3x - 12$ because $f(4) = 3 \cdot 4 - 12 = 0$. There is an interesting connection between the roots of a polynomial and its factors.

EXAMPLE 7

Let $f(x) = x^3 - 4x^2 + 2x + 3$.

(a) Show that 3 is a root of $f(x)$.

(b) Show that $x - 3$ is a factor of $f(x)$.

SOLUTION

(a) Evaluating $f(x)$ at 3 shows that

$$f(3) = 3^3 - 4(3^2) + 2(3) + 3 = 0.$$

Therefore, 3 is a root of $f(x)$.

(b) If $f(x)$ is divided by $x - 3$, then by the Division Algorithm, there is a quotient polynomial $q(x)$ such that

$$f(x) = (x - 3)q(x) + \text{remainder}.$$

The remainder Theorem shows that the remainder when $f(x)$ is divided by $x - 3$ is the number $f(3)$, which is 0, as we saw in part (a). Therefore,

$$f(x) = (x - 3)q(x) + 0 = (x - 3)q(x).$$

Thus, $x - 3$ is a factor of $f(x)$. [To determine the other factor, the quotient $q(x)$, you have to perform the division.] ■

Example 7 illustrates this fact, which can be proved by the same argument used in the example.

Factor Theorem

> The number c is a root of the polynomial $f(x)$ exactly when $x - c$ is a factor of $f(x)$.

EXAMPLE 8

The graph of $f(x) = 15x^3 - x^2 - 114x + 72$ in the standard viewing window (Figure 2–55 is obviously not complete but suggests that -3 is an x-intercept, and hence a root of $f(x)$. It is easy to verify that this is indeed the case.

$$f(-3) = 15(-3)^3 - (-3)^2 - 114(-3) + 72 = -405 - 9 + 342 + 72 = 0.$$

Since -3 is a root, $x - (-3) = x + 3$ is a factor of $f(x)$. Use synthetic or long division to verify that the other factor is $15x^2 - 46x + 24$. By factoring this quadratic, we obtain a complete factorization of $f(x)$.

$$f(x) = (x + 3)(15x^2 - 46x + 24) = (x + 3)(3x - 2)(5x - 12). \quad ■$$

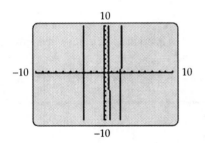

Figure 2–55

EXAMPLE 9

Find three polynomials of different degrees that have 1, 2, 3, and -5 as roots.

SOLUTION   A polynomial that has 1, 2, 3, and -5 as roots must have $x - 1$, $x - 2$, $x - 3$, and $x - (-5) = x + 5$ as factors. Many polynomials satisfy these conditions, such as

$$g(x) = (x - 1)(x - 2)(x - 3)(x + 5) = x^4 - x^3 - 19x^2 + 49x - 30$$

$$h(x) = 8(x - 1)(x - 2)(x - 3)^2(x + 5)$$

$$k(x) = 2(x + 4)^2(x - 1)(x - 2)(x - 3)(x + 5)(x^2 + x + 1).$$

Note that g has degree 4. When h is multiplied out, its leading term is $8x^5$, so h has degree 5. Similarly, k has degree 8 since its leading term is $2x^8$. ■

If a polynomial $f(x)$ has four roots, say a, b, c, d, then by the same argument used in Example 8, it must have

$$(x - a)(x - b)(x - c)(x - d)$$

as a factor. Since $(x - a)(x - b)(x - c)(x - d)$ has degree 4 (multiply it out—its leading term is x^4), $f(x)$ must have degree at least 4. In particular, this means that no polynomial of degree 3 can have four or more roots. A similar argument works in the general case.

Number of Roots

A polynomial of degree n has at most n distinct roots.

EXERCISES 2.9

In Exercises 1–10, determine whether the given algebraic expression is a polynomial. If it is, list its leading coefficient, constant term, and degree.

1. $1 + x^3$

2. -7

3. $(x - 1)(x^2 + 1)$

4. $7^x + 2x + 1$

5. $(x + \sqrt{3})(x - \sqrt{3})$

6. $x^3 + 3x^2 + \pi^3$

7. $x^3 + 3x^2 + \pi^x$

8. $4x^2 + 3\sqrt{x} + 5$

9. $\dfrac{7}{x^2} + \dfrac{5}{x} - 15$

10. $(x - 1)^k$ (where k is a fixed positive integer)

In Exercises 11–18, state the quotient and remainder when the first polynomial is divided by the second. Check your division by calculating (Divisor)(Quotient) + Remainder.

11. $3x^4 + 8x^2 - 6x + 1$; $x + 1$

12. $x^5 - x^3 + x - 5$; $x - 2$

13. $x^5 + 2x^4 - 6x^3 + x^2 - 5x + 1$; $x^3 + 1$

14. $2x^5 + 5x^4 + x^3 - 7x^2 - 13x + 12$; $x^2 + 2x + 3$

15. $2x^5 + 5x^4 + x^3 - 7x^2 - 13x + 12$; $2x^3 + x^2 - 7x + 4$

16. $3x^4 - 3x^3 - 11x^2 + 6x - 1$; $x^3 + x^2 - 2$

17. $5x^4 + 5x^2 + 5$; $x^2 - x + 1$

18. $x^5 - 1$; $x - 1$

In Exercises 19–22, determine whether the first polynomial is a factor of the second.

19. $x^2 + 5x - 1$; $x^3 + 2x^2 - 5x - 6$

20. $x^2 + 9$; $4x^5 + 13x^4 + 36x^3 + 108x^2 - 81$

21. $x^2 + 3x - 1$; $x^4 + 3x^3 - 2x^2 - 3x + 1$

22. $x^2 - 4x + 7$; $x^3 - 3x^2 - 3x + 9$

In Exercises 23–27, determine which of the given numbers are roots of the given polynomial.

23. $2, 3, -5, 1$; $g(x) = x^4 + 6x^3 - x^2 - 30x$

24. $1, 1/2, 2, -1/2, 1/3$; $f(x) = 6x^2 + x - 1$

25. $2\sqrt{2}, \sqrt{2}, -\sqrt{2}, 1, -1$; $h(x) = x^3 + x^2 - 8x - 8$

26. $\sqrt{3}, -\sqrt{3}, 1, -1$; $k(x) = 8x^3 - 12x^2 - 6x + 9$

27. $3, -3, 0$; $l(x) = x(x + 3)^{27}$

In Exercises 28–38, find the remainder when $f(x)$ is divided by $g(x)$, without using division.

28. $f(x) = x^2 - 1$; $g(x) = x - 1$

29. $f(x) = x^{10} + x^8$; $g(x) = x - 1$

30. $f(x) = x^6 - 10$; $g(x) = x + 2$

31. $f(x) = 3x^4 - 6x^3 + 2x - 1$; $g(x) = x + 3/2$

32. $f(x) = x^5 - 3x^2 + 2x - 1$; $g(x) = x - 3$

33. $f(x) = x^3 - 2x^2 + 8x - 4$; $g(x) = x + 2$

34. $f(x) = 10x^{70} - 8x^{60} + 6x^{40} + 4x^{32} - 2x^{15} + 5$; $g(x) = x - 1$

35. $f(x) = 2x^5 - \sqrt{3}x^4 + x^3 - \sqrt{3}x^2 + \sqrt{3}x - 100$; $g(x) = x - 10$

36. $f(x) = x^3 + 8x^2 - 29x + 44$; $g(x) = x + 11$

37. $f(x) = 2\pi x^5 - 3\pi x^4 + 2\pi x^3 - 8\pi x - 8\pi$; $g(x) = x - 20$

38. $f(x) = x^5 - 10x^4 + 20x^3 - 5x - 95$; $g(x) = x + 10$

In Exercises 39–46, use the Factor Theorem to determine whether or not $h(x)$ is a factor of $f(x)$.

39. $h(x) = x - 1$; $f(x) = x^5 + 1$

40. $h(x) = x - 1/2$; $f(x) = 2x^4 + x^3 + x - 3/4$

41. $h(x) = x + 3$; $f(x) = x^3 - 3x^2 - 4x - 12$

42. $h(x) = x + 1$; $f(x) = x^3 - 4x^2 + 3x + 8$

43. $h(x) = x - 1$; $f(x) = 14x^{99} - 65x^{56} + 51$

44. $h(x) = x - 2$; $f(x) = x^3 + x^2 - 4x + 4$

45. $h(x) = x - \sqrt{2}$; $f(x) = 3x^3 - 4x^2 - 6x + 8$

46. $h(x) = x - 2$; $f(x) = x^3 - \sqrt{2}x^2 - (6 + \sqrt{2})x + 6\sqrt{2}$

In Exercises 47–50, use the Factor Theorem and a calculator to factor the polynomial, as in Example 7.

47. $f(x) = 6x^3 - 7x^2 - 89x + 140$

48. $g(x) = x^3 - 5x^2 - 5x - 6$

49. $h(x) = 4x^4 + 4x^3 - 35x^2 - 36x - 9$

50. $f(x) = x^5 - 5x^4 - 5x^3 + 25x^2 + 6x - 30$

In Exercises 51–54, each graph is of a polynomial function f(x) of degree 5 whose leading coefficient is 1. The graph is not drawn to scale. Use the Factor Theorem to find the polynomial. [Hint: What are the roots of f(x)? What does the Factor Theorem tell you?]

51.

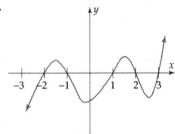

52.

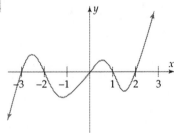

53.

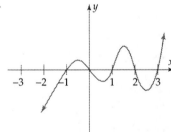

54.

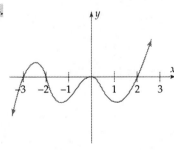

In Exercises 55–60, find a polynomial with the given degree n, the given roots, and no other roots.

55. $n = 3$;   roots $1, 7, -4$

56. $n = 3$;   roots $1, -1$

57. $n = 2$;   roots $1, -1$

58. $n = 1$;   root 5

59. $n = 6$;   roots $1, 2, \pi$

60. $n = 5$;   root 3

61. Find a polynomial function f of degree 3 such that

$$f(10) = 25$$

and the roots of $f(x)$ are 0, 5, and 8.

62. Find a polynomial function g of degree 4 such that the roots of g are $0, -1, 2, -3$, and $g(3) = 288$.

In Exercises 63–66, find a number k satisfying the given condition.

63. $x - 2$ is a factor of $x^3 + 3x^2 + kx - 2$.

64. $x - 3$ is a factor of $x^4 - 5x^3 - kx^2 + 18x + 18$.

65. $x - 1$ is a factor of $k^2x^4 - 2kx^2 + 1$.

66. $x + 2$ is a factor of $x^3 - kx^2 + 3x + 7k$.

67. Use the Factor Theorem to show that for every real number c, $x - c$ is *not* a factor of $x^4 + x^2 + 1$.

68. Let c be a real number and n a positive integer.

(a) Show that $x - c$ is a factor of $x^n - c^n$.

(b) If n is even, show that $x + c$ is a factor of $x^n - c^n$. [*Remember:* $x + c = x - (-c)$.]

69. (a) If c is a real number and n an odd positive integer, give an example to show that $x + c$ may not be a factor of $x^n - c^n$.

(b) If c and n are as in part (a), show that $x + c$ is a factor of $x^n + c^n$.

THINKERS

70. For what value of k is the difference quotient of

$$g(x) = kx^2 + 2x + 1$$

equal to $7x + 2 + 3.5h$?

71. For what value of k is the difference quotient of

$$f(x) = x^2 + kx$$

equal to $2x + 5 + h$?

72. Use the fact that $x - 2$ is a factor of $x^3 - 6x^2 + 9x - 2$ to find all the roots of

$$f(x) = x^3 - 6x^2 + 9x - 2.$$

73. Use the fact that $(x + 3)^2$ is a factor of $x^4 + 2x^3 - 91x^2 - 492x - 684$ to find all the roots of

$$f(x) = x^4 + 2x^3 - 91x^2 - 492x - 684.$$

2.10   Graphs of Polynomial Functions

Section Objectives   ■ Understand the properties of the graph of a polynomial.
■ Find a complete graph of a polynomial.
■ Use polynomial graphs in applications.

The graphs of first- and second-degree polynomial functions are straight lines and parabolas respectively (Sections 1.4 and 4.1). What happens when the degree is higher?

The simplest polynomial functions are those of the form $f(x) = ax^n$ (where a is a constant). Their graphs are of four types, as shown in the following chart.

GRAPH OF $f(x) = ax^n$

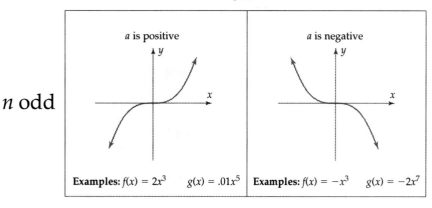

n odd

a is positive

a is negative

Examples: $f(x) = 2x^3$ $g(x) = .01x^5$ **Examples:** $f(x) = -x^3$ $g(x) = -2x^7$

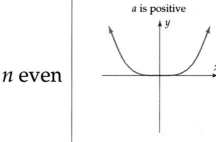

n even

a is positive

a is negative

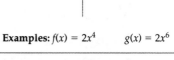

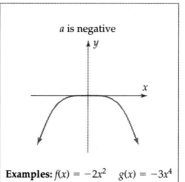

Examples: $f(x) = 2x^4$ $g(x) = 2x^6$ **Examples:** $f(x) = -2x^2$ $g(x) = -3x^4$

GRAPHING EXPLORATION

Verify the accuracy of the preceding summary by graphing each of the examples in the window with $-5 \le x \le 5$ and $-30 \le y \le 30$. What effect does increasing the value of n have on these graphs?

The graphs of more complicated polynomial functions can vary considerably in shape. Understanding the properties discussed below should assist you to interpret screen images correctly and to determine when a polynomial graph is complete.

CONTINUITY

Every polynomial graph is **continuous,** meaning that it is an unbroken curve, with no jumps, gaps, or holes. Furthermore, polynomial graphs have no sharp corners. Thus, neither of the graphs in Figure 2–56 is the graph of a polynomial function.

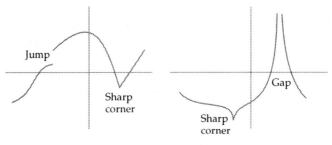

Figure 2–56

 SHAPE OF THE GRAPH WHEN $|x|$ IS LARGE

The shape of a polynomial graph at the far left and far right of the coordinate plane is easily determined by using our knowledge of graphs of functions of the form $f(x) = ax^n$.

EXAMPLE 1

Consider the function $f(x) = 2x^3 + x^2 - 6x$ and the function determined by its leading term $g(x) = 2x^3$.

GRAPHING EXPLORATION

Using the standard viewing window, graph f and g on the same screen.
Do the two graphs look different? Now graph f and g in the viewing window with $-20 \le x \le 20$ and $-10{,}000 \le y \le 10{,}000$. Do the graphs look almost the same?
Finally, graph f and g in the viewing window with

$$-100 \le x \le 100 \text{ and } -1{,}000{,}000 \le y \le 1{,}000{,}000.$$

Do the graphs look virtually identical?

The reason the answer to the last question is "yes" can be understood from this table.

x	-100	-50	70	100
$-6x$	600	300	-420	-600
x^2	10,000	2,500	4,900	10,000
$g(x) = 2x^3$	$-2{,}000{,}000$	$-250{,}000$	686,000	2,000,000
$f(x) = 2x^3 + x^2 - 6x$	$-1{,}989{,}400$	$-247{,}200$	690,480	2,009,400

It shows that when $|x|$ is large, the terms x^2 and $-6x$ are insignificant compared with $2x^3$ and barely affect the value of $f(x)$. Hence, the values of $f(x)$ and $g(x)$ are relatively close.   ■

Example 1 is typical of what happens in every case: When $|x|$ is very large, the highest power of x totally overwhelms all lower powers and plays the greatest role in determining the value of the function.

Behavior When
$|x|$ Is Large

> When $|x|$ is very large, the graph of a polynomial function closely resembles the graph of its highest degree term.
>
> In particular, when the polynomial function has odd degree, one end of its graph shoots upward and the other end downward.
>
> When the polynomial function has even degree, both ends of its graph shoot upward or both ends shoot downward.

EXAMPLE 2

Graph $f(x) = \dfrac{x^5}{120} - \dfrac{x^3}{6} + x$ and $g(x) = \dfrac{x^5}{120}$ on the same axes, first using the window $-4 \le x \le 4$ and then using the window $-12 \le x \le 12$ (Figure 2–57).

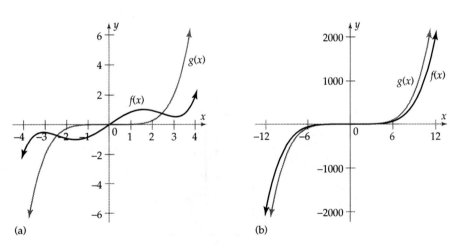

(a)   (b)

Figure 2–57

Notice how the first window shows that these are very different functions, but the second window shows that as $|x|$ gets larger, the graph of $\dfrac{x^5}{120} - \dfrac{x^3}{6} + x$ closely resembles the graph of $\dfrac{x^5}{120}$. If you were to graph these functions on the interval $-1000 \le x \le 1000$, you would be hard pressed to tell the difference between these curves.   ■

x-INTERCEPTS

As we saw in Section 4.3, the *x*-intercepts of the graph of a polynomial function are the real roots of the polynomial. Since a polynomial of degree n has at most n distinct roots (page 257), we have the following fact.

x-Intercepts

> The graph of a polynomial function of degree n meets the *x*-axis at most n times.

There is another connection between roots and graphs. For example, it is easy to see that the roots of

$$f(x) = (x + 3)^2(x + 1)(x - 1)^3$$

are -3, -1, and 1. We say that

-3 is a root of multiplicity 2;

-1 is a root of multiplicity 1;

1 is a root of multiplicity 3.

Observe that the graph of $f(x)$ in Figure 2–58 does not cross the *x*-axis at -3 (a root whose multiplicity is an *even* number) but does cross the *x*-axis at -1 and 1 (roots of *odd* multiplicity).

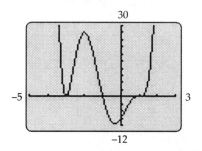

Figure 2–58

More generally, a number c is a **root of multiplicity** k of a polynomial $f(x)$ if $(x - c)^k$ is a factor of $f(x)$ and no higher power of $(x - c)$ is a factor, and we have this fact.

Multiplicity and Graphs

> Let c be a root of multiplicity k of a polynomial function f.
>
> If k is odd, the graph of f crosses the *x*-axis at c.
>
> If k is even, the graph of f touches, but does not cross, the *x*-axis at c.

EXAMPLE 3

It is a fact that $-x^4 + 2x^3 + 3x^2 - 4x - 4 = -(x + 1)^2 (x - 2)^2$. Use this fact to sketch the graph of

$$f(x) = -x^4 + 2x^3 + 3x^2 - 4x - 4$$

SOLUTION f has double roots at $x = -1$ and $x = 2$. The leading coefficient is negative and even, which tells us that both ends of the graph shoot downward. We find the *y*-intercept by observing that $f(0) = -4$. We obtain the graph shown in Figure 2–59 on the next page. ∎

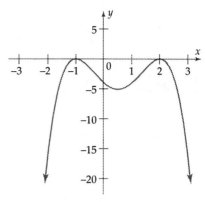

Figure 2–59

LOCAL EXTREMA

The term **local extremum** (plural, extrema) refers to either a local maximum or a local minimum, that is, a point where the graph is a peak or a valley.

GRAPHING EXPLORATION

Graph $f(x) = x^3 + 2x^2 - 4x - 3$ in the standard viewing window. What is the total number of peaks and valleys on the graph? What is the degree of $f(x)$?

Now graph $g(x) = x^4 - 3x^3 - 2x^2 + 4x + 5$ in the standard viewing window. What is the total number of peaks and valleys on the graph? What is the degree of $g(x)$?

The two polynomials you have just graphed are illustrations of the following fact, which is proved in calculus.

Local Extrema

A polynomial function of degree n has at most $n - 1$ local extrema. In other words, the total number of peaks and valleys on the graph is at most $n - 1$.

BENDING

A polynomial graph may bend upward or downward as indicated here by the vertical arrows (Figure 2–60):

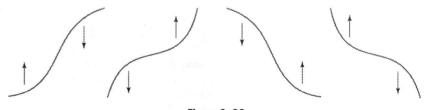

Figure 2–60

A point at which the graph changes from bending downward to bending upward (or vice versa) is called a **point of inflection.** The direction in which a graph bends may not always be clear on a calculator screen, and calculus is usually required to determine the exact location of points of inflection. The number of inflection points and hence the amount of bending in the graph are governed by these facts, which are proved in calculus.

Points of Inflection

> The graph of a polynomial function of degree n (with $n \geq 2$) has at most $n - 2$ points of inflection.
>
> The graph of a polynomial function of odd degree n (with $n \geq 3$) has at least one point of inflection.

Thus, the graph of a quadratic function (degree 2) has no points of inflection ($n - 2 = 2 - 2 = 0$), and the graph of a cubic has exactly one (since it has at least one and at most $3 - 2 = 1$). Figure 2–61 shows several cubic graphs, with their inflection point marked.

TECHNOLOGY TIP

Points of inflection may be found by using INFLC in the TI-86/89 GRAPH MATH menu.

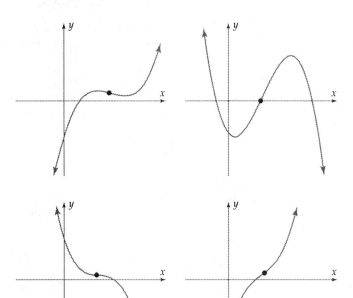

Figure 2–61

COMPLETE GRAPHS OF POLYNOMIAL FUNCTIONS

By using the facts discussed earlier, you can often determine whether or not the graph of a polynomial function is complete (that is, shows all the important features).

EXAMPLE 4

Find a complete graph of

$$f(x) = x^4 + 10x^3 + 21x^2 - 40x - 80.$$

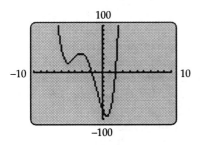

Figure 2–62

SOLUTION   Since $f(0) = -80$, the standard viewing window probably won't show a complete graph, so we try the window with

$$-10 \le x \le 10 \quad \text{and} \quad -100 \le y \le 100$$

and obtain Figure 2–62. The three peaks and valleys shown here are the only ones because a fourth-degree polynomial graph has at most three local extrema. There cannot be more x-intercepts than the two shown here because if the graph turned toward the x-axis farther out, there would be an additional peak, which is impossible. Finally, the outer ends of the graph resemble the graph of x^4, the highest-degree term (see the chart on page 270). Hence, Figure 2–62 includes all the important features of the graph and is therefore complete.   ∎

EXAMPLE 5

Find a complete graph of $f(x) = x^3 - 1.8x^2 + x + 2$.

SOLUTION   We first try the standard window (Figure 2–63). The graph is similar to the graph of the leading term $y = x^3$ but does not appear to have any local extrema. However, if you use the trace feature on the flat portion of the graph to the right of the x-axis, you see that the y-coordinates increase, then decrease, then increase (try it!). Zooming in on the portion of the graph between 0 and 1 (Figure 2–63), we see that the graph actually has a tiny peak and valley (the maximum possible number of local extrema for a cubic). So Figures 2–63 and 2–64 together provide a complete graph of f.   ∎

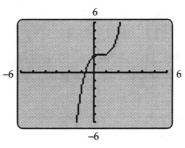

Figure 2–63

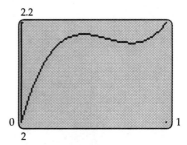

Figure 2–64

The following fact is proved in Exercise 59.

No nonconstant polynomial graph contains any horizontal line segments.

However, a calculator may erroneously show horizontal segments, as in Figure 2–63. So always investigate such segments, by using trace or zoom-in, to determine any hidden behavior, such as that in Example 5.

EXAMPLE 6

The graph of $f(x) = .01x^5 + x^4 - x^3 - 6x^2 + 5x + 4$ in the standard window is shown in Figure 2–65. Explain why this is *not* a complete graph and find a complete graph of f.

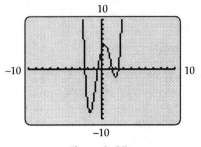

Figure 2–65

SOLUTION   When $|x|$ is large, the graph of f must resemble the graph of $y = .01x^5$, whose left end goes downward (see the chart on page 270). Since Figure 2–65 does not show this, it is not a complete graph. To have the same shape as the graph of $y = .01x^5$, the graph of f must turn downward and cross the x-axis somewhere to the left of the origin. Figure 2–65 shows three local extrema. Even without graphing, we can see that there must be one more peak (where the graph turns downward on the left), making a total of four local extrema (the most a fifth-degree polynomial can have), and another x-intercept, for a total of five. When these additional features are shown, we will have a complete graph.

GRAPHING EXPLORATION

Find a viewing window that includes the local maximum and x-intercept not shown in Figure 2–65. When you do, the scale will be such that the local extrema and x-intercepts shown in Figure 2–65 will no longer be visible.

Consequently, a complete graph of $f(x)$ requires several viewing windows in order to see all the important features.   ∎

The graphs obtained in Examples 4–6 were known to be complete because in each case, they included the maximum possible number of local extrema. In many cases, however, a graph may not have the largest possible number of peaks and valleys. In such cases, use any available information and try several viewing windows to obtain the most likely complete graph.

APPLICATIONS

The solution of many applied problems reduces to finding a local extremum of a polynomial function.

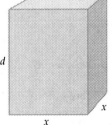

Figure 2–66

EXAMPLE 7

A rectangular box with a square base (Figure 2–66) is to be mailed. The sum of the height of the box and the perimeter of the base is to be 84 inches, the maximum allowable under postal regulations. What are the dimensions of the box with largest possible volume that meets these conditions?

SOLUTION   If the length of one side of the base is x, then the perimeter of the base (the sum of the length of its four sides) is $4x$. If the height of the box is d, then $4x + d = 84$, so $d = 84 - 4x$, and hence, the volume is

$$V = x \cdot x \cdot d = x \cdot x \cdot (84 - 4x) = 84x^2 - 4x^3.$$

The graph of the polynomial function $V(x) = 84x^2 - 4x^3$ in Figure 2–67 is complete (why?). However, the only relevant part of the graph in this situation is the portion with x and $V(x)$ positive (because x is a length and $V(x)$ is a volume). The graph of $V(x)$ has a local maximum between 10 and 20, and this local maximum value is the largest possible volume for the box.

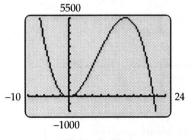

Figure 2–67

EXAMPLE 8

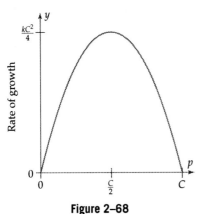

Figure 2–68

Assume we let some box-elder bugs loose in a neighborhood, and want to model their population growth. The "carrying capacity" of an environment is the number of box-elder bugs that it can support. According to one model, the rate at which a population grows is proportional to its size, and to the difference between that size and the environment's carrying capacity. We can write this model as an equation:

$$R = kP(C - P)$$

where R is the rate of growth, P is the population, C is the carrying capacity, and k is a constant of proportionality. If we multiply the equation out we get a polynomial, where P is our variable:

$$R = (-k)P^2 + (kC)P$$

The graph of this polynomial is given in Figure 2–68. If we wish to graph this equation on a calculator, we would have to choose sample values for C and k. ■

EXERCISES 2.10

In Exercises 1–6, decide whether the given graph could possibly be the graph of a polynomial function.

1.

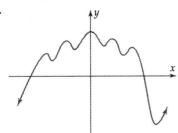

2.

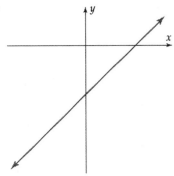

3.

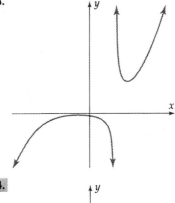

4.

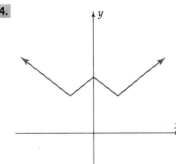

5.

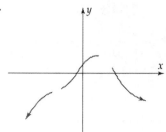

6.

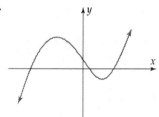

In Exercises 7–12, determine whether the given graph could possibly be the graph of a polynomial function of degree 3, of degree 4, or of degree 5.

7.

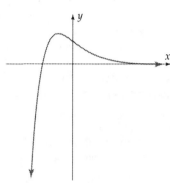

8.

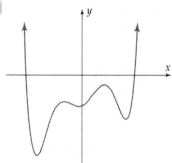

9.

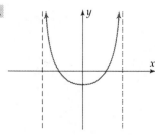

10.

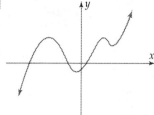

11.

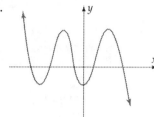

12.

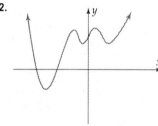

In Exercises 13 and 14, find a viewing window in which the graph of the given polynomial function f appears to have the same general shape as the graph of its leading term.

13. $f(x) = x^4 - 6x^3 + 9x^2 - 3$

14. $f(x) = x^3 - 5x^2 + 4x - 2$

In Exercises 15–18, a complete graph of a polynomial function is shown. List each root of the polynomial and state whether its multiplicity is even or odd.

15.

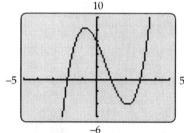

16.

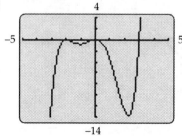

17.

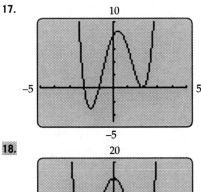

18.

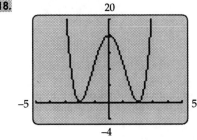

In Exercises 19–24, use your knowledge of polynomial graphs, not a calculator, to match the given function with its graph, which is one of (a)–(f).

(a)

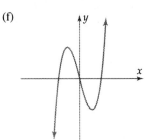

(b)

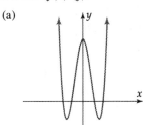

(c)

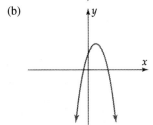

(d)

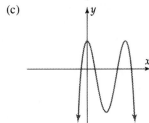

(e)

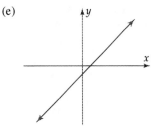

(f)

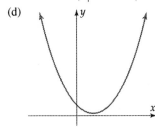

19. $f(x) = 2x - 3$

20. $g(x) = x^2 - 4x + 7$

21. $g(x) = x^3 - 4x$

22. $f(x) = x^4 - 5x^2 + 4$

23. $f(x) = -x^4 + 6x^3 - 9x^2 + 2$

24. $g(x) = -2x^2 + 3x + 1$

In Exercises 25–28, graph the function in the standard viewing window and explain why that graph cannot possibly be complete.

25. $f(x) = .01x^3 - .2x^2 - .4x + 7$

26. $g(x) = .01x^4 + .1x^3 - .8x^2 - .7x + 9$

27. $h(x) = .005x^4 - x^2 + 5$

28. $f(x) = .001x^5 - .01x^4 - .2x^3 + x^2 + x - 5$

In Exercises 29–32 find a single viewing window that shows a complete graph of the function.

29. $f(x) = x^3 + 8x^2 + 20x - 15$

30. $f(x) = 10x^3 - 12x^2 + 2x$

31. $f(x) = 10x^4 - 80x^3 + 239x^2 - 316x + 155$

32. $f(x) = 10x^4 - 80x^3 + 241x^2 - 324x + 163$

In Exercises 33–36, find a complete graph of the function and list the viewing window(s) that show this graph. (It may not be possible to obtain a complete graph in a single window.)

33. $f(x) = .1x^5 + 3x^4 - 4x^3 - 11x^2 + 3x + 5$

34. $f(x) = x^4 - 48x^3 - 101x^2 + 49x + 50$

35. $f(x) = .03x^3 - 1.5 x^2 - 200x$

36. $f(x) = .3x^5 + 2x^4 - 7x^3 + 2x^2$

37. (a) Explain why the graph of a cubic polynomial function has either two local extrema or none at all. [*Hint:* If it had only one, what would the graph look like when $|x|$ is very large?]

(b) Explain why the general shape of the graph of a cubic polynomial function must be one of the following:

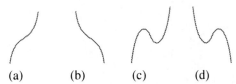

    (a)   (b)   (c)   (d)

38. The figure shows an incomplete graph of a fourth-degree even polynomial function f. (Even functions were defined in Special Topics 3.4.A.)

(a) Find the roots of f.
(b) Draw a complete graph of f.
(c) Explain why

$$f(x) = k(x - a)(x - b)(x - c)(x - d),$$

where a, b, c, d are the roots of f.

(d) Experiment with your calculator to find the value of k that produces the graph in the figure.
(e) List the approximate intervals on which f is increasing and those on which it is decreasing.

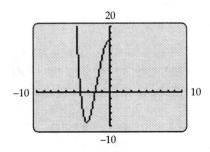

39. A complete graph of a polynomial function g is shown below.

(a) Is the degree of $g(x)$ even or odd?
(b) Is the leading coefficient of $g(x)$ positive or negative?
(c) What are the real roots of $g(x)$?
(d) What is the smallest possible degree of $g(x)$?

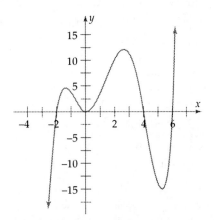

40. Do Exercise 39 for the polynomial function g whose complete graph is shown here.

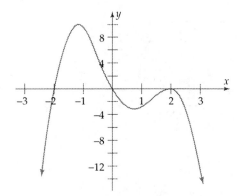

41. f is a third degree polynomial function whose leading coefficient is negative. Gordon graphs the function on his calculator, without being careful about choosing a window, and gets the plot shown below. Which of the patterns shown in Exercise 37 does this graph have?

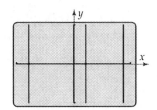

42. f is a fourth degree polynomial function. Madison graphs the function on her calculator, without being careful about choosing a window, and gets the plot shown below. Sketch the general shape of the graph and state whether the leading coefficient is positive or negative.

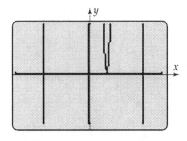

In Exercises 43–48, sketch a complete graph of the function. Label each x-intercept and the coordinates of each local extremum; find intercepts and coordinates exactly when possible and otherwise approximate them.

43. $f(x) = -x^3 + 3x^2 - 2$

44. $f(x) = .25x^4 + 2x^3 + 4x^2$

45. $f(x) = x^4 - 9x^3 + 30x^2 - 44x + 24$

46. $f(x) = 3x^3 - 18.5x^2 - 4.5x - 45$

47. $f(x) = x^5 - 3x^3 + x$

48. $f(x) = x^6 - 3x^3 + \dfrac{9}{4}$

49. The sales $f(x)$ of a certain product (in dollars) are related to the amount x (in thousands of dollars) spent on advertising by

$$f(x) = -3x^3 + 135x^2 + 3600x + 12{,}000$$
$$(0 \le x \le 40).$$

(a) Graph f in the window with $0 \le x \le 40$ and $0 \le y \le 180{,}000$ and verify that f is concave upward near the origin and concave downward near $x = 40$.

(b) Compute the average rate of change of $f(x)$ from $x = 0$ to $x = 15$ and from $x = 15$ to $x = 40$. What do these numbers tell you about the rate at which sales are increasing in each interval?

(c) This function has an inflection point at $x = 15$ (a fact you might want to verify if your calculator can find inflection points). Use the results of part (b) to explain why the inflection point is sometimes called the **point of diminishing returns**.

50. The profits (in thousands of dollars) from producing x hundred thousand tungsten darts are given by

$$g(x) = -x^3 + 27x^2 + 20x - 60 \qquad (0 \le x \le 20).$$

(a) Graph g in a window with $0 \le x \le 20$. If you have an appropriate calculator, verify that there is a point of inflection when $x = 9$.

(b) Verify that the point of inflection is the point of diminishing returns (see Exercise 49) by computing the average rate of change of profit from $x = 0$ to $x = 9$ and from $x = 9$ to $x = 20$.

51. When there are 22 apple trees per acre, the average yield has been found to be 500 apples per tree. For each additional tree planted per acre, the yield per tree decreases by 15 apples per tree. How many additional trees per acre should be planted to maximize the yield?

52. Name tags can be sold for $29 per thousand. The cost of manufacturing x thousand tags is $.001x^3 + .06x^2 - 1.5x$ dollars. Assuming that all tags manufactured are sold,

(a) What number of tags should be made to guarantee a maximum profit? What will that profit be?

(b) What is the largest number of tags that can be made without losing money?

53. The top of a 12-ounce can of soda pop is three times thicker than the sides and bottom (so that the flip-top opener will work properly), and the can has a volume of 355 cubic centimeters. What should the radius and height of the can be in order to use the least possible amount of metal? [Assume that the entire can is made from a single sheet of metal, with three layers being used for the top. Example 4 in Section 2.4 may be helpful.]

54. An open-top reinforced box is to be made from a 12-by-36-inch piece of cardboard as in Exercise 45 of Section 4.3. What size squares should be cut from the corners in order to have a box with maximum volume?

In calculus, you will learn that many complicated functions can be approximated by polynomials. For Exercises 55–58, use a

calculator to graph the function and the polynomial on the same axes in the given window, and determine where the polynomial is a good approximation.*

55. $f(x) = \sin(x)$, $p(x) = -\dfrac{1}{5040}x^7 + \dfrac{1}{120}x^5 - \dfrac{1}{6}x^3 + x$,
$-6 \le x \le 6$, $-4 \le y \le -4$

56. $f(x) = \dfrac{1}{1-x}$, $p(x) = x^7 + x^6 + x^5 + x^4 + x^3 + x^2 + x + 1$,
$-3 \le x \le 3$, $-6 \le y \le 6$

57. (a) $f(x) = e^x$, $p(x) = \dfrac{1}{5040}x^7 + \dfrac{1}{720}x^6 + \dfrac{1}{120}x^5 +$
$\dfrac{1}{24}x^4 + \dfrac{1}{6}x^3 + \dfrac{1}{2}x^2 + x + 1$, $-6 \le x \le 6$, $-3 \le y \le 10$

(b) $f(x) = e^x$, $p(x) = \dfrac{1}{5040}x^7 + \dfrac{1}{720}x^6 + \dfrac{1}{120}x^5 + \dfrac{1}{24}x^4 +$
$\dfrac{1}{6}x^3 + \dfrac{1}{2}x^2 + x + 1$, $-6 \le x \le 6$, $-50 \le y \le 400$

[*Hint:* On some calculators, the "e^x" key is labelled "exp(x)."]

58. $f(x) = \tan(x)$, $p(x) = \dfrac{17}{315}x^7 + \dfrac{2}{15}x^5 + \dfrac{1}{3}x^3 + x$, $-3 \le x \le 3$,
$-10 \le y \le 10$

THINKERS

59. (a) Graph $g(x) = .01x^3 - .06x^2 + .12x + 3.92$ in the viewing window with $-3 \le x \le 3$ and $0 \le y \le 6$ and verify that the graph appears to coincide with the horizontal line $y = 4$ between $x = 1$ and $x = 3$. In other words, it appears that every x with $1 \le x \le 3$ is a solution of the equation

$$.01x^3 - .06x^2 + .12x + 3.92 = 4.$$

Explain why this is impossible. Conclude that the actual graph is not horizontal between $x = 1$ and $x = 3$.

(b) Use the trace feature to verify that the graph is actually rising from left to right between $x = 1$ and $x = 3$. Find a viewing window that shows this.

(c) Show that it is not possible for the graph of a polynomial $f(x)$ to contain a horizontal segment. [*Hint:* A horizontal line segment is part of the horizontal line $y = k$ for some constant k. Adapt the argument in part (a), which is the case $k = 4$.]

60. (a) Let $f(x)$ be a polynomial of odd degree. Explain why $f(x)$ must have at least one real root. [*Hint:* Why must the graph of f cross the x-axis, and what does this mean?]

(b) Let $g(x)$ be a polynomial of even degree, with a negative leading coefficient and a positive constant term. Explain why $g(x)$ must have at least one positive and at least one negative root.

---

*You don't need to know what the SIN and e^x keys mean to do this exercise.

61. The graph of

$$f(x) = (x + 18)(x^2 - 20)(x - 2)^2(x - 10)$$

has x-intercepts at each of its roots, that is, at $x = -18$, $\pm\sqrt{20} \approx \pm4.472$, 2, and 10. It is also true that $f(x)$ has a relative minimum at $x = 2$.

(a) Draw the x-axis and mark the roots of $f(x)$. Then use the fact that $f(x)$ has degree 6 (why?) to sketch the general shape of the graph (as was done for cubics in Exercise 37).

(b) Now graph $f(x)$ in the standard viewing window. Does the graph resemble your sketch? Does it even show all the x-intercepts between -10 and 10?

(c) Graph $f(x)$ in the viewing window with $-19 \le x \le 11$ and $-10 \le y \le 10$. Does this window include all the x-intercepts as it should?

(d) List viewing windows that give a complete graph of $f(x)$.

62. (a) Graph $f(x) = x^3 - 4x$ in the viewing window with $-3 \le x \le 3$ and $-5 \le y \le 5$.

(b) Graph the difference quotient of $f(x)$ (with $h = .01$) on the same screen.

(c) Find the x-coordinates of the relative extrema of $f(x)$. How do these numbers compare with the x-intercepts of the difference quotient?

(d) Repeat this problem with the function $f(x) = x^4 - x^2$.

Chapter 3

NON-POLYNOMIAL FUNCTIONS

© Jeff Greenberg/PhotoEdit

Chapter Outline

Interdependence of Sections

3.1 Rational Functions

Section Objectives

- Find the domain of a rational function.
- Find the asymptotes of a linear rational function.
- Analyze the graph of a rational function algebraically and graphically.
- Use rational functions to solve applied problems.

A **rational function** is a function whose rule is the quotient of two polynomials, such as

$$f(x) = \frac{1}{x}, \qquad t(x) = \frac{4x - 3}{2x + 1}, \qquad k(x) = \frac{2x^3 + 5x + 2}{x^2 - 7x + 6}.$$

A polynomial function is defined for every real number, but the rational function $f(x) = g(x)/h(x)$ is defined only when its denominator is nonzero. Hence,

Domain

> The domain of the rational function $f(x) = \dfrac{g(x)}{h(x)}$ is the set of all real numbers that are *not* roots of the denominator $h(x)$.

For instance, the domain of

$$f(x) = \frac{x^2 + 3x + 1}{x^2 - x - 6}$$

can be found by determining the roots of the denominator. It factors as

$$x^2 - x - 6 = (x + 2)(x - 3),$$

so its roots are -2 and 3. Hence, the domain of f is the set of all real numbers except -2 and 3.

The key to understanding the behavior of rational numbers is the following fact from arithmetic.

The Big-Little Principle

If c is a number far from 0, then $1/c$ is a number close to 0. Conversely, if c is close to 0, then $1/c$ is far from 0. In less precise but more suggestive terms:

$$\frac{1}{\text{big}} = \text{little} \quad \text{and} \quad \frac{1}{\text{little}} = \text{big.}$$

For example, 5000 is big (far from 0), and $1/5000$ is little (close to 0). Similarly, $-1/1000$ is very close to 0, but

$$\frac{1}{-1/1000} = -1000$$

is far from 0. To see the role played by the Big-Little Principle, we examine two rational functions that are part of the catalog of basic functions.

EXAMPLE 1

Reciprocal Functions   Graph

$$f(x) = \frac{1}{x} \quad \text{and} \quad g(x) = \frac{1}{x^2}.$$

SOLUTION   Note that f and g are not defined when $x = 0$ (root of the denominator). The graphs are easily obtained, either by hand or by calculator (see Figures 3–1 and 3–2), and you should know their shapes by heart.   ∎

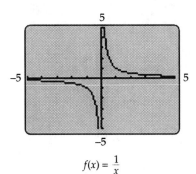

$$f(x) = \frac{1}{x}$$

Figure 3–1

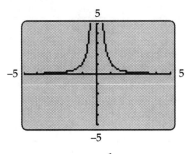

$$g(x) = \frac{1}{x^2}$$

Figure 3–2

The Big-Little Principle explains why these graphs have the shapes they do. When x is very close to 0, both $1/x$ and $1/x^2$ are very far from 0. That's why the graphs "explode" near the undefined place at $x = 0$, shooting sharply upward or downward on either side of the y-axis. We say that the y-axis is the **vertical asymptote** of the graph: The graph gets closer and closer to this line, but never touches it. In a rational function, a vertical asymptote can occur only where the function is not defined.

Similarly, when x is very far from 0, then $1/x$ and $1/x^2$ are very small numbers. So the farther you go from the origin, the closer the graphs get to the line $y = 0$ (the x-axis), which is called the **horizontal asymptote** of the graph.

EXAMPLE 2

Without using technology, describe the graphs of

(a) $h(x) = \dfrac{1}{x + 3}$ and   (b) $k(x) = \dfrac{1}{x^2 - 4x + 4}$.

SOLUTION

(a) Recall the graph of $f(x) = \dfrac{1}{x}$ in Figure 3–1, and note that

$$f(x + 3) = \frac{1}{x + 3} = h(x)$$

From Section 3.4, we know that the graph of h is the graph of f shifted horizontally 3 units to the left, as shown in Figure 3–3(a) on the next page. The vertical asymptote of this graph is at $x = -3$ [the root of the denominator of $h(x)$].

(b) To understand the graph of k, recall the graph of $g(x) = \dfrac{1}{x^2}$ in Figure 3–2 and factor the denominator of $k(x)$:

$$k(x) = \frac{1}{x^2 - 4x + 4} = \frac{1}{(x - 2)^2} = g(x - 2).$$

Thus, the graph of k is the graph of g shifted horizontally 2 units to the right, as shown in Figure 3–3(b). The vertical asymptote is at $x = 2$ [the root of the denominator of $k(x)$]. ∎

NOTE
The asymptotes are shown as dashed lines in Figure 4–35 and in the figures below. The asymptotes are included for easier visualization, but they are *not* part of the graph.

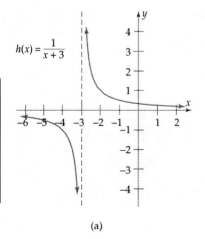

(a)

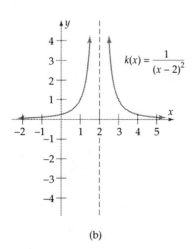

(b)

Figure 3–3

LINEAR RATIONAL FUNCTIONS

Next we consider the graphs of rational functions, where both the numerator and denominator are either constants or first-degree polynomials.

EXAMPLE 3

Find the asymptotes of the graph of

$$f(x) = \frac{x + 1}{2x - 4}$$

and graph the function.

SOLUTION   The function is not defined when $x = 2$ because the denominator is 0 there. When x is a number very close to 2, then

the numerator $x + 1$ is very close to 3;

the denominator $2x - 4$ is very close to 0.

Therefore,

$$f(x) = \frac{x + 1}{2x - 4} \approx \frac{3}{\text{little}} = \text{BIG (far from 0)}.$$

Consequently, the graph explodes near $x = 2$, as shown in the table and partial graph in Figure 3–4. The vertical line $x = 2$ is the vertical asymptote of the graph.

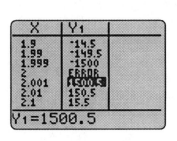

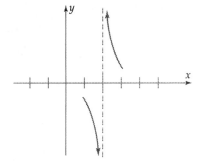

Figure 3–4

To determine the horizontal asymptote of the graph, we rewrite the rule of f like this:

$$f(x) = \frac{x + 1}{2x - 4} = \frac{\dfrac{x + 1}{x}}{\dfrac{2x - 4}{x}} = \frac{1 + \dfrac{1}{x}}{2 - \dfrac{4}{x}}.$$

As x gets larger in absolute value (far from 0), both $1/x$ and $4/x$ get very close to 0 by the Big-Little Principle. Consequently,

$$f(x) = \frac{1 + (1/x)}{2 - (4/x)}$$

gets very close to

$$\frac{1 + 0}{2 - 0} = \frac{1}{2}.$$

So when $|x|$ is large, the graph gets closer and closer to the horizontal line $y = 1/2$, but never touches it, as shown in Figure 3–5. Thus, the line $y = 1/2$ is the horizontal asymptote of the graph.

The preceding information, together with a few hand-plotted points, produces the graph in Figure 3–5.

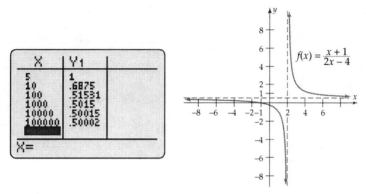

Figure 3–5

We can see this result in a different way. When x is very large, we can make the approximations $x + 1 \approx x$ and $2x - 4 \approx 2x$. Therefore, we have, for large x,

$$f(x) = \frac{x + 1}{2x - 4} \approx \frac{x}{2x} = \frac{1}{2}. \qquad \blacksquare$$

We can generalize the process used at the end of Example 3. If $f(x) = \dfrac{ax + b}{cx + d}$, with a and c non-zero, then for large $|x|$:

$$\frac{ax + b}{cx + d} \approx \frac{ax}{cx} = \frac{a}{c}.$$

We summarize below:

Linear Rational Functions

> The graph of $f(x) = \dfrac{ax + b}{cx + d}$ (with $c \neq 0$ and $ad \neq bc$) has two asymptotes:
>
> The vertical asymptote occurs at the root of the denominator.
>
> The horizontal asymptote is the line $y = a/c$.

Figure 3–6 shows some additional examples.

$$f(x) = \frac{-5x + 12}{2x - 4} \qquad\qquad k(x) = \frac{3x + 6}{x} = \frac{3x + 6}{1x + 0}$$

Vertical asymptote $x = 2$ Vertical asymptote $x = 0$

Horizontal asymptote $y = -\frac{5}{2}$ Horizontal asymptote $y = \frac{3}{1} = 3$

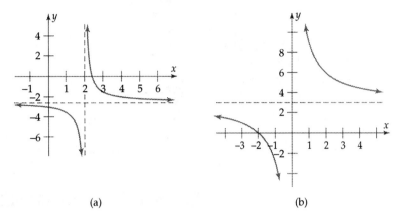

(a)   (b)

Figure 3–6

◤ RATIONAL FUNCTIONS AND TECHNOLOGY

Getting an accurate graph of a rational function on a calculator often depends on choosing an appropriate viewing window. For example, a TI-83+ produced the following graphs of

$$f(x) = \frac{x + 1}{2x - 4}$$

in Figure 3–7, two of which do not look like Figure 3–5 as they should.

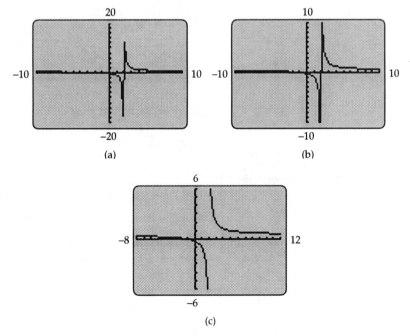

Figure 3–7

The vertical segments in graphs (a) and (b) are *not* representations of the vertical asymptote. They are a result of the calculator evaluating $f(x)$ just to the left of $x = 2$ and just to the right of $x = 2$ but not at $x = 2$ and then erroneously connecting these points with a near vertical segment that looks like an asymptote.

In the accurate graph (c), the calculator attempted to plot a point with $x = 2$ and, when it found that $f(2)$ was not defined, skipped a pixel and did not join the points on either side of the skipped one.

GRAPHING EXPLORATION

Find a viewing window that displays the graph of $f(x)$ in Figure 3–6(a), without any erroneous vertical line segments being shown. The Technology Tip in the margin may be helpful.

PROPERTIES OF RATIONAL GRAPHS

Here is a summary of the important characteristics of graphs of more complicated rational functions.

CONTINUITY AND SMOOTHNESS

There will be breaks in the graph of a rational function wherever the function is not defined. Between those breaks, the graph is a continuous unbroken curve. In addition, the graph has no sharp corners.

LOCAL MAXIMA AND MINIMA

The graph may have some local extrema (peaks and valleys), and calculus is needed to determine their exact location. There are no simple rules for the possible number of peaks and valleys as there were with polynomial functions.

INTERCEPTS

As with any function, the y-intercept of the graph of a rational function f occurs at $f(0)$, provided that f is defined at $x = 0$. The x-intercepts of the graph of any function f occur at each number c for which $f(c) = 0$. Now a fraction is 0 only when its numerator is 0 and its denominator is nonzero (since division by 0 is not defined). Thus,

Intercepts

> The x-intercepts of the graph of the rational function $f(x) = \dfrac{g(x)}{h(x)}$ occur at the numbers that are roots of the numerator $g(x)$ but *not* of the denominator $h(x)$.
>
> If f has a y-intercept, it occurs at $f(0)$.

For example, the graph of

$$f(x) = \frac{x^2 - x - 2}{x - 5}$$

has x-intercepts at $x = -1$ and $x = 2$ [which are the roots of $x^2 - x - 2 = (x + 1)(x - 2)$, but not of $x - 5$] and y-intercept at $y = 2/5$ (the value of f at $x = 0$).

VERTICAL ASYMPTOTES

In Example 3, we saw that the graph of

$$f(x) = \frac{x+1}{2x-4}$$

had a vertical asymptote at $x = 2$. Note that $x = 2$ is a root of the denominator $2x - 4$, but not of the numerator $x + 1$. The same thing occurs in the general case.

Vertical Asymptotes

> The function $f(x) = \dfrac{g(x)}{h(x)}$ has a vertical asymptote at every number that is a root of the denominator $h(x)$, but *not* of the numerator $g(x)$.

HOLES

When simplifying rational expressions, we often cancel factors, like so:

$$\frac{x^2 - 4}{x - 2} = \frac{(x + 2)(x - 2)}{x - 2} = x + 2.$$

But the functions given by

$$p(x) = \frac{x^2 - 4}{x - 2} \qquad \text{and} \qquad q(x) = x + 2$$

are *not* the same, because when $x = 2$,

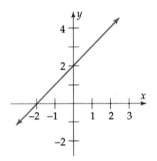

Figure 3–8

$$q(2) = 2 + 2 = 4, \qquad \text{but} \qquad p(2) = \frac{2^2 - 2}{2 - 2} = \frac{0}{0},$$

which is not defined. For any number other than 2, the two functions do have the same value, and hence, the same graph. The graph of $q(x) = x + 2$ is a straight line that includes the point $(2, 4)$, as shown in Figure 3–8. The graph of $p(x)$ is the same straight line, but with the point $(2, 4)$ omitted, so that the graph of p has a **hole** at $x = 2$ (indicated by an open circle in Figure 3–9). Note that the hole occurs at $x = 2$, which is a root of multiplicity 1 in both the numerator and the denominator of

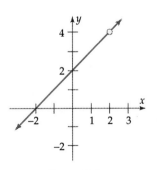

Figure 3–9

$$p(x) = \frac{x^2 - 4}{x - 2} = \frac{(x + 2)(x - 2)}{x - 2}.*$$

Similarly, the graph of $g(x) = \dfrac{x^2}{x^3}$ is the same as the graph of $f(x) = \dfrac{1}{x}$, except at $x = 0$, where neither function is defined. In this case, however, there is a vertical asymptote rather than a hole at $x = 0$ (see Figure 3–1 on page 289). Note that the vertical asymptote occurs at $x = 0$, which is a root of multiplicity 2 in the numerator, but of larger multiplicity 3 in the denominator. In general,

---

*Multiplicity of roots was discussed on page 273.

Holes

> Let $f(x) = \dfrac{g(x)}{h(x)}$ be a rational function and d a root of both $g(x)$ and $h(x)$. If the multiplicity of d as a root of $g(x)$ is greater than or equal to its multiplicity as a root of $h(x)$, then the graph of f has a hole at $x = d$. Otherwise, the graph has a vertical asymptote at $x = d$.

A calculator-drawn graph may not show holes where it should. If the calculator actually attempts to compute an undefined quantity, it indicates a hole by skipping a pixel; otherwise, it may erroneously show a continuous graph with no hole.

GRAPHING EXPLORATION

Graph $p(x) = \dfrac{x^2 - 4}{x - 2}$ with various viewing windows. Does your calculator display the hole at $x = 2$?

BEHAVIOR WHEN $|x|$ IS LARGE

The shape of a rational graph at the far left and far right (that is, when $|x|$ is large) can usually be found by algebraic analysis, as in the next example.

EXAMPLE 4

Determine the shape of the graph when $|x|$ is large for the following functions.

(a) $f(x) = \dfrac{7x^4 - 6x^3 + 4}{2x^4 + x^2}$ (b) $g(x) = \dfrac{x^2 - 2}{x^3 - 3x^2 + x - 3}$

(c) $h(x) = \dfrac{2x^3 - 5}{x + 3}$

SOLUTION

(a) When $|x|$ is very large, a polynomial function behaves in essentially the same way as its highest degree term, as we saw on page 272. Consequently, we have this approximation:

$$f(x) = \frac{7x^4 - 6x^3 + 4}{2x^4 + x^2} \approx \frac{7x^4}{2x^4} = \frac{7}{2} = 3.5.$$

Thus, when $|x|$ is large, the graph of $f(x)$ is very close to the horizontal line $y = 3.5$, which is a horizontal asymptote of the graph.

Confirm the last statement by graphing $f(x)$ and $y = 3.5$ in the window with $-10 \leq x \leq 10$ and $-2 \leq y \leq 12$.

(b) When $|x|$ is large, the graph of g closely resembles the graph of

$$y = \frac{x^2}{x^3} = \frac{1}{x}.$$

By the Big-Little Principle, $1/x$ is very close to 0 when $|x|$ is large. So the line $y = 0$ (that is, the x-axis) is the horizontal asymptote.

(c) When $|x|$ is large, the graph of g closely resembles the graph of

$$y = \frac{2x^3}{x} = 2x^2$$

In this case the Big-Little principle doesn't help us; when $|x|$ is large, so is $2x^2$. So all we know is that $h(x)$ eventually resembles the graph of $2x^2$. Special Topics 4.5.A discusses this case in more detail. ■

Arguments similar to those in the preceding example, using the highest-degree terms in the numerator and denominator, carry over to the general case and lead to this conclusion.

Horizontal Asymptotes

Let $f(x) = \dfrac{ax^n + \cdots}{cx^k + \cdots}$ be a rational function whose numerator has degree n and whose denominator has degree k.

If $n = k$, then the line $y = a/c$ is a horizontal asymptote.

If $n < k$, then the x-axis (the line $y = 0$) is a horizontal asymptote.

If $n > k$, then there is no horizontal asymptote.

 GRAPHS OF RATIONAL FUNCTIONS

The procedure for finding accurate graphs of rational functions is summarized here.

Graphing $f(x) = \dfrac{g(x)}{h(x)}$ **When**

Degree $g(x) \leq$ **Degree** $h(x)$

1. Analyze the function algebraically to determine its vertical asymptotes, holes, and intercepts.

2. Determine the horizontal asymptote of the graph when $|x|$ is large by using the facts in the box on the opposite page.

3. Use the preceding information to select an appropriate viewing window (or windows), to interpret the calculator's version of the graph (if necessary), and to sketch an accurate graph.

EXAMPLE 5

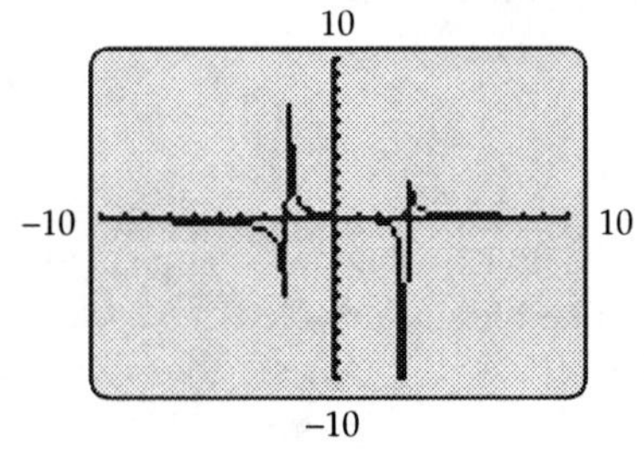

If you ignore the preceding advice and simply graph $f(x) = \dfrac{x-1}{x^2 - x - 6}$ in the standard viewing window, you get garbage (Figure 3–10). So let's try analyzing the function. We begin by factoring.

$$f(x) = \frac{x-1}{x^2 - x - 6} = \frac{x-1}{(x+2)(x-3)}.$$

The factored form allows us to read off the necessary information:

Vertical Asymptotes: $x = -2$ and $x = 3$ (roots of the denominator but not of the numerator).

Horizontal Asymptote: x-axis (because denominator has larger degree than the numerator).

Intercepts: y-intercept at $f(0) = \dfrac{0-1}{0^2 - 0 - 6} = \dfrac{1}{6}$; x-intercept at $x = 1$ (root of the numerator but not of the denominator).

Interpreting Figure 3–10 in light of this information suggests that a complete graph of f looks something like Figure 3–11.

Figure 3–10

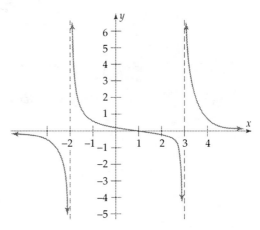

Figure 3–11

TECHNOLOGY TIP

A decimal window (with the *y*-range suitably adjusted) will usually produce an accurate graph of a rational function whose vertical asymptotes occur at numbers such as $x = -2.0$ or 3.7 or 4.1 that are within the *x*-range.

GRAPHING EXPLORATION

Find a viewing window in which the graph of *f* looks similar to Figure 3–11. The Technology Tip in the margin may be helpful.

■

NOTE

The graph of a rational function never touches a horizontal asymptote when *x* is large in absolute value. For smaller values of *x*, however, the graph may cross the asymptote, as in Example 5.

EXAMPLE 6

Graph

$$f(x) = \frac{2x^3}{x^3 + x^2 - 2x}$$

SOLUTION

We factor and then read off the necessary information:

$$f(x) = \frac{2x^3}{x^3 + x^2 - 2x} = \frac{2x^3}{x(x + 2)(x - 1)}.$$

Hole: $x = 0$ (root of multiplicity 3 in the denominator and a root of multiplicity 1 in the numerator; see page 295).

Vertical Asymptotes: $x = -2$ and $x = 1$ (roots of denominator that are not also roots of numerator).

Horizontal Asymptote: $y = 2/1 = 2$ (because numerator and denominator have the same degree; see the box on page 296).

Intercepts None: There is no *x*-intercept at 0, because even though $x = 0$ is a root of the numerator, it is *also* a root of the denominator. So $f(0)$ is not defined and there is no *y*-intercept.

Using this information and selecting a decimal viewing window that will accurately portray the graph near the vertical asymptotes, we obtain what seems to be a reasonably complete graph in Figure 3–12. The graph does not show the hole at $x = 0$. Also, the graph appears to be falling to the right of $x = 1$ as it approaches its horizontal asymptote, but this is not the case.

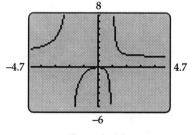

Figure 3–12

GRAPHING EXPLORATION

Graph *f* in this same viewing window and use the trace feature, beginning at approximately $x = 1.1$ and moving to the right. For what values of *x* is the graph above the horizontal asymptote $y = 2$? For what values of *x* is the graph below the horizontal asymptote?

The exploration indicates that there is some *hidden behavior* of the graph that is not visible in Figure 3–12.

GRAPHING EXPLORATION

To see this hidden behavior, graph both f and the line $y = 2$ in the viewing window with $1 \leq x \leq 50$ and $1.7 \leq y \leq 2.1$.

This Exploration shows that the graph has a local minimum near $x = 4$ and then stays below the asymptote, moving closer and closer to it as x takes larger values.   ∎

APPLICATIONS

Several applications of rational functions were considered in Section 2.4. Here is another one.

EXAMPLE 7

A cardboard box with a square base and a volume of 1000 cubic inches is to be constructed (Figure 3–13). The box must be at least 2 inches in height.

(a) What are the possible lengths for a side of the base if no more than 1100 square inches of cardboard can be used to construct the box?

(b) What is the least possible amount of cardboard that can be used?

(c) What are the dimensions of the box that uses the least possible amount of cardboard?

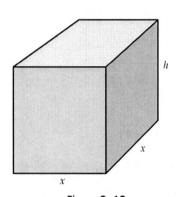

Figure 3–13

SOLUTION   The amount of cardboard needed is given by the surface area S of the box. From Figure 3–13, we have

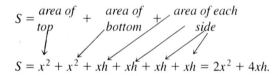

$$S = x^2 + x^2 + xh + xh + xh + xh = 2x^2 + 4xh.$$

Since the volume of the box is given by

$$\text{Length} \times \text{Width} \times \text{Height} = \text{Volume},$$

we have

$$x \cdot x \cdot h = 1000 \qquad \text{or, equivalently,} \qquad h = \frac{1000}{x^2}.$$

Substituting the above into the surface area formula allows us to express the surface area as a function of one variable, x:

$$S(x) = 2x^2 + 4xh = 2x^2 + 4x\left(\frac{1000}{x^2}\right) = 2x^2 + \frac{4000}{x} = \frac{2x^3 + 4000}{x}.$$

Although the rational function $S(x)$ is defined for all nonzero real numbers, x is a length here and must be positive. Furthermore, $x^2 \leq 500$ because if $x^2 > 500$, then $h = \frac{1000}{x^2}$ would be less than 2, contrary to specifications. Hence, the only values of x that make sense in this context are those with $0 < x \leq \sqrt{500}$. Since $\sqrt{500} \approx 22.4$, we choose the viewing window in Figure 3–14. For each point

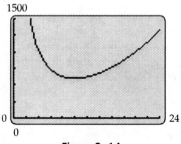

Figure 3–14

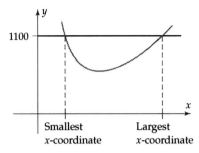

Figure 3–15

(x, y) on the graph, x is a possible side length for the base of the box, and y is the corresponding surface area.

(a) The points on the graph corresponding to the requirement that no more than 1100 square inches of cardboard be used are those whose y-coordinates are less than or equal to 1100. The x-coordinates of these points are the possible side lengths. The x-coordinates of the points where the graph of S meets the horizontal line y = 1100 are the smallest and largest possible values for x, as indicated in Figure 3–15.

GRAPHING EXPLORATION

Graph S(x) and y = 1100 on the same screen. Use an intersection finder to show that the possible side lengths that use no more than 1100 square inches of cardboard are those with 3.73 ≤ x ≤ 21.36.

(b) The least possible amount of cardboard corresponds to the point on the graph of S(x) with the smallest y-coordinate.

GRAPHING EXPLORATION

Show that the graph of S has a local minimum at the point (10.00, 600.00). Consequently, the least possible amount of cardboard is 600 square inches and this occurs when x = 10.

(c) When x = 10, h = 1000/10² = 10. So the dimensions of the box using the least amount of cardboard are 10 × 10 × 10. ■

EXERCISES 3.1

In Exercises 1–6, find the domain of the function. You may need to use some of the techniques of Section 4.3

1. $f(x) = \dfrac{2x}{3x - 4}$

2. $g(x) = \dfrac{x + 1}{2x^2 - x - 3}$

3. $h(x) = \dfrac{x^2 + 4}{x^2 + 9}$

4. $i(x) = \dfrac{x^4 + 2x^3}{x^5 - 81x}$

5. $j(x) = \dfrac{x}{\pi x^3 + \pi x^2 - 9\pi x - 9\pi}$

6. $k(x) = \dfrac{2}{x^5 + 4x^4 - 4}$

In Exercises 7–10, find equations of graphs with the given properties. Check your answer by graphing your function.

7. f has vertical asymptotes at x = 3 and x = −3, and a horizontal asymptote at y = 2

8. f has no vertical asymptotes, has a horizontal asymptote at the x axis, and goes through the point (0,2)

9. f has four vertical asymptotes, a horizontal asymptote at y = −1, goes through the point (0,4) and is an even function.

10. f has a vertical asymptote at x = 2, and a hole at x = 3.

In Exercises 11–14, use the graphs in Example 1 and the information in Section 3.4 to match the function with its graph, which is one of those shown here.

A.
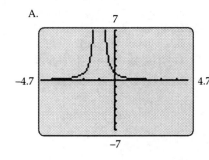

B.
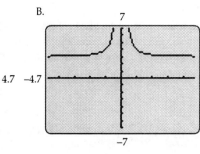

C.
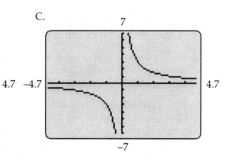

D.
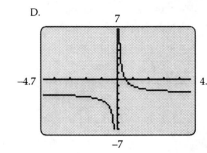

E.
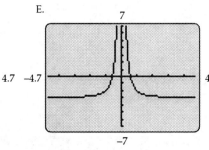

F.
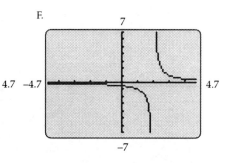

11. $f(x) = \dfrac{1}{x - 2}$

12. $g(x) = \dfrac{3}{x}$

13. $h(x) = \dfrac{1}{(x + 1)^2}$

14. $f(x) = \dfrac{1}{x^2} - 3$

In Exercises 15–18, use algebra to determine the location of the vertical asymptotes and holes in the graph of the function.

15. $f(x) = \dfrac{x^3 + 6x^2 + 11x + 6}{x^3 - x}$

16. $g(x) = \dfrac{x^2}{x^4 - x^2}$

17. $f(x) = \dfrac{x^2 + 8x + 2}{x^2 + 7x + 2}$

18. $g(x) = \dfrac{x^3 + 5x^2 + 8x + 4}{x^3 + 4x^2 + 5x + 2}$

In Exercises 19–24, find the horizontal asymptote, if any, of the graph of the given function. If there is a horizontal asymptote, find a viewing window in which the ends of the graph are within .1 of this asymptote.

19. $f(x) = \dfrac{x + 1}{x^6 + 20}$

20. $g(x) = \dfrac{3x^5 + 2x^4 + 1}{6x^5 + 8x^4 - 3x^2 + 2x + 1}$

21. $a(x) = \dfrac{x^5 - x^2 + x}{x^4 - 2x + 3}$

22. $m(x) = \dfrac{x^2 + 2x + 1}{x - 6}$

23. $f(x) = \dfrac{2x^3 + 4x^2 + 2x + 1}{3x^3 - 4x^2 - 2x}$

24. $r(x) = \dfrac{x^4 - 2x + 3}{x^5 - x^2 + x}$

In Exercises 25–36, analyze the function algebraically. List its vertical asymptotes, holes, y-intercept, and horizontal asymptote, if any. Then sketch a complete graph of the function.

25. $f(x) = \dfrac{1}{x - 2}$

26. $f(x) = \dfrac{-7}{x - 6}$

27. $f(x) = \dfrac{2x}{x + 1}$

28. $f(x) = \dfrac{2x - 3}{2x}$

29. $f(x) = \dfrac{x}{x(x - 2)(x - 3)}$

30. $f(x) = \dfrac{5x^2}{(x + 2)(x - 3)}$

31. $f(x) = \dfrac{2}{x^2 + 1}$

32. $f(x) = \dfrac{5}{(x + 1)^2(x - 4)}$

33. $f(x) = \dfrac{(x^2 + 6x + 5)(x + 5)}{(x + 5)^3(x - 1)}$

34. $f(x) = \dfrac{x^3 + 2x^2 - x - 2}{x^2 - x - 12}$

35. $f(x) = \dfrac{2x^3 + 3x^2 - 3x - 2}{x^3 + x^2 - 4x - 4}$

36. $f(x) = \dfrac{(x - 1)(x - 2)(x - 3)}{(4x + 1)}$

In Exercises 37–42, find a viewing window, or windows, that shows a complete graph of the function. Be alert for hidden behavior, such as that in Example 6.

37. $f(x) = \dfrac{x^3 + 4x^2 - 5x}{(x^2 - 4)(x^2 - 9)}$

38. $g(x) = \dfrac{x^4 + 2x^3 - 13x^2 + 10x}{x + 7}$

39. $h(x) = \dfrac{2x^2 - x - 6}{x^3 + x^2 - 6x}$

40. $f(x) = \dfrac{x^3 - x + 1}{x^4 - 2x^3 - 2x^2 + x - 1}$

41. $g(x) = \dfrac{x - 2}{x^3 - 11x^2 - x + 11}$

42. $h(x) = \dfrac{x^2 - 9}{x^3 + 2x^2 - 23x - 60}$

In Exercises 43–48, find and simplify the difference quotient of the function. [See Sections 3.2 and 3.6]

43. $f(x) = \dfrac{1}{x}$

44. $g(x) = \dfrac{2}{3x}$

45. $f(x) = \dfrac{3}{x - 2}$

46. $h(x) = \dfrac{1}{x^2}$

47. $g(x) = \dfrac{3}{x^2}$

48. $f(x) = \dfrac{m}{nx^2}$

49. (a) Use the difference quotient in Exercise 43 to determine the average rate of change of $f(x) = 1/x$ as x changes from 2 to 2.1, from 2 to 2.01, and from 2 to 2.001. Estimate the instantaneous rate of change of f at $x = 2$.

(b) Determine the average rate of change of $f(x) = 1/x$ as x changes from 3 to 3.1, from 3 to 3.01, and from 3 to 3.001. Estimate the instantaneous rate of change of f at $x = 3$.

(c) How are the instantaneous rates of change of f at $x = 2$ and $x = 3$ related to the values of the function $g(x) = -1/x^2$ at $x = 2$ and $x = 3$?

50. One way to limit current in a circuit is to add a "resistor." Resistance is measured in Ohms, and can never be negative. If two resistors are wired "in series" the total resistance is simply the sum $R_1 + R_2$.

It is more interesting if we wire them "in parallel."

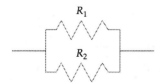

In that case we get: Total Resistance $= \dfrac{1}{\dfrac{1}{R_1} + \dfrac{1}{R_2}}$.

Assume that two resistors are wired in parallel and that R_1 is 5 Ohms.

(a) Write the total resistance as a rational function of R_2.

(b) If we allow R_2 to get larger and larger, the total resistance approaches a value. Compute that value.

(c) Is the total resistance defined if $R_2 = 0$?

(d) What happens to the total resistance if R_2 gets closer and closer to zero?

(e) Sketch a graph of total resistance vs. R_2.

51. (a) When $x \geq 0$, what rational function has the same graph as

$$f(x) = \frac{x - 1}{|x| - 2}?$$

[*Hint:* Use the definition of absolute value on page 9.]

(b) When $x < 0$, what rational function has the same graph as

$$f(x) = \frac{x - 1}{|x| - 2}?$$

[See the hint for part (a).]

(c) Use parts (a) and (b) to explain why the graph of

$$f(x) = \frac{x - 1}{|x| - 2}$$

has two vertical asymptotes. What are they? Confirm your answer by graphing the function.

52. Newton's law of gravitation states that every object in the universe attracts every other object, to some extent. If one object has mass a and the other has mass b then the force that they exert on each other is given by the equation $F = G\dfrac{ab}{d^2}$, where d is the distance between the objects, and G is a constant called, appropriately, the Gravitational Constant. We can approximate G rather well by $G \approx 6.673 \times 10^{-11}$. So if we put a 90 kilogram person about 2 meters from a 80 kilogram person, there would be a force of

$$(6.673 \times 10^{-11})\frac{(90)(80)}{2^2} \approx 1.201 \times 10^{-7} \text{ Newtons between}$$

them, or about .000000027 pounds.

(a) Use the force equation to determine what happens to the force between two objects as they get farther and farther apart.

(b) Use the force equation to determine what happens to the force between two objects as they get closer and closer together.

(c) The mass of the moon is approximately 7.36×10^{22} kilograms. The mass of the Earth is approximately 5.97×10^{24} kilograms. The distance from the moon to the Earth ranges from 357,643 km to 406,395 km. Draw a graph of the force that the Earth exerts on the moon versus their distance apart.

53. It costs 2.5 cents per square inch to make the top and bottom of the box in Example 7. The sides cost 1.5 cents per square inch. What are the dimensions of the cheapest possible box?

54. A box with a square base and a volume of 1000 cubic inches is to be constructed. The material for the top and bottom of the box costs \$3 per 100 square inches, and the material for the sides costs \$1.25 per 100 square inches.

(a) If x is the length of a side of the base, express the cost of constructing the box as a function of x.

(b) If the side of the base must be at least 6 inches long, for what value of x will the cost of the box be $7.50?

55. Our friend Joseph collects "action figures." In 1980, his annual action figure budget was $20, but it has gone up by $5 every year after that. The cost of action figures has risen as well. In 1980, they cost an average of $2 per figure, but that number has gone up by .25 every year after that.

(a) How many figures could Joseph buy in 1980?

(b) How many figures will he be able to buy in 2010?

(c) Write the number of figures he can buy in a given year as a function of time. Let $t = 0$ correspond to 1980.

(d) Graph the function you found in part (c). Use your graph to check your answer to part (b).

(e) Will he ever be able to buy 18? If so, when? Will he ever be able to buy 21? If so, when?

56. Pure alcohol is being added to 100 gallons of a coolant mixture that is 40% alcohol.

(a) Find the rule of the concentration function $c(x)$ that expresses the percentage of alcohol in the resulting mixture as a function of the number x of gallons of pure alcohol that are added. [*Hint:* The final mixture contains $100 + x$ gallons (why?). So $c(x)$ is the amount of alcohol in the final mixture divided by the total amount $100 + x$. How much alcohol is in the original 100-gallon mixture? How much is in the final mixture?]

(b) How many gallons of pure alcohol should be added to produce a mixture that is at least 60% alcohol and no more than 80% alcohol? Your answer will be a range of values.

(c) Determine algebraically the exact amount of pure alcohol that must be added to produce a mixture that is 70% alcohol.

57. A rectangular garden with an area of 200 square meters is to be located next to a building and fenced on three sides, with the building acting as a fence on the fourth side.

(a) If the side of the garden parallel to the building has length x meters, express the amount of fencing needed as a function of x.

(b) For what values of x will less than 60 meters of fencing be needed?

(c) What value of x will result in the least possible amount of fencing being used? What are the dimensions of the garden in this case?

58. A certain company has fixed costs of $40,000 and variable costs of $2.60 per unit.

(a) Let x be the number of units produced. Find the rule of the average cost function. [The average cost is the cost of the units divided by the number of units.]

(b) Graph the average cost function in a window with $0 \leq x \leq 100,000$ and $0 \leq y \leq 20$.

(c) Find the horizontal asymptote of the average cost function. Explain what the asymptote means in this situation. [How low can the average cost possibly be?]

59. Radioactive waste is stored in a cylindrical tank; the exterior has radius r and height h as shown in the figure. The sides, top, and bottom of the tank are 1 foot thick, and the tank has a volume of 150 cubic feet (including top, bottom, and walls).

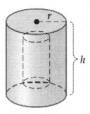

(a) Express the interior height h_1 (that is, the height of the storage area) as a function of h.

(b) Express the interior height as a function of r.

(c) Express the volume of the interior as a function of r.

(d) Explain why r must be greater than 2.

(e) What should the dimensions of the tank be in order for it to hold as much as possible?

60. The relationship between the fixed focal length F of a camera, the distance u from the object being photographed to the lens, and the distance v from the lens to the film is given by

$$\frac{1}{F} = \frac{1}{u} + \frac{1}{v}.$$

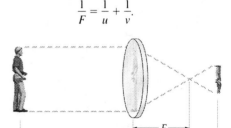

(a) If the focal length is 50 millimeters, express v as a function of u.

(b) What is the horizontal asymptote of the graph of the function in part (a)?

(c) Graph the function in part (a) when 50 millimeters $< u <$ 35,000 millimeters.

(d) When you focus the camera on an object, the distance between the lens and the film is changed. If the distance from the lens to the film changes by less than .1 millimeter, the object will remain in focus. Explain why you have more latitude in focusing on distant objects than on very close ones.

61. The formula for the gravitational acceleration (in units of meters per second squared) of an object relative to the earth is

$$g(r) = \frac{3.987 \times 10^{14}}{(6.378 \times 10^6 + r)^2},$$

where r is the distance in meters above the earth's surface.

(a) What is the gravitational acceleration at the earth's surface?

(b) Graph the function $g(r)$ for $r \geq 0$.

(c) Can you ever escape the pull of gravity? [Does the graph have any r-intercepts?]

3.2   Exponential Functions

Section Objectives
- Explore graphs of exponential functions.
- Use exponential functions to model growth and decay.
- Use the natural exponential function.

For each positive real number a there is a function (called the **exponential function with base a**) whose domain is all real numbers and whose rule is $f(x) = a^x$. For example,

$$f(x) = 10^x, \qquad g(x) = 2^x, \qquad h(x) = \left(\frac{1}{2}\right)^x, \qquad k(x) = \left(\frac{3}{2}\right)^x.$$

The graph of $f(x) = a^x$ is the next entry in the catalog of basic functions. To see how its graph depends on the size of the base a, do the following Graphing Exploration.

GRAPHING EXPLORATION

Using viewing window with $-3 \leq x \leq 7$ and $-2 \leq y \leq 18$, graph

$$f(x) = 1.3^x, \qquad g(x) = 2^x, \qquad \text{and} \qquad h(x) = 10^x$$

on the same screen. How is the steepness of the graph of $f(x) = a^x$ related to the size of a?

The Graphing Exploration illustrates these facts:

The Exponential Function
$$f(x) = a^x \, (a > 1)$$

When $a > 1$, the graph of $f(x) = a^x$ has the shape shown here and the properties listed below.

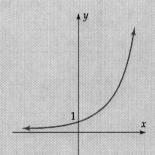

The graph is above the x-axis.   The negative x-axis is a horizontal
The y-intercept is 1.   asymptote.
$f(x)$ is an increasing function.   The larger the base a, the more steeply
                                     the graph rises to the right.

EXAMPLE 1

EXAMPLE 1

Graph $f(x) = 2^x$ and estimate the height of the graph when $x = 50$.

SOLUTION   A small portion of the graph is shown in Figure 3–16. If the x-axis were to be extended with the same scale, $x = 50$ would be at the right edge of the page. At that point, the height of the graph is $f(50) = 2^{50}$. Now the y-axis scale in Figure 3–16 is approximately 12 units to the inch, which is equivalent to 760,320 units per mile, as you can readily verify. Therefore, the height of the graph at $x = 50$ is

$$\frac{2^{50}}{760,320} = 1,480,823,741 \text{ MILES,}$$

which would put that part of the graph well beyond the planet Saturn!   ■

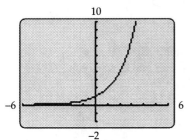

Figure 3–16

When the base a is between 0 and 1, then the graph of $f(x) = a^x$ has a different shape.

GRAPHING EXPLORATION

GRAPHING EXPLORATION

Using viewing window with $-4 \le x \le 4$ and $-1 \le y \le 4$, graph

$$f(x) = .2^x, \qquad g(x) = .4^x, \qquad h(x) = .6^x, \qquad \text{and} \qquad k(x) = .8^x$$

on the same screen. How is the steepness of the graph of $f(x) = a^x$ related to the size of a?

The exploration supports this conclusion.

The Exponential Function
$f(x) = a^x \, (0 < a < 1)$

When $0 < a < 1$, the graph of $f(x) = a^x$ has the shape shown here and the properties listed below.

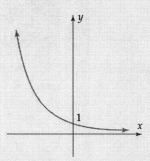

The graph is above the x-axis.   The positive x-axis is a horizontal
The y-intercept is 1.   asymptote.
$f(x)$ is a decreasing function.   The closer the base a is to 0, the more
    steeply the graph falls to the right.

EXAMPLE 2

Without graphing, describe the graph of $g(x) = 3^{-x}$.

SOLUTION   Note that

$$g(x) = 3^{-x} = (3^{-1})^x = \left(\frac{1}{3}\right)^x.$$

So $g(x)$ is an exponential function with a positive base less than 1. Its graph has the shape shown in the preceding box: It falls quickly to the right and rises very steeply to the left of the y-axis. ∎

GRAPHING EXPLORATION

Verify the analysis in Example 2 by graphing $g(x) = 3^{-x}$ in the viewing window with $-4 \le x \le 4$ and $-2 \le y \le 18$.

Exponential functions that model real-life situations generally have the form $f(x) = Pa^{kx}$, such as

$$f(x) = 5 \cdot 2^{.45x}, \qquad g(x) = 3.5(10^{-.03x}), \qquad h(x) = (-6)(1.076^{2x}).$$

Their graphs have the same basic shape as the graph of $f(x) = a^x$, but rise or fall at different rates, depending on the constants P, a, and k.

EXAMPLE 3

Figure 3–17 on the next page shows the graphs of

$$f(x) = 3^x, \qquad g(x) = 3^{.15x}, \qquad h(x) = 3^{.35x}, \qquad k(x) = 3^{-x}, \qquad p(x) = 3^{-.4x}.$$

Note how the coefficient of x determines the steepness of the graph. When this coefficient is positive, the graph rises, and when it is negative, the graph falls from left to right.

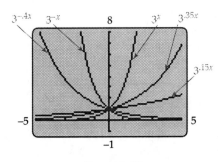

Figure 3–17

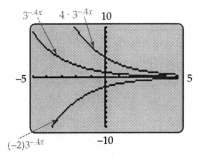

Figure 3–18

Figure 3–18 shows the graphs of

$$p(x) = 3^{-.4x}, \qquad q(x) = 4 \cdot 3^{-.4x}, \qquad r(x) = (-2)3^{-.4x}.$$

As we saw in Section 3.4, the graph of $q(x) = 4 \cdot 3^{-.4x}$ is the graph of $p(x) = 3^{-.4x}$ stretched away from the x-axis by a factor of 4. The graph of $r(x) = (-2)3^{-.4x}$ is the graph of $p(x) = 3^{-.4x}$ stretched away from the x-axis by a factor of 2 *and* reflected in the x-axis. ∎

EXPONENTIAL GROWTH

Exponential functions are useful for modeling situations in which a quantity increases by a fixed multiplier.

EXAMPLE 4

If you deposit $5000 in a savings account that pays 3% interest, compounded annually, how much money is in the account after nine years?

SOLUTION　　After one year, the account balance is

$$5000 + 3\% \text{ of } 5000 = 5000 + (.03)5000 = 5000(1 + .03)$$
$$= 5000(1.03) = \$5150.$$

The initial balance has grown by a factor of 1.03. If you leave the $5150 in the account, then at the end of the second year, the balance is

$$5150 + 3\% \text{ of } 5150 = 5150 + (.03)5150 = 5150(1 + .03) = 5150(1.03).$$

Once again, the amount at the beginning of the year has grown by a factor of 1.03. The same thing happens every year. A balance of P dollars at the beginning of the year grows to $P(1.03)$. So the balance grows like this:

$$\underset{\text{Year 1}}{5000} \to \underset{\text{Year 2}}{5000(1.03)} \to \underbrace{[5000(1.03)](1.03)}_{5000(1.03)^2} \to \underset{\text{Year 3}}{\underbrace{[5000(1.03)(1.03)](1.03)}_{5000(1.03)^3}} \to \cdots$$

Consequently, the balance at the end of year x is given by

$$f(x) = 5000 \cdot 1.03^x.$$

The balance at the end of nine years is $f(9) = 5000(1.03^9) = \$6523.87$ (rounded to the nearest penny). ∎

EXAMPLE 5

The world population in 1980 was about 4.5 billion people and has been increasing at approximately 1.5% per year.

(a) Estimate the world population in 2010.

(b) In what year will the population be double what it is in 2010?

SOLUTION

(a) The world population in 1981 was

$$4.5 + 1.5\% \text{ of } 4.5 = 4.5 + .015(4.5) = 4.5(1 + .015) = 4.5(1.015).$$

Similarly, in each successive year, the population increased by a factor of 1.015, so the population (in billions) in year x is given by

$$g(x) = 4.5(1.015^x),$$

where $x = 0$ corresponds to 1980. The year 2010 corresponds to $x = 30$, so the population then is $g(30) = 4.5(1.015^{30}) \approx 7.03$ billion people.

(b) Twice the population in 2010 is $2(7.03) = 14.06$ billion. We must find the number x such that $g(x) = 14.06$; that is, we must solve the equation

$$4.5(1.015^x) = 14.06.$$

This can be done with an equation solver or by graphical means, as in Figure 3–19, which shows the intersection point of $y = 4.5(1.015^x)$ and $y = 14.06$. The solution is $x \approx 76.5$, which corresponds to the year 2056. Thus, according to this model, the world population will double in your lifetime. This is what is meant by the population explosion. ∎

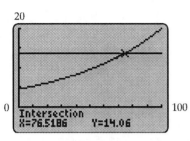

Figure 3–19

Examples 4 and 5 illustrate **exponential growth.** The functions developed there, $f(x) = 5000(1.03^x)$ and $g(x) = 4.5(1.015^x)$, are typical of the general case.

Exponential Growth

Exponential growth can be described by a function of the form

$$f(x) = Pa^x,$$

where $f(x)$ is the quantity at time x, P is the initial quantity (when $x = 0$) and $a > 1$ is the factor by which the quantity changes when x increases by 1.

If the quantity is growing at the rate r per time period, then $a = 1 + r$, and

$$f(x) = Pa^x = P(1 + r)^x.$$

EXAMPLE 6

At the beginning of an experiment, a culture contains 1000 bacteria. Five hours later, there are 7600 bacteria. Assuming that the bacteria grow exponentially, how many will there be after 24 hours?

SOLUTION The bacterial population is given by $f(x) = Pa^x$, where P is the initial population, a is the change factor, and x is the time in hours. We are given that $P = 1000$, so $f(x) = 1000a^x$. The next step is to determine a. Since there are 7600 bacteria when $x = 5$, we have

$$7600 = f(5) = 1000a^5,$$

so

$$1000\, a^5 = 7600$$

$$a^5 = 7.6$$

$$a = \sqrt[5]{7.6} = (7.6)^{.2}.$$

Therefore, the population function is $f(x) = 1000(7.6^{.2})^x = 1000 \cdot (7.6)^{.2x}$. After 24 hours, the bacteria population will be

$$f(24) = 1000(7.6)^{.2(24)} \approx 16{,}900{,}721. \qquad \blacksquare$$

EXPONENTIAL DECAY

In some situations, a quantity *decreases* by a fixed multiplier as time goes on.

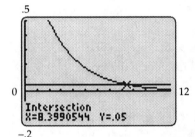

Figure 3–20

EXAMPLE 7

When tap water is filtered through a layer of charcoal and other purifying agents, 30% of the chemical impurities in the water are removed, and 70% remain. If the water is filtered through a second purifying layer, then the amount of impurities remaining is 70% of 70%, that is, $(.7)(.7) = .7^2 = .49$ or 49%. A third layer results in $.7^3$ of the impurities remaining. Thus, the function

$$f(x) = .7^x$$

gives the percentage of impurities remaining in the water after it passes through x layers of purifying material. How many layers are needed to ensure that 95% of the impurities are removed from the water?

SOLUTION   If 95% of the impurities are removed, then 5% will remain. Hence, we must find x such that $f(x) = .05$, that is, we must solve the equation $.7^x = .05$. This can be done numerically or graphically. Figure 3–20 shows that the solution is $x \approx 8.4$, so 8.4 layers of material are needed. $\blacksquare$

Example 7 illustrates **exponential decay.** Note that the impurities were removed at a rate of $30\% = .3$ and that the amount of impurities remaining in the water was changing by a factor of $1 - .30 = .7$. The same thing is true in the general case.

Exponential Decay

Exponential decay can be described by a function of the form

$$f(x) = Pa^x,$$

where $f(x)$ is the quantity at time x, P is the initial quantity (when $x = 0$) and $0 < a < 1$. Here, a is the factor by which the quantity changes when x increases by 1.

If the quantity is decaying at the rate r per time period, then $a = 1 - r$, and

$$f(x) = Pa^x = P(1 - r)^x.$$

GRAPHING EXPLORATION

Determine how many layers are needed to ensure that 99% of the impurities are removed.

One of the important uses of exponential functions is to describe radioactive decay. The **half-life** of a radioactive element is the time it takes a given quantity to decay to one-half of its original mass. The half-life depends only on the substance and not on the size of the sample. Exercise 82 proves the following result.

Radioactive
Decay

> The mass $M(x)$ of a radioactive element at time x is given by
>
> $$M(x) = c(.5^{x/h}),$$
>
> where c is the original mass and h is the half-life of the element.

EXAMPLE 8

Plutonium (^{239}Pu) has a half-life of 24,360 years. So the amount remaining from 1 kilogram after x years is given by

$$M(x) = 1(.5^{x/24360}) = (.5^{1/24360})^x \approx .99997^x.$$

Thus, M is an exponential function whose base is very close to 1. Its graph falls *very slowly* from left to right, as you can easily verify by graphing M in a window with $0 \leq x \leq 2000$. This means that even after an extremely long time, a substantial amount of plutonium will remain. In fact, most of the original kilogram is still there after *ten thousand years* because $M(10,000) \approx .75$ kg. This is the reason that nuclear waste disposal is such a serious problem. ∎

THE NUMBER e AND THE NATURAL EXPONENTIAL FUNCTION

There is an irrational number, denoted e, that arises naturally in a variety of phenomena and plays a central role in the mathematical description of the physical universe. Its decimal expansion begins

$$e = \mathbf{2.718281828459045} \ldots.$$

Your calculator has an e^x key that can be used to evaluate the **natural exponential function** $f(x) = e^x$. If you key in e^1, the calculator will display the first part of the decimal expansion of e.

The graph of $f(x) = e^x$ has the same shape as the graph of $g(x) = 2^x$ in Figure 3–16 but climbs more steeply.

TECHNOLOGY TIP

On most calculators, you use the e^x key, not the x^y or $\wedge$ keys to enter the function $f(x) = e^x$.

GRAPHING EXPLORATION

Graph $f(x) = e^x$, $g(x) = 2^x$, and $h(x) = 3^x$ on the same screen in a window with $-5 \leq x \leq 5$. The Technology Tip in the margin may be helpful.

EXAMPLE 9

Population Growth   If the population of the United States continues to grow as it has recently, then the approximate population of the United States (in millions) in year t will be given by the function

$$P(t) = 227e^{.0093t},$$

where 1980 corresponds to $t = 0$.

(a) Estimate the population in 2015.

(b) When will the population reach half a billion?

SOLUTION

(a) The population in 2015 (that is, $t = 35$) will be approximately

$$P(35) = 227e^{.0093(35)} \approx 314.3 \text{ million people.}$$

(b) Half a billion is 500 million people. So we must find the value of t for which $P(t) = 500$, that is, we must solve the equation

$$227e^{.0093t} = 500.$$

This can be done graphically by finding the intersection of the graph of $P(t)$ and the horizontal line $y = 500$, which occurs when $t \approx 84.9$ (Figure 3–21). Therefore, the population will reach half a billion late in the year 2064.   ∎

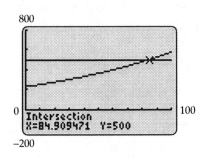

800

0

−200

Intersection
X=84.909471 Y=500

100

Figure 5–21

OTHER EXPONENTIAL FUNCTIONS

The population growth models in earlier examples do not take into account factors that may limit population growth in the future (wars, new diseases, etc.). Example 10 illustrates a function, called a **logistic model,** that is designed to model such situations more accurately.

EXAMPLE 10

Inhibited Population Growth   There is an upper limit on the fish population in a certain lake due to the oxygen supply, available food, etc. The population of fish in this lake at time t months is given by the function

$$p(t) = \frac{20{,}000}{1 + 24e^{-t/4}} \qquad (t \geq 0).$$

What is the upper limit on the fish population?

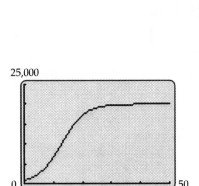

25,000

0
0

50

Figure 3–22

SOLUTION   The graph of $p(t)$ in Figure 3–22 suggests that the horizontal line $y = 20{,}000$ is a horizontal asymptote of the graph.

In other words, the fish population never goes above 20,000. You can confirm this algebraically by rewriting the rule of p in this form.

$$p(t) = \frac{20{,}000}{1 + 24e^{-t/4}} = \frac{20{,}000}{1 + \dfrac{24}{e^{t/4}}}.$$

When t is very large, so is $t/4$, which means that $e^{t/4}$ is huge. Hence, by the Big-Little Principle (page 288), $\dfrac{24}{e^{t/4}}$ is very close to 0, and $p(t)$ is very close to $\dfrac{20{,}000}{1 + 0} = 20{,}000$. Since $e^{t/4}$ is positive, the denominator of $p(t)$ is slightly bigger than 1, so $p(t)$ is always less than 20,000.   ∎

When a cable, such as a power line, is suspended between towers of equal height as in Figure 3–23, it forms a curve called a **catenary,** which is the graph of a function of the form

$$f(x) = A(e^{kx} + e^{-kx})$$

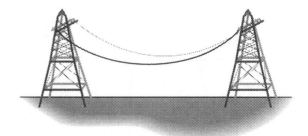

Figure 3–23

for suitable constants A and k. The Gateway Arch in St. Louis (Figure 3–24) has the shape of an inverted catenary, which was chosen because it evenly distributes the internal structural forces.

Figure 3–24

GRAPHING EXPLORATION

Graph each of the following functions in the window with $-5 \leq x \leq 5$ and $-10 \leq y \leq 80$.

$$y_1 = 10(e^{.4x} + e^{-.4x}), \qquad y_2 = 10(e^{.2x} + e^{-.2x}),$$
$$y_3 = 10(e^{.3x} + e^{-.3x}).$$

How does the coefficient of x affect the shape of the graph?

Predict the shape of the graph of $y = -y_1 + 80$. Confirm your answer by graphing.

EXERCISES 3.2

In Exercises 1–10, sketch a complete graph of the function.

1. $f(x) = 3^{-x}$

2. $f(x) = (1.001)^{-x}$

3. $g(x) = (5/2)^x$

4. $g(x) = (1.001)^x$

5. $h(x) = (1/\pi)^x$

6. $h(x) = (1/e)^{-x}$

7. $f(x) = 1 - 2^{-x}$

8. $g(x) = (1.2)^x + (.8)^{-x}$

9. $h(x) = 2^{x^2}$

10. $h(x) = 2^{-x^2}$

In Exercises 11–16, list the transformations needed to transform the graph of $h(x) = 2^x$ into the graph of the given function. [Section 3.4 may be helpful.]

11. $f(x) = 2^x - 5$

12. $g(x) = -(2^x)$

13. $k(x) = 3(2^x)$

14. $g(x) = 2^{x-1}$

15. $f(x) = 2^{x+2} - 5$

16. $g(x) = -5(2^{x-1}) + 7$

In Exercises 17 and 18, match the functions to the graphs. Assume $a > 1$ and $c > 1$.

17. $f(x) = a^x$
    $g(x) = a^{x+1}$
    $h(x) = a^x + 1$
    $j(x) = (a + 1)^x$

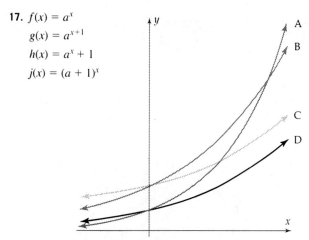

18. $f(x) = c^x$
    $g(x) = \left(\dfrac{1}{c}\right)^x$
    $h(x) = c^{1/x}$

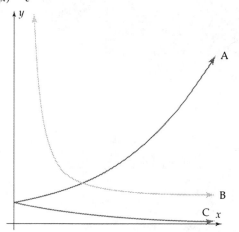

In Exercises 19–23, determine whether the function is even, odd, or neither (see Special Topics 3.4.A).

19. $f(x) = 10^x$

20. $g(x) = 2^x - x$

21. $f(x) = \dfrac{e^x + e^{-x}}{2}$

22. $f(x) = \dfrac{e^x - e^{-x}}{2}$

23. $f(x) = e^{-x^2}$

24. Use the Big-Little Principle to explain why $e^x + e^{-x}$ is approximately equal to e^x when x is large.

In Exercises 25–32, find the average rate of change of the function.

25. $f(x) = 3(4^x)$ as x goes from 1 to 3

26. $f(x) = 3(4^x)$ as x goes from 10 to 12

27. $g(x) = 3^{x^2 - x - 3}$ as x goes from -1 to 1

28. $h(x) = 2^x$ as x goes from 1 to 2

29. $h(x) = 2^x$ as x goes from 1 to 1.001

30. $h(x) = e^x$ as x goes from 1 to 2

31. $h(x) = e^x$ as x goes from 1 to 1.001

32. $f(x) = a^x$, $a > 0$, as x goes from 0 to 0.001

In Exercises 33–36, find the difference quotient of the function.

33. $f(x) = 10^x$

34. $g(x) = 5^{x^2}$

35. $f(x) = 2^x + 2^{-x}$

36. $f(x) = e^x - e^{-x}$

In Exercises 37–44, find a viewing window (or windows) that shows a complete graph of the function.

37. $k(x) = e^{-x}$

38. $f(x) = e^{-x^2}$

39. $f(x) = \dfrac{e^x + e^{-x}}{2}$

40. $h(x) = \dfrac{e^x - e^{-x}}{2}$

41. $g(x) = 2^x - x$

42. $k(x) = \dfrac{2}{e^x + e^{-x}}$

43. $f(x) = \dfrac{5}{1 + e^{-x}}$

44. $g(x) = \dfrac{10}{1 + 9e^{-x/2}}$

In Exercises 45–50, list all asymptotes of the graph of the function and the approximate coordinates of each local extremum.

45. $f(x) = x2^x$

46. $g(x) = x2^{-x}$

47. $h(x) = e^{x^2/2}$

48. $k(x) = 2^{x^2 - 6x + 2}$

49. $f(x) = e^{-x^2}$

50. $g(x) = -xe^{x^2/20}$

51. There is a colony of fruit flies in Andy's kitchen. Assume we can model the population t days from now by the function $p(t) = 100 \cdot (12)^{t/10}$. An average fruit fly is about .1 inches long.

    (a) How many fruit flies are currently in Andy's kitchen?
    (b) How many will there be at this time next week? In two weeks?
    (c) In how many days will the population reach 2500?
    (d) Is it realistic to assume that this model will remain valid for a year? Justify your answer. [*Hint:* According to the model, what will the population be in a year?]

52. If current rates of deforestation and fossil fuel consumption continue, then the amount of atmospheric carbon dioxide in parts per million (ppm) will be given by $f(x) = 375e^{.00609x}$, where $x = 0$ corresponds to 2000.*

    (a) What is the amount of carbon dioxide in 2003? In 2022?
    (b) In what year will the amount of carbon dioxide reach 500 ppm?

53. The pressure of the atmosphere $p(x)$ (in pounds per square inch) is given by

$$p(x) = ke^{-.0000425x},$$

---
*Based on projections from the International Panel on Climate Change.

where x is the height above sea level (in feet) and k is a constant.

(a) Use the fact that the pressure at sea level is 15 pounds per square inch to find k.
(b) What is the pressure at 5000 feet?
(c) If you were in a spaceship at an altitude of 160,000 feet, what would the pressure be?

54. (a) The function $g(t) = .6 - e^{-0.479t}$ gives the percentage of the United States population (expressed as a decimal) that has seen a new television show t weeks after it goes on the air. According to this model, what percentage of people have seen the show after 24 weeks?
(b) The show will be renewed if over half the population has seen it at least once. Approximately when will 50% of the people have seen the show?
(c) According to this model, when will 59.9% of the people have seen it? When will 60% have seen it?

55. According to data from the National Center for Health Statistics, the life expectancy at birth for a person born in a year x is approximated by the function

$$D(x) = \frac{79.257}{1 + 9.7135 \times 10^{24} \cdot e^{-.0304x}}$$

$$(1900 \le x \le 2050).$$

(a) What is the life expectancy of someone born in 1980? in 2000?
(b) In what year was life expectancy at birth 60 years?

56. The number of subscribers to basic cable TV (in millions) can be approximated by

$$g(x) = \frac{76.7}{1 + 16(.8444^x)},$$

where $x = 0$ corresponds to 1970.*

(a) Estimate the number of subscribers in 2005 and 2010.
(b) When does the number of subscribers reach 70 million?
(c) According to this model, will the number of subscribers ever each 90 million?

57. (a) The beaver population near a certain lake in year t is approximately

$$p(t) = \frac{2000}{1 + 199e^{-.5544t}}.$$

What is the population now ($t = 0$) and what will it be in 5 years?
(b) Approximately when will there be 1000 beavers?

58. The Gateway Arch (Figure 5–15) is 630 feet high and 630 feet wide at ground level. Suppose it were placed on a coordinate plane with the x-axis at ground level and the y-axis going through the center of the arch. Find a catenary

*Based on data from *The Cable TV Financial Datebook* and *The Pay TV Newsletter.*

function $g(x) = A(e^{kx} + e^{-kx})$ and a constant C such that the graph of the function $f(x) = g(x) + C$ provides a model of the arch. [*Hint:* Experiment with various values of A, k, C as in the Graphing Exploration on page 365. Many correct answers are possible.]

59. (a) A genetic engineer is growing cells in a fermenter. The cells multiply by splitting in half every 15 minutes. The new cells have the same DNA as the original ones. Complete the following table.

Time (hours)	Number of Cells
0	1
.25	2
.5	4
.75	
1	

(b) Write the rule of the function that gives the number of C cells at time t hours.

60. Do Exercise 59, using the following table, instead of the given one.

Time (hours)	Number of Cells
0	300
.25	600
.5	1200
.75	
1	

61. A weekly census of the tree-frog population in Frog Hollow State Park produces the following results.

Week	1	2	3	4	5	6
Population	18	54	162	486	1458	4374

(a) Find a function of the form $f(x) = Pa^x$ that describes the frog population at time x weeks.
(b) What is the growth factor in this situation (that is, by what number must this week's population be multiplied to obtain next week's population)?
(c) Each tree frog requires 10 square feet of space and the park has an area of 6.2 square miles. Will the space required by the frog population exceed the size of the park in 12 weeks? In 14 weeks? [Remember: 1 square mile = 5280^2 square feet.]

62. An eccentric billionaire offers you a job for the month of September. She says that she will pay you 2¢ on the first day, 4¢ on the second day, 8¢ on the third day, and so on, doubling your pay on each successive day.

(a) Let $P(x)$ denote your salary in *dollars* on day x. Find the rule of the function P.
(b) Would you be better off financially if instead you were paid $10,000 per day? [*Hint:* Consider $P(30)$.]

63. Take an ordinary piece of typing paper and fold it in half; then the folded sheet is twice as thick as the single sheet was. Fold it in half again so that it is twice as thick as before. Keep folding it in half as long as you can. Soon the folded paper will be so thick and small that you will be unable to continue, but suppose you could keep folding the paper as many times as you wanted. Assume that the paper is .002 inches thick.

(a) Make a table showing the thickness of the folded paper for the first four folds (with fold 0 being the thickness of the original unfolded paper).

(b) Find a function of the form $f(x) = Pa^x$ that describes the thickness of the folded paper after x folds.

(c) How thick would the paper be after 20 folds?

(d) How many folds would it take to reach the moon (which is 243,000 miles from the earth)? [*Hint:* One mile is 5280 feet.]

64. The figure is the graph of an exponential growth function $f(x) = Pa^x$.

(a) In this case, what is P? [*Hint:* What is $f(0)$?]

(b) Find the rule of the function f by finding a. [*Hint:* What is $f(2)$?]

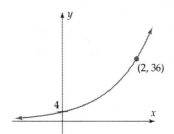

65. Suppose you invest $1200 in an account that pays 4% interest, compounded annually and paid from date of deposit to date of withdrawal.

(a) Find the rule of the function f that gives the amount you would receive if you closed the account after x years.

(b) How much would you receive after 3 years? After 5 years and 9 months?

(c) When should you close the account to receive $1850?

66. Anne now has a balance of $800 on her credit card, on which 1.5% interest per month is charged. Assume that she makes no further purchases or payments (and that the credit card company doesn't turn her account over to a bill collector).

(a) Find the rule of the function g that gives Anne's total credit card debt after x months.

(b) How much will Anne owe after one year? After two years?

(c) When will she owe twice the amount she owes now?

67. The population of Mexico was 100.4 million in 2000 and is expected to grow at the rate of 1.4% per year.

(a) Find the rule of the function f that gives Mexico's population (in millions) in year x, with $x = 0$ corresponding to 2000.

(b) Estimate Mexico's population in 2010.

(c) When will the population reach 125 million people?

68. The number of digital devices (such as MP3 players, hand-held computers, cell phones, and PCs) in the world was approximately .94 billion in 1999 and is growing at a rate of 28.3% a year.*

(a) Find the rule of a function that gives the number of digital devices (in billions) in year x, with $x = 0$ corresponding to 1999.

(b) Approximately how many digital devices will be in use in 2010?

(c) If this model remains accurate, when will the number of digital devices reach 6 billion?

69. The U.S. Census Bureau estimates that the Hispanic population in the United States will increase from 32.44 million in 2000 to 98.23 million in 2050.†

(a) Find an exponential function that gives the Hispanic population in year x, with $x = 0$ corresponding to 2000.

(b) What is the projected Hispanic population in 2010 and 2025?

(c) In what year will the Hispanic population reach 55 million?

70. The U.S. Department of Commerce estimated that there were 54 million Internet users in the United States in 1999 and 85 million in 2002.

(a) Find an exponential function that models the number of Internet users in year x, with $x = 0$ corresponding to 1999.

(b) For how long is this model likely to remain accurate? [*Hint:* The current U.S. population is about 305 million.]

71. At the beginning of an experiment, a culture contains 200 *H. pylori* bacteria. An hour later there are 205 bacteria. Assuming that the *H. pylori* bacteria grow exponentially, how many will there be after 10 hours? After 2 days?

72. The population of India was approximately 1030 million in 2001 and was 967 million in 1997. If the population continues to grow exponentially at the same rate, what will it be in 2010?

73. Kerosene is passed through a pipe filled with clay to remove various pollutants. Each foot of pipe removes 25% of the pollutants.

(a) Write the rule of a function that gives the percentage of pollutants remaining in the kerosene after it has passed through x feet of pipe. [See Example 7.]

(b) How many feet of pipe are needed to ensure that 90% of the pollutants have been removed from the kerosene?

74. If inflation runs at a steady 3% per year, then the amount a dollar is worth decreases by 3% each year.

(a) Write the rule of a function that gives the value of a dollar in year x.

(b) How much will the dollar be worth in 5 years? In 10 years?

(c) How many years will it take before today's dollar is worth only a dime?

75. You have 5 grams of carbon-14, whose half-life is 5730 years.

(a) Write the rule of the function that gives the amount of carbon-14 remaining after x years. [See the box preceding Example 8.]

(b) How much carbon-14 will be left after 4000 years? After 8000 years?

(c) When will there be just 1 gram left?

76. (a) The half-life of radium is 1620 years. If you start with 100 milligrams of radium, what is the rule of the function that gives the amount remaining after t years?

(b) How much radium is left after 800 years? After 1600 years? After 3200 years?

THINKERS

77. Find a function $f(x)$ with the property $f(r + s) = f(r)f(s)$ for all real numbers r and s.

78. Find a function $g(x)$ with the property $g(2x) = (g(x))^2$ for every real number x.

79. (a) Using the viewing window with $-4 \leq x \leq 4$ and $-1 \leq y \leq 8$, graph $f(x) = \left(\frac{1}{2}\right)^x$ and $g(x) = 2^x$ on the same screen. If you think of the y-axis as a mirror, how would you describe the relationship between the two graphs?

(b) Without graphing, explain how the graphs of $g(x) = 2^x$ and $k(x) = 2^{-x}$ are related.

80. Look back at Section 4.4, where the basic properties of graphs of polynomial functions were discussed. Then review the basic properties of the graph of $f(x) = a^x$ discussed in this section. Using these various properties, give an argument to show that for any fixed positive number $a(\neq 1)$, it is *not* possible to find a polynomial function

$g(x) = c_n x^n + \cdots + c_1 x + c_0$ such that $a^x = g(x)$ for *all* numbers x. In other words, *no exponential function is a polynomial function.* However, see Exercise 81.

81. Approximating exponential functions by polynomials. For each positive integer n, let f_n be the polynomial function whose rule is

$$f_n(x) = 1 + x + \frac{x^2}{2!} + \frac{x^3}{3!} + \frac{x^4}{4!} + \cdots + \frac{x^n}{n!},$$

where $k!$ is the product $1 \cdot 2 \cdot 3 \cdots k$.

(a) Using the viewing window with $-4 \leq x \leq 4$ and $-5 \leq y \leq 55$, graph $g(x) = e^x$ and $f_4(x)$ on the same screen. Do the graphs appear to coincide?

(b) Replace the graph of $f_4(x)$ by that of $f_5(x)$, then by $f_6(x)$, $f_7(x)$, and so on until you find a polynomial $f_n(x)$ whose graph appears to coincide with the graph of $g(x) = e^x$ in this viewing window. Use the trace feature to move from graph to graph at the same value of x to see how accurate this approximation is.

(c) Change the viewing window so that $-6 \leq x \leq 6$ and $-10 \leq y \leq 400$. Is the polynomial you found in part (b) a good approximation for $g(x)$ in this viewing window? What polynomial is?

82. This exercise provides a justification for the claim that the function $M(x) = c(.5)^{x/h}$ gives the mass after x years of a radioactive element with half-life h years. Suppose we have c grams of an element that has a half-life of 50 years. Then after 50 years, we would have $c\left(\frac{1}{2}\right)$ grams. After another 50 years, we would have half of that, namely, $c\left(\frac{1}{2}\right)\left(\frac{1}{2}\right) = c\left(\frac{1}{2}\right)^2$.

(a) How much remains after a third 50-year period? After a fourth 50-year period?

(b) How much remains after t 50-year periods?

(c) If x is the number of years, then $x/50$ is the number of 50-year periods. By replacing the number of periods t in part (b) by $x/50$, you obtain the amount remaining after x years. This gives the function $M(x)$ when $h = 50$. The same argument works in the general case (just replace 50 by h). Find $M(x)$.

3.3   Logarithmic Functions*

Section Objectives

■ Evaluate common and natural logarithms.

■ Translate logarithmic statements in exponential statements, and vice-versa.

■ Use the properties of logarithms.

■ Find the graphs of logarithmic functions.

*Section 3.7 (Inverse Functions) is a prerequisite for this section.

Roadmap

We begin with the only logarithms that are in widespread use, common and natural logarithms. Natural logarithms are emphasized because of their central role in calculus. Those who prefer to begin with logarithms to an arbitrary base b should cover Special Topics 3.4.A before reading this section.

The discovery of logarithms in the seventeenth century allowed scientists to perform many crucial computations that previously had been too difficult to be practical. Although computers now handle these computations, logarithms are still extremely useful in the sciences and engineering. Logarithmic functions provide excellent models of different phenomena, including sound volume, earthquake intensity, the perceived brightness of stars, computational complexity, the spread of certain kinds of diseases, the growth of rumors, and much more. Logarithms also have properties that make it possible to solve certain types of equations more easily.

COMMON LOGARITHMS

The exponential function $f(x) = 10^x$, whose graph is shown in Figure 3–25, is an increasing function and hence is one-to-one (as explained on page 219). Therefore, f has an inverse function g whose graph is the reflection of the graph of f in the line $y = x$ (see page 225), as shown in Figure 3–26.*

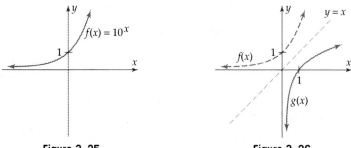

Figure 3–25   Figure 3–26

This inverse function g is called the **common logarithmic function.** The value of this function at the number x is denoted **log x** and called the **common logarithm** of the number x. Every calculator has a LOG key for evaluating the function $g(x) = \log x$. For instance,

$$\log .01 = -2, \qquad \log .6 = -.2218, \qquad \text{and} \qquad \log 10000 = 5^{\dagger}$$

As we saw in Section 3.7, the relationship between a function f and its inverse function g is given by

$$g(v) = u \qquad \text{exactly when} \qquad f(u) = v.$$

When $f(x) = 10^x$ and $g(x) = \log x$, this statement takes the following form.

Definition of Common Logarithms

Let u and v be real numbers, with $v > 0$. Then

$$\log v = u \qquad \text{exactly when} \qquad 10^u = v.$$

In other words,

log v is the exponent to which 10 must be raised to produce v.

---

*Parametric equations for the graph of $f(x) = 10^x$ can be obtained by letting

$$x = t \qquad \text{and} \qquad y = 10^t \quad (t \text{ any real number}).$$

As explained on page 224, parametric equations for the graph of the inverse function g can then be obtained by letting

$$x = 10^t \qquad \text{and} \qquad y = t \quad (t \text{ any real number}).$$

This trick will allow you to display the graphs of Figure 5–19 on your calculator in parametric mode.
†Here and below, all logarithms are rounded to four decimal places, and an equal sign is used rather than the more correct "approximately equal." The word "common" will be omitted except when it is necessary to distinguish these logarithms from other types that are introduced below.

EXAMPLE 1

Without using a calculator, find

(a) log 1000   (b) log 1   (c) log $\sqrt{10}$ (d) $\log\left(\dfrac{1}{\sqrt{10}}\right)$

SOLUTION

(a) To find log 1000, ask yourself, "What power of 10 equals 1000?" The answer is 3 because $10^3 = 1000$. Therefore, log 1000 = 3.

(b) To what power must 10 be raised to produce 1? Since $10^0 = 1$, we conclude that log 1 = 0.

(c) Log $\sqrt{10} = 1/2$ because $1/2$ is the exponent to which 10 must be raised to produce $\sqrt{10}$, that is $10^{1/2} = \sqrt{10}$.

(d) Log $\dfrac{1}{\sqrt{10}} = -1/2$ because $10^{-1/2} = \dfrac{1}{\sqrt{10}}$. ∎

EXAMPLE 2

Translate each of the following logarithmic statements into an equivalent exponential statement.

$$\log 29 = 1.4624 \qquad \log .47 = -.3279 \qquad \log (k + t) = d.$$

SOLUTION
Using the definition above, we have these translations.

Logarithmic Statement	Equivalent Exponential Statement
$\log 29 = 1.4624$	$10^{1.4624} = 29$
$\log .47 = -.3279$	$10^{-.3279} = .47$
$\log (k + t) = d$	$10^d = k + t$ ∎

EXAMPLE 3

Translate each of the following exponential statements into an equivalent logarithmic statement.

$$10^{5.5} = 316,227.766 \qquad 10^{.66} = 4.5708819 \qquad 10^{rs} = t$$

SOLUTION
Translate as follows.

Exponential Statement	Equivalent Logarithmic Statement
$10^{5.5} = 316,277.766$	$\log 316,277.766 = 5.5$
$10^{.66} = 4.5708819$	$\log 4.5708819 = .66$
$10^{rs} = t$	$\log t = rs$ ∎

EXAMPLE 4

Solve the equation log $x = 4$.

SOLUTION
log $x = 4$ is equivalent to $10^4 = x$. So the solution is $x = 10,000$. ∎

NATURAL LOGARITHMS

Common logarithms are closely related to the exponential function $f(x) = 10^x$. With the advent of calculus, however, it became clear that the most useful exponential function in science and engineering is $g(x) = e^x$. Consequently, a new type of logarithm, based on the number e instead of 10, was developed. This development is essentially a copy of what was done above, with some minor changes in notation.

The exponential function $f(x) = e^x$ whose graph is shown in Figure 3–27 is increasing and hence one-to-one, so f has an inverse function g whose graph is the reflection of the graph of f in the line $y = x$, as shown in Figure 3–28.

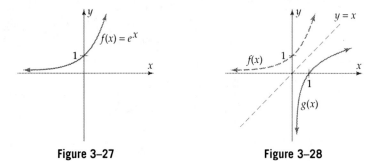

Figure 3–27   Figure 3–28

This inverse function g is called the **natural logarithmic function.** The value $g(x)$ of this function at a number x is denoted **ln x** and called the **natural logarithm** of the number x. Every calculator has an LN key for evaluating natural logarithms. For instance,

$$\ln .15 = -1.8971, \quad \ln 186 = 5.2257, \quad \text{and} \quad \ln 2.718 = .9999.$$

When the relationship of inverse functions (Section 3.7)

$$g(v) = u \qquad \text{exactly when} \qquad f(u) = v$$

is applied to the function $f(x) = e^x$ and its inverse $g(x) = \ln x$, it says the following.

Definition of
Natural Logarithms

> Let u and v be real numbers, with $v > 0$. Then
>
> $$\ln v = u \qquad \text{exactly when} \qquad e^u = v.$$
>
> In other words,
>
> $$\ln v \text{ is the exponent to which } e \text{ must be raised to produce } v.$$

EXAMPLE 5

Translate:

(a) $\ln 14 = 2.6391$ into an equivalent exponential statement.

(b) $e^{5.0626} = 158$ into an equivalent logarithmic statement.

SOLUTION

(a) Using the preceding definition, we see that $\ln 14 = 2.6391$ is equivalent to $e^{2.6391} = 14$.

(b) Similarly, $e^{5.0626} = 158$ is equivalent to $\ln 158 = 5.0626$. ∎

PROPERTIES OF LOGARITHMS

Since common and natural logarithms have almost identical definitions (just replace 10 by e), it is not surprising that they share the same essential properties. You don't need a calculator to understand these properties. You need only use the definition of logarithms or translate logarithmic statements into equivalent exponential ones (or vice versa).

EXAMPLE 6

What is $\ln(-10)$?

Translation: To what power must e be raised to produce -10?

Answer: The graph of $f(x) = e^x$ in Figure 3–27 shows that every power of e is *positive*. So e^x can *never* be -10 or any negative number or zero, and hence, $\ln(-10)$ is not defined. Similarly, $\log(-10)$ is not defined because every power of 10 is positive. Therefore,

$\ln v$ and $\log v$ are defined only when $v > 0$. ■

EXAMPLE 7

What is $\ln 1$?

Translation: To what power must e be raised to produce 1?

Answer: We know that $e^0 = 1$, which means that $\ln 1 = 0$. Combining this fact with Example 1(b), we have

$$\ln 1 = 0 \quad \text{and} \quad \log 1 = 0.$$ ■

EXAMPLE 8

What is $\ln e^9$?

Translation: To what power must e be raised to produce e^9?

Answer: Obviously, the answer is 9. So $\ln e^9 = 9$ and in general

$$\ln e^k = k \quad \text{for every real number } k.$$

Similarly,

$$\log 10^k = k \quad \text{for every real number } k$$

because k is the exponent to which 10 must be raised to produce 10^k. In particular, when $k = 1$, we have

$$\ln e = 1 \quad \text{and} \quad \log 10 = 1.$$ ■

EXAMPLE 9

Find $10^{\log 678}$ and $e^{\ln 678}$.

SOLUTION By definition, log 678 is the exponent to which 10 must be raised to produce 678. So if you raise 10 to this exponent, the answer will be 678, that is, $10^{\log 678} = 678$.* Similarly, ln 678 is the exponent to which e must be raised to produce 678, so that $e^{\ln 678} = 678$. The same argument works with any positive number v in place of 678:

$$e^{\ln v} = v \qquad \text{and} \qquad 10^{\log v} = v \quad \text{for every } v > 0. \qquad \blacksquare$$

The facts presented in the preceding examples may be summarized as follows.

Properties of Logarithms

Natural Logarithms	Common Logarithms
1. ln v is defined only when $v > 0$;	log v is defined only when $v > 0$.
2. ln $1 = 0$ and ln $e = 1$;	log $1 = 0$ and log $10 = 1$.
3. ln $e^k = k$ for every real number k;	log $10^k = k$ for every real number k.
4. $e^{\ln v} = v$ for every $v > 0$;	$10^{\log v} = v$ for every $v > 0$.

EXAMPLE 10

Applying Property 3 with $k = 2x^2 + 7x + 9$ shows that

$$\ln e^{2x^2+7x+9} = 2x^2 + 7x + 9. \qquad \blacksquare$$

EXAMPLE 11

Solve the equation $\ln(x + 1) = 2$.

SOLUTION Since $\ln(x + 1) = 2$, we have

$$e^{\ln(x+1)} = e^2.$$

Applying Property 4 with $v = x + 1$ shows that

$$x + 1 = e^{\ln(x+1)} = e^2$$
$$x = e^2 - 1 \approx 6.3891. \qquad \blacksquare$$

Property 4 has another interesting consequence. If a is any positive number, then $e^{\ln a} = a$. Hence, the rule of the exponential function $f(x) = a^x$ can be written as

$$f(x) = a^x = (e^{\ln a})^x = e^{(\ln a)x}.$$

---

*This is equivalent, in a sense, to answering the question "Who is the author whose name is Stephen King?" The answer is described in the question!

For example, $f(x) = 2^x = e^{(\ln 2)x} \approx e^{.6931x}$. Thus, we have this useful result.

Exponential Functions

Every exponential growth or decay function can be written in the form

$$f(x) = Pe^{kx},$$

where $f(x)$ is the amount at time x, P is the initial quantity, and k is positive for growth and negative for decay.

EXAMPLE 12

Write $f(x) = 3 \cdot 5^x$ in the form $f(x) = Pe^{kx}$.

SOLUTION
$$3 \cdot 5^x = 3 \cdot (e^{\ln 5})^x$$
$$= 3e^{\ln 5 \cdot x}$$
$$\approx 3e^{1.6094x}$$

■

GRAPHS OF LOGARITHMIC FUNCTIONS

Figure 3–29 shows the graphs of two more entries in the catalog of basic functions, $f(x) = \log x$ and $g(x) = \ln x$. Both are increasing functions with these four properties:

Domain: all positive real numbers   **x-intercept:** 1
Range: all real numbers   **Vertical Asymptote:** y-axis

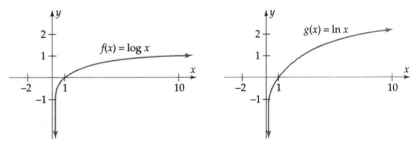

Figure 3–29

Calculators and computers do not accurately show that the y-axis is a vertical asymptote of these graphs. By evaluating the functions at very small numbers (such as $x = 1/10^{500}$), you can see that the graphs go lower and lower as x gets closer to 0. On a calculator, however, the graph will appear to end abruptly near the y-axis (try it!).

Some viewing windows may give the impression that logarithmic graphs (such as those in Figures 3–27 and 3–28) have horizontal asymptotes. Don't be fooled! These graphs have no horizontal asymptotes—the y-values get arbitrarily large.

EXAMPLE 13

Sketch the graph of $f(x) = \ln(x - 2)$.

SOLUTION   Using a calculator to graph $f(x) = \ln(x - 2)$, we obtain Figure 3–30, in which the graph appears to end abruptly near $x = 2$. Fortunately, however, we have read Section 3.4, so we know that this is *not* how the graph looks. From Section 3.4, we know that the graph of $f(x) = \ln(x - 2)$ is the graph of $g(x) = \ln x$ shifted horizontally 2 units to the right, as shown in Figure 3–31. In particular, the graph of f has a vertical asymptote at $x = 2$ and drops sharply downward there.   ∎

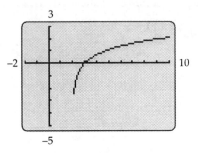

Figure 3–30   Figure 3–31

GRAPHING EXPLORATION

Graph $y_1 = \ln(x - 2)$ and $y_2 = -5$ in the same viewing window and verify that the graphs do not appear to intersect, as they should. Nevertheless, try to solve the equation $\ln(x - 2) = -5$ by finding the intersection point of y_1 and y_2. Some calculators will find the intersection point even through it does not show on the screen. Others produce an error message, in which case the SOLVER feature should be used instead of a graphical solution.

Although logarithms are only defined for positive numbers, many logarithmic functions include negative numbers in their domains.

EXAMPLE 14

Find the domain of each of the following functions.

(a) $f(x) = \ln(x + 4)$ (b) $g(x) = \log x^2$

SOLUTION

(a) $f(x) = \ln(x + 4)$ is defined only when $x + 4 > 0$, that is, when $x > -4$. So the domain of f consists of all real numbers greater than -4.

(b) Since $x^2 > 0$ for all nonzero x, the domain of $g(x) = \log x^2$ consists of all real numbers except 0.   ∎

GRAPHING EXPLORATION

Verify the conclusions of Example 14 by graphing each of the functions. What is the vertical asymptote of each graph?

EXERCISES 3.3

Unless stated otherwise, all letters represent positive numbers.

In Exercises 1–4, find the logarithm, without using a calculator.

1. $\log 10{,}000$
2. $\log .001$
3. $\log \dfrac{\sqrt{10}}{1000}$
4. $\log \sqrt[3]{.01}$

In Exercises 5–14, translate the given logarithmic statement into an equivalent exponential statement.

5. $\log 1000 = 3$
6. $\log .001 = -3$
7. $\log 750 = 2.88$
8. $\log (.8) = -.097$
9. $\ln 3 = 1.0986$
10. $\log (\log(x)) = 1$
11. $\ln .01 = -4.6052$
12. $\ln s = r$
13. $\ln (x^2 + 2y) = z + w$
14. $\log (a + c) = d$

In Exercises 15–24, translate the given exponential statement into an equivalent logarithmic statement.

15. $10^{-2} = .01$
16. $10^3 = 1000$
17. $10^{.4771} = 3$
18. $10^{3k} = 6r$
19. $e^{3.25} = 25.79$
20. $e^{3.14} = 23.1039$
21. $e^{12/7} = 5.5527$
22. $e^k = t$
23. $e^{2/r} = w$
24. $e^e = 15.1543$

In Exercises 25–36, evaluate the given expression without using a calculator.

25. $\log 10^{\sqrt{43}}$
26. $\log 10^{\sqrt[3]{r^2 - s^2}}$
27. $\ln e^{15}$
28. $e^{\ln \pi}$
29. $\ln \sqrt{e}$
30. $\ln \sqrt[5]{e}$
31. $e^{\ln 931}$
32. $\log (\log(10{,}000{,}000{,}000))$
33. $\ln e^{x+y}$
34. $\ln e^{x^2 + 2y}$
35. $e^{\ln x^2}$
36. $e^{\ln(\ln 2)}$

In Exercises 37–40, write the rule of the function in the form $f(x) = Pe^{kx}$. (See the discussion and box after Example 11.)

37. $f(x) = 4(25^x)$
38. $g(x) = 3.9(1.03^x)$
39. $g(x) = -16(30.5^x)$
40. $f(x) = -2.2(.75^x)$

In Exercises 41–42, write the rule of the function in the form $f(x) = a^x$. (See the discussion and box after Example 11.)

41. $g(x) = e^{-3x}$
42. $f(x) = e^{1.6094x}$

In Exercises 43–46, find the domain of the given function (that is, the largest set of real numbers for which the rule produces well-defined real numbers).

43. $f(x) = \ln (x + 1)$
44. $g(x) = \ln (x + 2)$
45. $h(x) = \log (-x)$
46. $k(x) = \log (\ln (2) - x)$

47. (a) Graph $y = x$ and $y = e^{\ln x}$ in separate viewing windows [or use a split-screen if your calculator has that feature]. For what values of x are the graphs identical?
    (b) Use the properties of logarithms to explain your answer in part (a).

48. (a) Graph $y = x$ and $y = \ln (e^x)$ in separate viewing windows [or a split-screen if your calculator has that feature]. For what values of x are the graphs identical?
    (b) Use the properties of logarithms to explain your answer in part (a).

49. Do the graphs of $f(x) = \log x^2$ and $g(x) = 2 \log x$ appear to be the same? How do they differ?

50. Do the graphs of $h(x) = \log x^3$ and $k(x) = 3 \log x$ appear to be the same?

In Exercises 51–56, list the transformations that will change the graph of $g(x) = \ln x$ into the graph of the given function. [Section 3.4 may be helpful.]

51. $f(x) = 2 \cdot \ln x$
52. $f(x) = \ln x - 7$
53. $h(x) = \ln (x - 4)$
54. $k(x) = \ln (x + 2)$
55. $h(x) = \ln (x + 3) - 4$
56. $k(x) = \ln (x - 2) + 2$

In Exercises 57–60, sketch the graph of the function.

57. $f(x) = \log (x - 3)$
58. $g(x) = 2 \ln x + 3$
59. $h(x) = -2 \log x$
60. $f(x) = \ln (-x) - 3$

In Exercises 61–68, find a viewing window (or windows) that shows a complete graph of the function.

61. $f(x) = \dfrac{x}{\ln x}$
62. $g(x) = \dfrac{\ln x}{x}$
63. $h(x) = \dfrac{\ln x^2}{x}$
64. $k(x) = e^{2/\ln x}$
65. $f(x) = 10 \log x - x$
66. $f(x) = \dfrac{\log x}{x}$
67. $l(x) = e^{e^x}$
68. $r(x) = \ln(e^x)$

In Exercises 69–72, find the average rate of change of the function.

69. $f(x) = \ln (x - 2)$, as x goes from 3 to 5.
70. $g(x) = x - \ln x$, as x goes from .5 to 1.

71. $g(x) = \log (x^2 + x + 1)$, as x goes from -5 to -3.

72. $f(x) = x \log |x|$, as x goes from 1 to 4.

73. (a) What is the average change of $f(t) = \ln t$, as t goes from 2 to $2 + h$?

(b) What is the average change of $f(t) = \ln t$, as t goes from 2 to $2 + h$ when h is .01? When h is .001? .0001? .00001?

(c) What is the average change of $f(t) = \ln t$, as t goes from 4 to $4 + h$ when h is .01? When h is .001? .0001? .00001?

(d) Approximate the average change of $f(t) = \ln t$, as t goes from 5 to $5 + h$ for very small values of h.

(e) Work some more examples like those above. What is the average rate of change of $f(t) = \ln t$, as t goes from x to $x + h$ for very small values of h?

74. (a) Find the average rate of change of $f(x) = \ln x^2$, as x goes from .5 to 2.

(b) Find the average rate of change of $g(x) = \ln (x - 3)^2$, as x goes from 3.5 to 5.

(c) What is the relationship between your answers in parts (a) and (b) and why is this so?

75. Show that $g(x) = \ln \left(\dfrac{x}{1 - x} \right)$ is the inverse function of

$f(x) = \dfrac{1}{1 + e^{-x}}$. (See Section 3.7.)

76. The doubling function $D(x) = \dfrac{\ln 2}{\ln (1 + x)}$ gives the years required to double your money when it is invested at interest rate x (expressed as a decimal), compounded annually.

(a) Find the time it takes to double your money at each of these interest rates: 4%, 6%, 8%, 12%, 18%, 24%, 36%.

(b) Round the answers in part (a) to the nearest year and compare them with these numbers: $72/4, 72/6, 72/8, 72/12, 72/18, 72/24, 72/36$. Use this evidence to state a rule of thumb for determining approximate doubling time, without using the function D. This rule of thumb, which has long been used by bankers, is called the **rule of 72.**

77. Suppose $f(x) = A \ln x + B$, where A and B are constants. If $f(1) = 10$ and $f(e) = 1$, what are A and B?

78. If $f(x) = A \ln x + B$ and $f(e) = 5$ and $f(e^2) = 8$, what are A and B?

79. The height h above sea level (in meters) is related to air temperature t (in degrees Celsius), the atmospheric pressure p (in centimeters of mercury at height h), and the atmospheric pressure c at sea level by

$$h = (30t + 8000) \ln (c/p).$$

If the pressure at the top of Mount Rainier is 44 centimeters on a day when sea level pressure is 75.126 centimeters and the temperature is 7°C, what is the height of Mount Rainier?

80. Mount Everest is 8850 meters high. What is the atmospheric pressure at the top of the mountain on a day when the temperature is -25°C and the atmospheric pressure at sea level is 75 centimeters? [See Exercise 79.]

81. Beef consumption in the United States (in billions of pounds) in year x can be approximated by the function

$$f(x) = -154.41 + 39.38 \ln x \qquad (x \geq 90).$$

where $x = 90$ corresponds to 1990.*

(a) How much beef was consumed in 1999 and in 2002?

(b) According to this model when will beef consumption reach 35 billion pounds per year?

82. Students in a precalculus class were given a final exam. Each month thereafter, they took an equivalent exam. The class average on the exam taken after t months is given by

$$F(t) = 82 - 8 \cdot \ln (t + 1).$$

(a) What was the class average after six months?

(b) After a year?

(c) When did the class average drop below 55?

83. One person with a flu virus visited the campus. The number T of days it took for the virus to infect x people was given by:

$$T = -.93 \ln \left[\frac{7000 - x}{6999x} \right].$$

(a) How many days did it take for 6000 people to become infected?

(b) After two weeks, how many people were infected?

84. The population of St. Petersburg, Florida (in thousands) can be approximated by the function

$$g(x) = -127.9 + 81.91 \ln x \qquad (x \geq 70),$$

where $x = 70$ corresponds to 1970.

(a) Estimate the population in 1995 and 2003.

(b) If this model remains accurate, when will the population be 260,000?

85. A bicycle store finds that the number N of bikes sold is related to the number d of dollars spent on advertising by $N = 51 + 100 \cdot \ln (d/100 + 2)$.

(a) How many bikes will be sold if nothing is spent on advertising? If $1000 is spent? If $10,000 is spent?

(b) If the average profit is $25 per bike, is it worthwhile to spend $1000 on advertising? What about $10,000?

(c) What are the answers in part (b) if the average profit per bike is $35?

86. Approximating Logarithmic Functions by Polynomials. For each positive integer n, let f_n be the polynomial function whose rule is

$$f_n(x) = x - \frac{x^2}{2} + \frac{x^3}{3} - \frac{x^4}{4} + \frac{x^5}{5} - \cdots \pm \frac{x^n}{n}$$

*Based on data from the U.S. Department of Agriculture.

where the sign of the last term is $+$ if n is odd and $-$ if n is even. In the viewing window with $-1 \le x \le 1$ and $-4 \le y \le 1$, graph $g(x) = \ln(1 + x)$ and $f_4(x)$ on the same screen. For what values of x does f_4 appear to be a good approximation of g?

87. Using the viewing window in Exercise 86, find a value of n for which the graph of the function f_n (as defined in Exercise 86) appears to coincide with the graph of $g(x) = \ln(1 + x)$. Use the trace feature to move from graph to graph to see how good this approximation actually is.

88. A *harmonic sum* is a sum of this form:
$$1 + \frac{1}{2} + \frac{1}{3} + \frac{1}{4} + \cdots + \frac{1}{k}.$$
(a) Compute $1 + \frac{1}{2} + \frac{1}{3} + \frac{1}{4}$, $1 + \frac{1}{2} + \frac{1}{3} + \frac{1}{4} + \frac{1}{5}$, and $1 + \frac{1}{2} + \frac{1}{3} + \frac{1}{4} + \frac{1}{5} + \frac{1}{6}$
(b) How many terms do you need in a harmonic sum for it to exceed three?
(c) It turns out to be hard to determine how many terms you would need for the sum to exceed 10. It will take

thousands of terms, more than you would want to plug into a calculator. Using calculus, we can derive this lower-bound formula: $\sum_{i=1}^{n} \frac{1}{i} > \ln n$. It means that the harmonic sum with n terms is always greater than $\ln n$. Use this formula to find a value of n such that the harmonic sum with n terms is greater than ten.
(d) Calculus also gives us an upper-bound formula:
$$\sum_{i=1}^{n} \frac{1}{i} < \ln n + 1.$$ Estimate the harmonic sum with 100,000 terms. How close is your estimate to the real number?

89. The ancient Sumerians started using a place-value system around 3000 BC. Assume that in 3000 BC you started adding
$$1 + \frac{1}{2} + \frac{1}{3} + \frac{1}{4} + \cdots$$ at the rate of ten additions per second.
(a) What would the value be today? Make your best guess.
(b) Use the upper-bound and lower-bound formulas given in Exercise 88 to estimate what the value would be today. Was your guess close?
(c) In what year are you guaranteed to be above 28.187?

3.4 Properties of Logs

Section Objectives ■ Use the Product, Quotient, and Power Laws for logarithms to simplify logarithmic expressions.
■ Use logarithms to solve applied problems.

Logarithms have several important properties beyond those presented in Section 5.3. These properties, which we shall call *logarithm laws,* arise from the fact that logarithms are exponents. Essentially, they are properties of exponents translated into logarithmic language.

The first law of exponents says that $b^m b^n = b^{m+n}$, or in words,

The exponent of a product is the sum of the exponents of the factors.

Since logarithms are just particular kinds of exponents, this statement translates as follows.

The logarithm of a product is the sum of the logarithms of the factors.

Here is the same statement in symbolic language.

Product Law for Logarithms

For all $v, w > 0$,
$$\ln(vw) = \ln v + \ln w$$
and
$$\log(vw) = \log v + \log w.$$

Before proving the Product Law, we illustrate it in the case when $v = 10^2$ and $w = 10^3$.

We have

$$\log v = \log 10^2 = 2 \qquad \text{and} \qquad \log w = \log 10^3 = 3,$$

so that

$$\log v + \log w = 2 + 3 = 5.$$

We also have

$$\log vw = \log(10^2 \, 10^3)$$
$$= \log(10^5) = 5.$$

Hence, $\log vw = \log v + \log w$ in this case.

Here is the formal proof of the Product Law for natural logarithms.

Proof   According to Property 4 of logarithms (in the box on page 380),

$$e^{\ln v} = v \qquad \text{and} \qquad e^{\ln w} = w.$$

Therefore, by the first law of exponents (with $m = \ln v$ and $n = \ln w$),

$$vw = e^{\ln v} e^{\ln w} = e^{\ln v + \ln w}.$$

So raising e to the exponent $(\ln v + \ln w)$ produces vw. But the definition of logarithm says that $\ln vw$ is the exponent to which e must be raised to produce vw. Therefore, we must have $\ln vw = \ln v + \ln w$. A similar argument works for common logarithms. ∎

EXAMPLE 1

A calculator shows that $\ln 7 = 1.9459$ and $\ln 9 = 2.1972$. Therefore,

$$\ln 63 = \ln (7 \cdot 9) = \ln 7 + \ln 9 = 1.9459 + 2.1972 = 4.1341. \quad \blacksquare$$

CALCULATOR EXPLORATION

We know that $5 \cdot 7 = 35$. Key in LOG(35) ENTER. Then key in LOG(5) + LOG(7) ENTER. The answers are the same by the Product Law. Do you get the same answer if you key in LOG(5) × LOG(7) ENTER?

EXAMPLE 2

Use the Product Law to write

(a) $\log (7xy)$ as a sum of three logarithms.

(b) $\log x^2 + \log y + 1$ as a single logarithm.

SOLUTION

(a) $\log (7xy) = \log 7x + \log y = \log 7 + \log x + \log y$

(b) Note that $\log 10 = 1$ (why?). Hence,

$$\log x^2 + \log y + 1 = \log x^2 + \log y + \log 10$$

$$= \log (x^2 y) + \log 10$$

$$= \log (10x^2 y). \quad \blacksquare$$

EXAMPLE 3

If a population of cells grows by a factor of ten every year, what do we know about the common logarithm of the population?

SOLUTION   Assume the population is P. Then, next year, the population will be $10P$. The logarithm of the population will be

$$\log (10P) = \log (10) + \log (P)$$
$$= 1 + \log (P).$$

So the logarithm of the population will increase by one every year. ∎

CAUTION

A common error in applying the Product Law for Logarithms is to write the *false* statement

$$\ln 7 + \ln 9 = \ln (7 + 9)$$
$$= \ln 16$$

instead of the correct statement

$$\ln 7 + \ln 9 = \ln (7 \cdot 9)$$
$$= \ln 63.$$

GRAPHING EXPLORATION

Illustrate the Caution in the margin graphically by graphing both

$$f(x) = \ln x + \ln 9 \qquad \text{and} \qquad g(x) = \ln (x + 9)$$

in the standard viewing window and verifying that the graphs are not the same. In particular, the functions have different values at $x = 7$.

The second law of exponents, namely, $b^m / b^n = b^{m-n}$, may be roughly stated in words as follows.

> The exponent of the quotient is the difference of exponents.

When the exponents are logarithms, this says

The logarithm of a quotient is the difference of the logarithms.

In other words,

Quotient Law for Logarithms

For all $v, w > 0$,

$$\ln \left(\frac{v}{w} \right) = \ln v - \ln w$$

and

$$\log \left(\frac{v}{w} \right) = \log v - \log w.$$

The proof of the Quotient Law is very similar to the proof of the Product Law (see Exercise 27).

```
log(297/39)
         .8816918423
log(297)-log(39)
         .8816918423
■
```

Figure 3–32

EXAMPLE 4

Figure 3–32 illustrates the Quotient Law by showing that

$$\log \left(\frac{297}{39} \right) = \log 297 - \log 39.$$ ∎

EXAMPLE 5

For any $w > 0$.

$$\ln\left(\frac{1}{w}\right) = \ln 1 - \ln w = 0 - \ln w = -\ln w$$

and

$$\log\left(\frac{1}{w}\right) = \log 1 - \log w = 0 - \log w = -\log w.$$

GRAPHING EXPLORATION

Illustrate the Caution graphically by graphing both $f(x) = \ln(x/3)$ and $g(x) = (\ln x)/(\ln 3)$ and verifying that the graphs are not the same at $x = 36$.

CAUTION

Do not confuse $\ln\left(\frac{v}{w}\right)$ with the quotient $\frac{\ln v}{\ln w}$. They are *different* numbers. For example,

$$\ln\left(\frac{36}{3}\right) = \ln(12) = 2.4849, \qquad \text{but} \qquad \frac{\ln 36}{\ln 3} = \frac{3.5835}{1.0986} = 3.2619.$$

The third law of exponents, namely, $(b^m)^k = b^{mk}$, can also be translated into logarithmic language.

Power Law for Logarithms

For all k and all $v > 0$,

$$\ln(v^k) = k(\ln v)$$

and

$$\log(v^k) = k(\log v).$$

Proof   Since $v = 10^{\log v}$ (why?), the third law of exponents (with $b = 10$ and $m = \log v$) shows that

$$v^k = (10^{\log v})^k = 10^{(\log v)k} = 10^{k(\log v)}.$$

So raising 10 to the exponent $k(\log v)$ produces v^k. But the exponent to which 10 must be raised to produce v^k is, by definition, $\log(v^k)$. Therefore, $\log(v^k) = k(\log v)$, and the proof is complete. A similar argument with e in place of 10 and "ln" in place of "log" works for natural logarithms. ∎

EXAMPLE 6

Express $\ln\sqrt{19}$ without radicals or exponents.

SOLUTION   First write $\sqrt{19}$ in exponent notation, then use the Power Law:

$$\ln\sqrt{19} = \ln 19^{1/2}$$

$$= \frac{1}{2}\ln 19 \qquad \text{or} \qquad \frac{\ln 19}{2}.$$

EXAMPLE 7

Express as a single logarithm: $\dfrac{\log(x^2 + 1)}{3} - \log x$.

SOLUTION

$$\frac{\log(x^2 + 1)}{3} - \log x = \frac{1}{3}\log(x^2 + 1) - \log x$$

$$= \log(x^2 + 1)^{1/3} - \log x \qquad \text{[Power Law]}$$

$$= \log \sqrt[3]{x^2 + 1} - \log x$$

$$= \log\left(\frac{\sqrt[3]{x^2 + 1}}{x}\right) \qquad \text{[Quotient Law]} \qquad ■$$

EXAMPLE 8

Express as a single logarithm: $\ln 3x + 4\ln x - \ln 3xy$.

SOLUTION

$$\ln 3x + 4 \cdot \ln x - \ln 3xy = \ln 3x + \ln x^4 - \ln 3xy \qquad \text{[Power Law]}$$

$$= \ln(3x \cdot x^4) - \ln 3xy \qquad \text{[Product Law]}$$

$$= \ln \frac{3x^5}{3xy} \qquad \text{[Quotient Law]}$$

$$= \ln \frac{x^4}{y} \qquad \text{[Cancel } 3x] \qquad ■$$

EXAMPLE 9

Simplify: $\ln\left(\dfrac{\sqrt{x}}{x}\right) + \ln \sqrt[4]{ex^2}$.

SOLUTION   Begin by changing to exponential notation.

$$\ln\left(\frac{x^{1/2}}{x}\right) + \ln(ex^2)^{1/4} = \ln(x^{-1/2}) + \ln(ex^2)^{1/4}$$

$$= -\frac{1}{2}\cdot \ln x + \frac{1}{4}\cdot \ln ex^2 \qquad \text{[Power Law]}$$

$$= -\frac{1}{2}\cdot \ln x + \frac{1}{4}(\ln e + \ln x^2) \qquad \text{[Product Law]}$$

$$= -\frac{1}{2}\cdot \ln x + \frac{1}{4}(\ln e + 2\cdot \ln x) \qquad \text{[Power Law]}$$

$$= -\frac{1}{2}\cdot \ln x + \frac{1}{4}\cdot \ln e + \frac{1}{2}\cdot \ln x$$

$$= \frac{1}{4}\cdot \ln e = \frac{1}{4} \qquad \text{[}\ln e = 1] \qquad ■$$

APPLICATIONS

Because logarithmic growth is slow, measurements on a logarithmic scale (that is, on a scale determined by a logarithmic function) can sometimes be deceptive.

EXAMPLE 10

Earthquakes   The magnitude $R(i)$ of an earthquake on the Richter scale is given by $R(i) = \log(i/i_0)$, where i is the amplitude of the ground motion of the earthquake and i_0 is the amplitude of the ground motion of the so-called zero earthquake.* A moderate earthquake might have 1000 times the ground motion of the zero earthquake (that is, $i = 1000i_0$). So its magnitude would be

$$\log(1000i_0/i_0) = \log 1000 = \log 10^3 = 3.$$

An earthquake with 10 times this ground motion (that is, $i = 10 \cdot 1000i_0 = 10{,}000i_0$) would have a magnitude of

$$\log(10{,}000i_0/i_0) = \log 10{,}000 = \log 10^4 = 4.$$

So a *tenfold* increase in ground motion produces only a one-point change on the Richter scale. In general,

> **Increasing the ground motion by a factor of 10^k increases the Richter magnitude by k units.**[†]

For instance, the 1989 World Series earthquake in San Francisco measured 7.0 on the Richter scale, and the great earthquake of 1906 measured 8.3. The difference of 1.3 points means that the 1906 quake was $10^{1.3} \approx 20$ times more intense than the 1989 one in terms of ground motion.   ∎

---

*The zero earthquake has ground motion amplitude of less than 1 micron on a standard seismograph 100 kilometers from the epicenter.

[†]*Proof:* If one quake has ground motion amplitude i and the other $10^k i$, then

$$R(10^k i) = \log(10^k i/i_0) = \log 10^k + \log(i/i_0)$$

$$= k + \log(i/i_0) = k + R(i).$$

 ## EXERCISES 3.4

In Exercises 1–10, write the given expression as a single logarithm.

1. $\ln x^2 + 3 \ln y$

2. $-5(\ln x) + \ln 4y - \ln 3z$

3. $\log(x^2 - 9) - \log(x + 3)$

4. $3(\log 2x) - 4[\log x - \log(y - 5)]$

5. $2(\ln x) - 3(\ln x^2 + \ln x)$

6. $-\log\left(\dfrac{3\sqrt{x}}{2}\right) - \log(\sqrt{5x})$

7. $3 \ln(e^2 - e) - 3$

8. $3 \log(7) - 4$

9. $\log(10x) + \log(20y) - 1$

10. $\ln(e^3 x^2) - \ln(ey^3) + 2$

In Exercises 11–16, let $u = \ln x$ and $v = \ln y$. Write the given expression in terms of u and v. For example,

$$\ln x^3 y = \ln x^3 + \ln y = 3 \ln x + \ln y = 3u + v.$$

11. $\ln(x^2 y^5)$

12. $\ln(x^4 y^3)$

13. $\ln(\sqrt{x} \cdot y^2)$

14. $\ln\left(\dfrac{\sqrt{xy}}{y^2}\right)$

15. $\ln\left(\sqrt[3]{x^2 \sqrt{y}}\right)$

16. $\ln\left(\dfrac{\sqrt[3]{x^2 y^2}}{x^5}\right)$

In Exercises 17–23, use graphical or algebraic means to determine whether the statement is true or false.

17. $\ln |x| = |\ln x|$?

18. $\ln\left(\dfrac{1}{x}\right) = \dfrac{1}{\ln x}$?

19. $\log x^5 = 5(\log x)$?

20. $e^{x \ln x} = x^x$ $(x > 0)$?

21. $\ln x^3 = (\ln x)^3$?

22. $\log \sqrt{x} = \sqrt{\log x}$?

23. $\ln (x + 5) = \ln(x) + \ln 5$?

In Exercises 24 and 25, find values of a and b for which the statement is false.

24. $\dfrac{\log a}{\log b} = \log\left(\dfrac{a}{b}\right)$

25. $\log (a + b) = \log a + \log b$

26. If $\ln b^{10} = 10$, what is b?

27. Prove the Quotient Law for Logarithms: For $v, w > 0$,
$\ln\left(\dfrac{v}{w}\right) = \ln v - \ln w$. (Use properties of exponents and the fact that $v = e^{\ln v}$ and $w = e^{\ln w}$.)

In Exercises 28–31, state the magnitude on the Richter scale of an earthquake that satisfies the given condition.

28. 100 times stronger than the zero quake.

29. $10^{4.7}$ times stronger than the zero quake.

30. 250 times stronger than the zero quake.

31. 1500 times stronger than the zero quake.

Exercises 32–35 deal with the energy intensity i of a sound, which is related to the loudness of the sound by the function $L(i) = 10 \cdot \log (i/i_0)$, where i_0 is the minimum intensity detectable by the human ear and $L(i)$ is measured in decibels. Find the decibel measure of the sound.

32. Ticking watch (intensity is 100 times i_0).

33. Soft music (intensity is 10,000 times i_0).

34. Loud conversation (intensity is 4 million times i_0).

35. Victoria Falls in Africa (intensity is 10 billion times i_0).

36. How much louder is the sound in Exercise 33 than the sound in Exercise 32?

37. The perceived loudness L of a sound of intensity I is given by $L = k \cdot \ln I$, where k is a certain constant. By how much must the intensity be increased to double the loudness? (That is, what must be done to I to produce $2L$?)

THINKERS

38. Compute each of the following pairs of numbers.

(a) $\log 18$ and $\dfrac{\ln 18}{\ln 10}$

(b) $\log 456$ and $\dfrac{\ln 456}{\ln 10}$

(c) $\log 8950$ and $\dfrac{\ln 8950}{\ln 10}$

(d) What do these results suggest?

39. Prove that for any positive number c, $\log c = \dfrac{\ln c}{\ln 10}$. [*Hint:* We know that $10^{\log c} = c$ (why?). Take natural logarithms on both sides and use a logarithm law to simplify and solve for $\log c$.]

40. Find each of the following logarithms.

(a) $\log 8.753$ (b) $\log 87.53$ (c) $\log 875.3$
(d) $\log 8753$ (e) $\log 87,530$
(f) How are the numbers $8.753, 87.53, \ldots, 87,530$ related to one another? How are their logarithms related? State a general conclusion that this evidence suggests.

41. Prove that for every positive number c, $\log c$ can be written in the form $k + \log b$, where k is an integer and $1 \le b < 10$. [*Hint:* Write c in scientific notation and use logarithm laws to express $\log c$ in the required form.]

42. A scientist is measuring the spread of a rumor over time. She notices a nice pattern when she graphs the natural logarithm of the number of people who know the rumor after t days:

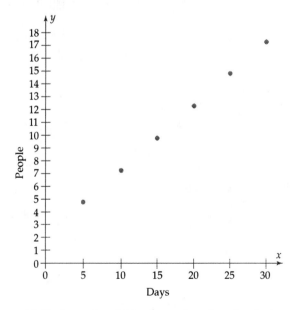

(a) Find a good model for the number of people who know the rumor at a given time t, where $0 \le t \le 30$

(b) A friend of the scientist wonders why she didn't just graph the number of people instead of the logarithm of the number of people. What was the advantage of using the logarithm in the graph?

43. Wayland and Christy have been tracking the number of cases of flu in their city:

Weeks since January 1	0	1	2	3	4	5	6
Number of cases	10	13	16	20	24	31	38

Wayland thinks this is exponential growth. Christy doesn't think so. After playing around with the data, they plot the points and still disagree.

(a) Plot the points. Do you agree with Wayland or with Christy?
(b) They create a new plot, this time using the natural logarithms of the number of cases. So they plot the points $(0, \ln(10))$, $(2, \ln(13))$, etc. As soon as they see this new plot, they agree! Construct this new plot.
(c) Who was right, Wayland or Christy? Why?

3.5 Trigonometric Functions

Section Objectives

■ Use the unit circle to define the sine, cosine and tangent functions.

■ Find the exact values of sine, cosine, and tangent at $\pi/3$, $\pi/4$, $\pi/6$, and integer multiples of these numbers.

■ Use the point-in-the-plane description to evaluate the trigonometric functions.

NOTE

If you have read Chapter 8, use Alternate Section 6.2 on page 452 in place of this section.

Roadmap

Instructors who wish to cover all six trigonometric functions simultaneously should incorporate Section 6.6 into Sections 6.2–6.4, as follows.

Subsection of Section 6.6	Cover at the end of
Part I	Section 6.2
Part II	Section 6.3
Part III	Section 6.4

Instructors who prefer to introduce triangle trigonometry early should consult the chart on page xiv.

Unlike most of the functions seen thus far, the definitions of the sine and cosine functions do not involve algebraic formulas. Instead, these functions are defined geometrically, using the unit circle.* Recall that the unit circle is the circle of radius 1 with center at the origin, whose equation is $x^2 + y^2 = 1$.

Both the sine and cosine functions have the set of all real numbers as domain. Their rules are given by the following three-step geometric process:

1. Given a real number t, construct an angle of t radians in standard position.

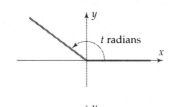

2. Find the coordinates of the point P where the terminal side of this angle meets the unit circle $x^2 + y^2 = 1$, say $P = (a, b)$.

3. The value of the **cosine function** at t (denoted $\cos t$) is the x-coordinate of P:

$$\cos t = a.$$

The value of the **sine function** at t (denoted $\sin t$) is the y-coordinate of P:

$$\sin t = b.$$

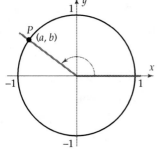

---

*If you have previously studied the trigonometry of triangles, the definition given here may not look familiar. If this is the case, just concentrate on this definition and don't worry about relating it to any definition you remember from the past. The connection between this definition and the trigonometry of triangles will be explained in Chapter 8.

Sine and Cosine

> If P is the point where the terminal side of an angle of t radians in standard position meets the unit circle, then
>
> $$P \text{ has coordinates } (\cos t, \sin t).$$

GRAPHING EXPLORATION

With your calculator in radian mode and parametric graphing mode, set the range values as follows:

$$0 \le t \le 2\pi, \quad -1.8 \le x \le 1.8, \quad -1.2 \le y \le 1.2^*$$

Then graph the curve given by the parametric equations

$$x = \cos t \quad \text{and} \quad y = \sin t.$$

The graph is the unit circle. Use the trace to move around the circle. At each point, the screen will display three numbers: the values of t, x, and y. For each t, the cursor is on the point where the terminal side of an angle of t radians meets the unit circle, so the corresponding x is the number $\cos t$ and the corresponding y is the number $\sin t$.

The **tangent function** is defined as the quotient of the sine and cosine functions. Its value at the number t, denoted $\tan t$, is given by

$$\tan t = \frac{\sin t}{\cos t}.$$

EXAMPLE 1

Evaluate the three trigonometric functions at

(a) $t = \pi$ (b) $t = \pi/2$.

SOLUTION

(a) Construct an angle of π radians, as in Figure 3–33. Its terminal side lies on the negative x-axis and intersects the unit circle at $P = (-1, 0)$. Hence,

$$\sin \pi = y\text{-coordinate of } P = 0$$
$$\cos \pi = x\text{-coordinate of } P = -1$$
$$\tan \pi = \frac{\sin \pi}{\cos \pi} = \frac{0}{-1} = 0$$

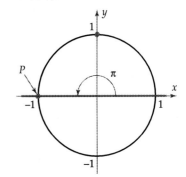

Figure 3–33

---

*Parametric graphing is explained in *Special Topics 3.3.A.* These settings give a square viewing window on calculators with a screen measuring approximately 95 by 63 pixels (such as TI-84+), and hence the unit circle will look like a circle. For wider screens, adjust the x range settings to obtain a square window.

(b) An angle of $\pi/2$ radians (Figure 3–34) has its terminal side on the positive y-axis and intersects the unit circle at $P = (0, 1)$.

$$\cos \frac{\pi}{2} = x\text{-coordinate of } P = 0$$

$$\sin \frac{\pi}{2} = y\text{-coordinate of } P = 1$$

$$\tan \frac{\pi}{2} = \frac{\sin (\pi/2)}{\cos (\pi/2)} = \frac{1}{0} \; undefined$$

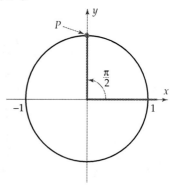

Figure 3–34 ■

The definitions of sine and cosine show that $\sin t$ and $\cos t$ are defined for every real number t. Example 1(b), however, shows that $\tan t$ is *not* defined when the x-coordinate of the point P is 0. This occurs when P has coordinates $(0, 1)$ or $(0, -1)$, that is, when $t = \pm\pi/2, \pm 3\pi/2, \pm 5\pi/2$, etc. Consequently, the domain (set of inputs) of each trigonometric function is as follows.

Function	Domain
$f(t) = \sin t$	All real numbers
$g(t) = \cos t$	All real numbers
$h(t) = \tan t$	All real numbers except $\pm\pi/2, \pm 3\pi/2, \pm 5\pi/2, \ldots$

In most cases, evaluating trigonometric functions is not as simple as in Example 1. Usually, you must use the SIN, COS, and TAN keys on a calculator (in radian mode) to approximate $\sin t$, $\cos t$, and $\tan t$, as illustrated in Figure 3–35.

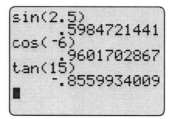

```
sin(2.5)
         .5984721441
cos(-6)
         .9601702867
tan(15)
        -.8559934009
```

Figure 3–35

EXAMPLE 2

When a baseball is hit by a bat, the horizontal distance d traveled by the ball is approximated by

$$d = \frac{v^2 \sin t \cos t}{16},$$

where the ball leaves the bat at an angle of t radians and has initial velocity v feet per second, as shown in Figure 3–36.

(a) How far does the ball travel when the initial velocity is 90 feet per second and $t = .7$?

(b) If the initial velocity is 105 feet per second and $t = 1$, how far does the ball travel?

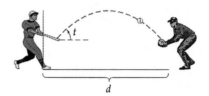

Figure 3–36

SOLUTION

(a) Let $v = 90$ and $t = .7$ in the formula for d. Then a calculator (in radian mode) shows that

$$d = \frac{v^2 \sin t \cos t}{16} = \frac{90^2 \sin .7 \cos .7}{16} \approx 249.44 \text{ feet.}$$

(b) Now let $v = 105$ and $t = 1$. Then

$$d = \frac{v^2 \sin t \cos t}{16} = \frac{105^2 \sin 1 \cos 1}{16} \approx 313.28. \qquad \blacksquare$$

SPECIAL VALUES

The trigonometric functions can be evaluated exactly at $t = \pi/3$, $t = \pi/4$, $t = \pi/6$, and any integer multiples of these numbers by using the following facts (which are explained in Examples 2–4 of the Geometry Review Appendix):*

A right triangle with hypotenuse 1 and angles of $\pi/6$ and $\pi/3$ radians has sides of lengths $1/2$ (opposite the angle of $\pi/6$) and $\sqrt{3}/2$ (opposite the angle of $\pi/3$).

A right triangle with hypotenuse 1 and two angles of $\pi/4$ radians has two sides of length $\sqrt{2}/2$.

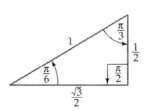

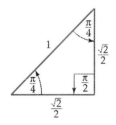

Figure 3–37

---

*Angles in the Geometry Review are given in degree measure: 60°, 45°, 30° instead of radian measure $\pi/3$, $\pi/4$, $\pi/6$, as is done here.

EXAMPLE 3

Evaluate the three trigonometric functions at $t = \pi/6$.

SOLUTION   Construct an angle of $\pi/6$ radians in standard position and let P be the point where its terminal side intersects the unit circle. Draw a vertical line from P to the x-axis, as shown in Figure 3–38, forming a right triangle that matches the first triangle in Figure 3–37. The sides of this triangle show that P has coordinates $(\sqrt{3}/2, 1/2)$. By the definition,

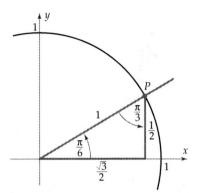

Figure 3–38

$$\sin \frac{\pi}{6} = y\text{-coordinate of } P = \frac{1}{2}$$

$$\cos \frac{\pi}{6} = x\text{-coordinate of } P = \frac{\sqrt{3}}{2}$$

$$\tan \frac{\pi}{6} = \frac{\sin(\pi/6)}{\cos(\pi/6)} = \frac{1/2}{\sqrt{3}/2} = \frac{1}{\sqrt{3}} = \frac{\sqrt{3}}{3}.$$

EXAMPLE 4

Evaluate the trigonometric functions at $t = \pi/4$.

SOLUTION   Construct an angle of $\pi/4$ radians in standard position whose terminal side intersects the unit circle at P. Draw a vertical line from P to the x-axis to form a right triangle that matches the second triangle in Figure 3–37. As Figure 3–39 shows, P has coordinates $(\sqrt{2}/2, \sqrt{2}/2)$ so that

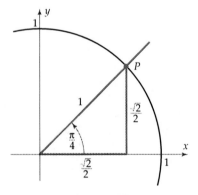

Figure 3–39

$$\sin \frac{\pi}{4} = y\text{-coordinate of } P = \frac{\sqrt{2}}{2}$$

$$\cos \frac{\pi}{4} = x\text{-coordinate of } P = \frac{\sqrt{2}}{2}$$

$$\tan \frac{\pi}{4} = \frac{\sin(\pi/6)}{\cos(\pi/6)} = \frac{\sqrt{2}/2}{\sqrt{2}/2} = 1.$$

EXAMPLE 5

Evaluate the trigonometric functions at $-5\pi/4$.

SOLUTION   Construct an angle of $-5\pi/4$ radians in standard position and let P be the point where the terminal side intersects the unit circle. Draw a vertical line from P to the x-axis, as shown in Figure 3–40, forming a right triangle that matches

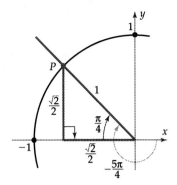

Figure 3–40

the second triangle in Figure 3–37. The sides of the triangle in Figure 3–40 show that P has coordinates $(-\sqrt{2}/2, \sqrt{2}/2)$. Hence,

$$\sin \frac{-5\pi}{4} = y\text{-coordinate of } P = \frac{\sqrt{2}}{2}$$

$$\cos \frac{-5\pi}{4} = x\text{-coordinate of } P = -\frac{\sqrt{2}}{2}$$

$$\tan \frac{-5\pi}{4} = \frac{\sin t}{\cos t} = \frac{\sqrt{2}/2}{-\sqrt{2}/2} = -1. \qquad \blacksquare$$

EXAMPLE 6

Evaluate the trigonometric functions at $11\pi/3$.

SOLUTION   Construct an angle of $11\pi/3$ radians in standard position and draw a vertical line from the x-axis to the point P where the terminal side of the angle meets the unit circle, as shown in Figure 3–41. The right triangle formed in this way matches the first triangle in Figure 3–37. The sides of the triangle in Figure 3–41 show that the coordinates of P are $(1/2, -\sqrt{3}/2)$. Therefore,

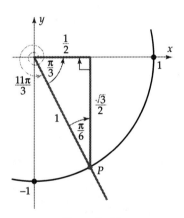

Figure 3–41

$$\sin \frac{11\pi}{3} = y\text{-coordinate of } P = -\frac{\sqrt{3}}{2}$$

$$\cos \frac{11\pi}{3} = x\text{-coordinate of } P = \frac{1}{2}$$

$$\tan \frac{11\pi}{3} = \frac{(\sin 11\pi/3)}{(\cos 11\pi/3)} = \frac{-\sqrt{3}/2}{1/2} = -\sqrt{3}. \qquad \blacksquare$$

POINT-IN-THE-PLANE DESCRIPTION OF TRIGONOMETRIC FUNCTIONS

In evaluating $\sin t$, $\cos t$ and $\tan t$, from the definition, we use the point where the unit circle intersects the terminal side of an angle of t radians in standard position. Here is an alternative method of evaluating the trigonometric functions that uses *any* point on the terminal side of the angle (except the origin); it is proved at the end of this section.

Point-in-the-Plane Description

Let t be a real number. Let (x, y) be any point (except the origin) on the terminal side of an angle of t radians in standard position. Then,

$$\sin t = \frac{y}{r} \qquad \cos t = \frac{x}{r} \qquad \tan t = \frac{y}{x}$$

where $r = \sqrt{x^2 + y^2}$ is the distance from (x, y) to the origin.

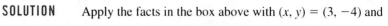

EXAMPLE 7

Figure 3–42 shows an angle of t radians in standard position. Evaluate the three trigonometric functions at t.

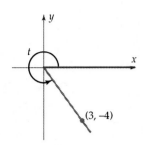

Figure 3–42

SOLUTION   Apply the facts in the box above with $(x, y) = (3, -4)$ and

$$r = \sqrt{x^2 + y^2} = \sqrt{3^2 + (-4)^2} = \sqrt{25} = 5.$$

Then we have

$$\sin t = \frac{y}{r} = \frac{-4}{5} = -\frac{4}{5}, \qquad \cos t = \frac{x}{r} = \frac{3}{5}, \qquad \tan t = \frac{y}{x} = \frac{-4}{3} = -\frac{4}{3}. \quad ■$$

EXAMPLE 8

The terminal side of a first-quadrant angle of t radians in standard position lies on the line with equation $2x - 3y = 0$. Evaluate the three trigonometric functions at t.

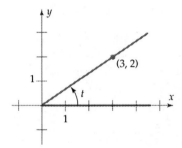

Figure 3–43

SOLUTION   Verify that the point $(3, 2)$ satisfies the equation and hence lies on the terminal side of the angle (Figure 3–43). Now we have

$$(x, y) = (3, 2) \qquad \text{and} \qquad r = \sqrt{x^2 + y^2} = \sqrt{3^2 + 2^2} = \sqrt{13}.$$

Therefore,

$$\sin t = \frac{y}{r} = \frac{2}{\sqrt{13}}, \qquad \cos t = \frac{x}{r} = \frac{3}{\sqrt{13}}, \qquad \tan t = \frac{y}{x} = \frac{2/\sqrt{13}}{3/\sqrt{13}} = \frac{2}{3}. \quad ■$$

Proof of the Point-in-the-Plane Description   Let Q be the point on the terminal side of the standard position angle of t radians and let P be the point where the terminal side meets the unit circle, as in Figure 3–44. The definition of sine and cosine shows that P has coordinates $(\cos t, \sin t)$. The distance formula shows that the segment OQ has length $\sqrt{x^2 + y^2}$, which we denote by r.

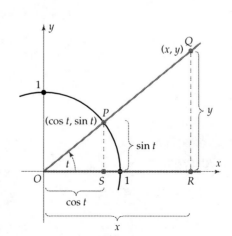

Figure 3–44

Both triangles QOR and POS are right triangles containing an angle of t radians. Therefore, these triangles are *similar*.* Consequently,

$$\frac{\text{length } OP}{\text{length } OQ} = \frac{\text{length } PS}{\text{length } QR} \quad \text{and} \quad \frac{\text{length } OP}{\text{length } OQ} = \frac{\text{length } OS}{\text{length } OR}.$$

Figure 3–40 shows what each of these lengths is. Hence,

$$\frac{1}{r} = \frac{\sin t}{y} \quad \text{and} \quad \frac{1}{r} = \frac{\cos t}{x}$$

$$r \sin t = y \qquad\qquad r \cos t = x$$

$$\sin t = \frac{y}{r} \qquad\qquad \cos t = \frac{x}{r}$$

Similar arguments work when the terminal side is not in the first quadrant. In every case, $\tan t = \dfrac{\sin t}{\cos t} = \dfrac{y/r}{x/r} = \dfrac{y}{x}$. This completes the proof of the statements in the box on page 447. ∎

---

*See the Geometry Review Appendix for the basic facts about similar triangles.

EXERCISES 3.5

Note: *Unless stated otherwise, all angles are in standard position.*

In Exercises 1–10, use the definition (not a calculator) to find the function value.

1. $\sin(3\pi/2)$ 2. $\sin(-\pi)$ 3. $\cos(3\pi/2)$

4. $\cos(-\pi/2)$ 5. $\tan(4\pi)$ 6. $\tan(-\pi)$

7. $\cos(-3\pi/2)$ 8. $\sin(9\pi/2)$ 9. $\cos(-11\pi/2)$

10. $\tan(-13\pi)$

In Exercises 11–14, assume that the terminal side of an angle of t radians passes through the given point on the unit circle. Find sin t, cos t, tan t.

11. $(-2/\sqrt{5}, 1/\sqrt{5})$ 12. $(1/\sqrt{10}, -3/\sqrt{10})$

13. $(-3/5, -4/5)$ 14. $(.6, -.8)$

In Exercises 15–29, find the exact value of the sine, cosine, and tangent of the number, without using a calculator.

15. $\pi/3$ 16. $2\pi/3$ 17. $7\pi/4$

18. $5\pi/4$ 19. $3\pi/4$ 20. $-7\pi/3$

21. $5\pi/6$ 22. 3π 23. $-23\pi/6$

24. $11\pi/6$ 25. $-19\pi/3$ 26. $-10\pi/3$

27. $-15\pi/4$ 28. $-25\pi/4$ 29. $-17\pi/2$

30. Fill the blanks in the following table. Write each entry as a fraction with denominator 2 and with a radical in the numerator. For example,

$$\sin\frac{\pi}{2} = 1 = \frac{\sqrt{4}}{2}.$$

Some students find the resulting pattern an easy way to remember these functional values.

t	0	$\pi/6$	$\pi/4$	$\pi/3$	$\pi/2$
$\sin t$					
$\cos t$					

In Exercises 31–36, write the expression as a single real number. Do not use decimal approximations. [Hint: Exercises 15–21 may be helpful.]

31. $\sin(\pi/3)\cos(\pi) + \sin(\pi)\cos(\pi/3)$

32. $\sin(\pi/6)\cos(\pi/2) - \cos(\pi/6)\sin(\pi/2)$

33. $\cos(\pi/2)\cos(\pi/4) - \sin(\pi/2)\sin(\pi/4)$

34. $\cos(2\pi/3)\cos(\pi) + \sin(2\pi/3)\sin(\pi)$

35. $\sin(3\pi/4)\cos(5\pi/6) - \cos(3\pi/4)\sin(5\pi/6)$

36. $\sin(-7\pi/3)\cos(5\pi/4) + \cos(-7\pi/3)\sin(5\pi/4)$

In Exercises 37–42, find sin t, cos t, tan t when the terminal side of an angle of t radians in standard position passes through the given point.

37. $(3, 5)$

38. $(-2, 1)$

39. $(-4, -5)$

40. $(3, -4)$

41. $(\sqrt{3}, -8)$

42. $(-2, \pi)$

In Exercises 43–46, use a calculator in radian mode.

43. When a plane flies faster than the speed of sound, the sound waves it generates trail the plane in a cone shape, as shown in the figure. When the bottom part of the cone hits the ground, you hear a sonic boom. The equation that describes this situation is

$$\sin\left(\frac{t}{2}\right) = \frac{w}{p},$$

where t is the radian measure of the angle of the cone, w is the speed of the sound wave, p is the speed of the plane, and $p > w$.

(a) Find the speed of the sound wave when the plane flies at 1200 mph and $t = .8$.

(b) Find the speed of the plane if the sound wave travels at 500 mph and $t = .7$.

44. Suppose the batter in Example 2 hits the ball with an initial velocity of 100 feet per second.

(a) Complete this table.

t	.5	.6	.7	.8	.9
d					

(b) By experimentation, find the value of t (to two decimal places) that produces the longest distance.

(c) If $t = 1.6$, what is d? Explain your answer.

45. The average daily temperature in St. Louis, Missouri (in degrees Fahrenheit), is approximated by the function

$$T(x) = 24.6 \sin(.522x - 2.1) + 56.3 \qquad (1 \le x < 13),$$

where $x = 1$ corresponds to January 1, $x = 2$ to February 1, etc.*

---

*Based on data from the National Climatic Data Center.

(a) Complete this table.

Date	Average Temperature
Jan. 1	
Mar. 1	
May 1	
July 1	
Sept. 1	
Nov. 1	

(b) Make a table that shows the average temperature every third day in June, beginning on June 1. [Assume that three days = 1/10 of a month.]

46. A regular polygon has n equal sides and n equal angles formed by the sides. For example, a regular polygon of three sides is an equilateral triangle, and a regular polygon of four sides is a square. If a regular polygon of n sides is circumscribed around a circle of radius r, as shown in the figure for $n = 4$ and $n = 5$, then the area of the polygon is given by

$$A = nr^2 \tan\left(\frac{\pi}{n}\right).$$

(a) Find the area of a regular polygon of 12 sides circumscribed around a circle of radius 5.

(b) Complete the following table for a regular polygon of n sides circumscribed around the unit circle (which, as you recall, has radius 1).

n	5	50	500	5000	10,000
Area					

(c) As n gets larger and larger, what number does the area get very close to? [*Hint:* What is the area of the unit circle?]

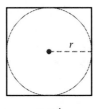

$n = 4$

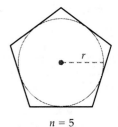

$n = 5$

In Exercises 47–54, find the average rate of change of the function over the given interval. Exact answers are required.

47. $f(t) = \cos t$ from $t = \pi/2$ to $t = \pi$

48. $g(t) = \sin t$ from $t = \pi/2$ to $t = \pi$

49. $g(t) = \sin t$ from $t = \pi/6$ to $t = 11\pi/3$

50. $h(t) = \tan t$ from $t = \pi/6$ to $t = 11\pi/3$

51. $f(t) = \cos t$ from $t = -5\pi/4$ to $t = \pi/4$

52. $g(t) = \sin t$ from $t = -5\pi/4$ to $t = \pi/4$

53. $h(t) = \tan t$ from $t = \pi/6$ to $t = \pi/3$

54. $f(t) = \cos t$ from $t = \pi/4$ to $t = \pi/3$

55. (a) Use a calculator to find the average rate of change of $g(t) = \sin t$ from 2 to $2 + h$, for each of these values of h: .01, .001, .0001, and .00001.

(b) Compare your answers in part (a) with the number $\cos 2$. What would you guess that the instantaneous rate of change of $g(t) = \sin t$ is at $t = 2$?

56. (a) Use a calculator to find the average rate of change of $f(t) = \cos t$ from 5 to $5 + h$, for each of these values of h: .01, .001, .0001, and .00001.

(b) Compare your answers in part (a) with the number $-\sin 5$. What would you guess that the instantaneous rate of change of $f(t) = \cos t$ is at $t = 5$?

In Exercises 57–62, assume that the terminal side of an angle of t radians in standard position lies in the given quadrant on the given straight line. Find sin t, cos t, tan t. [Hint: Find a point on the terminal side of the angle.]

57. Quadrant IV; line with equation $y = -2x$.

58. Quadrant III; line with equation $2y - 5x = 0$.

59. Quadrant IV; line through $(-3, 5)$ and $(-9, 15)$.

60. Quadrant III; line through the origin parallel to

$$7x - 2y = -6.$$

61. Quadrant II; line through the origin parallel to

$$2y + x = 6.$$

62. Quadrant I; line through the origin perpendicular to

$$3y + x = 6.$$

63. The values of $\sin t$, $\cos t$, and $\tan t$ are determined by the point (x, y) where the terminal side of an angle of t radians in standard position intersects the unit circle. The coordinates x and y are positive or negative, depending on what quadrant (x, y) lies in. For instance, in the second quadrant x is negative and y is positive, so that $\cos t$ (which is x by definition) is negative. Fill the blanks in this chart with the appropriate sign ($+$ or $-$).

Quadrant II $\pi/2 < t < \pi$		Quadrant I $0 < t < \pi/2$	
$\sin t$		$\sin t$	$+$
$\cos t$	$-$	$\cos t$	
$\tan t$		$\tan t$	

Quadrant III $\pi < t < 3\pi/2$		Quadrant IV $3\pi/2 < t < 2\pi$	
$\sin t$		$\sin t$	
$\cos t$		$\cos t$	
$\tan t$		$\tan t$	

64. (a) Find two numbers c and d such that

$$\sin(c + d) \neq \sin c + \sin d.$$

(b) Find two numbers c and d such that

$$\cos(c + d) \neq \cos c + \cos d.$$

In Exercises 65–70, draw a rough sketch to determine if the given number is positive.

65. $\sin 1$ [*Hint:* The terminal side of an angle of 1 radian lies in the first quadrant (why?), so any point on it will have a positive y-coordinate.]

66. $\cos 2$ **67.** $\tan 3$ **68.** $(\cos 2)(\sin 2)$

69. $\tan 1.5$ **70.** $\cos 3 + \sin 3$

In Exercises 71–76, find all the solutions of the equation.

71. $\sin t = 1$ **72.** $\cos t = -1$ **73.** $\tan t = 0$

74. $\sin t = -1$ **75.** $|\sin t| = 1$ **76.** $|\cos t| = 1$

THINKERS

77. Using only the definition and no calculator, determine which number is larger: $\sin(\cos 0)$ or $\cos(\sin 0)$.

78. With your calculator in radian mode and function graphing mode, graph the following functions on the same screen, using the viewing window with $0 \leq x \leq 2\pi$ and $-3 \leq y \leq 3$: $f(x) = \cos x^3$ and $g(x) = (\cos x)^3$. Are the graphs the same? What do you conclude about the statement $\cos x^3 = (\cos x)^3$?

79. Figure R is a diagram of a merry-go-round that includes horses A through F. The distance from the center P to A is 1 unit and the distance from P to D is 5 units. Define six functions as follows:

$$A(t) = \text{vertical distance from horse } A \text{ to the } x\text{-axis at}$$
$$\text{time } t \text{ minutes;}$$

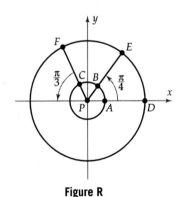

Figure R

and similarly for $B(t)$, $C(t)$, $D(t)$, $E(t)$, $F(t)$. The merry-go-round rotates counterclockwise at a rate of 1 revolution per minute, and the horses are in the positions shown in Figure R at the starting time $t = 0$. As the merry-go-round rotates, the horses move around the circles shown in Figure R.

(a) Show that $B(t) = A(t + 1/8)$ for every t.
(b) In a similar manner, express $C(t)$ in terms of the function $A(t)$.
(c) Express $E(t)$ and $F(t)$ in terms of the function $D(t)$.
(d) Explain why Figure S is valid and use it and similar triangles to express $D(t)$ in terms of $A(t)$.
(e) In a similar manner, express $E(t)$ and $F(t)$ in terms of $A(t)$.
(f) Show that $A(t) = \sin(2\pi t)$ for every t. [*Hint:* Exercises 57–64 in Section 6.1 may be helpful.]
(g) Use parts (a), (b), and (f) to express $B(t)$ and $C(t)$ in terms of the sine function.

(h) Use parts (d), (e), and (f) to express $D(t)$, $E(t)$, and $F(t)$ in terms of the sine function.

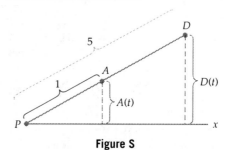

Figure S

Chapter 4

SOLVING EQUATIONS

© Rudi Von Briel/PhotoEdit

Chapter Outline

4.1 Solving Equations Algebraically

Section Objectives

- Understand the basic principles for solving equations.
- Solve linear equations.
- Solve quadratic equations by factoring, completing the square, or using the quadratic formula.
- Use the discriminant to determine the number of real solutions of a quadratic equation.
- Solve some types of higher-degree equations.
- Solve fractional equations.

This section deals with equations such as

$$3x - 6 = 7x + 4, \qquad x^2 - 5x + 6 = 0, \qquad 2x^4 - 13x^2 = 3.$$

A **solution** of an equation is a number that, when substituted for the variable x, produces a true statement.* For example, 5 is a solution of $3x + 2 = 17$ because $3 \cdot 5 + 2 = 17$ is a true statement. To **solve** an equation means to find all its solutions. Throughout this chapter, we shall deal only with **real solutions,** that is, solutions that are real numbers.

---

*Any letter may be used for the variable.

Two equations are said to be **equivalent** if they have the same solutions. For example, $3x + 2 = 17$ and $x - 2 = 3$ are equivalent because 5 is the only solution of each one.

Basic Principles for Solving Equations

> Performing any of the following operations on an equation produces an equivalent equation:
>
> 1. Add or subtract the same quantity from both sides of the equation.
>
> 2. Multiply or divide both sides of the equation by the same *nonzero* quantity.

The usual strategy in equation solving is to use these basic principles to transform a given equation into an equivalent one whose solutions are known.

A **first-degree,** or **linear, equation** is one that can be written in the form

$$ax + b = 0$$

for some constants a, b, with $a \neq 0$. Every first-degree equation has exactly one solution, which is easily found.

EXAMPLE 1

To solve $3x - 6 = 7x + 4$, we use the basic principles to transform this equation into an equivalent one whose solution is obvious:

$$3x - 6 = 7x + 4$$

Add 6 to both sides: $\qquad 3x = 7x + 10$

Subtract $7x$ from both sides: $\qquad -4x = 10$

Divide both sides by -4: $\qquad x = \dfrac{10}{-4} = -\dfrac{5}{2}.$

Since $-5/2$ is the only solution of this last equation, $-5/2$ is the only solution of the original equation, $3x - 6 = 7x + 4$. ∎

EXAMPLE 2

Solve the equation $a^2x + b^2y = 2$ for y.

SOLUTION Since we are to solve for y, we treat y as the variable and treat all other letters as constants. We begin by getting the y-term on one side and all other terms on the other side of the equation.

$$a^2x + b^2y = 2$$

Subtract a^2x from both sides: $\qquad b^2y = 2 - a^2x$

Divide both sides by b^2: $\qquad y = \dfrac{2 - a^2x}{b^2}$ ∎

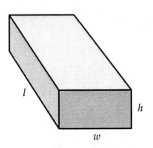

Figure 4–1

EXAMPLE 3

The surface area S of the rectangular box in Figure 4–1 is given by

$$2lh + 2lw + 2wh = S.$$

Solve this equation for h.

SOLUTION   Treat h as the variable and all the other letters as constants. First, get all the terms involving the variable h on one side of the equation and everything else on the other side.

$$2lh + 2lw + 2wh = S$$

Subtract $2lw$ from both sides: $$2lh + 2wh = S - 2lw$$

Factor out h on the left side: $$(2l + 2w)h = S - 2lw$$

Divide both sides by $(2l + 2w)$: $$h = \frac{S - 2lw}{2l + 2w}.$$ ∎

QUADRATIC EQUATIONS

A **second-degree,** or **quadratic, equation** is an equation that can be written in the form

$$ax^2 + bx + c = 0$$

for some constants a, b, c, with $a \neq 0$. There are several techniques for solving such equations. We begin with the **factoring method,** which makes use of this property of the real numbers:

Zero Products

> If a product of real numbers is zero, then at least one of the factors is zero; in other words,
>
> If $cd = 0$, then $c = 0$ or $d = 0$ (or both).

EXAMPLE 4

To solve $3x^2 - x = 10$, we first rearrange the terms to make one side 0 and then factor:

Subtract 10 from each side: $$3x^2 - x - 10 = 0$$

Factor left side: $$(3x + 5)(x - 2) = 0.$$

If a product of real numbers is 0, then at least one of the factors must be 0. So this equation is equivalent to

$$3x + 5 = 0 \qquad \text{or} \qquad x - 2 = 0$$
$$3x = -5 \qquad\qquad\qquad x = 2$$
$$x = -5/3$$

Therefore the solutions are $-5/3$ and 2. ∎

CAUTION

You cannot use the factoring method unless one side of the equation is 0. Otherwise, you'll get the wrong answer, as is the case here:

$$x^2 + 3x + 2 = 1$$
$$(x + 2)(x + 1) = 1$$
$$x + 2 = 1 \quad \text{or} \quad x + 1 = 1 \qquad \text{Mistake here!}$$
$$x = -1 \quad \text{or} \qquad x = 0$$

These are NOT solutions of the original equation, as you can easily verify.

There are two numbers whose square is 7, namely, $\sqrt{7}$ and $-\sqrt{7}$. So the solutions of $x^2 = 7$ are $\sqrt{7}$ and $-\sqrt{7}$, or in abbreviated form, $\pm\sqrt{7}$. The same argument works for any positive real number d:

The solutions of $x^2 = d$ are $\sqrt{d}$ and $-\sqrt{d}$.

The same reasoning enables us to solve other equations.

EXAMPLE 5

Solve: $(z - 2)^2 = 5$.

SOLUTION   The equation says that $z - 2$ is a number whose square is 5. Since there are only two numbers whose square is 5, namely, $\sqrt{5}$ and $-\sqrt{5}$, we must have

$$z - 2 = \sqrt{5} \qquad \text{or} \qquad z - 2 = -\sqrt{5}$$
$$z = \sqrt{5} + 2 \qquad\qquad\qquad z = -\sqrt{5} + 2.$$

In compact notation, the solutions of the equation are $\pm\sqrt{5} + 2$. ∎

We now use a slight variation of Example 5 to develop a method for solving quadratic equations that don't readily factor. Consider, for example, the expression $x^2 + 6x$. If you add 9, the result is a perfect square:

$$x^2 + 6x + 9 = (x + 3)^2$$

The process of adding a constant to produce a perfect square is called **completing the square.** Note that one-half the coefficient of x in $x^2 + 6x$ is $\frac{6}{2} = 3$. We added 9, which is 3^2, and the resulting perfect square was $(x + 3)^2$. The same idea works in the general case, as is proved in Exercise 94.

Completing the Square

| To change $x^2 + bx$ into a perfect square, add $\left(\dfrac{b}{2}\right)^2$. The resulting polynomial $x^2 + bx + \left(\dfrac{b}{2}\right)^2$ factors as $\left(x + \dfrac{b}{2}\right)^2$.

The following example shows how completing the square can be used to solve quadratic equations.

EXAMPLE 6

To solve $x^2 + 6x + 1 = 0$, we first rewrite the equation as $x^2 + 6x = -1$. Next we complete the square on the left side by adding the square of half the coefficient of x, namely, $(6/2)^2 = 9$. To have an equivalent equation, we must add 9 to *both* sides:

$$x^2 + 6x + 9 = -1 + 9$$

Factor left side: $\qquad (x + 3)^2 = 8.$

Thus $x + 3$ is a number whose square is 8. The only numbers whose squares equal 8 are $\sqrt{8}$ and $-\sqrt{8}$. So we must have

$$x + 3 = \sqrt{8} \qquad \text{or} \qquad x + 3 = -\sqrt{8}$$

$$x = \sqrt{8} - 3 \qquad \text{or} \qquad x = -\sqrt{8} - 3.$$

Therefore the solutions of the original equation are $\sqrt{8} - 3$ and $-\sqrt{8} - 3$ or, in more compact notation, $\pm\sqrt{8} - 3$. ∎

CAUTION

Completing the square only works when the coefficient of x^2 is 1. In an equation such as

$$5x^2 - x + 2 = 0,$$

you must first divide every term on both sides by 5 and *then* complete the square.

We can use the completing-the-square method to solve *any* quadratic equation:*

$$ax^2 + bx + c = 0$$

Divide both sides by a: $\qquad x^2 + \dfrac{b}{a}x + \dfrac{c}{a} = 0$

Subtract $\dfrac{c}{a}$ from both sides: $\qquad x^2 + \dfrac{b}{a}x = -\dfrac{c}{a}$

---

*If you have trouble following any step here, do it for a numerical example, such as the case when $a = 3, b = 11, c = 5$.

Add $\left(\dfrac{b}{2a}\right)^2$ to both sides:[*] $x^2 + \dfrac{b}{a}x + \left(\dfrac{b}{2a}\right)^2 = \left(\dfrac{b}{2a}\right)^2 - \dfrac{c}{a}$

Factor left side: $\left(x + \dfrac{b}{2a}\right)^2 = \left(\dfrac{b}{2a}\right)^2 - \dfrac{c}{a}$

Find common denominator
for right side: $\left(x + \dfrac{b}{2a}\right)^2 = \dfrac{b^2}{4a^2} - \dfrac{c}{a} = \dfrac{b^2 - 4ac}{4a^2}.$

Since the square of $x + \dfrac{b}{2a}$ equals $\dfrac{b^2 - 4ac}{4a^2}$, we must have

$$x + \frac{b}{2a} = \pm\sqrt{\frac{b^2 - 4ac}{4a^2}} = \pm\frac{\sqrt{b^2 - 4ac}}{2a}$$

Subtract $\dfrac{b}{2a}$ from
both sides: $x = \dfrac{-b}{2a} \pm \dfrac{\sqrt{b^2 - 4ac}}{2a} = \dfrac{-b \pm \sqrt{b^2 - 4ac}}{2a}.$

We have proved

**The Quadratic
Formula**

> The solutions of the quadratic equation $ax^2 + bx + c = 0$ are
> $$x = \frac{-b \pm \sqrt{b^2 - 4ac}}{2a}.$$

You should memorize the quadratic formula.

EXAMPLE 7

Solve $x^2 + 3 = -8x$.

SOLUTION   Rewrite the equation as $x^2 + 8x + 3 = 0$, and apply the quadratic formula with $a = 1$, $b = 8$, and $c = 3$:

$$x = \frac{-b \pm \sqrt{b^2 - 4ac}}{2a} = \frac{-8 \pm \sqrt{8^2 - 4 \cdot 1 \cdot 3}}{2 \cdot 1}$$

$$= \frac{-8 \pm \sqrt{52}}{2} = \frac{-8 \pm \sqrt{4 \cdot 13}}{2} = \frac{-8 \pm \sqrt{4}\sqrt{13}}{2}$$

$$= \frac{-8 \pm 2\sqrt{13}}{2} = -4 \pm \sqrt{13}.$$

The equation has two distinct real solutions, $-4 + \sqrt{13}$ and $-4 - \sqrt{13}$. ∎

---

[*]This is the square of half the coefficient of x.

EXAMPLE 8

Solve $x^2 - 194x + 9409 = 0$.

SOLUTION   Use a calculator and the quadratic formula with $a = 1$, $b = -194$, and $c = 9409$:

$$x = \frac{-b \pm \sqrt{b^2 - 4ac}}{2a} = \frac{-(-194) \pm \sqrt{(-194)^2 - 4 \cdot 1 \cdot 9409}}{2 \cdot 1}$$

$$= \frac{194 \pm \sqrt{37636 - 37636}}{2} = \frac{194 \pm 0}{2} = 97.$$

Thus, 97 is the only solution of the equation.   ■

EXAMPLE 9

Solve $2x^2 + x + 3 = 0$.

SOLUTION   Use the quadratic formula with $a = 2$, $b = 1$, and $c = 3$:

$$x = \frac{-b \pm \sqrt{b^2 - 4ac}}{2a} = \frac{-1 \pm \sqrt{1^2 - 4 \cdot 2 \cdot 3}}{2 \cdot 2} = \frac{-1 \pm \sqrt{1 - 24}}{4}$$

$$= \frac{-1 \pm \sqrt{-23}}{4}.$$

Since $\sqrt{-23}$ is not a real number, this equation has *no real solutions* (that is, no solutions in the real number system).   ■

The expression $b^2 - 4ac$ in the quadratic formula is called the **discriminant.** As the last three examples illustrate, the discriminant determines the *number* of real solutions of the equation $ax^2 + bx + c = 0$.

***Real Solutions of a
Quadratic Equation***

Discriminant $b^2 - 4ac$	Number of Real Solutions of $ax^2 + bx + c = 0$	Example
> 0	Two distinct real solutions	Example 7
$= 0$	One real solution	Example 8
< 0	No real solutions	Example 9

EXAMPLE 10

Use the discriminant to determine the number of real solutions of each of these equations.

(a) $4x^2 - 20x + 25 = 0$ (b) $7x^2 + 3 = 5x$ (c) $.5x^2 + 6x - 2 = 0$.

SOLUTION

(a) Here $a = 4$, $b = -20$, and $c = 25$. So the discriminant is

$$b^2 - 4ac = (-20)^2 - 4 \cdot 4 \cdot 25 = 400 - 400 = 0.$$

The equation has one real solution.

(b) First rewrite the equation as $7x^2 - 5x + 3 = 0$. The discriminant is

$$b^2 - 4ac = (-5)^2 - 4 \cdot 7 \cdot 3 = 25 - 84 = -59,$$

so the equation has no real solutions.

(c) The discriminant is $b^2 - 4ac = 6^2 - 4 \cdot (.5) \cdot (-2) = 36 + 4 = 40$. There are two real solutions. ∎

The quadratic formula and a calculator can be used to solve any quadratic equation with nonnegative discriminant.

EXAMPLE 11

The number of identity theft complaints (in thousands) in year x is approximated by

$$-5.5x^2 + 77.1x + 26.3 \qquad (0 \le x \le 9),$$

where x is the number of years since 2000.* Use the quadratic formula and a calculator to find the year in which there were 247,000 complaints.

SOLUTION   Complaints are measured in thousands, so we must solve

$$-5.5x^2 + 77.1x + 26.3 = 247.$$

Subtracting 247 from both sides produces the equivalent equation

$$-5.5x^2 + 77.1x - 220.7 = 0.$$

To solve this equation, we compute the radical part of the quadratic formula

$$\sqrt{b^2 - 4ac} = \sqrt{77.1^2 - 4(-5.5)(-220.7)}$$

and store the result in memory D. By the quadratic formula, the solutions of the equation are

$$x = \frac{-b \pm \sqrt{b^2 - 4ac}}{2a} = \frac{-b \pm D}{2a} = \frac{-77.1 \pm D}{2(-5.5)}.$$

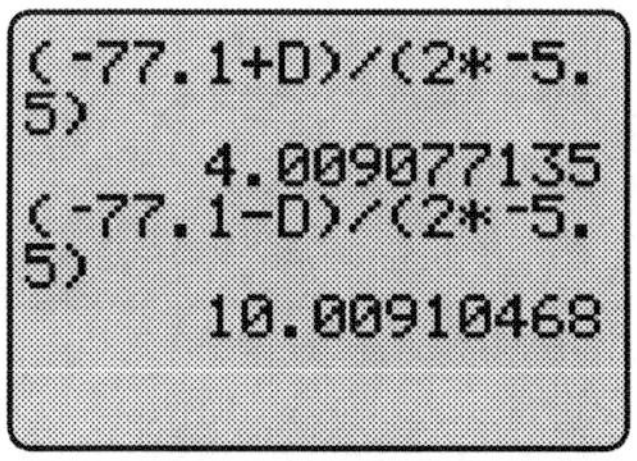

So the approximate solutions are

$$x = \frac{-77.1 + D}{2(-5.5)} \approx 4.009 \qquad \text{and} \qquad x = \frac{-77.1 - D}{2(-5.5)} \approx 10.009,$$

as shown in Figure 4–2. Since we are given that $0 \le x \le 9$, the only applicable solution here is $x \approx 4.009$, which corresponds to early 2004. ∎

```
(-77.1+D)/(2*-5.
5)
         4.009077135
(-77.1-D)/(2*-5.
5)
         10.00910468
```

Figure 4–2

---

*Based on data from the Identity Theft Clearinghouse of the Federal Trade Commission.

EXAMPLE 12

If an object is thrown upward, dropped, or thrown downward and travels in a straight line subject only to gravity (with wind resistance ignored), the height h of the object above the ground (in feet) after t seconds is given by

$$h = -16t^2 + v_0t + h_0,$$

where h_0 is the height of the object when $t = 0$ and v_0 is the initial velocity at time $t = 0$. The value of v_0 is taken as positive if the object moves upward and negative if it moves downward. If a baseball is thrown down from the top of a 640-foot-high building with an initial velocity of 52 feet per second, how long does it take to reach the ground?

SOLUTION   In this case, v_0 is -52 and h_0 is 640, so that the height equation is

$$h = -16t^2 - 52t + 640.$$

The object is on the ground when $h = 0$, so we must solve the equation

$$0 = -16t^2 - 52t + 640.$$

Using the quadratic formula and a calculator, we see that

$$t = \frac{-(-52) \pm \sqrt{(-52)^2 - 4(-16)(640)}}{2(-16)} = \frac{52 \pm \sqrt{43{,}664}}{-32} = \begin{cases} -8.15 \\ \text{or} \\ 4.90. \end{cases}$$

Only the positive answer makes sense in this case. So it takes about 4.9 seconds for the baseball to reach the ground. ∎

TECHNOLOGY TIP

Most calculators have built-in polynomial equation solvers that will solve quadratic and other polynomial equations. See Exercise 105.

HIGHER-DEGREE EQUATIONS

A **polynomial equation of degree n** is one that can be written in the form

$$a_nx^n + \cdots + a_3x^3 + a_2x^2 + a_1x + a_0 = 0,$$

where n is a positive integer, each a_i is a constant, and $a_n \neq 0$. For instance,

$$4x^6 - 3x^5 + x^4 + 7x^3 - 8x^2 + 4x + 9 = 0$$

is a polynomial equation of degree 6. As a general rule, polynomial equations of degree 3 and above are best solved by the numerical or graphical methods presented in Section 2.2. However, some such equations can be solved algebraically by making a suitable substitution, as we now see.

EXAMPLE 13

To solve $4x^4 - 13x^2 + 3 = 0$, substitute u for x^2 and solve the resulting quadratic equation:

$$4x^4 - 13x^2 + 3 = 0$$
$$4(x^2)^2 - 13x^2 + 3 = 0$$

$$\text{Let } u = x^2: \qquad 4u^2 - 13u + 3 = 0$$

$$(u - 3)(4u - 1) = 0$$

$$u - 3 = 0 \qquad \text{or} \qquad 4u - 1 = 0$$

$$u = 3 \qquad\qquad\qquad 4u = 1$$

$$u = \frac{1}{4}.$$

Since $u = x^2$, we see that

$$x^2 = 3 \qquad \text{or} \qquad x^2 = \frac{1}{4}$$

$$x = \pm\sqrt{3} \qquad\qquad x = \pm\frac{1}{2}.$$

Hence, the original equation has four solutions: $-\sqrt{3}, \sqrt{3}, -1/2, 1/2$.   ■

EXAMPLE 14

To solve $x^4 - 4x^2 + 1 = 0$, let $u = x^2$:

$$x^4 - 4x^2 + 1 = 0$$

$$u^2 - 4u + 1 = 0.$$

The quadratic formula shows that

$$u = \frac{-(-4) \pm \sqrt{(-4)^2 - 4 \cdot 1 \cdot 1}}{2 \cdot 1} = \frac{4 \pm \sqrt{12}}{2}$$

$$= \frac{4 \pm \sqrt{4 \cdot 3}}{2} = \frac{4 \pm \sqrt{4}\sqrt{3}}{2}$$

$$= \frac{4 \pm 2\sqrt{3}}{2} = 2 \pm \sqrt{3}.$$

Since $u = x^2$, we have the equivalent statements:

$$x^2 = 2 + \sqrt{3} \qquad \text{or} \qquad x^2 = 2 - \sqrt{3}$$

$$x = \pm\sqrt{2 + \sqrt{3}} \qquad\qquad x = \pm\sqrt{2 - \sqrt{3}}.$$

Therefore the original equation has four solutions.   ■

FRACTIONAL EQUATIONS

The first step in solving an equation that involves fractional expressions is to multiply both sides by a common denominator to eliminate the fractions. Then use the methods presented earlier in this chapter to solve the resulting equation. However, care must be used.

Multiplying both sides of an equation by a quantity involving the variable (which may be zero for some values) may lead to an **extraneous solution,** a number that does not satisfy the original equation.* To avoid errors in such situations, always check your solutions in the *original* equation.

---

*The second basic principle for solving equations (page 19) applies only to nonzero quantities.

EXAMPLE 15

Solve $\dfrac{x+2}{x-3} - \dfrac{7}{x+3} = \dfrac{30}{x^2-9}$.

SOLUTION Note that $(x-3)(x+3) = x^2 - 9$. Multiply both sides of the equation by $(x-3)(x+3)$ to eliminate the fractions.

$$\frac{x+2}{x-3}(x-3)(x+3) - \frac{7}{x+3}(x-3)(x+3) = \frac{30}{x^2-9}(x-3)(x+3)$$

Cancel common factors: $(x+2)(x+3) - 7(x-3) = 30$

Multiply out left side: $x^2 + 5x + 6 - 7x + 21 = 30$

Simplify: $x^2 - 2x + 27 = 30$

Subtract 30 from both sides: $x^2 - 2x - 3 = 0$

Factor: $(x-3)(x+1) = 0$

Zero Product Property: $x - 3 = 0 \quad \text{or} \quad x + 1 = 0$

$$x = 3 \qquad\qquad x = -1$$

So the *possible* solutions are 3 and -1. When 3 is substituted for x in the original equation, its first term becomes $\dfrac{3+3}{3-3} = \dfrac{6}{0}$, which is not defined. So 3 is *not* a solution of the original equation. Next we substitute -1 for x in the original equation and obtain:

Left side: $\dfrac{-1+2}{-1-3} - \dfrac{7}{-1+3} = \dfrac{1}{-4} - \dfrac{7}{2} = -\dfrac{1}{4} - \dfrac{14}{4} = -\dfrac{15}{4}$

Right side: $\dfrac{30}{(-1)^2-9} = \dfrac{30}{-8} = -\dfrac{15}{4}$.

So the left and right sides are equal. Therefore, -1 is the only solution of the original equation. ∎

EXAMPLE 16

The relationship between the focal length F of a digital camera lens, the distance u from the object being photographed to the lens, and the distance v from the lens to the camera's sensor is given by

$$\frac{1}{F} = \frac{1}{v} + \frac{1}{u}.$$

Express u in terms of F and v.

SOLUTION We must solve the equation for u. First we eliminate fractions by multiplying both sides by Fvu.

$$Fvu \cdot \frac{1}{F} = Fvu\left(\frac{1}{v} + \frac{1}{u}\right)$$

Distributive Law: $Fvu \cdot \dfrac{1}{F} = Fvu \cdot \dfrac{1}{v} + Fvu \cdot \dfrac{1}{u}$

Cancel:	$vu = Fu + Fv$
Subtract Fu from both sides:	$vu - Fu = Fv$
Distributive Law:	$(v - F)u = Fv$
Divide both sides by $v - F$:	$u = \dfrac{Fv}{v - F}.$ ∎

EXERCISES 4.1

In Exercises 1–6, solve the equation.

1. $3x + 2 = 26$

2. $\dfrac{y}{5} - 3 = 14$

3. $3x + 2 = 9x + 7$

4. $-7(t + 2) = 3(4t + 1)$

5. $\dfrac{3y}{4} - 6 = y + 2$

6. $2(1 + x) = 3x + 5$

In Exercises 7–12, solve the equation for the indicated variable.

7. $x = 3y - 5$ for y

8. $5x - 2y = 1$ for x

9. $A = \dfrac{h}{2}(b + c)$ for b

10. $V = \pi b^2 c$ for c

11. $V = \dfrac{\pi d^2 h}{4}$ for h

12. $\dfrac{1}{r} = \dfrac{1}{s} + \dfrac{1}{t}$ for r

In Exercises 13–22, solve the equation by factoring.

13. $x^2 - 8x + 15 = 0$

14. $x^2 - 5x + 6 = 0$

15. $x^2 - 5x = 14$

16. $x^2 + x = 20$

17. $2y^2 + 5y - 3 = 0$

18. $3t^2 - t - 2 = 0$

19. $4t^2 + 9t + 2 = 0$

20. $9t^2 + 2 = 11t$

21. $3u^2 - 4u = 4$

22. $5x^2 + 26x = -5$

In Exercises 23–26, solve the equation by completing the square.

23. $x^2 - 2x = 12$

24. $x^2 - 4x - 30 = 0$

25. $x^2 - x - 1 = 0$

26. $x^2 + 3x - 2 = 0$

In Exercises 27–32, find the number of real solutions of the equation by computing the discriminant.

27. $x^2 + 4x + 1 = 0$

28. $4x^2 - 4x - 3 = 0$

29. $9x^2 = 12x + 1$

30. $9t^2 + 15 = 30t$

31. $25t^2 + 49 = 70t$

32. $49t^2 + 5 = 42t$

In Exercises 33–42, use the quadratic formula to solve the equation.

33. $x^2 - 4x + 1 = 0$

34. $x^2 + 2x - 1 = 0$

35. $x^2 + 6x + 7 = 0$

36. $x^2 + 4x - 3 = 0$

37. $x^2 + 6 = 2x$

38. $x^2 + 11 = 6x$

39. $4x^2 + 4x = 7$

40. $4x^2 - 4x = 11$

41. $4x^2 - 8x + 1 = 0$

42. $2t^2 + 4t + 1 = 0$

In Exercises 43–52, solve the equation by any method.

43. $x^2 + 9x + 18 = 0$

44. $3t^2 - 11t - 20 = 0$

45. $4x(x + 1) = 1$

46. $25y^2 = 20y + 1$

47. $2x^2 = 7x + 15$

48. $2x^2 = 6x + 3$

49. $t^2 + 4t + 13 = 0$

50. $5x^2 + 2x = 2$

51. $\dfrac{7x^2}{3} = \dfrac{2x}{3} - 1$

52. $x^2 + \sqrt{2}x - 3 = 0$

In Exercises 53–56, use a calculator to find approximate solutions of the equation.

53. $4.42x^2 - 10.14x + 3.79 = 0$

54. $8.06x^2 + 25.8726x - 25.047256 = 0$

55. $3x^2 - 82.74x + 570.4923 = 0$

56. $7.63x^2 + 2.79x = 5.32$

In Exercises 57–64, find all real solutions of the equation exactly.

57. $y^4 - 7y^2 + 6 = 0$

58. $x^4 - 2x^2 + 1 = 0$

59. $x^4 - 2x^2 - 35 = 0$

60. $x^4 - 2x^2 - 24 = 0$

61. $2y^4 - 9y^2 + 4 = 0$

62. $6z^4 - 7z^2 + 2 = 0$

63. $10x^4 + 3x^2 = 1$

64. $6x^4 - 7x^2 = 3$

In Exercises 65–74, solve the equation and check your answers.

65. $\dfrac{1}{2t} - \dfrac{2}{5t} = \dfrac{1}{10t} - 1$

66. $\dfrac{1}{2} + \dfrac{2}{y} = \dfrac{1}{3} + \dfrac{3}{y}$

67. $\dfrac{2x - 7}{x + 4} = \dfrac{5}{x + 4} - 2$

68. $\dfrac{z + 4}{z + 5} = \dfrac{-1}{z + 5}$

69. $25x + \dfrac{4}{x} = 20$

70. $1 - \dfrac{3}{x} = \dfrac{40}{x^2}$

71. $\dfrac{2}{x^2} - \dfrac{5}{x} = 4$

72. $\dfrac{x}{x-1} + \dfrac{x+2}{x} = 3$

73. $\dfrac{4x^2 + 5}{3x^2 + 5x - 2} = \dfrac{4}{3x - 1} - \dfrac{3}{x + 2}$

74. $\dfrac{x + 3}{x - 2} - \dfrac{3}{x + 2} = \dfrac{20}{x^2 - 4}$

The gross federal debt y (in trillions of dollars) in year x is approximated by

$$y = .79x + 3.93 \quad (x \geq 3),$$

where x is the number of years after 2000. In Exercises 75–76, find the year in which the approximate federal debt is:*

75. $12.62 billion

76. $14.2 billion

The total health care expenditures E in the United States (in billions of dollars) can be approximated by

$$E = 73.04x + 625.6,$$

where x is the number of years since 1990.[†] Determine the year in which health care expenditures are at the given level.

77. $1794.25 billion

78. $1940.3 billion

In a simple model of the economy (by John Maynard Keynes), equilibrium between national output and national expenditures is given by the equilibrium equation

$$Y = C + I + G + (X - M),$$

where Y is the national income, C is consumption (which depends on national income), I is the amount of investment, G is government spending, X is exports, and M is imports (which also depend on national income). In Exercises 79 and 80, solve the equilibrium equation for Y under the given conditions.

79. $C = 120 + .9Y$, $M = 20 + .2Y$, $I = 140$, $G = 150$, and $X = 60$

80. $C = 60 + .85Y$, $M = 35 + .2Y$, $I = 95$, $G = 145$, and $X = 50$

In Exercises 81–84, use the height equation in Example 12. Note that an object that is dropped (rather than thrown downward) has initial velocity $v_0 = 0$.

81. How long does it take a baseball to reach the ground if it is dropped from the top of a 640-foot-high building? Compare with Example 12.

82. You are standing on a cliff that is 200 feet high. How long will it take a rock to reach the ground if

(a) you drop it?

(b) you throw it downward at an initial velocity of 40 feet per second?

(c) How far does the rock fall in 2 seconds if you throw it downward with an initial velocity of 40 feet per second?

83. A rocket is fired straight up from ground level with an initial velocity of 800 feet per second.

(a) How long does it take the rocket to rise 3200 feet?

(b) When will the rocket hit the ground?

84. A rocket loaded with fireworks is to be shot vertically upward from ground level with an initial velocity of 200 feet per second. When the rocket reaches a height of 400 feet on its upward trip the fireworks will be detonated. How many seconds after liftoff will this take place?

85. The atmospheric pressure a (in pounds per square foot) at height h thousand feet above sea level is approximately

$$a = .8315h^2 - 73.93h + 2116.1.$$

(a) Find the atmospheric pressure at sea level and at the top of Mount Everest, the tallest mountain in the world (29,035 feet*). [Remember that h is measured in thousands.]

(b) The atmospheric pressure at the top of Mount Rainier is 1223.43 pounds per square foot. How high is Mount Rainier?

86. Data from the U.S. Department of Health and Human Services indicates that the cumulative number N of reported cases of AIDS in the United States in year x can be approximated by the equation

$$N = 3362.1x^2 - 17,270.3x + 24,043,$$

where $x = 0$ corresponds to 1980. In what year did the total reach 550,000?

87. According to data from the U.S. Census Bureau, the population P of Cleveland, Ohio (in thousands) in year x can be approximated by $P = .08x^2 - 13.08x + 927$, where $x = 0$ corresponds to 1950. In what year in the past was the population about 804,200?

88. The number N of AIDS cases diagnosed to date (in thousands) is approximated by $N = -.37x^2 + 59.5x + 247.26$, where x is the number of years since 1990.[†] Assuming that this equation remains valid through 2011, determine when the number of diagnosed cases of AIDS was or will be

(a) 825,000

(b) 1.2 million

*Based on data and projections from the Congressional Budget Office in 2005.
[†]Based on data from the U.S. Centers for Medicare and Medicaid Services.

*Based on measurements in 1999 by climbers sponsored by the Boston Museum of Science and the National Geographic Society, using satellite-based technology.
[†]Based on data from the U.S. Department of Health and Human Services.

89. The number N of Walgreens drugstores in year x can be approximated by $N = 6.82x^2 - 1.55x + 666.8$, where $x = 0$ corresponds to 1980.* Determine when the number of stores was or will be

(a) 4240 (b) 5600 (c) 7000

90. The total resources T (in billions of dollars) of the Pension Benefit Guaranty Corporation, the government agency that insures pensions, can be approximated by the equation $T = -.26x^2 + 3.62x + 30.18$, where x is the number of years after 2000.† Determine when the total resources are at the given level.

(a) $42.5 billion
(b) $30 billion
(c) When will the Corporation be out of money ($T = 0$)?

91. According to data from the National Highway Traffic Safety Administration, the driver fatality rate D per 1000 licensed drivers every 100 million miles can be approximated by the equation $D = .0031x^2 - .291x + 7.1$, where x is the age of the driver.

(a) For what ages is the driver fatality rate about 1 death per 1000?
(b) For what ages is the rate three times greater than in part (a)?

92. The combined resistance of two resistors, with resistances R_1 and R_2 respectively, connected in parallel is given by $\dfrac{R_1 R_2}{R_1 + R_2}$. If the first resistor has 8 ohms resistance and the combined resistance is 4.8 ohms, what is the resistance of the second resistor?

93. The *cost-benefit equation* $\dfrac{18x}{100 - x} = D$ relates the cost D (in thousands of dollars) needed to remove x percent of a pollutant from the emissions of a factory. Find the percent of the pollutant removed when the following amounts are spent.

(a) $50,000 [Here $D = 50$]
(b) $100,000
(c) $200,000

94. (a) Let b be a real number. Multiply out the expression $\left(x + \dfrac{b}{2}\right)^2$.

(b) Explain why your computation in part (a) shows that this statement is true: If you add $\left(\dfrac{b}{2}\right)^2$ to the expression $x^2 + bx$, the resulting polynomial is a perfect square.

THINKERS

In Exercises 95–98, find a number k such that the given equation has exactly one real solution.

95. $x^2 + kx + 25 = 0$ **96.** $x^2 - kx + 49 = 0$

97. $kx^2 + 8x + 1 = 0$ **98.** $kx^2 + 24x + 16 = 0$

In Exercises 99–101, the discriminant of the equation $ax^2 + bx + c = 0$ (with a, b, c integers) is given. Use it to determine whether or not the solutions of the equation are rational numbers.

99. $b^2 - 4ac = 25$

100. $b^2 - 4ac = 0$

101. $b^2 - 4ac = 72$

102. Find the error in the following "proof" that $6 = 3$.

	$x = 3$
Multiply both sides by x:	$x^2 = 3x$
Subtract 9 from both sides:	$x^2 - 9 = 3x - 9$
Factor each side:	$(x - 3)(x + 3) = 3(x - 3)$
Divide both sides by $x - 3$:	$x + 3 = 3$
Since $x = 3$:	$3 + 3 = 3$
	$6 = 3$

103. Find a number k such that 4 and 1 are the solutions of $x^2 - 5x + k = 0$.

104. Suppose a, b, c are fixed real numbers such that $b^2 - 4ac \geq 0$. Let r and s be the solutions of

$$ax^2 + bx + c = 0.$$

(a) Use the quadratic formula to show that $r + s = -b/a$ and $rs = c/a$.
(b) Use part (a) to verify that $ax^2 + bx + c = a(x - r)(x - s)$.
(c) Use part (b) to factor $x^2 - 2x - 1$ and $5x^2 + 8x + 2$.

105. (a) Solve $x^2 + 5x + 2 = 0$ (exact answer required).

(b) If you have one of the calculators listed below, use its polynomial solver to solve the equation in part (a). Does your answer agree with the one in part (a)?

Calculator	Use this menu/choice
TI-84+	APPS/*PolySmlt**
TI-86	POLY†
TI-89	ALGEBRA/*Solve*‡
Casio 9850	EQUATION (Main Menu)
HP-39gs	MATH/POLYNOM/*Polyroot*§

(c) Use the solver to solve $3x^4 - 2x^3 - 5x^2 + 2x + 1 = 0$.

---

*Based on data from the Walgreen Company.
†Based on data from the Center on Federal Financial Institutions.

---

*If *PolySmlt* is not in the APPS menu, you can download it from TI.
†When asked for "order", enter the degree of the polynomial.
‡Syntax: Solve($x^2 + 5x + 2 = 0, x$)
§Syntax: Polyroot([1, 5, 2])

4.1.A   Absolute Value Equations

Section Objective ■ Solve absolute value equations algebraically.

If c is a real number, then by the definition of absolute value, $|c|$ is either c or $-c$ (whichever one is positive). This fact can be used to solve absolute value equations algebraically.

EXAMPLE 1

To solve $|3x - 4| = 8$, apply the fact stated above with $c = 3x - 4$. Then $|3x - 4|$ is either $3x - 4$ or $-(3x - 4)$, so

$$3x - 4 = 8 \qquad \text{or} \qquad -(3x - 4) = 8$$
$$3x = 12 \qquad\qquad\qquad -3x + 4 = 8$$
$$x = 4 \qquad\qquad\qquad\qquad -3x = 4$$
$$\qquad\qquad\qquad\qquad\qquad x = -4/3.$$

So there are two possible solutions of the original equation $|3x - 4| = 8$. You can readily verify that both 4 and $-4/3$ actually are solutions. ■

EXAMPLE 2

Solve $|x + 4| = 5x - 2$.

SOLUTION   The left side of the equation is either $x + 4$ or $-(x + 4)$ (why?). Hence,

$$x + 4 = 5x - 2 \qquad \text{or} \qquad -(x + 4) = 5x - 2$$
$$-4x + 4 = -2 \qquad\qquad\qquad -x - 4 = 5x - 2$$
$$-4x = -6 \qquad\qquad\qquad\qquad -6x = 2$$
$$x = \frac{-6}{-4} = \frac{3}{2} \qquad\qquad\qquad x = \frac{2}{-6} = -\frac{1}{3}.$$

We must check each of these possible solutions in the original equation,

$$|x + 4| = 5x - 2.$$

We see that $x = 3/2$ is a solution because

$$\left|\frac{3}{2} + 4\right| = \frac{11}{2} \qquad \text{and} \qquad 5\left(\frac{3}{2}\right) - 2 = \frac{11}{2}.$$

However, $x = -1/3$ is not a solution, since

$$\left|-\frac{1}{3} + 4\right| = \frac{11}{3} \qquad \text{but} \qquad 5\left(-\frac{1}{3}\right) - 2 = -\frac{11}{3}. \qquad ■$$

EXAMPLE 3

Solve the equation $|x^2 + 4x - 3| = 2$.

SOLUTION   The equation is equivalent to

$$x^2 + 4x - 3 = 2 \quad \text{or} \quad -(x^2 + 4x - 3) = 2$$
$$x^2 + 4x - 5 = 0 \qquad\qquad -x^2 - 4x + 3 = 2$$
$$-x^2 - 4x + 1 = 0$$
$$x^2 + 4x - 1 = 0.$$

The first of these equations can be solved by factoring and the second by the quadratic formula:

$$(x + 5)(x - 1) = 0 \quad \text{or} \quad x = \frac{-4 \pm \sqrt{4^2 - 4 \cdot 1 \cdot (-1)}}{2 \cdot 1}$$

$$x = -5 \quad \text{or} \quad x = 1 \qquad x = \frac{-4 \pm \sqrt{20}}{2} = \frac{-4 \pm 2\sqrt{5}}{2}$$

$$x = -2 + \sqrt{5} \quad \text{or} \quad x = -2 - \sqrt{5}.$$

Verify that all four of these numbers are solutions of the original equation.   ■

EXERCISES 4.1.A

In Exercises 1–12, find all real solutions of each equation.

1. $|2x + 3| = 9$

2. $|3x - 5| = 7$

3. $|6x - 9| = 0$

4. $|4x - 5| = -9$

5. $|2x + 3| = 4x - 1$

6. $|3x - 2| = 5x + 4$

7. $|x - 3| = x$

8. $|2x - 1| = 2x + 1$

9. $|x^2 + 4x - 1| = 4$

10. $|x^2 + 2x - 9| = 6$

11. $|x^2 - 5x + 1| = 3$

12. $|12x^2 + 5x - 7| = 4$

13. In statistical quality control, one needs to find the proportion of the product that is not acceptable. The upper and lower control limits are found by solving the following equation (in which $\bar{p}$ is the mean percent defective and n is the sample size) for *CL*.

$$|CL - \bar{p}| = 3\sqrt{\frac{\bar{p}(1 - \bar{p})}{n}}$$

Find the control limits when $\bar{p} = .02$ and $n = 200$.

4.1.B   Absolute Value Equations

Section Objectives
- ■ Set up and solve a direct variation equation.
- ■ Set up and solve an indirect variation equation.
- ■ Set up and solve combined variation equations.

If a plane flies 400 mph for t hours, then it travels a distance of $400t$ miles. So the distance d is related to the time t by the equation $d = 400t$. When time t increases, so does the distance d. We say that *d varies directly as t* and that the *constant of variation* is 400. Direct variation also occurs in other settings and is formally defined as follows.

Direct Variation

> Suppose the quantities u and v are related by the equation
>
> $$v = ku,$$
>
> where k is a nonzero constant. We say that v **varies directly as u** or that v **is directly proportional to u.** In this case, k is called the **constant of variation** or the **constant of proportionality.**

EXAMPLE 1

When you swim underwater, the pressure p varies directly with the depth d at which you swim. At a depth of 20 feet, the pressure is 8.6 pounds per square inch. What is the pressure at 65 feet deep?

SOLUTION The variation equation is $p = kd$ for some constant k. We first use the given information to find k. Since $p = 8.6$ when $d = 20$, we have

$$p = kd$$

$$8.6 = k(20)$$

$$k = \frac{8.6}{20} = .43.$$

Therefore, the variation equation is $p = .43d$. To find the pressure at 65 feet, substitute 65 for d in the equation:

$$p = .43d = .43(65) = 27.95 \text{ pounds per square inch.} \quad \blacksquare$$

The basic idea in direct variation is that the two quantities grow or shrink together. For instance, when $v = 3u$, then as u gets large, so does v. But two quantities can also be related in such a way that one grows as the other shrinks or vice versa. For example if $v = 5/u$, then when u is large (say, $u = 500$), v is small: $v = 5/500 = .01$. This is an example of *inverse variation.*

Inverse Variation

> Suppose the quantities u and v are related by the equation
>
> $$v = \frac{k}{u},$$
>
> where k is a nonzero constant. We say that v **varies inversely as u** or that v **is inversely proportional to u.** Once again, k is called the **constant of variation** or the **constant of proportionality.**

EXAMPLE 2

According to one of Parkinson's laws, the amount of time the Math Department spends discussing an item in its budget is inversely proportional to the cost of the item. If the department spent 40 minutes discussing the purchase of a copying machine for $2100, how much time will it spend discussing a $280 appropriation for the annual picnic?

SOLUTION Let t denote time (in minutes) and c the cost of an item. Then the variation equation is

$$t = \frac{k}{c}$$

for some constant k. We know that $t = 40$ when $c = 2100$. Substituting these numbers in the equation, we see that

$$40 = \frac{k}{2100}$$

$$k = 40 \cdot 2100 = 84,000.$$

So the variation equation is

$$t = \frac{84,000}{c}.$$

To find the time spent discussing the picnic, let $c = 280$. Hence,

$$t = \frac{84,000}{280} = 300 \text{ minutes } (= 5 \text{ hours!}). \qquad \blacksquare$$

The terminology of variation also applies to situations involving powers of variables, as illustrated in the following table.

Example	Terminology	General Case*
$y = 7x^4$	y varies directly as the fourth power of x. y is directly proportional to the fourth power of x. (Constant of variation is 7.)	$v = ku^n$
$A = \pi r^2$	A varies directly as the square of r. A is directly proportional to the square of r. (Constant of variation is π).	
$y = \dfrac{10}{x^3}$	y varies inversely as the cube of x. y is inversely proportional to the cube of x. (Constant of variation is 10.)	$v = \dfrac{k}{u^n}$
$W = \dfrac{3.48 \times 10^9}{d^2}$	W varies inversely as the square of d. W is inversely proportional to the square of d. (Constant of variation is 3.48×10^9.)	

EXAMPLE 3

The density of light I falling on an object (measured in lumens per square foot) is inversely proportional to the square of the distance d from the light source. If an object 2 feet from a standard 100-watt light bulb receives 34.82 lumens per square foot, how much light falls on an object 10 feet from this bulb?

SOLUTION The variation equation is

$$I = \frac{k}{d^2}$$

---

*k is a nonzero constant; u and v are variables.

for some constant k. Since $I = 34.82$, when $d = 2$, we have

$$34.82 = \frac{k}{2^2}$$

$$k = 34.82(4) = 139.28.$$

Therefore, the variation equation is

$$I = \frac{139.28}{d^2}.$$

So the light density at 10 feet is

$$I = \frac{139.28}{10^2} = 1.3928 \text{ lumens per square foot.} \qquad \blacksquare$$

In many situations, variation involves more than two variables. Typical terminology in such cases is illustrated in the following table.

Example	Terminology
$I = 100rt$	I varies jointly as r and t. I is jointly proportional to r and t.
$H = .06sd^3$	H varies jointly as s and the cube of d. H is jointly proportional to s and the cube of d.
$P = \dfrac{3T}{V}$	P varies directly as T and inversely as V. P is directly proportional to T and inversely proportional to V.
$S = \dfrac{2.5wt^2}{\ell}$	S varies directly as w and the square of t and inversely as ℓ. S is directly proportional to w and the square of t and inversely proportional to ℓ.

EXAMPLE 4

The electrical resistance R of wire (of uniform material) varies directly as the length L and inversely as the square of the diameter d. A 2-meter-long piece of wire with a diameter of 4.4 millimeters has a resistance of 500 ohms. What diameter wire should be used if a 10-meter piece is to have a resistance of 1300 ohms?

SOLUTION　The variation equation is

$$R = \frac{kL}{d^2}$$

for some constant k. So we substitute the known information ($R = 500$ when $L = 2$ and $d = 4.4$) and solve for k:

$$R = \frac{kL}{d^2}$$

$$500 = \frac{k \cdot 2}{(4.4)^2}$$

$$k = \frac{500(4.4)^2}{2} = 4840.$$

Hence, the equation is

$$R = \frac{4840L}{d^2}.$$

We must find d when $L = 10$ and $R = 1300$:

$$1300 = \frac{4840 \cdot 10}{d^2}$$

$$1300d^2 = 48{,}400$$

$$d^2 = \frac{48{,}400}{1300} \approx 37.2308.$$

Since the diameter is positive, we must have $d \approx \sqrt{37.2308} \approx 6.1$ mm. ∎

EXERCISES 4.1.B

In Exercises 1–6, express each geometric formula as a statement about variation by filling in the blanks in this sentence:

_____ varies _____ as _____;
the constant of variation is _____.

1. Area of a circle of radius r: $A = \pi r^2$.

2. Volume of a sphere of radius r: $V = \frac{4}{3}\pi r^3$.

3. Area of a rectangle of length l and width w: $A = lw$.

4. Area of a triangle of base b and height h: $A = \frac{bh}{2}$.

5. Volume of a right circular cone of base radius r and height h: $V = \frac{\pi r^2 h}{3}$.

6. Volume of a triangular cylinder of base b, height h, and length l: $V = \frac{1}{2}bhl$.

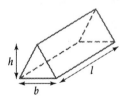

In Exercises 7–12, find the variation equation. Use k for the constant of variation.

7. a varies inversely as b.

8. r is proportional to t.

9. z varies jointly as x, y, and w.

10. The weight w of an object varies inversely as the square of the distance d from the object to the center of the earth.

11. The distance d one can see to the horizon varies directly as the square root of the height h above sea level.

12. The pressure p exerted on the floor by a person's shoe heel is directly proportional to the weight w of the person and inversely proportional to the square of the width r of the heel.

In Exercises 13–22, express the given statement as an equation and find the constant of variation.

13. v varies directly as u; $v = 8$ when $u = 2$.

14. v is directly proportional to u; $v = .4$ when $u = .8$.

15. v varies inversely as u; $v = 8$ when $u = 2$.

16. v is inversely proportional to u; $v = .12$ when $u = .1$.

17. t varies jointly as r and s; $t = 24$ when $r = 2$ and $s = 3$.

18. B varies inversely as u and v; $B = 4$ when $u = 1$ and $v = 3$.

19. w varies jointly as x and y^2; $w = 96$ when $x = 3$ and $y = 4$.

20. p varies directly as the square of z and inversely as r; $p = 32/5$ when $z = 4$ and $r = 10$.

21. T varies jointly as p and the cube of v and inversely as the square of u; $T = 24$ when $p = 3$, $v = 2$, and $u = 4$.

22. D varies jointly as the square of r and the square of s and inversely as the cube of t; $D = 18$ when $r = 4$, $s = 3$, and $t = 2$.

In Exercises 23–30, use an appropriate variation equation to find the required quantity.

23. If r varies directly as t, and $r = 6$ when $t = 3$, find r when $t = 2$.

24. If r is directly proportional to t, and $r = 4$ when $t = 2$, find t when $r = 2$.

25. If b varies inversely as x, and $b = 9$ when $x = 3$, find b when $x = 12$.

26. If b is inversely proportional to x, and $b = 10$ when $x = 4$, find x when $b = 12$.

27. Suppose w is directly proportional to the sum of u and the square of v. If $w = 200$ when $u = 1$ and $v = 7$, then find u when $w = 300$ and $v = 5$.

28. Suppose z varies jointly as x and y. If $z = 30$ when $x = 5$ and $y = 2$, then find x when $z = 45$ and $y = 3$.

29. Suppose r varies inversely as s and t. If $r = 12$ when $s = 3$ and $t = 1$, then find r when $s = 6$ and $t = 2$.

30. Suppose u varies jointly as r and s and inversely as t. If $u = 1.5$ when $r = 2$, $s = 3$, and $t = 4$, then find r when $u = 27$, $s = 9$, and $t = 5$.

31. A resident of Michigan whose taxable income was $24,000 dollars paid state income tax of $936 in 2005.* Use the fact that state income tax varies directly with the taxable income to determine the state tax paid by someone with a taxable income of $39,000.

32. By experiment, you discover that the amount of water that comes from your garden hose varies directly with the water pressure. A pressure of 10 pounds per square inch is needed to produce a flow of 3 gallons per minute.

    (a) What pressure is needed to produce a flow of 4.2 gallons per minute?
    (b) If the pressure is 5 pounds per square inch, what is the flow rate?

33. According to Hooke's law, the distance d that a spring stretches when an object is attached to it is directly proportional to the weight of the object. Suppose that the string stretches 15.75 inches when a 7-pound weight is attached. What weight is required to stretch the spring 27 inches?

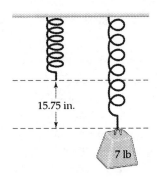

15.75 in.

7 lb

34. In a thunderstorm, there is a gap between the time you see the lightning and the time you hear the thunder. Your distance from the storm is directly proportional to the time interval between the lightning and the thunder. If you hear thunder from a storm that is 1.36 miles away 6.6 seconds after you see lightning, how far away is a storm for which the time gap between lightning and thunder is 12 seconds?

35. At a fixed temperature, the pressure of an enclosed gas is inversely proportional to its volume. The pressure is 50 kilograms per square centimeter when the volume is 200 cubic centimeters. If the gas is compressed to 125 cubic centimeters, what is the pressure?

36. The electrical resistance in a piece of wire of a given length and material varies inversely as the square of the diameter of the wire. If a wire of diameter .01 cm has a resistance of

.4 ohm, what is the resistance of a wire of the same length and material but with diameter .025 cm?

37. The distance traveled by a falling object (subject only to gravity, with wind resistance ignored) is directly proportional to the square of the time it takes to fall that far. If an object falls 100 feet in 2.5 seconds, how far does it fall in 5 seconds?

38. The weight of an object varies inversely with the square of its distance from the center of the earth. Assume that the radius of the earth is 3960 miles. If an astronaut weighs 180 pounds on the surface of the earth, what does that astronaut weigh when traveling 300 miles above the surface of the earth?

39. The weight of a cylindrical can of Glop varies jointly as the height and the square of the base radius. The weight is 250 ounces when the height is 20 inches and the base radius is 5 inches. What is the height when the weight is 960 ounces and the base radius is 8 inches?

40. The force of the wind blowing directly on a flat surface varies directly with the area of the surface and the square of the velocity of the wind. A 10 mile an hour (mph) wind blowing on a wooden gate that measures 3 by 6 feet exerts a force of 15 pounds. What is the force on a 1.5 by 2 foot traffic sign from a 50 mph wind?

41. The force needed to keep a car from skidding on a circular curve varies inversely as the radius of the curve and jointly as the weight of the car and the square of the speed. It takes 1500 kilograms of force to keep a 1000-kilogram car from skidding on a curve of radius 200 meters at a speed of 50 kilometers per hour. What force is needed to keep the same car from skidding on a curve of radius 320 meters at 100 kilometers per hour?

42. Boyle's law states that the volume of a given mass of gas varies directly as the temperature and inversely as the pressure. If a gas has a volume of 14 cubic inches when the temperature is 40° and the pressure is 280 pounds per square inch, what is the volume at a temperature of 50° and pressure of 175 pounds per square inch?

43. The maximum safe load that a rectangular beam can support varies directly with the width w and the square of the height h, and inversely with the length l of the beam. A 6-foot-long beam that is 2 inches high and 4 inches wide has a maximum safe load of 1000 pounds.

    (a) What is the maximum safe load for a 10-foot-long beam that is 4 inches high and 4 inches wide?
    (b) How long should a 4 inch by 4 inch beam be to safely support a 6000-pound load?

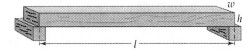

w

h

l

---

44. The period of a pendulum is the time it takes for the pendulum to make one complete swing (going both left and right) and return to its starting point. The period P varies directly with the *square root* of the length l of the pendulum.

(a) Write the variation equation that describes this situation, using k for the constant of variation.
(b) What happens to the period if the length of the pendulum is quadrupled?

4.2 Real Roots of Polynomials

Section Objectives

■ Use the Rational Root Test to find the rational roots of a polynomial.
■ Use the Bounds Test and a graphing calculator to find an interval that contains all the real roots of a polynomial.

Finding the real roots of polynomials is the same as solving polynomial equations. The root of a first-degree polynomial, such as $5x - 3$, can be found by solving the equation $5x - 3 = 0$. Similarly, the roots of any second-degree polynomial can be found by using the quadratic formula (Section 1.2). Although the roots of higher-degree polynomials can always be approximated graphically as in Section 2.2, it is better to find exact solutions, if possible.

RATIONAL ROOTS

When a polynomial has integer coefficients, all of its **rational roots** (roots that are rational numbers) can be found exactly by using the following result.

The Rational Root Test

If a rational number r/s (in lowest terms) is a root of the polynomial

$$a_n x^n + \cdots + a_1 x + a_0,$$

where the coefficients $a_n, \ldots, a_1, a_0$ are integers with $a_n \neq 0$, $a_0 \neq 0$, then

r is a factor of the constant term a_0 and
s is a factor of the leading coefficient a_n.

The test states that every rational root must satisfy certain conditions.* By finding all the numbers that satisfy these conditions, we produce a list of *possible* rational roots. Then we must evaluate the polynomial at each number on the list to see whether the number actually is a root. This testing process can be considerably shortened by using a calculator, as in the next example.

EXAMPLE 1

Find the rational roots of

$$f(x) = 2x^4 + x^3 - 17x^2 - 4x + 6.$$

SOLUTION If $f(x)$ has a rational root r/s, then by the Rational Root Test r must be a factor of the constant term 6. Therefore, r must be one of ± 1, ± 2, ± 3,

---

*Since the proof of the Rational Root Test sheds no light on how the test is actually used to solve equations, it will be omitted.

or ± 6 (the only factors of 6). Similarly, s must be a factor of the leading coefficient 2, so s must be one of ± 1 or ± 2 (the only factors of 2). Consequently, the only *possibilities* for r/s are

$$\frac{\pm 1}{\pm 1}, \frac{\pm 2}{\pm 1}, \frac{\pm 3}{\pm 1}, \frac{\pm 6}{\pm 1}, \frac{\pm 1}{\pm 2}, \frac{\pm 2}{\pm 2}, \frac{\pm 3}{\pm 2}, \frac{\pm 6}{\pm 2}.$$

Eliminating duplications from this list, we see that the only *possible* rational roots are

$$1, -1, 2, -2, 3, -3, 6, -6, \frac{1}{2}, -\frac{1}{2}, \frac{3}{2}, -\frac{3}{2}.$$

Now graph $f(x)$ in a viewing window that includes all of these numbers on the x-axis, say $-7 \le x \le 7$ and $-5 \le y \le 5$ (Figure 4–3 on the next page). A complete graph isn't necessary, since we are interested only in the x-intercepts.

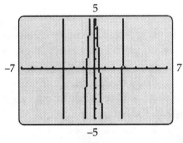

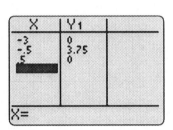

Figure 4–3   Figure 4–4

Figure 4–3 shows that the only numbers on our list that could possibly be roots (x-intercepts) are -3, $-1/2$, and $1/2$, so these are the only ones that need be tested. We use the table feature to evaluate $f(x)$ at these three numbers (Figure 4–4). The table shows that -3 and $1/2$ are the only rational roots of $f(x)$. Its other roots (x-intercepts) in Figure 4–3 must be irrational numbers. ∎

ROOTS AND THE FACTOR THEOREM

Once some roots of a polynomial have been found, the Factor Theorem can be used to factor the polynomial, which may lead to additional roots.

EXAMPLE 2

Find all the roots of $f(x) = 2x^4 + x^3 - 17x^2 - 4x + 6$.

SOLUTION   In Example 1, we saw that -3 and $1/2$ are the rational roots of $f(x)$. By the Factor Theorem, $x - (-3) = x + 3$ and $x - 1/2$ are factors of $f(x)$. Using synthetic or long division twice, we have

$$2x^4 + x^3 - 17x^2 - 4x + 6 = (x + 3)(2x^3 - 5x^2 - 2x + 2)$$

$$= (x + 3)(x - .5)(2x^2 - 4x - 4).$$

The remaining roots of $f(x)$ are the roots of $2x^2 - 4x - 4$, that is, the solutions of

$$2x^2 - 4x - 4 = 0$$

$$x^2 - 2x - 2 = 0.$$

They are easily found by the quadratic formula.

$$x = \frac{-(-2) \pm \sqrt{(-2)^2 - 4 \cdot 1 \cdot (-2)}}{2 \cdot 1}$$

$$= \frac{2 \pm \sqrt{12}}{2} = \frac{2 \pm 2\sqrt{3}}{2} = 1 \pm \sqrt{3}.$$

Therefore, $f(x)$ has rational roots -3 and $1/2$, and irrational roots $1 + \sqrt{3}$ and $1 - \sqrt{3}$. ∎

EXAMPLE 3

Factor $f(x) = 2x^5 - 10x^4 + 7x^3 + 13x^2 + 3x + 9$ completely.

SOLUTION   We begin by finding as many roots of $f(x)$ as we can. By the Rational Root Test, every rational root is of the form r/s where $r = \pm 1, \pm 3$, or ± 9 and $s = \pm 1$ or ± 2. Thus, the possible rational roots are

$$\pm 1, \quad \pm 3, \quad \pm 9, \quad \pm\frac{1}{2}, \quad \pm\frac{3}{2}, \quad \pm\frac{9}{2}.$$

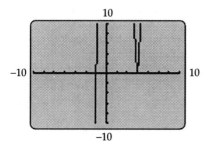

Figure 4–5

The partial graph of $f(x)$ in Figure 4–5 shows that the only possible roots (x-intercepts) are -1 and 3. You can easily verify that both -1 and 3 are roots of $f(x)$.

Since -1 and 3 are roots, $x - (-1) = x + 1$ and $x - 3$ are factors of $f(x)$ by the Factor Theorem. Division shows that

$$f(x) = 2x^5 - 10x^4 + 7x^3 + 13x^2 + 3x + 9$$
$$= (x + 1)(2x^4 - 12x^3 + 19x^2 + 3x + 9)$$
$$= (x + 1)(x - 3)(2x^3 - 6x^2 + x - 3).$$

The other roots of $f(x)$ are the roots of $g(x) = 2x^3 - 6x^2 + x - 3$. We first check for rational roots of $g(x)$. Since every root of $g(x)$ is also a root of $f(x)$ (why?), the only possible rational roots of $g(x)$ are -1 and 3 [the rational roots of $f(x)$]. We have

$$g(-1) = 2(-1)^3 - 6(-1)^2 + (-1) - 3 = 12;$$
$$g(3) = 2(3^3) - 6(3^2) + 3 - 3 = 0.$$

So -1 is not a root, but 3 is a root of $g(x)$. By the Factor Theorem, $x - 3$ is a factor of $g(x)$. Division shows that

$$f(x) = (x + 1)(x - 3)(2x^3 - 6x^2 + x - 3)$$
$$= (x + 1)(x - 3)(x - 3)(2x^2 + 1).$$

Since $2x^2 + 1$ has no real roots, it cannot be factored. So the factorization of $f(x)$ is complete. ∎

BOUNDS

The polynomial $f(x)$ in Example 2 had degree 4 and had four real roots. Since a polynomial of degree n has at most n roots, we know that we found all the roots of $f(x)$. In other cases, however, special techniques may be needed to guarantee that we have found all the roots.

EXAMPLE 4

Prove that all the real roots of

$$g(x) = x^5 - 2x^4 - x^3 + 3x + 1$$

lie between -1 and 3. Then find all the real roots of $g(x)$.

SOLUTION   We first prove that $g(x)$ has no root larger than 3, as follows. Use synthetic division to divide $g(x)$ by $x - 3$.*

$$
\begin{array}{r|rrrrrr}
3 & 1 & -2 & -1 & 0 & 3 & 1 \\
  &   & 3 & 3 & 6 & 18 & 63 \\
\hline
  & 1 & 1 & 2 & 6 & 21 & \boxed{64}
\end{array}
$$

Thus, the quotient is $x^4 + x^3 + 2x^2 + 6x + 21$, and the remainder is 64. Applying the Division Algorithm, we have

$$f(x) = (x - 3)(x^4 + x^3 + 2x^2 + 6x + 21) + 64.$$

When $x > 3$, then the factor $x - 3$ is positive, and the quotient

$$x^4 + x^3 + 2x^2 + 6x + 21$$

is also positive (because all its coefficients are). The remainder 64 is also positive. Therefore, $f(x)$ is positive whenever $x > 3$. In particular, $f(x)$ is never zero when $x > 3$, and so there are no roots of $f(x)$ greater than 3.

Now we show that $g(x)$ has no root less than -1. Divide $g(x)$ by

$$x - (^-1) = x + 1:$$

$$
\begin{array}{r|rrrrrr}
-1 & 1 & -2 & -1 & 0 & 3 & 1 \\
   &   & -1 & 3 & -2 & 2 & -5 \\
\hline
   & 1 & -3 & 2 & -2 & 5 & \boxed{-4}
\end{array}
$$

Read off the quotient and remainder and apply the Division Algorithm:

$$f(x) = (x + 1)(x^4 - 3x^3 + 2x^2 - 2x + 5) - 4.$$

When $x < -1$, then the factor $x + 1$ is negative. When x is negative, its odd powers are negative and its even powers are positive. Consequently, the quotient $x^4 - 3x^3 + 2x^2 - 2x + 5$ is positive (because the odd powers of x are multiplied by negative coefficients). The product of the positive quotient with the negative factor $x + 1$ is negative. The remainder -4 is also negative. Hence, $f(x)$ is negative whenever $x < -1$. So there are no real roots less than -1. Therefore, all the real roots of $g(x)$ lie between -1 and 3.

Finally, we find the roots of $g(x) = x^5 - 2x^4 - x^3 + 3x + 1$. The only possible rational roots are ± 1 (why?) and it is easy to verify that neither is actually a root. The graph of $g(x)$ in Figure 4–6 shows that there are exactly three real roots (x-intercepts) between -1 and 3. Since all the real roots of $g(x)$ lie between -1 and 3, $g(x)$ has only these three real roots. They are readily approximated by a root finder:

$$x \approx -.3361, \qquad x \approx 1.4268, \qquad \text{and} \qquad x \approx 2.2012. \qquad ■$$

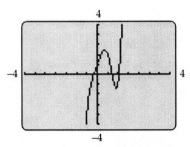

Figure 4–6

*If you haven't read Special Topics 4.2.A, use long division to find the quotient and remainder.

Suppose $f(x)$ is a polynomial and r and s are real numbers with $r < s$. If all the real roots of $f(x)$ are between r and s, we say that r is a **lower bound** and s is an **upper bound** for the real roots of $f(x)$.* Example 4 shows that -1 is a lower bound and 3 is an upper bound for the real roots of $g(x) = x^5 - 2x^4 - x^3 + 3x + 1$.

If you know lower and upper bounds for the real roots of a polynomial, you can usually determine the number of real roots the polynomial has, as we did in Example 4. The technique used in Example 4 to test possible lower and upper bounds works in the general case:

Bounds Test

Let $f(x)$ be a polynomial with positive leading coefficient.

If $d > 0$ and every number in the last row in the synthetic division of $f(x)$ by $x - d$ is nonnegative,[†] then d is an upper bound for the real roots of $f(x)$.

If $c < 0$ and the numbers in the last row of the synthetic division of $f(x)$ by $x - c$ are alternately positive and negative [with 0 considered as either][‡] then c is a lower bound for the real roots of $f(x)$.

NOTE

When the last row of the synthetic division by $x - d$ is nonnegative, then d is definitely an upper bound. But if the last row contains some negative entries, no conclusion can be drawn from the Bounds Test [d might or might not be an upper bound]. In such a case, try a larger number in place of d.

Analogous remarks apply to lower bounds.

EXAMPLE 5

Find all real roots of

$$f(x) = x^7 - 6x^6 + 9x^5 + 7x^4 - 28x^3 + 33x^2 - 36x + 20.$$

SOLUTION   By the Rational Root Test, the only possible roots are

$$\pm 1, \quad \pm 2, \quad \pm 4, \quad \pm 5, \quad \pm 10, \quad \text{and} \quad \pm 20.$$

The graph of $f(x)$ in Figure 4–7 is hard to read but shows that the possible roots are quite close to the origin. Changing the window (Figure 4–8), we see that the only numbers on the list that could possibly be roots (x-intercepts) are 1 and 2. You can easily verify that both 1 and 2 are roots of $f(x)$.

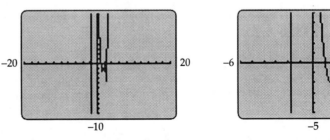

Figure 4–7   Figure 4–8

---

*The bounds are not unique. Any number smaller than r is also a lower bound, and any number larger than s is also an upper bound.

[†]Equivalently, all the coefficients of the quotient and the remainder are nonnegative.

[‡]Equivalently, the coefficients of the quotient are altenatively positive and negative, with the last one and the remainder having opposite signs.

In Figures 4–7 and 4–8, all the real roots of $f(x)$ lie between -2 and 6, which suggests that these numbers might be lower and upper bounds for the real roots of $f(x)$.* The Bounds Test shows that this is indeed the case:

$-2 \rfloor$	1	-6	9	7	-28	33	-36	20
		-2	16	-50	86	-116	172	-272
	1	-8	25	-43	58	-86	136	$\lfloor -252 \rfloor$

Alternating Signs
-2 is a lower bound

$6 \rfloor$	1	-6	9	7	-28	33	-36	20
		6	0	54	366	2028	12,366	73,980
	1	0	9	61	338	2061	12,330	$\lfloor 74,000 \rfloor$

All Nonnegative
6 is an upper bound

Therefore, the four x-intercepts in Figure 4–8 are the only real roots of $f(x)$. We have seen that two of these are the rational roots, 1 and 2. A root finder shows that the other roots are $x \approx -1.7913$ and $x \approx 2.7913$.   ∎

SUMMARY

The examples above illustrate the following guidelines for finding all the real roots of a polynomial $f(x)$.

1. Use the Rational Root Test to find all the rational roots of $f(x)$. [*Examples 1, 3, 5*]

2. Write $f(x)$ as the product of linear factors (one for each rational root) and another factor $g(x)$. [*Examples 2, 3*]

3. If $g(x)$ has degree 2, find its roots by factoring or the quadratic formula. [*Example 2*]

4. If $g(x)$ has degree 3 or more, use the Bounds Test, if possible, to find lower and upper bounds for the roots of $g(x)$ and approximate the remaining roots graphically. [*Examples 4, 5*]

Shortcuts and variations are always possible. For instance, if the graph of a cubic shows three x-intercepts, then it has three real roots (the maximum possible) and there is no point in finding bounds on the roots. In order to find as many roots as possible exactly in guideline 4, check to see if the rational roots of $f(x)$ are also roots of $g(x)$ and factor $g(x)$ accordingly, as in Example 3.

TECHNOLOGY TIP

The polynomial solvers on TI-86/89 and HP-39gs can find or approximate all the roots of a polynomial simultaneously. The solver on Casio 9850 is limited to polynomials of degree 2 or 3.

EXERCISES 4.2

Directions: *When asked to find the roots of a polynomial, find exact roots whenever possible and approximate the other roots. In Exercises 1–15, find all the rational roots of the polynomial.*

1. $x^3 - 3x^2 - x + 3$

2. $x^3 - x^2 - 3x + 3$

3. $x^3 - 3x^2 - 6x + 8$

4. $3x^3 + 17x^2 + 35x + 25$

5. $6x^3 - 11x^2 - 19x - 6$

6. $x^4 - x^2 - 2$

7. $f(x) = 2x^5 - 3x^4 - 11x^3 + 6x^2$ [*Hint:* The Rational Root Test can only be used on polynomials with nonzero constant terms. Factor $f(x)$ as a product of a power of x and a polynomial $g(x)$ with nonzero constant term. Then use the Rational Root Test on $g(x)$.]

---

*If you are wondering why we don't test 3, 4, or 5 as upper bounds, we did—but the Bounds Test is inconclusive for these numbers, as you can easily verify. See the Note at the top of page.

8. $2x^6 - 3x^5 - 7x^4 - 6x^3$

9. $f(x) = \frac{1}{12}x^3 - \frac{1}{12}x^2 - \frac{2}{3}x + 1$ [*Hint:* The Rational Root

Test can only be used on polynomials with integer coefficients. Note that $f(x)$ and $12f(x)$ have the same roots (why?).]

10. $\frac{1}{2}x^4 + \frac{5}{2}x^3 + 3x^2 - 2x - 4$

11. $\frac{1}{3}x^3 - \frac{5}{6}x^2 - \frac{1}{6}x + 1$

12. $\frac{1}{3}x^7 - \frac{1}{2}x^6 - \frac{1}{6}x^5 + \frac{1}{6}x^4$

13. $.1x^3 - 1.9x + 3$ **14.** $.05x^3 + .45x^2 - .4x + 1$

15. $x^{10} - 10x^9 + 45x^8 - 120x^7 + 210x^6 - 252x^5 + 210x^4 - 120x^3 + 45x^2 - 10x + 1$

In Exercises 16–22, factor the polynomial as a product of linear factors and a factor $g(x)$ such that $g(x)$ is either a constant or a polynomial that has no rational roots.

16. $x^{15} - x - 1$ **17.** $2x^3 - 2x^2 + 3x - 3$

18. $12x^3 - 10x^2 + 6x - 2$ **19.** $x^6 - 4x^5 + 3x^4 - 12x^3$

20. $x^5 - 2x^4 + 2x^3 - 3x + 2$

21. $x^5 - 6x^4 + 5x^3 + 34x^2 - 84x + 56$

22. $x^5 + 4x^3 + x^2 + 6x$

In Exercises 23–28, use the Bounds Test to find lower and upper bounds for the real roots of the polynomial.

23. $x^3 + 2x^2 - 7x + 20$ **24.** $x^3 - 15x^2 - 16x + 12$

25. $x^3 - 5x^2 + 5x + 3$ **26.** $x^4 - 2x^3 - 3x^2 + 4x + 4$

27. $-x^5 - 5x^4 + 9x^3 + 18x^2 - 68x + 176$ [*Hint:* The Bounds Test applies only to polynomials with positive leading coefficient. The polynomial $f(x)$ has the same roots as $-f(x)$ (why?).]

28. $-.002x^3 - 5x^2 + 8x - 3$

In Exercises 29–40, find all real roots of the polynomial.

29. $2x^3 - x^2 - 13x - 6$ **30.** $t^4 - 3t^3 + 5t^2 - 9t + 6$

31. $6x^3 - 13x^2 + x + 2$ **32.** $z^3 + z^2 + 2z + 2$

33. $x^4 + x^3 - 19x^2 + 32x - 12$

34. $3x^6 - 7x^5 - 22x^4 + 8x^3$

35. $2x^5 - x^4 - 10x^3 + 5x^2 + 12x - 6$

36. $x^{10} - 10x^9 + 45x^8 - 120x^7 + 210x^6 - 252x^5 + 210x^4 - 120x^3 + 45x^2 - 10x + 1$

37. $x^6 - 3x^5 - 4x^4 - 9x^2 + 27x + 36$

38. $x^5 + 8x^4 + 20x^3 + 9x^2 - 27x - 27$

39. $x^4 - 48x^3 - 101x^2 + 49x + 50$

40. $3x^7 + 8x^6 - 13x^5 - 36x^4 - 10x^3 + 21x^2 + 41x + 10$

41. (a) Show that $\sqrt{2}$ is an irrational number. [*Hint:* $\sqrt{2}$ is a root of $x^2 - 2$. Does this polynomial have any rational roots?]

(b) Show that $\sqrt{3}$ is irrational.

(c) What would happen if you tried to use the techniques from the previous parts of this question to show $\sqrt{4}$ is irrational?

42. Graph $f(x) = .001x^3 - .199x^2 - .23x + 6$ in the standard viewing window.

(a) How many roots does $f(x)$ appear to have? Without changing the viewing window, explain why $f(x)$ must have an additional root. [*Hint:* Each root corresponds to a factor of $f(x)$. What does the rest of the factorization consist of?]

(b) Find all the roots of $f(x)$.

43. According to data from the FBI, the number of people murdered each year per 100,000 can be approximated by the polynomial function

$$f(x) = -.0002724x^5 + .005237x^4 - .03027x^3 + .1069x^2 - .9062x + 9.003$$
$$(0 \le x \le 10)$$

where $x = 0$ corresponds to 1995.

(a) What was the murder rate in 2000 and in 2003?

(b) According to this model, in what year was the murder rate 7 people per 100,000?

(c) According to this model, in what year between 1995 and 2005 was the murder rate the highest?

(d) According to this model, in what year between 1995 and 2005 was the murder rate the lowest? (Be careful! This one isn't immediate.)

(e) According to this model, during what time interval between 1995 and 2005 was the murder rate increasing?

44. During the first 150 hours of an experiment, the growth rate of a bacteria population at time t hours is

$$g(t) = -.0003t^3 + .04t^2 + .3t + .2 \text{ bacteria per hour.}$$

(a) What is the growth rate at 50 hours? At 100 hours?

(b) What is the growth rate at 145 hours? What does this mean?

(c) At what time is the growth rate 0?

(d) At what time is the growth rate -50 bacteria per hour?

(e) At what time does the highest growth rate occur?

45. An open-top reinforced box is to be made from a 12- by 36-inch piece of cardboard by cutting along the marked lines, discarding the shaded pieces, and folding as shown in the figure. If the box must be less than 2.5 inches high, what size squares should be cut from the corners in order for the box to have a volume of 448 cubic inches?

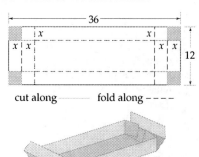

cut along ———— fold along ----

46. A box with a lid is to be made from a 48- by 24-inch piece of cardboard by cutting and folding, as shown in the figure. If the box must be at least 6 inches high, what size squares should be cut from the two corners in order for the box to have a volume of 1000 cubic inches?

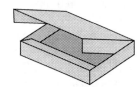

47. In a sealed chamber where the temperature varies, the instantaneous rate of change of temperature with respect to time over an 11-day period is given by

$$F(t) = .0035t^4 - .4t^2 - .2t + 6,$$

where time is measured in days and temperature in degrees Fahrenheit (so that rate of change is in degrees per day).

(a) At what rate is the temperature changing at the beginning of the period ($t = 0$)? At the end of the period ($t = 11$)?

(b) When is the temperature increasing at a rate of 4°F per day?

(c) When is the temperature decreasing at a rate of 3°F per day?

(d) When is the temperature decreasing at the fastest rate?

48. (a) If c is a root of

$$f(x) = 5x^4 - 4x^3 + 3x^2 - 4x + 5,$$

show that $1/c$ is also a root.

(b) Do part (a) with $f(x)$ replaced by

$$g(x) = 2x^6 + 3x^5 + 4x^4 - 5x^3 + 4x^2 + 3x + 2.$$

(c) Let $f(x) = a_{12}x^{12} + a_{11}x^{11} + \cdots + a_2x^2 + a_1x + a_0$. What conditions must the coefficients a_i satisfy in order that this statement be true: If c is a root of $f(x)$, then $1/c$ is also a root?

49. According to the "modified logistic growth" model, the rate at which a population of bunnies grows is a function of x, the number of bunnies there already are:

$$f(x) = k(-x^3 + x^2(T + C) - CTx) \text{ bunnies/year}$$

where C is the "carrying capacity" of the bunnies' environment, T is the "threshold population" of bunnies necessary for them to thrive and survive, and k is a positive constant that can be determined experimentally. If $f(x)$ is big, that means the bunny population is growing quickly. If $f(x)$ is negative, it means the bunny population is declining.

(a) Why can we assume $T < C$?

(b) What is happening to the bunny population if x is between T and C?

(c) What is happening to the bunny population if $x < T$?

(d) What is happening to the bunny population if $x > C$?

(e) Factor $k(-x^3 + x^2(T + C) - CTx)$

(f) What bunny populations will remain stable (unchanging)?

4.3   Radical Equations

■ Use algebraic and graphical methods to solve radical equations.

Section Objectives ■ Solve applied problems that involve radicals.

The algebraic solution of equations involving radicals depends on this fact: If two quantities are equal, say,

$$x - 2 = 3,$$

then their squares are also equal:

$$(x - 2)^2 = 9.$$

Thus,

every solution of $x - 2 = 3$ is also a solution of $(x - 2)^2 = 9$.

But *be careful:* This works only in one direction. For instance, -1 is a solution of $(x - 2)^2 = 9$, but not of $x - 2 = 3$. This is an example of the Power Principle.

Power Principle

> If both sides of an equation are raised to the same positive integer power, then every solution of the original equation is also a solution of the new equation. But the new equation may have solutions that are *not* solutions of the original one.

Consequently, if you raise both sides of an equation to a power, you must *check your solutions* in the *original* equation. Graphing provides a quick way to eliminate most extraneous solutions. But only an algebraic computation can confirm an exact solution.

EXAMPLE 1

Solve $5 + \sqrt{3x - 11} = x$.

SOLUTION   We first rearrange terms to get the radical expression alone on one side.

$$\sqrt{3x - 11} = x - 5.$$

Then we square both sides and solve the resulting equation.

$$(\sqrt{3x - 11})^2 = (x - 5)^2$$
$$3x - 11 = x^2 - 10x + 25$$
$$0 = x^2 - 13x + 36$$
$$0 = (x - 4)(x - 9)$$
$$x - 4 = 0 \quad \text{or} \quad x - 9 = 0$$
$$x = 4 \qquad\qquad x = 9.$$

These are *possible* solutions. We must check each one in the original equation. If $x = 9$ we have

Left side: $5 + \sqrt{3x - 11}$ Right side: x
$5 + \sqrt{3 \cdot 9 - 11}$ 9
$5 + \sqrt{16}$
9

Hence, $x = 9$ is a solution of the original equation. When we try the same calculations with $x = 4$, we obtain

Left side: $5 + \sqrt{3x - 11}$ Right side: x
$5 + \sqrt{3 \cdot 4 - 11}$ 4
$5 + \sqrt{1}$
6

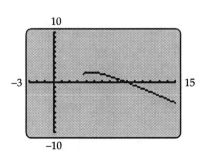

Figure 4–9

The two sides are not the same, so $x = 4$ is not a solution of the original equation.

These results can be confirmed graphically by graphing $y = 5 + \sqrt{3x - 11} - x$, as in Figure 4–9. The x-intercepts of this graph are the solutions of the equation (why?). There is an x-intercept at $x = 9$, but none at $x = 4$, indicating that $x = 9$ is a solution and $x = 4$ is not.   ■

EXAMPLE 2

Solve $\sqrt{2x - 3} - \sqrt{x + 7} = 2$.

SOLUTION   We first rearrange terms so that one side contains only a single radical term.

$$\sqrt{2x - 3} = \sqrt{x + 7} + 2.$$

Then we square both sides and simplify.

$$(\sqrt{2x - 3})^2 = (\sqrt{x + 7} + 2)^2$$

$$2x - 3 = (\sqrt{x + 7})^2 + 2 \cdot 2 \cdot \sqrt{x + 7} + 2^2$$

$$2x - 3 = x + 7 + 4\sqrt{x + 7} + 4$$

$$x - 14 = 4\sqrt{x + 7}.$$

Now we square both sides and solve the resulting equation.

$$(x - 14)^2 = (4\sqrt{x + 7})^2$$

$$x^2 - 28x + 196 = 4^2 \cdot (\sqrt{x + 7})^2$$

$$x^2 - 28x + 196 = 16(x + 7)$$

$$x^2 - 28x + 196 = 16x + 112$$

$$x^2 - 44x + 84 = 0$$

$$(x - 2)(x - 42) = 0$$

$$x - 2 = 0 \qquad \text{or} \qquad x - 42 = 0$$

$$x = 2 \qquad\qquad\qquad x = 42.$$

Substituting 2 and 42 in the left side of the original equation shows that

$$\sqrt{2 \cdot 2 - 3} - \sqrt{2 + 7} = \sqrt{1} - \sqrt{9} = 1 - 3 = -2;$$

$$\sqrt{2 \cdot 42 - 3} - \sqrt{42 + 7} = \sqrt{81} - \sqrt{49} = 9 - 7 = 2.$$

Therefore, 42 is the only solution of the equation.   ■

Many radical equations are not amenable to algebraic techniques. In such cases, graphical or numerical means must be used to approximate the solutions.

EXAMPLE 3

Solve $\sqrt[5]{x^2 - 6x + 2} = x - 4$.

SOLUTION   If we raise both sides of the equation to the fifth power, we obtain

$$x^2 - 6x + 2 = (x - 4)^5.$$

Unfortunately, this equation is not readily solvable, even if we multiply out the right hand side. The best we can do is to approximate the solutions. We can do this graphically as follows: We rewrite the equation as

$$\sqrt[5]{x^2 - 6x + 2} - x + 4 = 0,$$

then the solutions are the x-intercepts of the graph of

$$h(x) = \sqrt[5]{x^2 - 6x + 2} - x + 4$$

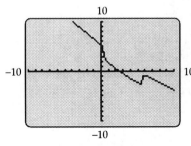

Figure 4–10

(see Figure 4–10). Alternatively, we can graph $f(x) = \sqrt[5]{x^2 - 6x + 2}$ and

$$g(x) = x - 4$$

on the same screen and find the x-coordinate of their intersection (Figure 4–11).

Equations involving rational exponents can be solved graphically, provided that the function to be graphed is entered properly. Many such equations can also be solved algebraically by making an appropriate substitution.

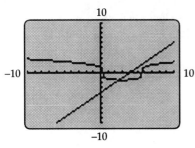

Figure 4–11

GRAPHING EXPLORATION

Use a root finder in Figure 4–10 or an intersection finder in Figure 4–11 to verify that $x \approx 2.534$ is the solution of the equation.

■

EXAMPLE 4

Solve $x^{2/3} - 2x^{1/3} - 15 = 0$ both algebraically and graphically.

SOLUTION

Algebraic: Let $u = x^{1/3}$, rewrite the equation, and solve:

$$x^{2/3} - 2x^{1/3} - 15 = 0$$

$$(x^{1/3})^2 - 2x^{1/3} - 15 = 0$$

$$u^2 - 2u - 15 = 0$$

$$(u + 3)(u - 5) = 0$$

$$u + 3 = 0 \qquad \text{or} \qquad u - 5 = 0$$

$$u = -3 \qquad\qquad u = 5$$

$$x^{1/3} = -3 \qquad\qquad x^{1/3} = 5.$$

Cubing both sides of these last equations shows that

$$(x^{1/3})^3 = (-3)^3 \qquad \text{or} \qquad (x^{1/3})^3 = 5^3$$

$$x = -27 \qquad\qquad x = 125.$$

Since we cubed both sides, we must check these numbers in the original equation. Verify that both *are* solutions.

Graphical: Graph the function $f(x) = x^{2/3} - 2x^{1/3} - 15$ and find the x-intercepts, namely, $x = -27$ and $x = 125$. The only difficulty is the one mentioned in the Note on page 344. Depending on your calculator, you might have to enter the function f in one of these forms:

$$f(x) = (x^2)^{1/3} - 2x^{1/3} - 15 \qquad \text{or} \qquad f(x) = (x^{1/3})^2 - 2x^{1/3} - 15.$$

Otherwise, the calculator might not produce a graph when x is negative. Your result should resemble Figure 4–12.

■

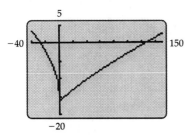

Figure 4–12

EXAMPLE 5

Hoa, who is standing at point A on the bank of a 2.5-kilometer-wide river wants to reach point B, 15 kilometers downstream on the opposite bank. She plans to row to a point C on the opposite shore and then run to B, as shown in Figure 4–13. She can row at a rate of 4 kilometers per hour and can run at 8 kilometers per hour.

(a) If her trip took 3 hours, how far from B did she land?

(b) How far from B should she land to make the time for the trip as short as possible?

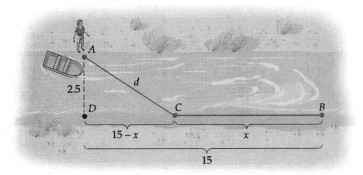

Figure 4–13

SOLUTION   Let x be the distance that Hoa ran from C to B. Using the basic formula for distance, we have

$$\text{Rate} \times \text{Time} = \text{Distance}$$

$$\text{Time} = \frac{\text{Distance}}{\text{Rate}} = \frac{x}{8}.$$

Similarly, the time required to row distance d is

$$\text{Time} = \frac{\text{Distance}}{\text{Rate}} = \frac{d}{4}.$$

Since $15 - x$ is the distance from D to C, the Pythagorean Theorem applied to right triangle ADC shows that

$$d^2 = (15 - x)^2 + 2.5^2 \qquad \text{or, equivalently,} \qquad d = \sqrt{(15 - x)^2 + 6.25}.$$

Therefore, the total time for the trip is given by

$$T(x) = \text{Rowing time} + \text{Running time} = \frac{d}{4} + \frac{x}{8} = \frac{\sqrt{(x - 15)^2 + 6.25}}{4} + \frac{x}{8}.$$

(a) If the trip took 3 hours, then $T(x) = 3$, and we must solve the equation

$$\frac{\sqrt{(x - 15)^2 + 6.25}}{4} + \frac{x}{8} = 3.$$

Using the viewing window with $0 \le x \le 15$ and $-2 \le y \le 2$, graph the function

$$f(x) = \frac{\sqrt{(x-15)^2 + 6.25}}{4} + \frac{x}{8} - 3$$

and use a root finder to find its x-intercept (the solution of the equation).

This Graphing Exploration shows that Hoa should land approximately 6.74 kilometers from B to make the trip in 3 hours.

(b) To find the shortest possible time, we must find the value of x that makes

$$T(x) = \frac{\sqrt{(x-15)^2 + 6.25}}{4} + \frac{x}{8}$$

as small as possible.

Using the viewing window with $0 \le x \le 15$ and $0 \le y \le 4$, graph $T(x)$ and use a minimum finder to verify that the lowest point on the graph (that is, the point with the y-coordinate $T(x)$ as small as possible) is approximately $(13.56, 2.42)$.

Therefore, the shortest time for the trip will be 2.42 hours and will occur if Hoa rows to a point 13.56 kilometers from B. ∎

EXERCISES 4.3

In Exercises 1–26, find all real solutions of each equation. Find exact solutions when possible and approximate ones otherwise.

1. $\sqrt{x+2} = 3$
2. $\sqrt{x-7} = 4$
3. $\sqrt{4x+9} = 0$
4. $\sqrt{4x+9} = -1$
5. $\sqrt[3]{5-11x} = 3$
6. $\sqrt[3]{6x-10} = 2$
7. $\sqrt[3]{x^2-1} = 2$
8. $(x-2)^{2/3} = 9$
9. $\sqrt{x^2-x-1} = 1$
10. $\sqrt{x^2-5x+4} = 2$
11. $\sqrt{x+7} = x-5$
12. $\sqrt{x+5} = x-1$
13. $(3x^2+7x-2)^{1/2} = x+1$
14. $\sqrt{4x^2-10x+5} = x-3$
15. $(x^3+x^2-4x+5)^{1/3} = x+1$
16. $\sqrt[3]{x^3-6x^2+2x+3} = x-1$
17. $\sqrt[5]{9-x^2} = x^2+1$
18. $(x^3-x+1)^{1/4} = x^2-1$
19. $\sqrt[3]{x^5-x^3-x} = x+2$
20. $\sqrt{x^3+2x^2-1} = x^3+2x-1$

21. $\sqrt{x^2+x-1} = \sqrt{14-x}$
22. $\sqrt[3]{x^3+3x} = \sqrt[3]{3x^2+1}$
23. $\sqrt{5x+6} = 3 + \sqrt{x+3}$
24. $\sqrt{3y+1} - 1 = \sqrt{y+4}$
25. $\sqrt{2x-5} = 1 + \sqrt{x-3}$
26. $\sqrt{x-3} + \sqrt{x+5} = 4$

27. The surface area S of the right circular cone in the figure is given by $S = \pi r \sqrt{r^2 + h^2}$. What radius should be used to produce a cone of height 5 inches and surface area 100 square inches?

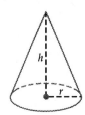

28. What is the radius of the base of a cone whose surface area is 18π square centimeters and whose height is 4 cm?

29. Find the radius of the base of a conical container whose height is $1/3$ of the radius and whose volume is 180 cubic inches. [*Note:* The volume of a cone of radius r and height h is $\pi r^2 h/3$.]

30. The surface area of the right square pyramid in the figure is given by $S = b\sqrt{b^2 + 4h^2}$. If the pyramid has height 10 feet and surface area 100 square feet, what is the length of a side b of its base?

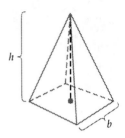

In Exercises 31–34, assume that all letters represent positive numbers and solve each equation for the required letter.

31. $A = \sqrt{1 + \dfrac{a^2}{b^2}}$ for b

32. $T = 2\pi\sqrt{\dfrac{m}{g}}$ for g

33. $y = \dfrac{1}{\sqrt{1 - x^2}}$

34. $R = \sqrt{d^2 + k^2}$ for d

In Exercises 35–42, solve each equation algebraically.

35. $x - 4x^{1/2} + 4 = 0$ [*Hint:* Let $u = x^{1/2}$.]

36. $x - x^{1/2} - 12 = 0$

37. $2x - 8\sqrt{x} - 24 = 0$

38. $3x - 11\sqrt{x} - 4 = 0$

39. $x^{2/3} + 3x^{1/3} + 2 = 0$ [*Hint:* Let $u = x^{1/3}$.]

40. $x^{4/3} - 4x^{2/3} + 3 = 0$

41. $x^{1/2} - x^{1/4} - 2 = 0$ [*Hint:* Let $u = x^{1/4}$.]

42. $x^{1/3} + x^{1/6} - 2 = 0$

In Exercises 43–46, solve each equation graphically.

43. $x^{3/5} - 2x^{2/5} + x^{1/5} - 6 = 0$

44. $x^{5/3} + x^{4/3} - 3x^{2/3} + x = 5$

45. $x^{-3} + 2x^{-2} - 4x^{-1} + 5 = 0$

46. $x^{-2/3} - 3x^{-1/3} = 4$

47. A rope is to be stretched at uniform height from a tree to a 35-foot-long fence, which is 20 feet from the tree, and then to the side of a building at a point 30 feet from the fence, as shown in the figure.

(a) If 63 feet of rope is to be used, how far from the building wall should the rope meet the fence?

(b) How far from the building wall should the rope meet the fence if as little rope as possible is to be used?

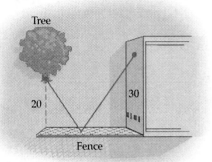

48. Anne is standing on a straight road and wants to reach her helicopter, which is located 2 miles down the road from her, a mile from the road in a field (see the figure). She can run 5 miles per hour on the road and 3 miles per hour in the field. She plans to run down the road, then cut diagonally across the field to reach the helicopter.

(a) If she reaches the helicopter in exactly 42 minutes (.7 hours) where did she leave the road?

(b) Where should she leave the road to reach the helicopter as soon as possible?

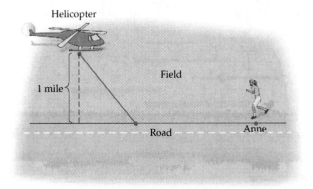

49. A power plant is located on the bank of a river that is $\frac{1}{2}$ mile wide. Wiring is to be laid across the river and then along the shore to a substation 8 miles downstream, as shown in the figure. It costs $12,000 per mile for underwater wiring and $8000 per mile for wiring on land. If $72,000 is to be spent on the project, how far from the substation should the wiring come to shore?

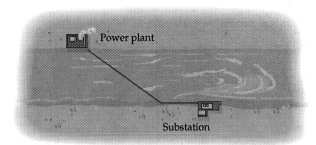

50. A spotlight is to be placed on a building wall to illuminate a bench that is 32 feet from the base of the wall. The intensity I of the light at the bench is known to be x/d^3, where x is the height of the spotlight above the ground and d is the distance from the bench to the spotlight.

(a) Express I as a function of x. [It may help to draw a picture.]

(b) How high should the spotlight be in order to provide maximum illumination at the bench?

51. If an object is dropped from a height h_0 feet, it will take $\frac{1}{4}\sqrt{h_0}$ seconds to hit the ground, assuming that h_0 is small enough that air resistance is negligible.

(a) We wish to make a movie by dropping a running camcorder off of a building. From how high would we have to drop it to make a 10-second film?

(b) How long would the camera take to hit the ground if dropped off of the Sears Tower in Chicago? (See example 4 of Section 1.1.)

52. In an attempt to steady a tottering, old, statue, two ropes are tied to the top, and secured firmly to the ground. The first rope winds up three feet from the base of the statue. The second rope winds up five feet from the base of the statue. If 10 total feet of rope are used, how tall is the statue?

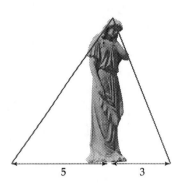

5   3

4.4   Linear and Rational Inequalities

Section Objectives

- Solve linear inequalities algebraically.
- Solve polynomial inequalities algebraically and graphically.
- Solve quadratic and factorable inequalities.
- Solve rational inequalities algebraically and graphically.

Inequalities may be solved by using algebraic or geometric methods, both of which are discussed here. Whenever possible, we shall use algebra to obtain exact solutions. When algebraic methods are too difficult, approximate graphical solutions will be found. The basic tools for working with inequalities are the following principles.

Basic Principles for Solving Inequalities

Performing any of the following operations on an inequality produces an equivalent inequality:*

1. Add or subtract the same quantity on both sides of the inequality.

2. Multiply or divide both sides of the inequality by the same *positive* quantity.

3. Multiply or divide both sides of the inequality by the same *negative* quantity and *reverse the direction of the inequality.*

---

*Two inequalities are **equivalent** if they have the same solutions.

*Basic Principles
for Solving Inequalities*

> Performing any of the following operations on an inequality produces an equivalent inequality:*
>
> 1. Add or subtract the same quantity on both sides of the inequality.
>
> 2. Multiply or divide both sides of the inequality by the same *positive* quantity.
>
> 3. Multiply or divide both sides of the inequality by the same *negative* quantity and *reverse the direction of the inequality.*

Note principle 3 carefully. It says, for example, that if you multiply both sides of $-3 < 5$ by -2, the equivalent inequality is $6 > -10$ (direction of inequality is reversed).

LINEAR INEQUALITIES

EXAMPLE 1

Solve $3x + 2 > 8$.

SOLUTION   We use the basic principles to transform the inequality into one whose solutions are obvious.

$$3x + 2 > 8$$

Subtract 2 from both sides: $\qquad 3x > 6$

Divide both sides by 3: $\qquad x > 2$

Therefore, the solutions are all real numbers greater than 2. In interval notation, we say the solutions are the numbers in the interval $(2, \infty)$. ∎

EXAMPLE 2

Solve $5x + 3 \le 6 + 7x$.

SOLUTION   We again use the basic principles to transform the inequality into one whose solutions are obvious.

$$5x + 3 \le 6 + 7x$$

Subtract 7x from both sides: $\qquad -2x + 3 \le 6$

Subtract 3 from both sides: $\qquad -2x \le 3$

Divide both sides by -2 and reverse the direction of the inequality: $\qquad x \ge -3/2$

Therefore, the solutions are all real numbers greater than or equal to $-3/2$, that is, the interval $[-3/2, \infty)$. ∎

EXAMPLE 3

A solution of the inequality $2 \leq 3x + 5 < 2x + 11$ is any number that is a solution of *both* of these inequalities:

$$2 \leq 3x + 5 \quad \text{and} \quad 3x + 5 < 2x + 11.$$

Each of these inequalities can be solved by the methods used earlier. For the first one, we have

$$2 \leq 3x + 5$$

Subtract 5 from both sides: $\quad -3 \leq 3x$

Divide both sides by 3: $\quad -1 \leq x.$

The second inequality is solved similarly:

$$3x + 5 < 2x + 11$$

Subtract 5 from both sides. $\quad 3x < 2x + 6$

Subtract $2x$ from both sides: $\quad x < 6.$

The solutions of the original inequality are the numbers x that satisfy *both* $-1 \leq x$ *and* $x < 6$, that is, all x with $-1 \leq x < 6$. Thus, the solutions are the numbers in the interval $[-1, 6)$, as shown in Figure 4–14. ∎

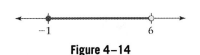

Figure 4–14

CAUTION

All inequality signs in an inequality should point in the same direction. *Don't* write things like $4 < x > 2$ or $-3 \geq x < 5$.

EXAMPLE 4

When solving the inequality $4 < 3 - 5x < 18$, in which the variable appears only in the middle part, you can proceed as follows.

$$4 < 3 - 5x < 18$$

Subtract 3 from each part: $\quad 1 < -5x < 15$

Divide each part by -5 and reverse the directions of the inequalities: $\quad -\dfrac{1}{5} > x > -3.$

Reading this last inequality from right to left we see that

$$-3 < x < -1/5,$$

so the solutions are the numbers in the interval $(-3, -1/5)$.

POLYNOMIAL INEQUALITIES

Although the basic principles play a role in the solution of nonlinear inequalities, the key to solving such inequalities is this geometric fact.

> **The graph of $y = f(x)$ lies above the x-axis exactly when $f(x) > 0$ and below the x-axis exactly when $f(x) < 0$.**

Consequently, the solutions of $f(x) > 0$ are the numbers x for which the graph of f lies above the x-axis and the solutions $f(x) < 0$ are the numbers x for which the graph of f lies below the x-axis.

EXAMPLE 5

Solve $2x^3 - 15x < x^2$.

SOLUTION   We replace the inequality by an equivalent one,

$$2x^3 - x^2 - 15x < 0,$$

and consider the graph of the function $f(x) = 2x^3 - x^2 - 15x$ (Figure 4–53). Since $f(x)$ factors as

$$f(x) = 2x^3 - x^2 - 15x = x(2x^2 - x - 15) = x(2x + 5)(x - 3),$$

its roots (the x-intercepts of its graph) are $x = 0$, $x = -5/2$, and $x = 3$. The graph of $f(x) = 2x^3 - x^2 - 15x$ in Figure 4–15 is complete (why?) and lies below the x-axis when $x < -5/2$ or $0 < x < 3$. Therefore, the solutions of

$$2x^3 - x^2 - 15x < 0,$$

and hence of the original inequality, are all numbers x such that $x < -5/2$ or $0 < x < 3$. ∎

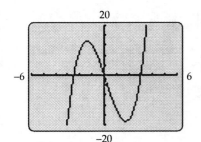

Figure 4–15

EXAMPLE 6

Solve $2x^3 - x^2 - 15x \geq 0$.

SOLUTION   Figure 4–15 shows that the solutions of $2x^3 - x^2 - 15x > 0$ (that is, the numbers x for which the graph of $f(x) = 2x^3 - x^2 - 15x$ lies above the x-axis) are all x such that $-5/2 < x < 0$ or $x > 3$. The solutions of the equation $2x^3 - x^2 - 15x = 0$ are the roots of $f(x) = 2x^3 - x^2 - 15x$, namely, 0, $-5/2$, and 3 as we saw in Example 5. Therefore, the solutions of the given inequality are all numbers x such that $-5/2 \leq x \leq 0$ or $x \geq 3$. ∎

When the roots of a polynomial $f(x)$ cannot be determined exactly, a root finder can be used to approximate them and to find approximate solutions of the inequalities $f(x) > 0$ and $f(x) < 0$.

EXAMPLE 7

Solve $x^4 + 10x^3 + 21x^2 + 8 > 40x + 88$.

SOLUTION   This inequality is equivalent to

$$x^4 + 10x^3 + 21x^2 - 40x - 80 > 0.$$

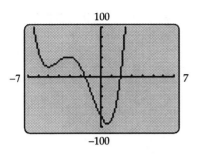

Figure 4–16

The graph $f(x) = x^4 + 10x^3 + 21x^2 - 40x - 80$ in Figure 4–16 is complete (why?) and shows that $f(x)$ has two roots, one between -2 and -1 and the other near 2.

GRAPHING EXPLORATION

Use a root finder to show that the approximate roots of $f(x)$ are -1.53 and 1.89.

Therefore, the approximate solutions of the inequality (the numbers x for which the graph is above the x-axis) are all numbers x such that $x < -1.53$ or $x > 1.89$.   ■

CAUTION

Do not attempt to write the solution in Example 7, namely, "$x < -1.53$ or $x > 1.89$" as a single inequality. If you do, the result will be a *nonsense statement* such as $-1.53 > x > 1.89$ (which says, among other things, that $-1.53 > 1.89$).

QUADRATIC AND FACTORABLE INEQUALITIES

The preceding examples show that solving a polynomial inequality depends only on knowing the roots of a polynomial and the places where its graph is above or below the x-axis. In the case of quadratic inequalities or completely factored polynomial inequalities, a calculator is not needed to determine this information.

EXAMPLE 8

The solutions of $2x^2 + 3x - 4 \le 0$ are the numbers x at which the graph of $f(x) = 2x^2 + 3x - 4$ lies on or below the x-axis. The points where the graph meets the x-axis are the roots of $f(x) = 2x^2 + 3x - 4$, which can be found by means of the quadratic formula:

$$x = \frac{-3 \pm \sqrt{3^2 - 4 \cdot 2(-4)}}{2 \cdot 2} = \frac{-3 \pm \sqrt{41}}{4}.$$

From Section 4.1, we know that the graph of $f(x)$ is an upward-opening parabola, so the graph must have the general shape shown in Figure 4–17.

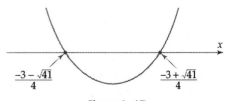

Figure 4–17

The graph lies below the x-axis between the two roots. Therefore, the solutions of the original inequality are all numbers x such that

$$\frac{-3 - \sqrt{41}}{4} \leq x \leq \frac{-3 + \sqrt{41}}{4}.$$ ∎

EXAMPLE 9

Solve $(x + 15)(x - 2)^6(x - 10) \leq 0$.

SOLUTION   The roots of $f(x) = (x + 15)(x - 2)^6(x - 10)$ are easily read from the factored form: $-15, 2$, and 10. So we need only determine where the graph of $f(x)$ is on or below the x-axis. To do this without a calculator, note that the three roots of $f(x)$ divide the x-axis into four intervals:

$$x < -15, \qquad -15 < x < 2, \qquad 2 < x < 10, \qquad x > 10.$$

For each of these intervals, we shall determine whether the graph is above or below the x-axis.

Consider, for example, the interval between the roots 2 and 10. The graph of $f(x)$ touches the x-axis at $x = 2$ and $x = 10$ but does not touch the axis at any point in between, since the only other root (x-intercept) is -15. Since a polynomial graph is continuous—it has no gaps or holes—the graph of $f(x)$ cannot "jump over" the x-axis between $x = 2$ and $x = 10$. It must be either entirely above the x-axis there or entirely below it.

To determine which is the case, choose any number between 2 and 10, say, $x = 4$, and test $f(4)$.

$$f(4) = (4 + 15)(4 - 2)^6(4 - 10) = 19(2^6)(-6).$$

You don't even have to finish the computation to see that $f(4)$ is a negative number. Therefore, the point $(4, f(4))$ on the graph of $f(x)$ lies below the x-axis. Since one point of the graph between 2 and 10 lies below the x-axis, the entire graph must be below the x-axis between 2 and 10.

The location of the graph on the other intervals can be determined similarly, by choosing a test number in each interval, as summarized in this chart.

Interval	$x < -15$	$-15 < x < 2$	$2 < x < 10$	$x > 10$
Test number in this interval	-20	0	4	11
Value of $f(x)$ at test number	$(-5)(-22)^6(-30)$	$15(-2)^6(-10)$	$19(2^6)(-6)$	$26(9^6)(1)$
Sign of $f(x)$ at test number	$+$	$-$	$-$	$+$
Graph	Above x-axis	Below x-axis	Below x-axis	Above x-axis

The last line of the chart shows that the intervals where the graph is below the x-axis are $-15 < x < 2$ and $2 < x < 10$. Since the graph touches the x-axis at the roots $-15, 2$, and 10, the solutions of the original inequality (the numbers x for which the graph is on or below the x-axis) are all numbers x such that $-15 \leq x \leq 10$.   ∎

The procedures used in Examples 5–9 may be summarized as follows.

Solving Polynomial Inequalities

1. Write the inequality in one of these forms:
$$f(x) > 0, \qquad f(x) \geq 0, \qquad f(x) < 0, \qquad f(x) \leq 0.$$

2. Determine the roots of $f(x)$, exactly if possible, approximately otherwise.

3. Use a calculator (as in Examples 5–7), your knowledge of quadratic functions (as in Example 8), or a sign chart (as in Example 9) to determine whether the graph of $f(x)$ is above or below the x-axis on each of the intervals determined by the roots.

4. Use the information in step 3 to find the solutions of the inequality.

RATIONAL INEQUALITIES

Rational inequalities are solved in essentially the same way that polynomial inequalities are solved, with one difference. The graph of a rational function may cross the x-axis at an x-intercept, but there is another possibility: The graph may be above the x-axis on one side of a vertical asymptote and below it on the other side (see, for instance, Examples 5–6 in Section 4.5). Since the x-intercepts of the graph of the rational function $g(x)/h(x)$ are determined by the roots of its numerator $g(x)$ and the vertical asymptotes by the roots of its denominator $h(x)$, all of these roots must be considered in determining the solution of an inequality involving $g(x)/h(x)$.

EXAMPLE 10

Solve $\dfrac{x}{x-1} > -6$.

SOLUTION   There are three ways to solve this inequality.

Geometric: The fastest way to get an approximate solution is to replace the given inequality by an equivalent one,

$$\frac{x}{x-1} + 6 > 0.$$

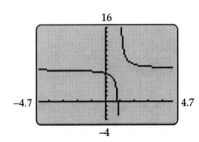

Figure 4–18

and graph the function $f(x) = \dfrac{x}{x-1} + 6$ as in Figure 4–18.

The graph is above the x-axis everywhere except between the x-intercept and the vertical asymptote $x = 1$. Using a root finder, we see that the x-intercept is approximately .857. Therefore, the approximate solutions of the original inequality are all numbers x such that $x < .857$ or $x > 1$.

Algebraic/Geometric: Proceed as above, but rewrite the rule of the function f as a single rational expression before graphing.

$$f(x) = \frac{x}{x-1} + 6 = \frac{x}{x-1} + \frac{6(x-1)}{x-1} = \frac{x + 6x - 6}{x-1} = \frac{7x-6}{x-1}.$$

When the rule of f is written in this form, it is easy to see that the x-intercept of the graph (the root of the numerator) is $x = 6/7$ (whose decimal approximation begins .857). Therefore, the exact solutions of the original inequality (the numbers x for which the graph in Figure 4–56 is above the x-axis) are all numbers x such that $x < 6/7$ or $x > 1$.

Algebraic: Write the rule of the function f as a single rational expression $f(x) = \dfrac{7x - 6}{x - 1}$. The roots of the numerator and denominator (6/7 and 1) divide the x-axis into three intervals. Use test numbers and a sign chart instead of graphing to determine the location of the graph on each interval:*

Interval	$x < 6/7$	$6/7 < x < 1$	$x > 1$
Test number in this interval	0	.9	2
Value of $f(x)$ at test number	$\dfrac{7 \cdot 0 - 6}{0 - 1}$	$\dfrac{7(.9) - 6}{.9 - 1}$	$\dfrac{7 \cdot 2 - 6}{2 - 1}$
Sign of $f(x)$ at test number	+	−	+
Graph	Above x-axis	Below x-axis	Above x-axis

The last line of the chart shows that the solutions of the original inequality (the numbers x for which the graph is above the x-axis) are all such that $x < 6/7$ or $x > 1$. ■

The algebraic technique of writing the left side of the inequality as a single rational expression is useful whenever the resulting numerator has low degree (so that its roots can be found exactly), but can usually be omitted when the roots of the numerator must be approximated.

CAUTION

Don't treat rational inequalities as if they are equations, as in this *incorrect* "solution" of the preceding example:

$$\frac{x}{x - 1} > -6$$

$$x > -6(x - 1) \quad \text{[Both sides multiplied by } x - 1]$$

$$x > -6x + 6$$

$$7x > 6$$

$$x > \frac{6}{7}$$

According to this, the inequality has no negative solution and $x = 1$ is a solution, but as we saw in Example 10, *every* negative number is a solution and $x = 1$ is not.[†]

---

*The justification for this approach is essentially the same as that in Example 9: Because f is continuous everywhere that it is defined, the graph can change from one side of the x-axis to the other only at x-intercepts or vertical asymptotes, so testing one number in each interval is sufficient to determine the side on which the graph lies.
[†]The source of the error is multiplying by $x - 1$. This quantity is negative for some values of x and positive for others. To do this calculation correctly, you must consider two separate cases and reverse the direction of the inequality when $x - 1$ is negative.

APPLICATIONS

EXAMPLE 11

A computer store has determined that the cost C of ordering and storing x laser printers is given by

$$C = 2x + \frac{300,000}{x}.$$

If the delivery truck can bring at most 450 printers per order, how many printers should be ordered at a time to keep the cost below \$1600?

SOLUTION   To find the values of x that make C less than 1600, we must solve the inequality

$$2x + \frac{300,000}{x} < 1600 \qquad \text{or, equivalently,} \qquad 2x + \frac{300,000}{x} - 1600 < 0.$$

We shall solve this inequality graphically, although it can also be solved algebraically. In this context, the only solutions that make sense are those between 0 and 450. So we choose the viewing window in Figure 4–19 and graph

$$f(x) = 2x + \frac{300,000}{x} - 1600.$$

Figure 4–19 is consistent with the fact that $f(x)$ has a vertical asymptote at $x = 0$ and shows that the desired solutions (numbers where the graph is below the x-axis) are all numbers x between the root and 450. A root finder shows that the root is $x \approx 300$. In fact, this is the exact root, since a simple computation shows that $f(300) = 0$. (Do it!) Therefore, to keep costs under \$1600, x printers should be ordered each time, with $300 < x \leq 450$. ∎

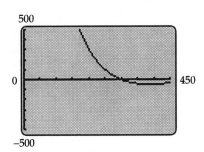

Figure 4–19

EXERCISES 4.4

In Exercises 1–20, solve the inequality and express your answer in interval notation.

1. $2x + 4 \leq 7$

2. $4x - 3 > -12$

3. $3 - 5x < 13$

4. $2 - 3x < 11$

5. $6x + 3 \leq x - 5$

6. $5x + 3 \leq 2x + 7$

7. $5 - 7x < 2x - 4$

8. $8 - 4x > 7x + 2$

9. $2 < 3x - 4 < 8$

10. $4 < 9x + 2 < 10$

11. $0 < 5 - 2x \leq 11$

12. $-4 \leq 7 - 3x < 0$

13. $5x + 6(-8x - 1) < 2(x - 1)$

14. $x + 3(x - 5) \geq 3x + 2(x + 1)$

15. $\dfrac{x + 1}{2} - 3x \leq \dfrac{x + 5}{3}$

16. $\dfrac{x - 1}{4} + 2x \geq \dfrac{2x - 1}{3} + 2$

17. $2x + 3 \leq 5x + 6 < -3x + 7$

18. $2x - 1 < x + 4 < 9x + 2$

19. $3 - x < 2x + 1 \leq 3x - 4$

20. $2x + 5 \leq 4 - 3x < 1 - 4x$

In Exercises 21–24, a, b, c, and d are positive constants. Solve the inequality for x.

21. $ax - b < c$

22. $d - cx > a$

23. $0 < x - c < a$

24. $-d < x - c < d$

In Exercises 25–46, solve the inequality. Find exact solutions when possible and approximate ones otherwise.

25. $x^2 - 4x + 3 \leq 0$

26. $x^2 - 7x + 10 \leq 0$

27. $8 + x - x^2 \leq 0$

28. $x^2 + 8x + 20 \geq 0$

29. $x^3 - x \geq 0$

30. $x^3 + 2x^2 + x > 0$

31. $x^3 + 3x^2 - x - 3 < 0$

32. $x^4 - 14x^3 + 48x^2 \geq 0$

33. $x^4 - 5x^2 + 4 < 0$

34. $x^4 - 10x^2 + 9 \leq 0$

35. $2x^4 + 3x^3 < 2x^2 + 4x - 2$

36. $x^5 + 5x^4 > 4x^3 - 3x^2 + 2$

37. $\dfrac{3x + 1}{2x - 4} > 0$

38. $\dfrac{2x^2 + x - 1}{x^2 - 4x + 4} \geq 0$

39. $\dfrac{x - 2}{x - 1} < 1$

40. $\dfrac{-x + 5}{2x + 3} \geq 2$

41. $\dfrac{2}{x + 3} \geq \dfrac{1}{x - 1}$

42. $\dfrac{1}{x - 1} < \dfrac{-1}{x + 2}$

43. $\dfrac{x^3 - 3x^2 + 5x - 29}{x^2 - 7} > 3$

44. $\dfrac{x^4 - 3x^3 + 2x^2 + 2}{x - 2} > 15$

45. $\dfrac{2x^2 + 6x - 8}{2x^2 + 5x - 3} < 1$ [Be alert for hidden behavior.]

46. $\dfrac{1}{x^2 + x - 6} + \dfrac{x - 2}{x + 3} > \dfrac{x + 3}{x - 2}$

In Exercises 47–48, solve the inequality using the method of Example 9.

47. $x(x - 1)^3 (x - 2)^4 \geq 0$

48. $x^4 - 5x^3 + 9x^2 - 7x + 2 < 0$

   [*Hint:* First find the rational roots; then factor.]

In Exercises 49–51, read the solution of the inequality from the given graph.

49. $3 - 2x < .8x + 7$

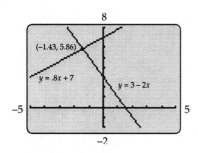

50. $8 - |7 - 5x| > 3$

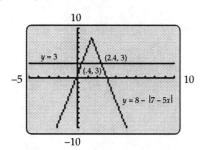

51. $x^2 + 3x + 1 \geq 4$

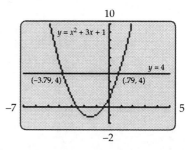

52. The graphs of the revenue and cost functions for a manufacturing firm are shown in the figure.

   (a) What is the break-even point?

   (b) Shade in the region representing profit.

   (c) What does the y-intercept of the cost graph represent? Why is the y-intercept of the revenue graph 0?

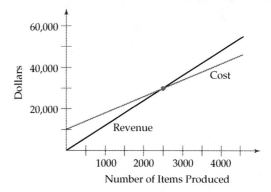

53. One freezer costs \$723.95 and uses 90 kilowatt hours (kwh) of electricity each month. A second freezer costs \$600 and uses 100 kwh of electricity each month. The expected life of each freezer is 12 years. What is the minimum electric rate (in *cents* per kwh) for which the 12-year total cost (purchase price + electricity costs) will be less for the first freezer?

54. A business executive leases a car for \$300 per month. She decides to lease another brand for \$250 per month but has to pay a penalty of \$1000 for breaking the first lease. How long must she keep the second car to come out ahead?

55. A sales agent is given a choice of two different compensation plans. The first plan has no salary, but a 10% commission on total sales. The second plan has a salary of \$3000 per month, plus a 2% commission on total sales. What range of monthly sales will make the first plan a better choice for the sales agent?

56. A developer subdivided 60 acres of a 100-acre tract, leaving 20% of the 60 acres as a park. Zoning laws require that at least 25% of the total tract be set aside for parks. For financial reasons, the developer wants to have no more than 30% of the tract as parks. How many one-quarter-acre lots can the developer sell in the remaining 40 acres and still meet the requirements for the whole tract?

57. Emma and Aidan currently pay $60 per month for phone service from AT&T. This fee gets them 900 minutes per month. They look at their phone bills and realize that, at most, they talk for 100 minutes per month. They find out that they can go with Virgin Mobile and pay 18 cents per minute. If they choose to switch services, they will have to buy two new phones at $40 each, and pay a $175 "cancellation fee" to AT&T.

 (a) Assuming that they talk for 100 minutes per month, how many months would they have to talk before they would be saving money?

 (b) Assume they make the switch, and talk between zero and 100 minutes per month. What is the range of possible savings?

58. How many gallons of a 12% salt solution should be added to 10 gallons of an 18% salt solution to produce a solution whose salt content is between 14% and 16%?

59. Find all pairs of numbers that satisfy these two conditions: Their sum is 20, and the sum of their squares is less than 362.

60. The length of a rectangle is 6 inches longer than its width. What are the possible widths if the area of the rectangle is at least 667 square inches?

61. It costs a craftsman $5 in materials to make a medallion. He has found that if he sells the medallions for $50 - x$ dollars each, where x is the number of medallions produced each week, then he can sell all that he makes. His fixed costs are $350 per week. If he wants to sell all he makes and show a profit each week, what are the possible numbers of medallions he should make?

62. A retailer sells file cabinets for $80 - x$ dollars each, where x is the number of cabinets she receives from the supplier each week. She pays $10 for each file cabinet and has fixed costs of $600 per week. How many file cabinets should she order from the supplier each week to guarantee that she makes a profit?

In Exercises 63–66, you will need the formula for the height h of an object above the ground at time t seconds:

$$h = -16t^2 + v_0 t + h_0;$$

this formula was explained on page 249.

63. A toy rocket is fired straight up from ground level with an initial velocity of 80 feet per second. During what time interval will it be at least 64 feet above the ground?

64. A projectile is fired straight up from ground level with an initial velocity of 72 feet per second. During what time interval is it at least 37 feet above the ground?

65. A ball is dropped from the roof of a 120-foot-high building. During what time period will it be strictly between 56 feet and 39 feet above the ground?

66. A ball is thrown straight up from a 40-foot-high tower with an initial velocity of 56 feet per second.

 (a) During what time interval is the ball at least 8 feet above the ground?

 (b) During what time interval is the ball between 53 feet and 80 feet above the ground?

67. (a) Solve the inequalities $x^2 < x$ and $x^2 > x$.

 (b) Use the results of part (a) to show that for any nonzero real number c with $|c| < 1$, it is always true that $c^2 < |c|$.

 (c) Use the results of part (a) to show that for any nonzero real number c with $|c| > 1$, it is always true that $c^2 > c$.

68. (a) If $0 < a \leq b$, prove that $1/a \geq 1/b$.

 (b) If $a \leq b < 0$, prove that $1/a \geq 1/b$.

 (c) If $a < 0 < b$, how are $1/a$ and $1/b$ related?

THINKERS

In Exercises 69–77, solve the inequality.

69. $4x - 5 \geq 4x + 2$ **70.** $3x - 4 < 3x - 4$

71. $3x - 4 \geq 3x - 4$ **72.** $(x - \pi)^2 \geq 0$

73. $(x + 2)^2(x - 3)^2 < 0$ **74.** $(2x - 5)^2 > 0$

75. $(x + 1)^2 < 0$ **76.** $3 < 6x + 6 < 2$

77. $8 \leq 4x - 2 \leq 8$

78. We know that for large values of x, we can approximate $x^2 - 2x^2 + x - 1$ by using x^3.

 (a) Compute the percent error in this approximation when $x = 50$ and when $x = 100$.

 (b) For what positive values of x is the error less than 10%?

4.5   Absolute Value Inequalities

Section Objective ■ Solve absolute value inequalities algebraically and graphically.

Polynomial and rational inequalities involving absolute value can be solved graphically, just as was done earlier: Rewrite the inequality in an equivalent form that has 0 on the right side of the inequality sign; then graph the function whose rule is given by the left side and determine where the graph is above or below the x-axis.

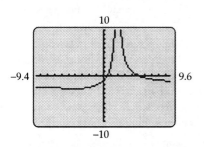

Figure 4–20

EXAMPLE 1

Solve $\left|\dfrac{x+4}{x-2}\right| > 3$

SOLUTION   We use the equivalent inequality

$$\left|\frac{x+4}{x-2}\right| - 3 > 0$$

and graph the function $f(x) = \left|\dfrac{x+4}{x-2}\right| - 3$ (Figure 4–20). The graph is above the x-axis between the two x-intercepts, which can be found algebraically or graphically.

GRAPHING EXPLORATION

Verify that the x-intercepts are $x = 1/2$ and $x = 5$.

Since $f(x)$ is not defined at $x = 2$ (where the graph has a vertical asymptote), the solutions of the original inequality are all x such that $1/2 < x < 2$ or $2 < x < 5$. ∎

EXAMPLE 2

Solve $|x^4 + 2x^2 - x + 2| < 11x$.

SOLUTION   We determine the numbers for which the graph of

$$f(x) = |x^4 + 2x^2 - x + 2| - 11x$$

lies below the x-axis. (Why?) Convince yourself that the graph of $f(x)$ in Figure 4–21 is complete.

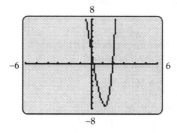

Figure 4–21

A root finder shows that the approximate x-intercepts are $x = .17$ and $x = 1.92$. Therefore, the approximate solutions of the original inequality (the numbers where the graph is below the x-axis) are all x such that $.17 < x < 1.92$. ∎

◢ ALGEBRAIC METHODS

Most linear and quadratic inequalities involving absolute values can be solved exactly by algebraic means. In fact, this is often the easiest way to solve such inequalities. The key to the algebraic method is the fact that the absolute value of a number can be interpreted as distance on the number line. For example, the inequality $|r| \leq 5$ states that the distance from r to 0 (namely, $|r|$) is 5 units or less. A glance at the number line in Figure 4–22 shows that these are the numbers r with $-5 \leq r \leq 5$.

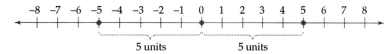

Figure 4–22

Similarly, the numbers r such that $|r| \geq 5$ are those whose distance to 0 is 5 or more units, that is, the numbers r with $r \leq -5$ or $r \geq 5$. This argument works with any positive number k in place of 5 and proves the following facts (which are also true with $<$ and $>$ in place of $\leq$ and $\geq$).

Absolute Value Inequalities

> Let k be a positive number and r any real number.
>
> $$|r| \leq k \quad \text{is equivalent to} \quad -k \leq r \leq k.$$
>
> $$|r| \geq k \quad \text{is equivalent to} \quad r \leq -k \quad \text{or} \quad r \geq k.$$

EXAMPLE 3

To solve $|3x - 7| \leq 11$, apply the first fact in the box, with $3x - 7$ in place of r and 11 in place of k, and obtain this equivalent inequality: $-11 \leq 3x - 7 \leq 11$. Then

Add 7 to each part: $-4 \leq 3x \leq 18$

Divide each part by 3: $-4/3 \leq x \leq 6$.

Therefore, the solutions of the original inequality are all numbers in the interval $[-4/3, 6]$. ∎

EXAMPLE 4

To solve $|5x + 2| > 3$, apply the second fact in the box, with $5x + 2$ in place of r, and 3 in place of k, and $>$ in place of $\geq$. This produces the equivalent statement:

$$5x + 2 < -3 \quad \text{or} \quad 5x + 2 > 3$$
$$5x < -5 \qquad\qquad 5x > 1$$
$$x < -1 \quad \text{or} \quad x > 1/5.$$

Therefore, the solutions of the original inequality are the numbers in *either* of the intervals $(-\infty, -1)$ or $(1/5, \infty)$, as shown in Figure 4–23. ∎

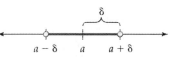

Figure 4–23

EXAMPLE 5

If a and δ are real numbers with δ positive, then the inequality $|x - a| < \delta$ is equivalent to $-\delta < x - a < \delta$. Adding a to each part shows that

$$a - \delta < x < a + \delta \text{ as shown in Figure 4–24}.$$ ∎

Figure 4–24

EXAMPLE 6

To solve $\left|x^2 - x - 4\right| \geq 2$, we use the fact in the box on the preceding page to replace it by an equivalent inequality:

$$x^2 - x - 4 \leq -2 \qquad \text{or} \qquad x^2 - x - 4 \geq 2,$$

which is the same as

$$x^2 - x - 2 \leq 0 \qquad \text{or} \qquad x^2 - x - 6 \geq 0.$$

The solutions are all numbers that are solutions of *either one* of the two inequalities. To solve the first of these inequalities, note that the graph of

$$f(x) = x^2 - x - 2 = (x + 1)(x - 2)$$

is an upward-opening parabola that crosses the x-axis at -1 and 2 (the roots of $f(x)$). Therefore, the solutions of

$$x^2 - x - 2 \leq 0$$

(the numbers for which the graph of $f(x)$ is on or below the x-axis) are all x with $-1 \leq x \leq 2$. The second inequality above, $x^2 - x - 6 \geq 0$, is solved similarly.

GRAPHING EXPLORATION

What is the shape of the graph of $g(x) = x^2 - x - 6$ and what are its x-intercepts?

This Graphing Exploration shows that the solutions of the second inequality (the numbers for which the graph of $g(x)$ is on or above the x-axis) are all x with $x \leq -2$ or $x \geq 3$.

Consequently, the solutions of the original inequality are all numbers x such that $x \leq -2$ or $-1 \leq x \leq 2$ or $x \geq 3$, as shown in Figure 4–25. ∎

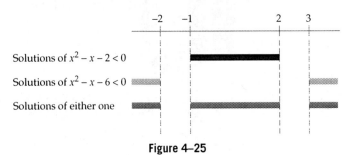

Figure 4–25

EXERCISES 4.5

In Exercises 1–30, solve the inequality. Find exact solutions when possible and approximate ones otherwise.

1. $|3x + 2| \leq 2$

2. $|4x + 2| < 8$

3. $|3 - 2x| < 2/3$

4. $|4 - 5x| \leq 4$

5. $|5x + 2| \geq \dfrac{3}{4}$

6. $|5 - 2x| > 7$

7. $\left|\dfrac{12}{5} + 2x\right| > \dfrac{1}{4}$

8. $\left|\dfrac{5}{6} + 3x\right| < \dfrac{7}{6}$

9. $\left|\dfrac{x - 1}{x + 2}\right| \leq 3$

10. $\left|\dfrac{x + 1}{3x + 5}\right| < 2$

11. $\left|\dfrac{1 - 4x}{2 + 3x}\right| < 1$

12. $\left|\dfrac{3x + 1}{1 - 2x}\right| \geq 2$

13. $|x^2 - 2| < 1$

14. $|x^2 - 4| \le 3$

15. $|x^2 - 2| > 4$

16. $\left| \dfrac{1}{x^2 - 1} \right| \le 2$

17. $|x^2 + x - 1| \ge 1$

18. $|x^2 + 3x - 4| < 6$

19. $|x^5 - x^3 + 1| < 2$

20. $|4x - x^3| > 1$

21. $|x^4 - x^3 + x^2 - x + 1| > 4$

22. $|x^3 - 6x^2 + 4x - 5| < 3$

23. $\dfrac{x + 2}{|x - 3|} \le 4$

24. $\dfrac{x^2 - 9}{|x^2 - 4|} < -2$

25. $\left| \dfrac{2x^2 + 2x - 12}{x^3 - x^2 + x - 2} \right| > 2$

26. $\left| \dfrac{x^2 - x - 2}{x^2 + x - 2} \right| > 3$

27. $|x^2 - 3x + 2| \ge 0$

28. $|x^2 - 3x + 2| > 0$

29. $|x^2 - 3x + 2| \le 0$

30. $|x^2 - 3x + 2| < 0$

THINKERS

31. Let E be a fixed real number. Show that every solution of $|x - 3| < E/5$ is also a solution of $|(5x - 4) - 11| < E$.

32. Let a and b be fixed real numbers with $a < b$. Show that the solutions of

$$\left| x - \frac{a + b}{2} \right| < \frac{b - a}{2}$$

are all x with $a < x < b$.

33. A factory manufactures iron rods. The customer specifies the length of the rod, and the factory produces the desired item. Obviously, they aren't going to be able to make the length *exact*, but they guarantee that the manufactured rod will be within 1 millimeter of the requested length.

   (a) If a customer orders a rod of length 3 meters, what is the range of acceptable lengths of rod for the factory to produce?
   (b) If a customer orders a rod of length δ meters, what is the acceptable range? Write your answer as a single absolute value inequality, and label all variables you use.

4.6   The Number *e*

Section Objective ■ Apply compound interest formulas to financial situations.

When money earns compound interest, as in Example 4 on page 360, the exponential growth function can be described as follows.

Compound Interest Formula

If P dollars is invested at interest rate r per time period (expressed as a decimal), then the amount A after t periods is

$$A = P(1 + r)^t$$

EXAMPLE 1

Suppose you borrow $50 from your friendly neighborhood loan shark, who charges 18% interest per week. How much do you owe after one year (assuming that he lets you wait that long to pay)?

SOLUTION   You use the compound interest formula with $P = 50$, $r = .18$, and $t = 52$ (because interest is compounded weekly and there are 52 weeks in a year). So you figure that you owe

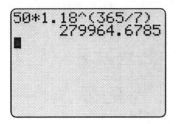

Figure 4–26

$$A = P(1 + r)^t = 50(1 + .18)^{52} = 50 \cdot 1.18^{52} = \$273,422.58.^*$$

When you try to pay the loan shark this amount, however, he points out that a 365-day year has more than 52 weeks, namely, $\frac{365}{7} = 52\frac{1}{7}$ weeks. So you recalculate with $t = 365/7$ (and careful use of parentheses, as shown in Figure 4–26) and find that you actually owe

$$A = P(1 + r)^t = 50(1 + .18)^{365/7} = 50 \cdot 1.18^{365/7} = \$279,964.68.$$

Ouch!   ∎

As Example 1 illustrates, the compound interest formula can be used even when the number of periods t is not an integer. You must also learn how to read "financial language" to apply the formula correctly, as shown in the following example.

EXAMPLE 2

Determine the amount a \$3500 investment is worth after three and a half years at the following interest rates:

(a) 6.4% compounded annually;

(b) 6.4% compounded quarterly;

(c) 6.4% compounded monthly.

SOLUTION

(a) Using the compound interest formula with $P = 3500$, $r = .064$, and $t = 3.5$, we have

$$A = 3500(1 + .064)^{3.5} = \$4348.74.$$

(b) "6.4% interest, compounded quarterly" means that the interest period is one-fourth of a year and the interest rate per period is $.064/4 = .016$. Since there are four interest periods per year, the number of periods in 3.5 years is $4(3.5) = 14$, so

$$A = 3500\left(1 + \frac{.064}{4}\right)^{14} = 3500(1 + .016)^{14} = \$4370.99.$$

(c) Similarly, "6.4% compounded monthly" means that the interest period is one month (1/12 of a year) and the interest rate per period is $.064/12$. The number of periods (months) in 3.5 years is 42, so

$$A = 3500\left(1 + \frac{.064}{12}\right)^{42} = \$4376.14.$$

Note that the more often interest is compounded, the larger the final amount   ∎

---

*Here and below, all financial answers are rounded to the nearest penny.

EXAMPLE 3

If $5000 is invested at 6.5% annual interest, compounded monthly, how long will it take for the investment to double?

SOLUTION

The compound interest formula (with $P = 5000$ and $r = .065/12$) shows that the amount in the account after t months is $5000\left(1 + \dfrac{.065}{12}\right)^t$. We must find the value of t such that

$$5000\left(1 + \frac{.065}{12}\right)^t = 10{,}000.$$

Algebraic methods for solving this equation will be considered in Section 5.5. For now, we use technology.

GRAPHING EXPLORATION

Solve the equation, either by using an equation solver, or by graphical means as follows. Graph

$$y = 5000\left(1 + \frac{.065}{12}\right)^t - 10{,}000$$

in a viewing window with $0 \le t \le 240$ (that's 20 years) and find the t-intercept.

The exploration shows that it will take 128.3 months (approximately 10.7 years) for the investment to double. ∎

EXAMPLE 4

What interest rate, compounded annually, is needed for a $16,000 investment to grow to $50,000 in 18 years?

SOLUTION

In the compound interest formula, we have $A = 50{,}000$, $P = 16{,}000$ and $t = 18$. We must find r in the equation

$$16{,}000(1 + r)^{18} = 50{,}000.$$

The equation can be solved numerically with an equation solver or by one of the following methods.

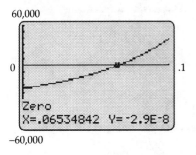

Figure 4–27

Graphical: Rewrite the equation as $16{,}000(1 + r)^{18} - 50{,}000 = 0$. Then the solution is the r-intercept of the graph of $y = 16{,}000(1 + r)^{18} - 50{,}000$, as shown in Figure 4–27.

Algebraic:

$$16{,}000(1 + r)^{18} = 50{,}000$$

Divide both sides by 16,000: $\qquad (1 + r)^{18} = \dfrac{50{,}000}{16{,}000} = 3.125$

Take 18th roots on both sides: $\qquad \sqrt[18]{(1 + r)^{18}} = \sqrt[18]{3.125}$

$$1 + r = \sqrt[18]{3.125}$$

$$r = \sqrt[18]{3.125} - 1 \approx .06535.$$

So the necessary interest rate is about 6.535%. ∎

 ## CONTINUOUS COMPOUNDING AND THE NUMBER *e*

As a general rule, the more often interest is compounded, the better off you are, as we saw in Example 2. But there is, alas, a limit.

EXAMPLE 5

The Number *e* You have $1 to invest for 1 year. The Exponential Bank offers to pay 100% annual interest, compounded n times per year and rounded to the nearest penny. You may pick any value you want for n. We have already seen that the larger n is, the more money you wind up earning. How large should you choose n in order to make your $1 grow to $5?

SOLUTION Since interest rate is compounded n times per year and the annual rate is 100% ($= 1.00$), the interest rate per period is $r = 1/n$ and the number of periods in 1 year is n. According to the formula, the amount at the end of the year will be $A = \left(1 + \dfrac{1}{n}\right)^{n}$. Here's what happens for various values of n:

Interest Is Compounded	$n =$	$\left(1 + \dfrac{1}{n}\right)^{n} =$
Annually	1	$(1 + \frac{1}{1})^{1} = 2$
Semiannually	2	$(1 + \frac{1}{2})^{2} = 2.25$
Quarterly	4	$(1 + \frac{1}{4})^{4} \approx 2.4414$
Monthly	12	$(1 + \frac{1}{12})^{12} \approx 2.6130$
Daily	365	$(1 + \frac{1}{365})^{365} \approx 2.71457$
Hourly	8760	$(1 + \frac{1}{8760})^{8760} \approx 2.718127$
Every minute	525,600	$(1 + \frac{1}{525{,}600})^{525{,}600} \approx 2.7182792$
Every second	31,536,000	$(1 + \frac{1}{31{,}536{,}000})^{31{,}536{,}000} \approx 2.7182818$

Since interest is rounded to the nearest penny, your dollar will grow no larger than $2.72, no matter how big n is. You will not be able to make your dollar grow to $5 at that interest rate. ∎

The last entry in the preceding table, 2.7182818, is the number *e* to seven decimal places. This is just one example of how *e* arises naturally in real-world situations. In calculus, it is provided that *e* is the *limit* of $\left(1 + \dfrac{1}{n}\right)^n$, meaning that as *n* gets larger and larger, $\left(1 + \dfrac{1}{n}\right)^n$ gets closer and closer to *e*.

GRAPHING EXPLORATION

Confirm this fact graphically by graphing the function

$$f(x) = \left(1 + \frac{1}{x}\right)^x$$

and the horizontal line $y = e$ in the viewing window with $0 \le x \le 5000$ and $-1 \le y \le 4$ and noting that the two graphs appear to be identical.

When interest is compounded *n* times per year for larger and larger values of *n*, as in Example 5, we say that the interest is **continuously compounded.** In this terminology, Example 5 says that \$1 will grow to \$2.72 in 1 year at an interest rate of 100% compounded continuously. A similar argument with more realistic interest rates (see Exercise 30) produces the following result (Example 5 is the case when $P = 1$, $r = 1$, and $t = 1$).

Continuous Compounding

> If *P* dollars is invested at interest rate *r*, compounded continuously, then the amount *A* after *t* years is
>
> $$A = Pe^{rt}.$$

EXAMPLE 6

If \$3800 is invested in a CD with a 3.8% interest rate, compounded continuously, find:

(a) The amount in the account after seven and a half years.

(b) The number of years for the account balance to reach \$5000.

SOLUTION

(a) Apply the continuous compounding formula with $P = 3800$, $r = .038$, and $t = 7.5$.

$$A = 3800e^{(.038)7.5} = 3800e^{.285} \approx \$5053.10.$$

(b) We must solve the equation

$$3800e^{.038t} = 5000, \qquad \text{or, equivalently,} \qquad 3800e^{.038t} - 5000 = 0.$$

GRAPHING EXPLORATION

Solve the equation graphically and verify that it will take a bit more than seven years for the investment to be worth \$5000.

EXERCISES 4.6

1. If $1,000 is invested at 8%, find the value of the investment after 5 years if interest is compounded

(a) annually.   (b) quarterly.   (c) monthly.
(d) weekly.

2. If $2500 is invested at 11.5%, what is the value of the investment after 10 years if interest is compounded

(a) annually?   (b) monthly?   (c) daily?

In Exercises 3–10, determine how much money will be in a savings account if the initial deposit was $500 and the interest rate is:

3. 3% compounded annually for 8 years.

4. 3% compounded annually for 10 years.

5. 3% compounded quarterly for 10 years.

6. 2.5% compounded annually for 20 years.

7. 2.477% compounded quarterly for 20 years.

8. 2.469% compounded continuously for 20 years.

9. 3% compounded continuously for 10 years, 7 months.

10. 3% compounded continuously for 30 years.

*A sum of money P that can be deposited today to yield some larger amount A in the future is called the **present value** of A. In Exercises 11–14, find the present value of the given amount A. [Hint: Substitute A, the interest rate per period r, and the number t of periods in the compound interest formula and solve for P.]*

11. $5000 at 6% compounded annually for 7 years.

12. $3500 at 5.5% compounded annually for 4 years.

13. $4800 at 7.2% compounded quarterly for 5 years.

14. $7400 at 5.9% compounded quarterly for 8 years.

15. You are to receive an insurance settlement in the amount of $8000. Because of various bureaucratic delays, it will take you about three years to collect your money.

(a) Assuming that your bank offers you an interest rate of 4 percent, compounded continuously, what is the present value of your settlement?

(b) If your insurance agent offers you $7050, payable immediately, to give up the settlement, is it best to take the deal?

16. You win a lawsuit, and the defendant is ordered to pay you $5000, and has up to eight years to pay you. We can assume that the defendant will probably wait until the last possible minute to give you your check.

(a) If you can get an interest rate of 3.75 percent on your money, compounded continuously, what is the present value of the money in question?

(b) If the defendant offers you $4000 (paid immediately) to forgive the debt, is it best to take the deal?

17. You have $10,000 to invest for two years. Fund A pays 13.2% interest, compounded annually. Fund B pays 12.7% interest, compounded quarterly. Fund C pays 12.6% interest, compounded monthly. Which fund will return the most money?

18. If you invest $7400 for five years, are you better off with an interest rate of 5% compounded quarterly or 4.8% compounded continuously?

19. If you borrow $1200 at 14% interest, compounded monthly, and pay off the loan (principal and interest) at the end of two years, how much interest will you have paid?

20. A developer borrows $150,000 at 6.5% interest, compounded quarterly, and agrees to pay off the loan in four years. How much interest will she owe?

21. A manufacturer has settled a lawsuit out of court by agreeing to pay $1.5 million four years from now. At this time, how much should the company put in an account paying 6.4% annual interest, compounded monthly, to have $1.5 million in four years? [*Hint:* See Exercises 11–14.]

22. Lisa Chow wants to have $30,000 available in five years for a down payment on a house. She has inherited $25,000. How much of the inheritance should be invested at 5.7% annual interest, compounded quarterly, to accumulate the $30,000?

23. If an investment of $1000 grows to $1407.10 in seven years with interest compounded annually, what is the interest rate?

24. If an investment of $2000 grows to $2700 in three and a half years, with an annual interest rate that is compounded quarterly, what is the annual interest rate?

25. If you put $3000 in a savings account today, what interest rate (compounded annually) must you receive in order to have $4000 after five years?

26. If interest is compounded continuously, what annual rate must you receive if your investment of $1500 is to grow to $2100 in six years?

27. At an interest rate of 8% compounded annually, how long will it take to double an investment of

(a) $100   (b) $500   (c) $1200?
(d) What conclusion about doubling time do parts (a)–(c) suggest?

28. At an interest rate of 6% compounded annually, how long will it take to double an investment of P dollars?

29. How long will it take to double an investment of $500 at 7% annual interest, compounded continuously?

THINKERS

30. This exercise provides an illustration of why the continuous compounding formula (page 373) is valid, using a realistic interest rate. We shall determine the value of $4000 deposited for three years at 5% interest compounded n times per year for larger and larger values of n. In this case, the interest rate per period is $.05/n$ and the number of periods in three years is $3n$. So the amount in the account at the end of three years is:

$$A = 4000\left(1 + \frac{.05}{n}\right)^{3n} = 4000\left[\left(1 + \frac{.05}{n}\right)^{n}\right]^{3}.$$

(a) Fill in the missing entries in the following table.

n	$\left(1 + \dfrac{.05}{n}\right)^{n}$
1,000	
10,000	
500,000	
1,000,000	
5,000,000	
10,000,000	

(b) Compare the entries in the second column of the table with the number $e^{.05}$ and fill the blank in the following sentence:

As n gets larger and larger, the value of $\left(1 + \dfrac{.05}{n}\right)^{n}$

gets closer and closer to the number _____.

(c) Use you answer to part (b) to fill the blank in the following sentence:

As n gets larger and larger, the value of

$$A = 4000\left[\left(1 + \frac{.05}{n}\right)^{n}\right]^{3}$$

gets closer and closer to _____.

(d) Compare your answer in part (c) to the value of the investment given by the continuous compounding formula.

31. Municipal bonds are investments issued by cities, states, or counties that wish to raise money to build things like schools, highways and hospitals. You buy a bond for a certain amount, and you get an interest payment every six months. Then, at a certain time (the "maturity date") you get your principal (the amount you paid for the bond) back. For example, if you bought a $10000 bond with a 10% interest rate, you would get payments of $500 every six months for a while, and then you would get a payment for $10500 back at the maturity date.

(a) In 2007 Sioux City, Iowa issued $5000 bonds for their community school district at an interest rate of 3.63%. The maturity date is October 1, 2012. The interest was to be paid every April 1 and October 1. If you bought one of these bonds on April 1, 2007, and held it until the maturity date, how much total interest will you have earned?

(b) What if, instead of buying the Sioux City bond, you could buy a CD (Certificate of Deposit) from a local bank that paid 3.4%, compounded semi-annually. Again, assuming you were going to save $5000 from April 1, 2007 though October 1, 2012, which would be the better choice and why?

(c) As discussed above, when you buy the Sioux City municipal bond, you are getting a payment every six months. What if you took those interest payments, and put them in a bank account that pays 3% interest, compounded semi-annually? Now how much total interest will you have earned on October 1, 2012? Would you make more money doing this, or buying the CD?

4.7   Exponential and Log Equations

Section Objectives
■ Solve exponential and logarithmic equations algebraically.
■ Use exponential and logarithmic equations to solve applied problems.

Most of the exponential and logarithmic equations solved by graphical means earlier in this chapter could also have been solved algebraically. The algebraic techniques for solving such equations are based on the properties of logarithms.

EXPONENTIAL EQUATIONS

The easiest exponential equations to solve are those in which both sides are powers of the same base.

EXAMPLE 1

Solve $8^{x} = 2^{x+1}$.

SOLUTION   Using the fact that $8 = 2^3$, we rewrite the equation as follows.

$$8^x = 2^{x+1}$$
$$(2^3)^x = 2^{x+1}$$
$$2^{3x} = 2^{x+1}$$

Since the powers of 2 are equal, the exponents must be the same, that is,

$$3x = x + 1$$
$$2x = 1$$
$$x = \frac{1}{2}.$$ ∎

When different bases are involved in an exponential equation, a different solution technique is needed.

EXAMPLE 2

Solve $5^x = 2$.

SOLUTION

Take logarithms on each side:* $\ln 5^x = \ln 2$

Use the Power Law: $x(\ln 5) = \ln 2$

Divide both sides by ln 5: $x = \dfrac{\ln 2}{\ln 5} \approx \dfrac{.6931}{1.6094} \approx .4307.$

Remember: $\dfrac{\ln 2}{\ln 5}$ is neither $\ln \dfrac{2}{5}$ nor $\ln 2 - \ln 5$. ∎

EXAMPLE 3

Solve $2^{4x-1} = 3^{1-x}$,

SOLUTION

Take logarithms of each side: $\ln 2^{4x-1} = \ln 3^{1-x}$

Use the Power Law: $(4x - 1)(\ln 2) = (1 - x)(\ln 3)$

Multiply out both sides: $4x(\ln 2) - \ln 2 = \ln 3 - x(\ln 3)$

Rearrange terms: $4x(\ln 2) + x(\ln 3) = \ln 2 + \ln 3$

Factor left side: $(4 \cdot \ln 2 + \ln 3)x = \ln 2 + \ln 3$

Divide both sides by $(4 \cdot \ln 2 + \ln 3)$: $x = \dfrac{\ln 2 + \ln 3}{4 \cdot \ln 2 + \ln 3} \approx .4628.$ ∎

 ## APPLICATIONS OF EXPONENTIAL EQUATIONS

As we saw in Section 5.2, the mass of a radioactive element at time x is given by

$$M(x) = c(.5^{x/h}),$$

where c is the initial mass and h is the half-life of the element.

---

*We shall use natural logarithms, but the same techniques are valid for logarithms to other bases (Exercise 34).

EXAMPLE 4

After 43 years, a 20-milligram sample of strontium-90 (^{90}Sr) decays to 6.071 mg. What is the half-life of strontium-90?

SOLUTION   The mass of the sample at time x is given by

$$f(x) = 20(.5^{x/h}),$$

where h is the half-life of strontium-90. We know that $f(x) = 6.071$ when $x = 43$, that is, $6.071 = 20(.5^{43/h})$. We must solve this equation for h.

Divide both sides by 20:	$\dfrac{6.071}{20} = .5^{43/h}$
Take logarithms on both sides:	$\ln \dfrac{6.071}{20} = \ln .5^{43/h}$
Use the Power Law:	$\ln \dfrac{6.071}{20} = \dfrac{43}{h} \ln .5$
Multiply both sides by h:	$h \ln \dfrac{6.071}{20} = 43 \ln .5$
Divide both sides by $\ln \dfrac{6.071}{20}$:	$h = \dfrac{43 \ln .5}{\ln(6.071/20)} \approx 25.$

Therefore, strontium-90 has a half-life of 25 years. ∎

EXAMPLE 5

When a living organism dies, its carbon-14 decays. The half-life of carbon-14 is 5730 years. If the skeleton of a mastodon has lost 58% of its original carbon-14, when did the mastodon die?*

SOLUTION   Time is measured from the death of the mastodon. The amount of carbon-14 left in the skeleton at time x is given by

$$M(x) = c(.5^{x/5730}),$$

where c is the original mass of carbon-14. The skeleton has lost 58% of c, that is, $.58c$. So the present value of $M(x)$ is $c - .58c = .42c$, and we have

$$M(x) = c(.5^{x/5730})$$

$$.42c = c(.5^{x/5730})$$

$$.42 = .5^{x/5730}.$$

The solution of this equation is the time elapsed from the mastodon's death to the present. It can be solved as above.

$$\ln .42 = \ln (.5)^{x/5730}$$

$$\ln .42 = \frac{x}{5730} (\ln .5)$$

---

*Archeologists can determine how much carbon-14 has been lost by a technique that involves measuring the ratio of carbon-14 to carbon-12 in the skeleton.

$$5730(\ln .42) = x(\ln .5)$$

$$x = \frac{5730(\ln .42)}{\ln .5} \approx 7171.32.$$

Therefore, the mastodon died approximately 7200 years ago.   ■

EXAMPLE 6

A certain bacteria is known to grow exponentially, with the population at time t given by a function of the form $g(t) = Pe^{kt}$, where P is the original population and k is the continuous growth rate. A culture shows 1000 bacteria present. Seven hours later, there are 5000.

(a) Find the continuous growth rate k.

(b) Determine when the population will reach one billion.

SOLUTION

(a) The original population is $P = 1000$, so the growth function is $g(t) = 1000e^{kt}$. We know that $g(7) = 5000$, that is,

$$1000e^{k \cdot 7} = 5000.$$

To determine the growth rate, we solve this equation for k.

Divide both sides by 1000:	$e^{7k} = 5$
Take logarithms of both sides:	$\ln e^{7k} = \ln 5$
Use the Power Law:	$7k \ln e = \ln 5.$

Since $\ln e = 1$ (why?), this equation becomes

$$7k = \ln 5$$

Divide both sides by 7: $k = \dfrac{\ln 5}{7} \approx .22992.$

Therefore, the growth function is $g(t) \approx 1000e^{.22992t}$.

(b) The population will reach one billion when $g(t) = 1{,}000{,}000{,}000$, that is, when

$$1000e^{.22992t} = 1{,}000{,}000{,}000.$$

So we solve this equation for t:

Divide both sides by 1000:	$e^{.22992t} = 1{,}000{,}000$
Take logarithms on both sides:	$\ln e^{.22992t} = \ln 1{,}000{,}000$
Use the Power Law:	$.22992t \ln e = \ln 1{,}000{,}000$
Remember $\ln e = 1$:	$.22992t = \ln 1{,}000{,}000$
Divide both sides by .22992:	$t = \dfrac{\ln 1{,}000{,}000}{.22992} \approx 60.09.$

Therefore, it will take a bit more than 60 hours for the culture to grow to one billion.   ■

EXAMPLE 7

Inhibited Population Growth   The population of fish in a lake at time t months is given by the function

$$p(t) = \frac{20{,}000}{1 + 24e^{-t/4}}.$$

How long will it take for the population to reach 15,000?

SOLUTION   We must solve this equation for t.

$$15{,}000 = \frac{20{,}000}{1 + 24e^{-t/4}}$$

$$15{,}000(1 + 24e^{-t/4}) = 20{,}000$$

$$1 + 24e^{-t/4} = \frac{20{,}000}{15{,}000} = \frac{4}{3}$$

$$24e^{-t/4} = \frac{1}{3}$$

$$e^{-t/4} = \frac{1}{3} \cdot \frac{1}{24} = \frac{1}{72}$$

$$\ln e^{-t/4} = \ln \left(\frac{1}{72}\right)$$

$$\left(-\frac{t}{4}\right)(\ln e) = \ln 1 - \ln 72$$

$$-\frac{t}{4} = -\ln 72 \qquad \text{[ln } e = 1 \text{ and ln } 1 = 0]$$

$$t = 4(\ln 72) \approx 17.1067.$$

So the population reaches 15,000 in a little over 17 months.   ■

LOGARITHMIC EQUATIONS

Equations that involve only logarithmic terms may be solved by using the following fact, which is proved in Exercise 33 (and is valid with log replaced by ln).

If $\log u = \log v$, then $u = v$.

EXAMPLE 8

Solve $\log (3x + 2) + \log (x + 2) = \log (7x + 6)$.

SOLUTION   First we write the left side as a single logarithm.

$$\log (3x + 2) + \log (x + 2) = \log (7x + 6)$$

Use the Product Law: $\log[(3x + 2)(x + 2)] = \log (7x + 6)$

Multiply out left side: $\log (3x^2 + 8x + 4) = \log (7x + 6).$

Since the logarithms are equal, we must have

$$3x^2 + 8x + 4 = 7x + 6$$

Subtract $7x + 6$ from both sides: $3x^2 + x - 2 = 0$

Factor: $(3x - 2)(x + 1) = 0$

$$3x - 2 = 0 \qquad \text{or} \qquad x + 1 = 0$$

$$3x = 2 \qquad\qquad\qquad x = -1$$

$$x = \frac{2}{3}$$

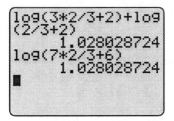

Figure 4–28

Thus, $x = 2/3$ and $x = -1$ are the *possible* solutions and must be checked in the *original* equation. When $x = 2/3$, both sides of the original equation have the same value, as shown in Figure 4–28. So $2/3$ is a solution. When $x = -1$, however, the right side of the equation is

$$\log (7x + 6) = \log [7(-1) + 6] = \log (-1),$$

which is not defined. So -1 is not a solution. ■

Equations that involve both logarithmic and constant terms may be solved by using the basic property of logarithms (see page 380).

(∗) $$10^{\log v} = v \quad \text{and} \quad e^{\ln v} = v.$$

EXAMPLE 9

Solve $7 + 2 \log 5x = 11$.

SOLUTION   We start by getting all the logarithmic terms on one side and the constant on the other.

Subtract 7 from both sides:	$2 \log 5x = 4$
Divide both sides by 2:	$\log 5x = 2.$

We know that if two quantities are equal, say $a = b$, then $10^a = 10^b$. We use this fact here, with the two sides of the preceding equation as a and b.

Exponentiate both sides:	$10^{\log 5x} = 10^2$
Use the basic logarithm property (∗):	$5x = 100$
Divide both sides by 5:	$x = 20.$

Verify that 20 is actually a solution of the original equation. ■

EXAMPLE 10

Solve $\ln (x - 3) = 5 - \ln (x - 3)$.

SOLUTION   We proceed as in Example 9, but since the base for these logarithms is e, we use e rather than 10 when we exponentiate.

	$\ln (x - 3) = 5 - \ln (x - 3)$
Add $\ln (x - 3)$ to both sides:	$2 \ln (x - 3) = 5$
Divide both sides by 2:	$\ln (x - 3) = \dfrac{5}{2}$
Exponentiate both sides:	$e^{\ln(x-3)} = e^{5/2}$
Use the basic property of logarithms (∗):	$x - 3 = e^{5/2}$
Add 3 to both sides:	$x = e^{5/2} + 3 \approx 15.1825.$

This is the only possibility for a solution. A calculator shows that it actually is a solution of the original equation. ■

EXAMPLE 11

Solve $\log (x - 16) = 2 - \log (x - 1)$.

SOLUTION

$$\log (x - 16) = 2 - \log (x - 1)$$

Add $\log (x - 1)$ to both sides: $\qquad \log (x - 16) + \log (x - 1) = 2$

Use the Product Law: $\qquad \log [(x - 16)(x - 1)] = 2$

Multiply out left side: $\qquad \log (x^2 - 17x + 16) = 2$

Exponentiate both sides: $\qquad 10^{\log (x^2 - 17x + 16)} = 10^2$

Use the basic logarithm property (∗): $\qquad x^2 - 17x + 16 = 100$

Subtract 100 from both sides: $\qquad x^2 - 17x - 84 = 0$

Factor: $\qquad (x + 4)(x - 21) = 0$

$$x + 4 = 0 \quad \text{or} \quad x - 21 = 0$$

$$x = -4 \quad \text{or} \quad x = 21.$$

You can easily verify that 21 is a solution of the original equation, but -4 is not [when $x = -4$, then $\log (x - 16) = \log (-20)$, which is not defined]. ∎

EXAMPLE 12

To solve $\log (x + 5) = 1 - \log (x - 2)$,

Rearrange terms: $\qquad \log (x + 5) + \log (x - 2) = 1$

Use the Product Law: $\qquad \log [(x + 5)(x - 2)] = 1$

$$\log (x^2 + 3x - 10) = 1$$

Exponentiate both sides: $\qquad 10^{\log (x^2 + 3x - 10)} = 10^1$

Use the basic logarithm property (∗): $\qquad x^2 + 3x - 10 = 10$

$$x^2 + 3x - 20 = 0.$$

This equation can be solved with the quadratic formula.

$$x = \frac{-3 \pm \sqrt{3^2 - 4 \cdot 1 \cdot (-20)}}{2 \cdot 1} = \frac{-3 \pm \sqrt{89}}{2}.$$

An easy way to verify that

$$x = \frac{-3 + \sqrt{89}}{2}$$

is a solution is to store this number in your calculator as A and then evaluate both sides of the original equation at $x = A$, as shown in Figure 4–29. The other possibility, however, is not a solution because

$$x = \frac{-3 - \sqrt{89}}{2}$$

is negative, so $\log (x - 2)$ is not defined. ∎

```
(-3+√(89))/2→A
          3.216990566
log(A+5)
           .9147127884
1-log(A-2)
           .9147127884
■
```

Figure 4–29

EXAMPLE 13

The number of pounds of fish (in billions) used for human consumption in the United States in year x is approximated by the function

$$f(x) = 10.57 + 1.75 \ln x,$$

where $x = 5$ corresponds to 1995.*

(a) How many pounds of fish were used in 2004?

(b) When will fish consumption reach 16 billion pounds?

SOLUTION

(a) Since 2004 corresponds to $x = 14$, we evaluate $f(x)$ at 14.

$$f(14) = 10.57 + 1.75 \ln 14 \approx 15.19 \text{ billion pounds.}$$

(b) Fish consumption is 16 billion pounds when $f(x) = 16$, so we must solve the equation

$$10.57 + 1.75 \ln x = 16$$

Subtract 10.57 from both sides:	$1.75 \ln x = 5.43$
Divide both sides by 1.75:	$\ln x = \dfrac{5.43}{1.75}$
Exponentiate both sides:	$e^{\ln x} = e^{5.43/1.75}$
Use the basic property of logarithms (∗):	$x \approx 22.26.$

Since $x = 22$ corresponds to 2012, fish consumption will reach 16 billion pounds in 2012. ∎

---

*Based on data from the U.S. National Oceanic and Atmospheric Administration and the National Marine Fisheries Service.

EXERCISES 4.7

In Exercises 1–8, solve the equation without using logarithms.

1. $3^x = 81$
2. $5^x - 2 = 23$
3. $3^{x+1} = 9^{5x}$
4. $3^{7x} = 9^{2x-5}$
5. $3^{5x}9^{x^2} = 27$
6. $7^{x^2+3x} = 1/49$
7. $9^{x^2} = 3^{-5x-2}$
8. $5^{2x^2+3x} = 25^{6-x}$

In Exercises 9–22, solve the equation. First express your answer in terms of natural logarithms (for instance, $x = (2 + \ln 5)/(\ln 3)$). Then use a calculator to find an approximation for the answer.

9. $3^x = 5$
10. $2^x = 9$
11. $2^x = 3^{x-1}$
12. $9^{x-1} = 8^{x-3}$
13. $3^{1-2x} = 5^{x+5}$
14. $2^{1-3x} = 7^{x+3}$
15. $2^{1-3x} = 3^{x+1}$
16. $5^{x+3} = 2^x$
17. $e^{2x} = 5$
18. $e^{-9x} = 3$
19. $6e^{-1.4x} = 21$
20. $27e^{-x/4} = 67.5$
21. $2.1e^{(x/2)\ln 3} = 5$
22. $2.7e^{(-x/3)\ln 7} = 21$

In Exercises 23–29, solve the equation for x by first making an appropriate substitution, as in the Hint for Exercise 23.

23. $9^x - 4 \cdot 3^x + 3 = 0$ [*Hint:* Let $u = 3^x$ and note that $9^x = (3^2)^x = 3^{2x} = (3^x)^2$. Hence, the equation becomes $u^2 - 4u + 3 = 0$. Solve this equation for u. In each solution, replace u by 3^x and solve for x.]
24. $25^x - 8 \cdot 5^x = -12$
25. $e^{2x} - 5e^x + 6 = 0$ [*Hint:* Let $u = e^x$.]

26. $3e^{2x} - 16e^x + 5 = 0$ **27.** $6e^{2x} - 16e^x = 6$

28. $6e^{2x} + 7e^x = 10$ **29.** $4^x + 6 \cdot 4^{-x} = 5$

In Exercises 30–32, solve the equation for x.

30. $\dfrac{e^x + e^{-x}}{e^x - e^{-x}} = t$ **31.** $\dfrac{e^x - e^{-x}}{2} = t$

32. $\dfrac{e^x - e^{-x}}{e^x + e^{-x}} = t$

33. (a) Prove that if $\ln u = \ln v$, then $u = v$. [*Hint:* Property (∗) on page 404.]
    (b) Is it always the case that if $u = v$ then $\ln u = \ln v$? Why or why not?

34. (a) Solve $7^x = 3$, using natural logarithms. Leave your answer in logarithmic form; don't approximate with a calculator.
    (b) Solve $7^x = 3$, using common (base 10) logarithms. Leave your answer in logarithmic form.
    (c) Use the change of base formula in Special Topics 5.4.A to show that your answers in parts (a) and (b) are the same.

In Exercises 35–44, solve the equation as in Example 8.

35. $\ln (3x - 5) = \ln 11 + \ln 2$

36. $\log (3x + 8) = \log (2x + 1) + \log 3$

37. $\log (3x - 1) + \log 2 = \log 4 + \log (x + 2)$

38. $\ln (2x - 1) - \ln 2 = \ln (3x + 6) - \ln 6$

39. $2 \ln x = \ln 36$

40. $2 \log x = 3 \log 9$

41. $\ln x + \ln (x + 1) = \ln 3 + \ln 4$

42. $\ln (5x - 2) + \ln x = \ln 3$

43. $\ln x = \ln 3 - \ln (x + 5)$

44. $\ln (3x - 4) + \ln x = \ln e$

In Exercises 45–52, solve the equation.

45. $\ln (x + 9) - \ln x = 1$

46. $\ln (3x + 5) - 1 = \ln (2x - 3)$

47. $\log x + \log (x - 3) = 1$

48. $\log (x - 4) + \log (x - 1) = 1$

49. $\log \sqrt{x^2 - 1} = 2$

50. $\log \sqrt[5]{x^2 + 15x} = 2/5$

51. $\ln (x^2 + 1) - \ln (x - 1) = 1 + \ln (x + 1)$

52. $\dfrac{\ln (2x + 1)}{\ln (3x - 1)} = 2$

Exercises 53–62 deal with radioactive decay and the function $M(x) = c(.5^{x/h})$; see Examples 4 and 5.

53. A sample of 300 grams of uranium decays to 200 grams in .26 billion years. Find the half-life of uranium.

54. It takes 1000 years for a sample of 300 mg of radium-226 to decay to 195 mg. Find the half-life of radium-226.

55. A 3-gram sample of an isotope of sodium decays to 1 gram in 23.7 days. Find the half-life of the isotope of sodium.

56. The half-life of cobalt-60 is 5.3 years. How long will it take for 100 grams to decay to 33 grams?

57. After six days a sample of radon-222 decayed to 33.6% of its original mass. Find the half-life of radon-222. [*Hint:* When $x = 6$, then $M(x) = .336P$.]

58. Krypton-85 loses 6.44% of its mass each year. What is its half-life?

59. How old is a piece of ivory that has lost 36% of its carbon-14?

60. How old is a mummy that has lost 62% of its carbon-14?

61. A Native American mummy was found recently. If it has lost 26.4% of its carbon-14, approximately how long ago did the Native American die?

62. How old is a wooden statue that has only one-third of its original carbon-14?

Exercises 63–68 deal with the compound interest formula $A = P(1 + r)^t$, which was discussed in Special Topics 5.2.A.

63. At what annual rate of interest should $1000 be invested so that it will double in 10 years if interest is compounded quarterly?

64. How long does it take $500 to triple if it is invested at 6% compounded: (a) annually, (b) quarterly, (c) daily?

65. (a) How long will it take to triple your money if you invest $500 at a rate of 5% per year compounded annually?
    (b) How long will it take at 5% compounded quarterly?

66. At what rate of interest (compounded annually) should you invest $500 if you want to have $1500 in 12 years?

67. How much money should be invested at 5% interest, compounded quarterly, so that 9 years later the investment will be worth $5000? This amount is called the **present value** of $5000 at 5% interest.

68. Find a formula that gives the time needed for an investment of P dollars to double, if the interest rate is r% compounded annually. [*Hint:* Solve the compound interest formula for t, when $A = 2P$.]

Exercises 69–76 deal with functions of the form $f(x) = Pe^{kx}$, where k is the continuous exponential growth rate (see Example 6).

69. The present concentration of carbon dioxide in the atmosphere is 364 parts per million (ppm) and is increasing exponentially at a continuous yearly rate of .4% (that is, $k = .004$). How many years will it take for the concentration to reach 500 ppm?

70. The amount P of ozone in the atmosphere is currently decaying exponentially each year at a continuous rate of $\frac{1}{4}\%$ (that is, $k = -.0025$). How long will it take for half the ozone to disappear (that is, when will the amount be $P/2$)? [Your answer is the half-life of ozone.]

71. The population of Brazil increased from 151 million in 1990 to 180 million in 2002.*

(a) At what continuous rate was the population growing during this period?

(b) Assuming that Brazil's population continues to increase at this rate, when will it reach 250 million?

72. Between 1996 and 2004, the number of United States subscribers to cell-phone plans has grown nearly exponentially. In 1996 there were 44,043,000 subscribers and in 2004 there were 182,140,000[†].

(a) What is the continuous growth rate of the number of cell-phone subscribers?

(b) In what year were there 60,000,000 cell-phone subscribers?

(c) Assuming that this rate continuous, in what year will there be 350,000,000 subscribers?

(d) In 2007 the United States population was approximately 300 million. Is your answer to part (c) realistic? If not, what could have gone wrong?

73. The probability P percent of having an accident while driving a car is related to the alcohol level of the driver's blood by the formula $P = e^{kt}$, where k is a constant. Accident statistics show that the probability of an accident is 25% when the blood alcohol level is $t = .15$.

(a) Find k. [Use $P = 25$, not .25.]

(b) At what blood alcohol level is the probability of having an accident 50%?

74. Under normal conditions, the atmospheric pressure (in millibars) at height h feet above sea level is given by $P(h) = 1015e^{-kh}$, where k is a positive constant.

(a) If the pressure at 18,000 feet is half the pressure at sea level, find k.

(b) Using the information from part (a), find the atmospheric pressure at 1000 feet, 5000 feet, and 15,000 feet.

75. One hour after an experiment begins, the number of bacteria in a culture is 100. An hour later, there are 500.

(a) Find the number of bacteria at the beginning of the experiment and the number three hours later.

(b) How long does it take the number of bacteria at any given time to double?

76. If the population at time t is given by $S(t) = ce^{kt}$, find a formula that gives the time it takes for the population to double.

77. The spread of a flu virus in a community of 45,000 people is given by the function

$$f(t) = \frac{45,000}{1 + 224e^{-.899t}},$$

where $f(t)$ is the number of people infected in week t.

(a) How many people had the flu at the outbreak of the epidemic? After three weeks?

(b) When will half the town be infected?

78. The beaver population near a certain lake in year t is approximately

$$p(t) = \frac{2000}{1 + 199e^{-.5544t}}.$$

(a) When will the beaver population reach 1000?

(b) Will the population ever reach 2000? Why?

79. Assume that you watched 1000 hours of television this year, and will watch 750 hours next year, and will continue to watch 75% as much every year thereafter.

(a) In what year will you be down to ten hours per year?

(b) In what year would you be down to one hour per year?

80. In the year 2009, Olivia's bank balance is $1000. In the year 2010, her balance is $1100.

(a) If her balance is growing exponentially, in what year will it reach $2500?

(b) If her balance is instead growing linearly, in what year will it reach $2500?

THINKERS

81. According to one theory of learning, the number of words per minute N that a person can type after t weeks of practice is given by $N = c(1 - e^{-kt})$, where c is an upper limit that N cannot exceed and k is a constant that must be determined experimentally for each person.

(a) If a person can type 50 wpm (words per minute) after four weeks of practice and 70 wpm after eight weeks, find the values of k and c for this person. According to the theory, this person will never type faster than c wpm.

(b) Another person can type 50 wpm after four weeks of practice and 90 wpm after eight weeks. How many weeks must this person practice to be able to type 125 wpm?

82. Kate has been offered two jobs, each with the same starting salary of $32,000 and identical benefits. Assuming satisfactory performance, she will receive a $1600 raise each year at the Great Gizmo Company, whereas the Wonder Widget Company will give her a 4% raise each year.

(a) In what year (after the first year) would her salary be the same at either company? Until then, which company pays better? After that, which company pays better?

(b) Answer the questions in part (a) assuming that the annual raise at Great Gizmo is $2000.

4.8   Solving Equations Graphically

Section Objectives
- Use technology to solve equations graphically and numerically.
- Solve equations by the intercept method.
- Solve equations the intersection method.
- Use an equation solver to solve equations numerically.
- Learn strategies for solving radical and fractional equations with technology.

Algebraic techniques can be used to solve linear, quadratic, and some higher-degree equations, as we saw in Section 1.2. For many other equations, however, graphical and numerical approximation methods are the only practical alternatives. These methods are based on a connection between equations and graphs that we now examine.

Recall that the x-intercepts of the graph of

$$y = x^4 - 4x^3 + 3x^2 - x - 2$$

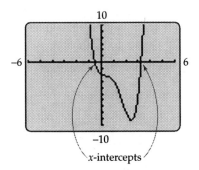

Figure 4–30

are the x-coordinates of the points where the graph intersects the x-axis (see Figure 4–30). Since points on the x-axis have 0 second coordinates, the x-intercepts are found algebraically by setting $y = 0$ and solving for x, that is, by solving the equation

$$x^4 - 4x^3 + 3x^2 - x - 2 = 0.$$

Graphical equation solving amounts to running this in the opposite direction: An equation is solved by finding the x-intercepts, as illustrated in the next example.

EXAMPLE 1

Solve $x^4 - 4x^3 + 3x^2 - x - 2 = 0$ graphically.

SOLUTION   As we have just seen, the solutions are the x-intercepts of the graph of

$$y = x^4 - 4x^3 + 3x^2 - x - 2.$$

These x-intercepts may be found by graphing the equation and using the graphical root finder, as in Figure 4–31. (See the Technology Tip in the margin.)

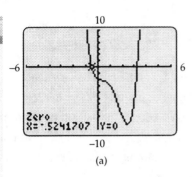
(a)

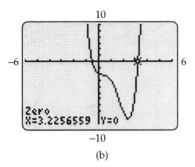
(b)

Figure 4–31

Therefore, the approximate solutions of the original equation are $x \approx -.5242$ and $x \approx 3.2257$. ∎

The process in Example 1 works in the general case as well.

The Intercept Method

To solve a one-variable equation of the form,

$$\text{Expression in } x = 0,$$

1. Graph the two-variable equation

    $$y = \text{expression in } x.$$

2. Use a graphical root finder to determine the *x*-intercepts of the graph.

The *x*-intercepts are the real solutions of the equation.

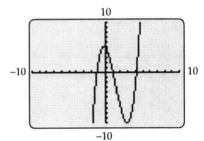

Figure 4–32

EXAMPLE 2

Solve $x^3 - 4x^2 - 2x + 5 = 0$.

SOLUTION   We graph $y = x^3 - 4x^2 - 2x + 5$ (Figure 4–32) and see that it has three *x*-intercepts. So the equation has three real solutions. A root finder shows that one solution is $x \approx -1.1926$ (Figure 4–33 on the next page). ∎

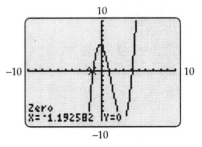

Figure 4–33

Use your graphical root finder to find the other two solutions (*x*-intercepts) of the equation in Example 2.

 THE INTERSECTION METHOD

The next examples illustrate an alternative graphical method, which is sometimes more convenient for solving equations.

EXAMPLE 3

Solve $|x^2 - 4x - 3| = x^3 + x - 6$.

SOLUTION   Let $y_1 = |x^2 - 4x - 3|$ and $y_2 = x^3 + x - 6$, and graph both equations on the same screen (Figure 4–34). Consider the point where the two graphs intersect. Since it is on the graph of y_1, its second coordinate is $|x^2 - 4x - 3|$, and since it is also on the graph of y_2, its second coordinate is $x^3 + x - 6$. So for this number x, we must have $|x^2 - 4x - 3| = x^3 + x - 6$. In other words, *the x-coordinate of the intersection point is the solution of the equation.*

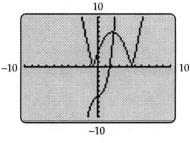

Figure 4–34

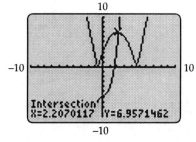

Figure 4–35

TECHNOLOGY TIP

The graphical intersection finder is in the same menu/submenu as the root finder. It is labeled *Intersection*, *Intersect*, *Isect*, or *ISCT*.

This coordinate can be approximated by using a graphical intersection finder (see the Technology Tip in the margin), as shown in Figure 4–35. Therefore, the solution of the original equation is $x \approx 2.207$. ∎

GRAPHING EXPLORATION

Show that the equation $x^2 - 2x - 6 = \sqrt{2x + 7}$ has two real solutions by graphing the left and right sides in the standard window and counting the number of intersection points. The positive solution is $x \approx 4.3094$. Find the negative solution.

The technique used in Example 3 and the preceding exploration works in the general case

The Intersection Method

To solve an equation of the form

$$\text{First expression in } x = \text{Second expression in } x,$$

1. Set y_1 equal to the left side and y_2 equal to the right side.

2. Graph y_1 and y_2 on the same screen.

3. Use a graphical intersection finder to find the x-coordinate of each point where the graphs intersect.

These x-coordinates are the real solutions of the equation.

EXAMPLE 4

According to data from the U.S. Census Bureau, the approximate population y (in millions) of Detroit is given by

$$y = (-6.985 \times 10^{-7})x^4 + (9.169 \times 10^{-5})x^3 - .00373x^2 + .0268x + 1.85,$$

where $x = 0$ corresponds to 1950. The approximate population of San Diego during the same period is given by

$$y = (-6.216 \times 10^{-6})x^3 + (4.569 \times 10^{-4})x^2 + .01035x + .346.$$

(a) Approximately when did the two cities have the same population?

(b) In what year was the population of Detroit about 1,500,000?

SOLUTION

(a) The populations of the two cities are equal when

$$(-6.985 \times 10^{-7})x^4 + (9.169 \times 10^{-5})x^3 - .00373x^2 + .0268x + 1.85$$
$$= (-6.216 \times 10^{-6})x^3 + (4.569 \times 10^{-4})x^2 + .01035x + .346.$$

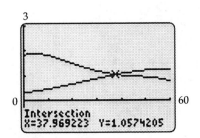

Figure 4–36

We solve this equation by graphing the left side as y_1 and the right side as y_2 and finding the intersection point, as in Figure 4–36. Rounding the x-coordinate to the nearest year ($x \approx 38$), we see that the populations were equal around 1988.

(b) To find when the population of Detroit was 1,500,000 (that is, 1.5 million), we must solve the equation

$$(-6.985 \times 10^{-7})x^4 + (9.169 \times 10^{-5})x^3 - .00373x^2 + .0268x + 1.85 = 1.5.$$

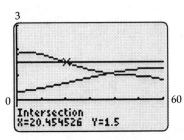

Figure 4–37

Since the left side of this equation has already been graphed as y_1, we need only graph $y_3 = 1.5$ on the same screen and find the intersection point of y_1 and y_3, as in Figure 4–37. The solution $x \approx 20.45$ shows that Detroit had a population of 1.5 million in 1970.   ∎

NUMERICAL METHODS

In addition to graphical tools for solving equations, calculators and computer algebra systems have **equation solvers** that can find or approximate the solutions of most equations. On most calculators, the solver finds one solution at a time. You must enter the equation and an initial guess and possibly an interval in which to search. A few calculators (such as TI-89) and most computer systems have **one-step equation solvers** that will find or approximate all the solutions in a single step. Check you calculator instruction manual or your computer's help menu for directions on using these solvers.

TECHNOLOGY TIP

To call up the equation solver, use this menu/choice:

TI-84+: MATH/*Solver*
TI-86: SOLVER (keyboard)
TI-89: ALGEBRA/*Solve*
HP-39gs: APLET/*Solve*
Casio: EQUA (Main Menu)/*Solver*

EXAMPLE 5

Use an equation solver to solve

$$\frac{5}{\sqrt{x^2 + 1}} = \frac{x^4}{x + 5}.$$

SOLUTION   On the TI-84+ solver, the equation must be put in the form $\dfrac{5}{\sqrt{x^2 + 1}} - \dfrac{x^4}{x + 5} = 0$. When asked to find a solution in the interval $-10 \le x \le 10$, with an initial guess of 1, the solver found the one in Figure 4–38. We changed the initial guess to -1 to produce the solution in Figure 4–39.*

The one-step solver on a TI-89 produced both solutions of the equation (Figure 4–40).

The first solution in Figure 4–40 was found on Maple with the command

fsolve(5/sqrt(x^2 + 1) − x^4/(x + 5) = 0, x);

and the second was found by changing the search interval to $-10 \le x \le 0$, with the command

fsolve(5/sqrt(x^2 + 1) − x^4/(x + 5) = 0, x, x = −10. . 0).   ∎

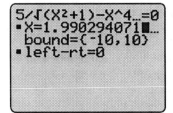

Figure 4–38

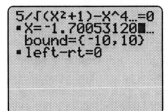

Figure 4–39

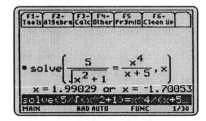

Figure 4–40

---

*In some cases, you may also have to change the search interval to find additional solutions.

Several calculators and many computer algebra systems also have **polynomial solvers,** one-step solvers designed specifically for polynomial equations; you need only enter the degree and coefficients of the polynomial. A few of these (such as Casio 9850) are limited to equations of degree 2 and 3. Directions for using polynomial solvers on calculators are in Exercise 105 on page 31. Computer users should check the help menu for the proper syntax.

EXAMPLE 6

Use a polynomial solver to solve

$$4x^5 - 12x^3 + 8x - 1 = 0.$$

SOLUTION   We enter the degree and the coefficients of the equation in the polynomial solver (Figure 4–41) and press SOLVE to obtain the five solutions (Figure 4–42).* The fsolve command on Maple also produced all five solutions. ∎

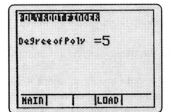
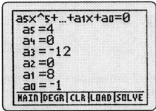
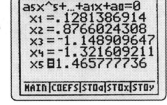

Figure 4–41   **Figure 4–42**

STRATEGIES FOR SPECIAL CASES

Because of various technological shortcomings, some equations are easier to solve if an indirect approach is used.

EXAMPLE 7

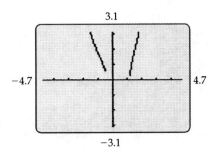

Figure 4–43

Solve $\sqrt{x^4 + x^2 - 2x - 1} = 0$.

SOLUTION   The graph of $y = \sqrt{x^4 + x^2 - 2x - 1}$ in Figure 2–37 does not even appear to touch the x-axis (although it actually does touch at two places). Consequently, some solvers and graphical root finders will return an error message (check yours). Even if your root finder or solver can handle this equation, it may fail in other similar situations. So the best approach is to use the following fact:

The only number whose square root is 0 is 0 itself.

---

*This illustrates the procedure for TI-84+ and 86. For HP-39gs, see Exercise 105 on page 31.

Thus, $\sqrt{x^4 + x^2 - 2x - 1} = 0$ exactly when $x^4 + x^2 - 2x - 1 = 0$. So you need only solve the polynomial equation

$$x^4 + x^2 - 2x - 1 = 0,$$

which is easily done on any calculator or computer. In fact, if you have a polynomial or one-step solver, you can find all the solutions at once, which is faster than solving the original equation with a root finder or other solvers.

GRAPHING EXPLORATION

If you have a polynomial or one-step solver, use it to find all the real solutions of $x^4 + x^2 - 2x - 1 = 0$ at once. Otherwise, graph $y = x^4 + x^2 - 2x - 1$ and use the graphical root finder to obtain the solutions one at a time. Verify that the real solutions of this equation, and hence, of the original one, are $x \approx -.4046978$ and $x \approx 1.1841347$.

■

The technique used in Example 7 is recommended for all similar situations.

Radical Equations

To solve an equation of the form

$$\sqrt{\text{Expression in } x} = 0,$$

set the expression under the radical equal to 0 and solve the resulting equation.

EXAMPLE 8

Solve

$$\frac{2x^2 + x - 1}{9x^2 - 9x + 2} = 0.$$

SOLUTION   If you graph

$$y = \frac{2x^2 + x - 1}{9x^2 - 9x + 2},$$

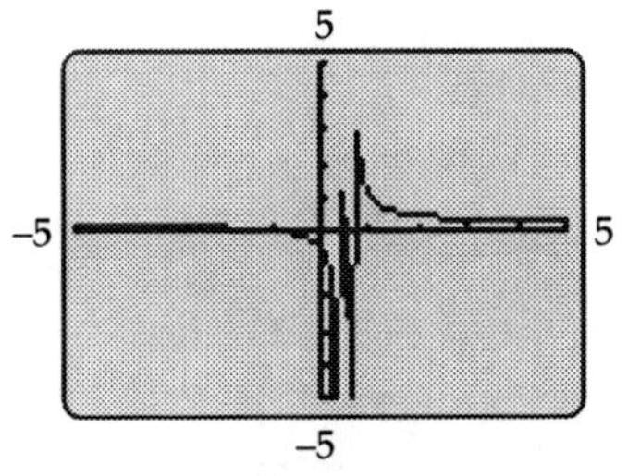

you may get "garbage," as in Figure 4–44. You could experiment with other viewing windows, but it's easier to use this fact:

**A fraction is 0 exactly when its numerator is 0 and
its denominator is nonzero.**

To find where the numerator is 0, we need only solve $2x^2 + x - 1 = 0$. This is easily done algebraically.*

$$2x^2 + x - 1 = 0$$

$$(2x - 1)(x + 1) = 0$$

$$x = 1/2 \quad \text{or} \quad x = -1$$

You can readily verify that neither of these numbers make the denominator 0. Hence, the solutions of the original equation are $1/2$ and -1.   ■

Figure 4–44

---

*In other cases, you may need technology to solve the numerator equation.

Example 8 illustrates a useful technique.

Fractional Equations

To solve an equation of the form

$$\text{Fraction} = 0,$$

set the numerator equal to 0 and solve the resulting equation. The solutions that do *not* make the denominator of the fraction 0 are the solutions of the original equation.*

CHOOSING A SOLUTION METHOD

We have seen that equations can be solved by algebraic, graphical, and numerical methods. Each method has both advantages and disadvantages, as summarized in the table.

Solution Method	Advantages	Possible Disadvantages
Algebraic	Produces exact solutions. Easiest method for most linear and quadratic equations.	May be difficult or impossible to use with complicated equations.
Graphical Root Finder or Intersection Finder	Works well for a large variety of equations. Gives visual picture of the location of the solutions.	Solutions may be approximations. Finding a useable viewing window may take a lot of time.
Numerical Equation Solvers		Solutions may be approximations.
Polynomial solver	Fast and easy.	Works only for polynomial equations.
One-step solver	Fast and easy.	May miss some solutions or be unable to solve certain equations.
Other solvers		May require a considerable amount of work to find the particular solution you want.

The choice of solution method is up to you. In the rest of this book, we normally use algebraic means for solving linear and quadratic equations because this is often the fastest and most accurate method. Naturally, any such equation can also be solved graphically or numerically (and you may want to do that as a check against errors). Except in special cases, graphical and numerical methods will normally be used for more complicated equations.

---

*A number that makes *both* numerator and denominator 0 is *not* a solution of the original equation because 0/0 is not defined.

EXERCISES 4.8

In Exercises 1–6, determine graphically the number of solutions of the equation, but don't solve the equation. You may need a viewing window other than the standard one to find all the x-intercepts.

1. $x^5 + 5 = 3x^4 + x$

2. $x^3 + 5 = 3x^2 + 24x$

3. $x^7 - 10x^5 + 15x + 10 = 0$

4. $x^5 + 36x + 25 = 13x^3$

5. $x^4 + 500x^2 - 8000x = 16x^3 - 32,000$

6. $6x^5 + 80x^3 + 45x^2 + 30 = 45x^4 + 86x$

In Exercises 7–20, use graphical approximation (a root finder or an intersection finder) to find a solution of the equation in the given open interval.

7. $x^3 + 4x^2 + 10x + 15 = 0$; $(-3, -2)$

8. $x^3 + 9 = 3x^2 + 6x$; $(1, 2)$

9. $x^4 + x - 3 = 0$; $(-\infty, 0)$

10. $x^5 + 5 = 3x^4 + x$; $(2, \infty)$

11. $\sqrt{x^4 + x^3 - x - 3} = 0$; $(-\infty, 0)$

12. $\sqrt{8x^4 - 14x^3 - 9x^2 + 11x - 1} = 0$; $(-\infty, 0)$

13. $\sqrt{\dfrac{2}{5}x^5 + x^2 - 2x} = 0$; $(0, \infty)$

14. $\sqrt{x^4 + x^2 - 3x + 1} = 0$; $(0, 1)$

15. $x^2 = \sqrt{x + 5}$; $(-2, -1)$

16. $\sqrt{x^2 - 1} - \sqrt{x + 9} = 0$; $(3, 4)$

17. $\dfrac{2x^5 - 10x + 5}{x^3 + x^2 - 12x} = 0$; $(1, \infty)$

18. $\dfrac{3x^5 - 15x + 5}{x^7 - 8x^5 + 2x^2 - 5} = 0$; $(1, \infty)$

19. $\dfrac{x^3 - 4x + 1}{x^2 + x - 6} = 0$; $(-\infty, 0)$

20. $\dfrac{4}{x + 2} - \dfrac{3}{x + 1} = 0$; $(0, \infty)$ [*Hint:* Write the left side as a single fraction.]

In Exercises 21–34, use algebraic, graphical, or numerical methods to find all real solutions of the equation, approximating when necessary.

21. $2x^3 - 4x^2 + x - 3 = 0$

22. $6x^3 - 5x^2 + 3x - 2 = 0$

23. $x^5 - 6x + 6 = 0$

24. $x^3 - 3x^2 + x - 1 = 0$

25. $10x^5 - 3x^2 + x - 6 = 0$

26. $\dfrac{1}{4}x^4 - x - 4 = 0$

27. $2x - \dfrac{1}{2}x^2 - \dfrac{1}{12}x^4 = 0$

28. $\dfrac{1}{4}x^4 + \dfrac{1}{3}x^2 + 3x - 1 = 0$

29. $\dfrac{5x}{x^2 + 1} - 2x + 3 = 0$

30. $\dfrac{2x}{x + 5} = 1$

31. $|x^2 - 4| = 3x^2 - 2x + 1$

32. $|x^3 + 2| = 5 + x - x^2$

33. $\sqrt{x^2 + 3} = \sqrt{x - 2} + 5$

34. $\sqrt{x^3 + 2} = \sqrt{x + 5} + 4$

In Exercises 35–40, find an exact solution of the equation in the given open interval. (For example, if the graphical approximation of a solution begins .3333, check to see whether 1/3 is the exact solution. Similarly, $\sqrt{2} \approx 1.414$; so if your approximation begins 1.414, check to see whether $\sqrt{2}$ is a solution.)

35. $3x^3 - 2x^2 + 3x - 2 = 0$; $(0, 1)$

36. $4x^3 - 3x^2 - 3x - 7 = 0$; $(1, 2)$

37. $12x^4 - x^3 - 12x^2 + 25x - 2 = 0$; $(0, 1)$

38. $8x^5 + 7x^4 - x^3 + 16x - 2 = 0$; $(0, 1)$

39. $4x^4 - 13x^2 + 3 = 0$; $(1, 2)$

40. $x^3 + x^2 - 2x - 2 = 0$; $(1, 2)$

Exercises 41–46 deal with exponential, logarithmic, and trigonometric equations, which will be dealt with in later chapters. If you are familiar with these concepts, solve each equation graphically or numerically.

41. $10^x - \dfrac{1}{4}x = 28$

42. $e^x - 6x = 5$

43. $x + \sin\left(\dfrac{x}{2}\right) = 4$

44. $x^3 + \cos\left(\dfrac{x}{3}\right) = 5$

45. $5 \ln x + x^3 - x^2 = 5$

46. $\ln x - x^2 + 3 = 0$

47. According to data from the U.S. Department of Education, the average cost y of tuition and fees at four-year public colleges and universities in year x is approximated by

$$y = \sqrt{180,115x^2 + 2,863,851x + 11,383,876}$$

where $x = 0$ corresponds to 2000. If this model continues to be accurate, in what year will tuition and fees reach \$7000? Round your answer to the nearest year.

48. Use the information in Example 4 to determine the year in which the population of San Diego reached 1.1 million people.

49. According to data from the U.S. Department of Health and Human Services, the cumulative number y of AIDS cases (in thousands) as of year x is approximated by

$$y = .004x^3 - 1.367x^2 + 54.35x + 569.72 \quad (0 \le x < 11),$$

where $x = 0$ corresponds to 1995.

(a) When did the cumulative number of cases reach 944,000?

(b) If this model remains accurate after 2006, in what year will the cumulative number of cases reach 1.1 million?

50. The enrollment in public high schools (in millions of students) in year x is approximated by

$$y = -.000035606x^4 + .0021x^3 - .02714x^2 - .12059x + 14.2996 \qquad (0 \le x < 35),$$

where $x = 0$ corresponds to 1975.* During the current century, when was enrollment 13.9 million students?

51. In Example 4 of Section 1.1 (page 9), a formula is given for determining how far you can see from a given height. Suppose you are on a cruise ship and that you can see the top of a lighthouse 12 miles away. About how high above water level are you?

52. According to the U.S. Centers for Medicare and Medicaid Services, total medical expenditures (in billions of dollars) in the United States in year x are expected to be given by

$$y = -.035x^4 + 1.01x^3 - 4.91x^2 + 126.94x + 1309.6,$$

where $x = 0$ corresponds to 2000. When will expenditures be $2.6 trillion?

53. When is the population of China expected to reach 1.4 billion people? [*Hint:* The equation that estimates the population of China is in Exercise 28 of Section 2.1 (page 89).]

54. (a) How many real solutions does the equation

$$.2x^5 - 2x^3 + 1.8x + k = 0$$

have when $k = 0$?
    (b) How many real solutions does it have when $k = 1$?
    (c) Is there a value of k for which the equation has just one real solution?
    (d) Is there a value of k for which the equation has no real solutions?

---

*Based on data from the National Center for Educational Statistics.

Chapter 5

SOLVING SYSTEMS OF EQUATIONS

© DEA/A. RIZZI/ Getty Images

Chapter Outline

Interdependence of Sections

5.1   Linear Equations in Two Variables

Section Objectives

- Solve systems of linear equations graphically.
- Use the substitution method to solve systems of linear equations.
- Use the elimination method to solve systems of linear equations.
- Identify inconsistent and dependent systems.
- Use systems of linear equations to solve applied problems.

Systems of linear equations in two variables may be solved graphically or algebraically. The geometric method is similar to what we have done previously.

EXAMPLE 1

Solve this system graphically.

$$2x - y = 1$$
$$3x + 2y = 4.$$

SOLUTION   First, we solve each equation for y.

$$2x - y = 1 \qquad\qquad 3x + 2y = 4$$
$$-y = -2x + 1 \qquad\qquad 2y = -3x + 4$$
$$y = 2x - 1 \qquad\qquad y = \frac{-3x + 4}{2}.$$

Next, we graph both equations on the same screen (Figure 5–1). As we saw in Section 1.4, each graph is a straight line, and every point on the graph represents a solution of the equation. Therefore, the solution of the system is given by the coordinates of the point that lies on both lines. An intersection finder (Figure 5–2) shows that the approximate coordinates of this point are

$$x \approx .85714286 \qquad \text{and} \qquad y \approx .71428571. \qquad\qquad\blacksquare$$

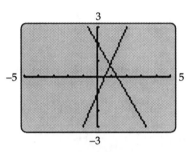

Figure 5–1

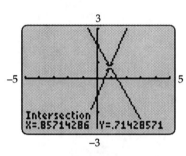

Figure 5–2

As is shown in Example 1, the solutions of a system of linear equations are determined by the points where their graphs intersect. There are exactly three geometric possibilities for two lines in the plane: They are parallel, they intersect at a single point, or they coincide, as illustrated in Figure 5–3. Each of these possibilities leads to a different number of solutions for the system.

Number of Solutions of a System

A system of two linear equations in two variables must have

No solutions *or*

Exactly one solution *or*

An infinite number of solutions.

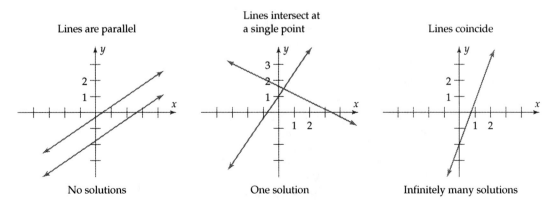

Figure 5–3

THE SUBSTITUTION METHOD

When you use a calculator to solve systems graphically, you may have to settle for an approximate solution, as we did in Example 1. Algebraic methods, however, produce exact solutions. Furthermore, algebraic methods are often as easy to implement as graphical ones, so we shall use them, whenever practical, to obtain exact solutions. One algebraic method is **substitution,** which is explained in the next example.

EXAMPLE 2

Use substitution to find the exact solution of the system from Example 1.

$$2x - y = 1$$
$$3x + 2y = 4.$$

SOLUTION   Any solution of this system must satisfy the first equation, $2x - y = 1$. Solving this equation for y, as in Example 1, shows that

$$y = 2x - 1.$$

Substituting this expression for y in the second equation, we have

$$3x + 2y = 4$$
$$3x + 2(2x - 1) = 4$$
$$3x + 4x - 2 = 4$$
$$7x = 6$$
$$x = 6/7.$$

Therefore, every solution of the original system must have $x = 6/7$. But when $x = 6/7$, we see from the first equation that

$$2x - y = 1$$
$$2\left(\frac{6}{7}\right) - y = 1$$
$$\frac{12}{7} - y = 1$$
$$-y = -\frac{12}{7} + 1$$
$$y = \frac{12}{7} - 1 = \frac{5}{7}.$$

(We would also have found that $y = 5/7$ if we had substituted $x = 6/7$ in the second equation.) Consequently, the exact solution of the original system is $x = 6/7, y = 5/7$. ∎

CAUTION

To guard against arithmetic mistakes, you should always *check your answers* by substituting them into *all* the equations of the original system. We have in fact checked the answers in all the examples, but these checks are omitted to save space.

When using the substitution method, you may solve either of the given equations for either one of the variables and then substitute that result in the other equation. In Example 2, we solved for y in the first equation because that avoided the fractional expression that would have occurred if we had solved for x or had solved the second equation for x or y.

THE ELIMINATION METHOD

The **elimination method** of solving systems of linear equations is often more convenient than substitution. It depends on this fact.

Multiplying both sides of an equation by a nonzero constant does not change the solutions of the equation.

For example, the equation $x + 3 = 5$ has the same solution as $2x + 6 = 10$ (the first equation multiplied by 2). The elimination method also uses this fact from basic algebra:

If $A = B$ and $C = D$, then $A + C = B + D$ and $A - C = B - D$.

EXAMPLE 3

Solve this system using the elimination method:

$$x - 3y = 4$$
$$2x + y = 1.$$

SOLUTION   We replace the first equation by an equivalent one (that is, one with the same solutions).

$$-2x + 6y = -8 \qquad \text{[First equation multiplied by } -2\text{]}$$
$$2x + y = 1.$$

The multiplier -2 was chosen so that the coefficients of x in the two equations would be negatives of each other. Any solution of this last system must also be a solution of the sum of the two equations.

$$-2x + 6y = -8$$
$$\underline{2x + y = 1}$$
$$7y = -7. \qquad \text{[The first variable has been eliminated]}$$

Solving this last equation, we see that $y = -1$. Substituting this value in the first of the original equations shows that

$$x - 3(-1) = 4$$
$$x = 1.$$

Therefore, $x = 1$, $y = -1$ is the solution of the original system.   ■

EXAMPLE 4

Solve the following system:

$$5x - 3y = 3$$
$$3x - 2y = 1.$$

SOLUTION   Any solution of the above system must also be a solution of this system:

$$10x - 6y = \quad 6 \quad \text{[First equation multiplied by 2]}$$

$$-9x + 6y = -3. \quad \text{[Second equation multiplied by } -3]$$

The multipliers 2 and -3 were chosen so that the coefficients of y in the new equations would be negatives of each other. Any solution of this last system must also be a solution of the equation obtained by adding these two equations.

$$10x - 6y = \quad 6$$
$$\underline{-9x + 6y = -3}$$
$$x = \quad 3. \quad \text{[The second variable has been eliminated]}$$

Substituting $x = 3$ in the first of the original equations shows that

$$5(3) - 3y = 3$$

$$-3y = -12$$

$$y = 4.$$

Therefore, the solution of the original system is $x = 3$, $y = 4$.   ∎

EXAMPLE 5

To solve the system

$$2x - 3y = 5$$

$$4x - 6y = 1,$$

we multiply the first equation by -2 and add.

$$-4x + 6y = -10$$
$$\underline{4x - 6y = \quad 1}$$
$$0 \qquad = -9.$$

Since $0 = -9$ is always false, the original system cannot possibly have any solutions. A system with no solution is said to be **inconsistent.**   ∎

GRAPHING EXPLORATION

Confirm the result of Example 5 geometrically by graphing the two equations in the system. Do these lines intersect, or are they parallel?

EXAMPLE 6

To solve the system

$$3x - \quad y = 2$$

$$6x - 2y = 4$$

we multiply the first equation by 2 to obtain the following system.

$$6x - 2y = 4$$
$$6x - 2y = 4.$$

The two equations are identical. So the solutions of this system are the same as the solutions of the single equation $6x - 2y = 4$, which can be rewritten as

$$2y = 6x - 4$$
$$y = 3x - 2.$$

This equation, and hence the original system, has infinitely many solutions. They can be described as follows: Choose any real number for x, say, $x = b$. Then $y = 3x - 2 = 3b - 2$. So the solutions of the system are all pairs of numbers of the form

$$x = b, \qquad y = 3b - 2, \quad \text{where } b \text{ is any real number.}$$

A system such as this is said to be **dependent.**   ∎

Some nonlinear systems can be solved by replacing them with equivalent linear systems.

EXAMPLE 7

Solve the following system:

$$\frac{1}{x} + \frac{3}{y} = -1$$
$$\frac{2}{x} - \frac{1}{y} = 5.$$

SOLUTION   We wish to transform this system into a linear one. We let $u = 1/x$ and $v = 1/y$ so that the system becomes

$$u + 3v = -1$$
$$2u - v = 5.$$

We can solve this system by multiplying the first equation by -2 and adding it to the second equation.

$$-2u - 6v = 2$$
$$\underline{2u - v = 5}$$
$$-7v = 7$$
$$v = -1.$$

Substituting $v = -1$ in the equation $u + 3v = -1$, we see that

$$u = -3v - 1 = -3(-1) - 1 = 2.$$

Consequently, the possible solution of the original system is

$$x = \frac{1}{u} = \frac{1}{2} \qquad \text{and} \qquad y = \frac{1}{v} = \frac{1}{(-1)} = -1.$$

You should substitute this possible solution in both equations of the original system to check that it is actually a solution of the system.   ∎

APPLICATIONS

Producers are happy to supply items at a high price, but if they do, the consumers' demand for them may be low. At lower prices, more items will be demanded, but if the price is too low, producers may not want to supply the items. The **equilibrium price** is the price at which the number of items demanded by consumers is the same as the number supplied by producers. The number of items demanded and supplied at the equilibrium price is the **equilibrium quantity.**

EXAMPLE 8

The consumer demand for a certain type of floor tile is related to its price by the equation $p = 60 - .75x$, where p is the price (in dollars) at which x thousand boxes of tile will be demanded. The supply of these tiles is related to their price by the equation $p = .8x + 5.75$, where p is the price at which x thousand boxes will be supplied by the producer. Find the equilibrium quantity and the equilibrium price.

SOLUTION   We must find the values of x and p that satisfy both the supply and demand equations. In other words, we must solve this system:

$$p = 60 - .75x$$

$$p = .8x + 5.75.$$

Algebraic Method.   Since both equations are already solved for p, we use substitution. Substituting the value of p given by the first equation into the second, we obtain

$$60 - .75x = .8x + 5.75$$

Subtract $.8x$ from both sides: $60 - 1.55x = 5.75$

Subtract 60 from both sides: $-1.55x = -54.25$

Divide both sides by -1.55: $x = \dfrac{-54.25}{-1.55} = 35.$

We can determine p by substituting $x = 35$ in either equation, say, the first one.

$$p = 60 - .75x$$

$$p = 60 - .75(35) = 33.75.$$

Therefore, the equilibrium quantity is 35,000 boxes (x is measured in thousands), and the equilibrium price is $33.75 per box.

Graphical Method.   We graph the two equations in the form $y = 60 - .75x$ and $y = .8x + 5.75$ on the same screen and find their intersection point (Figure 5–4). The intersection point (35, 33.75) is called the **equilibrium point.** Its first coordinate is the equilibrium quantity, and its second coordinate is the equilibrium price.   ■

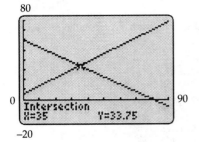

Figure 5–4

EXAMPLE 9

575 people attend a ball game, and total ticket sales are $2575. If adult tickets cost $5 and children's tickets cost $3, how many adults attended the game? How many children?

SOLUTION   Let x be the number of adults, and let y be the number of children. Then,

Number of adults + Number of children = Total attendance

$$x + y = 575.$$

We can obtain a second equation by using the information about ticket sales.

Adult ticket sales   +   Children ticket sales   = Total ticket sales

$$\left(\begin{array}{c}\text{Price} \\ \text{per} \\ \text{ticket}\end{array}\right) \times \left(\begin{array}{c}\text{Number} \\ \text{of} \\ \text{adults}\end{array}\right) + \left(\begin{array}{c}\text{Price} \\ \text{per} \\ \text{ticket}\end{array}\right) \times \left(\begin{array}{c}\text{Number} \\ \text{of} \\ \text{children}\end{array}\right) = 2575$$

$$5x \quad + \quad 3y \qquad\qquad = 2575.$$

To find x and y, we need only solve this system of equations:

$$x + \ \ y = \ \ 575$$
$$5x + 3y = 2575.$$

Multiplying the first equation by -3 and adding, we have

$$-3x - 3y = -1725$$
$$\underline{5x + 3y = \ \ \ 2575}$$
$$2x \qquad = \ \ \ \ 850$$
$$x = \ \ \ \ 425.$$

So 425 adults attended the game. The number of children was

$$y = 575 - x = 575 - 425 = 150.$$ ∎

EXAMPLE 10

A plane flies 3000 miles from San Francisco to Boston in 5 hours, with a tailwind all the way. The return trip on the same route, now with a headwind, takes 6 hours. Assuming that both remain constant, find the speed of the plane and the speed of the wind.

SOLUTION   Let x be the plane's speed, and let y be the wind speed (both in miles per hour). Then on the trip to Boston with a tailwind,

$\quad x + y =$ actual speed of the plane (wind and plane go in same direction).

On the return trip against a headwind,

$\quad x - y =$ actual speed of plane (wind and plane go in opposite directions).

Using the basic rate/distance equation, we have

Trip to Boston	**Return Trip**
time × rate = distance	time × rate = distance

$$5(x + y) = 3000 \qquad\qquad 6(x - y) = 3000$$

$$5x + 5y = 3000 \qquad\qquad 6x - 6y = 3000$$

$$x + y = 600 \qquad\qquad\quad x - y = 500$$

Thus, we need only solve this system of equations:

$$x + y = 600$$

$$x - y = 500.$$

Adding the two equations shows that

$$2x = 1100$$

$$x = 550.$$

Substituting this result in the first equation, we have

$$550 + y = 600$$

$$y = 50.$$

Thus, the plane's speed is 550 mph, and the wind speed is 50 mph.   ■

EXAMPLE 11

How many pounds of tin and how many pounds of copper should be added to 1000 pounds of an alloy that is 10% tin and 30% copper to produce a new alloy that is 27.5% tin and 35% copper?

SOLUTION   Let x be the number of pounds of tin and y the number of pounds of copper to be added to the 1000 pounds of the old alloy. Then there will be $1000 + x + y$ pounds of the new alloy. We first find the *amounts* of tin and copper in the new alloy.

	Pounds in old alloy	+ Pounds added	= Pounds in new alloy
Tin	10% of 1000 +	x	= $100 + x$
Copper	30% of 1000 +	y	= $300 + y$

Now consider the *percentages* of tin and copper in the new alloy.

	Percentage in new alloy	×	Total weight of new alloy	= Pounds in new alloy
Tin	27.5%	of	$1000 + x + y$	= $.275(1000 + x + y)$
Copper	35%	of	$1000 + x + y$	= $.35(1000 + x + y)$

The two ways of computing the weight of each metal in the alloy must produce the same result, that is,

$$100 + x = .275(1000 + x + y) \quad \text{[pounds of tin]}$$

$$300 + y = .35(1000 + x + y). \quad \text{[pounds of copper]}$$

Multiplying out the right sides and rearranging terms produces this system of equations:

$$.725x - .275y = 175$$

$$-.35x + .65y = 50.$$

Multiplying the first equation by .65 and the second by .275 and adding the results, we have

$$.47125x - .17875y = 113.75$$

$$\underline{-.09625x + .17875y = 13.75}$$

$$.37500x \qquad\quad = 127.50$$

$$x = 340.$$

Substituting this in the first equation and solving for y shows that $y = 260$. Therefore, 340 pounds of tin and 260 pounds of copper should be added. ∎

EXERCISES 5.1

In Exercises 1–6, determine whether the given values of x, y, and z are a solution of the system of equations.

1. $x = -1, y = 3$

$2x + y = 1$

$-3x + 2y = 9$

2. $x = -2, y = 5$

$2x + 3y = 11$

$x - 2y = -12$

3. $x = 2, y = -1$

$\dfrac{1}{3}x + \dfrac{1}{2}y = \dfrac{1}{6}$

$\dfrac{1}{2}x + \dfrac{1}{3}y = \dfrac{2}{3}$

4. $x = .3, y = .7$

$4x - 1.2y = .36$

$3.1x + 2y = 4.7$

5. $x = \dfrac{1}{3}, y = 2, z = -1$

$3x - y + 2z = 1$

$4y - 3z = 5$

$3z = 3$

6. $x = 3, y = -\dfrac{5}{4}, z = \dfrac{3}{4}$

$4x - 6y + 10z = 27$

$4x + 8y - 28z = -19$

$x + 4y - 8z = -8$

In Exercises 7–14, use substitution to solve the system.

7. $x + 3y = 6$

$3x - y = 2$

8. $2x - 3y = 6$

$5x + 7y = 2$

9. $3x - 2y = 4$

$2x + y = -1$

10. $5x - 3y = 1$

$5x - 2y = -7$

11. $r + s = 0$

$r - s = 5$

12. $t = 7u - 4$

$t = 5u + 6$

13. $x + y = c + d$ (where c, d are constants)

$x - y = 2c - d$

14. $x - 2y = 2c + 5d$ (where c, d are constants)

$3x - y = c - 2d$

In Exercises 15–30, use the elimination method to solve the system.

15. $2x - 2y = 12$

$-2x + 3y = 10$

16. $4x - 3y = 10$

$7x + 4y = -1$

17. $x + 3y = -1$

$2x - y = 5$

18. $3x - 2y = -12$

$x + 5y = 13$

19. $2x + 3y = 15$

$8x + 12y = 40$

20. $2x - 3y = 7$

$6x - 9y = 1$

21. $4x - 5y = 2$

$12x - 15y = 6$

22. $5x - 2y = 1$

$15x - 6y = 3$

23. $\dfrac{x}{3} - \dfrac{y}{2} = -3$

$\dfrac{2x}{5} + \dfrac{y}{5} = -2$

24. $\dfrac{5x}{7} + \dfrac{3y}{7} = 1$

$x + \dfrac{2y}{3} = 1$

25.
$$\frac{x+y}{4} - \frac{x-y}{3} = 1$$
$$\frac{x+y}{4} + \frac{x-y}{2} = 9$$

26.
$$\frac{x-y}{3} + \frac{x+y}{5} = \frac{2}{3}$$
$$\frac{x-3y}{4} - \frac{2x-y}{5} = \frac{3}{8}$$

27.
$$\frac{1}{x} - \frac{3}{y} = 2$$
$$\frac{2}{x} + \frac{1}{y} = 3$$

28.
$$\frac{3}{x} + \frac{2}{y} = -7$$
$$\frac{1}{x} - \frac{4}{y} = -14$$

29.
$$\frac{2}{x} + \frac{3}{y} = 8$$
$$\frac{3}{x} - \frac{1}{y} = 1$$

30.
$$\frac{3}{x-7} + \frac{2}{y-4} = 7$$
$$\frac{5}{x-7} - \frac{1}{y-4} = 3$$
$$\left[\text{Hint: Let } u = \frac{1}{x-7} \text{ and } v = \frac{1}{y-4}. \right]$$

31. The population y in year x of Philadelphia and Houston is approximated by these equations:

Philadelphia: $7.96x + y = 1588.47$
Houston: $-26.67x + y = 1644.64$,

where $x = 0$ corresponds to 1990 and y is in thousands.*

(a) How can you tell from the equation whether a city's population was increasing or decreasing since 1990?
(b) According to this model, in what year did the two cities have the same population?

32. The cost of bread, y, in dollars per pound, is approximated by these equations:*

White Bread: $-.0071t + y = .982$
Whole Wheat: $.014t + y = 1.360$,

where t is the number of years since 2000. According to this model, in what year will white bread and wheat bread cost the same?

33. On the basis of data from 2000–2004, the median income y in year x for men and women is approximated by these equations:

Men: $135x + y = 31,065$
Women: $-29.31x + 3y = 42,908$

where $x = 0$ corresponds to 2000 and y is in constant 2004 dollars.* If the equations remain valid in the future, when will the median income of men and women be the same?

34. The death rate per 100,000 population y in year x for heart disease and cancer is approximated by these equations:

Heart Disease: $6.9x + 2y = 728.4$
Cancer: $-1.3x + y = 167.5$,

where $x = 0$ corresponds to 1970.* If the equations remain accurate, when will the death rates for heart disease and cancer be the same?

In Exercises 35 and 36, solve the system of equations.

35. $ax + by = r$ (where a, b, c, d, r, s are
$cx + dy = s$ constants and $ad - bc \neq 0$)

36. $ax + by = ab$ (where a, b are nonzero constants)
$bx - ay = ab$

37. Let c be any real number. Show that this system has exactly one solution.
$$x + 2y = c$$
$$6x - 3y = 4.$$

38. (a) Find the values of c for which this system has an infinite number of solutions.
$$2x - 4y = 6$$
$$-3x + 6y = c.$$
(b) Find the values of c for which the system in part (a) has no solutions.

In Exercises 39 and 40, find the values of c and d for which both given points lie on the given straight line.

39. $cx + dy = 2$; (0, 4) and (2, 16)

40. $cx + dy = -6$; (1, 3) and (−2, 12)

In Exercises 41–44, find the equilibrium quantity and the equilibrium price. In the supply and demand equations, p is price (in dollars) and x is quantity (in thousands).

41. Supply: $p = .85x$
Demand: $p = 40 - 1.15x$

42. Supply: $p = 1.4x - .6$
Demand: $p = -2x + 3.2$

43. Supply: $p = 300 - 30x$
Demand: $p = 80 + 25x$

44. Supply: $p = 181 - .01x$
Demand: $p = 52 + .02x$

45. A 200-seat theater charges $8 for adults and $5 for children. If all seats were filled and the total ticket income was $1,435, how many adults and how many children were in the audience?

46. A theater charges $50 for main floor seats and $15 for balcony seats. If all seats are sold, the ticket income is $27,000. At one show, 25% of the main floor seats and 40% of the balcony seats were sold, and ticket income was $8,550. How many seats are on the main floor and how many are in the balcony?

47. A boat made a 4-mile trip upstream against a constant current in 15 minutes. The return trip at the same constant speed with the same current took 12 minutes. What is the speed of the boat and what is the speed of the current?

48. A plane flying into a headwind travels 2000 miles in 4 hours and 24 minutes. The return flight along the same route with a tailwind takes 4 hours. Find the wind speed and the plane's speed (assuming that both are constant).

49. At a certain store, cashews cost $4.40/pound and peanuts cost $1.20/pound. If you want to buy exactly 6 pounds of nuts for $12 dollars, how many pounds of each kind of nuts should you buy?

50. How many cubic centimeters (cm^3) of a solution that is 20% acid and of another solution that is 45% acid should be mixed to produce 100 cm^3 of a solution that is 30% acid?

51. How many grams of a 50%-silver alloy should be mixed with a 75%-silver alloy to obtain 40 grams of a 60%-silver alloy?

52. A winemaker has two large casks of wine. One wine is 8% alcohol, and the other is 18% alcohol. How many liters of each wine should be mixed to produce 30 liters of wine that is 12% alcohol?

53. Bill and Ann plan to install a heating system for their swimming pool. Since gas is not available, they have a choice of electric or solar heat. They have gathered the following cost information.

System	Installation Costs	Monthly Operational Cost
Electric	$2,000	$80
Solar	$14,000	$9.50

(a) Ignoring changes in fuel prices, write a linear equation for each heating system that expresses its total cost y in terms of the number of *years* x of operation.

(b) What is the five-year total cost of electric heat? Of solar heat?

(c) In what year will the total cost of the two heating systems be the same? Which is the cheaper system before that time? After that time?

54. A toy company makes Boomie Babies, as well as collector cases for each Boomie Baby. To make x cases cost the company $5000 in fixed overhead, plus $7.50 per case. An outside supplier has offered to produce any desired volume of cases for $8.20 per case.

(a) Write an equation that expresses the company's cost to make x cases itself.

(b) Write an equation that expresses the cost of buying x cases from the outside supplier.

(c) Graph both equations on the same axes and determine when the two costs are the same.

(d) When should the company make the cases themselves and when should they buy them from the outside supplier?

55. When Neil Simon planned to open his play *London Suite,* his producer, Emanuel Azenberg, made the following cost and revenue estimates for opening on Broadway or off Broadway.*

	On Broadway	Off Broadway
Initial cost to open[†]	$1,295,000	$440,000
Weekly costs[†]	$206,500	$82,000
Weekly revenue	$250,500	$109,000

For a production on Broadway that runs x weeks, find a linear equation that gives the

(a) total revenue R;
(b) total cost C;
(c) total profit P.
(d) Do parts (a)–(c) for an off-Broadway production.
(e) After how many weeks will the on-Broadway profit equal the off-Broadway profit? What is the profit then?
(f) When would it be better to open off Broadway rather than on Broadway?

56. A store sells their 80-GB iPods for $350, and their 30-GB iPods for $250. Their total iPod inventory would sell for $15,250. During a recent month, the store actually sold half of the 80-GB iPods and two-thirds of their 30-GB iPods, taking in a total of $9,000. How many of each kind did they have at the beginning of the month?

*Exercises 57–60 deal with the **break-even point**, which is the point at which revenue equals cost.*

57. The cost C of making x hedge trimmers is given by $C = 45x + 6000$. Each hedge trimmer can be sold for $60.

(a) Find an equation that expresses the revenue R from selling x hedge trimmers.

(b) How many hedge trimmers must be sold for the company to break even?

58. The cost C of making x cases of pet food is given by $C = 100x + 2600$. Each case of 100 boxes sells for $120.

(a) Find an equation that expresses the revenue from selling x cases.

(b) How many cases must be sold for the company to break even?

*Albert Goetz, "Basic Economics: Calculating against Theatrical Disaster," *Mathematics Teacher* 89, no. 1 (January 1996) © 1996. Reprinted with permission of the National Councils of Teachers of Mathematics. All rights reserved.
[†]Initial cost includes sets, costumes, rehearsals, etc. Weekly expenses include theater rent, salaries, advertising, etc.

59. A firm is developing a new product. The marketing department estimates that no more than 450 units can be sold. Costs for producing x units are expected to be given by $C = 80x + 7500$, and revenues are given by $R = 95x$. You are the manager who must determine whether or not to produce the product. What is your decision? Why?

60. Do Exercise 59 when costs are given by

$$C = 1750x + 96{,}175,$$

and revenue is given by $R = 1975x$; no more than 800 units can be produced.

61. An investor has part of her money in an account that pays 9% annual interest and the rest in an account that pays 11% annual interest. If she has $8000 less in the higher-paying account than in the lower-paying one and her total annual interest income is $2010, how much does she have invested in each account?

62. Joyce has money in two investment funds. Last year, the first fund paid a dividend of 8%, the second paid a dividend of 2%, and Joyce received a total of $780. This year, the first fund paid a 10% dividend, the second paid only 1%, and Joyce received $810. How much money does she have invested in each fund?

63. The table shows the percentages of men and women in the labor force who are college graduates in selected years.*

Year	1992	1995	1997	1998	1999	2000	2005	2006
Men	27.5	29.7	29.2	29.6	30.5	30.9	32.1	32.5
Women	25.0	26.6	28.0	28.6	29.5	29.8	32.8	33.5

(a) Use linear regression (with $x = 0$ corresponding to 1990) to find an equation that gives the percentage of men in the labor force in year x who are college graduates.

(b) Do part (a) for women.

(c) When did the percentage of women equal that of men?

64. The table shows the number of passenger cars (in thousands) imported into the United States from Japan and Canada in selected years.*

Year	1995	1996	1997	1998	1999	2000
Japan	1114.4	1190.9	1387.8	1456.1	1707.3	1839.1
Canada	1552.7	1690.7	1731.2	1837.6	2170.4	2138.8

(a) Use linear regression to find an equation that approximates the number y of cars imported from Japan in year x, with $x = 5$ corresponding to 1995.

(b) Do part (a) for Canada.

(c) If these models remain accurate, in what year will the imports from Japan and Canada be the same? Approximately how many cars will be imported that year?

65. A machine in a pottery factory takes 3 minutes to form a bowl and 2 minutes to form a plate. The material for a bowl costs $.25, and the material for a plate costs $.20. If the machine runs for 8 hours straight and exactly $44 is spent for material, how many bowls and plates can be produced?

66. Because Chevrolet and Saturn produce cars in the same price range, Chevrolet's sales are a function not only of Chevy prices (x), but of Saturn prices (y) as well. Saturn prices are related similarly to both Saturn and Chevy prices. Suppose General Motors forecasts the demand z_1 for Chevrolets and the demand z_2 for Saturns to be given by

$$z_1 = 68{,}000 - 6x + 4y \quad \text{and} \quad z_2 = 42{,}000 + 3x - 3y.$$

Solve this system of equations and express

(a) the price x of Chevrolets as a function of z_1 and z_2;

(b) the price y of Saturns as a function of z_1 and z_2.

---

*U.S. Bureau of Labor Statistics.

*U.S. Census Bureau, Foreign Trade Division.

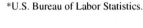

5.2   Nonlinear Equations

Section Objectives
- Solve systems of nonlinear equations algebraically and graphically.
- Use systems of nonlinear equations to solve applied problems.

Some systems that include nonlinear equations can be solved algebraically.

EXAMPLE 1

Solve the system

$$-2x + y = -1$$

$$xy = 3.$$

SOLUTION   Solve the first equation for y:

$$y = 2x - 1$$

and substitute this into the second equation:

$$xy = 3$$
$$x(2x - 1) = 3$$
$$2x^2 - x = 3$$
$$2x^2 - x - 3 = 0$$
$$(2x - 3)(x + 1) = 0$$
$$2x - 3 = 0 \quad \text{or} \quad x + 1 = 0$$
$$x = 3/2 \qquad\qquad x = -1.$$

Using the equation $y = 2x - 1$ to find the corresponding values of y, we see that

$$\text{If } x = \frac{3}{2}, \quad \text{then } y = 2\left(\frac{3}{2}\right) - 1 = 2.$$

$$\text{If } x = -1, \quad \text{then } y = 2(-1) - 1 = -3.$$

Therefore, the solutions of the system are $x = 3/2, y = 2$, and $x = -1, y = -3$.

■

EXAMPLE 2

Solve the system

$$x^2 + y^2 = 8$$
$$x^2 - y = 6.$$

SOLUTION   Solve the second equation for y, obtaining $y = x^2 - 6$, and substitute this into the first equation.

$$x^2 + y^2 = 8$$
$$x^2 + (x^2 - 6)^2 = 8$$
$$x^2 + x^4 - 12x^2 + 36 = 8$$
$$x^4 - 11x^2 + 28 = 0$$
$$(x^2 - 4)(x^2 - 7) = 0$$
$$x^2 - 4 = 0 \quad \text{or} \quad x^2 - 7 = 0$$
$$x^2 = 4 \qquad\qquad x^2 = 7$$
$$x = \pm 2 \qquad\qquad x = \pm\sqrt{7}.$$

Using the equation $y = x^2 - 6$ to find the corresponding values of y, we find that the solutions of the system are

$$x = 2, y = -2; \quad x = -2, y = -2; \quad x = \sqrt{7}, y = 1;$$
$$x = -\sqrt{7}, y = 1.$$

■

Algebraic techniques were successful in Examples 1 and 2 because substitution led to equations whose solutions could be found exactly. When this is not the case, graphical methods are needed. The solutions of a system of equations are the points that are on the graphs of all the equations in the system. They can be approximated with a graphical intersection finder.

EXAMPLE 3

Solve the system

$$y = x^4 - 4x^3 + 9x - 1$$
$$y = 3x^2 - 3x - 7.$$

SOLUTION   If you try substitution on this system, say, by substituting the expression for y from the first equation into the second, you obtain

$$x^4 - 4x^3 + 9x - 1 = 3x^2 - 3x - 7$$
$$x^4 - 4x^3 - 3x^2 + 12x + 6 = 0.$$

This fourth-degree equation cannot be readily solved algebraically, so a graphical approach is appropriate.

Graph both equations of the original system on the same screen. In the viewing window of Figure 5–5, the graphs intersect at three points. However, the graphs seem to be getting closer together as they run off the screen at the top right, which suggests that there may be another intersection point.

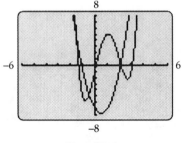

Figure 5–5

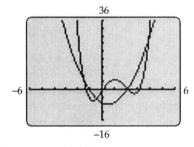

Figure 5–6

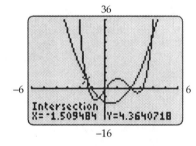

Figure 5–7

The larger window in Figure 5–6 shows four intersection points. There cannot be any more because, as we saw in the previous paragraph, the intersection points (solutions of the system) correspond to the solutions of a fourth-degree polynomial equation, which has a maximum of four solutions. An intersection finder (Figure 5–7) shows that one of the approximate solutions of the system is

$$x = -1.509484, \qquad y = 4.3640718.$$

GRAPHING EXPLORATION

Graph the two equations in the viewing window of Figure 5–6 and use your intersection finder to approximate the other three solutions of this system.

SYSTEMS WITH SECOND-DEGREE EQUATIONS

Solving systems of equations graphically depends on our ability to graph each equation in the system. With some equations of higher degree, this may require special techniques.

EXAMPLE 4

Solve this system graphically.

$$x^2 - 4x - y + 1 = 0$$

$$10x^2 + 25y^2 = 100.$$

SOLUTION   It's easy to graph the first equation, since it can be rewritten as $y = x^2 - 4x + 1$. To graph the second equation, we must first solve for y.

$$10x^2 + 25y^2 = 100$$

$$25y^2 = 100 - 10x^2$$

$$y^2 = \frac{100 - 10x^2}{25}$$

$$y = \sqrt{\frac{100 - 10x^2}{25}} \quad \text{or} \quad y = -\sqrt{\frac{100 - 10x^2}{25}}.$$

TECHNOLOGY TIP

On most calculators, you can graph both of these functions at once by keying in

$$y = \{1, -1\}\sqrt{\frac{100 - 10x^2}{25}}.$$

By graphing both these functions on the same screen (see the Technology Tip), we obtain the complete graph of the equation $10x^2 + 25y^2 = 100$, as shown in Figure 5–8. The graphs of both equations in the system are shown in Figure 5–9.

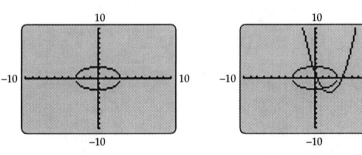

Figure 5–8   Figure 5–9

The two intersection points (solutions of the system) in Figure 5–9 can now be determined by an intersection finder.

$$x = -.2348, y = 1.9945 \quad \text{and} \quad x = .9544, y = -1.9067. \quad \blacksquare$$

EXAMPLE 5

To solve the system

$$-4x^2 + 24xy + 3y^2 - 48 = 0$$

$$16x^2 + 24xy + 9y^2 + 100x + 50y + 100 = 0,$$

we must express each equation in terms of functions in order to graph it. The first equation may be rewritten as

$$3y^2 + (24x)y + (-4x^2 - 48) = 0.$$

This is a quadratic equation of the form $ay^2 + by + c = 0$, with

$$a = 3, \qquad b = 24x, \qquad c = -4x^2 - 48,$$

and hence can be solved by using the quadratic formula.

$$y = \frac{-b \pm \sqrt{b^2 - 4ac}}{2a}$$

$$y = \frac{-24x \pm \sqrt{(24x)^2 - 4 \cdot 3 \cdot (-4x^2 - 48)}}{2 \cdot 3}$$

$$= \frac{-24x \pm \sqrt{(24x)^2 - 12(-4x^2 - 48)}}{6}.$$

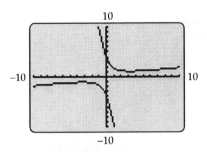

Figure 5–10

Consequently, the graph of the first equation can be obtained by graphing both of these functions on the same screen (Figure 5–10).

(∗)
$$y = \frac{-24x + \sqrt{(24x)^2 - 12(-4x^2 - 48)}}{6}.$$

$$y = \frac{-24x - \sqrt{(24x)^2 - 12(-4x^2 - 48)}}{6}.$$

The second equation can also be solved for y by rewriting it as follows.

$$16x^2 + 24xy + 9y^2 + 100x + 50y + 100 = 0$$

$$9y^2 + (24xy + 50y) + (16x^2 + 100x + 100) = 0$$

$$9y^2 + (24x + 50)y + (16x^2 + 100x + 100) = 0.$$

Now apply the quadratic formula with $a = 9$, $b = 24x + 50$, and $c = 16x^2 + 100x + 100$.

$$y = \frac{-b \pm \sqrt{b^2 - 4ac}}{2a}$$

$$= \frac{-(24x + 50) \pm \sqrt{(24x + 50)^2 - 4 \cdot 9(16x^2 + 100x + 100)}}{2 \cdot 9}.$$

TECHNOLOGY TIP

TI-84+/86 users can save keystrokes by entering the first equation of (∗) as y_1 and then using the RCL key to copy the text of y_1 to y_2. On TI-89, use COPY and PASTE in place of RCL. Then only one sign needs to be changed to make y_2 into the second equation to be graphed.

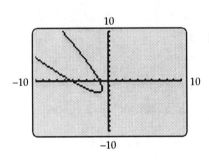

Figure 5–11

Thus, the graph of the second equation (Figure 5–11) consists of the graphs of these two functions.

(∗∗)
$$y = \frac{-(24x + 50) + \sqrt{(24x + 50)^2 - 36(16x^2 + 100x + 100)}}{18}$$

$$y = \frac{-(24x + 50) - \sqrt{(24x + 50)^2 - 36(16x^2 + 100x + 100)}}{18}.$$

By graphing both equations (that is, all four functions shown in (∗) and (∗∗)), we obtain Figure 5–12. Then an intersection finder shows that the solutions of the system (points of intersection) are

$$x = -3.623, y = -1.113 \qquad \text{and} \qquad x = -.943, y = -1.833. \qquad \blacksquare$$

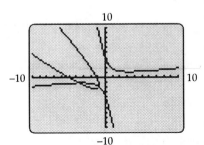

Figure 5–12

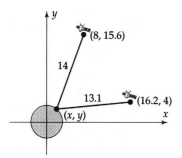

Figure 5–13

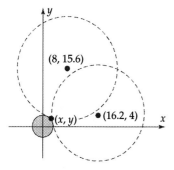

Figure 5–14

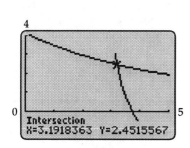

Figure 5–15

APPLICATIONS

EXAMPLE 6

Suppose the earth is a flat, circular disc of radius 4000 miles, centered at the origin of a two-dimensional coordinate system in which 1 unit represents 1000 miles. Figure 5–13 (which is not to scale) shows a GPS device at point (x, y) and two satellites at $(8, 15.6)$ and $(16.2, 4)$. Radio signals show that the distances of the satellites to (x, y) are 14 thousand and 13.1 thousand miles respectively, as shown in the figure. What are the coordinates of the device?

SOLUTION The distance from (x, y) to $(8, 15.6)$ is 14. By the distance formula,

$$\sqrt{(x - 8)^2 + (y - 15.6)^2} = 14$$

Square both sides: $(x - 8)^2 + (y - 15.6)^2 = 14^2.$

Thus, (x, y) lies on the circle with center $(8, 15.6)$ and radius 14. Similarly, since the distance from (x, y) to $(16.2, 4)$ is 13.1,

$$\sqrt{(x - 16.2)^2 + (y - 4)^2} = 13.1$$

$$(x - 16.2)^2 + (y - 4)^2 = 13.1^2.$$

So (x, y) also lies on the circle with center $(16.2, 4)$ and radius 13.1.

Therefore, (x, y) is one of the intersection points of these two circles, as shown in Figure 5–14*. We must find this intersection point, that is, solve the system

$$(x - 8)^2 + (y - 15.6)^2 = 14^2$$

$$(x - 16.2)^2 + (y - 4)^2 = 13.1^2.$$

To solve this system graphically, we first solve each equation for y.

$$(x - 8)^2 + (y - 15.6)^2 = 14^2$$

$$(y - 15.6)^2 = 14^2 - (x - 8)^2$$

$$y - 15.6 = \pm\sqrt{14^2 - (x - 8)^2}$$

$$y = \sqrt{14^2 - (x - 8)^2} + 15.6 \quad \text{or} \quad y = -\sqrt{14^2 - (x - 8)^2} + 15.6.$$

A similar computation with the equation $(x - 16.2)^2 + (y - 4)^2 = 13.1^2$ shows

$$y = \sqrt{13.1^2 - (x - 16.2)^2} + 4 \quad \text{or} \quad y = -\sqrt{13.1^2 - (x - 16.2)^2} + 4.$$

Graphing the four preceding equations should produce something similar to Figure 5–14. Because of limited resolution, however, a graphing calculator will show only parts of the circles (try it!). Fortunately, we are interested only in the intersection point closest to the origin. Using an intersection finder in the partial graph in Figure 5–15, shows that this point is

$$(x, y) \approx (3.1918, 2.4516). \qquad \blacksquare$$

---

*In our actual three-dimensional world, the GPS location would be an intersection point of three or more spheres, i.e., a solution of a system of three or more second-degree equations in three variables.

EXAMPLE 7

A 52-foot-long piece of wire is to be cut into three pieces, two of which are the same length. The two equal pieces are to be bent into squares and the third piece into a circle. What should the length of each piece be if the total area enclosed by the two squares and the circle is 100 square feet?

SOLUTION   Let x be the length of each piece of wire that is to be bent into a square, and let y be the length of the piece that is to be bent into a circle. Since the original wire is 52 feet long,

$$x + x + y = 52 \qquad \text{or, equivalently,} \qquad y = 52 - 2x.$$

If a piece of wire of length x is bent into a square, the side of the square will have length $x/4$ and hence the area of the square will be $(x/4)^2 = x^2/16$. The remaining piece of wire will be made into a circle of circumference (length) y. Since the circumference is 2π times the radius (that is, $y = 2\pi r$), the circle has radius $r = y/2\pi$. Therefore, the area of the circle is

$$\pi r^2 = \pi \left(\frac{y}{2\pi}\right)^2 = \frac{\pi y^2}{4\pi^2} = \frac{y^2}{4\pi}.$$

The sum of the areas of the two squares and the circle is 100, that is,

$$\frac{x^2}{16} + \frac{x^2}{16} + \frac{y^2}{4\pi} = 100$$

$$\frac{y^2}{4\pi} = 100 - \frac{2x^2}{16}$$

$$y^2 = 4\pi\left(100 - \frac{x^2}{8}\right).$$

Therefore, the lengths x and y are solutions of this system of equations.

$$y = 52 - 2x$$

$$y^2 = 4\pi\left(100 - \frac{x^2}{8}\right).$$

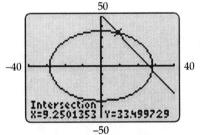

Figure 5–16

The system may be solved either algebraically or graphically, using Figure 5–16. Since x and y are lengths, both must be positive. Consequently, we need only consider the intersection point in the first quadrant. An intersection finder shows that its coordinates are $x \approx 9.25$, $y \approx 33.50$. Therefore, the wire should be cut into two 9.25-foot pieces and one 33.5-foot piece. ∎

EXERCISES 5.2

In Exercises 1–12, solve the system algebraically.

1. $x^2 - y = 0$
    $-2x + y = 3$

2. $x^2 - y = 0$
    $3x + y = 18$

3. $x^2 - y = 0$
    $x + 2y = 5$

4. $x^2 - y = 0$
    $x + 5y = 7$

5. $x + y = 10$
     $xy = 21$

6. $2x + y = 5$
    $xy = 3$

7. $xy + y^2 = 9$
    $x - 2y = 6$

8. $xy + 3x^2 = -2$
    $4x + y = 1$

9. $x^2 + y^2 - 4x - 4y = -4$
   $x - y = 2$

10. $x^2 + y^2 - 4x - y = -1$
    $x + 3y = 2$

11. $x^2 + y^2 = 25$ 12. $x^2 + y^2 = 4$
    $x^2 + y = 19$ $x^2 - y = 10$

In Exercises 13–28, solve the system by any means.

13. $y = x^3 - 3x^2 + 4$
    $y = -.5x^2 + 3x - 2$

14. $y = -x^3 + 5x^2 + x - 4$
    $y = 3x^2 - 2$

15. $y = x^3 - 3x + 2$
    $y = \dfrac{3}{x^2 + 3}$

16. $y = .5x^4 + x^2 - 5$
    $y = x^3 + 2x^2 - 3x + 2$

17. $y = x^3 + x + 1$
    $y = \sin x$

18. $y = x^3 + 2x^2 - 1$
    $y = \cos x$

19. $25x^2 - 16y^2 = 400$
    $-9x^2 + 4y^2 = -36$

20. $5x^2 + 8y^2 = 100$
    $2x^2 - 4y^2 = 1$

21. $3x^2 + 4y^2 - 18x + 14y = 1$
    $x - y = 3$

22. $3x^2 + 6y^2 = 40$
    $2x - y = 3$

23. $x^2 + 4xy + 4y^2 - 30x - 90y + 450 = 0$
    $x^2 + x - y + 1 = 0$

24. $4x^2 + xy - 4y^2 - 2x + 3y + 50 = 0$
    $x^2 - 3x - y = 0$

25. $4x^2 - 6xy + 2y^2 - 3x + 10y = 6$
    $4x^2 + y^2 = 64$

26. $4x^2 + xy + y^2 - x + 2y - 3 = 0$
    $3x^2 + 5xy + y^2 + 3x - 4y + 6 = 0$

27. $x^2 + 3xy + y^2 = 2$
    $3x^2 - 5xy + 3y^2 = 7$

28. $\qquad 2x^2 - 8xy + 8y^2 + 2x - 5 = 0$
    $16x^2 - 24xy + 9y^2 + 100x - 200y + 100 = 0$

29. Suppose that the first satellite in Example 6 is located at (2.7, 15.9) and is 12.7 thousand miles from the GPS device. If the second satellite is at (13.9, 9.9) and is 13.3 thousand miles from the device, what are the coordinates of the device?

30. Internet sales of apparel (in billions of dollars) are projected to be given by

$$f(x) = .38x^2 - .35x + 4.85.$$

where $x = 2$ corresponds to 2002.* Similarly, sales of computer-related items are projected to be given by

$$g(x) = -.17x^2 + 2.73x + 2.71.$$

In what year were Internet sales of apparel and computer-related items at the same level?

31. A rectangular box (including top) with square ends and a volume of 16 cubic meters is to be constructed from 40 square meters of cardboard. What should its dimensions be?

32. A rectangular sheet of metal is to be rolled into a circular tube. If the tube is to have a surface area (excluding ends) of 210 square inches and a volume of 252 cubic inches, what size sheet of metal should be used?

33. Find two real numbers whose sum is -17 and whose product is 52.

34. Find two real numbers whose sum is 34.5 and whose product is 297.

35. Find two real numbers whose difference is 25.75 and whose product is 127.5.

36. Find two real numbers whose sum is 3 such that the sum of their squares is 369.

37. Find two real numbers whose sum is 2 such that the difference of their squares is 60.

38. Find the dimensions of a rectangular room whose perimeter is 58 feet and whose area is 204 square feet.

39. Find the dimensions of a rectangular room whose perimeter is 53 feet and whose area is 165 square feet.

40. A rectangle has area 120 square inches and a diagonal of length 17 inches. What are its dimensions?

41. A right triangle has area 225 square centimeters and a hypotenuse of length 35 centimeters. To the nearest tenth of a centimeter, how long are the legs of the triangle?

42. Find the equation of the straight line that intersects the parabola $y = x^2$ *only* at the point (3, 9). [*Hint:* What condition on the discriminant guarantees that a quadratic equation has exactly one real solution?]

---

*Based on data from Forrester Research.

5.3   Large Systems of Linear Equations

Section Objectives

■ Use Gaussian elimination to solve large systems of linear equations.
■ Use matrix methods to solve systems of linear equations.
■ Identify matrices that are in row echelon or reduced row echelon form.
■ Use the Gauss-Jordan method to solve systems of linear equations.
■ Identify inconsistent and dependent systems.
■ Use systems of linear equations to solve applied problems.

Systems of linear equations in three variables can be interpreted geometrically as the intersection of planes. However, algebraic methods are the only practical means to solve such systems or ones with more variables. Large systems can be solved by **Gaussian elimination,*** which is an extension of the elimination method used in Section 11.1.

Two systems of equations are said to be **equivalent** if they have the same solutions. The basic idea of Gaussian elimination is to transform a given system into an equivalent system that can easily be solved. There are several operations on a system of equations that leave the solutions to the system unchanged and, hence, produce an equivalent system. The first one is to

Interchange any two equations in the system,

which obviously won't affect the solutions of the system. The second is to

Multiply an equation in the system by a nonzero constant.

This does not change the solutions of the equation and therefore does not change the solutions of the system. To understand how the next operation works, we shall examine an earlier example from a different viewpoint.

EXAMPLE 1

In Example 3 of Section 11.1, we solved the system

$$x - 3y = 4$$
$$2x + y = 1$$

by multiplying the first equation by -2 and adding it to the second to eliminate the variable x.

$$-2x + 6y = -8 \qquad \text{[}-2 \text{ times first equation]}$$
$$\underline{2x + y = 1} \qquad \text{[Second equation]}$$
$$7y = -7. \qquad \text{[Sum of second equation and } -2 \text{ times first equation]}$$

---

*Named after the German mathematician K. F. Gauss (1777–1855).

We then solved this last equation for y and substituted the answer, $y = -1$, in the original first equation to find that $x = 1$. What we did, in effect, was

> **Replace the original system by the following system, in which x has been eliminated from the second equation; then solve this new system.**

$$(*) \qquad \begin{aligned} x - 3y &= 4 \qquad \text{[First equation]}\\ 7y &= -7. \qquad \text{[Sum of second equation and } -2 \text{ times first equation]} \end{aligned}$$

The solution of system $(*)$ is easily seen to be $y = -1$, $x = 1$, and you can readily verify that this is the solution of the original system. So the two systems are equivalent. [*Note:* We are not claiming that the second equations in the two systems have the same solutions—they don't—but only that the two *systems* have the same solutions.] ∎

Example 1 is an illustration of the third of the following operations.

Elementary Operations

Performing any of the following operations on a system of equations produces an equivalent system.

1. Interchange any two equations in the system.

2. Replace an equation in the system by a nonzero constant multiple of itself.

3. Replace an equation in the system by the sum of itself and a constant multiple of another equation in the system.

The next example shows how elementary operations can be used to transform a system into an equivalent system that can be solved.

EXAMPLE 2

Solve the system

$$\begin{aligned} x + 4y - 3z &= 1 \qquad \text{[Equation } A\text{]}\\ -3x - 6y + z &= 3 \qquad \text{[Equation } B\text{]}\\ 2x + 11y - 5z &= 0. \qquad \text{[Equation } C\text{]} \end{aligned}$$

SOLUTION We first use elementary operations to produce an equivalent system in which the variable x has been eliminated from the second and third equations.

To eliminate x from equation B, replace equation B by the sum of itself and 3 times equation A.

$$\begin{array}{rl} \text{[3 times } A\text{]} & 3x + 12y - 9z = 3\\ \text{[}B\text{]} & \underline{-3x - 6y + z = 3}\\ & 6y - 8z = 6 \end{array}$$

$$\begin{aligned} x + 4y - 3z &= 1 \qquad \text{[}A\text{]}\\ 6y - 8z &= 6 \qquad \text{[Sum of } B \text{ and 3 times } A\text{]}\\ 2x + 11y - 5z &= 0. \qquad \text{[}C\text{]} \end{aligned}$$

To eliminate x from equation C, we replace equation C by the sum of itself and -2 times equation A.

$$\begin{array}{rl} \text{[-2 times A]} & -2x - 8y + 6z = -2 \\ \text{[C]} & \underline{2x + 11y - 5z = 0} \\ & 3y + z = -2 \end{array}$$

$$\begin{aligned} x + 4y - 3z &= 1 \\ 6y - 8z &= 6 \\ 3y + z &= -2. \quad \text{[Sum of C and -2 times A]} \end{aligned}$$

The next step is to eliminate the y term in one of the last two equations. This can be done by replacing the second equation by the sum of itself and -2 times the third equation.

$$\begin{aligned} x + 4y - 3z &= 1 \\ -10z &= 10 \quad \begin{array}{l}\text{[Sum of second equation and}\\ \text{-2 times third equation]}\end{array} \\ 3y + z &= -2. \end{aligned}$$

Finally, interchange the last two equations.

$$(*) \qquad \begin{aligned} x + 4y - 3z &= 1 \\ 3y + z &= -2 \\ -10z &= 10. \end{aligned}$$

This last system, which is equivalent to the original one, is easily solved. The last equation shows that

$$-10z = 10 \qquad \text{or, equivalently,} \qquad z = -1.$$

Substituting $z = -1$ in the second equation shows that

$$\begin{aligned} 3y + z &= -2 \\ 3y + (-1) &= -2 \\ 3y &= -1 \\ y &= -\frac{1}{3}. \end{aligned}$$

Substituting $y = -1/3$ and $z = -1$ in the first equation yields

$$\begin{aligned} x + 4y - 3z &= 1 \\ x + 4\left(-\frac{1}{3}\right) - 3(-1) &= 1 \\ x &= 1 + \frac{4}{3} - 3 = -\frac{2}{3}. \end{aligned}$$

Therefore, the original system has just one solution: $x = -2/3$, $y = -1/3$, $z = -1$. ∎

The process used to solve the final system $(*)$ in Example 2 is called **back substitution** because you begin with the last equation and work back to the first. It works because system $(*)$ is in **triangular form:** The first variable in the first equation, x, does not appear in any subsequent equation; the first variable in the second equation, y, does not appear in any subsequent equation, and so on. It can be shown that the procedure in Example 2 works in every case.

Gaussian Elimination

> Any system of linear equations can be transformed into an equivalent system in triangular form by using a finite number of elementary operations. If the system has solutions, they can then be found by back substitution in the triangular form system.

Most people prefer to use a calculator or computer to solve large systems of equations. However, the system solvers on some calculators are limited (see the Technology Tip in the margin). So we now develop a version of Gaussian elimination that works with all systems and is easily implemented on a calculator.

MATRIX METHODS

When solving systems by hand, a lot of time is wasted copying the x's, y's, z's, and so on. This fact suggests a shorthand system for representing a system of equations. For example, the system

$$
\begin{aligned}
x + 2y + 3z &= -2 \\
2x + 6y + z &= 2 \\
3x + 3y + 10z &= -2
\end{aligned}
$$

(*)

can be represented by the following rectangular array of numbers, consisting of the coefficients of the variables and the constants on the right of the equal sign, arranged in the same order in which they appear in the system.

$$
\left(\begin{array}{ccc|c}
1 & 2 & 3 & -2 \\
2 & 6 & 1 & 2 \\
3 & 3 & 10 & -2
\end{array}\right)
$$

This array is called the **augmented matrix** of the system. It has three horizontal **rows** and four vertical **columns.**

EXAMPLE 3

Use the matrix form of the preceding system (*) to solve the system.

SOLUTION   To solve the system in its original equation form, we would use elementary operations to eliminate the x terms from the last two equations, and then eliminate the y term from the last equation. With matrices, we do essentially the same thing, with the elementary operations on equations being replaced by the corresponding **row operations** on the augmented matrix in order to make certain

---

*If it's not in the APPS menu, it can be downloaded from TI.

entries in the first and second columns 0. Here is a side-by-side development of the two solution methods.

Equation Method	**Matrix Method**

Equation Method

Replace the second equation by the sum of itself and -2 times the first equation:

$$x + 2y + 3z = -2$$
$$2y - 5z = 6$$
$$3x + 3y + 10z = -2$$

Replace the third equation by the sum of itself and -3 times the first equation:

$$x + 2y + 3z = -2$$
$$2y - 5z = 6$$
$$-3y + z = 4$$

Multiply the second equation by $1/2$ (so that y has coefficient 1):

$$x + 2y + 3z = -2$$
$$y - \frac{5}{2}z = 3$$
$$-3y + z = 4$$

Replace the third equation by the sum of itself and 3 times the second equation:

$$x + 2y + 3z = -2$$
$$y - \frac{5}{2}z = 3$$
$$-\frac{13}{2}z = 13$$

Finally, multiply the last equation by $-2/13$:*

$$x + 2y + 3z = -2$$
$$(**) \qquad y - \frac{5}{2}z = 3$$
$$z = -2$$

Matrix Method

Replace the second row by the sum of itself and -2 times the first row:

$$\begin{pmatrix} 1 & 2 & 3 & | & -2 \\ 0 & 2 & -5 & | & 6 \\ 3 & 3 & 10 & | & -2 \end{pmatrix}$$

Replace the third row by the sum of itself and -3 times the first row:

$$\begin{pmatrix} 1 & 2 & 3 & | & -2 \\ 0 & 2 & -5 & | & 6 \\ 0 & -3 & 1 & | & 4 \end{pmatrix}$$

Multiply the second row by $1/2$:

$$\begin{pmatrix} 1 & 2 & 3 & | & -2 \\ 0 & 1 & -\frac{5}{2} & | & 3 \\ 0 & -3 & 1 & | & 4 \end{pmatrix}$$

Replace the third row by the sum of itself and 3 times the second row:

$$\begin{pmatrix} 1 & 2 & 3 & | & -2 \\ 0 & 1 & -\frac{5}{2} & | & 3 \\ 0 & 0 & -\frac{13}{2} & | & 13 \end{pmatrix}$$

Finally, multiply the last row by $-2/13$:

$$\begin{pmatrix} 1 & 2 & 3 & | & -2 \\ 0 & 1 & -\frac{5}{2} & | & 3 \\ 0 & 0 & 1 & | & -2 \end{pmatrix}$$

---

*This step isn't necessary, but it is often convenient to have 1 as the coefficient of the first variable in each equation.

System (∗∗) is easily solved. The third equation shows that $z = -2$, and substituting this in the second equation shows that

$$y - \frac{5}{2}(-2) = 3$$

$$y = 3 - 5 = -2.$$

Substituting $y = -2$ and $z = -2$ in the first equation yields

$$x + 2(-2) + 3(-2) = -2$$

$$x = -2 + 4 + 6 = 8.$$

Therefore, the only solution of the original system is $x = 8$, $y = -2$, $z = -2$. ∎

When using matrix notation, row operations replace elementary operations on equations, as shown in Example 3. The solution process ends when you reach a matrix, (and corresponding system), such as the final matrix in Example 1:

$$(\ast\ast) \qquad \begin{pmatrix} 1 & 2 & 3 & -2 \\ 0 & 1 & -\dfrac{5}{2} & 3 \\ 0 & 0 & 1 & -2 \end{pmatrix} \qquad \begin{aligned} x + 2y + 3z &= -2 \\ y - \frac{5}{2}z &= 3 \\ z &= -2. \end{aligned}$$

The final matrix should satisfy these conditions:

All rows consisting entirely of zeros (if any) are at the bottom.

The first nonzero entry in each nonzero row is a 1 (called a **leading 1**).

Each leading 1 appears to the right of leading 1's in any preceding rows.

Such a matrix is said to be in **row echelon form.**

Most calculators have a key that uses row operations to put a given matrix into row echelon form (see the Technology Tip in the margin). For example, using the TI-84+ REF key on the first matrix in Example 3 produced this row echelon matrix and corresponding system of equations.

$$\begin{pmatrix} 1 & 1 & \dfrac{10}{3} & -\dfrac{2}{3} \\ 0 & 1 & -\dfrac{17}{12} & \dfrac{5}{6} \\ 0 & 0 & 1 & -2 \end{pmatrix} \qquad \begin{aligned} x + y + \frac{10}{3}z &= -\frac{2}{3} \\ y - \frac{17}{12}z &= \frac{5}{6} \\ z &= -2. \end{aligned}$$

Because the calculator used a different sequence of row operations than was used in Example 3, it produced a row echelon matrix (and corresponding system) that differs from matrix (∗∗) above. You can easily verify, however, that the preceding system has the same solutions as system (∗∗), namely,

$$x = 8, \quad y = -2, \quad z = -2.$$

TECHNOLOGY TIP

To put a matrix in row echelon form, use REF in this menu/submenu:

TI-84+: MATRIX/MATH

TI-86: MATRIX/OPS

TI-89: MATH/MATRIX

Casio and HP-39gs users should consult the Technology Tip after Example 5.

EXAMPLE 4

Solve the system

$$\begin{aligned} x + y + 2z &= 1 \\ 2x + 4y + 5z &= 2 \\ 3x + 5y + 7z &= 4. \end{aligned}$$

SOLUTION   If you try to use a systems equation solver on a calculator, you may get an error message. So we form the augmented matrix and reduce it to row echelon form either by hand or by using the REF key. A TI-86 produced the row echelon matrix in Figure 5–17.

```
ref A▶Frac
    [[1 5/3 7/3 4/3]
     [0 1   1/2 1/2]
     [0 0    0   1 ]]
```

Figure 5–17

Look at the last row of the matrix in Figure 5–17; it represents the equation

$$0x + 0y + 0z = 1.$$

Since this equation has no solutions (the left side is always 0 and the right side is always 1), neither does the original system. Such a system is said to be **inconsistent.** ∎

THE GAUSS-JORDAN METHOD

Gaussian elimination on a calculator is an efficient method of solving systems of equations but may involve some messy calculations when you solve the final triangular form system by hand. Most hand computations can be eliminated by using a slight variation, known as the **Gauss-Jordan method,** * which is illustrated in the next example.

EXAMPLE 5

Use the Gauss-Jordan method to solve this system.

$$x - y + 5z = -6$$
$$3x + 3y - z = 10$$
$$x - 5y + 8z = -17$$
$$x + 3y + 2z = 5.$$

SOLUTION   The augmented matrix of the system is shown in Figure 5–18, and an equivalent row echelon matrix (obtained by using the REF and FRAC keys) is shown in Figure 5–19.

$$\begin{pmatrix} 1 & -1 & 5 & -6 \\ 3 & 3 & -1 & 10 \\ 1 & -5 & 8 & -17 \\ 1 & 3 & 2 & 5 \end{pmatrix}$$

Figure 5–18

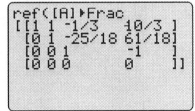

Figure 5–19

*This method was developed by the German engineer Wilhelm Jordan (1842–1899).

At this point in Gaussian elimination, we would use back substitution to solve the triangular form system represented by the last matrix in Figure 11–19. In the Gauss-Jordan method, however, additional elimination of variables replaces back substitution. Look at the leading 1 in the third row (shown in color).

$$\begin{pmatrix} 1 & 1 & -\dfrac{1}{3} & \dfrac{10}{3} \\ 0 & 1 & -\dfrac{25}{18} & \dfrac{61}{18} \\ 0 & 0 & 1 & -1 \\ 0 & 0 & 0 & 0 \end{pmatrix}.$$

In Gauss-Jordan elimination, we make the entries above this leading 1 into 0's.

Replace the second row by the sum of itself and 25/18 times the third row:

$$\begin{pmatrix} 1 & 1 & -\dfrac{1}{3} & \dfrac{10}{3} \\ 0 & 1 & 0 & 2 \\ 0 & 0 & 1 & -1 \\ 0 & 0 & 0 & 0 \end{pmatrix}$$

Replace the first row by the sum of itself and 1/3 times the third row:

$$\begin{pmatrix} 1 & 1 & 0 & 3 \\ 0 & 1 & 0 & 2 \\ 0 & 0 & 1 & -1 \\ 0 & 0 & 0 & 0 \end{pmatrix}$$

Now consider the leading 1 in the second row (shown in color), and make the entry above it 0.

Replace the first row by the sum of itself and -1 times the second row:

$$\begin{pmatrix} 1 & 0 & 0 & 1 \\ 0 & 1 & 0 & 2 \\ 0 & 0 & 1 & -1 \\ 0 & 0 & 0 & 0 \end{pmatrix}$$

This last matrix represents the following system, whose solution is obvious:

$$\begin{aligned} x &= 1 \\ y &= 2 \\ z &= -1. \end{aligned}$$

∎

TECHNOLOGY TIP

To put a matrix in reduced row echelon form, use RREF in this menu/submenu:

TI-84+: MATRIX/MATH

TI-86: MATRIX/OPS

TI-89: MATH/MATRIX

HP-39gs: MATH/MATRIX

RREF programs for Casio are in the Program Appendix.

A row echelon form matrix, such as the last one in Example 5, in which any column containing a leading 1 has 0's in all other positions, is said to be in **reduced row echelon form.** The goal in the Gauss-Jordan method is to use row operations to put a given augmented matrix into reduced row echelon form (from which the solutions can be read immediately, as in Example 5).

As a general rule, Gaussian elimination (matrix version) is the method of choice when working by hand, (the additional row operations needed to put a matrix in reduced row echelon form are usually more time-consuming—and error-prone—than back substitution). With a calculator or computer, however, it's better to find a reduced row echelon matrix for the system. You can do this in one step on a calculator by using the RREF key (see the Technology Tip in the margin).

EXAMPLE 6

Solve this system.

$$2x + 5y + z + 3w = 0$$
$$2y - 4z + 6w = 0$$
$$2x + 17y - 23z + 40w = 0.$$

SOLUTION   A system such as this, in which all the constants on the right side are zero, is called a **homogeneous system.** Every homogeneous system has at least one solution, namely, $x = 0$, $y = 0$, $z = 0$, $w = 0$, which is called the **trivial solution.** The issue with homogeneous systems is whether or not they have any nonzero solutions. The augmented matrix of the system is shown in Figure 5–20, and an equivalent reduced row echelon form matrix is shown in Figure 5–21.*

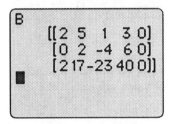

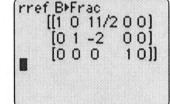

| Figure 5–20 | Figure 5–21 |

The system corresponding to the reduced echelon form matrix in Figure 5–21 is

$$x + \frac{11}{2}z = 0$$
$$y - 2z = 0$$
$$w = 0.$$

The second equation shows that

$$y = 2z.$$

This equation has an infinite number of solutions, for instance,

$$z = 1, y = 2 \quad \text{or} \quad z = 3, y = 6 \quad \text{or} \quad z = -2.5, y = -5.$$

In fact, for each real number t, there is a solution: $z = t$, $y = 2t$. Substituting $z = t$ into the first equation shows that

$$x + \frac{11}{2}t = 0$$
$$x = -\frac{11}{2}t.$$

Therefore, this system, and hence the original one, has an infinite number of solutions, one for each real number t.

$$x = -\frac{11}{2}t, \qquad y = 2t, \qquad z = t, \qquad w = 0.$$

A system with infinitely many solutions, such as this one, is said to be **dependent.**

∎

TECHNOLOGY TIP

If the TI-84 + PolySmlt solver displays the message

   "No Solutions Found",

press the RREF key at the bottom of the screen to display the reduced row echelon matrix of the system, from which you can determine the solutions, if any.

---

*When dealing with homogeneous systems, it's not really necessary to include the last column of zeros, as is done here, because row operations do not change this column.

APPLICATIONS

In calculus, it is sometimes necessary to write a complicated rational expression as the sum of simpler ones. One technique for doing this involves systems of equations.

> **NOTE**
>
> Every system that has more variables than equations (as in Example 6) is dependent, but other systems may be dependent as well.

EXAMPLE 7

Find constants A, B, and C such that

$$\frac{2x^2 + 15x + 10}{(x - 1)(x + 2)^2} = \frac{A}{x - 1} + \frac{B}{x + 2} + \frac{C}{(x + 2)^2}.$$

SOLUTION Multiply both sides of the equation by the common denominator $(x - 1)(x + 2)^2$ and collect like terms on the right side.

$$\begin{aligned}
2x^2 + 15x + 10 &= A(x + 2)^2 + B(x - 1)(x + 2) + C(x - 1) \\
&= A(x^2 + 4x + 4) + B(x^2 + x - 2) + C(x - 1) \\
&= Ax^2 + 4Ax + 4A + Bx^2 + Bx - 2B + Cx - C \\
&= (A + B)x^2 + (4A + B + C)x + (4A - 2B - C).
\end{aligned}$$

Since the polynomials on the left and right sides of the last equation are equal, their coefficients must be equal term by term, that is,

$$A + B = 2 \qquad \text{[Coefficients of } x^2\text{]}$$

$$4A + B + C = 15 \qquad \text{[Coefficients of } x\text{]}$$

$$4A - 2B - C = 10. \qquad \text{[Constant terms]}$$

We can consider this as a system of equations with unknowns A, B, C. The augmented matrix of the system is shown in Figure 5–22, and an equivalent reduced row echelon form matrix is shown in Figure 5–23.

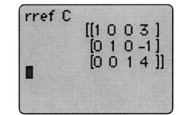

```
C
   [[1  1  0  2 ]
    [4  1  1  15]
    [4 -2 -1 10]]
```

Figure 5–22

```
rref C
        [[1 0 0  3 ]
         [0 1 0 -1]
         [0 0 1  4 ]]
```

Figure 5–23

The solutions of the system can be read from the reduced row echelon form matrix in Figure 5–23.

$$A = 3, \qquad B = -1, \qquad C = 4.$$

Therefore,

$$\frac{2x^2 + 15x + 10}{(x - 1)(x + 2)^2} = \frac{3}{x - 1} + \frac{-1}{x + 2} + \frac{4}{(x + 2)^2}.$$

The right side of this equation is called the **partial fraction decomposition** of the fraction on the left side.

EXAMPLE 8

Charlie is starting a small business and borrows $10,000 on three different credit cards, with annual interest rates of 18%, 15%, and 9%, respectively. He borrows three times as much on the 15% card as on the 18% card, and his total annual interest on all three cards is $1244.25. How much did he borrow on each credit card?

SOLUTION   Let x be the amount on the 18% card, let y be the amount on the 15% card, and let z be the amount on the 9% card. Then $x + y + z = 10,000$. Furthermore,

$$\underset{\begin{array}{c}\text{Interest on}\\\text{18\% card}\end{array}}{} + \underset{\begin{array}{c}\text{Interest on}\\\text{15\% card}\end{array}}{} + \underset{\begin{array}{c}\text{Interest on}\\\text{9\% card}\end{array}}{} = \underset{\begin{array}{c}\text{Total}\\\text{interest}\end{array}}{}$$

$$.18x \quad + \quad .15y \quad + \quad .09z \quad = 1244.25.$$

Finally, we have

$$\underset{\begin{array}{c}\text{Amount on}\\\text{15\% card}\end{array}}{} = \underset{\begin{array}{c}\text{3 times amount}\\\text{on 18\% card}\end{array}}{}$$

$$y = 3x,$$

which is equivalent to $3x - y = 0$. Therefore, we must solve this system of equations.

$$\begin{aligned} x + \quad y + \quad z &= 10,000 \\ .18x + .15y + .09z &= 1,244.25 \\ 3x - \quad y \qquad\quad &= 0, \end{aligned}$$

whose augmented matrix is

$$\begin{pmatrix} 1 & 1 & 1 & 10,000 \\ .18 & .15 & .09 & 1,244.25 \\ 3 & -1 & 0 & 0 \end{pmatrix}.$$

CALCULATOR EXPLORATION

Enter this matrix in your calculator. Use row operations or the RREF key to put it in reduced row echelon form. Read the solutions of the system from this last matrix.

The Calculator Exploration shows that Charlie borrowed $1275 on the 18% card, $3825 on the 15% card, and $4900 on the 9% card.   ∎

The preceding examples illustrate the following fact, whose proof is omitted.

Number of Solutions of a System

Any system of linear equations must have

No solutions (an inconsistent system) *or*

Exactly one solution *or*

An infinite number of solutions (a dependent system).

EXERCISES 5.3

In Exercises 1–4, write the augmented matrix of the system.

1. $2x - 3y + 4z = 1$
$x + 2y - 6z = 0$
$3x - 7y + 4z = -3$

2. $4x + y + z + 7w = 4$
$x - 4y \quad - 3w = 0$
$5x \quad - 5z + 10w = -3$

3. $2x - \dfrac{5}{2}y + \dfrac{2}{3}z = 0$

$x - \dfrac{1}{4}y + 4z = 0$

$\quad - 3y + \dfrac{1}{2}z = 0$

4. $x + 7y - \dfrac{2}{5}z + \dfrac{5}{6}w = 0$

$\dfrac{1}{8}x - y - 8z \qquad = 1$

$\qquad \dfrac{2}{3}y - 5z + \quad w = -2$

$\dfrac{1}{6}x + 4y + \dfrac{2}{7}z \qquad = 3$

In Exercises 5–8, the augmented matrix of a system of equations is given. Express the system in equation notation.

5. $\begin{pmatrix} 3 & -5 & 4 \\ 9 & 7 & 2 \end{pmatrix}$

6. $\begin{pmatrix} 2 & -3 & 5 & 0 \\ 7 & 0 & -1 & 5 \end{pmatrix}$

7. $\begin{pmatrix} 1 & 0 & 1 & 0 & 1 \\ 1 & -1 & 4 & -2 & 3 \\ 4 & 2 & 5 & 0 & 2 \end{pmatrix}$

8. $\begin{pmatrix} -1 & 0 & 2 & 6 \\ 0 & 5 & -4 & 1 \\ 8 & -2 & 3 & 4 \end{pmatrix}$

In Exercises 9–12, the reduced row echelon form of the augmented matrix of a system of equations is given. Find the solutions of the system.

9. $\begin{pmatrix} 1 & 0 & 0 & 0 & 3/2 \\ 0 & 1 & 0 & 0 & 5 \\ 0 & 0 & 1 & 0 & -2 \\ 0 & 0 & 0 & 1 & 0 \end{pmatrix}$

10. $\begin{pmatrix} 1 & 0 & 0 & 0 & -1 \\ 0 & 1 & 0 & 0 & 3 \\ 0 & 0 & 1 & 0 & 1 \\ 0 & 0 & 0 & 0 & 1 \end{pmatrix}$

11. $\begin{pmatrix} 1 & 0 & 0 & 2 & 3 \\ 0 & 1 & 0 & 3 & 5 \\ 0 & 0 & 1 & 0 & 2 \\ 0 & 0 & 0 & 0 & 0 \end{pmatrix}$

12. $\begin{pmatrix} 1 & 0 & 0 & -2 \\ 0 & 1 & 0 & 3 \\ 0 & 0 & 1 & 0 \\ 0 & 0 & 0 & 0 \end{pmatrix}$

In Exercises 13–16, use Gaussian elimination to solve the system.

13. $-x + 3y + 2z = 0$
$2x - y - z = 3$
$x + 2y + 3z = 0$

14. $2x - 3y + 2z = 8$
$3x + 2y + z = 3$
$x + 2y + 3z = 1$

15. $x + y + z = 1$
$x - 2y + 2z = 4$
$2x - y + 3z = 5$

16. $2x \quad - z = 3$
$8x + y + 4z = -1$
$4x + y + 6z = -7$

In Exercises 17–20, use the Gauss-Jordan method to solve the system.

17. $x - 2y + 4z = 6$
$x + y + 13z = 6$
$-2x + 6y - z = -10$

18. $5x - 2y - 3z = 31$
$2x + y - 7z = -10$
$x + y + 2z = 3$

19. $x + y + z = 200$
$x - 2y \quad = 0$
$2x + 3y + 5z = 600$
$2x - y + z = 200$

20. $2x - 4y + z = 2$
$x + y - 5z = 3$

In Exercises 21–36, solve the system.

21. $11x + 10y + 9z = 5$
$x + 2y + 3z = 1$
$3x + 2y + z = 1$

22. $2x + y = -1$
$x - 3y = 5$
$3x + 5y = -7$

23. $5x - y = 7$
$x + y = 5$
$4x - 2y = 2$

24. $6x + 2y - z = 4$
$3x \quad - 2z = 0$
$3x - 8y - 14z = -1$

25. $x - 4y - 13z = 4$
$x - 2y - 3z = 2$
$-3x + 5y + 4z = 2$

26. $3x - y + 4z = -2$
$4x - 2y \quad = 2$
$2x - y + 8z = 2$

27. $4x + y + 3z = 7$
$x - y + 2z = 3$
$3x + 2y + z = 4$

28. $2x + 5y + 3z = -5$
$5x - 8y - 2z = -2$
$x - 18y - 8z = 8$

29. $x + y + z = 0$
$3x - y + z = 0$
$-5x - y + z = 0$

30. $3x - y + 4z = 0$
$-x - y - 3z = 0$
$2x + y + 5z = 0$

31.
$$2x + y + 3z - 2w = -6$$
$$4x + 3y + z - w = -2$$
$$x + y + z + w = -5$$
$$-2x - 2y + 2z + 2w = -10$$

32.
$$x + 7y - z + 2w = 24$$
$$5x - 3y - 8z = 7$$
$$x + 4y + 7z + w = 6$$
$$3y + 4z - w = -2$$

33.
$$x - 2y - z - 3w = -3$$
$$-x + y + z = 0$$
$$4y + 3z - 2w = -1$$
$$2x - 2y + w = 1$$

34.
$$2x - 7y - 2z + 2w = -6$$
$$3x + 2y - z = 14$$
$$x + 4y + 7z + 3w = 4$$
$$x - 3y - 4z - w = 1$$

35.
$$\frac{3}{x} - \frac{1}{y} + \frac{4}{z} = -13$$
$$\frac{1}{x} + \frac{2}{y} - \frac{1}{z} = 12$$
$$\frac{4}{x} - \frac{1}{y} + \frac{3}{z} = -7$$

[*Hint:* Let $u = 1/x$, $v = 1/y$, $w = 1/z$.]

36.
$$\frac{1}{x+1} - \frac{2}{y-3} + \frac{3}{z-2} = 4$$
$$\frac{5}{y-3} - \frac{10}{z-2} = -5$$
$$\frac{-3}{x+1} + \frac{4}{y-3} - \frac{1}{z-2} = -2$$

[*Hint:* Let $u = 1/(x+1)$, $v = 1/(y-3)$, $w = 1/(z-2)$.]

Exercises 37–40, solve the system. [*Note: The REF and RREF keys on some calculators produce an error message when there are more rows than columns in a matrix, in which case you will have to solve the system by some other means.*]

37.
$$2x - y = 1$$
$$3x + y = 2$$
$$4x - 2y = 2$$
$$5x + 5y = 4$$

38.
$$x + y = 3$$
$$-x + 2y = 3$$
$$5x - y = 3$$
$$-7x + 5y = 3$$

39.
$$x + 2y = 3$$
$$2x + 3y = 4$$
$$3x + 4y = 5$$
$$4x + 5y = 6$$

40.
$$x - y = 2$$
$$x + y = 4$$
$$2x + 3y = 9$$
$$3x - 2y = 6$$

In Exercises 41–46, find the constants A, B, and C.

41. $\dfrac{4x}{(x-1)(x+3)} = \dfrac{A}{x-1} + \dfrac{B}{x+3}$

42. $\dfrac{1}{(x+1)(x-1)} = \dfrac{A}{x+1} + \dfrac{B}{x-1}$

43. $\dfrac{2x+1}{(x+2)(x-3)^2} = \dfrac{A}{x+2} + \dfrac{B}{x-3} + \dfrac{C}{(x-3)^2}$

44. $\dfrac{x^2 - x - 21}{(2x-1)(x^2+4)} = \dfrac{A}{2x-1} + \dfrac{Bx+C}{x^2+4}$

45. $\dfrac{5x^2+1}{(x+1)(x^2-x+1)} = \dfrac{A}{x+1} + \dfrac{Bx+C}{x^2-x+1}$

46. $\dfrac{x-2}{(x+4)(x^2+2x+2)} = \dfrac{A}{x+4} + \dfrac{Bx+C}{x^2+2x+2}$

47. Lillian borrows $10,000. She borrows some from her friend at 8% annual interest, twice as much as that from her bank at 9%, and the remainder from her insurance company at 5%. She pays a total of $830 in interest for the first year. How much did she borrow from each source?

48. An investor puts a total of $25,000 into three very speculative stocks. She invests some of it in Crystalcomp and $2000 more than one-half that amount in Flyboys. The remainder is invested in Zumcorp. Crystalcomp rises 16% in value, Flyboys rises 20%, and Zumcorp rises 18%. Her investment in the three stocks is now worth $29,440. How much was originally invested in each stock?

49. An investor has $70,000 invested in a mutual fund, bonds, and a fast food franchise. She has twice as much invested in bonds as in the mutual fund. Last year the mutual fund paid a 2% dividend, the bonds paid 10%, and the fast food franchise paid 6%; her dividend income was $4800. How much is invested in each of the three investments?

50. Tickets to a band concert cost $2 for children, $3 for teenagers, and $5 for adults. 570 people attended the concert and total ticket receipts were $1950. Three-fourths as many teenagers as children attended. How many children, adults, and teenagers attended?

51. The table shows the calories, sodium, and protein in one cup of various kinds of soup.

	Progresso Roasted Chicken Rotini	Healthy Choice Hearty Chicken	Campbell's Chunky Chicken Noodle
Calories	100	130	130
Sodium (mg)	970	480	880
Protein (g)	6	8	8

How many cups of each kind of soup should be mixed together to produce ten servings of soup, each of which provides 203 calories, 1190 milligrams of sodium, and

12.4 grams of protein? What is the serving size (in cups)? (*Hint:* In ten servings, there must be 2030 calories, 11,900 milligrams of sodium, and 124 grams of protein.)

52. The table shows the calories, sodium, and fat in one ounce of various snack foods (all produced by Planters).

	Cashews	Dry Roasted Honey Peanuts	Cajun Crunch Trail Mix
Calories	170	150	160
Sodium (mg)	115	110	270
Fat (g)	14	12	11

How many ounces of each kind of snack should be combined to produce ten servings, each of which provides 220 calories, 188 milligrams of sodium, and 17.4 grams of fat? What is the serving size?

53. Comfort Systems, Inc., sells three models of humidifiers. The bedroom model weighs 10 pounds and comes in an 8-cubic-foot box; the living-room model weighs 20 pounds and comes in an 8-cubic-foot box; the whole-house model weighs 60 pounds and comes in a 28-cubic-foot box. Each of the company's delivery vans has 248 cubic feet of space and can hold a maximum of 440 pounds. For a van to be as fully loaded as possible, how many of each model should it carry?

54. Peanuts cost $3 per pound, almonds cost $4 per pound, and cashews costs $8 per pound. How many pounds of each should be used to produce 140 pounds of a mixture costing $6 per pound, in which there are twice as many peanuts as almonds?

Exercises 55 and 56 deal with computer-aided tomography (CAT) scanners that take X-rays of body parts from different directions to create a picture of a cross section of the body.* The amount by which the X-ray energy decreases (measured in linear-attenuation units) indicates whether the X-ray has passed through healthy tissue, tumorous tissue, or bone, according to the following table.

Tissue Type	Linear-Attenuation Units
Healthy	.1625–.2977
Tumorous	.2679–.3930
Bone	.3857–.5108

**Exercises 55 and 56 are based on D. Jabon, G. Nord, B. W. Wilson, and P. Coffman, "Medical Applications of Linear Equations," *Mathematics Teacher* 89, no. 5 (May 1996).*

The body part being scanned is divided into cells. The total linear-attenuation value is the sum of the values for each cell the X-ray passes through. In the figure for Exercise 55, for example, let a, b, and c be the values for cells A, B, and C, respectively; then the attenuation value for X-ray 3 is b + c.

55. (a) In the figure, find the linear-attenuation values for X-rays 1 and 2.
  (b) If the total linear-attenuation values for X-rays 1, 2, and 3 are .75, .60, and .54, respectively, set up and solve a system of three equations in a, b, c.
  (c) What kind of tissue are cells A, B, and C?

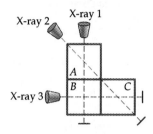

56. Four X-ray beams are aimed at four cells, as shown in the figure.

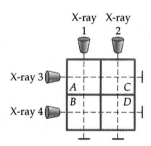

(a) If the total linear-attenuation values for X-rays 1, 2, 3, and 4 are .60, .75, .65, and .70, respectively, is there enough information to determine the values of a, b, c, and d? Explain.
(b) If an additional X-ray beam is added, with a linear-attenuation value of .85, as shown in the figure below, can the values of a, b, c, and d be determined? If so, what are they? What can be said about cells A, B, C, and D?

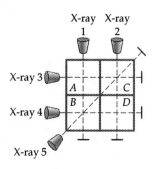

57. A furniture manufacturer has 1950 machine hours available each week in the cutting department, 1490 hours in the assembly department, and 2160 in the finishing department. Manufacturing a chair requires .2 hours of cutting, .3 hours of assembly, and .1 hours of finishing. A chest requires .5 hours of cutting, .4 hours of assembly, and .6 hours of finishing. A table requires .3 hours of cutting, .1 hours of assembly, and .4 hours of finishing. How many chairs, chests, and tables should be produced to use all the available production capacity?

58. A stereo equipment manufacturer produces three models of speakers, R, S, and T, and has three kinds of delivery vehicles: trucks, vans, and station wagons. A truck holds two boxes of model R, one of model S, and three of model T. A van holds one box of model R, three of model S, and two of model T. A station wagon holds one box of model R, three of model S, and one of model T. If 15 boxes of model R, 20 boxes of model S, and 22 boxes of model T are to be delivered, how many vehicles of each type should be used so that all operate at full capacity?

59. The diagram shows the traffic flow at four intersections during a typical one-hour period. The streets are all one-way, as indicated by the arrows. To adjust the traffic lights to avoid congestion, engineers must determine the possible values of x, y, z, and t.

   (a) Write a system of linear equations that describes congestion-free traffic flow. [*Hint:* 600 cars per hour come down Euclid to intersection A, and 400 come down 4th Avenue to intersection A. Also, x cars leave intersection A on Euclid, and t cars leave on 4th Avenue. To avoid congestion, the number of cars leaving the intersection must be the same as the number entering, that is, $x + t = 600 + 400$. Use intersections B, C, and D to find three more equations.]
   (b) Solve the system in part (a), which is dependent. Express your answers in terms of the variable t.

   (c) Find the largest and smallest number of cars that can leave the given intersection on the given street: A on 4th Avenue, A on Euclid, C on 5th Avenue, and C on Chester.

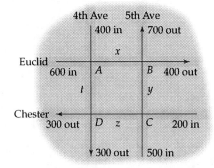

60. The diagram shows the traffic flow at four intersections during rush hour, as in Exercise 59.

   (a) What are the possible values of x, y, z, and t in order to avoid any congestion? [Express your answers in terms of t.]
   (b) What are the possible values of t?

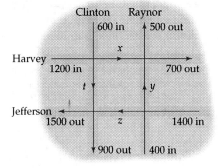

INTRODUCTION TO TRIGONOMETRY

Chapter Outline

Interdependence of Sections

6.1   Angles and Their Measurement

Section Objectives
- ■ Use basic terminology to describe angles.
- ■ Learn radian measure for angles
- ■ Convert the measure of an angle from radians to degree and vice versa.

In trigonometry an **angle** is formed by rotating a half-line around its endpoint (the **vertex**), as shown in Figure 6–1, where the arrow indicates the direction of rotation. The position of the half-line at the beginning is the **initial side,** and its final position is the **terminal side** of the angle.

---

*Parts of Section 6.6 may be covered much earlier; see the Roadmap at the beginning of Section 6.2.
†In fact, "trigonometry" means "triangle measurement."

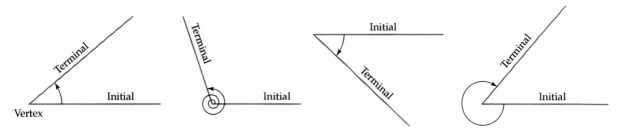

Figure 6–1

Figure 6–2 shows that different angles (that is, angles obtained by different rotations) may have the same initial and terminal side.* Such angles are said to be **coterminal.**

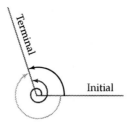

Figure 6–2

An angle in the coordinate plane is said to be in **standard position** if its vertex is at the origin and its initial side on the positive x-axis, as in Figure 6–3. When measuring angles in standard position, we use positive numbers for angles obtained by counterclockwise rotation (**positive angles**) and negative numbers for ones obtained by clockwise rotation (**negative angles**).

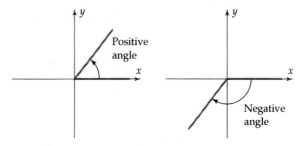

Figure 6–3

The classical unit for angle measurement is the **degree** (in symbols, °), as explained in the Geometry Review Appendix. You should be familiar with the positive angles in standard position shown in Figure 6–4 on the next page. Note that a 360° angle corresponds to one full revolution and thus is coterminal with an angle of 0°.

---

*They are *not* the same angle, however. For instance, both $\frac{1}{2}$ turn and $1\frac{1}{2}$ turns put a circular faucet handle in the same position, but the water flow is quite different.

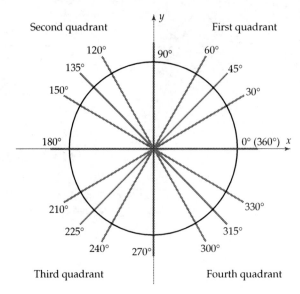

Figure 6–4

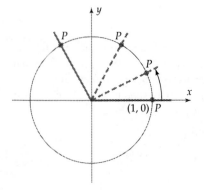

Figure 6–5

RADIAN MEASURE

Because it simplifies many formulas in calculus and physics, a different unit of angle measurement is used in mathematical and scientific applications. Recall that the unit circle is the circle of radius 1 with center at the origin; its equation is $x^2 + y^2 = 1$. When a positive angle in standard position is formed by rotating the initial side (the positive x-axis) counterclockwise, then the point $P = (1, 0)$ moves along the unit circle, as in Figure 6–5. The **radian measure** of the angle is defined to be

> **the distance traveled along the unit circle by the point P as it moves from its starting position on the initial side to its final position on the terminal side of the angle.**

The radian measure of a negative angle in standard position is found in the same way, except that you move clockwise along the unit circle. Figure 6–6 shows angles of 3.75, 7, and −2 radians, respectively.

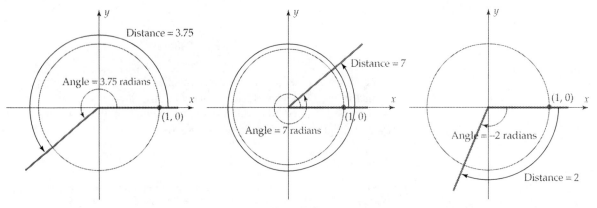

Figure 6–6

To become comfortable with radian measure, think of the terminal side of the angle revolving around the origin: When it makes one full revolution, it produces an angle of 2π radians (because the circumference of the unit circle is 2π). When it makes half a revolution, it forms an angle whose radian measure is $1/2$ of 2π, that is, π radians, and so on, as illustrated in Figure 6–7 and the table below.

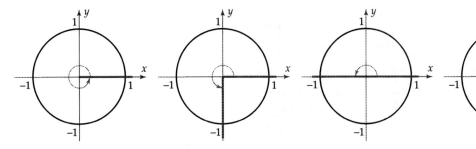

1 revolution	3/4 revolution	1/2 revolution	$1\frac{1}{4}$ revolutions
2π radians	$\frac{3}{4} \cdot 2\pi = \frac{3\pi}{2}$ radians	$\frac{1}{2} \cdot 2\pi = \pi$ radians	$\frac{5}{4} \cdot 2\pi = \frac{5\pi}{2}$ radians

Figure 6–7

Terminal Side	Radian Measure of Angle	Equivalent Degree Measure
1 revolution	2π	$360°$
$\frac{7}{8}$ revolution	$\frac{7}{8} \cdot 2\pi = \frac{7\pi}{4}$	$\frac{7}{8} \cdot 360 = 315°$
$\frac{3}{4}$ revolution	$\frac{3}{4} \cdot 2\pi = \frac{3\pi}{2}$	$\frac{3}{4} \cdot 360 = 270°$
$\frac{2}{3}$ revolution	$\frac{2}{3} \cdot 2\pi = \frac{4\pi}{3}$	$\frac{2}{3} \cdot 360 = 240°$
$\frac{1}{2}$ revolution	$\frac{1}{2} \cdot 2\pi = \pi$	$\frac{1}{2} \cdot 360 = 180°$
$\frac{1}{3}$ revolution	$\frac{1}{3} \cdot 2\pi = \frac{2\pi}{3}$	$\frac{1}{3} \cdot 360 = 120°$
$\frac{1}{4}$ revolution	$\frac{1}{4} \cdot 2\pi = \frac{\pi}{2}$	$\frac{1}{4} \cdot 360 = 90°$
$\frac{1}{6}$ revolution	$\frac{1}{6} \cdot 2\pi = \frac{\pi}{3}$	$\frac{1}{6} \cdot 360 = 60°$
$\frac{1}{8}$ revolution	$\frac{1}{8} \cdot 2\pi = \frac{\pi}{4}$	$\frac{1}{8} \cdot 360 = 45°$
$\frac{1}{12}$ revolution	$\frac{1}{12} \cdot 2\pi = \frac{\pi}{6}$	$\frac{1}{12} \cdot 360 = 30°$

Although equivalent degree measures are given in the table, you should learn to "think in radians" as much as possible rather than mentally translating from radians to degrees.

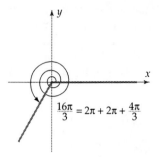

$$\frac{16\pi}{3} = 2\pi + 2\pi + \frac{4\pi}{3}$$

Figure 6–8

EXAMPLE 1

To construct an angle of $16\pi/3$ radians in standard position, note that

$$\frac{16\pi}{3} = \frac{6\pi}{3} + \frac{6\pi}{3} + \frac{4\pi}{3} = 2\pi + 2\pi + \frac{4\pi}{3}.$$

So the terminal side must be rotated counterclockwise through two complete revolutions (each full-circle revolution is 2π radians) and then rotated an additional $2/3$ of a revolution (since $4\pi/3$ is $2/3$ of a complete revolution of 2π radians), as shown in Figure 6–8.   ∎

EXAMPLE 2

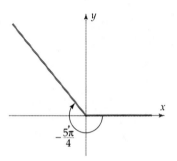

Figure 6–9

Since $-5\pi/4 = -\pi - \pi/4$, an angle of $-5\pi/4$ radians in standard position is obtained by rotating the terminal side *clockwise* for half a revolution (π radians) plus an additional $1/8$ of a revolution (since $\pi/4$ is $1/8$ of a full-circle revolution of 2π radians), as shown in Figure 6–9.   ∎

Consider an angle of t radians in standard position (Figure 6–10). Since 2π radians corresponds to a full revolution of the terminal side, this angle has the same terminal side as an angle of $t + 2\pi$ radians or $t - 2\pi$ radians or $t + 4\pi$ radians.

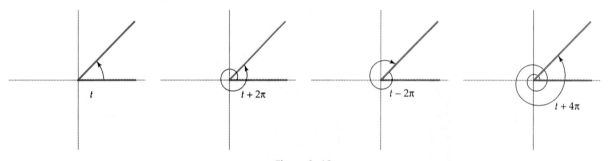

Figure 6–10

The same thing is true in general.

Coterminal Angles

Increasing or decreasing the radian measure of an angle by an integer multiple of 2π results in a coterminal angle.

EXAMPLE 3

Find angles in standard position that are coterminal with an angle of

(a) $23\pi/5$ radians

(b) $-\pi/12$ radians.

SOLUTION

(a) We can subtract 2π to obtain a coterminal angle whose measure is

$$\frac{23\pi}{5} - 2\pi = \frac{23\pi}{5} - \frac{10\pi}{5} = \frac{13\pi}{5} \text{ radians,}$$

or we can subtract 4π to obtain a coterminal angle of measure

$$\frac{23\pi}{5} - 4\pi = \frac{3\pi}{5} \text{ radians.}$$

Subtracting 6π produces a coterminal angle of

$$\frac{23\pi}{5} - 6\pi = -\frac{7\pi}{5} \text{ radians.}$$

(b) An angle of $\dfrac{-\pi}{12}$ radians is coterminal with an angle of

$$-\frac{\pi}{12} + 2\pi = \frac{23\pi}{12} \text{ radians}$$

and with an angle of

$$-\frac{\pi}{12} - 2\pi = -\frac{25\pi}{12} \text{ radians.} \qquad ■$$

RADIAN/DEGREE CONVERSION

Although we shall generally work with radians, it may occasionally be necessary to convert from radian to degree measure or vice versa. The key to doing this is the fact that

(∗) $\pi\ radians = 180°.$

Dividing both sides of (∗) by π shows that

$$1 \text{ radian} = \frac{180}{\pi} \text{ degrees} \approx 57.3°,$$

and dividing both sides of (∗) by 180 shows that

$$1° = \frac{\pi}{180} \text{ radians} \approx .0175 \text{ radians.}$$

Consequently, we have these rules.

Radian/Degree Conversion

> To convert radians to degrees, multiply by $\dfrac{180}{\pi}$.
>
> To convert degrees to radians, multiply by $\dfrac{\pi}{180}$.

EXAMPLE 4

Find the degree measure of the angles with radian measure:

(a) 2.4 radians   (b) $\pi/60$ radians   (c) $-.3$ radians.

SOLUTION   In each case, multiply the given radian measure by $\dfrac{180}{\pi}$.

(a) $2.4\left(\dfrac{180}{\pi}\right) = \dfrac{432}{\pi} \approx 137.51°.$

(b) $\dfrac{\pi}{60}\left(\dfrac{180}{\pi}\right) = \dfrac{180}{60} = 3°.$

(c) $(-.3)\left(\dfrac{180}{\pi}\right) = \dfrac{-54}{\pi} \approx -17.19°.$ ■

EXAMPLE 5

Find the radian measure of the angles with degree measure:

(a) 12°   (b) −150°   (c) 236°

SOLUTION   In each case, multiply by $\dfrac{\pi}{180}$.

(a) $12\left(\dfrac{\pi}{180}\right) = \dfrac{\pi}{15}$ radians.

(b) $-150\left(\dfrac{\pi}{180}\right) = \dfrac{-5\pi}{6}$ radians.

(c) $236\left(\dfrac{\pi}{180}\right) = \dfrac{59\pi}{45} \approx 4.12$ radians. ■

EXERCISES 6.1

In Exercises 1–5, find the radian measure of the angle in standard position formed by rotating the terminal side by the given amount.

1. 1/9 of a circle
2. 1/24 of a circle
3. 1/18 of a circle
4. 1/72 of a circle
5. 1/36 of a circle

6. State the radian measure of *every* standard position angle in the figure.*

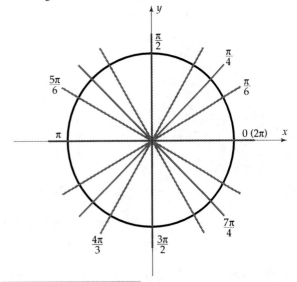

In Exercises 7–10, estimate the radian measure of the angle.

7.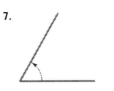

8.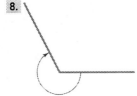

9.

10.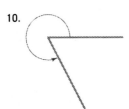

In Exercises 11–14, find the radian measure of four angles in standard position that are coterminal with the angle in standard position whose measure is given.

11. $\pi/4$
12. $7\pi/5$
13. $-\pi/6$
14. $-9\pi/7$

In Exercises 15–18, determine whether or not the given angles in standard position are coterminal.

15. $\dfrac{5\pi}{12}, \dfrac{17\pi}{12}$

16. $\dfrac{7\pi}{6}, -\dfrac{5\pi}{6}$

17. 117°, 837°

18. 170°, −550°

*This is the same diagram that appears in Figure 6–4 on page 430, showing positive angles in standard position.

In Exercises 19–26, find the radian measure of an angle in standard position that has measure between 0 and 2π and is coterminal with the angle in standard position whose measure is given.

19. $-\pi/3$ 20. $-3\pi/4$ 21. $19\pi/4$

22. $16\pi/3$ 23. $-7\pi/5$ 24. $45\pi/8$

25. 7 26. 18.5

In Exercises 27–38, convert the given degree measure to radians.

27. $6°$ 28. $-10°$ 29. $-12°$

30. $36°$ 31. $75°$ 32. $-105°$

33. $135°$ 34. $-165°$ 35. $-225°$

36. $252°$ 37. $930°$ 38. $-585°$

In Exercises 39–50, convert the given radian measure to degrees.

39. $\pi/5$ 40. $-\pi/6$ 41. $-\pi/10$

42. $2\pi/5$ 43. $3\pi/4$ 44. $-5\pi/3$

45. $\pi/45$ 46. $-\pi/60$ 47. $-5\pi/12$

48. $7\pi/15$ 49. $27\pi/5$ 50. $-41\pi/6$

In Exercises 51–56, determine the positive radian measure of the angle that the second hand of a clock traces out in the given time.

51. 40 seconds   52. 50 seconds

53. 35 seconds   54. 2 minutes and 15 seconds.

55. 3 minutes and 25 seconds   56. 1 minute and 55 seconds

In Exercises 57–64, a wheel is rotating around its axle. Find the angle (in radians) through which the wheel turns in the given time when it rotates at the given number of revolutions per minute (rpm). Assume that $t > 0$ and $k > 0$.

57. 3.5 minutes, 1 rpm   58. t minutes, 1 rpm

59. 1 minute, 2 rpm   60. 3.5 minutes, 2 rpm

61. 4.25 minutes, 5 rpm   62. t minutes, 5 rpm

63. 1 minute, k rpm   64. t minutes, k rpm

6.2 Trigonometric Identities

Section Objectives

■ Learn how functional notation is used with trigonometric functions.

■ Apply the rules of algebra to trigonometric functions.

■ Use the Pythagorean identity to evaluate and simplify trigonometric expressions.

■ Use the periodic identities to evaluate trigonometric expressions.

■ Use the negative angle identities to evaluate and simplify trigonometric expressions.

Roadmap

Section 8.1 may be covered at this point by instructors who prefer to introduce right triangle trigonometry early.

In the previous section, we concentrated on evaluating the trigonometric functions. In this section, the emphasis is on the algebra of such functions. When dealing with trigonometric functions, two conventions are normally observed:

1. **Parentheses are omitted whenever no confusion can result.**

   For example,

$\sin(t)$	is written	$\sin t$
$-(\cos(5t))$	is written	$-\cos 5t$
$4(\tan t)$	is written	$4 \tan t$.

On the other hand, parentheses *are* needed to distinguish

$$\cos(t + 3) \qquad \text{from} \qquad \cos t + 3,$$

because the first one says, "Add 3 to t and take the cosine of the result," but the second one says, "Take the cosine of t and add 3 to the result." When $t = 5$, for example, these are different numbers, as shown in Figure 6–11.*

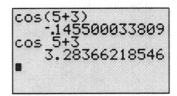

Figure 6–11

2. **When dealing with powers of trigonometric functions, positive exponents are written between the function symbol and the variable.**

For example,

$$(\cos t)^3 \qquad \text{is written} \qquad \cos^3 t$$

$$(\sin t)^4 (\tan 7t)^2 \qquad \text{is written} \qquad \sin^4 t \tan^2 7t.$$

Furthermore,

$$\sin t^3 \qquad \text{means} \qquad \sin(t^3) \qquad [\textit{not} \ (\sin t)^3 \qquad \text{or} \qquad \sin^3 t]$$

For instance, when $t = 4$, we have Figure 6–12.

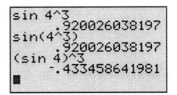

Figure 6–12

Except for these two conventions and the Caution in the margin, the algebra of trigonometric functions is just like the algebra of other functions. They may be added, subtracted, multiplied, composed, etc.

EXAMPLE 1

If $f(t) = \sin^2 t + \tan t$ and $g(t) = \tan^3 t + 5$, then the product function fg is given by the rule

$$(fg)(t) = f(t)g(t) = (\sin^2 t + \tan t)(\tan^3 t + 5)$$

$$= \sin^2 t \tan^3 t + 5 \sin^2 t + \tan^4 t + 5 \tan t.$$

*Figures 6–38 and 6–39 show a TI-86 screen.

TECHNOLOGY TIP

TI-84+ and HP-39gs automatically insert an opening parenthesis when the COS key is pushed. The display COS(5 + 3 is interpreted as COS(5 + 3). If you want cos 5 + 3, you must insert a parenthesis after the 5: COS(5) + 3.

CAUTION

Convention 2 is not used when the exponent is −1. For example, $\sin^{-1} t$ does *not* mean $(\sin t)^{-1}$ or $1/(\sin t)$; it has an entirely different meaning that will be discussed in Section 7.4. Similar remarks apply to $\cos^{-1} t$ and $\tan^{-1} t$.

TECHNOLOGY TIP

Calculators do not use convention 2. To obtain $\sin^3 4$, you must enter $(\sin 4)^3$.

EXAMPLE 2

Factor $2 \cos^2 t - 5 \cos t - 3$.

SOLUTION   You can do this directly, but it may be easier to understand if you make a substitution. Let $u = \cos t$, then

$$2 \cos^2 t - 5 \cos t - 3 = 2(\cos t)^2 - 5 \cos t - 3$$
$$= 2u^2 - 5u - 3$$
$$= (2u + 1)(u - 3)$$
$$= (2 \cos t + 1)(\cos t - 3). \qquad \blacksquare$$

EXAMPLE 3

If $f(t) = \cos^2 t - 9$ and $g(t) = \cos t + 3$, then the quotient function f/g is given by the rule

$$\left(\frac{f}{g}\right)(t) = \frac{f(t)}{g(t)} = \frac{\cos^2 t - 9}{\cos t + 3} = \frac{(\cos t + 3)(\cos t - 3)}{\cos t + 3} = \cos t - 3. \qquad \blacksquare$$

CAUTION

You are dealing with *functional notation* here, so the symbol sin t is a *single entity*, as are cos t and tan t. Don't try some nonsensical "canceling" operation, such as

$$\frac{\sin t}{\cos t} = \frac{\sin}{\cos} \qquad \text{or} \qquad \frac{\cos t^2}{\cos t} = \frac{\cos t}{\cos} = t.$$

EXAMPLE 4

If $f(t) = \sin t$ and $g(t) = t^2 + 3$, then the composite function $g \circ f$ is given by the rule

$$(g \circ f)(t) = g(f(t)) = g(\sin t) = \sin^2 t + 3.$$

The composite function $f \circ g$ is given by the rule

$$(f \circ g)(t) = f(g(t)) = f(t^2 + 3) = \sin(t^2 + 3).$$

The parentheses are crucial here because $\sin(t^2 + 3)$ is *not* the same function as $\sin t^2 + 3$. For instance, a calculator in radian mode shows that for $t = 5$,

$$\sin(5^2 + 3) = \sin(25 + 3) = \sin 28 \approx .2709,$$

whereas

$$\sin 5^2 + 3 = \sin 25 + 3 \approx (-.1324) + 3 = 2.8676. \qquad \blacksquare$$

THE PYTHAGOREAN IDENTITY

Trigonometric functions have numerous interrelationships that are usually expressed as *identities*. An **identity** is an equation with this property: For every value of the variable for which both sides of the equation are defined, the equation is true. Here is one of the most important trigonometric identities.

Pythagorean Identity

For every real number t,

$$\sin^2 t + \cos^2 t = 1.$$

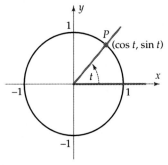

Figure 6–13

Proof   For each real number t, the point P, where the terminal side of an angle of t radians intersects the unit circle, has coordinates $(\cos t, \sin t)$, as in Figure 6–13. Since P lies on the unit circle, its coordinates must satisfy the equation of the unit circle: $x^2 + y^2 = 1$, that is, $\cos^2 t + \sin^2 t = 1$. ∎

GRAPHING EXPLORATION

Recall that the graph of $y = 1$ is a horizontal line through $(0, 1)$. Verify the Pythagorean identity by graphing the equation

$$y = (\sin x)^2 + (\cos x)^2$$

in the window with $-10 \le x \le 10$ and $-3 \le y \le 3$ and using the trace feature.

EXAMPLE 5

If $\pi/2 < t < \pi$ and $\sin t = 2/3$, find $\cos t$ and $\tan t$.

SOLUTION   By the Pythagorean identity,

$$\cos^2 t = 1 - \sin^2 t = 1 - \left(\frac{2}{3}\right)^2 = 1 - \frac{4}{9} = \frac{5}{9}.$$

So there are two possibilities:

$$\cos t = \sqrt{5/9} = \sqrt{5}/3 \qquad \text{or} \qquad \cos t = -\sqrt{5/9} = -\sqrt{5}/3.$$

Since $\pi/2 < t < \pi$, $\cos t$ is negative (see Exercise 63 on page 451). Therefore, $\cos t = -\sqrt{5}/3$, and

$$\tan t = \frac{\sin t}{\cos t} = \frac{2/3}{-\sqrt{5}/3} = \frac{-2}{\sqrt{5}} = \frac{-2\sqrt{5}}{5}.$$ ∎

EXAMPLE 6

The Pythagorean identity is valid for *any* number t. For instance, if $t = 3k + 7$, then $\sin^2(3k + 7) + \cos^2(3k + 7) = 1$. ∎

EXAMPLE 7

To simplify the expression $\tan^2 t \cos^2 t + \cos^2 t$, we use the definition of tangent and the Pythagorean identity:

$$\tan^2 t \cos^2 t + \cos^2 t = \frac{\sin^2 t}{\cos^2 t}\cos^2 t + \cos^2 t$$

$$= \sin^2 t + \cos^2 t = 1. \qquad \blacksquare$$

For every real number t, the point $(\cos t, \sin t)$ is on the unit circle, as illustrated in Figure 6–13. Since the coordinates of any point on the unit circle are between -1 and 1, we have this useful fact:

Range of Sine and Cosine

For every real number t

$$-1 \le \sin t \le 1$$

and

$$-1 \le \cos t \le 1.$$

As we shall see in Section 6.4,

The range of the tangent function consists of all real numbers.

You can confirm this fact by doing the following Exploration.

CALCULATOR EXPLORATION

Use the table feature to evaluate $\tan\left(\dfrac{\pi}{2} + x\right)$ when $x = .01, .001, .0001$, and so on. What does this suggest about the outputs of the tangent function? Now evaluate when $x = -.01, -.001, -.0001$, and so on, and answer the same question.

PERIODICITY IDENTITIES

Let t be any real number and construct two angles in standard position of measure t and $t + 2\pi$ radians, respectively, as shown in Figure 6–14. As we saw in Section 6.1, both of these angles have the same terminal side. Therefore, the point P where the terminal side meets the unit circle is the *same* in both cases.

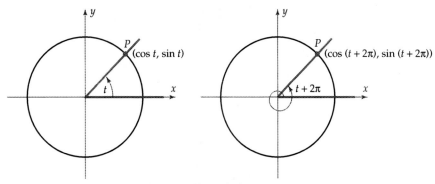

Figure 6–14

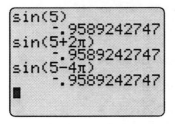

Figure 6–15

Therefore, the coordinates of P are the same, that is,

$$\sin t = \sin(t + 2\pi) \qquad \text{and} \qquad \cos t = \cos(t + 2\pi).$$

Furthermore, since an angle of t radians has the same terminal side as angles of radian measure $t \pm 2\pi, t \pm 4\pi, t \pm 6\pi$, and so forth, the same argument shows that

$$\sin t = \sin(t \pm 2\pi) = \sin(t \pm 4\pi) = \sin(t \pm 6\pi) = \cdots$$

$$\cos t = \cos(t \pm 2\pi) = \cos(t \pm 4\pi) = \cos(t \pm 6\pi) = \cdots$$

as illustrated (for $t = 5$) in Figure 6–15.

There is a special name for functions that repeat their values at regular intervals. A function f is said to be **periodic** if there is a positive constant k such that $f(t) = f(t + k)$ for every number t in the domain of f. There will be more than one constant k with this property; the smallest one is called the **period** of the function f. We have just seen that sine and cosine are periodic with $k = 2\pi$. Exercises 69 and 70 show that 2π is the smallest such positive constant k. Therefore, we have the following.

Period of Sine and Cosine

> The sine and cosine functions are periodic with period 2π: For every real number t,
>
> $$\sin t = \sin(t \pm 2\pi) = \sin(t \pm 4\pi) = \sin(t \pm 6\pi) = \cdots$$
>
> and
>
> $$\cos t = \cos(t \pm 2\pi) = \cos(t \pm 4\pi) = \cos(t \pm 6\pi) = \cdots$$

EXAMPLE 8

As we saw in Examples 3 and 5 of Section 6.2, $\sin \dfrac{\pi}{6} = \dfrac{1}{2}$ and $\cos\left(-\dfrac{5\pi}{4}\right) = -\dfrac{\sqrt{2}}{2}$. Use these facts to find

(a) $\sin \dfrac{13\pi}{6}$ (b) $\cos\left(-\dfrac{29\pi}{4}\right)$.

SOLUTION   The key is to write the given number as a sum in which one summand is an even multiple of π, and then apply a periodicity identity.

(a)
$$\sin\frac{13\pi}{6} = \sin\left(\frac{\pi}{6} + \frac{12\pi}{6}\right)$$

$$= \sin\left(\frac{\pi}{6} + 2\pi\right)$$

$$= \sin\left(\frac{\pi}{6}\right) = \frac{1}{2} \qquad \text{[Periodicity Identity]}$$

(b)
$$\cos\left(-\frac{29\pi}{4}\right) = \cos\left(-\frac{5\pi}{4} - \frac{24\pi}{4}\right)$$

$$= \cos\left(-\frac{5\pi}{4} - 6\pi\right)$$

$$= \cos\left(-\frac{5\pi}{4}\right) = -\frac{\sqrt{2}}{2} \qquad \text{[Periodicity Identity]}$$

The tangent function is also periodic (see Exercise 36), but its period is π rather than 2π, that is,

$$\tan(t + \pi) = \tan t \quad \text{for every real number } t,$$

as we shall see in Section 6.4.

NEGATIVE ANGLE IDENTITIES

GRAPHING EXPLORATION

(a) In a viewing window with $-2\pi \le x \le 2\pi$, graph $y_1 = \sin x$ and $y_2 = \sin(-x)$ on the same screen. Use trace to move along $y_1 = \sin x$. Stop at a point and note its y-coordinate. Use the up or down arrow to move vertically to the graph of $y_2 = \sin(-x)$. The x-coordinate remains the same, but the y-coordinate is different. How are the two y-coordinates related? Is one the negative of the other? Repeat the procedure for other points. Are the results the same?

(b) Now graph $y_1 = \cos x$ and $y_2 = \cos(-x)$ on the same screen. How do the graphs compare?

(c) Repeat part (a) for $y_1 = \tan x$ and $y_2 = \tan(-x)$. Are the results similar to those for sine?

The preceding Graphing Exploration suggests the truth of the following statement.

Negative Angle Identities

For every real number t,

$$\sin(-t) = -\sin t$$

$$\cos(-t) = \cos t$$

$$\tan(-t) = -\tan t.$$

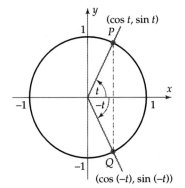

Figure 6–16

Proof   Consider angles of t radians and $-t$ radians in standard position, as in Figure 6–16. By the definition of sine and cosine, P has coordinates $(\cos t, \sin t)$, and Q has coordinates $(\cos(-t), \sin(-t))$. As Figure 6–16 suggests, P and Q lie on the same vertical line. Therefore, they have the same first coordinate, that is, $\cos(-t) = \cos t$. As the figure also suggests, P and Q lie at equal distances from the x-axis.* So the y-coordinate of Q must be the negative of the y-coordinate of P, that is, $\sin(-t) = -\sin t$. Finally, by the definition of the tangent function and the two identities just proved, we have

$$\tan(-t) = \frac{\sin(-t)}{\cos(-t)} = \frac{-\sin t}{\cos t} = -\frac{\sin t}{\cos t} = -\tan t. \quad \blacksquare$$

EXAMPLE 9

In Example 3 of Section 6.2, we showed that

$$\sin \frac{\pi}{6} = \frac{1}{2}, \qquad \cos \frac{\pi}{6} = \frac{\sqrt{3}}{2}, \qquad \tan \frac{\pi}{6} = \frac{\sqrt{3}}{3}.$$

---

*These facts can be proved by using congruent triangles. (See Exercise 13 in the Geometry Review Appendix.)

Using the negative angle identities, we have

$$\sin\left(-\frac{\pi}{6}\right) = -\sin\frac{\pi}{6} = -\frac{1}{2}, \qquad \cos\left(-\frac{\pi}{6}\right) = \cos\frac{\pi}{6} = \frac{\sqrt{3}}{2},$$

$$\tan\left(-\frac{\pi}{6}\right) = -\tan\frac{\pi}{6} = -\frac{\sqrt{3}}{3}.$$ ∎

EXAMPLE 10

To simplify $(1 + \sin t)(1 + \sin(-t))$, we use the negative angle identity and the Pythagorean identity.

$$(1 + \sin t)(1 + \sin(-t)) = (1 + \sin t)(1 - \sin t)$$
$$= 1 - \sin^2 t$$
$$= \cos^2 t.$$ ∎

EXERCISES 6.2

In Exercises 1–4, find the rule of the product function fg.

1. $f(t) = 3\sin t;$ $g(t) = \sin t + 2\cos t$

2. $f(t) = 5\tan t;$ $g(t) = \tan^3 t - 1$

3. $f(t) = 3\sin^2 t;$ $g(t) = \sin t + \tan t$

4. $f(t) = \sin 2t + \cos^4 t;$ $g(t) = \cos 2t + \cos^2 t$

In Exercises 5–14, factor the given expression.

5. $\cos^2 t - 4$ **6.** $25 - \tan^2 t$

7. $\sin^2 t - \cos^2 t$ **8.** $\sin^3 t - \sin t$

9. $\tan^2 t + 6\tan t + 9$ **10.** $\cos^2 t - \cos t - 2$

11. $6\sin^2 t - \sin t - 1$ **12.** $\tan t \cos t + \cos^2 t$

13. $\cos^4 t + 4\cos^2 t - 5$ **14.** $3\tan^2 t + 5\tan t - 2$

In Exercises 15–18, find the rules of the composite functions f∘g and g∘f.

15. $f(t) = \cos t;$ $g(t) = 2t + 4$

16. $f(t) = \sin t + 2;$ $g(t) = t^2$

17. $f(t) = \tan(t + 3);$ $g(t) = t^2 - 1$

18. $f(t) = \cos^2(t - 2);$ $g(t) = 5t + 2$

In Exercises 19–24, determine if it is possible for a number t to satisfy the given conditions. [Hint: Think Pythagorean.]

19. $\sin t = 5/13$ and $\cos t = 12/13$

20. $\sin t = -2$ and $\cos t = 1$

21. $\sin t = -1$ and $\cos t = 1$

22. $\sin t = 1/\sqrt{2}$ and $\cos t = -1/\sqrt{2}$

23. $\sin t = 1$ and $\tan t = 1$

24. $\cos t = 8/17$ and $\tan t = 15/8$

In Exercises 25–28, use the Pythagorean identity to find sin t.

25. $\cos t = -.5$ and $\pi < t < 3\pi/2$

26. $\cos t = -3/\sqrt{10}$ and $\pi/2 < t < \pi$

27. $\cos t = 1/2$ and $0 < t < \pi/2$

28. $\cos t = 2/\sqrt{5}$ and $3\pi/2 < t < 2\pi$

In Exercises 29–35, assume that sin t = 3/5 and $0 < t < \pi/2$. Use identities in the text to find the number.

29. $\sin(-t)$ **30.** $\sin(t + 10\pi)$ **31.** $\sin(2\pi - t)$

32. $\cos t$ **33.** $\tan t$ **34.** $\cos(-t)$

35. $\tan(2\pi - t)$

36. (a) Show that $\tan(t + 2\pi) = \tan t$ for every t in the domain of $\tan t$. [*Hint:* Use the definition of tangent and some identities proved in the text.]
(b) Verify that it appears true that $\tan(x + \pi) = \tan x$ for every t in the domain by using your calculator's table feature to make a table of values for $y_1 = \tan(x + \pi)$ and $y_2 = \tan x$.

In Exercises 37–42, assume that

$$\cos t = -2/5 \quad and \quad \pi < t < 3\pi/2.$$

Use identities to find the number.

37. $\sin t$ **38.** $\tan t$ **39.** $\cos(2\pi - t)$

40. $\cos(-t)$ **41.** $\sin(4\pi + t)$ **42.** $\tan(4\pi - t)$

In Exercises 43–46, assume that

$$\sin(\pi/8) = \frac{\sqrt{2 - \sqrt{2}}}{2}$$

and use identities to find the exact functional value.

43. $\cos(\pi/8)$ **44.** $\tan(\pi/8)$

45. $\sin(17\pi/8)$ **46.** $\tan(-15\pi/8)$

In Exercises 47–58, use algebra and identities in the text to simplify the expression. Assume all denominators are nonzero.

47. $(\sin t + \cos t)(\sin t - \cos t)$

48. $(\sin t - \cos t)^2$ **49.** $\tan t \cos t$

50. $(\sin t)/(\tan t)$ **51.** $\sqrt{\sin^3 t \cos t} \sqrt{\cos t}$

52. $(\tan t + 2)(\tan t - 3) - (6 - \tan t) + 2 \tan t$

53. $\left(\dfrac{4 \cos^2 t}{\sin^2 t}\right)\left(\dfrac{\sin t}{4 \cos t}\right)^2$

54. $\dfrac{5 \cos t}{\sin^2 t} \cdot \dfrac{\sin^2 t - \sin t \cos t}{\sin^2 t - \cos^2 t}$

55. $\dfrac{\cos^2 t + 4 \cos t + 4}{\cos t + 2}$

56. $\dfrac{\sin^2 t - 2 \sin t + 1}{\sin t - 1}$

57. $\dfrac{1}{\cos t} - \sin t \tan t$

58. $\dfrac{1 - \tan^2 t}{1 + \tan^2 t} + 2 \sin^2 t$

59. The average monthly temperature in Cleveland, Ohio is approximated by

$$f(t) = 22.7 \sin(.52x - 2.18) + 49.6,$$

where $t = 1$ corresponds to January, $t = 2$ to February, and so on.

(a) Construct a table of values ($t = 1, 2, \ldots, 12$) for the function $f(t)$ and another table for $f(t + 12.083)$.

(b) Based on these tables would you say that the function f is (approximately) periodic? If so, what is the period? Is this reasonable?

60. A typical healthy person's blood pressure can be modeled by the periodic function

$$f(t) = 22 \cos(2.5\pi t) + 95,$$

where t is time (in seconds) and $f(t)$ is in millimeters of mercury. Which one of .5, .8, or 1 appears to be the period of this function?

61. The percentage of the face of the moon that is illuminated (as seen from earth) on day t of the lunar month is given by

$$g(t) = .5\left(1 - \cos \frac{2\pi t}{29.5}\right).$$

(a) What percentage of the face of the moon is illuminated on day 0? Day 10? Day 22?

(b) Construct appropriate tables to confirm that g is a periodic function with period 29.5 days.

(c) When does a full moon occur ($g(t) = 1$)?

In Exercises 62–67, show that the given function is periodic with period less than 2π. [Hint: Find a positive number k with $k < 2\pi$ such that $f(t + k) = f(t)$ for every t in the domain of f.]

62. $f(t) = \sin 2t$

63. $f(t) = \cos 3t$

64. $f(t) = \sin 4t$

65. $f(t) = \sin(\pi t)$

66. $f(t) = \cos(3\pi t/2)$

67. $f(t) = \tan 2t$

68. Fill the blanks with "even" or "odd" so that the resulting statement is true. Then prove the statement by using an appropriate identity. [*Hint: Special Topics* 3.4.A may be helpful.]

(a) $f(t) = \sin t$ is an _____ function.

(b) $g(t) = \cos t$ is an _____ function.

(c) $h(t) = \tan t$ is an _____ function.

(d) $f(t) = t \sin t$ is an _____ function.

(e) $g(t) = t + \tan t$ is an _____ function.

69. Here is a proof that the cosine function has period 2π. We saw in the text that $\cos(t + 2\pi) = \cos t$ for every t. We must show that there is no positive number smaller than 2π with this property. Do this as follows:

(a) Find all numbers k such that $0 < k < 2\pi$ and $\cos k = 1$. [*Hint:* Draw a picture and use the definition of the cosine function.]

(b) Suppose k is a number such that $\cos(t + k) = \cos t$ for every number t. Show that $\cos k = 1$. [*Hint:* Consider $t = 0$.]

(c) Use parts (a) and (b) to show that there is no positive number k less than 2π with the property that $\cos(t + k) = \cos t$ for *every* number t. Therefore, $k = 2\pi$ is the smallest such number, and the cosine function has period 2π.

70. Here is proof that the sine function has period 2π. We saw in the text that $\sin(t + 2\pi) = \sin t$ for every t. We must show that there is no positive number smaller than 2π with this property. Do this as follows:

(a) Find a number t such that $\sin(t + \pi) \neq \sin t$.

(b) Find all numbers k such that $0 < k < 2\pi$ and $\sin k = 0$. [*Hint:* Draw a picture and use the definition of the sine function.]

(c) Suppose k is a number such that $\sin(t + k) = \sin t$ for every number t. Show that $\sin k = 0$. [*Hint:* Consider $t = 0$.]

(d) Use parts (a)–(c) to show that there is no positive number k less than 2π with the property that $\sin(t + k) = \sin t$ for *every* number t. Therefore, $k = 2\pi$ is the smallest such number, and the sine function has period 2π.

6.3   Trigonometric Graphs

Section Objectives   ■ Analyze the graphs of the sine, cosine, and tangent functions.
■ Derive the graphs of other trigonometric functions from the graphs of sine, cosine, and tangent.
■ Explore trigonometric identities graphically.

Although a graphing calculator will quickly sketch the graphs of the sine, cosine, and tangent functions, it will not give you much insight into why these graphs have the shapes they do and why these shapes are important. So the emphasis here is on the connection between the definition of these functions and their graphs.

As t Increases	The Point P Moves	The y-coordinate of $P(= \sin t)$	Rough Sketch of the Graph
from 0 to $\frac{\pi}{2}$	from (1, 0) to (0, 1)	increases from 0 to 1	
from $\frac{\pi}{2}$ to π	from (0, 1) to (−1, 0)	decreases from 1 to 0	
from π to $\frac{3\pi}{2}$	from (−1, 0) to (0, −1)	decreases from 0 to −1	
from $\frac{3\pi}{2}$ to 2π	from (0, −1) to (1, 0)	increases from −1 to 0	

If P is the point where the unit circle meets the terminal side of an angle of t radians, then the y-coordinate of P is the number sin t. As shown in the chart on the facing page, we can get a rough sketch of the graph of $f(t) = \sin t$ by watching the y-coordinate of P.

GRAPHING EXPLORATION

Your calculator can provide a dynamic simulation of this process. Put it in parametric graphing mode and set the range values as follows:

$$0 \le t \le 6.28 \quad -1 \le x \le 6.28 \quad -2.5 \le y \le 2.5.$$

On the same screen, graph the two functions given by

$$x_1 = \cos t, \quad y_1 = \sin t \quad \text{and} \quad x_2 = t, \quad y_2 = \sin t.$$

Using the trace feature, move the cursor along the first graph (the unit circle). Stop at a point on the circle, and note the value of t and the y-coordinate of the point. Then switch the trace to the second graph (the sine function) by using the up or down cursor arrows. The value of t remains the same. What are the x- and y-coordinates of the new point? How does the y-coordinate of the new point compare with the y-coordinate of the original point on the unit circle?

To complete the graph of the sine function, note that as t goes from 2π to 4π, the point P on the unit circle *retraces* the path it took from 0 to 2π, so *the same wave shape will repeat* on the graph. The same thing happens when t goes from 4π to 6π, or from -2π to 0, and so on. This repetition of the same pattern is simply the graphical expression of the fact that the sine function has period 2π: For any number t, the points

$$(t, \sin t) \quad \text{and} \quad (t + 2\pi, \sin(t + 2\pi))$$

on the graph have the same second coordinate.

A graphing calculator or some point plotting with an ordinary calculator now produces the graph of $f(t) = \sin t$ (Figure 6–17).

TECHNOLOGY TIP

Calculators have built-in windows for trigonometric functions, in which the x-axis tick marks are at intervals of $\pi/2$.
Choose TRIG or ZTRIG in this menu:

TI: ZOOM

HP-39gs: VIEWS

Casio: V-WINDOW

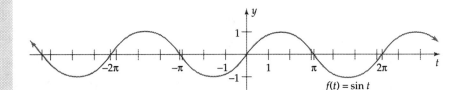

$f(t) = \sin t$

Figure 6–17

NOTE

Throughout this chapter, we use t as the variable for trigonometric functions to avoid any confusion with the x's and y's that are part of the definition of these functions. For calculator graphing in "function mode," however, you must use x as the variable: $f(x) = \sin x$, $g(x) = \cos x$, etc.

The graph of the sine function and the techniques of Section 3.4 can be used to graph other trigonometric functions.

EXAMPLE 1

The graph of $h(t) = 3 \sin t$ is the graph of $f(t) = \sin t$ stretched away from the horizontal axis by a factor of 3, as shown in Figure 6–18. ■

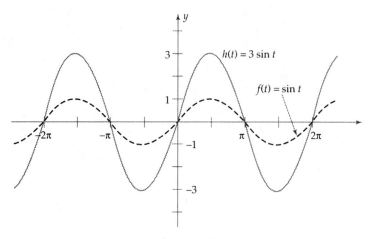

Figure 6–18

EXAMPLE 2

The graph of $k(t) = -\frac{1}{2} \sin t$ is the graph of $f(t) = \sin t$ shrunk by a factor of $1/2$ toward the horizontal axis and then reflected in the horizontal axis, as shown in Figure 6–19. ■

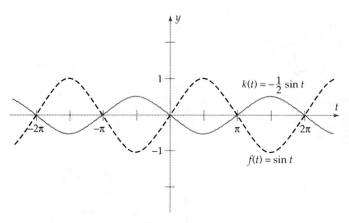

Figure 6–19

GRAPH OF THE COSINE FUNCTION

To obtain the graph of $g(t) = \cos t$, we follow the same procedure as with sine, except that we now watch the x-coordinate of P (which is $\cos t$).

As t Increases	The Point P Moves	The x-coordinate of P ($= \cos t$)	Rough Sketch of the Graph
from 0 to $\frac{\pi}{2}$	from (1, 0) to (0, 1)	decreases from 1 to 0	
from $\frac{\pi}{2}$ to π	from (0, 1) to (−1, 0)	decreases from 0 to −1	
from π to $\frac{3\pi}{2}$	from (−1, 0) to (0, −1)	increases from −1 to 0	
from $\frac{3\pi}{2}$ to 2π	from (0, −1) to (1, 0)	increases from 0 to 1	

As t takes larger values, P begins to retrace its path around the unit circle, so the graph of $g(t) = \cos t$ repeats the same wave pattern, and similarly for negative values of t. So the graph looks like Figure 6–20.

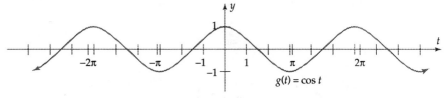

Figure 6–20

For a dynamic simulation of the cosine graphing process described above, see Exercise 69.

The techniques of Section 3.4 can be used to graph variations of the cosine function.

EXAMPLE 3

The graph of $h(t) = 4 \cos t$ is the graph of $g(t) = \cos t$ stretched away from the horizontal axis by a factor of 4, as shown in Figure 6–21.   ∎

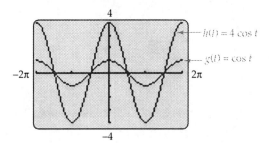

Figure 6–21

EXAMPLE 4

The graph of $k(t) = -2 \cos t + 3$ is the graph of $g(t) = \cos t$ stretched away from the horizontal axis by a factor of 2, reflected in the horizontal axis, and shifted vertically 3 units upward as shown in Figure 6–22.   ∎

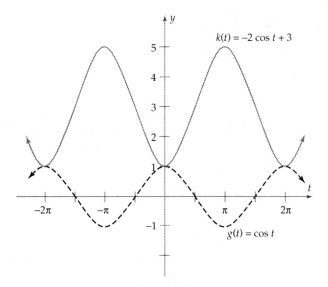

Figure 6–22

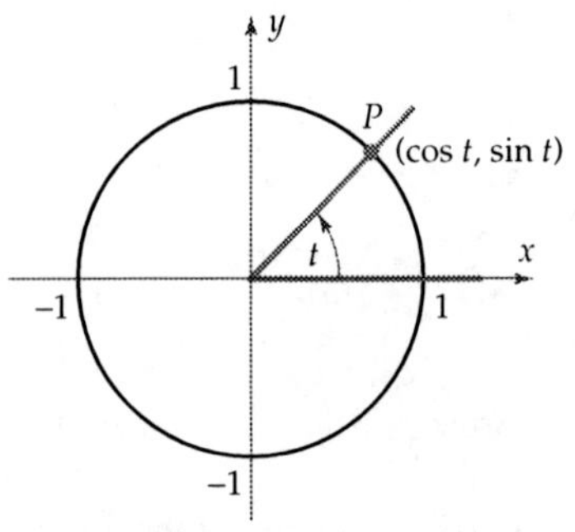

GRAPH OF THE TANGENT FUNCTION

To determine the shape of the graph of $h(t) = \tan t$, we use an interesting connection between the tangent function and straight lines. As shown in Figure 6–23, the point P where the terminal side of an angle of t radians in standard position meets the unit circle has coordinates $(\cos t, \sin t)$. We can use this point and the point $(0, 0)$ to compute the *slope* of the terminal side.

$$\text{slope} = \frac{\sin t - 0}{\cos t - 0} = \frac{\sin t}{\cos t} = \tan t$$

Figure 6–23

Therefore, we have the following.

**Slope and
Tangent**

The slope of the terminal side of an angle of t radians in standard position is the number $\tan t$.

The graph of $h(t) = \tan t$ can now be sketched by watching the slope of the terminal side of an angle of t radians, as t takes different values. Recall that the more steeply a line rises from left to right, the larger its slope. Similarly, lines that fall from left to right have negative slopes that increase in absolute value as the line falls more steeply.

As t Changes	The Terminal Side of the Angle Moves	Its Slope ($\tan t$)	Rough Sketch of the Graph
from 0 to $\frac{\pi}{2}$	from horizontal upward toward vertical	increases from 0 in the positive direction and keeps getting larger	
from 0 to $-\frac{\pi}{2}$	from horizontal downward toward vertical	decreases from 0 in the negative direction and keeps getting larger in absolute value	

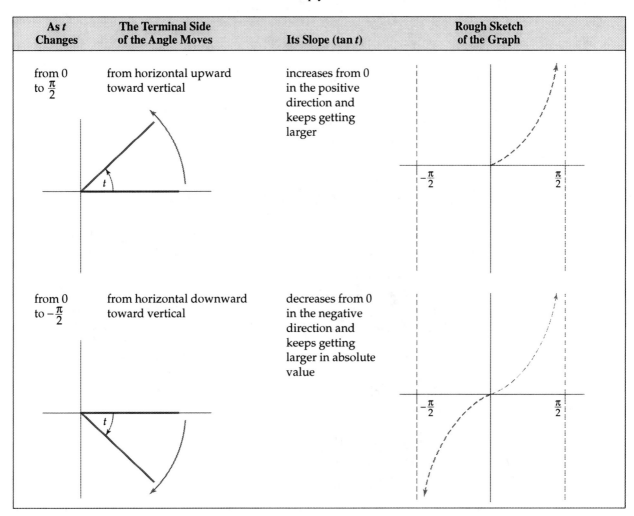

When $t = \pm\pi/2$, the terminal side of the angle is vertical, and hence its slope is not defined. This corresponds to the fact that the tangent function is not defined when $t = \pm\pi/2$. The vertical lines through $\pm\pi/2$ are vertical asymptotes of the graph: It gets closer and closer to these lines but never touches them.

As t goes from $\pi/2$ to $3\pi/2$, the terminal side goes from almost vertical with negative slope to horizontal to almost vertical with positive slope (draw a picture), exactly as it does between $-\pi/2$ and $\pi/2$. So the graph repeats the same pattern. The same thing happens between $3\pi/2$ and $5\pi/2$, between $-3\pi/2$ and $-\pi/2$, etc. Therefore, the entire graph looks like Figure 6–24 on the next page.

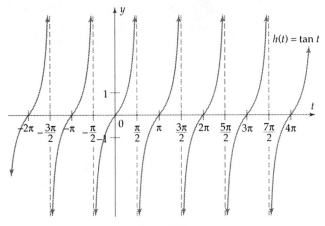

Figure 6–24

Because calculators sometimes do not graph accurately across vertical asymptotes, the graph may look slightly different on a calculator screen (with vertical line segments where the asymptotes should be).

The graph of the tangent function repeats the same pattern at intervals of length π. This means that the tangent function repeats its values at intervals of π.

Period of
Tangent

> The tangent function is periodic with period π: For every real number t in its domain,
>
> $$\tan(t \pm \pi) = \tan t.$$

EXAMPLE 5

As we saw in Section 3.4, the graph of

$$k(t) = \tan\left(t - \frac{\pi}{2}\right)$$

is the graph of $h(t) = \tan t$ shifted horizontally $\pi/2$ units to the right (Figure 6–25). ∎

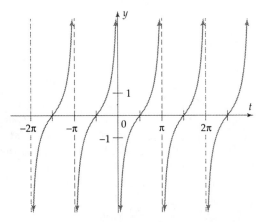

Figure 6–25

GRAPHS AND IDENTITIES

Graphing calculators can be used to identify equations that could possibly be identities. A calculator cannot *prove* that such an equation is an identity; but it can provide evidence that it *might* be one. On the other hand, a calculator *can* prove that a particular equation is *not* an identity.

EXAMPLE 6

Which of the following equations could possibly be an identity?

(a) $\cos\left(\dfrac{\pi}{2} + t\right) = \sin t$ (b) $\cos\left(\dfrac{\pi}{2} - t\right) = \sin t$

SOLUTION

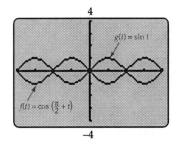

Figure 6–26

(a) Consider the functions $f(t) = \cos\left(\dfrac{\pi}{2} + t\right)$ and $g(t) = \sin t$, whose rules are given by the two sides of the equation

$$\cos\left(\frac{\pi}{2} + t\right) = \sin t.$$

If this equation is an identity, then $f(t) = g(t)$ for every real number t, and hence, f and g have the same graph. But the graphs of f and g on the interval $[-2\pi, 2\pi]$ (Figure 6–26) are obviously different. Therefore, this equation is *not* an identity.

(b) We can test this equation in the same manner. The graph of the left side, that is, the graph of

$$h(t) = \cos\left(\frac{\pi}{2} - t\right),$$

in Figure 6–27 appears to be the same as the graph of $g(t) = \sin t$ on the interval $[-2\pi, 2\pi]$ (Figure 6–26). To check this, do the Graphing Exploration in the margin.

GRAPHING EXPLORATION

Graph $h(t) = \cos\left(\dfrac{\pi}{2} - t\right)$ and $g(t) = \sin t$ on the same screen and use the trace feature to confirm that the graphs appear to be identical.

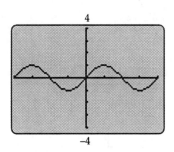

Figure 6–27

The fact that the graphs appear to be identical means that the two functions have the same value at every number t that the calculator computed in making the graphs (at least 95 numbers). This evidence strongly suggests that the equation

$\cos\left(\dfrac{\pi}{2} - t\right) = \sin t$ is an identity, but does not prove it. All we can say at this point is that the equation possibly is an identity. ∎

> **CAUTION**
>
> Do not assume that two graphs that look the same on a calculator screen actually are the same. Depending on the viewing window, two graphs that are actually quite different may appear to be identical. See Exercises 61, 62, and 64–67 for some examples.

EXERCISES 6.3

In Exercises 1–6, use the graphs of the sine and cosine functions to find all the solutions of the equation.

1. $\sin t = 0$ **2.** $\cos t = 0$ **3.** $\sin t = 1$

4. $\sin t = -1$ **5.** $\cos t = -1$ **6.** $\cos t = 1$

In Exercises 7–10, find tan t, where the terminal side of an angle of t radians lies on the given line.

7. $y = 11x$ **8.** $y = 1.5x$ **9.** $y = 1.4x$ **10.** $y = .32x$

In Exercises 11–22, list the transformations needed to change the graph of f(t) into the graph of g(t). [See Section 3.4.]

11. $f(t) = \sin t;$ $g(t) = \sin t + 3$

12. $f(t) = \cos t;$ $g(t) = \cos t - 2$

13. $f(t) = \cos t;$ $g(t) = -\cos t$

14. $f(x) = \sin t;$ $g(t) = -3 \sin t$

15. $f(t) = \tan t;$ $g(t) = \tan t + 5$

16. $f(t) = \tan t;$ $g(t) = -\tan t$

17. $f(t) = \cos t;$ $g(t) = 3 \cos t$

18. $f(t) = \sin t;$ $g(t) = -2 \sin t$

19. $f(t) = \sin t;$ $g(t) = 3 \sin t + 2$

20. $f(t) = \cos t;$ $g(t) = 5 \cos t + 3$

21. $f(t) = \sin t;$ $g(t) = \sin(t - 2)$

22. $f(t) = \cos t;$ $g(t) = 3 \cos(t + 2) - 3$

In Exercises 23–30 match the function with its graph, which is one of A–J below. [Note: the tangent graphs have erroneous vertical lines where the vertical asymptotes should be.]

23. $f(t) = 4 \sin t$ **24.** $g(t) = -\tan t$ **25.** $h(t) = 3 \tan t$ **26.** $k(t) = 2 - \sin t$

27. $f(t) = 2 \cos t$ **28.** $g(t) = -2 \sin t$ **29.** $h(t) = \cos t + 2$ **30.** $k(t) = 2 - 2 \sin t$

A.
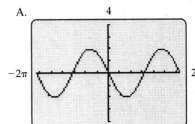

B.
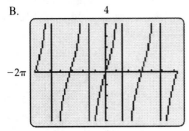

C.
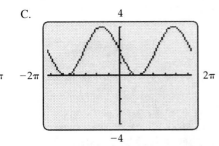

D.
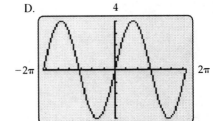

E.
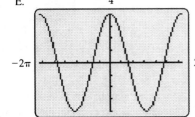

F.
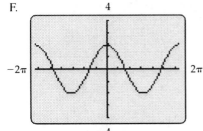

G.

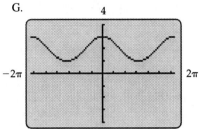

H.

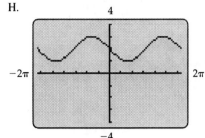

I.

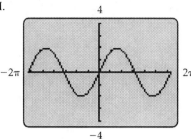

J.

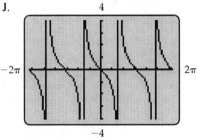

In Exercises 31–38, use the graphs of the trigonometric functions to determine the number of solutions of the equation between 0 and 2π.

31. $\sin t = 3/5$ [*Hint:* How many points on the graph of $f(t) = \sin t$ between $t = 0$ and $t = 2\pi$ have second coordinate $3/5$?]

32. $\cos t = -1/4$ **33.** $\tan t = 4$

34. $\cos t = 2/3$ **35.** $\sin t = -1/2$

36. $\sin t = k$, where k is a nonzero constant such that $-1 < k < 1$.

37. $\cos t = k$, where k is a constant such that $-1 < k < 1$.

38. $\tan t = k$, where k is any constant.

In Exercises 39–50, use graphs to determine whether the equation could possibly be an identity or definitely is not an identity.

39. $\sin(-t) = -\sin t$

40. $\cos(-t) = \cos t$

41. $\sin^2 t + \cos^2 t = 1$

42. $\sin(t + \pi) = -\sin t$

43. $\sin t = \cos(t - \pi/2)$

44. $\sin^2 t - \tan^2 t = -(\sin^2 t)(\tan^2 t)$

45. $\dfrac{\sin t}{1 + \cos t} = \tan t$

46. $\dfrac{\cos t}{1 - \sin t} = \dfrac{1}{\cos t} + \tan t$

47. $\cos\left(\dfrac{\pi}{2} + t\right) = -\sin t$

48. $\sin\left(\dfrac{\pi}{2} + t\right) = -\cos t$

49. $(1 + \tan t)^2 = \dfrac{1}{\cos t}$

50. $(\cos^2 t - 1)(\tan^2 t + 1) = -\tan^2 t$

In Exercises 51–54, determine if the graph appears to be the graph of a periodic function. If it is, state the period.

51.

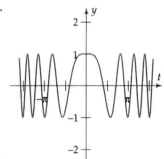

52.

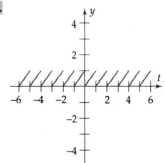

53.

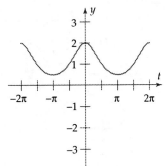

54.

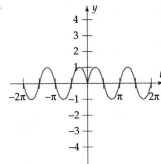

In Exercises 55–60, graph the function. Does the function appear to be periodic? If so, what is the period?

55. $f(t) = \cos |t|$

56. $f(t) = |\cos t|$

57. $g(t) = \sin |t|$

58. $g(t) = |\sin t|$

59. $h(t) = \tan |t|$

60. $h(t) = |\tan t|$

THINKERS

Exercises 61–64, explore various ways in which a calculator can produce inaccurate graphs of trigonometric functions. These exercises also provide examples of two functions, with different graphs, whose graphs appear identical in certain viewing windows.

61. Choose a viewing window with $-3 \le y \le 3$ and $0 \le x \le k$, where k is chosen as follows.

Width of Screen	k
95 pixels (TI-83/84+)	188π
127 pixels (TI-86, Casio)	252π
131 pixels (HP-39gs)	260π
159 pixels (TI-89)	316π

(a) Graph $y = \cos x$ and the constant function $y = 1$ on the same screen. Do the graphs look identical? Are the functions the same?

(b) Use the trace feature to move the cursor along the graph of $y = \cos x$, starting at $x = 0$. For what values of x did the calculator plot points? [*Hint:* $2\pi \approx 6.28$.] Use this information to explain why the two graphs look identical.

62. Using the viewing window in Exercise 61, graph $y = \tan x + 2$ and $y = 2$ on the same screen. Explain why the graphs look identical even though the functions are not the same.

63. The graph of $g(x) = \cos x$ is a series of repeated waves (see Figure 6–47). A full wave (from the peak, down to the trough, and up to the peak again) starts at $x = 0$ and finishes at $x = 2\pi$.

(a) How many full waves will the graph make between $x = 0$ and $x = 502.65$ ($\approx 80 \cdot 2\pi$)?

(b) Graph $g(t) = \cos t$ in a viewing window with $0 \le t \le 502.65$. How many full waves are shown on the graph? Is your answer the same as in part (a)? What's going on?

64. Find a viewing window in which the graphs of $y = \cos x$ and $y = .54$ appear identical. [*Hint:* See the chart in Exercise 61 and note that $\cos 1 \approx .54$.]

Exercises 65–68 provide further examples of functions with different graphs, whose graphs appear identical in certain viewing windows.

65. *Approximating trigonometric functions by polynomials.* For each odd positive integer n, let f_n be the function whose rule is

$$f_n(t) = t - \frac{t^3}{3!} + \frac{t^5}{5!} - \frac{t^7}{7!} + \cdots - \frac{t^n}{n!}.$$

Since the signs alternate, the sign of the last term might be $+$ instead of $-$, depending on what n is. Recall that $n!$ is the product of all integers from 1 to n; for instance, $5! = 1 \cdot 2 \cdot 3 \cdot 4 \cdot 5 = 120$.

(a) Graph $f_7(t)$ and $g(t) = \sin t$ on the same screen in a viewing window with $-2\pi \le t \le 2\pi$. For what values of t does f_7 appear to be a good approximation of g?

(b) What is the smallest value of n for which the graphs of f_n and g appear to coincide in this window? In this case, determine how accurate the approximation is by finding $f_n(2)$ and $g(2)$.

66. For each even positive integer n, let f_n be the function whose rule is

$$f_n(t) = 1 - \frac{t^2}{2!} + \frac{t^4}{4!} - \frac{t^6}{6!} + \frac{t^8}{8!} - \cdots + \frac{t^n}{n!}.$$

(The sign of the last term may be $-$ instead of $+$, depending on what n is.)

(a) In a viewing window with $-2\pi \le t \le 2\pi$, graph f_6, f_{10}, and f_{12}.

(b) Find a value of n for which the graph of f_n appears to coincide (in this window) with the graph of a well-known trigonometric function. What is the function?

67. Find a rational function whose graph appears to coincide with the graph of $h(t) = \tan t$ when

$$-2\pi \leq t \leq 2\pi.$$

[*Hint:* Exercises 65 and 66.]

68. Find a periodic function whose graph consists of "square waves." [*Hint:* Consider the sum

$$\sin \pi t + \frac{1}{3} \sin 3\pi t + \frac{1}{5} \sin 5\pi t + \frac{1}{7} \sin 7\pi t + \cdots.]$$

69. With your calculator in parametric graphing mode and the range values

$$0 \leq t \leq 6.28 \qquad -1 \leq x \leq 6.28 \qquad -2.5 \leq y \leq 2.5,$$

graph the following two functions on the same screen:

$$x_1 = \cos t, \ y_1 = \sin t \qquad \text{and} \qquad x_2 = t, \ y_2 = \cos t.$$

Using the trace feature, move the cursor along the first graph (the unit circle). Stop at a point on the circle, note the value of t and the x-coordinate of the point. Then switch the trace to the second graph (the cosine function) by using the up or down cursor arrows. The value of t remains the same. How does the y-coordinate of the new point compare with the x-coordinate of the original point on the unit circle? Explain what's going on.

70. (a) Judging from their graphs, which of the functions $f(t) = \sin t$, $g(t) = \cos t$, and $h(t) = \tan t$ appear to be even functions? Which appear to be odd functions?
(b) Confirm your answers in part (a) algebraically by using appropriate identities from Section 6.3.

6.4 Periodic Graphs

Section Objectives

■ Identify the period, amplitude, and phase shift of the functions
$f(t) = A \sin(bt + c)$ and $g(t) = A \cos(bt + c)$

■ Explore simple harmonic motion.

We now analyze functions whose rule is of the form

$$f(t) = A \sin(bt + c) \qquad \text{or} \qquad g(t) = A \cos(bt + c),$$

where A, b, and c are constants. Many periodic phenomena can be modeled by such functions, as we shall see below.

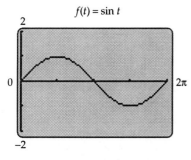

$f(t) = \sin t$

Figure 6–28

PERIOD

The functions $f(t) = \sin t$ and $g(t) = \cos t$ have period 2π, so each of their graphs makes one full wave between 0 and 2π. The sine wave begins on the horizontal axis, rises to height 1, falls to -1, and returns to the axis (Figure 6–28). The cosine wave between 0 and 2π begins at height 1, falls to -1, and rises to height 1 again (Figure 6–29).

$g(t) = \cos t$

Figure 6–29

GRAPHING EXPLORATION

Graph the following functions, one at a time, in a viewing window with $0 \leq t \leq 2\pi$. Determine the number of complete waves in each graph and the period of the function (the length of one wave).

$$f(t) = \sin 2t, \qquad g(t) = \cos 3t, \qquad h(x) = \sin 4t, \qquad k(x) = \cos 5t.$$

This exploration suggests the following.

Period

> If $b > 0$, then the graph of either
>
> $$f(t) = \sin bt \qquad \text{or} \qquad g(t) = \cos bt$$
>
> makes b complete waves between 0 and 2π. Hence, each function has period $2\pi/b$.

Although we arrived at this statement by generalizing from several graphs, it can also be explained algebraically.

EXAMPLE 1

The graph of $g(t) = \cos t$ makes one complete wave as t takes values from 0 to 2π. Similarly, the graph of $k(t) = \cos 3t$ will complete one wave as the quantity $3t$ takes values from 0 to 2π. However,

$$3t = 0 \text{ when } t = 0 \qquad \text{and} \qquad 3t = 2\pi \text{ when } t = 2\pi/3.$$

So the graph of $k(t) = \cos 3t$ makes one complete wave between $t = 0$ and $t = 2\pi/3$, as shown in Figure 6–30, and hence k has period $2\pi/3$. Similarly, the graph makes a complete wave from $t = 2\pi/3$ to $t = 4\pi/3$ and another one from $t = 4\pi/3$ to $t = 2\pi$, as shown in Figure 6–57. ∎

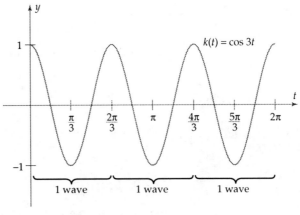

Figure 6–30

EXAMPLE 2

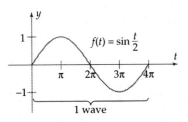

Figure 6–31

According to the box above, the function $f(t) = \sin \frac{1}{2}t$ has period $\dfrac{2\pi}{1/2} = 4\pi$. Its graph makes *half* a wave from $t = 0$ to $t = 2\pi$ (just as $\sin t$ does from $t = 0$ to $t = \pi$) and the other half of the wave from $t = 2\pi$ to $t = 4\pi$, as shown in Figure 6–31. ∎

EXAMPLE 3

Except over *very* tiny intervals, your calculator is incapable of accurately graphing $f(t) = \sin bt$ or $g(t) = \cos bt$ when b is large. For instance, we know that the graph of

$$f(t) = \sin 500t$$

should show 500 complete waves between 0 and 2π. Depending on the model, however, your calculator will produce either garbage (Figure 6–32) or a graph with far fewer than 500 waves (Figure 6–33). For the reason why, see Exercises 59 and 60. ∎

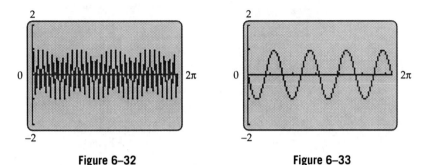

Figure 6–32   **Figure 6–33**

AMPLITUDE

As we saw in Section 3.4, multiplying the rule of a function by a positive constant has the effect of stretching its graph away from or shrinking it toward the horizontal axis.

EXAMPLE 4

The function $g(t) = 7 \cos 3t$ is just the function $k(t) = \cos 3t$ multiplied by 7. Consequently, the graph of g is just the graph of k (which was obtained in Example 1) stretched away from the horizontal axis by a factor of 7, as shown in Figure 6–34.

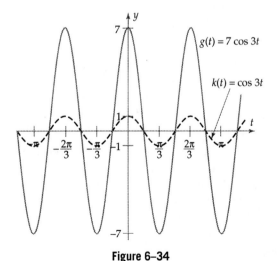

Figure 6–34

Stretching the graph affects only the height of the waves, not the period of the function: Both graphs have period $2\pi/3$, and each full wave has length $2\pi/3$. ∎

The waves of the graph of $g(t) = 7 \cos 3t$ in Figure 6–34 rise 7 units above the t-axis and drop 7 units below the axis. More generally, the waves of the graph of $f(t) = A \sin bt$ or $g(t) = A \cos bt$ move a distance of $|A|$ units above and below the t-axis, and we say that these functions have **amplitude** $|A|$. In summary, we have the following.

Amplitude and Period

> If $A \neq 0$ and $b > 0$, then each of the functions
> $$f(t) = A \sin bt \qquad \text{or} \qquad g(t) = A \cos bt$$
> has amplitude $|A|$ and period $2\pi/b$.

EXAMPLE 5

The function $f(t) = -2 \sin 4t$ has amplitude $|-2| = 2$ and period $2\pi/4 = \pi/2$. So the graph consists of waves of length $\pi/2$ that rise and fall between -2 and 2. But be careful: The waves in the graph of $2 \sin 4t$ (like the waves of $\sin t$) begin at height 0, rise, and then fall. But the graph of $f(t) = -2 \sin 4t$ is the graph of $2 \sin 4t$ reflected in the horizontal axis (see page 184). So its waves start at height 0, move *downward,* and then rise, as shown in Figure 6–35. ∎

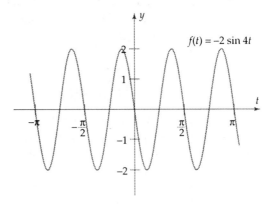

Figure 6–35

PHASE SHIFT

Next, we consider horizontal shifts. As we saw in Section 3.4, the graph of $\sin(t - 3)$ is the graph of $\sin t$ shifted 3 units to the right, and the graph of $\sin(t + 3)$ is the graph of $\sin t$ shifted 3 units to the left.

EXAMPLE 6

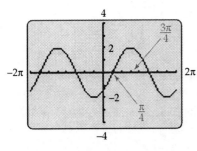

Figure 6–36

(a) Find a sine function whose graph looks like Figure 6–36.

(b) Find a cosine function whose graph looks like Figure 6–36.

SOLUTION

(a) Since each wave has height 2, Figure 6–36 looks like the graph of $2 \sin t$ shifted $\pi/4$ units to the right (so that a sine wave starts at $t = \pi/4$). Since the graph of $2 \sin(t - \pi/4)$ is the graph of $2 \sin t$ shifted $\pi/4$ units to the right (see page 181), we conclude that Figure 6–36 closely resembles the graph of $f(t) = 2 \sin(t - \pi/4)$.

(b) Figure 6–36 also looks like the graph of $2 \cos t$ shifted $3\pi/4$ units to the right (so that a cosine wave starts at $t = 3\pi/4$). Hence, Figure 6–36 could also be the graph of $g(t) = 2 \cos(t - 3\pi/4)$. ∎

EXAMPLE 7

(a) Find the amplitude and the period of

$$f(t) = 3 \sin(2t + 5).$$

(b) Do the same for the function $f(t) = A \sin(bt + c)$, where A, b, c are constants.

SOLUTION   The analysis of $f(t) = 3 \sin(2t + 5)$ is in the left-hand column below, and the analysis of the general case $f(t) = A \sin(bt + c)$ is in the right-hand column. Observe that exactly the same procedure is used in both cases: Just change 3 to A, 2 to b, and 5 to c.

(a) Rewrite the rule of $f(t) = 3 \sin(2t + 5)$ as

$$f(t) = 3 \sin(2t + 5) = 3 \sin\left(2\left(t + \frac{5}{2}\right)\right).$$

Thus, the rule of f can be obtained from the rule of the function $k(t) = 3 \sin 2t$ by replacing t with $t + \frac{5}{2}$. Therefore, the graph of f is just the graph of k shifted horizontally 5/2 units to the left, as shown in Figure 6–37.

Hence, $f(t) = 3 \sin(2t + 5)$ has the same amplitude as $k(t) = 3 \sin 2t$, namely, 3, and the same period, namely, $2\pi/2 = \pi$.

On the graph of $k(t) = 3 \sin 2t$, a wave begins when $t = 0$. On the graph of

$$f(t) = 3 \sin 2\left(t + \frac{5}{2}\right),$$

the shifted wave begins when $t + 5/2 = 0$, that is, when $t = -5/2$.

(b) Rewrite the rule of $f(t) = A \sin(bt + c)$ as

$$f(t) = A \sin(bt + c) = A \sin\left(b\left(t + \frac{c}{b}\right)\right).$$

Thus, the rule of f can be obtained from the rule of the function $k(t) = A \sin bt$ by replacing t with $t + \frac{c}{b}$. Therefore, the graph of f is just the graph of k shifted horizontally by c/b units.

Hence, $f(t) = A \sin(bt + c)$ has the same amplitude as $k(t) = A \sin bt$, namely, $|A|$, and the same period, namely, $2\pi/b$.

On the graph of $k(t) = A \sin bt$, a wave begins when $t = 0$. On the graph of

$$f(t) = A \sin b\left(t + \frac{c}{b}\right),$$

the shifted wave begins when $t + c/b = 0$, that is, when $t = -c/b$. ∎

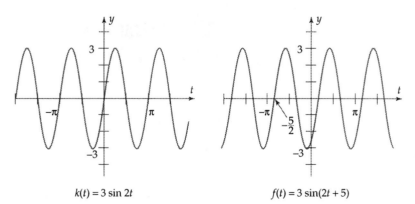

$$k(t) = 3 \sin 2t \qquad\qquad f(t) = 3 \sin(2t + 5)$$

Figure 6–37

We say that the function $f(t) = A \sin(bt + c)$ has **phase shift** $-c/b$. A similar analysis applies to the function $g(t) = \cos(bt + c)$ and leads to this conclusion.

Amplitude, Period,
and Phase Shift

> If $A \neq 0$ and $b > 0$, then each of the functions
>
> $$f(t) = A \sin(bt + c) \qquad \text{and} \qquad g(t) = A \cos(bt + c)$$
>
> has
>
> $$\text{amplitude } |A|, \qquad \text{period } 2\pi/b, \qquad \text{phase shift } -c/b.$$
>
> A wave of the graph begins at $t = -c/b$.

EXAMPLE 8

Describe the graph of $g(t) = 2\cos(3t - 4)$.

SOLUTION   The rule of g can be rewritten as

$$g(t) = 2\cos(3t + (-4)).$$

This is the case described in the preceding box with $A = 2$, $b = 3$, and $c = -4$. Therefore, the function g has

$$\text{amplitude } |A| = |2| = 2, \qquad \text{period } \frac{2\pi}{b} = \frac{2\pi}{3},$$

$$\text{phase shift } -\frac{c}{b} = -\frac{-4}{3} = \frac{4}{3}.$$

Hence, the graph of g consists of waves of length of $2\pi/3$ that run vertically between 2 and -2. A wave begins at $t = 4/3$.

GRAPHING EXPLORATION

Verify the accuracy of this analysis by graphing $y = 2\cos(3t - 4)$ in the viewing window with $-2\pi \leq t \leq 2\pi$ and $-3 \leq y \leq 3$.

■

Many other types of trigonometric graphs, including those consisting of waves of varying height and length, are considered in Special Topics 6.5.A.

APPLICATIONS

The sine and cosine functions, or variations of them, can be used to describe many different phenomena.

EXAMPLE 9

A typical person's blood pressure can be modeled by the function

$$f(t) = 22\cos(2.5\pi t) + 95,$$

where t is time (in seconds) and $f(t)$ is in millimeters of mercury. The highest pressure (systolic) occurs when the heart beats, and the lowest pressure (diastolic)

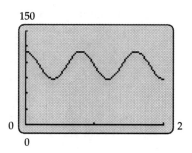

Figure 6–38

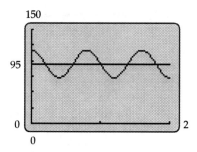

Figure 6–39

occurs when the heart is at rest between beats. The blood pressure is the ratio systolic/diastolic.

(a) Graph the blood pressure function over a period of two seconds and determine the person's blood pressure.

(b) Find the person's pulse rate (number of heartbeats per minute).

SOLUTION

(a) The graph of f is shown in Figure 6–38. The systolic pressure occurs at each local maximum of the graph and the diastolic pressure at each local minimum. Their heights can be determined by using our knowledge of periodic functions. The graph of f is the graph of $22 \cos(2.5\pi t)$ shifted upward by 95 units (as explained in Section 3.4). Since the amplitude of $22 \cos(2.5\pi t)$ is 22, its graph rises 22 units above and falls 22 units below the x-axis. When this graph is shifted 95 units upward, it rises and falls 22 units above and below the horizontal line $y = 95$ (see Figure 6–39), that is

from a high of $95 + 22 = 117$ to a low of $95 - 22 = 73$.

In other words, the systolic pressure is 117 and the diastolic pressure is 73. So the person's blood pressure is 117/73.

GRAPHING EXPLORATION

Use a maximum/minimum finder to confirm that the local maxima of the graph in Figure 6–65 occur when $y = 117$ and the local minima when $y = 73$.

(b) The time between heartbeats is the horizontal distance between peaks of the graph, that is, the period of the function. The period of $\cos(2.5\pi t)$ is

$$\frac{2\pi}{b} = \frac{2\pi}{2.5\pi} = .8 \text{ second.}$$

Since one minute is 60 seconds, the number of beats per minute (pulse rate) is

$$\frac{60}{.8} = 75. \qquad \blacksquare$$

EXAMPLE 10

A wheel of radius 2 centimeters is rotating counterclockwise at 3 radians per second. A free-hanging rod 10 centimeters long is connected to the edge of the wheel at point P and remains vertical as the wheel rotates (Figure 6–40). Assuming that the center of the wheel is at the origin and that P is at $(2, 0)$ at time $t = 0$, find a function that describes the y-coordinate of the tip E of the rod at time t.

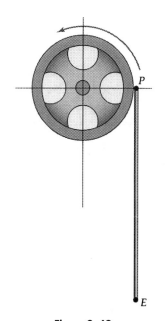

Figure 6–40

SOLUTION   The wheel is rotating at 3 radians per second, so after t seconds, the point P has moved through an angle of $3t$ radians and is 2 units from the

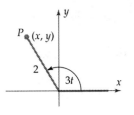

Figure 6–41

origin, as shown in Figure 6–41. By the point-in-the-plane description, the coordinates (x, y) of P satisfy

$$\frac{x}{2} = \cos 3t \qquad \frac{y}{2} = \sin 3t$$

$$x = 2 \cos 3t \qquad y = 2 \sin 3t.$$

Since E lies 10 centimeters directly below P, its y-coordinate is 10 less than the y-coordinate of P. Hence, the function giving the y-coordinate of E at time t is

$$f(t) = y - 10 = 2 \sin 3t - 10. \qquad ■$$

EXAMPLE 11

Suppose that a weight hanging from a spring is set in motion by an upward push (Figure 6–42) and that it takes 5 seconds for it to move from its equilibrium position to 8 centimeters above, then drop to 8 centimeters below, and finally return to its equilibrium position. [We consider an idealized situation in which the spring has perfect elasticity and friction, air resistance, etc., are negligible.]

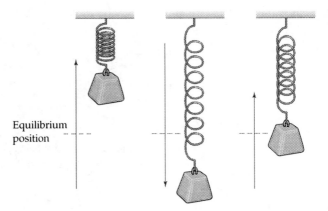

Figure 6–42

Let $h(t)$ denote the distance of the weight above $(+)$ or below $(-)$ its equilibrium position at time t. Then $h(t)$ is 0 when $t = 0$. As t runs from 0 to 5, $h(t)$ increases from 0 to 8, decreases to -8, and increases again to 0. In the next 5 seconds, it repeats the same pattern, and so on. Thus, the graph of h has some kind of wave shape. Two possibilities are shown in Figure 6–43.

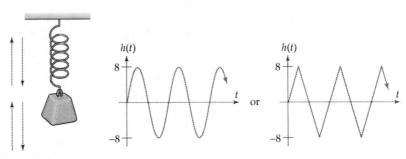

Figure 6–43

Careful physical experimentation suggests that the left-hand curve in Figure 6–43, which resembles the sine graphs studied earlier, is a reasonably accurate model of this process. Facts from physics, calculus, and differential equations show that the rule of the function h is the form $h(t) = A \sin(bt + c)$ for some constants A, b, c. Since the amplitude of h is 8, its period is 5, and its phase shift is 0, the constants A, b, and c must satisfy

$$A = 8, \qquad \frac{2\pi}{b} = 5, \qquad -\frac{c}{b} = 0$$

or, equivalently,

$$A = 8 \qquad b = \frac{2\pi}{5}, \qquad c = 0.$$

Therefore, the motion of the moving spring can be described by the function

$$h(t) = A \sin(bt + c) = 8 \sin\left(\frac{2\pi}{5}t + 0\right) = 8 \sin \frac{2\pi t}{5}. \qquad \blacksquare$$

Motion that can be described by a function of the form $f(t) = A \sin(bt + c)$ or $f(t) = A \cos(bt + c)$ is called **simple harmonic motion.** Many kinds of physical motion are simple harmonic motions. Other periodic phenomena, such as sound waves, are more complicated to describe. Their graphs consist of waves of varying amplitude. Such graphs are discussed in Special Topics 6.5.A.

EXAMPLE 12*

The table shows the average monthly temperature in Cleveland, OH, based on 30 years of data from the National Climatic Data Center. Since average temperatures are not likely to vary much from year to year, the data essentially repeats the same pattern in subsequent years. So a periodic model is appropriate.

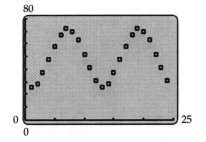

Figure 6–44

Month	Temperature (°F)	Month	Temperature (°F)
Jan	25.7	Jul	71.9
Feb	28.4	Aug	70.2
Mar	37.5	Sep	63.3
Apr	47.6	Oct	52.2
May	58.5	Nov	41.8
Jun	67.5	Dec	31.1

The data for a two-year period is plotted in Figure 6–44 (with $x = 1$ corresponding to January, $x = 2$ to February, and so on).[†] The sine regression feature on a calculator produces this model from the 24 data points:

$$y = 22.7 \sin(.5219x - 2.1842) + 49.5731.$$

The period of this function is $2\pi/.5219 \approx 12.04$ slightly off from the 12-month period we would expect. However, its graph in Figure 6–45 appears to fit the data well. $\blacksquare$

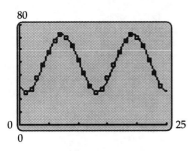

Figure 6–45

---

*Skip this example if you haven't read Sections 2.5 and 5.5 on regression.
[†]The reasons why a two-year period is used are considered in Exercises 62 and 63.

EXERCISES 6.4

In Exercises 1–7, state the amplitude, period, and phase shift of the function.

1. $g(t) = 3 \sin(2t - \pi)$ 2. $h(t) = -6 \cos(4t - \pi/4)$

3. $q(t) = -5 \sin(5t + 1/5)$

4. $g(t) = 97 \cos(14t + 5)$

5. $f(t) = \cos 2\pi t$ 6. $k(t) = \cos(2\pi t/3)$

7. $p(t) = 6 \cos(3\pi t + 1)$

8. (a) What is the period of $f(t) = \sin 2\pi t$?
   (b) For what values of t (with $0 \le t \le 2\pi$) is $f(t) = 0$?
   (c) For what values of t (with $0 \le t \le 2\pi$) is $f(t) = 1$? or $f(t) = -1$?

In Exercises 9–14, give the rule of a periodic function with the given numbers as amplitude, period, and phase shift (in this order).

9. $3, \pi/4, \pi/5$ 10. $4, 5, 0$ 11. $3/4, 2, 0$

12. $4/5, 3, 1$ 13. $7, 5/3, -\pi/2$ 14. $18, 3, -6$

In Exercises 15–18, state the rule of a function of the form $f(t) = A \sin bt$ or $g(t) = A \cos bt$ whose graph appears to be identical to the given graph.

15.

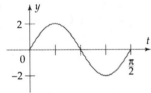

16.

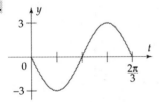

17.

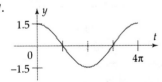

18.

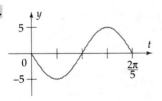

In Exercises 19–22,
(a) *State the period of the function.*
(b) *Describe the graph of the function between 0 and 2π.*
(c) *Find a viewing window that accurately shows exactly four complete waves of the graph.*

19. $f(t) = \sin 200t$ 20. $f(t) = \sin 600t$

21. $g(t) = \cos 900t$ 22. $g(t) = \cos 575t$

In Exercises 23–26,
(a) *State the rule of a function of the form*
$$f(t) = A \sin(bt + c)$$
whose graph appears to be identical with the given graph.
(b) *State the rule of a function of the form*
$$g(t) = A \cos(bt + c)$$
whose graph appears to be identical with the given graph.

23.

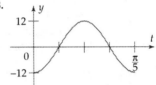

24.

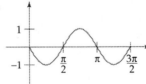

25.

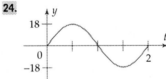

26.

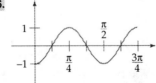

In Exercises 27–32, sketch a complete graph of the function.

27. $k(t) = -3 \sin t$ 28. $y(t) = -2 \cos 3t$

29. $p(t) = -\dfrac{1}{2} \sin 2t$ 30. $q(t) = \dfrac{2}{3} \cos \dfrac{3}{2}t$

31. $h(t) = 3 \sin(2t + \pi/2)$ 32. $p(t) = 3 \cos(3t - \pi)$

In Exercises 33–36, graph the function over the interval $[0, 2\pi)$ and determine the location of all local maxima and minima. [This can be done either graphically or algebraically.]

33. $f(t) = \frac{1}{2}\sin\left(t - \frac{\pi}{3}\right)$

34. $g(t) = 2\sin(2t/3 - \pi/9)$

35. $f(t) = -2\sin(3t - \pi)$

36. $h(t) = \frac{1}{2}\cos\left(\frac{\pi}{2}t - \frac{\pi}{8}\right) + 1$

In Exercises 37–40, graph $f(t)$ in a viewing window with $-2\pi \le t \le 2\pi$. Use a maximum finder and a root finder to determine constants A, b, c such that the graph of $f(t)$ appears to coincide with the graph of $g(t) = A\sin(bt + c)$.

37. $f(t) = 3\sin t + 2\cos t$

38. $f(t) = -5\sin t + 3\cos t$

39. $f(t) = 3\sin(4t + 2) + 2\cos(4t - 1)$

40. $f(t) = 2\sin(3t - 5) - 3\cos(3t + 2)$

In Exercises 41 and 42, explain why there could not possibly be constants A, b, and c such that the graph of $g(t) = A\sin(bt + c)$ coincides with the graph of $f(t)$.

41. $f(t) = \sin 2t + \cos 3t$

42. $f(t) = 2\sin(3t - 1) + 3\cos(4t + 1)$

43. Do parts (a) and (b) of Example 9 for a person whose blood pressure is given by

$$g(t) = 21\cos(2.5\pi t) + 113.$$

According to current guidelines, someone with systolic pressure above 140 or diastolic pressure above 90 has high blood pressure and should see a doctor about it. What would you advise the person in this case?

44. Find the function in Example 10 if the wheel has a radius of 13 centimeters and the rod is 18 centimeters long.

45. The volume $V(t)$ of air (in cubic inches) in an adult's lungs t seconds after exhaling is approximately

$$V(t) = 55 + 24.5\sin\left(\frac{\pi x}{2} - \frac{\pi}{2}\right).$$

(a) Find the maximum and minimum amount of air in the lungs.
(b) How often does the person exhale?
(c) How many breaths per minute does the person take?

46. The brightness of the binary star Beta Lyrae (as seen from the earth) varies. Its visual magnitude $M(t)$ after t days is approximately

$$M(t) = .55\cos(.97t) + 3.85.$$

The visual magnitude scale is reversed from what you would expect: The lower the number, the brighter the star. With this in mind, answer the following questions.

(a) Graph the function M when $0 \le t \le 21$.
(b) What is the visual magnitude when the star is brightest? When it is dimmest?
(c) What is the period of the magnitude (the interval between its brightest times)?

47. The current generated by an AM radio transmitter is given by a function of the form $f(t) = A\sin 2000\pi mt$, where $550 \le m \le 1600$ is the location on the broadcast dial and t is measured in seconds. For example, a station at 980 on the AM dial has a function of the form

$$f(t) = A\sin 2000\pi(980)t = A\sin 1{,}960{,}000\pi t.$$

Sound information is added to this signal by varying (modulating) A, that is, by changing the amplitude of the waves being transmitted. (*AM* means "amplitude modulation.") For a station at 980 on the dial, what is the period of function f? What is the frequency (number of complete waves per second)?

48. The number of hours of daylight in Winnipeg, Manitoba, can be approximated by

$$d(t) = 4.15\sin(.0172t - 1.377) + 12,$$

where t is measured in days, with $t = 1$ being January 1.

(a) On what day is there the most daylight? The least? How much daylight is there on these days?
(b) On which days are there 11 hours or more of daylight?
(c) What do you think the period of this function is? Why?

49. The original Ferris wheel, built by George Ferris for the Columbian Exposition of 1893, was much larger and slower than its modern counterparts: It had a diameter of 250 feet and contained 36 cars, each of which held 60 people; it made one revolution every 10 minutes. Imagine that the Ferris wheel revolves counterclockwise in the x-y plane with its center at the origin. A car had coordinates $(125, 0)$ at time $t = 0$. Find the rule of a function that gives the y-coordinate of the car at time t.

50. Do Exercise 49 if the wheel turns at 2 radians per minute and the car is at $(0, -125)$ at time $t = 0$.

51. A circular wheel of radius 1 foot rotates counterclockwise. A 4-foot-long rod has one end attached to the edge of this wheel and the other end to the base of a piston (see the figure). It transfers the rotary motion of the wheel into a back-and-forth linear motion of the piston. If the wheel is rotating at 10 revolutions per second, point W is at $(1, 0)$ at time $t = 0$, and point P is always on the x-axis, find the rule of a function that gives the x-coordinate of P at time t.

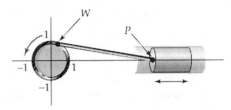

52. Do Exercise 51 if the wheel has a radius of 2 feet, rotates at 50 revolutions per second, and is at $(2, 0)$ when $t = 0$.

In Exercises 53–56, suppose there is a weight hanging from a spring (under the same idealized conditions as described in Example 11). The weight is given a push to start it moving. At any time t, let $h(t)$ be the height (or depth) of the weight above (or below) its equilibrium point. Assume that the maximum distance the weight moves in either direction from the equilibrium point is 6 centimeters and that it moves through a complete cycle every 4 seconds. Express $h(t)$ in terms of the sine or cosine function under the stated conditions.

53. Initial push is *upward* from the equilibrium point.

54. Initial push is *downward* from the equilibrium point. [*Hint:* What does the graph of $A \sin bt$ look like when $A < 0$?]

55. Weight is pulled 6 centimeters above equilibrium, and the initial movement (at $t = 0$) is downward. [*Hint:* Think cosine.]

56. Weight is pulled 6 centimeters below equilibrium, and the initial movement is upward.

57. A pendulum swings uniformly back and forth, taking 2 seconds to move from the position directly above point A to the position directly above point B.

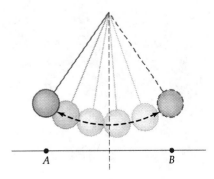

The distance from A to B is 20 centimeters. Let $d(t)$ be the horizontal distance from the pendulum to the (dashed) center line at time t seconds (with distances to the right of the line measured by positive numbers and distances to the left by negative ones). Assume that the pendulum is on the center line at time $t = 0$ and moving to the right. Assume that the motion of the pendulum is simple harmonic motion. Find the rule of the function $d(t)$.

58. The diagram shows a merry-go-round that is turning counterclockwise at a constant rate, making 2 revolutions in 1 minute. On the merry-go-round are horses A, B, C, and D at 4 meters from the center and horses E, F, and G at 8 meters from the center. There is a function $a(t)$ that gives the distance the horse A is from the y-axis (this is the x-coordinate of the position A is in) as a function of time t (measured in minutes). Similarly, $b(t)$ gives the x-coordinate for B as a function of time, and so on. Assume that the diagram shows the situation at time $t = 0$.

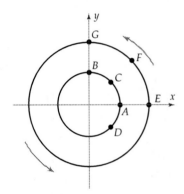

(a) Which of the following functions does $a(t)$ equal?

$$4 \cos t, \quad 4 \cos \pi t, \quad 4 \cos 2t, \quad 4 \cos 2\pi t,$$
$$4 \cos \left(\tfrac{1}{2}t\right), \quad 4 \cos \left((\pi/2)t\right), \quad 4 \cos 4\pi t$$

Explain.

(b) Describe the functions $b(t)$, $c(t)$, $d(t)$, and so on using the cosine function:

$$b(t) = \underline{\quad}, c(t) = \underline{\quad}, d(t) = \underline{\quad}.$$
$$e(t) = \underline{\quad}, f(t) = \underline{\quad}, g(t) = \underline{\quad}.$$

(c) Suppose the x-coordinate of a horse S is given by the function $4 \cos(4\pi t - (5\pi/6))$ and the x-coordinate of another horse T is given by $8 \cos(4\pi t - (\pi/3))$. Where are these horses located in relation to the rest of the horses? Mark the positions of T and S at $t = 0$ into the figure.

Exercises 59–60 explore various ways in which a calculator can produce inaccurate or misleading graphs of trigonometric functions.

59. (a) If you were going to draw a rough picture of a full wave of the sine function by plotting some points and connecting them with straight-line segments, approximately how many points would you have to plot?

(b) If you were drawing a rough sketch of the graph of $f(t) = \sin 100t$ when $0 \le t \le 2\pi$, according to the method in part (a), approximately how many points would have to be plotted?

(c) How wide (in pixels) is your calculator screen? Your answer to this question is the maximum number of points that your calculator plots when graphing any function.

(d) Use parts (a)–(c) to explain why your calculator cannot possibly produce an accurate graph of $f(t) = \sin 100t$ in any viewing window with $0 \le t \le 2\pi$.

60. (a) Using a viewing window with $0 \le t \le 2\pi$, use the trace feature to move the cursor along the horizontal axis. [On some calculators, it may be necessary to graph $y = 0$ to do this.] What is the distance between one pixel and the next (to the nearest hundredth)?

(b) What is the period of $f(t) = \sin 300t$? Since the period is the length of one full wave of the graph, approximately how many waves should there be between two adjacent pixels? What does this say about the possibility of your calculator's producing an accurate graph of this function between 0 and 2π?

61. The table below shows the number of unemployed people in the labor force (in millions) for 1984–2005.*

(a) Sketch a scatter plot of the data, with $x = 0$ corresponding to 1980.

(b) Does the data appear to be periodic? If so, find an appropriate model.

(c) Do you think this model is likely to be accurate much beyond 2005? Why?

Year	Unemployed
1984	8.539
1985	8.312
1986	8.237
1987	7.425
1988	6.701
1989	6.528
1990	7.047
1991	8.628
1992	9.613
1993	8.940
1994	7.996

Year	Unemployed
1995	7.404
1996	7.236
1997	6.739
1998	6.210
1999	5.880
2000	5.692
2001	6.801
2002	8.378
2003	8.774
2004	8.149
2005	7.591

In Exercises 62 and 63, do the following.

(a) Use 12 data points (with $x = 1$ corresponding to January) to find a periodic model of the data.

*U.S. Bureau of Labor Statistics.

(b) What is the period of the function found in part (a)? Is this reasonable?

(c) Plot 24 data points (two years) and graph the function from part (a) on the same screen. Is the function a good model in the second year?

(d) Use the 24 data points in part (c) to find another periodic model for the data.

(e) What is the period of the function in part (d)? Does its graph fit the data well?

62. The table shows the average monthly temperature in Chicago, IL, based on data from 1971 to 2000.*

Month	Temperature (°F)
Jan	22.0
Feb	27.0
Mar	37.3
Apr	47.8
May	58.7
Jun	68.2
Jul	73.3
Aug	71.7
Sep	63.8
Oct	52.1
Nov	39.3
Dec	27.4

63. The table shows the average monthly precipitation (in inches) in San Francisco, CA, based on data from 1971 to 2000.†

Month	Precipitation
Jan	4.45
Feb	4.01
Mar	3.26
Apr	1.17
May	.38
Jun	.11
Jul	.03
Aug	.07
Sep	.2
Oct	1.04
Nov	2.49
Dec	2.89

*National Climatic Data Center.
†National Climatic Data Center.

THINKERS

64. On the basis of the results of Exercises 37–42, under what conditions on the constants a, k, h, d, r, s does it appear that the graph of

$$f(t) = a \sin(kt + h) + d \cos(rt + s)$$

coincides with the graph of the function

$$g(t) = A \sin(bt + c)?$$

65. A grandfather clock has a pendulum length of k meters and its swing is given (as in Exercise 57) by the function

$$f(t) = .25 \sin(\omega t), \text{ where}$$

$$\omega = \sqrt{\frac{9.8}{k}}.$$

(a) Find k such that the period of the pendulum is 2 seconds.

(b) The temperature in the summer months causes the pendulum to increase its length by .01%. How much time will the clock lose in June, July, and August? [*Hint:* These three months have a total of 92 days (7,948,800 seconds). If k is increased by .01%, what is $f(2)$?]

6.5   Other Trigonometric Functions

Section Objectives
- Define and graph the cotangent, secant and cosecant functions.
- Use the point-in-the-plane description of these functions.
- Apply the periodicity and Pythagorean identities for these functions.

This section introduces three more trigonometric functions. It is divided into three parts, each of which may be covered earlier, as shown in the table.

Subsection of Section 6.6	May be covered at the end of
Part I	Section 6.2
Part II	Section 6.3
Part III	Section 6.4

PART I: Definitions and Descriptions

The three remaining trigonometric functions are defined in terms of sine and cosine, as follows.

Definition of Cotangent, Secant, and Cosecant Functions

Name of Function	Value of Function at t Is Denoted	Rule of Function
contangent	cot t	$\cot t = \dfrac{\cos t}{\sin t}$
secant	sec t	$\sec t = \dfrac{1}{\cos t}$
cosecant	csc t	$\csc t = \dfrac{1}{\sin t}$

The domain of each function consists of all real numbers for which the denominator is not 0. The graphs of the sine and cosine function in Section 6.4 show that $\sin t = 0$ only when $t = 0$, $\pm \pi$, $\pm 2\pi$, $\pm 3\pi$, . . . and $\cos t = 0$ only when $t = \pm \pi/2$, $\pm 3\pi/2$, $\pm 5\pi/2$, ... So the domains of cotangent, secant, and cosecant are as follows.

Function	Domain
$f(t) = \cot t$	All real numbers except 0, $\pm \pi$, $\pm 2\pi$, $\pm 3\pi$, . . .
$g(t) = \sec t$	All real numbers except $\pm \pi/2$, $\pm 3\pi/2$, $\pm 5\pi/2$, . . .
$h(t) = \csc t$	All real numbers except 0, $\pm \pi$, $\pm 2\pi$, $\pm 3\pi$, . . .

The values of these functions may be approximated on a calculator by using the SIN and COS keys. For instance,

$$\cot(-3.1) = \frac{\cos(-3.1)}{\sin(-3.1)} \approx 24.0288, \qquad \sec 7 = \frac{1}{\cos 7} \approx 1.3264,$$

$$\csc 18.5 = \frac{1}{\sin 18.5} \approx -2.9199.$$

The cotangent function can also be evaluated with the TAN key, by using this fact:

$$\cot t = \frac{\cos t}{\sin t} = \frac{1}{\dfrac{\sin t}{\cos t}} = \frac{1}{\tan t}.^*$$

For example,

$$\cot(-5) = \frac{1}{\tan(-5)} \approx .2958.$$

CAUTION

The calculator keys labeled SIN^{-1}, COS^{-1}, and TAN^{-1} do *not* denote the functions $1/\sin t$, $1/\cos t$, and $1/\tan t$. For instance, if you key in

$$COS^{-1} \quad 7 \quad ENTER$$

you will get an error message, not the number sec 7, and if you key in

$$TAN^{-1} \quad -5 \quad ENTER$$

you will obtain -1.3734, which is *not* $\cot(-5)$.

EXAMPLE 1

A batter hits a baseball. The ball is three feet above the ground and leaves the bat with an initial velocity of 100 feet per second at an angle of t radians from the horizontal. According to physics, the ball reaches a maximum height of

$$\frac{156.25 \tan^2 t}{\sec^2 t} + 3 \text{ feet.}^*$$

What is the maximum height of the ball when it leaves the bat at an angle of .6 radians?

---

*This identity is valid except for $t = \pm \pi/2$, $\pm 3\pi/2$, $\pm 5\pi/2$, ... At these values, $\cos t = 0$ and $\sin t = \pm 1$, so $\cot t = 0$, but $\tan t$ is not defined.

*Wind resistance is ignored here.

SOLUTION   Use a calculator to evaluate the formula for $t = .6$. The maximum height is

$$\frac{156.25 \tan^2 .6}{\sec^2 .6} + 3 = \frac{156.25 \tan^2 .6}{\dfrac{1}{\cos^2 .6}} + 3 = 156.25(\tan .6)^2(\cos .6)^2 + 3$$

$$\approx 52.816 \text{ feet.} \qquad \blacksquare$$

These new trigonometric functions may be evaluated exactly at any integer multiple of $\pi/3$, $\pi/4$, or $\pi/6$.

EXAMPLE 2

Evaluate the cotangent, secant, and cosecant functions at $t = \pi/3$.

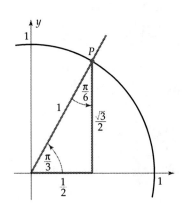

Figure 6–46

SOLUTION   Let P be the point where the terminal side of an angle of $\pi/3$ radians in standard position meets the unit circle (Figure 6–46). Draw the vertical line from P to the x-axis, forming a right triangle with hypotenuse 1, angles of $\pi/3$ and $\pi/6$ radians, and sides of lengths of $1/2$ and $\sqrt{3}/2$ as explained on page 445. Then P has coordinates $(1/2, \sqrt{3}/2)$, and by definition,

$$\sin \frac{\pi}{3} = y\text{-coordinate of } P = \sqrt{3}/2,$$

$$\cos \frac{\pi}{3} = x\text{-coordinate of } P = 1/2.$$

Therefore,

$$\csc \frac{\pi}{3} = \frac{1}{\sin(\pi/3)} = \frac{1}{\sqrt{3}/2} = \frac{2}{\sqrt{3}} = \frac{2\sqrt{3}}{3},$$

$$\sec \frac{\pi}{3} = \frac{1}{\cos(\pi/3)} = \frac{1}{1/2} = 2,$$

$$\cot \frac{\pi}{3} = \frac{\cos(\pi/3)}{\sin(\pi/3)} = \frac{1/2}{\sqrt{3}/2} = \frac{1}{\sqrt{3}} = \frac{\sqrt{3}}{3}. \qquad \blacksquare$$

ALTERNATE DESCRIPTIONS

The point-in-the-plane description of sine, cosine, and tangent readily extends to these new functions.

Point-in-the-Plane Description

Let t be a real number and (x, y) any point (except the origin) on the terminal side of an angle of t radians in standard position. Let

$$r = \sqrt{x^2 + y^2}.$$

Then,

$$\cot t = \frac{x}{y}, \qquad \sec t = \frac{r}{x}, \qquad \csc t = \frac{r}{y}$$

for each number t in the domain of the given function.

These statements are proved by using the similar descriptions of sine and cosine. For instance,

$$\cot t = \frac{\cos t}{\sin t} = \frac{x/r}{y/r} = \frac{x}{y}.$$

The proofs of the other statements are similar.

EXAMPLE 3

Evaluate all six trigonometric functions at $t = 3\pi/4$.

SOLUTION   The terminal side of an angle of $3\pi/4$ radians in standard position lies on the line $y = -x$, as shown in Figure 6–47. We shall use the point $(-1, 1)$ on this line to compute the function values. In this case,

$$r = \sqrt{x^2 + y^2} = \sqrt{(-1)^2 + 1^2} = \sqrt{2}.$$

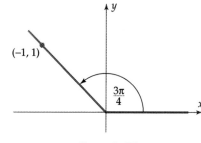

(–1, 1)

$\frac{3\pi}{4}$

Figure 6–47

Therefore,

$$\sin \frac{3\pi}{4} = \frac{y}{r} = \frac{1}{\sqrt{2}} = \frac{\sqrt{2}}{2} \qquad \cos \frac{3\pi}{4} = \frac{x}{r} = \frac{-1}{\sqrt{2}} = \frac{-\sqrt{2}}{2}$$

$$\tan \frac{3\pi}{4} = \frac{y}{x} = \frac{1}{-1} = -1 \qquad \csc \frac{3\pi}{4} = \frac{r}{y} = \frac{\sqrt{2}}{1} = \sqrt{2}$$

$$\sec \frac{3\pi}{4} = \frac{r}{x} = \frac{\sqrt{2}}{-1} = -\sqrt{2} \qquad \cot \frac{3\pi}{4} = \frac{x}{y} = \frac{-1}{1} = -1.$$ ∎

PART II: Algebra and Identities

We begin by noting the relationship between the cotangent and tangent functions.

Reciprocal
Identities

> The cotangent and tangent functions are reciprocals; that is,
>
> $$\cot t = \frac{1}{\tan t} \qquad \text{and} \qquad \tan t = \frac{1}{\cot t}$$
>
> for every number t in the domain of both functions.

The first of these identities was proved on page 497, and the second is proved similarly (Exercise 49).

Period of Secant,
Cosecant, Cotangent

The secant and cosecant functions are periodic with period 2π and the cotangent function is periodic with period π. In symbols,

$$\sec(t + 2\pi) = \sec t, \qquad \csc(t + 2\pi) = \csc t,$$

$$\cot(t + \pi) = \cot t$$

for every number t in the domain of the given function.

The proof of these statements uses the fact that each of these functions is the reciprocal of a function whose period is known. For instance,

$$\csc(t + 2\pi) = \frac{1}{\sin(t + 2\pi)} = \frac{1}{\sin t} = \csc t,$$

$$\cot(t + \pi) = \frac{1}{\tan(t + \pi)} = \frac{1}{\tan t} = \cot t.$$

The other details are left as an exercise.

Pythagorean
Identities

For every number t in the domain of both functions,

$$1 + \tan^2 t = \sec^2 t$$

and

$$1 + \cot^2 t = \csc^2 t.$$

Proof By the definitions of the functions and the Pythagorean identity $(\sin^2 t + \cos^2 t = 1)$, we have

$$1 + \tan^2 t = 1 + \frac{\sin^2 t}{\cos^2 t} = \frac{\cos^2 t + \sin^2 t}{\cos^2 t} = \frac{1}{\cos^2 t} = \left(\frac{1}{\cos t}\right)^2 = \sec^2 t.$$

The second identity is proved similarly. ∎

EXAMPLE 4

Simplify the expression $\dfrac{30\cos^3 t \sin t}{6\sin^2 t \cos t}$, assuming that $\sin t \neq 0$, $\cos t \neq 0$.

SOLUTION

$$\frac{30\cos^3 t \sin t}{6\sin^2 t \cos t} = \frac{5\cos^3 t \sin t}{\cos t \sin^2 t} = \frac{5\cos^2 t}{\sin t} = 5\frac{\cos t}{\sin t}\cos t = 5\cot t \cos t. \quad\blacksquare$$

EXAMPLE 5

Assume that $\cos t \neq 0$ and simplify $\cos^2 t + \cos^2 t \tan^2 t$.

SOLUTION

$$\cos^2 t + \cos^2 t \tan^2 t = \cos^2 t (1 + \tan^2 t) = \cos^2 t \sec^2 t = \cos^2 t \cdot \frac{1}{\cos^2 t} = 1. \quad \blacksquare$$

EXAMPLE 6

If $\tan t = 3/4$ and $\sin t < 0$, find $\cot t$, $\cos t$, $\sin t$, $\sec t$, and $\csc t$.

SOLUTION   First we have $\cot t = 1/\tan t = 1/(3/4) = 4/3$. Next we use the Pythagorean identity to obtain

$$\sec^2 t = 1 + \tan^2 t = 1 + \left(\frac{3}{4}\right)^2 = 1 + \frac{9}{16} = \frac{25}{16}$$

$$\sec t = \pm\sqrt{\frac{25}{16}} = \pm\frac{5}{4}$$

$$\frac{1}{\cos t} = \pm\frac{5}{4} \quad \text{or, equivalently,} \quad \cos t = \pm\frac{4}{5}.$$

Since $\sin t$ is given as negative and $\tan t = \sin t/\cos t$ is positive, $\cos t$ must be negative. Hence, $\cos t = -4/5$. Consequently,

$$\frac{3}{4} = \tan t = \frac{\sin t}{\cos t} = \frac{\sin t}{(-4/5)}$$

so

$$\sin t = \left(-\frac{4}{5}\right)\left(\frac{3}{4}\right) = -\frac{3}{5}.$$

Therefore,

$$\sec t = \frac{1}{\cos t} = \frac{1}{(-4/5)} = -\frac{5}{4} \quad \text{and} \quad \csc t = \frac{1}{\sin t} = \frac{1}{(-3/5)} = -\frac{5}{3}. \quad \blacksquare$$

PART III: Graphs

The graph of the secant function is shown in red in Figure 6–48.

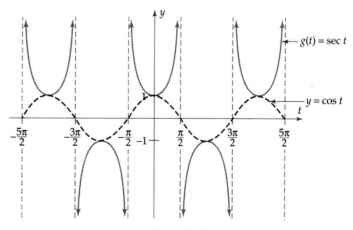

Figure 6–48

The shape of the secant graph can be understood by looking at the graph of cosine (blue in Figure 6–48) and noting these facts:

1. $\sec t = 1/\cos t$ is not defined when $\cos t = 0$, that is, when $t = \pm \pi/2$, $\pm 3\pi/2$, $\pm 5\pi/2$, and so on.

2. The graph of $\sec t$ has a vertical asymptote at $t = \pm \pi/2$, $\pm 3\pi/2$, $\pm 5\pi/2$, ... The reason is that when $\cos t$ is close to 0 (graph close to t-axis), then $\sec t = 1/\cos t$ is very large in absolute value,* so its graph is far from the axis.

3. When $\cos t$ is near 1 or -1 (that is, when t is near 0, $\pm \pi$, $\pm 2\pi$, $\pm 3\pi$, ...), then so is $\sec t = 1/\cos t$.

The graphs of $h(t) = \csc t = 1/\sin t$ and $f(t) = \cot t = 1/\tan t$ can be obtained in a similar fashion (Figure 6–49).

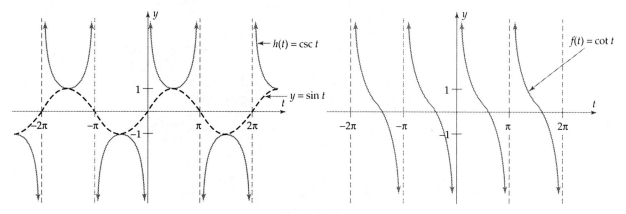

Figure 6–49

*See the Big-Little Principle on page 288.

EXERCISES 6.5

Note: The arrangement of the exercises corresponds to the subsections of this section.

Part I: Definitions and Descriptions

In Exercises 1–6, determine the quadrant containing the terminal side of an angle of t radians in standard position under the given conditions.

1. $\cos t > 0$ and $\sin t < 0$

2. $\sin t < 0$ and $\tan t > 0$

3. $\sec t < 0$ and $\cot t < 0$

4. $\csc t < 0$ and $\sec t > 0$

5. $\sec t > 0$ and $\cot t < 0$

6. $\sin t > 0$ and $\sec t < 0$

In Exercises 7–16, evaluate all six trigonometric functions at t, where the given point lies on the terminal side of an angle of t radians in standard position.

7. $(3, 4)$

8. $(0, 6)$

9. $(-5, 12)$

10. $(-2, -3)$

11. $(-1/5, 1)$

12. $(4/5, -3/5)$

13. $(\sqrt{2}, \sqrt{3})$

14. $(-2\sqrt{3}, \sqrt{3})$

15. $(1 + \sqrt{2}, 3)$

16. $(1 + \sqrt{3}, 1 - \sqrt{3})$

17. Suppose the batter in Example 1 hits a popup (the ball leaves the bat at an angle of 1.4 radians). What is the maximum height of the ball?

Exercises 18–20 deal with the path of a projectile (such as a baseball, a rocket, or an arrow). If the projectile is fired with an initial velocity of v feet per second at angle of t radians and its initial height is k feet, then the path of the projectile is given by

$$y = \left(\frac{-16}{v^2} \sec^2 t\right)x^2 + (\tan t)x + k.*$$

You can think of the projectile as being fired in the direction of the x-axis from the point (0, k) on the y-axis.

18. (a) Find a viewing window that shows the path of a projectile that is fired from a 20-foot high platform at an initial velocity of 120 feet per second at an angle of .8 radians.
(b) What is the maximum height reached by the projectile?
(c) How far down range does the projectile hit the ground?

19. Do Exercise 18 for a projectile that is fired from ground level at an initial velocity of 80 feet per second at an angle of .4 radians.

20. Do Exercise 18 for a projectile that is fired from a 40-foot high platform at an initial velocity of 125 feet per second at an angle of 1.2 radians.

In Exercises 21–25, evaluate all six trigonometric functions at the given number without using a calculator.

21. $\frac{4\pi}{3}$ **22.** $-\frac{7\pi}{6}$ **23.** $\frac{7\pi}{4}$

24. $\frac{11\pi}{3}$ **25.** $\frac{-11\pi}{4}$

26. Fill in the missing entries in the following table. Give exact answers, not decimal approximations.

27. Find the average rate of change of $f(t) = \cot t$ from $t = 1$ to $t = 3$.

28. Find the average rate of change of $g(t) = \csc t$ from $t = 2$ to $t = 3$.

29. (a) Find the average rate of change of $f(t) = \tan t$ from $t = 2$ to $t = 2 + h$, for each of these values of h: .01, .001, .0001, and .00001.
(b) Compare your answers in part (a) with the number $(\sec 2)^2$. What would you guess that the instantaneous rate of change of $f(t) = \tan t$ is at $t = 2$?

Part II: Algebra and Identities

In Exercises 30–36, perform the indicated operations, then simplify your answers by using appropriate definitions and identities.

30. $\tan t (\cos t - \csc t)$ **31.** $\cos t \sin t (\csc t + \sec t)$

32. $(1 + \cot t)^2$ **33.** $(1 - \sec t)^2$

34. $(\sin t - \csc t)^2$

35. $(\cot t - \tan t)(\cot^2 t + 1 + \tan^2 t)$

36. $(\sin t + \csc t)(\sin^2 t + \csc^2 t - 1)$

In Exercises 37–42, factor and simplify the given expression.

37. $\sec t \csc t - \csc^2 t$ **38.** $\tan^2 t - \cot^2 t$

39. $\tan^4 t - \sec^4 t$ **40.** $4 \sec^2 t + 8 \sec t + 4$

41. $\cos^3 t - \sec^3 t$ **42.** $\csc^4 t + 4 \csc^2 t - 5$

In Exercises 43–48, simplify the given expression. Assume that all denominators are nonzero and all quantities under radicals are nonnegative.

43. $\frac{\cos^2 t \sin t}{\sin^2 t \cos t}$ **44.** $\frac{\sec^2 t + 2 \sec t + 1}{\sec t}$

45. $\frac{4 \tan t \sec t + 2 \sec t}{6 \sin t \sec t + 2 \sec t}$ **46.** $\frac{\sec^2 t \csc t}{\csc^2 t \sec t}$

47. $(2 + \sqrt{\tan t})(2 - \sqrt{\tan t})$

t	0	$\frac{\pi}{6}$	$\frac{\pi}{4}$	$\frac{\pi}{3}$	$\frac{\pi}{2}$	$\frac{2\pi}{3}$	$\frac{3\pi}{4}$	$\frac{5\pi}{6}$	π	$\frac{3\pi}{2}$
sin t										
cos t										
tan t					—					—
cot t	—							—		
sec t					—					—
csc t	—								—	

*Wind resistance is ignored in this equation.

48. $\dfrac{6 \tan t \sin t - 3 \sin t}{9 \sin^2 t + 3 \sin t}$

In Exercises 49–54, prove the given identity.

49. $\tan t = \dfrac{1}{\cot t}$ [Hint: See page 497.]

50. $\sec(t + 2\pi) = \sec t$ [Hint: See page 500.]

51. $1 + \cot^2 t = \csc^2 t$ [Hint: Look at the proof of the similar identity on page 500]

52. $\cot(-t) = -\cot t$ [Hint: Express the left side in terms of sine and cosine; then use the negative angle identities and express the result in terms of cotangent.]

53. $\sec(-t) = \sec t$ [Adapt the hint for Exercise 52.]

54. $\csc(-t) = -\csc t$

In Exercises 55–60, find the values of all six trigonometric functions at t if the given conditions are true.

55. $\cos t = -1/2$ and $\sin t > 0$
[Hint: $\sin^2 t + \cos^2 t = 1$.]

56. $\cos t = \dfrac{1}{2}$ and $\sin t < 0$

57. $\cos t = 0$ and $\sin t = 1$

58. $\sin t = -2/3$ and $\sec t > 0$

59. $\sec t = -13/5$ and $\tan t < 0$

60. $\csc t = 8$ and $\cos t < 0$

Part III: Graphs

In Exercises 61–64, use graphs to determine whether the equation could possibly be an identity or is definitely not an identity.

61. $\tan t = \cot\left(\dfrac{\pi}{2} - t\right)$ **62.** $\dfrac{\cos t}{\cos(t - \pi/2)} = \cot t$

63. $\dfrac{\sin t}{1 - \cos t} = \cot t$

64. $\dfrac{\sec t + \csc t}{1 + \tan t} = \csc t$

65. Show graphically that the equation $\sec t = t$ has infinitely many solutions, but none between $-\pi/2$ and $\pi/2$.

THINKERS

66. In the diagram of the unit circle in the figure, find six line segments whose respective lengths are $\sin t$, $\cos t$, $\tan t$, $\cot t$, $\sec t$, $\csc t$. [Hint: $\sin t = $ length CA. Why? Note that OC has length 1 and various right triangles in the figure are similar.]

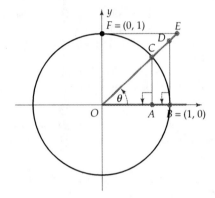

67. In the figure for Exercise 66, find the following areas in terms of θ.

(a) triangle OCA
(b) triangle ODB
(c) circular segment OCB

Chapter 7

TRIGONOMETRIC IDENTITIES

© Stefano Torrione/Getty Images

Chapter Outline

Interdependence of Sections

7.1   Addition and Subtraction

Section Objectives

■ Use the addition and subtraction identities to evaluate trigonometric functions.

■ Use the addition and subtraction identities to prove other identities.

■ Use the cofunction identities to prove other identities.

A common student ERROR is to write

$$\sin\left(x + \frac{\pi}{6}\right) = \sin x + \sin \frac{\pi}{6} = \sin x + \frac{1}{2}.$$

GRAPHING EXPLORATION

Verify graphically that the equation above is NOT an identity by graphing $y = \sin(x + \pi/6)$ and $y = \sin x + 1/2$ on the same screen.

The exploration shows that "$\sin(x + y) = \sin x + \sin y$" is NOT an identity (because it's false when $y = \pi/6$). There is an identity that enables us to express $\sin(x + y)$, but it is a bit more complicated, as we now see.

Addition and Subtraction Identities

$$\sin(x + y) = \sin x \cos y + \cos x \sin y$$

$$\sin(x - y) = \sin x \cos y - \cos x \sin y$$

$$\cos(x + y) = \cos x \cos y - \sin x \sin y$$

$$\cos(x - y) = \cos x \cos y + \sin x \sin y$$

The addition and subtraction identities are probably the most important of all the trigonometric identities. Before reading their proofs at the end of this section, you should become familiar with the examples and special cases below.

EXAMPLE 1

Use the addition and subtraction identities to find the *exact* values of

(a) $\sin\left(\dfrac{\pi}{12}\right)$ (b) $\cos\left(\dfrac{7\pi}{12}\right)$.

SOLUTION   The key here is to write $\pi/12$ and $7\pi/12$ as a sum or difference of two numbers whose sine and cosine are known.

(a) Note that

$$\frac{\pi}{12} = \frac{4\pi}{12} - \frac{3\pi}{12} = \frac{\pi}{3} - \frac{\pi}{4}.$$

we apply the subtraction identity for sine with $x = \pi/3$ and $y = \pi/4$.

$$\sin\left(\frac{\pi}{12}\right) = \sin\left(\frac{\pi}{3} - \frac{\pi}{4}\right)$$

$$= \sin\frac{\pi}{3}\cos\frac{\pi}{4} - \cos\frac{\pi}{3}\sin\frac{\pi}{4}$$

$$= \frac{\sqrt{3}}{2} \cdot \frac{\sqrt{2}}{2} - \frac{1}{2} \cdot \frac{\sqrt{2}}{2}$$

$$= \frac{\sqrt{3}\sqrt{2}}{4} - \frac{\sqrt{2}}{4} = \frac{\sqrt{6}}{4} - \frac{\sqrt{2}}{4} = \frac{\sqrt{6} - \sqrt{2}}{4}$$

(b) In this case, we see that $\dfrac{7\pi}{12} = \dfrac{4\pi}{12} + \dfrac{3\pi}{12} = \dfrac{\pi}{3} + \dfrac{\pi}{4}$. So we apply the addition identity for cosine with $x = \pi/3$ and $y = \pi/4$.

$$\cos\left(\frac{7\pi}{12}\right) = \cos\left(\frac{\pi}{3} + \frac{\pi}{4}\right)$$

$$= \cos\frac{\pi}{3}\cos\frac{\pi}{4} - \sin\frac{\pi}{3}\sin\frac{\pi}{4}$$

$$= \frac{1}{2} \cdot \frac{\sqrt{2}}{2} - \frac{\sqrt{3}}{2} \cdot \frac{\sqrt{2}}{2}$$

$$= \frac{\sqrt{2}}{4} - \frac{\sqrt{3}\sqrt{2}}{4} = \frac{\sqrt{2}}{4} - \frac{\sqrt{6}}{4} = \frac{\sqrt{2} - \sqrt{6}}{4}. \qquad \blacksquare$$

EXAMPLE 2

Find $\sin(\pi - y)$.

SOLUTION   Apply the subtraction identity for sine with $x = \pi$.

$$\sin(\pi - y) = \sin \pi \cos y - \cos \pi \sin y$$
$$= (0)(\cos y) - (-1)(\sin y)$$
$$= \sin y. \qquad \blacksquare$$

EXAMPLE 3

Show that the difference quotient of the function $f(x) = \sin x$ is given by:

$$\frac{f(x + h) - f(x)}{h} = \sin x \left(\frac{\cos h - 1}{h} \right) + \cos x \left(\frac{\sin h}{h} \right).$$

[This fact is needed in calculus.]

SOLUTION   Use the addition identity for $\sin(x + y)$ with $y = h$.

$$\frac{f(x + h) - f(x)}{h} = \frac{\sin(x + h) - \sin x}{h}$$

$$= \frac{\sin x \cos h + \cos x \sin h - \sin x}{h}$$

$$= \frac{\sin x(\cos h - 1) + \cos x \sin h}{h}$$

$$= \sin x \left(\frac{\cos h - 1}{h} \right) + \cos x \left(\frac{\sin h}{h} \right). \qquad \blacksquare$$

EXAMPLE 4

Prove the identity:

$$\frac{\cos(x + y)}{\cos x \cos y} = 1 - \tan x \tan y.$$

SOLUTION   Begin with the left side and apply the addition identity for cosine to the numerator.

$$\frac{\cos(x + y)}{\cos x \cos y} = \frac{\cos x \cos y - \sin x \sin y}{\cos x \cos y}$$

$$= \frac{\cos x \cos y}{\cos x \cos y} - \frac{\sin x \sin y}{\cos x \cos y}$$

$$= 1 - \frac{\sin x}{\cos x} \cdot \frac{\sin y}{\cos y} = 1 - \tan x \tan y. \qquad \blacksquare$$

EXAMPLE 5

Prove that

$$\cos x \cos y = \frac{1}{2}[\cos(x + y) + \cos(x - y)].$$

SOLUTION   We begin with the more complicated right side and use the addition and subtraction identities for cosine to transform it into the left side.

$$\frac{1}{2}[\cos(x + y) + \cos(x - y)] = \frac{1}{2}[(\cos x \cos y - \sin x \sin y)$$
$$+ (\cos x \cos y + \sin x \sin y)]$$
$$= \frac{1}{2}(\cos x \cos y + \cos x \cos y)$$
$$= \frac{1}{2}(2 \cos x \cos y) = \cos x \cos y. \quad \blacksquare$$

The addition and subtraction identities for sine and cosine can be used to obtain the following identities, as outlined in Exercise 38.

Addition and Subtraction Identities for Tangent

$$\tan(x + y) = \frac{\tan x + \tan y}{1 - \tan x \tan y}$$

$$\tan(x - y) = \frac{\tan x - \tan y}{1 + \tan x \tan y}$$

It is sometimes convenient to say that x is a number *in the first quadrant* if $0 < x < \pi/2$, that x is a number *in the second quadrant* if $\pi/2 < x < \pi$, and so on.

EXAMPLE 6

Suppose x is a number in the first quadrant and y is a number in the third quadrant. If $\sin x = 3/4$ and $\cos y = -1/3$, find the exact values of $\sin(x + y)$ and $\tan(x + y)$ and determine in which quadrant $x + y$ lies.

SOLUTION   We want to apply the addition identities for sine and tangent. To do so we must first find $\cos x$, $\tan x$, $\sin y$ and $\tan y$. Using the Pythagorean identity and the fact that $\cos x$ and $\tan x$ are positive when $0 < x < \pi/2$, we have

$$\cos x = \sqrt{1 - \sin^2 x} = \sqrt{1 - \left(\frac{3}{4}\right)^2} = \sqrt{1 - \frac{9}{16}} = \sqrt{\frac{7}{16}} = \frac{\sqrt{7}}{4},$$

$$\tan x = \frac{\sin x}{\cos x} = \frac{3/4}{\sqrt{7}/4} = \frac{3}{4} \cdot \frac{4}{\sqrt{7}} = \frac{3}{\sqrt{7}} = \frac{3\sqrt{7}}{7}.$$

Since y lies between π and $3\pi/2$, its sine is negative; hence,

$$\sin y = -\sqrt{1 - \cos^2 y} = -\sqrt{1 - \left(-\frac{1}{3}\right)^2} = -\sqrt{\frac{8}{9}} = -\frac{\sqrt{8}}{3} = -\frac{2\sqrt{2}}{3},$$

$$\tan y = \frac{\sin y}{\cos y} = \frac{-2\sqrt{2}/3}{-1/3} = \frac{-2\sqrt{2}}{3} \cdot \frac{3}{-1} = 2\sqrt{2}.$$

The addition identities for sine and tangent now show that

$$\sin(x + y) = \sin x \cos y + \cos x \sin y$$

$$= \frac{3}{4} \cdot \frac{-1}{3} + \frac{\sqrt{7}}{4} \cdot \frac{-2\sqrt{2}}{3} = \frac{-3}{12} - \frac{2\sqrt{14}}{12} = \frac{-3 - 2\sqrt{14}}{12},$$

$$\tan(x + y) = \frac{\tan x + \tan y}{1 - \tan x \tan y}$$

$$= \frac{\dfrac{3\sqrt{7}}{7} + 2\sqrt{2}}{1 - \left(\dfrac{3\sqrt{7}}{7}\right)(2\sqrt{2})} = \frac{\dfrac{3\sqrt{7} + 14\sqrt{2}}{7}}{\dfrac{7 - 6\sqrt{14}}{7}} = \frac{3\sqrt{7} + 14\sqrt{2}}{7 - 6\sqrt{14}}.$$

The numerator of $\sin(x + y)$ is negative and the denominator of $\tan(x + y)$ is negative, as you can easily verify, so the sine and tangent of $x + y$ are negative numbers. The fourth quadrant is the only one in which both sine and tangent are negative (see the sign chart in Exercise 63 on page 451). Hence, $x + y$ must be in the fourth quadrant, that is, in the interval $(3\pi/2, 2\pi)$. ∎

COFUNCTION IDENTITIES

Other special cases of the addition and subtraction identities are the cofunction identities:

Cofunction Identities

$\sin x = \cos\left(\dfrac{\pi}{2} - x\right)$	$\cos x = \sin\left(\dfrac{\pi}{2} - x\right)$
$\tan x = \cot\left(\dfrac{\pi}{2} - x\right)$	$\cot x = \tan\left(\dfrac{\pi}{2} - x\right)$
$\sec x = \csc\left(\dfrac{\pi}{2} - x\right)$	$\csc x = \sec\left(\dfrac{\pi}{2} - x\right)$

The first confunction identity is proved by using the identity for $\cos(x - y)$ with $\pi/2$ in place of x and x in place of y.

$$\cos\left(\frac{\pi}{2} - x\right) = \cos\frac{\pi}{2}\cos x + \sin\frac{\pi}{2}\sin x = (0)(\cos x) + (1)(\sin x) = \sin x.$$

Since the first cofunction identity is valid for *every* number x, it is also valid with the number $\pi/2 - x$ in place of x.

$$\sin\left(\frac{\pi}{2} - x\right) = \cos\left[\frac{\pi}{2} - \left(\frac{\pi}{2} - x\right)\right] = \cos x.$$

Thus, we have proved the second cofunction identity. The others now follow from these two. For instance,

$$\tan\left(\frac{\pi}{2} - x\right) = \frac{\sin[(\pi/2) - x]}{\cos[(\pi/2) - x]} = \frac{\cos x}{\sin x} = \cot x.$$

EXAMPLE 7

Verify that $\dfrac{\cos(x - \pi/2)}{\cos x} = \tan x$.

SOLUTION   Beginning on the left side, we see that the term $\cos(x - \pi/2)$ looks almost, but not quite, like the term $\cos(\pi/2 - x)$ in the cofunction identity. But note that $-(x - \pi/2) = \pi/2 - x$. Therefore,

$$\frac{\cos\left(x - \dfrac{\pi}{2}\right)}{\cos x} = \frac{\cos\left[-\left(x - \dfrac{\pi}{2}\right)\right]}{\cos x} \qquad \text{[Negative angle identity with } x - \dfrac{\pi}{2} \text{ in place of } x]$$

$$= \frac{\cos\left(\dfrac{\pi}{2} - x\right)}{\cos x}$$

$$= \frac{\sin x}{\cos x} \qquad \text{[Cofunction identity]}$$

$$= \tan x. \qquad \text{[Reciprocal identity]} \qquad \blacksquare$$

PROOF OF THE ADDITION AND SUBTRACTION IDENTITIES

We first prove the subtraction identity for cosine:

$$\cos(x - y) = \cos x \cos y + \sin x \sin y.$$

If $x = y$, then this is true by the Pythagorean identity:

$$\cos(x - x) = \cos 0 = 1 = \cos^2 x + \sin^2 x = \cos x \cos x + \sin x \sin x.$$

Next we prove the identity in the case when $x > y$. Let P be the point where the terminal side of an angle of x radians in standard position meets the unit circle and let Q be the point where the terminal side of an angle of y radians in standard position meets the circle, as shown in Figure 7–1. According to the definitions of sine and cosine, P has coordinates $(\cos x, \sin x)$ and Q has coordinates $(\cos y, \sin y)$.

Using the distance formula, we have

Distance from P to Q

$$= \sqrt{(\cos x - \cos y)^2 + (\sin x - \sin y)^2}$$

$$= \sqrt{\cos^2 x - 2 \cos x \cos y + \cos^2 y + \sin^2 x - 2 \sin x \sin y + \sin^2 y}$$

$$= \sqrt{(\cos^2 x + \sin^2 x) + (\cos^2 y + \sin^2 y) - 2 \cos x \cos y - 2 \sin x \sin y}$$

$$= \sqrt{1 + 1 - 2 \cos x \cos y - 2 \sin x \sin y}$$

$$= \sqrt{2 - 2 \cos x \cos y - 2 \sin x \sin y}.$$

The angle QOP formed by the two terminal sides has radian measure $x - y$ (Figure 7.1). Rotate this angle clockwise until side OQ lies on the horizontal axis, as shown in Figure 7–2. Angle QOP is now in standard position, and its terminal side meets the unit circle at P. Since angle QOP has radian measure $x - y$, the

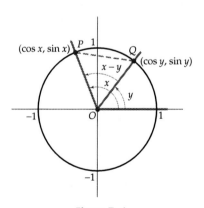

Figure 7–1

definitions of sine and cosine show that the point P, in this new location, has co-ordinates $(\cos(x - y), \sin(x - y))$. Q now has coordinates $(1, 0)$.

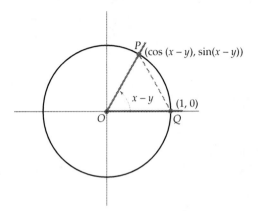

Figure 7–2

Using the coordinates of P and Q *after* the angle is rotated shows that

$$\text{Distance from } P \text{ to } Q = \sqrt{[\cos(x - y) - 1]^2 + [\sin(x - y) - 0]^2}$$

$$= \sqrt{\cos^2(x - y) - 2\cos(x - y) + 1 + \sin^2(x - y)}$$

$$= \sqrt{\cos^2(x - y) + \sin^2(x - y) - 2\cos(x - y) + 1}$$

$$= \sqrt{1 - 2\cos(x - y) + 1} \qquad \text{[Pythagorean identity]}$$

$$= \sqrt{2 - 2\cos(x - y)}.$$

The two expressions for the distance from P to Q must be equal. Hence,

$$\sqrt{2 - 2\cos(x - y)} = \sqrt{2 - 2\cos x \cos y - 2\sin x \sin y}.$$

Squaring both sides of this equation and simplifying the result yields

$$2 - 2\cos(x - y) = 2 - 2\cos x \cos y - 2\sin x \sin y$$

$$-2\cos(x - y) = -2(\cos x \cos y + \sin x \sin y)$$

$$\cos(x - y) = \cos x \cos y + \sin x \sin y.$$

This completes the proof of the subtraction identity for cosine when $x > y$. If $y > x$, then the proof just given is valid with the roles of x and y interchanged; it shows that

$$\cos(y - x) = \cos y \cos x + \sin y \sin x$$

$$= \cos x \cos y + \sin x \sin y.$$

The negative angle identity with $x - y$ in place of x shows that

$$\cos(x - y) = \cos[-(x - y)] = \cos(y - x).$$

Combining this fact with the previous one shows that

$$\cos(x - y) = \cos x \cos y + \sin x \sin y$$

in this case also. Therefore, the subtraction identity for cosine is proved.

Next, we prove the addition identity for cosine:

$$\mathbf{\cos(x + y) = \cos x \cos y - \sin x \sin y.}$$

The proof uses the subtraction identity for cosine just proved and the fact that $x + y = x - (-y)$.

$$\cos(x + y) = \cos[x - (-y)]$$

$$= \cos x \cos(-y) + \sin x \sin(-y) \qquad \text{[Subtraction identity for cosine]}$$

$$= \cos x \cos y + \sin x(-\sin y) \qquad \text{[Negative angle identities]}$$

$$= \cos x \cos y - \sin x \sin y.$$

The proofs of the addition and subtraction identities for sine are in Exercises 36 and 37.

EXERCISES 7.1

In Exercises 1–12, find the exact value.

1. $\cos \dfrac{\pi}{12}$ **2.** $\tan \dfrac{\pi}{12}$ **3.** $\sin \dfrac{5\pi}{12}$

4. $\cos \dfrac{5\pi}{12}$ **5.** $\cot \dfrac{5\pi}{12}$ **6.** $\sin \dfrac{7\pi}{12}$

7. $\tan \dfrac{7\pi}{12}$ **8.** $\sin \dfrac{11\pi}{12}$ **9.** $\cos \dfrac{11\pi}{12}$

10. $\sin 75°$ [*Hint:* $75° = 45° + 30°$.]*

11. $\sin 105°$*   **12.** $\cos 165°$*

In Exercises 13–18, rewrite the given expression in terms of $\sin x$ *and* $\cos x$.

13. $\sin\left(\dfrac{\pi}{2} + x\right)$ **14.** $\cos\left(x + \dfrac{\pi}{2}\right)$ **15.** $\cos\left(x - \dfrac{3\pi}{2}\right)$

16. $\csc\left(x + \dfrac{\pi}{2}\right)$ **17.** $\sec(x - \pi)$ **18.** $\cot(x + \pi)$

In Exercises 19–24, simplify the given expression.

19. $\sin 3 \cos 5 - \cos 3 \sin 5$

20. $\sin 37° \sin 53° - \cos 37° \cos 53°$*

21. $\cos(x + y) \cos y + \sin(x + y) \sin y$

22. $\sin(x - y) \cos y + \cos(x - y) \sin y$

23. $\cos(x + y) - \cos(x - y)$

24. $\sin(x + y) - \sin(x - y)$

25. If $\sin x = \dfrac{1}{3}$ and $0 < x < \dfrac{\pi}{2}$, then $\sin\left(\dfrac{\pi}{4} + x\right) = ?$

26. If $\cos x = -\dfrac{1}{4}$ and $\dfrac{\pi}{2} < x < \pi$, then $\cos\left(\dfrac{\pi}{6} - x\right) = ?$

27. If $\cos x = -\dfrac{1}{5}$ and $\pi < x < \dfrac{3\pi}{2}$, then $\sin\left(\dfrac{\pi}{3} - x\right) = ?$

28. If $\sin x = -\dfrac{3}{4}$ and $\dfrac{3\pi}{2} < x < 2\pi$, then $\cos\left(\dfrac{\pi}{4} + x\right) = ?$

*Skip Exercises 10–12 and 20 if you haven't read Section 8.1.

In Exercises 29–32, assume that $\sin x = .8$ *and* $\sin y = \sqrt{.75}$ *and that x and y lie between* 0 *and* $\pi/2$. *Evaluate the given expressions.*

29. $\sin(x + y)$ **30.** $\cos(x - y)$

31. $\sin(x - y)$ **32.** $\tan(x + y)$

33. The figure shows an angle of t radians. Prove that for any number x,

$$5 \sin(x + t) = 3 \sin x + 4 \cos x.$$

34. The figure shows an angle of t radians. Prove that for any number y,

$$13 \cos(t - y) = 12 \cos y + 5 \sin y.$$

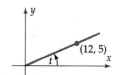

35. If $f(x) = \cos x$ and h is a fixed nonzero number, prove that:

$$\dfrac{f(x + h) - f(x)}{h} = \cos x\left(\dfrac{\cos h - 1}{h}\right) - \sin x\left(\dfrac{\sin h}{h}\right).$$

36. Prove the subtraction identity for sine:

$$\sin(x - y) = \sin x \cos y - \cos x \sin y.$$

[*Hint:* Use the first cofunction identity*

$$\sin(x - y) = \cos\left[\dfrac{\pi}{2} - (x - y)\right] = \cos\left[\left(\dfrac{\pi}{2} - x\right) + y\right]$$

and the addition identity for cosine.]

*The cofunction identity may be validly used here because its proof on page 527 depends only on the subtraction identity for cosine which was proved in the text.

37. Prove the addition identity for sine:

$$\sin(x + y) = \sin x \cos y + \cos x \sin y.$$

[*Hint:* You may assume Exercise 36. Use the same method by which the addition identity for cosine was obtained from the subtraction identity for cosine in the text.]

38. Prove the addition and subtraction identities for the tangent function (page 526). [*Hint:*

$$\tan(x + y) = \frac{\sin(x + y)}{\cos(x + y)}.$$

Use the addition identities on the numerator and denominator; then divide both numerator and denominator by $\cos x \cos y$ and simplify.]

In Exercises 39–44, prove the identity.

39. $\dfrac{\cos(x - y)}{\cos x \cos y} = 1 + \tan x \tan y$

40. $\dfrac{\sin(x + y)}{\sin x \sin y} = \cot x + \cot y$

41. $\dfrac{\sin(x - y)}{\sin x \sin y} = \cot y - \cot x$

42. $\dfrac{\cos(x - y)}{\sin x \sin y} = 1 + \cot x \cot y$

43. $\dfrac{\sin(x + y)}{\sin x \cos y} = 1 + \cot x \tan y$

44. $\dfrac{\sin(x - y)}{\sin x \cos y} = 1 - \cot x \tan y$

45. If x is in the first and y is in the second quadrant, $\sin x = 24/25$, and $\sin y = 4/5$, find the exact value of $\sin(x + y)$ and $\tan(x + y)$ and the quadrant in which $x + y$ lies.

46. If x and y are in the second quadrant, $\sin x = 1/3$, and $\cos y = -3/4$, find the exact value of $\sin(x + y)$, $\cos(x + y)$, $\tan(x + y)$, and find the quadrant in which $x + y$ lies.

47. If x is in the first and y is in the second quadrant, $\sin x = 4/5$, and $\cos y = -12/13$, find the exact value of $\cos(x + y)$ and $\tan(x + y)$ and the quadrant in which $x + y$ lies.

48. If x is in the fourth and y is in the first quadrant, $\cos x = 1/3$, and $\cos y = 2/3$, find the exact value of $\sin(x - y)$ and $\tan(x - y)$ and the quadrant in which $x - y$ lies.

49. Express $\sin(u + v + w)$ in terms of sines and cosines of u, v, and w. [*Hint:* First apply the addition identity with $x = u + v$ and $y = w$.]

50. Express $\cos(x + y + z)$ in terms of sines and cosines of x, y, and z.

51. If $x + y = \pi/2$, show that $\sin^2 x + \sin^2 y = 1$.

52. Prove that $\cot(x + y) = \dfrac{\cot x \cot y - 1}{\cot x + \cot y}$.

In Exercises 53–64, prove the identity.

53. $\sin(x - \pi) = -\sin x$

54. $\cos(x - \pi) = -\cos x$

55. $\cos(\pi - x) = -\cos x$

56. $\tan(\pi - x) = -\tan x$

57. $\sin(x + \pi) = -\sin x$

58. $\cos(x + \pi) = -\cos x$

59. $\tan(x + \pi) = \tan x$

60. $\sin x \cos y = \frac{1}{2}[\sin(x + y) + \sin(x - y)]$

61. $\sin x \sin y = \frac{1}{2}[\cos(x - y) - \cos(x + y)]$

62. $\cos x \sin y = \frac{1}{2}[\sin(x + y) - \sin(x - y)]$

63. $\cos(x + y)\cos(x - y) = \cos^2 x \cos^2 y - \sin^2 x \sin^2 y$

64. $\sin(x + y)\sin(x - y) = \sin^2 x \cos^2 y - \cos^2 x \sin^2 y$

In Exercises 65–74, determine graphically whether the equation could possibly be an identity (by choosing a numerical value for y and graphing both sides). If it could, prove that it is.

65. $\dfrac{\cos(x - y)}{\sin x \cos y} = \cot x + \tan y$

66. $\dfrac{\cos(x + y)}{\sin x \cos y} = \cot x - \tan y$

67. $\sin(x - y) = \sin x - \sin y$

68. $\cos(x + y) = \cos x + \cos y$

69. $\dfrac{\sin(x + y)}{\sin(x - y)} = \dfrac{\tan x + \tan y}{\tan x - \tan y}$

70. $\dfrac{\sin(x + y)}{\sin(x - y)} = \dfrac{\cot y + \cot x}{\cot y - \cot x}$

71. $\dfrac{\cos(x + y)}{\cos(x - y)} = \dfrac{\cot x + \tan y}{\cot x - \tan y}$

72. $\dfrac{\cos(x - y)}{\cos(x + y)} = \dfrac{\cot y + \tan x}{\cot y - \tan x}$

73. $\tan(x + y) = \tan x + \tan y$

74. $\cot(x - y) = \cot x - \cot y$

7.2 Other Identities

Section Objectives
■ Use the double-angle, power-reducing, and half-angle identities to evaluate and simplify trigonometric functions.
■ Use the product-to-sum and sum-to-product identities to prove other identities.

We now present a variety of identities that are special cases of the addition and subtraction identities of Section 7.2, beginning with

Double-Angle Identities

$$\sin 2x = 2 \sin x \cos x$$

$$\cos 2x = \cos^2 x - \sin^2 x$$

$$\tan 2x = \frac{2 \tan x}{1 - \tan^2 x}$$

Proof Let $x = y$ in the addition identities:

$$\sin 2x = \sin(x + x) = \sin x \cos x + \cos x \sin x = 2 \sin x \cos x,$$

$$\cos 2x = \cos(x + x) = \cos x \cos x - \sin x \sin x = \cos^2 x - \sin^2 x,$$

$$\tan 2x = \tan(x + x) = \frac{\tan x + \tan x}{1 - \tan x \tan x} = \frac{2 \tan x}{1 - \tan^2 x}.$$ ■

EXAMPLE 1

If $\pi < x < 3\pi/2$ and $\cos x = -8/17$, find $\sin 2x$ and $\cos 2x$, and show that $5\pi/2 < 2x < 3\pi$.

SOLUTION To use the double-angle identities, we first must determine $\sin x$. It can be found by using the Pythagorean identities.

$$\sin^2 x = 1 - \cos^2 x = 1 - \left(-\frac{8}{17}\right)^2 = 1 - \frac{64}{289} = \frac{225}{289}.$$

Since $\pi < x < 3\pi/2$, we know $\sin x$ is negative. Therefore,

$$\sin x = -\sqrt{\frac{225}{289}} = -\frac{15}{17}.$$

We now substitute these values in the double-angle identities.

$$\sin 2x = 2 \sin x \cos x = 2\left(-\frac{15}{17}\right)\left(-\frac{8}{17}\right) = \frac{240}{289} \approx .83$$

$$\cos 2x = \cos^2 x - \sin^2 x = \left(-\frac{8}{17}\right)^2 - \left(-\frac{15}{17}\right)^2$$

$$= \frac{64}{289} - \frac{225}{289} = -\frac{161}{289} \approx -.56.$$

Since $\pi < x < 3\pi/2$, we know that $2\pi < 2x < 3\pi$. The calculations above show that at $2x$, sine is positive and cosine is negative. This can occur only if $2x$ lies between $5\pi/2$ and 3π. ■

EXAMPLE 2

Express the rule of the function $f(x) = \sin 3x$ in terms of $\sin x$ and constants.

SOLUTION   We first use the addition identity for $\sin(x + y)$ with $y = 2x$.

$$f(x) = \sin 3x = \sin(x + 2x) = \sin x \cos 2x + \cos x \sin 2x.$$

Next apply the double-angle identities for $\cos 2x$ and $\sin 2x$.

$$f(x) = \sin 3x = \sin x \cos 2x + \cos x \sin 2x$$

$$= \sin x(\cos^2 x - \sin^2 x) + \cos x(2 \sin x \cos x)$$

$$= \sin x \cos^2 x - \sin^3 x + 2 \sin x \cos^2 x$$

$$= 3 \sin x \cos^2 x - \sin^3 x.$$

Finally, use the Pythagorean identity.

$$f(x) = \sin 3x = 3 \sin x \cos^2 x - \sin^3 x = 3 \sin x(1 - \sin^2 x) - \sin^3 x$$

$$= 3 \sin x - 3 \sin^3 x - \sin^3 x = 3 \sin x - 4 \sin^3 x.$$ ■

The double-angle identity for $\cos 2x$ can be rewritten in several useful ways. For instance, we can use the Pythagorean identity in the form of $\cos^2 x = 1 - \sin^2 x$ to obtain:

$$\cos 2x = \cos^2 x - \sin^2 x = (1 - \sin^2 x) - \sin^2 x = 1 - 2 \sin^2 x.$$

Similarly, using the Pythagorean identity in the form $\sin^2 x = 1 - \cos^2 x$, we have:

$$\cos 2x = \cos^2 x - \sin^2 x = \cos^2 x - (1 - \cos^2 x) = 2 \cos^2 x - 1.$$

In summary:

More Double-Angle Identities

$$\cos 2x = 1 - 2 \sin^2 x$$

$$\cos 2x = 2 \cos^2 x - 1$$

EXAMPLE 3

Prove that

$$\frac{1 - \cos 2x}{\sin 2x} = \tan x.$$

SOLUTION   The first identity in the preceding box and the double-angle identity for sine show that

$$\frac{1 - \cos 2x}{\sin 2x} = \frac{1 - (1 - 2\sin^2 x)}{2\sin x \cos x} = \frac{2\sin^2 x}{2\sin x \cos x} = \frac{\sin x}{\cos x} = \tan x. \qquad \blacksquare$$

If we solve the first equation in the preceding box for $\sin^2 x$ and the second one for $\cos^2 x$, we obtain a useful alternate form for these identities.

Power-Reducing Identities

$$\sin^2 x = \frac{1 - \cos 2x}{2}$$

$$\cos^2 x = \frac{1 + \cos 2x}{2}$$

EXAMPLE 4

Express the rule of the function $f(x) = \sin^4 x$ in terms of constants and first powers of the cosine function.

SOLUTION   We begin by applying the power-reducing identity.

$$f(x) = \sin^4 x = \sin^2 x \sin^2 x = \frac{1 - \cos 2x}{2} \cdot \frac{1 - \cos 2x}{2}$$

$$= \frac{1 - 2\cos 2x + \cos^2 2x}{4}.$$

Next we apply the power-reducing identity for cosine to $\cos^2 2x$. Note that this means using $2x$ in place of x in the identity.

$$\cos^2 2x = \frac{1 + \cos 2(2x)}{2} = \frac{1 + \cos 4x}{2}.$$

Finally, we substitute this last result in the expression for $\sin^4 x$ above.

$$f(x) = \sin^4 x = \frac{1 - 2\cos 2x + \cos^2 2x}{4} = \frac{1 - 2\cos 2x + \dfrac{1 + \cos 4x}{2}}{4}$$

$$= \frac{1}{4} - \frac{1}{2}\cos 2x + \frac{1}{8}(1 + \cos 4x)$$

$$= \frac{3}{8} - \frac{1}{2}\cos 2x + \frac{1}{8}\cos 4x. \qquad \blacksquare$$

HALF-ANGLE IDENTITIES

If we use the power-reducing identity with $x/2$ in place of x, we obtain

$$\sin^2\left(\frac{x}{2}\right) = \frac{1 - \cos 2\left(\frac{x}{2}\right)}{2} = \frac{1 - \cos x}{2}.$$

Consequently, we must have

$$\sin\left(\frac{x}{2}\right) = \pm\sqrt{\frac{1 - \cos x}{2}}.$$

This proves the first of the half-angle identities.

Half-Angle Identities

$$\sin\frac{x}{2} = \pm\sqrt{\frac{1 - \cos x}{2}} \qquad \cos\frac{x}{2} = \pm\sqrt{\frac{1 + \cos x}{2}}$$

$$\tan\frac{x}{2} = \pm\sqrt{\frac{1 - \cos x}{1 + \cos x}}$$

The half-angle identity for cosine is derived from a power-reducing identity, as was the half-angle identity for sine. The half-angle identity for tangent then follows immediately since $\tan(x/2) = \sin(x/2)/\cos(x/2)$. In all cases, *the sign in front of the radical depends on the quadrant in which $x/2$ lies.*

EXAMPLE 5

Find the exact value of

(a) $\cos\dfrac{5\pi}{8}$ (b) $\sin\dfrac{\pi}{12}$.

SOLUTION

(a) Since $\dfrac{5\pi}{8} = \dfrac{1}{2}\left(\dfrac{5\pi}{4}\right) = \dfrac{5\pi/4}{2}$, we use the half-angle identity with $x = 5\pi/4$ and the fact that $\cos(5\pi/4) = -\sqrt{2}/2$. The sign chart in Exercise 63 on page 451 shows that $\cos(5\pi/8)$ is negative because $5\pi/8$ is in the second quadrant. So we use the negative sign in front of the radical.

$$\cos\frac{5\pi}{8} = \cos\frac{5\pi/4}{2} = -\sqrt{\frac{1 + \cos(5\pi/4)}{2}}$$

$$= -\sqrt{\frac{1 + (-\sqrt{2}/2)}{2}} = -\sqrt{\frac{(2 - \sqrt{2})/2}{2}}$$

$$= -\sqrt{\frac{2 - \sqrt{2}}{4}}$$

$$= \frac{-\sqrt{2 - \sqrt{2}}}{2}.$$

(b) Since $\dfrac{\pi}{12} = \dfrac{1}{2}\left(\dfrac{\pi}{6}\right) = \dfrac{\pi/6}{2}$ and $\pi/12$ is in the first quadrant, where sine is positive, we have

$$\sin\frac{\pi}{12} = \sin\frac{\pi/6}{2} = \sqrt{\frac{1 - \cos(\pi/6)}{2}}$$

$$= \sqrt{\frac{1 - \sqrt{3}/2}{2}} = \sqrt{\frac{(2 - \sqrt{3})/2}{2}} = \sqrt{\frac{2 - \sqrt{3}}{4}}$$

$$= \frac{\sqrt{2 - \sqrt{3}}}{2}$$ ∎

Example 5(b) shows that

$$\sin\frac{\pi}{12} = \frac{\sqrt{2 - \sqrt{3}}}{2}.$$

On the other hand, in Example 1(a) of Section 7.2 we proved that

$$\sin\frac{\pi}{12} = \frac{\sqrt{6} - \sqrt{2}}{4}.$$

So we can conclude that

$$\frac{\sqrt{2 - \sqrt{3}}}{2} = \frac{\sqrt{6} - \sqrt{2}}{4},$$

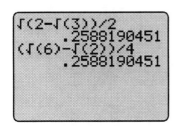

Figure 7–3

a fact that can readily be confirmed by a calculator (Figure 7–3). The moral here is that there may be several correct ways to express the exact value of a trigonometric function.

The problem of determining signs in the half-angle formulas can be eliminated with tangent by using these identities.

Half-Angle Identities for Tangent

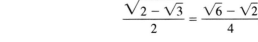

$$\tan\frac{x}{2} = \frac{1 - \cos x}{\sin x}$$

$$\tan\frac{x}{2} = \frac{\sin x}{1 + \cos x}$$

Proof   In the identity

$$\tan x = \frac{1 - \cos 2x}{\sin 2x},$$

which was proved in Example 3, replace x by $x/2$.

$$\tan\left(\frac{x}{2}\right) = \frac{1 - \cos 2(x/2)}{\sin 2(x/2)} = \frac{1 - \cos x}{\sin x}.$$

The second identity in the box is proved in Exercise 89.   ■

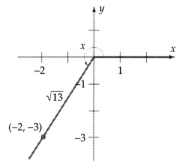

Figure 7–4

EXAMPLE 6

If $\tan x = \dfrac{3}{2}$ and $\pi < x < \dfrac{3\pi}{2}$, find $\tan \dfrac{x}{2}$.

SOLUTION   The terminal side of an angle of x radians in standard position lies in the third quadrant, as shown in Figure 7–4. The tangent of the angle in standard position whose terminal side passes through the point $(-2, -3)$ is $\dfrac{-3}{-2} = \dfrac{3}{2}$. Since there is only one angle in the third quadrant with tangent $3/2$, the point $(-2, -3)$ must lie on the terminal side of the angle of x radians.

Since the distance from $(-2, -3)$ to the origin is

$$\sqrt{(-2 - 0)^2 + (-3 - 0)^2} = \sqrt{13},$$

we have

$$\sin x = \frac{-3}{\sqrt{13}} \qquad \text{and} \qquad \cos x = \frac{-2}{\sqrt{13}}.$$

Therefore, by the first of the half-angle identities for tangent

$$\tan \frac{x}{2} = \frac{1 - \cos x}{\sin x} = \frac{1 - \left(\dfrac{-2}{\sqrt{13}}\right)}{\dfrac{-3}{\sqrt{13}}} = \frac{\dfrac{\sqrt{13} + 2}{\sqrt{13}}}{\dfrac{-3}{\sqrt{13}}} = -\frac{\sqrt{13} + 2}{3}. \quad ■$$

SUM/PRODUCT IDENTITIES

The following identities were proved in Example 5 and Exercises 60–62 of Section 7.2.

Product to Sum Identities

$$\sin x \cos y = \frac{1}{2}[\sin(x + y) + \sin(x - y)]$$

$$\sin x \sin y = \frac{1}{2}[\cos(x - y) - \cos(x + y)]$$

$$\cos x \cos y = \frac{1}{2}[\cos(x + y) + \cos(x - y)]$$

$$\cos x \sin y = \frac{1}{2}[\sin(x + y) - \sin(x - y)]$$

EXAMPLE 7

Express $\sin(3x)\cos(5x)$ as a sum or difference of trigonometric functions.

SOLUTION   We use the first product to sum identity, with $3x$ in place of x and $5x$ in place of y.

$$\sin(3x)\cos(5x) = \frac{1}{2}[\sin(3x + 5x) + \sin(3x - 5x)]$$

$$= \frac{1}{2}[\sin(8x) + \sin(-2x)]$$

$$= \frac{1}{2}[\sin(8x) - \sin(2x)] \qquad \text{[Negative angle identity]}$$

$$= \frac{1}{2}\sin(8x) - \frac{1}{2}\sin(2x) \qquad\qquad\blacksquare$$

If we use the first product to sum identity with $\frac{1}{2}(x + y)$ in place of x and $\frac{1}{2}(x - y)$ in place of y, we obtain

$$\sin\left[\frac{1}{2}(x + y)\right]\cos\left[\frac{1}{2}(x - y)\right] = \frac{1}{2}\left[\sin\left(\frac{1}{2}(x + y) + \frac{1}{2}(x - y)\right)\right.$$
$$\left. + \sin\left(\frac{1}{2}(x + y) - \frac{1}{2}(x - y)\right)\right]$$

$$= \frac{1}{2}(\sin x + \sin y).$$

Multiplying both sides of the last equation by 2 produces the first of the following identities.

Sum to Product Identities

$$\sin x + \sin y = 2\sin\left(\frac{x + y}{2}\right)\cos\left(\frac{x - y}{2}\right)$$

$$\sin x - \sin y = 2\cos\left(\frac{x + y}{2}\right)\sin\left(\frac{x - y}{2}\right)$$

$$\cos x + \cos y = 2\cos\left(\frac{x + y}{2}\right)\cos\left(\frac{x - y}{2}\right)$$

$$\cos x - \cos y = -2\sin\left(\frac{x + y}{2}\right)\sin\left(\frac{x - y}{2}\right)$$

The last three sum to product identities are proved in the same way as the first. (See Exercises 59–61.)

EXAMPLE 8

Express $\cos(7x) + \cos(3x)$ as a product of trigonometric functions.

SOLUTION   We use the third sum to product identity with $7x$ in place of x and $3x$ in place of y.

$$\cos(7x) + \cos(3x) = 2\cos\left(\frac{7x + 3x}{2}\right)\cos\left(\frac{7x - 3x}{2}\right)$$

$$= 2\cos\left(\frac{10x}{2}\right)\cos\left(\frac{4x}{2}\right)$$

$$= 2\cos(5x)\cos(2x) \qquad\qquad\blacksquare$$

EXAMPLE 9

Prove the identity

$$\frac{\sin t + \sin 3t}{\cos t + \cos 3t} = \tan 2t.$$

SOLUTION Using the first factoring identity with $x = t$ and $y = 3t$ yields

$$\sin t + \sin 3t = 2 \sin\left(\frac{t + 3t}{2}\right)\cos\left(\frac{t - 3t}{2}\right) = 2 \sin 2t \cos(-t).$$

Similarly,

$$\cos t + \cos 3t = 2 \cos\left(\frac{t + 3t}{2}\right)\cos\left(\frac{t - 3t}{2}\right) = 2 \cos 2t \cos(-t),$$

so

$$\frac{\sin t + \sin 3t}{\cos t + \cos 3t} = \frac{2 \sin 2t \cos(-t)}{2 \cos 2t \cos(-t)} = \frac{\sin 2t}{\cos 2t} = \tan 2t. \qquad \blacksquare$$

EXERCISES 7.2

In Exercises 1–7, find sin 2x, cos 2x, and tan 2x under the given conditions.

1. $\sin x = \frac{5}{13} \quad \left(0 < x < \frac{\pi}{2}\right)$

2. $\sin x = -\frac{4}{5} \quad \left(\pi < x < \frac{3\pi}{2}\right)$

3. $\cos x = -\frac{3}{5} \quad \left(\pi < x < \frac{3\pi}{2}\right)$

4. $\cos x = -\frac{1}{3} \quad \left(\frac{\pi}{2} < x < \pi\right)$

5. $\tan x = \frac{3}{4} \quad \left(\pi < x < \frac{3\pi}{2}\right)$

6. $\tan x = -\frac{3}{2} \quad \left(\frac{\pi}{2} < x < \pi\right)$

7. $\csc x = 4 \quad \left(0 < x < \frac{\pi}{2}\right)$

8. A batter hits a baseball that is caught by a fielder. If the ball leaves the bat at an angle of θ radians to the horizontal, with an initial velocity of v feet per second, then the approximate horizontal distance d traveled by the ball is given by

$$d = \frac{v^2 \sin \theta \cos \theta}{16}.$$

(a) Use an identity to show that

$$d = \frac{v^2 \sin 2\theta}{32}.$$

(b) If the initial velocity is 115 ft/second, what angle θ will produce the maximum distance? [*Hint:* Use part (a). For what value of θ is sin 2θ as large as possible?]

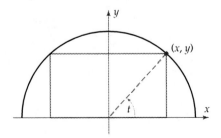

9. A rectangle is inscribed in a semicircle of radius 3 inches and the radius to the corner makes an angle of t radians with the horizontal, as shown in the figure.

(a) Express the horizontal length, vertical height, and area of the rectangle in terms of x and y.

(b) Express x and y in terms of sine and cosine.

(c) Use parts (a) and (b) and suitable identities to show that the area A of the rectangle is given by

$$A = 9 \sin 2t.$$

10. In Exercise 9, what angle will produce a rectangle with largest possible area? What is this maximum area?

In Exercises 11–26, use the half-angle identities to evaluate the given expression exactly.

11. $\cos \dfrac{\pi}{8}$ 12. $\tan \dfrac{\pi}{8}$ 13. $\sin \dfrac{3\pi}{8}$ 14. $\cos \dfrac{3\pi}{8}$

15. $\tan \dfrac{\pi}{12}$ 16. $\sin \dfrac{5\pi}{8}$ 17. $\cos \dfrac{\pi}{12}$ 18. $\tan \dfrac{5\pi}{8}$

19. $\sin \dfrac{7\pi}{8}$ 20. $\cos \dfrac{7\pi}{8}$ 21. $\tan \dfrac{7\pi}{8}$ 22. $\cot \dfrac{\pi}{8}$

23. $\cos \dfrac{\pi}{16}$ [*Hint:* Exercise 11]   24. $\sin \dfrac{\pi}{16}$

25. $\sin \dfrac{\pi}{24}$ [*Hint:* Exercise 17]   26. $\cos \dfrac{\pi}{24}$

In Exercises 27–32, find $\sin \dfrac{x}{2}$, $\cos \dfrac{x}{2}$, and $\tan \dfrac{x}{2}$ under the given conditions.

27. $\cos x = .4 \quad \left(0 < x < \dfrac{\pi}{2}\right)$

28. $\sin x = .6 \quad \left(\dfrac{\pi}{2} < x < \pi\right)$

29. $\sin x = -\dfrac{3}{5} \quad \left(\dfrac{3\pi}{2} < x < 2\pi\right)$

30. $\cos x = .8 \quad \left(\dfrac{3\pi}{2} < x < 2\pi\right)$

31. $\tan x = \dfrac{1}{2} \quad \left(\pi < x < \dfrac{3\pi}{2}\right)$

32. $\cot x = 1 \quad \left(-\pi < x < -\dfrac{\pi}{2}\right)$

In Exercises 33–38, write each expression as a sum or difference.

33. $\sin 4x \cos 6x$ 34. $\sin 5x \sin 7x$

35. $\cos 2x \cos 4x$ 36. $\sin 3x \cos 5x$

37. $\sin 17x \sin(-3x)$ 38. $\cos 13x \cos(-5x)$

In Exercises 39–44, write each expression as a product.

39. $\sin 3x + \sin 5x$ 40. $\cos 2x + \cos 6x$

41. $\sin 9x - \sin 5x$ 42. $\cos 5x - \cos 7x$

43. $\cos 2x + \cos 5x$ 44. $\sin 4x + \sin 3x$

In Exercises 45–50, assume $\sin x = .6$ and $0 < x < \pi/2$ and evaluate the given expression.

45. $\sin 2x$ 46. $\cos 4x$ 47. $\cos 2x$ 48. $\sin 4x$

49. $\sin \dfrac{x}{2}$ 50. $\cos \dfrac{x}{2}$

51. Express $\cos 3x$ in terms of $\cos x$.

52. (a) Express the rule of the function $f(x) = \cos^3 x$ in terms of constants and first powers of the cosine function as in Example 4.
   (b) Do the same for $f(x) = \cos^4 x$.

In Exercises 53–58, simplify the given expression.

53. $\dfrac{\sin 2x}{2 \sin x}$ 54. $1 - 2 \sin^2\left(\dfrac{x}{2}\right)$

55. $2 \cos 2y \sin 2y$ (Think!)

56. $\cos^2\left(\dfrac{x}{2}\right) - \sin^2\left(\dfrac{x}{2}\right)$ 57. $(\sin x + \cos x)^2 - \sin 2x$

58. $2 \sin x \cos^3 x - 2 \sin^3 x \cos x$

In Exercises 59–61, prove the given sum to product identity. [Hint: See the proof on page 541.]

59. $\sin x - \sin y = 2 \cos\left(\dfrac{x+y}{2}\right)\sin\left(\dfrac{x-y}{2}\right)$

60. $\cos x + \cos y = 2 \cos\left(\dfrac{x+y}{2}\right)\cos\left(\dfrac{x-y}{2}\right)$

61. $\cos x - \cos y = -2 \sin\left(\dfrac{x+y}{2}\right)\sin\left(\dfrac{x-y}{2}\right)$

62. When you press a key on a touch-tone phone, the key emits two tones that combine to produce the sound wave
$$f(t) = \sin(2\pi Lt) + \sin(2\pi Ht),$$
Where t is in seconds, L is the low frequency tone for the row the key is in, and H is the high frequency tone for the column the key is in, as shown in the diagram below. For example, pressing 2 produces the sound wave $f(t) = \sin[2\pi(697)t] + \sin[2\pi(1336)t]$.

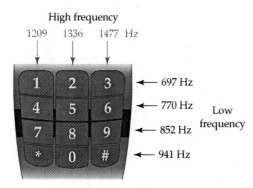

(a) Write the function that gives the sound wave produced by pressing the 6 key.
(b) Express the 6 key function in part (a) as the product of a sine and a cosine function.

In Exercises 63–76, determine graphically whether the equation could possibly be an identity. If it could, prove that it is.

63. $\sin 16x = 2 \sin 8x \cos 8x$ 64. $\cos 8x = \cos^2 4x - \sin^2 4x$

65. $\cos^4 x - \sin^4 x = \cos 2x$ 66. $\sec 2x = \dfrac{1}{1 - 2 \sin^2 x}$

67. $\cos 4x = 2\cos 2x - 1$ **68.** $\sin^2 x = \cos^2 x - 2\sin x$

69. $\dfrac{1 + \cos 2x}{\sin 2x} = \cot x$ **70.** $\sin 2x = \dfrac{2\cot x}{\csc^2 x}$

71. $\sin 3x = (\sin x)(3 - 4\sin^2 x)$

72. $\sin 4x = (4\cos x \sin x)(1 - 2\sin^2 x)$

73. $\cos 2x = \dfrac{2\tan x}{\sec^2 x}$

74. $\cos 3x = (\cos x)(3 - 4\cos^2 x)$

75. $\csc^2\left(\dfrac{x}{2}\right) = \dfrac{2}{1 - \cos x}$

76. $\sec^2\left(\dfrac{x}{2}\right) = \dfrac{2}{1 + \cos x}$

In Exercises 77 and 78, the graph of the left side of the expression is shown. Fill the blank on the right side with a simple trigonometric expression and prove that the resulting equation is an identity. [Hint: What trigonometric function has a graph that closely resembles the given one?]

77. $\dfrac{\sin 5x - \sin 3x}{2\cos 4x} = $ ____

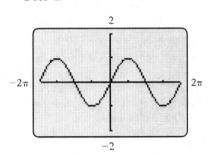

78. $\dfrac{\sin 5x + \sin 3x}{2\sin 4x} = $ ____

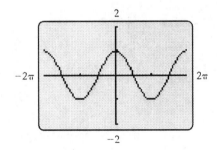

In Exercises 79–82, fill the blank on the right side with a simple trigonometric expression and prove that the resulting equation is an identity. [Hint: Exercises 77 and 78.]

79. $\dfrac{\cos x + \cos 3x}{2\cos 2x} = $ ____   **80.** $\dfrac{\cos 4x - \cos 6x}{\sin 4x + \sin 6x} = $ ____

81. $\dfrac{\sin 3x - \sin x}{\cos x + \cos 3x} = $ ____   **82.** $\dfrac{\cos x + \cos 3x}{\sin x - \sin 3x} = $ ____

In Exercises 83–88, prove the identity.

83. $\dfrac{\sin x - \sin 3x}{\cos x + \cos 3x} = -\tan x$ **84.** $\dfrac{\sin x - \sin 3x}{\cos x - \cos 3x} = -\cot 2x$

85. $\dfrac{\sin 4x + \sin 6x}{\cos 4x - \cos 6x} = \cot x$

86. $\dfrac{\cos 8x + \cos 4x}{\cos 8x - \cos 4x} = -\cot 6x \cot 2x$

87. $\dfrac{\sin x + \sin y}{\cos x - \cos y} = -\cot\left(\dfrac{x - y}{2}\right)$

88. $\dfrac{\sin x - \sin y}{\cos x + \cos y} = \tan\left(\dfrac{x - y}{2}\right)$

89. (a) Prove that $\dfrac{1 - \cos x}{\sin x} = \dfrac{\sin x}{1 + \cos x}$.

(b) Use part (a) and the half-angle identity proved in the text to prove that

$$\tan\frac{x}{2} = \frac{\sin x}{1 + \cos x}.$$

90. To avoid a steep hill, a road is being built in straight segments from P to Q and from Q to R; it makes a turn of t radians at Q, as shown in the figure. The distance from P to S is 40 miles, and the distance from R to S is 10 miles. Use suitable trigonometric functions to express:

(a) c in terms of b and t [*Hint:* Place the figure on a coordinate plane with P and Q on the x-axis, with Q at the origin. Then what are the coordinates of R?]

(b) b in terms of t

(c) a in terms of t [*Hint:* $a = 40 - c$; use parts (a) and (b).]

(d) Use parts (b) and (c) and a suitable identity to show that the length $a + b$ of the road is

$$40 + 10\tan\frac{t}{2}.$$

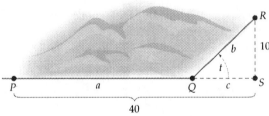

91. Find the exact value of $\cos\dfrac{\pi}{32}$. [*Hint:* Exercise 23.]

92. (a) List the exact values of $\cos\dfrac{\pi}{4}$, $\cos\dfrac{\pi}{8}$, $\cos\dfrac{\pi}{16}$, and $\cos\dfrac{\pi}{32}$. [*Hint:* Exercises 11, 23 and 91.]

(b) Based on the pattern you see in the answers to part (a) make a conjecture about the exact value of $\cos\dfrac{\pi}{64}$. Use a calculator to support your answer.

(c) Make a conjecture about the exact value of $\cos\dfrac{\pi}{128}$ and support the truth of your conjecture with a calculator.

(d) What do you think the exact value of $\cos\dfrac{\pi}{256}$ is?

7.3 Inverse Trigonometric Functions

Section Objectives
- ■ Evaluate the inverse sine, cosine, and tangent functions.
- ■ Investigate the properties of the inverse trigonometric functions.
- ■ Prove identities involving inverse trigonometric functions.
- ■ Use inverse trigonometric functions to to solve applied problems.

Before reading this section, you should review the concept of an inverse function (Section 3.7). As explained there, a function f has an inverse function only when its graph passes the Horizontal Line Test:

No horizontal line intersects the graph of f more than once.

The graphs of the sine, cosine, and tangent functions certainly do not have this property. However, functions that are closely related to them (same rules but smaller domains) *do* have inverse functions.

The **restricted sine function** is defined as follows:

$$\text{Domain: } [-\pi/2, \pi/2] \qquad \text{Rule: } f(x) = \sin x.$$

Its graph in Figure 7–5 shows that for each number v between -1 and 1, there is exactly one number u between $-\pi/2$ and $\pi/2$ such that $\sin u = v$.

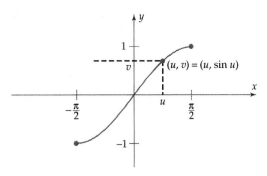

Figure 7–5

Since the graph of the restricted sine function passes the horizontal line test, we know that it has an inverse function. This inverse function is called the **inverse sine** (or **arcsine**) **function** and is denoted by $g(x) = \sin^{-1}x$ or $g(x) = \arcsin x$. The domain of the inverse sine function is the interval $[-1, 1]$, and its rule is as follows.

Inverse Sine Function

For each v with $-1 \le v \le 1$,

$\sin^{-1}v = $ the unique number u between $-\pi/2$ and $\pi/2$ whose sine is v;

that is,

$$\sin^{-1}v = u \qquad \text{exactly when} \qquad \sin u = v.$$

EXAMPLE 1

Find

(a) $\sin^{-1}(1/2)$ (b) $\sin^{-1}(-\sqrt{2}/2)$.

SOLUTION

(a) $\text{Sin}^{-1}(1/2)$ is the one number between $-\pi/2$ and $\pi/2$ whose sine is $1/2$. From our study of special values, we know that $\sin \pi/6 = 1/2$, and $\pi/6$ is between $-\pi/2$ and $\pi/2$. Hence, $\sin^{-1}(1/2) = \pi/6$.

(b) $\text{Sin}^{-1}(-\sqrt{2}/2) = -\pi/4$ because $\sin(-\pi/4) = -\sqrt{2}/2$ and $-\pi/4$ is between $-\pi/2$ and $\pi/2$. ∎

EXAMPLE 2

Except for special values (as in Example 1), you should use the SIN^{-1} key (labeled ASIN on some calculators) in *radian mode* to evaluate the inverse sine function. For instance,

$$\sin^{-1}(-.67) \approx -.7342 \qquad \text{and} \qquad \sin^{-1}(.42) \approx .4334.$$ ∎

EXAMPLE 3

If you key in SIN^{-1} 2 ENTER, you will get an error message, because 2 is not in the domain of the inverse sine function.* ∎

CAUTION

The notation $\sin^{-1}x$ is *not* exponential notation. It does *not* mean either $(\sin x)^{-1}$ or $\dfrac{1}{\sin x}$. For instance, Example 1 shows that

$$\sin^{-1}(1/2) = \pi/6 \approx .5236,$$

but

$$\left(\sin \frac{1}{2}\right)^{-1} = \frac{1}{\sin \dfrac{1}{2}} \approx \frac{1}{.4794} \approx 2.0858.$$

Suppose $-1 \le v \le 1$ and $\sin^{-1}v = u$. Then by the definition of the inverse sine function, we know that $-\pi/2 \le u \le \pi/2$ and $\sin u = v$. Therefore,

$$\sin^{-1}(\sin u) = \sin^{-1}(v) = u \qquad \text{and} \qquad \sin(\sin^{-1}v) = \sin u = v.$$

This shows that the restricted sine function and the inverse sine function have the usual "round-trip properties" of inverse functions. In summary,

Properties of Inverse Sine

$$\sin^{-1}(\sin u) = u \qquad \text{if} \qquad -\frac{\pi}{2} \le u \le \frac{\pi}{2}$$

$$\sin(\sin^{-1}v) = v \qquad \text{if} \qquad -1 \le v \le 1$$

---

*TI-85/86 and HP-39gs display the complex number $(1.5707\cdots, -1.3169\cdots)$ for $\sin^{-1}(2)$. For our purposes, this is equivalent to an error message, since we deal only with functions whose values are real numbers.

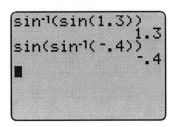

Figure 7–6

A calculator can illustrate the identities in the preceding box, as shown in Figure 7–6. Nevertheless, when special values are involved, you should be able to deal with them by hand.

EXAMPLE 4

Find   (a) $\sin^{-1}(\sin \pi/6)$ (b) $\sin^{-1}(\sin 5\pi/6)$.

SOLUTION

(a) We know that $\sin \pi/6 = 1/2$. Hence,

$$\sin^{-1}\left(\sin \frac{\pi}{6}\right) = \sin^{-1}\left(\frac{1}{2}\right) = \frac{\pi}{6}$$

because $\pi/6$ is the number between $-\pi/2$ and $\pi/2$ whose sine is $1/2$.

(b) We also have $\sin 5\pi/6 = 1/2$, so the expression $\sin^{-1}(\sin 5\pi/6)$ is defined. However,

$$\sin^{-1}\left(\sin \frac{5\pi}{6}\right) \quad \text{is NOT equal to} \quad \frac{5\pi}{6}$$

because the identity in the box on page 546 is valid only when u is between $-\pi/2$ and $\pi/2$. Using the result of part (a), we see that

$$\sin^{-1}\left(\sin \frac{5\pi}{6}\right) = \sin^{-1}\left(\frac{1}{2}\right) = \frac{\pi}{6}.$$ ■

EXAMPLE 5

Find the exact value of $\tan\left[\sin^{-1}\left(\dfrac{5}{9}\right)\right]$.

SOLUTION   Let $\sin^{-1}\left(\dfrac{5}{9}\right) = t$. We must find $\tan t$, so we construct an angle of t radians in standard position (Figure 7–7). Let (x, y) be the point on the terminal side of the angle that is 9 units from the origin. By the point-in-the plane description, we have

$$\sin t = \frac{y}{9} \quad \text{and} \quad \tan t = \frac{y}{x}.$$

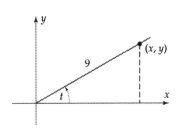

Figure 7–7

Consequently,

$$\frac{y}{9} = \sin t = \sin\left[\sin^{-1}\left(\frac{5}{9}\right)\right] = \frac{5}{9}.$$

The first and last terms of this equation show that $y = 5$. Applying the Pythagorean Theorem to the right triangle in Figure 7–7, we see that

$$x^2 + 5^2 = 9^2$$
$$x^2 + 25 = 81$$
$$x^2 = 56$$
$$x = \sqrt{56}.$$

Therefore,

$$\tan\left[\sin^{-1}\left(\frac{5}{9}\right)\right] = \tan t = \frac{y}{x} = \frac{5}{\sqrt{56}}.$$ ■

Recall that the graph of the inverse function of f can be obtained in two ways: Reverse the coordinates of each point on the graph of f or, equivalently, reflect the graph of f in the line $y = x$, as explained on pages 224–225. In summary,

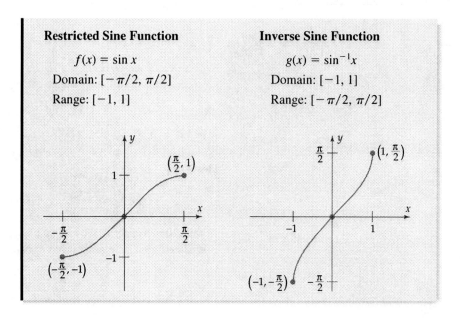

Restricted Sine Function

$$f(x) = \sin x$$
Domain: $[-\pi/2, \pi/2]$
Range: $[-1, 1]$

Inverse Sine Function

$$g(x) = \sin^{-1}x$$
Domain: $[-1, 1]$
Range: $[-\pi/2, \pi/2]$

THE INVERSE COSINE FUNCTION

The **restricted cosine function** is defined as follows:

Domain: $[0, \pi]$ Rule: $f(x) = \cos x$.

Its graph in Figure 7–8 shows that for each number v between -1 and 1, there is exactly one number u between 0 and π such that $\cos u = v$.

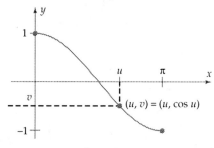

Figure 7–8

Since the graph of the restricted cosine function passes the Horizontal Line Test, we know that it has an inverse function. This inverse function is called the **inverse cosine (or arccosine) function** and is denoted by $h(x) = \cos^{-1}x$ or $h(x) = \arccos x$. The domain of the inverse cosine function is the interval $[-1, 1]$, and its rule is as follows.

Inverse Cosine Function

For each v with $-1 \leq v \leq 1$,

$\cos^{-1}v =$ the unique number u between 0 and π whose cosine is v;

that is,

$$\cos^{-1}v = u \qquad \text{exactly when} \qquad \cos u = v.$$

The inverse cosine function has these properties:

$$\cos^{-1}(\cos u) = u \qquad \text{if} \qquad 0 \leq u \leq \pi;$$

$$\cos(\cos^{-1}v) = v \qquad \text{if} \qquad -1 \leq v \leq 1.$$

CAUTION

$\cos^{-1}x$ does *not* mean $(\cos x)^{-1}$, or $1/\cos x$.

EXAMPLE 6

Find   (a) $\cos^{-1}(1/2)$ (b) $\cos^{-1}(0)$ (c) $\cos^{-1}(-.63)$.

SOLUTION

(a) $\text{Cos}^{-1}(1/2) = \pi/3$ since $\pi/3$ is the unique number between 0 and π whose cosine is $1/2$.

(b) $\text{Cos}^{-1}(0) = \pi/2$ because $\cos \pi/2 = 0$ and $0 \leq \pi/2 \leq \pi$.

(c) The COS^{-1} key on a calculator in *radian mode* shows that $\cos^{-1}(-.63) \approx 2.2523$. ∎

EXAMPLE 7

Write $\sin(\cos^{-1}v)$ as an algebraic expression in v.

SOLUTION $\text{Cos}^{-1}v = u$, where $\cos u = v$ and $0 \leq u \leq \pi$. Hence, $\sin u$ is non-negative, and by the Pythagorean identity, $\sin u = \sqrt{\sin^2 u} = \sqrt{1 - \cos^2 u}$. Also, $\cos^2 u = v^2$. Therefore,

$$\sin(\cos^{-1}v) = \sin u = \sqrt{1 - \cos^2 u} = \sqrt{1 - v^2}.$$ ∎

EXAMPLE 8

Prove the identity $\sin^{-1}x + \cos^{-1}x = \pi/2$.

SOLUTION   Suppose $\sin^{-1}x = u$, with $-\pi/2 \leq u \leq \pi/2$. Verify that $0 \leq \pi/2 - u \leq \pi$ (Exercise 24). Then we have

$$\sin u = x \qquad \text{[Definition of inverse sine]}$$

$$\cos\left(\frac{\pi}{2} - u\right) = x \qquad \text{[Cofunction identity]}$$

$$\cos^{-1}x = \frac{\pi}{2} - u. \qquad \text{[Definition of inverse cosine]}$$

Therefore,

$$\sin^{-1}x + \cos^{-1}x = u + \left(\frac{\pi}{2} - u\right) = \frac{\pi}{2}. \qquad \blacksquare$$

EXAMPLE 9

Prove that

$$\sin(\cos^{-1}x) = \cos(\sin^{-1}x).$$

SOLUTION   By the identity in Example 8,

$$\sin(\cos^{-1}x) = \sin\left(\frac{\pi}{2} - \sin^{-1}x\right)$$

$$= \cos(\sin^{-1}x) \qquad \text{[Cofunction identity]} \qquad \blacksquare$$

The graph of the inverse cosine function is the reflection of the graph of the restricted cosine function in the line $y = x$, as shown below.

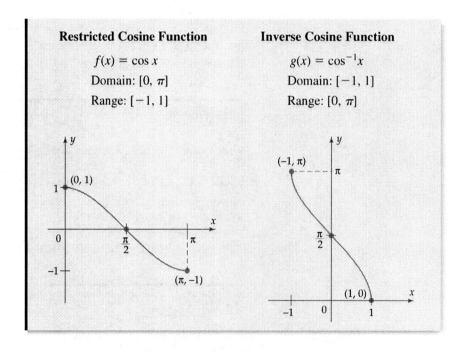

THE INVERSE TANGENT FUNCTION

The **restricted tangent function** is defined as follows:

$$\text{Domain: } (-\pi/2, \pi/2) \qquad \text{Rule: } f(x) = \tan x.$$

Its graph in Figure 7–9 shows that for every real number v, there is exactly one number u between $-\pi/2$ and $\pi/2$ such that $\tan u = v$.

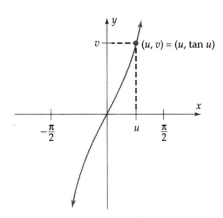

Figure 7–9

Since the graph of the restricted tangent function passes the horizontal line test, we know that it has an inverse function. This inverse function is called the **inverse tangent** (or **arctangent**) **function** and is denoted by $g(x) = \tan^{-1}x$ or $g(x) = \arctan x.$ The domain of the inverse tangent function is the set of all real numbers, and its rule is as follows.

Inverse Tangent Function

For each real number v,

$\tan^{-1}v$ = the unique number u between $-\pi/2$ and $\pi/2$ whose tangent is v;

that is,

$$\tan^{-1}v = u \qquad \text{exactly when} \qquad \tan u = v.$$

The inverse tangent function has these properties:

$$\tan^{-1}(\tan u) = u \qquad \text{if} \qquad -\frac{\pi}{2} < u < \frac{\pi}{2};$$

$$\tan(\tan^{-1}v) = v \qquad \text{for every number } v.$$

CAUTION

$\tan^{-1}x$ does *not* mean $(\tan x)^{-1}$, or $1/\tan x.$

EXAMPLE 10

$\text{Tan}^{-1}1 = \pi/4$ because $\pi/4$ is the unique number between $-\pi/2$ and $\pi/2$ such that $\tan \pi/4 = 1.$ A calculator in *radian mode* shows that $\tan^{-1}(136) \approx 1.5634.$ ∎

EXAMPLE 11

Find the exact value of $\cos[\tan^{-1}(\sqrt{5}/2)].$

SOLUTION   Consider an angle of u radians in standard position whose terminal side passes through $(2, \sqrt{5})$, as in Figure 7–10. By the point-in-the-plane description,

$$\tan u = \sqrt{5}/2.$$

Since u is between $-\pi/2$ and $\pi/2$ and $\tan u = \sqrt{5}/2$, we must have

$$u = \tan^{-1}(\sqrt{5}/2).$$

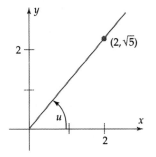

Figure 7–10

Furthermore, the distance from $(2, \sqrt{5})$ to the origin is

$$\sqrt{(2-0)^2 + (\sqrt{5}-0)^2} = \sqrt{4+5} = 3,$$

so

$$\cos u = 2/3.$$

Therefore,

$$\cos[\tan^{-1}(\sqrt{5}/2)] = \cos u = 2/3. \qquad \blacksquare$$

The graph of the inverse tangent function is the reflection of the graph of the restricted tangent function in the line $y = x$, as shown below.

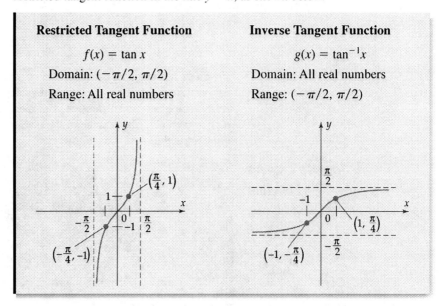

Restricted Tangent Function

$$f(x) = \tan x$$

Domain: $(-\pi/2, \pi/2)$

Range: All real numbers

Inverse Tangent Function

$$g(x) = \tan^{-1} x$$

Domain: All real numbers

Range: $(-\pi/2, \pi/2)$

EXAMPLE 12

A 26-foot high movie screen is located 12 feet above the ground, as shown in Figure 7–11. Assume that when you are seated your eye is 4 feet above the ground.

(a) Express the angle of t radians as a function of your distance x from the wall holding the screen.

(b) How far should you be from the wall to make t as large as possible?

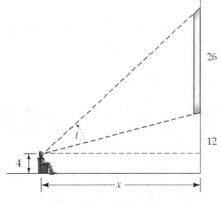

Figure 7–11

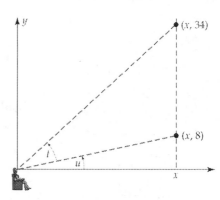

Figure 7–12

SOLUTION

(a) Imagine that the x-axis is at your eye level with your eye at the origin. Since your eye is 4 feet above the ground, the bottom of the screen is 8 feet above your eye level and the situation looks like Figure 7–12. The point-in-the-plane description shows that

$$\tan u = \frac{8}{x} \quad \text{and} \quad \tan(u + t) = \frac{34}{x}.$$

Hence,

$$u = \tan^{-1}\frac{8}{x} \quad \text{and} \quad u + t = \tan^{-1}\frac{34}{x},$$

so that

$$t = (u + t) - u = \tan^{-1}\frac{34}{x} - \tan^{-1}\frac{8}{x}.$$

(b) We graph the function $t = \tan^{-1}\frac{34}{x} - \tan^{-1}\frac{8}{x}$ and use a maximum finder to determine that t is largest when $x \approx 16.5$ feet (Figure 7–13). ■

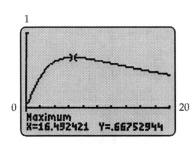

Figure 7–13

EXERCISES 7.3

In Exercises 1–14, find the exact functional value without using a calculator.

1. $\sin^{-1}1$
2. $\cos^{-1}0$
3. $\tan^{-1}(-1)$
4. $\sin^{-1}(-1)$
5. $\cos^{-1}1$
6. $\tan^{-1}1$
7. $\tan^{-1}(\sqrt{3}/3)$
8. $\cos^{-1}(\sqrt{3}/2)$
9. $\sin^{-1}(-\sqrt{2}/2)$
10. $\sin^{-1}(\sqrt{3}/2)$
11. $\tan^{-1}(-\sqrt{3})$
12. $\cos^{-1}(-\sqrt{2}/2)$
13. $\cos^{-1}\left(-\frac{1}{2}\right)$
14. $\sin^{-1}\left(-\frac{1}{2}\right)$

In Exercises 15–23, use a calculator in radian mode to approximate the functional value.

15. $\sin^{-1}.35$
16. $\cos^{-1}.76$
17. $\tan^{-1}(-3.256)$
18. $\sin^{-1}(-.795)$
19. $\sin^{-1}(\sin 7)$ [The answer is *not* 7.]
20. $\cos^{-1}(\cos 3.5)$
21. $\tan^{-1}[\tan(-4)]$
22. $\sin^{-1}[\sin(-2)]$
23. $\cos^{-1}[\cos(-8.5)]$
24. Let u be a number such that

$$-\frac{\pi}{2} \le u \le \frac{\pi}{2}.$$

Prove that

$$0 \le \frac{\pi}{2} - u \le \pi.$$

25. Given that $u = \sin^{-1}(-\sqrt{3}/2)$, find the exact value of $\cos u$ and $\tan u$.

26. Given that $u = \tan^{-1}(4/3)$, find the exact value of $\sin u$ and $\sec u$.

In Exercises 27–48, find the exact functional value without using a calculator.

27. $\sin^{-1}(\cos 0)$
28. $\cos^{-1}(\sin \pi/6)$
29. $\cos^{-1}(\sin 4\pi/3)$
30. $\tan^{-1}(\cos \pi)$
31. $\sin^{-1}(\cos 7\pi/6)$
32. $\cos^{-1}(\tan 7\pi/4)$
33. $\sin^{-1}(\sin 2\pi/3)$ (See Exercise 19.)
34. $\cos^{-1}(\cos 5\pi/4)$
35. $\cos^{-1}[\cos(-\pi/6)]$
36. $\tan^{-1}[\tan(-4\pi/3)]$
37. $\sin[\cos^{-1}(3/5)]$ (See Example 11.)
38. $\tan[\sin^{-1}(3/5)]$
39. $\cos[\tan^{-1}(-3/4)]$
40. $\cos[\sin^{-1}(12/13)]$
41. $\tan[\cos^{-1}(5/13)]$
42. $\sin[\tan^{-1}(12/5)]$
43. $\cos[\sin^{-1}(\sqrt{3}/5)]$
44. $\tan[\sin^{-1}(\sqrt{7}/12)]$
45. $\sin[\cos^{-1}(3/\sqrt{13})]$
46. $\tan[\cos^{-1}(8/9)]$
47. $\sin[\tan^{-1}(\sqrt{5}/10)]$
48. $\cos[\tan^{-1}(3/7)]$

In Exercises 49–55, write the expression as an algebraic expression in v, as in Example 7.

49. $\cos(\sin^{-1}v)$
50. $\tan(\cos^{-1}v)$
51. $\tan(\sin^{-1}v)$
52. $\sin(\tan^{-1}v)$
53. $\cos(\tan^{-1}v)$
54. $\sin(2\sin^{-1}v)$
55. $\sin(2\cos^{-1}v)$

In Exercises 56–58, prove the identity.

56. $\tan(\sin^{-1}v) = \cot(\cos^{-1}v)$
57. $\tan(\cos^{-1}v) = \cot(\sin^{-1}v)$
58. $\sec(\sin^{-1}v) = \csc(\cos^{-1}v)$

In Exercises 59–62, graph the function.

59. $f(x) = \cos^{-1}(x + 1)$ **60.** $g(x) = \tan^{-1}x + \pi$

61. $h(x) = \sin^{-1}(\sin x)$ **62.** $k(x) = \sin(\sin^{-1}x)$

63. In an alternating current circuit, the voltage is given by the formula

$$V = V_{\max} \cdot \sin(2\pi ft + \phi),$$

where $V_{\max}$ is the maximum voltage, f is the frequency (in cycles per second), t is the time in seconds, and ϕ is the phase angle.

(a) If the phase angle is 0, solve the voltage equation for t.
(b) If $\phi = 0$, $V_{\max} = 20$, $V = 8.5$, and $f = 120$, find the smallest positive value of t.

64. Calculus can be used to show that the area A between the x-axis and the graph of $y = \dfrac{1}{x^2 + 1}$ from $x = a$ to $x = b$ is given by

$$A = \tan^{-1} b - \tan^{-1} a.$$

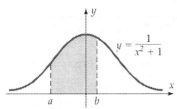

Find the area A when
(a) $a = 0$ and $b = 1$ (b) $a = -1$ and $b = 2$
(c) $a = -2.5$ and $b = -.5$.

Note: *Example 12 may be helpful for Exercises 65–71.*

65. A model plane 40 feet above the ground is flying away from an observer.

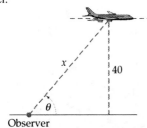

(a) Express the angle of elevation θ of the plane as a function of the distance x from the observer to the plane.
(b) What is θ when the plane is 250 feet away from the observer?

66. Suppose that another model plane is flying while attached to the ground by a 100 foot long wire that is always kept taut. Let h denote the height of the plane above the ground and θ the radian measure of the angle the wire makes with the ground. (The figure for Exercise 65 is the case when $x = 100$ and $h = 40$.)

(a) Express θ as a function of the height h.
(b) What is θ when the plane is 55 feet above the ground?
(c) When $\theta = 1$ radian, how high is the plane?

67. A rocket is fired straight up. The line of sight from an observer 4 miles away makes an angle of t radians with the horizontal.

(a) Express t as a function of the height h of the rocket.
(b) Find t when the rocket is .25 mile, 1 mile, and 2 miles high respectively.
(c) When $t = .4$ radian, how high is the rocket?

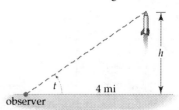

68. A cable from the top of a 60-foot high tower is to be attached to the ground x feet from the base of the tower.

(a) If the cable makes an angle of t radians with the ground when attached, express t as a function of x. [*Hint:* Select a coordinate system in which both x and t are positive, or use Section 8.1.]
(b) What is t when the distance $x = 40$ feet? When $x = 70$ feet? When $x = 100$ feet?
(c) If $t = \pi/5$, how far is the end of the cable from the base of the tower?

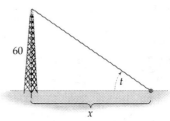

69. Suppose that the movie screen in Example 12 is 24 feet high and is 10 feet above the ground and that the eye level of the watcher is 4 feet above the ground.

(a) Express the angle t at the watcher's eye as a function of her distance x from the wall holding the screen.
(b) At what distance from the screen is the angle t as large as possible?

70. Section 8.1 is a prerequisite for this exercise. A camera on a 5-foot-high tripod is placed in front of a 6-foot-high picture that is mounted 3 feet above the floor.

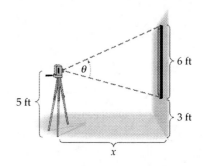

(a) Express angle θ as a function of the distance x from the camera to the wall.

(b) The photographer wants to use a particular lens, for which $\theta = 36°$ ($\pi/5$ radians). How far should she place the camera from the wall to be sure that the entire picture will show in the photograph?

71. A 15-foot-wide highway sign is placed 10 feet from a road, perpendicular to the road (see figure). A spotlight at the edge of the road is aimed at the sign.

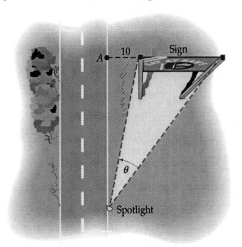

(a) Express θ as a function of the distance x from point A to the spotlight.

(b) How far from point A should the spotlight be placed so that the angle θ is as large as possible?

72. Show that the restricted secant function, whose domain consists of all numbers x such that $0 \le x \le \pi$ and $x \ne \pi/2$, has an inverse function. Sketch its graph.

73. Show that the restricted cosecant function, whose domain consists of all numbers x such that $-\pi/2 \le x \le \pi/2$ and $x \ne 0$, has an inverse function. Sketch its graph.

74. Show that the restricted cotangent function, whose domain is the interval $(0, \pi)$, has an inverse function. Sketch its graph.

75. Show that the inverse cosine function actually has the two properties listed in the box on page 549.

76. Show that the inverse tangent function actually has the two properties listed in the box on page 551.

In Exercises 77–84, prove the identity.

77. $\sin^{-1}(-x) = -\sin^{-1}x$ [*Hint:* Let $u = \sin^{-1}(-x)$ and show that $\sin^{-1}x = -u$.]

78. $\tan^{-1}(-x) = -\tan^{-1}x$

79. $\cos^{-1}(-x) = \pi - \cos^{-1}x$ [*Hint:* Let $u = \cos^{-1}(-x)$ and show that $0 \le \pi - u \le \pi$; use the identity

$$\cos(\pi - u) = -\cos u.]$$

80. $\sin^{-1}(\cos x) = \pi/2 - x \quad (0 \le x \le \pi)$

81. $\tan^{-1}(\cot x) = \pi/2 - x \quad (0 < x < \pi)$

82. $\tan^{-1}x + \tan^{-1}\left(\dfrac{1}{x}\right) = \dfrac{\pi}{2}$

83. $\sin^{-1}x = \tan^{-1}\left(\dfrac{x}{\sqrt{1 - x^2}}\right) \quad (-1 < x < 1)$

[*Hint:* Let $u = \sin^{-1}x$ and show that $\tan u = x/\sqrt{1 - x^2}$. Since $\sin u = x$, $\cos u = \pm\sqrt{1 - x^2}$. Show that in this case, $\cos u = \sqrt{1 - x^2}$.]

84. $\cos^{-1}x = \dfrac{\pi}{2} - \tan^{-1}\left(\dfrac{x}{\sqrt{1 - x^2}}\right) \quad (-1 < x < 1)$

[*Hint:* See Example 8 and Exercise 83.]

85. Is it true that $\tan^{-1}x = \dfrac{\sin^{-1}x}{\cos^{-1}x}$? Justify your answer.

86. Using the viewing window with $-2\pi \le x \le 2\pi$ and $-4 \le y \le 4$ graph the functions $f(x) = \cos(\cos^{-1}x)$ and $g(x) = \cos^{-1}(\cos x)$. How do you explain the shapes of the two graphs?

7.4 Trigonometric Equations

Section Objectives
■ Solve basic trigonometric equations.
■ Solve other trigonometric equations.

Any equation that involves trigonometric functions can be solved graphically, and many can be solved algebraically. Unlike the equations solved previously, trigonometric equations typically have an infinite number of solutions. In most cases, these solutions can be systematically determined by using periodicity, as we now see.

BASIC EQUATIONS

We begin with **basic equations,** such as

$$\sin x = .39, \qquad \cos x = .2, \qquad \tan x = -3.$$

Basic equations can be solved by the methods illustrated in Examples 1–3.

EXAMPLE 1

Solve $\tan x = 2$.

SOLUTION   The equation can be solved graphically by graphing $y = \tan x$ and $y = 2$ on the same coordinate axes and finding the intersection points. The x-coordinate of every such point is a number whose tangent is 2, that is, a solution of the equation.

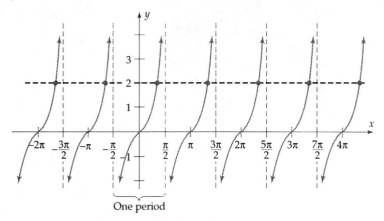

Figure 7–14

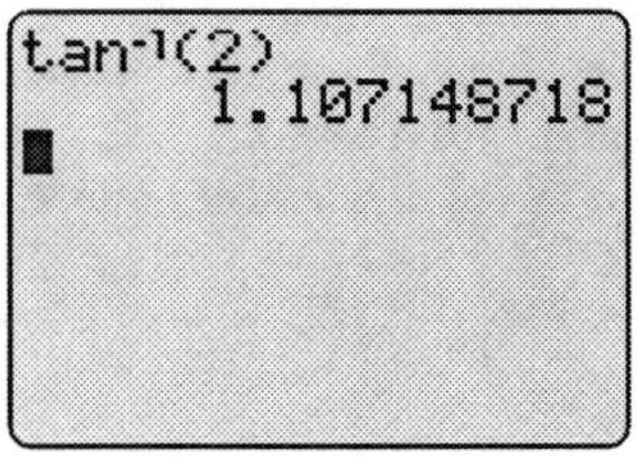

Figure 7–14 shows that there is exactly one solution in each period of $\tan x$. The solution between $-\pi/2$ and $\pi/2$ could be found graphically, but it's faster to compute $\tan^{-1} 2$ on a calculator.* The calculator then displays the number between $-\pi/2$ and $\pi/2$ whose tangent is 2, namely, $x = 1.1071$, as shown in Figure 7–15.† Since the tangent graph repeats its pattern with period π, all the other solutions differ from this one by an integer multiple of π. Thus, all the solutions are

$$1.1071, \qquad 1.1071 \pm \pi, \qquad 1.1071 \pm 2\pi, \qquad 1.1071 \pm 3\pi, \qquad \text{etc.}$$

These solutions are customarily written like this:

$$x = 1.1071 + k\pi \quad (k = 0, \pm 1, \pm 2, \pm 3, \ldots). \qquad \blacksquare$$

tan⁻¹(2)
       1.107148718

Figure 7–15

EXAMPLE 2

Solve $\tan^{-1} x = 1$.

SOLUTION   We can construct a picture of the situation by replacing the horizontal blue line through 2 in Figure 7–14 by a horizontal line through 1. As in

---

*Unless stated otherwise, radian mode is used throughout this section.
†You need not have read about inverse trigonometric functions in Section 7.4 to understand this section. Here the calculator's $\tan^{-1}$ key is used only to produce one number with the given tangent, and similarly for the $\sin^{-1}$ and $\cos^{-1}$ keys.

Example 1, there is just one solution between $-\pi/2$ and $\pi/2$. Our knowledge of special values tells us that this solution is $x = \pi/4$ (because $\tan(\pi/4) = 1$ by Example 4 of Section 6.2). Since the tangent function has period π, the other solutions differ from $x = \pi/4$ by integer multiples of π. So all solutions are given by

$$x = \frac{\pi}{4} + k\pi \quad (k = 0, \pm 1, \pm 2, \pm 3, \ldots).$$ ∎

The techniques illustrated in Examples 1 and 2 apply in the general case.

Solving
tan x = c

If c is any real number, then the equation

$$\tan x = c$$

can be solved as follows.

1. Find one solution u by using your knowledge of special values or by computing $\tan^{-1} c$ on a calculator.

2. Then all solutions are given by

$$x = u + k\pi \, (k = 0, \pm 1, \pm 2, \pm 3, \ldots).$$

Solving basic sine equations is similar to solving basic tangent equations, but involves one additional step, as illustrated in the next example.

EXAMPLE 3

Solve $\sin x = -.75$

SOLUTION The solutions are the x-coordinates of the points where the graphs of $y = \sin x$ and $y = -.75$ intersect (why?). Note that there are exactly two solutions in every period of $\sin x$ (for instance, between $-\pi/2$ and $3\pi/2$).

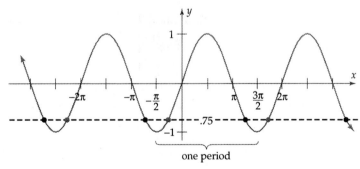

Figure 7–16

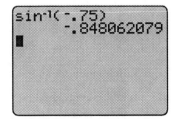

Figure 7–17

Figure 7–16 shows that there is one solution between $-\pi/2$ and $\pi/2$. It can be found by computing $\sin^{-1}(-.75)$ on a calculator. The calculator displays the number between $-\pi/2$ and $\pi/2$ whose sine is $-.75$, namely $x = -.8481$, as shown in Figure 7–17. Since the sine graph repeats is pattern with period 2π, all of the following numbers are also solutions:

$$-.8481, \qquad -.8481 \pm 2\pi, \qquad -.8481 \pm 4\pi, \qquad -.8481 \pm 6\pi, \qquad \text{etc.}$$

These solutions correspond to the red intersection points in Figure 7–16, each of which is 2π units from the next red point. As you can see, there are still more solutions (corresponding to the blue points). One of them can be found by using the identity that was proved in Example 2 of Section 7.2:

$$\sin(\pi - x) = \sin x.$$

Applying this identity with the solution $x = -.8481$ shows that

$$\sin[\pi - (-.8481] = \sin(-.8481) = -.75.$$

In other words, $\pi - (-.8481) = 3.9897$ is also a solution of $\sin x = -.75$. The other solutions of the equation are

$$3.9897, \qquad 3.9897 \pm 2\pi, \qquad 3.9897 \pm 4\pi, \qquad 3.9897 \pm 6\pi, \qquad \text{etc.,}$$

corresponding to the blue intersection points in Figure 7–16, each of which is 2π units from the next blue point. Therefore, all the solutions of $\sin x = -0.75$ are

$$x = -.8481 + 2k\pi \qquad \text{and} \qquad x = 3.9897 + 2k\pi$$

$$(k = 0, \pm 1, \pm 2, \pm 3, \ldots).$$ ∎

The solution methods of Example 3 extend to the general case.

Solving $\sin x = c$

If c is a number between -1 and 1, then the equation

$$\sin x = c$$

can be solved as follows.*

1. Find one solution u by using your knowledge of special values or by computing $\sin^{-1} c$ on a calculator.

2. A second solution is $\pi - u$.

3. All solutions are given by

$$x = u + 2k\pi \quad \text{and} \quad x = (\pi - u) + 2k\pi \qquad (k = 0, \pm 1, \pm 2, \pm 3, \ldots).$$

EXAMPLE 4

Solve $\sin v = \sqrt{2}/2$ without using a calculator.

SOLUTION   Our knowledge of special values shows that $v = \pi/4$ is one solution (see Example 4 of Section 6.2). Hence, a second solution is

$$\pi - v = \pi - \frac{\pi}{4} = \frac{3\pi}{4},$$

and all solutions are

$$v = \frac{\pi}{4} + 2k\pi \qquad \text{and} \qquad v = \frac{3\pi}{4} + 2k\pi \qquad (k = 0, \pm 1, \pm 2, \pm 3, \ldots).$$ ∎

---

*Equations of the form $\sin x = c$, with $|c| > 1$, have no solutions because the values of sine are always between -1 and 1, as we saw in Chapter 6.

Solving basic cosine equations is similar to solving basic sine equations, except that a different identity must be used to find the second solution.

EXAMPLE 5

Solve $\cos x = \sqrt{3}/2$.

SOLUTION   By graphing $y = \cos x$ and $y = \sqrt{3}/2$ on the same screen (Figure 7–18), we see that there are two solutions of the equation between $-\pi$ and π (one full period of cosine). The positive solution could be approximated by computing $\cos^{-1}(\sqrt{3}/2)$ on a calculator. However, our knowledge of special values provides an exact solution. Example 3 of Section 6.2 shows that $\cos(\pi/6) = \sqrt{3}/2$. So one solution of the equation is $x = \pi/6$. The negative angle identity $\cos(-x) = \cos x$ shows that the second solution is $x = -\pi/6$, because

$$\cos\left(-\frac{\pi}{6}\right) = \cos\left(\frac{\pi}{6}\right) = \frac{\sqrt{3}}{2}.$$

Since the interval $[-\pi, \pi]$ is one full period of cosine, all the solutions of the equation are

$$x = \frac{\pi}{6} + 2k\pi \quad \text{and} \quad x = -\frac{\pi}{6} + 2k\pi \quad (k = 0, \pm 1, \pm 2, \pm 3, \ldots). \quad \blacksquare$$

In the general case, we have the following result.

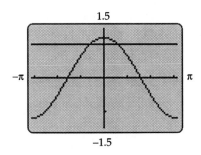

1.5

−π   π

−1.5

Figure 7–18

**Solving
$\cos x = c$**

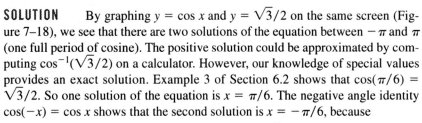

If c is a number between -1 and 1, then the equation

$$\cos x = c$$

can be solved as follows.*

1. Find one solution u by using your knowledge of special values or by computing $\cos^{-1}c$ on a calculator.

2. A second solution is $-u$.

3. All solutions are given by

$$x = u + 2k\pi \quad \text{and} \quad x = -u + 2k\pi \quad (k = 0, \pm 1, \pm 2, \pm 3, \ldots).$$

EXAMPLE 6

Find all solutions of $\sec x = 8$ in the interval $[0, 2\pi)$.

SOLUTION   Note that $\sec x = 8$ exactly when

$$\frac{1}{\cos x} = 8 \quad \text{or, equivalently,} \quad \cos x = \frac{1}{8} = .125.$$

Since $\cos^{-1}(.125) = 1.4455$, the solutions of $\cos x = .125$, and hence of $\sec x = 8$, are

$$x = 1.4455 + 2k\pi \quad \text{and} \quad x = -1.4455 + 2k\pi$$
$$(k = 0, \pm 1, \pm 2, \pm 3, \ldots).$$

---

*Equations of the form $\cos x = c$, with $|c| > 1$, have no solutions because the values of cosine are always between -1 and 1, as we saw in Chapter 6.

Of these solutions, the two between 0 and 2π are

$$x = 1.4455 \quad \text{and} \quad x = -1.4455 + 2\pi = 4.8377.$$ ■

ALGEBRAIC SOLUTION OF OTHER TRIGONOMETRIC EQUATIONS

Many trigonometric equations can be solved algebraically by using substitution, factoring, the quadratic formula, and identities to reduce the problem to an equivalent one that involves only basic equations.

EXAMPLE 7

Solve exactly: $\sin 2x = \sqrt{2}/2$.

SOLUTION   First, let $v = 2x$ and solve the basic equation $\sin v = \sqrt{2}/2$. As we saw in Example 4, the solutions are

$$v = \frac{\pi}{4} + 2k\pi \quad \text{and} \quad v = \frac{3\pi}{4} + 2k\pi \quad (k = 0, \pm 1, \pm 2, \pm 3, \ldots).$$

Since $v = 2x$, each of these solutions leads to a solution of the original equation.

$$2x = v = \frac{\pi}{4} + 2k\pi \quad \text{or, equivalently,} \quad x = \frac{1}{2}\left(\frac{\pi}{4} + 2k\pi\right) = \frac{\pi}{8} + k\pi.$$

Similarly,

$$2x = v = \frac{3\pi}{4} + 2k\pi \quad \text{or, equivalently,} \quad x = \frac{1}{2}\left(\frac{3\pi}{4} + 2k\pi\right) = \frac{3\pi}{8} + k\pi.$$

Therefore, all solutions of $\sin 2x = \sqrt{2}/2$ are given by

$$x = \frac{\pi}{8} + k\pi \quad \text{and} \quad x = \frac{3\pi}{8} + k\pi \quad (k = 0, \pm 1, \pm 2, \pm 3, \ldots).$$

The fact that the solutions are obtained by adding multiples of π rather than 2π is a reflection of the fact that the period of $\sin 2x$ is π. ■

EXAMPLE 8

Solve $-10 \cos^2 x - 3 \sin x + 9 = 0$.

SOLUTION   We first use the Pythagorean identity to rewrite the equation in terms of the sine function.

$$-10 \cos^2 x - 3 \sin x + 9 = 0$$

$$-10(1 - \sin^2 x) - 3 \sin x + 9 = 0$$

$$-10 + 10 \sin^2 x - 3 \sin x + 9 = 0$$

$$10 \sin^2 x - 3 \sin x - 1 = 0.$$

Now factor the left side:*

$$(2 \sin x - 1)(5 \sin x + 1) = 0$$

$$2 \sin x - 1 = 0 \qquad \text{or} \qquad 5 \sin x + 1 = 0$$

$$2 \sin x = 1 \qquad\qquad\qquad 5 \sin x = -1$$

$$\sin x = 1/2 \qquad\qquad\qquad \sin x = -1/5 = -.2.$$

Each of these basic equations is readily solved. We note that $\sin(\pi/6) = 1/2$, so $x = \pi/6$ and $x = \pi - \pi/6 = 5\pi/6$ are solutions of the first one. Since $\sin^{-1}(-.2) = -.2014$, both $x = -.2014$ and $x = \pi - (-.2014) = 3.3430$ are solutions of the second equation. Therefore, all solutions of the original equation are given by

$$x = \frac{\pi}{6} + 2k\pi, \qquad x = \frac{5\pi}{6} + 2k\pi,$$

$$x = -.2014 + 2k\pi, \qquad x = 3.3430 + 2k\pi,$$

where $k = 0, \pm 1, \pm 2, \pm 3, \ldots$.   ■

EXAMPLE 9

Solve $\sec^2 x + 5 \tan x = -2$.

SOLUTION   We use the Pythagorean identity $\sec^2 x = 1 + \tan^2 x$ to obtain an equivalent equation.

$$\sec^2 x + 5 \tan x = -2$$

$$\sec^2 x + 5 \tan x + 2 = 0$$

$$(1 + \tan^2 x) + 5 \tan x + 2 = 0$$

$$\tan^2 x + 5 \tan x + 3 = 0.$$

If we let $u = \tan x$, this last equation becomes $u^2 + 5u + 3 = 0$. Since the left side does not readily factor, we use the quadratic formula to solve the equation.

$$u = \frac{-5 \pm \sqrt{5^2 - 4 \cdot 1 \cdot 3}}{2} = \frac{-5 \pm \sqrt{13}}{2}.$$

Since $u = \tan x$, the original equation is equivalent to

$$\tan x = \frac{-5 + \sqrt{13}}{2} \approx -.6972 \qquad \text{or} \qquad \tan x = \frac{-5 - \sqrt{13}}{2} \approx -4.3028.$$

Solving these basic equations as above, we find that $x = -.6089$ is a solution of the first and $x = -1.3424$ is a solution of the second. Hence, the solutions of the original equation are

$$x = -.6089 + k\pi \qquad \text{and} \qquad x = -1.3424 + k\pi$$

$$(k = 0, \pm 1, \pm 2, \pm 3, \ldots).$$ ■

---

*The factorization may be easier to see if you first substitute v for $\sin x$, so that $10 \sin^2 x - 3 \sin x - 1$ becomes $10v^2 - 3v - 1 = (2v - 1)(5v + 1)$.

EXAMPLE 10

Solve $5 \cos x + 3 \cos 2x = 3$.

SOLUTION   We use the double-angle identity: $\cos 2x = 2 \cos^2 x - 1$ as follows.

$$5 \cos x + 3 \cos 2x = 3$$

Use double-angle identity: $5 \cos x + 3(2 \cos^2 x - 1) = 3$

Multiply out left side: $5 \cos x + 6 \cos^2 x - 3 = 3$

Rearrange terms: $6 \cos^2 x + 5 \cos x - 6 = 0$

Factor left side: $(2 \cos x + 3)(3 \cos x - 2) = 0$

$$2 \cos x + 3 = 0 \quad \text{or} \quad 3 \cos x - 2 = 0$$

$$2 \cos x = -3 \qquad\qquad 3 \cos x = 2$$

$$\cos x = -\frac{3}{2} \qquad\qquad \cos x = \frac{2}{3}.$$

The equation $\cos x = -3/2$ has no solutions because $\cos x$ always lies between -1 and 1. A calculator shows that the solutions of $\cos x = 2/3$ are

$$x = .8411 + 2k\pi \qquad \text{and} \qquad x = -.8411 + 2k\pi$$

$$(k = 0, \pm 1, \pm 2, \pm 3, \ldots).$$ ∎

GRAPHICAL SOLUTION METHOD

When the techniques of the preceding examples are inadequate, trigonometric equations may be solved by the following graphical procedure.

Graphical Method for Solving Trigonometric Equations

1. Write the equation in the form $f(x) = 0$.

2. Determine the period of p of $f(x)$.

3. Graph $f(x)$ over an interval of length p.

4. Use a graphical root finder to determine the x-intercepts of the graph in this interval.

5. For each x-intercept u, all of the numbers

$$u + kp \qquad (k = 0, \pm 1, \pm 2, \pm 3, \ldots)$$

are solutions of the equation.

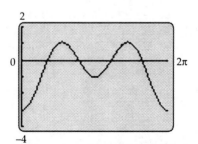

Figure 7–19

EXAMPLE 11

Solve $3 \sin^2 x - \cos x - 2 = 0$.

SOLUTION   Both sine and cosine have period 2π, so $f(x) = 3 \sin^2 x - \cos x - 2$ also has period 2π. Figure 7–19 shows one full period of the graph of f. A graphical root finder shows that the four x-intercepts (solutions of the equation) in this window are

$$x = 1.1216, \quad x = 2.4459, \quad x = 3.8373, \quad x = 5.1616.$$

Since the graph repeats its pattern to the left and right, the other x-intercepts (solutions) will differ from these four by multiples of 2π. For instance, in addition to the solution $x = 1.1216$, each of the following is a solution.

$$x = 1.1216 \pm 2\pi, \quad x = 1.1216 \pm 4\pi, \quad x = 1.1216 \pm 6\pi, \text{ etc.}$$

A similar analysis applies to the other solutions between 0 and 2π. Hence, all solutions of the equation are given by

$$x = 1.1216 + 2k\pi, \quad x = 2.4459 + 2k\pi, \quad x = 3.8373 + 2k\pi,$$

$$x = 5.1616 + 2k\pi, \quad \text{where } k = 0, \pm 1, \pm 2, \pm 3, \dots. \quad ■$$

EXAMPLE 12

Solve $\tan x = 3 \sin 2x$.

SOLUTION   We first rewrite the equation as

$$\tan x - 3 \sin 2x = 0.$$

Both $\tan x$ and $\sin 2x$ have period π (see pages 472 and 478). Hence, the function given by the left side of the equation, $f(x) = \tan x - 3 \sin 2x$, also has period π. The graph of f on the interval $[0, \pi)$ (Figure 7–20) shows an erroneous vertical line segment at $x = \pi/2$, where tangent is not defined, as well as x-intercepts at the endpoints of the interval. Consequently, we use the more easily read graph f in Figure 7–21, which uses the interval $(-\pi/2, \pi/2)$.

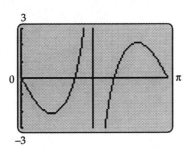

Figure 7–20

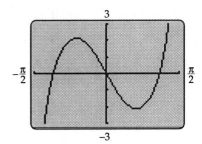

Figure 7–21

Even without the graph, we can verify that there is an x-intercept at the origin because

$$f(0) = \tan 0 - 3 \sin(2 \cdot 0) = 0.$$

A root finder shows that the other two x-intercepts in Figure 7–22 are

$$x = -1.1503 \quad \text{and} \quad x = 1.1503.$$

Since $f(x)$ has period π, all solutions of the equation are given by

$$x = -1.1503 + k\pi, \quad x = 0 + k\pi, \quad x = 1.1503 + k\pi$$

$$(k = 0, \pm 1, \pm 2, \pm 3, \dots). \quad ■$$

EXERCISES 7.4

In all exercises, find exact solutions if possible (as in Examples 2, 4, 5, and 7) and approximate ones otherwise. When a calculator is used, round your answers (but not any intermediate results) to four decimal places.

In Exercises 1–10, find all solutions of the equation.

1. $\sin x = .465$

2. $\sin x = .682$

3. $\cos x = -.564$

4. $\cos x = -.371$

5. $\tan x = -.354$

6. $\tan x = 10$

7. $\cot x = 2.3$ [Remember: $\cot x = 1/\tan x$.]

8. $\cot x = -3.5$ 9. $\sec x = -1.6$

10. $\csc x = 6.4$

In Exercises 11–14, approximate all solutions in $[0, 2\pi)$ of the given equation.

11. $\sin x = .119$ 12. $\cos x = .958$

13. $\tan x = 4$ 14. $\tan x = 18$

In Exercises 15–24, use your knowledge of special values to find the exact solutions of the equation.

15. $\sin x = \sqrt{3}/2$ 16. $2\cos x = \sqrt{2}$

17. $\tan x = -\sqrt{3}$ 18. $\tan x = 1$

19. $2\cos x = -\sqrt{3}$ 20. $\sin x = 0$

21. $2\sin x + 1 = 0$ 22. $\csc x = \sqrt{2}$

23. $\csc x = 2$ 24. $-2\sec x = 4$

In Exercises 25–34, find all angles θ with $0° \leq \theta < 360°$ that are solutions of the given equation. [Hint: Put your calculator in degree mode and replace π by $180°$ in the solution algorithms for basic equations.]

25. $\tan \theta = 7.95$ 26. $\tan \theta = 69.4$

27. $\cos \theta = -.42$ 28. $\cot \theta = -2.4$

29. $2\sin^2\theta + 3\sin\theta + 1 = 0$

30. $4\cos^2\theta + 4\cos\theta - 3 = 0$

31. $\tan^2\theta - 3 = 0$

32. $2\sin^2\theta = 1$

33. $4\cos^2\theta + 4\cos\theta + 1 = 0$

34. $\sin^2\theta - 3\sin\theta = 10$

At the instant you hear a sonic boom from an airplane overhead, your angle of elevation α to the plane is given by the equation $\sin \alpha = 1/m$, where m is the Mach number for the speed of the plane (Mach 1 is the speed of sound, Mach 2.5 is 2.5 times the speed of sound, etc.). In Exercises 35–38, find the angle of elevation (in degrees) for the given Mach number. Remember that an angle of elevation must be between $0°$ and $90°$.

35. $m = 1.1$ 36. $m = 1.6$

37. $m = 2$ 38. $m = 2.4$

When a light beam passes from one medium to another (for instance, from air to water), it changes both its speed and direction. According to Snell's Law of Refraction,

$$\frac{\sin \theta_1}{\sin \theta_2} = \frac{v_1}{v_2},$$

where v_1 is the speed of light in the first medium, v_2 its speed in the second medium, θ_1 the angle of incidence, and θ_2 the angle of refraction, as shown in the figure. The number v_1/v_2 is called the index of refraction. Use this information to do Exercises 39–42.

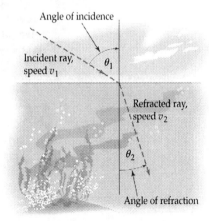

39. The index of refraction of light passing from air to water is 1.33. If the angle of incidence is $38°$, find the angle of refraction.

40. The index of refraction of light passing from air to ordinary glass is 1.52. If the angle of incidence is $17°$, find the angle of refraction.

41. The index of refraction of light passing from air to dense glass is 1.66. If the angle of incidence is $24°$, find the angle of refraction.

42. The index of refraction of light passing from air to quartz is 1.46. If the angle of incidence is $50°$, find the angle of refraction.

In Exercises 43–52, use an appropriate substitution (as in Example 7) to find all solutions of the equation.

43. $\sin 2x = -\sqrt{3}/2$

44. $\cos 2x = \sqrt{2}/2$

45. $2 \cos \dfrac{x}{2} = \sqrt{2}$

46. $2 \sin \dfrac{x}{3} = 1$

47. $\tan 3x = -\sqrt{3}$

48. $5 \sin 2x = 2$

49. $5 \cos 3x = -3$

50. $2 \tan 4x = 16$

51. $4 \tan \dfrac{x}{2} = 8$

52. $5 \sin \dfrac{x}{4} = 4$

Exercises 53–60, deal with a circle of radius r and a central angle of t radians, $(0 < t < \pi)$, as shown in the figure. The length L of the chord determined by the angle and the area A of the shaded segment are given by

$$L = 2r \sin \frac{t}{2} \quad \text{and} \quad A = \frac{r^2}{2}(t - \sin t).$$

(See Exercise 108 for a proof of the first of these formulas.)

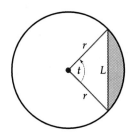

In Exercises 53–56, find the radian measure of the angle and the area of the segment under the given conditions.

53. $r = 5$ and $L = 8$

54. $r = 8$ and $L = 5$

55. $r = 1$ and $L = 1.5$

56. $r = 10$ and $L = 12$.

In Exercises 57–60, find the radian measure of the angle and the length L of the chord under the given conditions.

57. $r = 10$ and $A = 50$

58. $r = 1$ and $A = .5$

59. $r = 8$ and $A = 20$

60. $r = 5$ and $A = 2$

Exercises 61 and 62 deal with a rectangle inscribed in the segment of the graph of $f(x) = 2 \cos 2x$ shown in the figure.

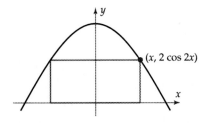

61. (a) Find a formula for the area of the rectangle in terms of x. [*Hint:* The length is $2x$.]

(b) For what values of x does the rectangle have an area of 1 square unit?

62. Use the formula in Exercise 61(a) to determine the value of x that determines the rectangle with the largest possible area. What is this maximum area?

In Exercises 63–88, use factoring, the quadratic formula, or identities to solve the equation. Find all solutions in the interval $[0, 2\pi)$.

63. $3 \sin^2 x - 8 \sin x - 3 = 0$

64. $5 \cos^2 x + 6 \cos x = 8$

65. $2 \tan^2 x + 7 \tan x + 5 = 0$

66. $3 \sin^2 x + 2 \sin x = 5$

67. $\cot x \cos x = \cos x$ [Be careful; see Exercise 109.]

68. $\tan x \cos x = \cos x$

69. $\cos x \csc x = 2 \cos x$

70. $\tan x \sec x + 3 \tan x = 0$

71. $4 \sin x \tan x - 3 \tan x + 20 \sin x - 15 = 0$
[*Hint:* One factor is $\tan x + 5$.]

72. $25 \sin x \cos x - 5 \sin x + 20 \cos x = 4$

73. $\sin^2 x + 2 \sin x - 2 = 0$

74. $\cos^2 x + 5 \cos x = 1$

75. $\tan^2 x + 1 = 3 \tan x$

76. $4 \cos^2 x - 2 \cos x = 1$

77. $2 \tan^2 x - 1 = 3 \tan x$

78. $6 \sin^2 x + 4 \sin x = 1$

79. $\sin^2 x + 3 \cos^2 x = 0$

80. $\sec^2 x - 2 \tan^2 x = 0$

81. $\sin 2x + \cos x = 0$

82. $\cos 2x - \sin x = 1$

83. $9 - 12 \sin x = 4 \cos^2 x$

84. $\sec^2 x + \tan x = 3$

85. $\cos^2 x - \sin^2 x + \sin x = 0$

86. $2 \tan^2 x + \tan x = 5 - \sec^2 x$

87. $\sin \dfrac{x}{2} = 1 - \cos x$

88. $4 \sin^2 \left(\dfrac{x}{2}\right) + \cos^2 x = 2$

In Exercises 89–100, solve the equation graphically.

89. $4 \sin 2x - 3 \cos 2x = 2$

90. $5 \sin 3x + 6 \cos 3x = 1$

91. $3 \sin^3 2x = 2 \cos x$

92. $\sin^2 2x - 3 \cos 2x + 2 = 0$

93. $\tan x + 5 \sin x = 1$

94. $2 \cos^2 x + \sin x + 1 = 0$

95. $\cos^3 x - 3 \cos x + 1 = 0$

96. $\tan x = 3 \cos x$

97. $\cos^4 x - 3 \cos^3 x + \cos x = 1$

98. $\sec x + \tan x = 3$

99. $\sin^3 x + 2 \sin^2 x - 3 \cos x + 2 = 0$

100. $\csc^2 x + \sec x = 1$

101. The number of hours of daylight in Detroit on day t of a non–leap year (with $t = 0$ being January 1) is given by the function

$$d(t) = 3 \sin\left[\frac{2\pi}{365}(t - 80)\right] + 12.$$

(a) On what days of the year are there exactly 11 hours of daylight?

(b) What day has the maximum amount of daylight?

102. A weight hanging from a spring is set into motion (see Figure 6–69 on page 484), moving up and down. Its distance (in centimeters) above or below the equilibrium point at time t seconds is given by

$$d = 5(\sin 6t - 4 \cos 6t).$$

At what times during the first 2 seconds is the weight at the equilibrium position ($d = 0$)?

In Exercises 103–106, use the following fact: When a projectile (such as a ball or a bullet) leaves its starting point at angle of elevation θ with velocity v, the horizontal distance d it travels is given by the equation

$$d = \frac{v^2}{32} \sin 2\theta,$$

where d is measured in feet and v in feet per second. Note that the horizontal distance traveled may be the same for two different angles of elevation, so some of these exercises may have more than one correct answer.

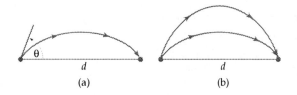

(a)   (b)

103. If muzzle velocity of a rifle is 300 feet per second, at what angle of elevation (in radians) should it be aimed for the bullet to hit a target 2500 feet away?

104. Is it possible for the rifle in Exercise 103 to hit a target that is 3000 feet away? [At what angle of elevation would it have to be aimed?]

105. A fly ball leaves the bat at a velocity of 98 mph and is caught by an outfielder 288 feet away. At what angle of elevation (in degrees) did the ball leave that bat?

106. An outfielder throws the ball at a speed of 75 mph to the catcher who is 200 feet away. At what angle of elevation was the ball thrown?

THINKERS

107. Under what conditions (on the constant) does a basic equation involving the sine and cosine function have *no* solutions?

108. Prove the formula $L = 2r \sin \dfrac{t}{2}$ used in Exercises 53–60 as follows.

(a) Construct the perpendicular line from the center of the circle to the chord PQ, as shown in the figure. Verify that triangles OCP and OCQ are congruent. [*Hint:* Angles P and Q are equal by the Isosceles Triangle Theorem,* and in each triangle, angle C is a right angle (why?). Use the Congruent Triangles Theorem.*]

(b) Use part (a) to explain why angle POC measures $t/2$ radians.

(c) Show that the length of PC is $r \sin \dfrac{t}{2}$.

(d) Use the fact that PC and QC have the same length to conclude that the length L of PC is

$$L = 2r \sin \frac{t}{2}.$$

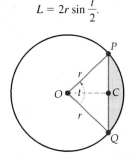

109. What is wrong with this so-called solution?

$$\sin x \tan x = \sin x$$

$$\tan x = 1$$

$$x = \frac{\pi}{4} \quad \text{or} \quad \frac{5\pi}{4}.$$

[*Hint:* Solve the original equation by moving all terms to one side and factoring. Compare your answers with the ones above.]

110. Let n be a fixed positive integer. Describe *all* solutions of the equation $\sin nx = 1/2$. [*Hint:* See Exercises 43–52.]

---

*See the Geometry Review Appendix.

Chapter 8

RIGHT TRIANGLE TRIGONOMETRY

© Jerry Kobalenko/ Getty Images

Chapter Outline

8.1   Right Triangle & Solving Right Triangles

Section Objectives
- Evaluate trigonometric functions of angles.
- Use right triangles to evaluate trigonometric functions.
- Solve right triangles.

> **NOTE**
>
> If you have not read Chapter 6, use Alternate Section 8.1 on page 584 in place of this section.

Trigonometric functions were defined in Chapter 6 as functions whose domains consist of real numbers. In the classical approach, however, the domains of the trigonometric functions consist of *angles*. In other words, instead of starting with a number t and then moving to an angle of t radians, we start directly with the angle, as summarized here.

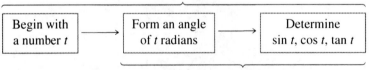

In this chapter (and hereafter, whenever convenient), we shall take this classical approach and begin with angles. From there on, everything is essentially the same. The *values* of the trigonometric functions are still *numbers* and are obtained as before. For example, the point-in-the-plane description now reads as follows.

Point-in-the-Plane Description

Let θ be an angle in standard position and let (x, y) be any point (except the origin) on the terminal side of θ. Let $r = \sqrt{x^2 + y^2}$. Then, the values of the six trigonometric functions of the angle θ are given by

$$\sin \theta = \frac{y}{r} \qquad \cos \theta = \frac{x}{r} \qquad \tan \theta = \frac{y}{x}$$

$$\csc \theta = \frac{r}{y} \qquad \sec \theta = \frac{r}{x} \qquad \cot \theta = \frac{x}{y}$$

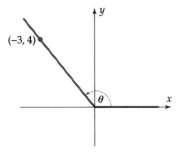

Figure 8–1

EXAMPLE 1

Evaluate the six trigonometric functions at the angle θ shown in Figure 8–1.

SOLUTION   We use $(-3, 4)$ as the point (x, y), so

$$r = \sqrt{x^2 + y^2} = \sqrt{9 + 16} = \sqrt{25} = 5.$$

Thus,

$$\sin \theta = \frac{y}{r} = \frac{4}{5} \qquad \cos \theta = \frac{x}{r} = \frac{-3}{5} \qquad \tan \theta = \frac{y}{x} = \frac{4}{-3}$$

$$\csc \theta = \frac{r}{y} = \frac{5}{4} \qquad \sec \theta = \frac{r}{x} = \frac{5}{-3} \qquad \cot \theta = \frac{x}{y} = \frac{-3}{4}.$$ ∎

DEGREES AND RADIANS

Angles can be measured in either degrees or radians. If radian measure is used (as was the case in Chapter 6), then everything is the same as before. For example, sin 30 denotes the sine of an angle of 30 radians.

But when angles are measured in degrees (as will be done in the rest of this chapter), new notation is needed. To denote the value of the sine function at an angle of 30 *degrees,* we write

$$\sin 30° \qquad \text{[note the degree symbol]}$$

The degree symbol here is essential for avoiding error. For example, an angle of 30 degrees is the same as an angle of $\pi/6$ radians. Therefore,

$$\sin 30° = \sin \pi/6 = 1/2$$

This is *not* the same as sin 30 (the sine of an angle of 30 *radians*); a calculator in radian mode shows that $\sin 30 \approx -.988$.

The various identities proved in earlier sections are valid for angles measured in degrees, provided that π radians is replaced by $180°$. For any angle θ measured in degrees for which the functions are defined, the following identities hold.

Identities for Angles Measured in Degrees

Periodicity Identities

$$\sin(\theta + 360°) = \sin\theta \qquad \csc(\theta + 360°) = \csc\theta$$
$$\cos(\theta + 360°) = \cos\theta \qquad \sec(\theta + 360°) = \sec\theta$$
$$\tan(\theta + 180°) = \tan\theta \qquad \cot(\theta + 180°) = \cot\theta$$

Pythagorean Identities

$$\sin^2\theta + \cos^2\theta = 1 \qquad 1 + \tan^2\theta = \sec^2\theta \qquad 1 + \cot^2\theta = \csc^2\theta$$

Negative Angle Identities

$$\sin(-\theta) = -\sin\theta \qquad \cos(-\theta) = \cos\theta \qquad \tan(-\theta) = -\tan\theta$$

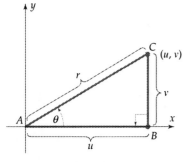

Figure 8–2

RIGHT TRIANGLE DESCRIPTION OF TRIGONOMETRIC FUNCTIONS

For angles between $0°$ and $90°$, the trigonometric functions may be evaluated by using right triangles as follows. Suppose θ is an angle in a right triangle. Place the triangle so that angle θ is in standard position, with the hypotenuse as its terminal side, as shown in Figure 8–2.

Denote the length of the side AB (the one *adjacent* to angle θ) by u and the length of side BC (the one *opposite* angle θ) by v. Then the coordinates of C are (u, v). Let r be the length of the *hypotenuse AC* (the distance from (u, v) to the origin). Then the point-in-the-plane description shows that

$$\sin\theta = \frac{v}{r} = \frac{\text{length of opposite side}}{\text{length of hypotenuse}}, \qquad \cos\theta = \frac{u}{r} = \frac{\text{length of adjacent side}}{\text{length of hypotenuse}},$$

$$\tan\theta = \frac{v}{u} = \frac{\text{length of opposite side}}{\text{length of adjacent side}},$$

and similarly for the other trigonometric functions. These facts can be summarized as follows.

Right Triangle Description

Consider a right triangle containing an angle θ.

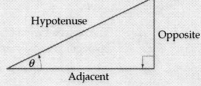

The values of the six trigonometric functions of the angle θ are given by

$$\sin\theta = \frac{\text{opposite}}{\text{hypotenuse}} \qquad \cos\theta = \frac{\text{adjacent}}{\text{hypotenuse}} \qquad \tan\theta = \frac{\text{opposite}}{\text{adjacent}}$$

$$\csc\theta = \frac{\text{hypotenuse}}{\text{opposite}} \qquad \sec\theta = \frac{\text{hypotenuse}}{\text{adjacent}} \qquad \cot\theta = \frac{\text{adjacent}}{\text{opposite}}$$

This description of the trigonometric functions has the advantage of being independent of both the unit circle and the coordinate system in the plane.

EXAMPLE 2

Evaluate sin θ, cos θ, and tan θ for the angle θ shown in Figure 8–3.

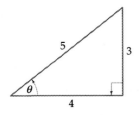

Figure 8–3

SOLUTION   The side opposite angle θ has length 3, and the side adjacent to angle θ has length 4. Hence,

$$\sin \theta = \frac{\text{length of side opposite angle } \theta}{\text{length of hypotenuse}} = \frac{3}{5}$$

$$\cos \theta = \frac{\text{length of side adjacent to angle } \theta}{\text{length of hypotenuse}} = \frac{4}{5}$$

$$\tan \theta = \frac{\text{length of side opposite angle } \theta}{\text{length of side adjacent to angle } \theta} = \frac{3}{4}.$$ ∎

EXAMPLE 3

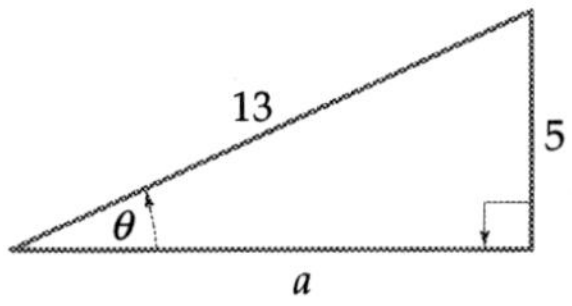

Evaluate sin θ, cos θ, and tan θ when θ is the angle shown in Figure 8–4.

Figure 8–4

SOLUTION   First, we find the length of the third side a by using the Pythagorean Theorem.

$$a^2 + 5^2 = 13^2$$

Multiply out terms: $a^2 + 25 = 169$

Subtract 25 from both sides: $a^2 = 144$

Take square roots on both sides.* $a = \sqrt{144} = 12.$

Now we can calculate the values of the trigonometric functions.

$$\sin \theta = \frac{\text{opposite}}{\text{hypotenuse}} = \frac{5}{13}, \qquad \cos \theta = \frac{\text{adjacent}}{\text{hypotenuse}} = \frac{12}{13},$$

$$\tan \theta = \frac{\text{opposite}}{\text{adjacent}} = \frac{5}{12}.$$ ∎

Unless you are given an appropriate triangle, whose sides are known (or can be computed) as in Example 3, it may be difficult to find the exact values of the trigonometric functions at an angle θ. Fortunately, however, your calculator can provide good approximations, as illustrated in Figure 8–5 on the next page.

---

*The equation $a^2 = 144$ has two solutions, 12 and -12, but only the positive one applies here since a is the side of a triangle.

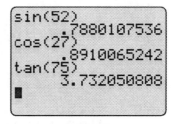

```
sin(52)
        .7880107536
cos(27)
        .8910065242
tan(75)
        3.732050808
■
```

Figure 8–5

In a few cases, however, we can find the exact values of sine, cosine, and tangent.

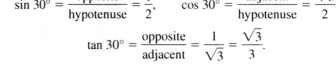

EXAMPLE 4

Evaluate $\sin \theta$, $\cos \theta$, $\tan \theta$ when (a) $\theta = 30°$ (b) $\theta = 60°$.

SOLUTION

(a) Consider a 30°-60°-90° triangle whose hypotenuse has length 2. As explained in Example 3 of the Geometry Review Appendix, the side opposite the 30° angle must have length 1 (half the hypotenuse) and the side adjacent to this angle must have length $\sqrt{3}$, as shown in Figure 8–6. According to the right triangle description,

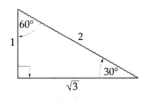

Figure 8–6

$$\sin 30° = \frac{\text{opposite}}{\text{hypotenuse}} = \frac{1}{2}, \qquad \cos 30° = \frac{\text{adjacent}}{\text{hypotenuse}} = \frac{\sqrt{3}}{2},$$

$$\tan 30° = \frac{\text{opposite}}{\text{adjacent}} = \frac{1}{\sqrt{3}} = \frac{\sqrt{3}}{3}.$$

(b) The same triangle can be used to evaluate the trigonometric functions at 60°. In this case, the opposite side has length $\sqrt{3}$ and the adjacent side has length 1. Therefore,

$$\sin 60° = \frac{\text{opposite}}{\text{hypotenuse}} = \frac{\sqrt{3}}{2}, \qquad \cos 60° = \frac{\text{adjacent}}{\text{hypotenuse}} = \frac{1}{2},$$

$$\tan 60° = \frac{\text{opposite}}{\text{adjacent}} = \frac{\sqrt{3}}{1} = \sqrt{3}. \qquad ■$$

EXAMPLE 5

Evaluate $\sin 45°$, $\cos 45°$, $\tan 45°$.

SOLUTION   Consider a 45°-45°-90° triangle whose sides each have length 3 (Figure 8–7). According to the Pythagorean Theorem, the hypotenuse d satisfies

$$d^2 = 3^2 + 3^2 = 18,$$

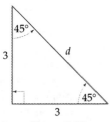

Figure 8–7

so

$$d = \sqrt{18} = \sqrt{9 \cdot 2} = \sqrt{9}\sqrt{2} = 3\sqrt{2}.$$

Therefore,

$$\sin 45° = \frac{\text{opposite}}{\text{hypotenuse}} = \frac{3}{3\sqrt{2}} = \frac{1}{\sqrt{2}} = \frac{\sqrt{2}}{2}$$

$$\cos 45° = \frac{\text{adjacent}}{\text{hypotenuse}} = \frac{3}{3\sqrt{2}} = \frac{1}{\sqrt{2}} = \frac{\sqrt{2}}{2}$$

$$\tan 45° = \frac{\text{opposite}}{\text{adjacent}} = \frac{3}{3} = 1.$$

■

SOLVING RIGHT TRIANGLES

Many applications of trigonometry involve **"solving a triangle."** This means finding the lengths of all three sides and the measures of all three angles when only some of these quantities are given. Solving the right triangles depends on this fact.

> **The right angle description of a trigonometric function (such as sin θ = opposite/hypotenuse) relates three quantities: the angle θ and two sides of the right triangle.**

When two of these three quantities are known, then the third can always be found.

EXAMPLE 6

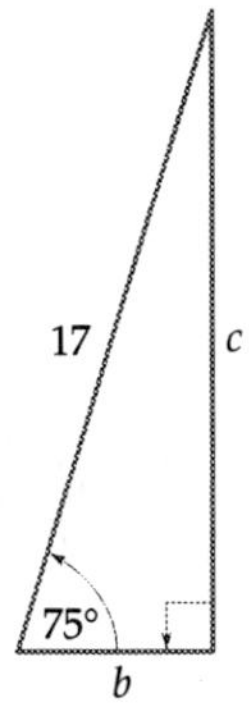

Figure 8–8

Find the lengths of sides b and c in the right triangle shown in Figure 8–8.

SOLUTION   Since the side c is opposite the 75° angle and the hypotenuse is 17, we have

$$\sin 75° = \frac{\text{opposite}}{\text{hypotenuse}} = \frac{c}{17}.$$

We can solve this equation for c.

$$\frac{c}{17} = \sin 75°$$

Multiply both sides by 17: $c = 17 \sin 75°$

Use a calculator (in degree mode) to evaluate sin 75°: $c \approx 17(.9659) \approx 16.42.$

Side b can now be found by the Pythagorean Theorem or by using the fact that

$$\cos 75° = \frac{\text{adjacent}}{\text{hypotenuse}} = \frac{b}{17}.$$

Solving this equation and using a calculator shows that

$$\frac{b}{17} = \cos 75°$$

$$b = 17 \cos 75° \approx 17(.2588) \approx 4.40.$$

■

EXAMPLE 7

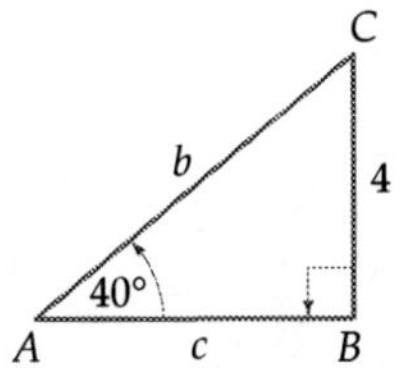

Figure 8–9

Solve the right triangle in Figure 8–9.

SOLUTION   We must find the measure of $\angle C$ and the lengths of sides b and c. Since the sum of the angles of a triangle is 180°, we have

$$40° + 90° + \angle C = 180°$$

$$\angle C = 180° - 40° - 90° = 50°.$$

Furthermore, Figure 8–9 shows that

$$\sin A = \frac{4}{b}$$

Since $A = 40°$: $\quad \sin 40° = \dfrac{4}{b}$

Multiply both sides by b: $\quad b \sin 40° = 4$

Divide both sides by $\sin 40°$: $\quad b = \dfrac{4}{\sin 40°} \approx 6.22.$

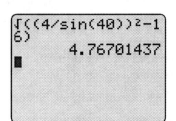

Figure 8–10

Now side c can be found by using the Pythagorean Theorem.

$$4^2 + c^2 = b^2$$

$$c^2 = b^2 - 16$$

$$c = \sqrt{b^2 - 16} = \sqrt{\left(\frac{4}{\sin 40°}\right)^2 - 16}.$$

A calculator shows that $c \approx 4.77$ (Figure 8–10). ∎

CALCULATOR EXPLORATION

In Example 7, use the approximation $b \approx 6.22$ and the Pythagorean Theorem to find c. Is your answer the same as the length of c found in Figure 8–10? Why not? The moral here is: Don't use approximations in intermediate steps if you can avoid it. However, rounding your final answer is usually appropriate.

EXAMPLE 8

Find the degree measure of the angle θ in Figure 8–11.

SOLUTION We first note that

$$\cos \theta = \frac{\text{adjacent}}{\text{hypotenuse}} = \frac{4}{5} = .8.$$

Before calculators were available, θ was found by using a table of cosine values, as follows: Look through the column of cosine values for the closest one to .8, then look in the first column for the corresponding value of θ. You can do the same thing by having your calculator generate a table for $y_1 = \cos x$, as in Figure 8–12. The closest entry to .8 in the cosine (y_1) column is .79968, which corresponds to an angle of 36.9°. Hence, $\theta \approx 36.9°$.

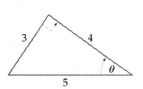

Figure 8–11

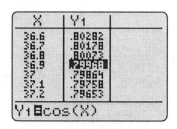

Figure 8–12

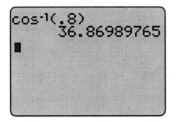

Figure 8–13

A faster, more accurate method of finding θ is to use the COS^{-1} key on your calculator (labeled ACOS on some models). When you key in COS^{-1} .8, as in Figure 8–13, the calculator produces an acute angle whose cosine is .8, namely, $\theta \approx 36.8699°$. Thus, the COS^{-1} key provides the electronic equivalent of searching the cosine table, without actually having to construct the table. ∎

NOTE

In this chapter, we shall use the COS^{-1} key, and the analogous keys SIN^{-1} and TAN^{-1}, as they were used in the preceding example: as a way to find an angle θ in a triangle, when $\sin \theta$ or $\cos \theta$ or $\tan \theta$ is known. The other uses of these keys are discussed in Section 7.4, which deals with the inverse functions of sine, cosine, and tangent.

EXAMPLE 9

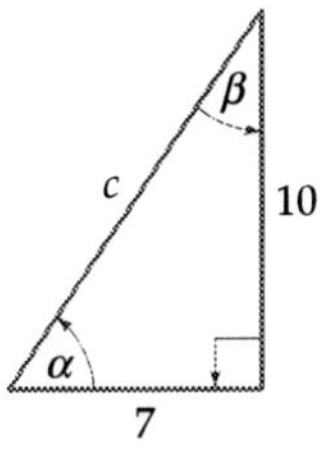

Without using the Pythagorean Theorem, find angles α and β and side c of the triangle in Figure 8–14. Make your answers as accurate as your technology allows.

SOLUTION   We first note that

$$\tan \alpha = \frac{\text{opposite}}{\text{adjacent}} = \frac{10}{7}.$$

Figure 8–14

We use the TAN^{-1} key on a calculator to approximate α and store the result

$$\alpha \approx 55.0079798°$$

in memory A (Figure 8–15).* Since the sum of the angles of a triangle is 180°, we have

$$\alpha + \beta + 90° = 180°$$
$$\beta = 180° - 90° - \alpha.$$

Using a calculator and the stored value of α, we see that $\beta \approx 34.9920202°$ (Figure 8–16).

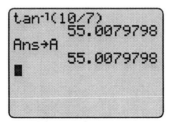

Figure 8–15

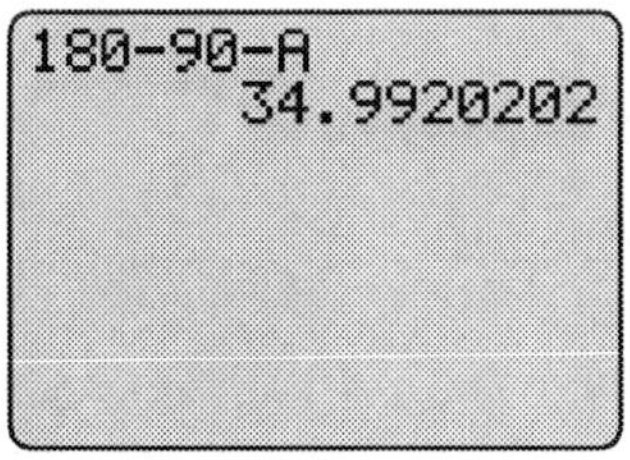

Figure 8–16

---

*We are using a TI-84+. Other calculators and computer programs may give answers with a different degree of accuracy. For instance, a TI-89 gives $\alpha \approx 55.0079798014°$.

Finally, we use the fact that

$$\sin \alpha = \frac{\text{opposite}}{\text{hypotenuse}} = \frac{10}{c}.$$

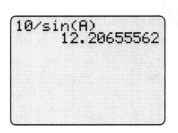

Figure 8–17

Multiplying both ends of this equation by c shows that

$$c \sin \alpha = 10$$

$$c = \frac{10}{\sin \alpha}.$$

Using a calculator and the stored value of α, we find that $c \approx 12.20655562$ (Figure 8–17). ■

EXERCISES 8.1

Directions: *When solving triangles here, all decimal approximations should be rounded off to one decimal place at the end of the computation.*

In Exercises 1–6, *evaluate the trigonometric functions at the angle (in standard position) whose terminal side contains the given point.*

1. $(2, 3)$ **2.** $(4, -2)$ **3.** $(-3, 7)$

4. $(\sqrt{2}, \sqrt{3})$ **5.** $(-3, -\sqrt{2})$ **6.** $(3, -5)$

In Exercises 7–12, *find* $\sin \theta$, $\cos \theta$, $\tan \theta$.

7.

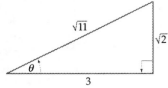

8.

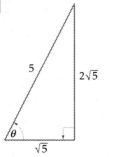

9.

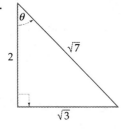

10.

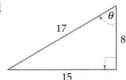

11.

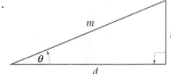

12.

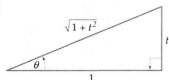

In Exercises 13–18, *find side c of the right triangle in the figure under the given conditions.*

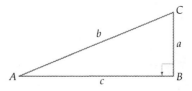

13. $\cos A = 12/13$ and $b = 39$

14. $\sin C = 3/4$ and $b = 12$

15. $\tan A = 5/12$ and $a = 15$

16. $\sec A = 2$ and $b = 8$

17. $\cot A = 6$ and $a = 1.4$

18. $\csc C = 1.5$ and $b = 4.5$

In Exercises 19–24, find the length h of the side of the right triangle, without using a calculator.

19.

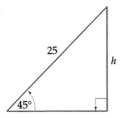

20.

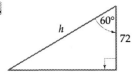

21.

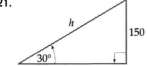

22.

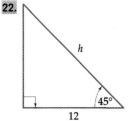

23.

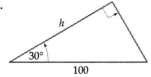

24.

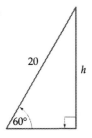

In Exercises 25–28, find the required side without using a calculator.

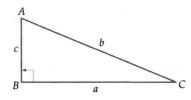

25. $a = 4$ and angle A measures 60°; find c.

26. $c = 5$ and angle A measures 60°; find a.

27. $c = 10$ and angle A measures 30°; find a.

28. $a = 12$ and angle A measures 30°; find c.

In Exercises 29–36, use the figure for Exercises 25–28. Solve the right triangle under the given conditions.

29. $b = 10$ and $\angle C = 40°$

30. $c = 12$ and $\angle C = 37°$

31. $a = 16$ and $\angle A = 14°$

32. $a = 8$ and $\angle A = 40°$

33. $c = 5$ and $\angle A = 65°$

34. $c = 4$ and $\angle C = 28°$

35. $b = 3.5$ and $\angle A = 72°$

36. $a = 4.2$ and $\angle C = 33°$

In Exercises 37–40, find angle θ.

37.

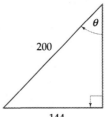

38.

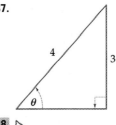

39.

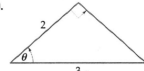

40.

In Exercises 41–48, use the figure for Exercises 25–28 to find angles A and C under the given conditions.

41. $a = 8$ and $c = 15$

42. $b = 14$ and $c = 5$

43. $a = 7$ and $b = 10$

44. $a = 7$ and $c = 3$

45. $b = 18$ and $c = 12$

46. $a = 4$ and $b = 9$

47. $a = 2.5$ and $c = 1.4$

48. $b = 3.7$ and $c = 2.2$

49. Let θ be an acute angle with sides a and b in a triangle, as in the figure below.

   (a) Find the area of the triangle (in terms of h and a).
   (b) Find $\sin\theta$.
   (c) Use part (b) to show that $h = b\sin\theta$.
   (d) Use parts (a) and (c) to show that the area A of a triangle in which an acute angle θ has sides a and b is

$$A = \frac{1}{2}ab\sin\theta.$$

In Exercises 50–54, use the result of Exercise 49 to find the area of the given triangle.

50.

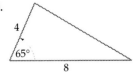

51.

52.

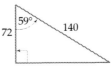

53.

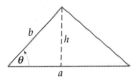

54.

55. Let θ and α be acute angles of a right triangle, as shown in the figure.

   (a) Find $\sin\theta$ and $\cos\alpha$.
   (b) Explain why $\theta + \alpha = 90°$.
   (c) Use parts (a) and (b) to conclude that for any acute angle θ,

$$\cos(90° - \theta) = \sin\theta.$$

56. (a) Using the figure for Exercise 55, find $\cos\theta$ and $\sin\alpha$.
   (b) Use part (a) and part (b) of Exercise 55 to show that for any acute angle θ,

$$\sin(90° - \theta) = \cos\theta.$$

This equation and the one in Exercise 55(c) are called *cofunction identities*.

8.1 *ALTERNATE* Right Triangle & Solving Right Triangles

Section Objectives
- Use right triangles to evaluate the trigonometric functions of acute angles.
- Use the point-in-the-plane description to evaluate trigonometric functions of any angle.

NOTE
If you have read Chapter 6, omit this section. If you have not read Chapter 6, use this section in place of Section 8.1.

Before reading this section, it might be a good idea to read the Geometry Review Appendix, which presents the basic facts about angles and triangles that frequently are used here. In particular, recall that a **right triangle** is one that contains a **right angle**, that is, an angle of 90°. An **acute angle** is an angle whose measure is less than 90°. Consider the right triangles in Figure 8–18, each of which has an acute angle of θ degrees.

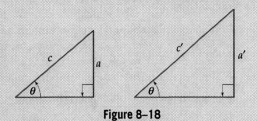

Figure 8–18

Since the sum of the angles of any triangle is 180°, we see that the third angle in each of these triangles has the same measure, namely, $180° - 90° - \theta$. Thus, both triangles have equal corresponding angles and, therefore, are similar. Consequently, by the Ratios Theorem of the Geometry Review Appendix, we know that the ratio of corresponding sides is the same, that is

$$\frac{a}{c} = \frac{a'}{c'}.$$

Each of these fractions is the ratio

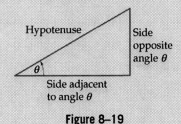

Figure 8–19

$$\frac{\text{length of the side opposite angle } \theta}{\text{length of the hypotenuse}},$$

as indicated in Figure 8–19. Consequently, *this ratio depends only on the angle θ* and *not* on the size of the triangle. Similar remarks apply to the ratios of other sides of the triangle in Figure 8–19 and make it possible to define three new functions. For each function, the input is an acute angle θ, and the corresponding output is a ratio of sides in any right triangle containing angle θ, as summarized here.

Trigonometric Functions of Acute Angles

Name of Function	Abbre-viation	Rule of Function
sine	sin	$\sin \theta = \dfrac{\text{length of side opposite angle } \theta}{\text{length of hypotenuse}}$
cosine	cos	$\cos \theta = \dfrac{\text{length of side adjacent to angle } \theta}{\text{length of hypotenuse}}$
tangent	tan	$\tan \theta = \dfrac{\text{length of side opposite angle } \theta}{\text{length of side adjacent to angle } \theta}$

NOTE

Now turn to page 577 and begin reading at Example 2. When you have finished Example 9 on page 582, return here and continue reading below. [If you prefer, you can delay reading the material below until Section 8.3, where it will first be used.]

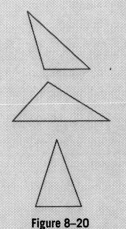

Figure 8–20

The preceding discussion applies only to right triangles. The next step is to learn how to solve other triangles, such as those in Figure 8–20. To do this, we must find a description of the trigonometric functions that is not limited to acute angles of a right triangle. First, we introduce some terminology.

An angle in the coordinate plane is said to be in **standard position** if its vertex is at the origin and one of its sides (which we call the **initial side**) is on the positive x-axis, as shown in Figure 8–21. The other side of the angle will be called its **terminal side.**

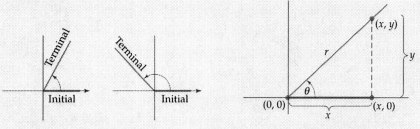

Figure 8–21   Figure 8–22

Let θ be an acute angle in standard position. Choose any point (x, y) on the terminal side of θ (except the origin) and consider the right triangle with vertices $(0, 0)$, $(x, 0)$, and (x, y) shown in Figure 8–22.

The legs of this triangle have lengths x and y, respectively. The distance formula shows that the hypotenuse has length

$$\sqrt{(x - 0)^2 + (y - 0)^2} = \sqrt{x^2 + y^2},$$

which we denote by r. The triangle shows that

$$\sin \theta = \frac{y}{r} \qquad \cos \theta = \frac{x}{r} \qquad \tan \theta = \frac{y}{x}.$$

We now have a description of the trigonometric functions in terms of the coordinate plane rather than right triangles. Furthermore, this description makes sense for *any* angle. Consequently, we make the following definition.

**Point-in-the-Plane
Description**

Let θ be an angle in standard position and (x, y) any point (except the origin) on its terminal side. Then the trigonometric functions are defined by these rules:

$$\sin \theta = \frac{y}{r}, \qquad \cos \theta = \frac{x}{r}, \qquad \tan \theta = \frac{y}{x} \quad (x \neq 0),$$

where $r = \sqrt{x^2 + y^2}$ is the distance from (x, y) to the origin.

The discussion preceding the box shows that when θ is an acute angle, these definitions produce the same numbers for $\sin \theta$, $\cos \theta$, and $\tan \theta$ as does the right triangle definition on page 585. It can be shown that the values of the trigonometric functions of θ are independent of the point that is chosen on the terminal side (just as the definition for acute angles is independent of the size of the right triangle).

EXAMPLE 10

Find $\sin \theta$, $\cos \theta$, and $\tan \theta$ for the angle θ shown in Figure 8–23.

SOLUTION   Since $(-5, 7)$ is on the terminal side of θ, we apply the definitions in the preceding box with $(x, y) = (-5, 7)$ and

$$r = \sqrt{x^2 + y^2} = \sqrt{(-5)^2 + 7^2} = \sqrt{74}:$$

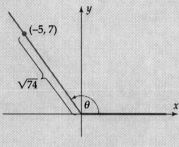

$$\sin \theta = \frac{y}{r} = \frac{7}{\sqrt{74}}$$

$$\cos \theta = \frac{x}{r} = \frac{-5}{\sqrt{74}}$$

$$\tan \theta = \frac{y}{x} = \frac{7}{-5} = -\frac{7}{5}.$$

Figure 8–23

For most angles, we use a calculator in degree mode to approximate the values of the trigonometric functions, as in Figure 8–24. But there are a few angles for which we can compute the exact values of the trigonometric functions.

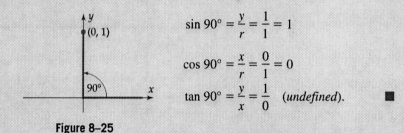

```
sin(125)
          .8191520443
cos(178)
         -.999390827
tan(98)
          -7.115369722
■
```

Figure 8–24

EXAMPLE 11

Find the exact values of the trigonometric functions at $\theta = 90°$.

SOLUTION   We use the point $(0, 1)$ on the terminal side of an angle of $90°$ in standard position (Figure 8–25). In this case, $r = \sqrt{x^2 + y^2} = \sqrt{0^2 + 1^2} = 1$, so

$$\sin 90° = \frac{y}{r} = \frac{1}{1} = 1$$

$$\cos 90° = \frac{x}{r} = \frac{0}{1} = 0$$

$$\tan 90° = \frac{y}{x} = \frac{1}{0} \quad (undefined).$$

Figure 8–25

The last part of Example 11 shows that the domain of the tangent function excludes $90°$, whereas the domains of sine and cosine include all angles.

EXAMPLE 12

Find the exact values of $\sin 135°$, $\cos 135°$, and $\tan 135°$.

SOLUTION   Construct an angle of $135°$ in standard position and let P be the point on the terminal side that is 1 unit from the origin (Figure 8–26 on the next page). Draw a vertical line from P to the x-axis, forming a right triangle with hypotenuse 1 and two angles of $45°$. Each side of this triangle has length $\sqrt{2}/2$, as explained in Example 2 of the Geometry Review Appendix. Therefore, the coordinates of P are $(-\sqrt{2}/2, \sqrt{2}/2)$, and we have

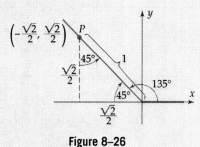

$$\sin 135° = \frac{y}{r} = \frac{\sqrt{2}/2}{1} = \frac{\sqrt{2}}{2}$$

$$\cos 135° = \frac{x}{r} = \frac{-\sqrt{2}/2}{1} = -\frac{\sqrt{2}}{2}$$

$$\tan 135° = \frac{y}{x} = \frac{\sqrt{2}/2}{-\sqrt{2}/2} = -1.$$

Figure 8–26

EXERCISES ALTERNATE 8.1

Use the exercises for Section 8.1 on page 582.

8.2 Applications

Section Objective ■ Use right triangle trigonometry to solve applied problems.

The following examples illustrate a variety of practical applications of triangle trigonometry.

EXAMPLE 1

Lola and her sister Harper see a tree on the river's edge directly opposite them. They walk along the riverbank for 120 feet and note that the angle formed by their path and a line to the tree measures 70°, as indicated in Figure 8–27. How wide is the river?

SOLUTION   Using the right triangle whose one leg is the width w of the river and whose other leg is the 120-foot path on this side of the river, we see that

$$\tan 70° = \frac{\text{opposite}}{\text{adjacent}} = \frac{w}{120}.$$

Solving this equation for w, we have

$$w = 120 \tan 70° \approx 329.7.$$

So the river is about 330 feet wide.   ■

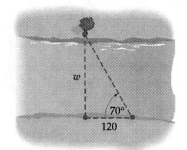

Figure 8–27

EXAMPLE 2

A plane takes off, making an angle of 18° with the ground. After the plane travels three miles along this flight path, how high (in feet) is it above the ground?

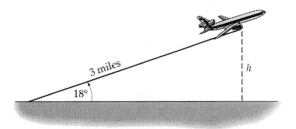

Figure 8–28

SOLUTION   Figure 8–28 shows that

$$\sin 18° = \frac{\text{opposite}}{\text{hypotenuse}} = \frac{h}{3}$$

Multiply both sides by 3: $h = 3 \sin 18° \approx .92705$ miles.

Since there are 5280 feet in a mile, the height of the plane in feet is

$$h = .92705 \cdot 5280 \approx 4894.8 \text{ feet.} \quad \blacksquare$$

EXAMPLE 3

According to the safety sticker on an extension ladder, the distance from the foot of the ladder to the base of the wall on which it leans should be one-fourth of the length of the ladder. If the ladder is in this position, what angle does it make with the ground?

SOLUTION   Let c be the distance from the foot of the ladder to the base of the wall. Then the ladder's length is $4c$, as shown in Figure 8–29. If θ is the angle the ladder makes with the ground, then

$$\cos \theta = \frac{\text{adjacent}}{\text{hypotenuse}} = \frac{c}{4c} = \frac{1}{4}.$$

Using the COS^{-1} key, we find that $\theta \approx 75.52°$, as shown in Figure 8–30. $\blacksquare$

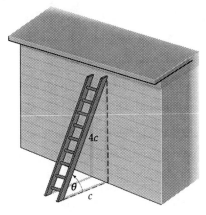

Figure 8–29

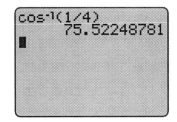

Figure 8–30

In many practical applications, one uses the angle between the horizontal and some other line (for instance, the line of sight from an observer to a distant object). This angle is called the **angle of elevation** or the **angle of depression,** depending on whether the line is above or below the horizontal, as shown in Figure 8–31.

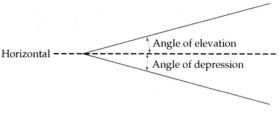

Horizontal

Angle of elevation

Angle of depression

Figure 8–31

EXAMPLE 4

A surveyor stands on one edge of a ravine. By using the method in Example 1, she determines that the ravine is 125 feet wide. She then determines that the angle of depression from the edge where she is standing to a point on the bottom of the ravine is 57.5°, as shown in Figure 8–32 (which is not to scale). How deep is the ravine?

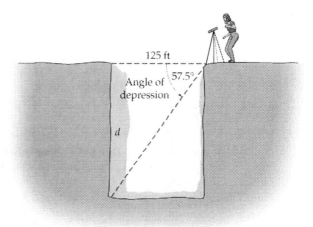

125 ft

Angle of
depression

57.5°

d

Figure 8–32

SOLUTION   From Figure 8–32, we see that

$$\tan 57.5° = \frac{\text{opposite}}{\text{adjacent}} = \frac{d}{125}$$

Multiply both sides by 125: $\qquad\qquad d = 125 \tan 57.5°$

$$d \approx 196.21 \text{ feet} \qquad\blacksquare$$

EXAMPLE 5

A wire is to be stretched from the top of a 10-meter-high building to a point on the ground. From the top of the building, the angle of depression to the ground point is 22°. How long must the wire be?

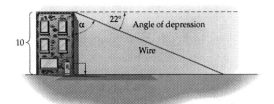

Figure 8–33

SOLUTION   Figure 8–33 shows that the sum of the angle of depression and the angle α is 90°. Hence, α measures $90° - 22° = 68°$. We know the length of the side of the triangle adjacent to the angle α and must find the hypotenuse w (the length of the wire). Using the cosine function, we see that

$$\cos 68° = \frac{\text{adjacent}}{\text{hypotenuse}} = \frac{10}{w}$$

$$w = \frac{10}{\cos 68°} \approx 26.7 \text{ meters.} \qquad \blacksquare$$

EXAMPLE 6

A large American flag flies from a pole on top of the Terminal Tower in Cleveland (Figure 8–34). At a point 203 feet from the base of the tower, the angle of elevation to the bottom of the flag pole is 74°, and the angle of elevation to the top of the pole is 75.285°. To the nearest foot, how long is the flagpole?

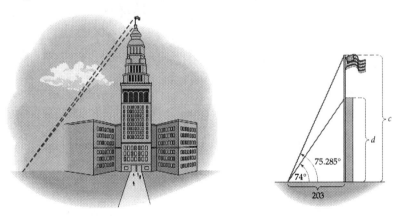

Figure 8–34   Figure 8–35

SOLUTION   By abstracting the given information, we see that there are two right triangles, as shown in Figure 8–35 (which is not to scale). The length of the flagpole is $c - d$. We can use the two triangles to find c and d.

Larger Triangle

$$\frac{c}{203} = \frac{\text{opposite}}{\text{adjacent}} = \tan 75.285°$$

$$c = 203 \tan 75.285° \approx 773$$

Smaller Triangle

$$\frac{d}{203} = \frac{\text{opposite}}{\text{adjacent}} = \tan 74°$$

$$d = 203 \tan 74° \approx 708$$

As shown in Figure 8–36, the length of the flagpole is

$$c - d \approx 773 - 708 = 65 \text{ feet.} \qquad \blacksquare$$

```
203tan(75.285)-2
03tan(74)
          65.02034083
■
```

Figure 8–36

EXAMPLE 7

Phil Embree stands on the edge of one bank of a canal and observes a lamp post on the edge of the other bank of the canal. His eye level is 152 centimeters above the ground (approximately 5 feet). The angle of elevation from eye level to the top of the lamp post is 12°, and the angle of depression from eye level to the bottom of the lamp post is 7°, as shown in Figure 8–37. How wide is the canal? How high is the lamp post?

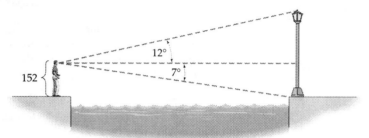

Figure 8–37

SOLUTION   Abstracting the essential information, we obtain the diagram in Figure 8–38.

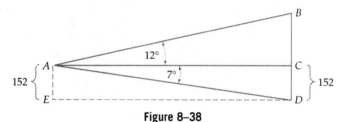

Figure 8–38

We must find the height of the lamp post BD and the width of the canal AC (or ED). The eye level height AE of the observer is 152 centimeters. Since AC and ED are parallel, CD also has length 152 centimeters. In right triangle ACD, we know the angle of 7° and the side CD opposite it. We must find the adjacent side AC. The tangent function is needed.

$$\tan 7° = \frac{\text{opposite}}{\text{adjacent}} = \frac{152}{AC} \qquad \text{or, equivalently,} \qquad AC = \frac{152}{\tan 7°}$$

$$AC = \frac{152}{\tan 7°} \approx 1237.94 \text{ centimeters.}$$

So the canal is approximately 12.3794 meters* wide (about 40.6 feet). Now using right triangle ACB, we see that

$$\tan 12° = \frac{\text{opposite}}{\text{adjacent}} = \frac{BC}{AC} \approx \frac{BC}{1237.94}$$

or, equivalently,

$$BC \approx 1237.94(\tan 12°) \approx 263.13 \text{ centimeters.}$$

Therefore, the height of the lamp post BD is $BC + CD \approx 263.13 + 152 = 415.13$ centimeters or, equivalently, 4.1513 meters.   ∎

---

*Remember, 100 centimeters = 1 meter.

EXERCISES 8.2

In Exercises 1–4, solve the right triangle.

1.

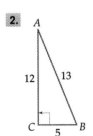

2.

3.

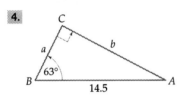

4.

5. What is the width of the river in Example 1 if the angle to the tree is 40° (and all the other information is the same)?

6. Suppose the plane in Example 2 takes off at an angle of 5° and travels along this path for one mile. How high (in feet) is the plane above the ground?

7. Suppose you have a 24-foot-long ladder and you ignore the safety advice in Example 3 by placing the foot of the ladder 9 feet from the base of the wall. What angle does the ladder make with the ground?

8. The surveyor in Example 4 stands at the edge of another ravine, which is known to be 115 feet wide. She notes that the angle of depression from the edge she is standing on to the bottom of the oposite side is 64.3°. How deep is this ravine?

9. How long a wire is needed in Example 5 if the angle of depression is 25.8°?

10. Suppose that the flagpole on the Terminal Tower (Example 6) has been replaced. Now from a point 240 feet from the base of the tower, the angle of elevation to the bottom of the flagpole is 71.3°, and the angle of elevation to the top of the pole is 72.9°. To the nearest foot, how long is the new flagpole?

11. A 20-foot-long ladder leans on a wall of a building. The foot of the ladder makes an angle of 50° with the ground.

How far above the ground does the top of the ladder touch the wall?

12. A pilot flying at an altitude of 14,500 feet notes that his angle of depression to the control tower of a nearby airport is 15°. If the plane continues flying at this altitude toward the control tower, how far must it travel before it is directly over the tower?

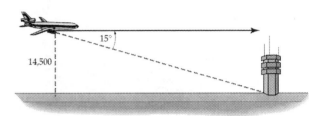

13. A straight road leads from an ocean beach into the nearby hills. The road has a constant upward grade of 3°. After taking this road for one mile, how high above sea level (in feet) are you?

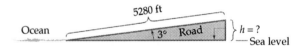

14. If you travel the road in Exercise 13 for a mile and a half, how high above sea level are you?

15. A powerful searchlight projects a beam of light vertically upward so that it shines on the bottom of a cloud. A clinometer, 600 feet from the searchlight, measures the angle θ, as shown in the figure. If θ measures 80°, how high is the cloud?

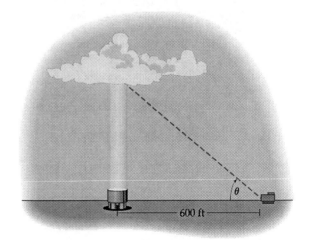

16. A wire from the top of a TV tower to the ground makes an angle of 49.5° with the ground and touches ground 225 feet from the base of the tower. How high is the tower?

17. Find the distance across the pond (from *B* to *C*) if *AC* is 110 feet and angle *A* measures 38°.

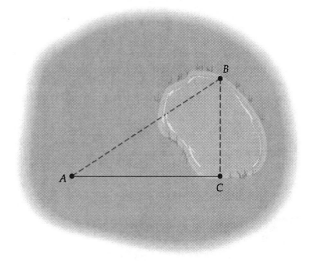

18. The Seattle Space Needle casts a 225-foot-long shadow. If the angle of elevation from the tip of the shadow to the top of the Space Needle is 69.6°, how high is the Space Needle?

19. Batman is on the edge of a 200-foot-deep chasm and wants to jump to the other side. A tree on the edge of the chasm is directly across from him. He walks 20 feet to his right and notes that the angle to the tree is 54°. His jet belt enables him to jump a maximum of 24 feet. How wide is the chasm, and is it safe for Batman to jump?

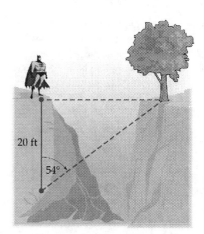

20. From the top of a 130-foot-high lighthouse, the angle of depression to a boat in Lake Erie is 2.5°. How far is the boat from the lighthouse?

21. If you stand upright on a mountainside that makes a 62° angle with the horizontal and stretch your arm straight out at shoulder height, you may be able to touch the mountain (as shown in the figure). Can a person with an arm reach of 27 inches, whose shoulder is five feet above the ground, touch the mountain?

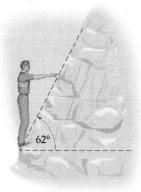

22. Alice is flying a kite. Her hand is three feet above ground level and is holding the end of a 300-foot-long kite string, which makes an angle of 57° with the horizontal. How high is the kite above the ground?

23. It is claimed that the Ohio Turnpike never has an uphill grade of more than 3°. How long must a straight uphill segment of the road be to allow a vertical rise of 450 feet?

24. A swimming pool is three feet deep in the shallow end. The bottom of the pool has a steady downward drop of 12°. If the pool is 50 feet long, how deep is it at the deep end?

25. Consider a 16-foot-long drawbridge on a medieval castle, as shown in the figure. The royal army is engaged in ignominious retreat. The king would like to raise the end of the drawbridge 8 feet off the ground so that Sir Rodney can jump onto the drawbridge and scramble into the castle while the enemy's cavalry are held at bay. Through how much of an angle must the drawbridge be raised for the end of it to be 8 feet off the ground?

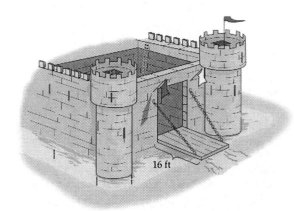

26. Through what angle must the drawbridge in Exercise 25 be raised in order that its end be directly above the center of the moat?

27. A buoy in the ocean is observed from the top of a 40-meter-high radar tower on shore. The angle of depression from the top of the tower to the base of the buoy is 6.5°. How far is the buoy from the base of the radar tower?

28. A 150-foot-long ramp connects a ground-level parking lot with the entrance of a building. If the entrance is 8 feet above the ground, what angle does the ramp make with the ground?

29. A plane flies a straight course. On the ground directly below the flight path, observers two miles apart spot the plane at the same time. The plane's angle of elevation is 46° from one observation point and 71° from the other. How high is the plane?

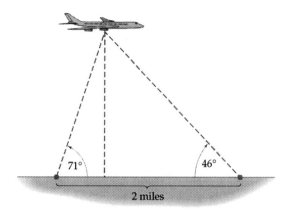

30. A man stands 20 feet from a statue. The angle of elevation from his eye level to the top of the statue is 30°, and the angle of depression to the base of the statue is 15°. How tall is the statue?

31. Two boats lie on a straight line with the base of a lighthouse. From the top of the lighthouse (21 meters above water level), it is observed that the angle of depression of the nearer boat is 53° and the angle of depression of the farther boat is 27°. How far apart are the boats?

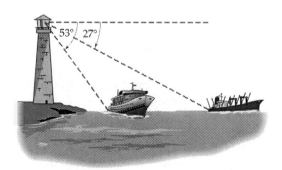

32. A rocket shoots straight up from the launchpad. Five seconds after liftoff, an observer two miles away notes that the rocket's angle of elevation is 3.5°. Four seconds later, the angle of elevation is 41°. How far did the rocket rise during those four seconds?

33. From a 35-meter-high window, the angle of depression to the top of a nearby streetlight is 55°. The angle of depression to the base of the streetlight is 57.8°. How high is the streetlight?

34. A plane takes off at an angle of 6° traveling at the rate of 200 feet/second. If it continues on this flight path at the same speed, how many minutes will it take to reach an altitude of 8000 feet?

35. A car on a straight road passes under a bridge. Two seconds later an observer on the bridge, 20 feet above the road, notes that the angle of depression to the car is 7.4°. How fast (in miles per hour) is the car traveling? [*Note:* 60 mph is equivalent to 88 feet/second.]

36. A plane passes directly over your head at an altitude of 500 feet. Two seconds later, you observe that its angle of elevation is 42°. How far did the plane travel during those two seconds?

37. Laura Bernett is 5 ft-4 inches tall. She stands 10 feet from a streetlight and casts a 4-foot-long shadow. How tall is the streetlight? What is angle θ?

38. One plane flies straight east at an altitude of 31,000 feet. A second plane is flying west at an altitude of 14,000 feet on a course that lies directly below that of the first plane and directly above the straight road from Thomasville to Johnsburg. As the first plane passes over Thomasville, the second is passing over Johnsburg. At that instant, both planes spot a beacon next to the road between Thomasville to Johnsburg. The angle of depression from the first plane to the beacon is 61°, and the angle of depression from the second plane to the beacon is 34°. How far is Thomasville from Johnsburg?

39. A schematic diagram of a pedestrian overpass is shown in the figure. If you walk on the overpass from one end to the other, how far have you walked?

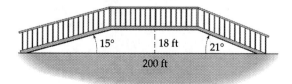

40. A 5-inch-high plastic beverage glass has a 2.5-inch-diameter base. Its sides slope outward at a 4° angle as shown. What is the diameter of the top of the glass?

41. In aerial navigation, directions are given in degrees clockwise from north. Thus, east is 90°, south is 180°, and so on, as shown in the figure. A plane travels from an airport for 200 miles in the direction 300°. How far west of the airport is the plane then?

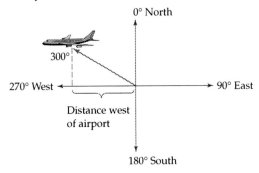

42. A plane travels at a constant 300 mph in the direction 65° (see Exercise 41).

(a) How far east of its starting point is the plane after half an hour?

(b) How far north of its starting point is the plane after 2 hours and 24 minutes?

43. A closed 60-foot-long drawbridge is 24 feet above water level. When open, the bridge makes an angle of 33° with the horizontal.

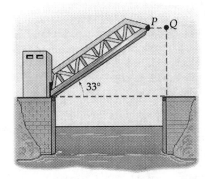

(a) How high is the tip P of the open bridge above the water?

(b) When the bridge is open, what is the distance from P to Q?

THINKERS

44. A gutter is to be made from a strip of metal 24 inches wide by bending up the sides to form a trapezoid.

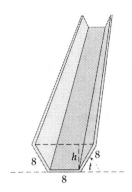

(a) Express the area of the cross section of the gutter as a function of the angle t. [*Hint:* The area of a trapezoid with bases b and b' and height h is $h(b + b')/2$.]

(b) For what value of t will this area be as large as possible?

45. The cross section of a tunnel is a semicircle with radius 10 meters. The interior walls of the tunnel form a rectangle.

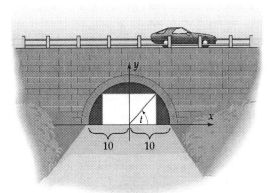

(a) Express the area of the rectangular cross section of the tunnel opening as a function of angle t.

(b) For what value of t is the cross-sectional area of the tunnel opening as large as possible? What are the dimensions of the tunnel opening in this case?

46. A spy plane on a practice run over the Midwest takes a picture that shows Cleveland, Ohio, on the eastern horizon and St. Louis, Missouri, 520 miles away, on the western horizon (the figure is not to scale). Assuming that the radius of the earth is 3950 miles, how high was the plane when the picture was taken? [*Hint:* The sight lines from the plane to the horizons are tangent to the earth, and a tangent line to a circle is perpendicular to the radius at that point. The arc of the earth between St. Louis and Cleveland is 520 miles long. Use this fact and the arc length formula to find angle θ (your answers will be in radians). Note that $\alpha = \theta/2$ (why?).]

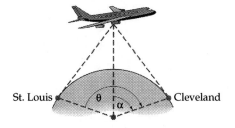

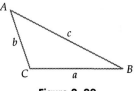

St. Louis θ α Cleveland

47. A 50-foot-high flagpole stands on top of a building. From a point on the ground, the angle of elevation of the top of the pole is 43°, and the angle of elevation of the bottom of the pole is 40°. How high is the building?

48. Two points on level ground are 500 meters apart. The angles of elevation from these points to the top of a nearby hill are 52° and 67°, respectively. The two points and the ground level point directly below the top of the hill lie on a straight line. How high is the hill?

8.3 The Law of Cosines

Section Objectives
- Use the Law of Cosines to solve oblique triangles.
- Use the Law of Cosines to solve applied problems.

Figure 8–39

We now consider the solution of *oblique* triangles (ones that don't contain a right angle). We shall use **standard notation** for triangles: Each vertex is labeled with a capital letter, and the length of the side opposite that vertex is denoted by the same letter in lower case, as shown in Figure 8–39. The letter A will also be used to label the *angle* at vertex A and similarly for B and C. So we shall make statements such as $A = 37°$ or $\cos B = .326$.

The first fact needed to solve oblique triangles is the Law of Cosines, whose proof is given at the end of this section.

Law of Cosines

In any triangle ABC, with sides of lengths a, b, c, as in Figure 8–39,

$$a^2 = b^2 + c^2 - 2bc \cos A$$
$$b^2 = a^2 + c^2 - 2ac \cos B$$
$$c^2 = a^2 + b^2 - 2ab \cos C$$

You need only memorize one of these equations since each of them provides essentially the same information: a description of one side of a triangle in terms of the angle opposite it and the other two sides.

NOTE

When C is a right angle, then c is the hypotenuse and

$$\cos C = \cos 90° = 0.$$

In this case, the third equation in the Law of Cosines becomes the Pythagorean Theorem:

$$c^2 = a^2 + b^2.$$

So the Pythagorean Theorem is a special case of the Law of Cosines.

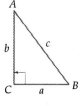

EXAMPLE 1

If the triangle in Figure 8–39 has $a = 7$, $c = 15$ and $B = 60°$, find b.

SOLUTION   Using the second equation in the Law of Cosines, we have

$$b^2 = a^2 + c^2 - 2ac \cos B$$
$$= 7^2 + 15^2 - 2 \cdot 7 \cdot 15 \cos 60°$$
$$= 49 + 225 - 210 \cos 60°$$
$$= 274 - 210 \cdot \frac{1}{2}$$
$$b^2 = 169$$

Hence, $b = \sqrt{169} = 13$. ∎

Sometimes it is more convenient to use the Law of Cosines in a slightly different form. To do this we solve the first equation in the Law of Cosines for $\cos A$.

$$a^2 = b^2 + c^2 - 2bc \cos A$$

Add $2bc \cos A$ to both sides: $2bc \cos A + a^2 = b^2 + c^2$

Subtract a^2 from both sides: $2bc \cos A = b^2 + c^2 - a^2$

Divide both sides by $2bc$: $\cos A = \dfrac{b^2 + c^2 - a^2}{2bc}$

So we have the following result.

Law of Cosines: Alternate Form

> In any triangle ABC, with sides of lengths a, b, c, as in Figure 8–39,
>
> $$\cos A = \frac{b^2 + c^2 - a^2}{2bc}.$$

The other two equations can be similarly rewritten. In this form, the Law of Cosines provides a description of each angle of a triangle in terms of the three sides. Consequently, the Law of Cosines can be used to solve triangles in these cases:

1. Two sides and the angle between them are known (SAS).
2. Three sides are known (SSS).

EXAMPLE 2

SAS   Solve triangle ABC in Figure 8–40.

SOLUTION   We have $a = 16$, $b = 10$, and $C = 110°$. The right side of the third equation in the Law of Cosines involves only these known quantities. Hence,

$$c^2 = a^2 + b^2 - 2ab \cos C$$
$$c^2 = 16^2 + 10^2 - 2 \cdot 16 \cdot 10 \cos 110°$$
$$c^2 \approx 256 + 100 - 320(-.342) \approx 465.4.*$$

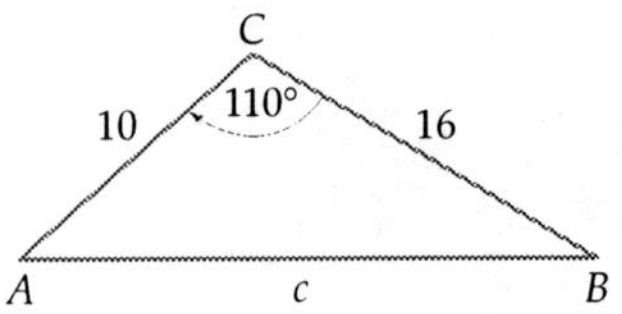

Figure 8–40

*Throughout this chapter, all decimals are printed in rounded-off form for reading convenience, but no rounding is done in the actual computation until the final answer is obtained.

Therefore, $c \approx \sqrt{465.4} \approx 21.6$. Now use the alternate form of the Law of Cosines.

$$\cos A = \frac{b^2 + c^2 - a^2}{2bc}$$

$$\approx \frac{10^2 + (21.6)^2 - 16^2}{2 \cdot 10 \cdot 21.6} \approx .7172.$$

A calculator (in degree mode) shows that $\cos^{-1}(.7172) \approx 44.2°$. So $A \approx 44.2°$ is an angle with cosine .7172. Hence,

$$B = 180° - A - C$$

$$\approx 180° - 44.2° - 110° = 25.8°. \qquad \blacksquare$$

EXAMPLE 3

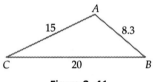

Figure 8–41

SSS   Find the angles of triangle ABC in Figure 8–41.

SOLUTION   In this case, $a = 20$, $b = 15$, and $c = 8.3$. By the alternate form of the Law of Cosines,

$$\cos A = \frac{b^2 + c^2 - a^2}{2bc}$$

$$= \frac{15^2 + 8.3^2 - 20^2}{2 \cdot 15 \cdot 8.3} = \frac{-106.11}{249} \approx -.4261.$$

The COS^{-1} key shows that $A \approx 115.2°$. Similarly, the alternate form of the Law of Cosines yields

$$\cos B = \frac{a^2 + c^2 - b^2}{2ac}$$

$$\cos B = \frac{20^2 + 8.3^2 - 15^2}{2 \cdot 20 \cdot 8.3} = \frac{243.89}{332} \approx .7346$$

$$B \approx 42.7°.$$

Therefore, $C \approx 180° - 115.2° - 42.7° = 22.1°.$ $\qquad \blacksquare$

EXAMPLE 4

Two trains leave a station on different tracks. The tracks make an angle of 125° with the station as vertex. The first train travels at an average speed of 100 kilometers per hour, and the second travels at an average speed of 65 kilometers per hour. How far apart are the trains after 2 hours?

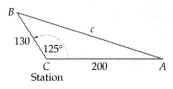

Figure 8-42

SOLUTION   The first train A traveling at 100 kilometers per hour for 2 hours goes a distance of $100 \times 2 = 200$ kilometers. The second train B travels a distance of $65 \times 2 = 130$ kilometers. So we have the situation shown in Figure 8–42.

By the Law of Cosines,

$$c^2 = a^2 + b^2 - 2ab \cos C$$

$$= 130^2 + 200^2 - 2 \cdot 130 \cdot 200 \cos 125°$$

$$= 56{,}900 - 52{,}000 \cos 125° \approx 86{,}725.97$$

$$c \approx \sqrt{86{,}725.97} = 294.5 \text{ kilometers.}$$

The trains are 294.5 kilometers apart after 2 hours.   ■

EXAMPLE 5

A small powerboat leaves Chicago and sails 35 miles due east on Lake Michigan. It then changes course 59° northward, heading for Grand Haven, Michigan, as shown in Figure 8–43. After traveling 60 miles on this course, how far is the boat from Chicago?

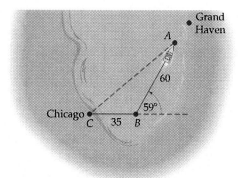

Figure 8-43

SOLUTION   Figure 8–43 shows that

$$B + 59° = 180°$$

$$B = 180° - 59° = 121°.$$

We must find the side of the triangle opposite angle B. By the Law of Cosines,

$$b^2 = a^2 + c^2 - 2ac \cos B$$

$$b^2 = 35^2 + 60^2 - 2 \cdot 35 \cdot 60 \cos 121°$$

$$b^2 \approx 6988.1599$$

$$b \approx \sqrt{6988.1599} \approx 83.5952.$$

So the boat is about 83.6 miles from Chicago.   ■

EXAMPLE 6

A sculpture is being placed in front of a new office building. The sculpture consists of two steel beams of lengths 10 and 12 feet, respectively, and a 15.2-foot cable, as shown in Figure 8–44. If the 10-foot beam makes an angle of 50° with the ground, what angle does the 12-foot beam make with the ground?

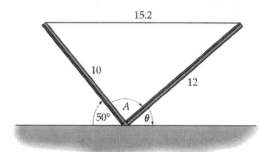

Figure 8–44

SOLUTION   We must find the measure of angle θ. As you can see in Figure 8–44,

$$50° + A + \theta = 180°.$$

We first find the measure of angle A and then solve this equation for θ. The triangle formed by the beams and cable has sides of lengths 10, 12, and 15.2, with angle A opposite the 15.2-foot side. By the alternate form of the Law of Cosines,

$$\cos A = \frac{10^2 + 12^2 - 15.2^2}{2 \cdot 10 \cdot 12} = .054.$$

Figure 8–45

Hence, the measure of angle A is about 86.9° (Figure 8–45). Therefore,

$$50° + A + \theta = 180°$$
$$50° + 86.9° + \theta = 180°$$
$$\theta = 180° - 50° - 86.9° = 43.1°. \quad \blacksquare$$

EXAMPLE 7

A 100-foot-tall antenna tower is to be placed on a hillside that makes an angle of 12° with the horizontal. It is to be anchored by two cables from the top of the tower to points 85 feet uphill and 95 feet downhill from the base. How much cable is needed?

SOLUTION   The situation is shown in Figure 8–46 on the next page.

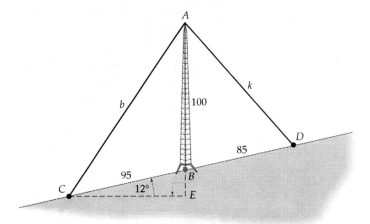

Figure 8–46

In triangle BEC, angle E is a right angle and by hypothesis, angle C measures $12°$. Since the sum of the angles of a triangle is $180°$, we must have

$$\measuredangle CBE = 180° - (90° + 12°) = 78°.$$

As shown in the figure, the sum of angles CBE and CBA is a straight angle ($180°$). Hence,

$$\measuredangle CBA = 180° - 78° = 102°.$$

Apply the Law of Cosines to triangle ABC.

$$b^2 = a^2 + c^2 - 2ac \cos B$$
$$b^2 = 95^2 + 100^2 - 2 \cdot 95 \cdot 100 \cos 102°$$
$$= 9025 + 10{,}000 - 19{,}000 \cos 102°$$
$$\approx 22{,}975.32.$$

Therefore, the length of the downhill cable is $b \approx \sqrt{22{,}975.32} \approx 151.58$ feet.

To find the length of the uphill cable, note that the sum of angles CBA and DBA is a straight angle, so

$$\measuredangle DBA = 180° - \measuredangle CBA = 180° - 102° = 78°.$$

Applying the Law of Cosines to triangle DBA, we have

$$k^2 = 85^2 + 100^2 - 2 \cdot 85 \cdot 100 \cos 78°$$
$$= 7225 + 10{,}000 - 17{,}000 \cos 78° \approx 13{,}690.50.$$

Hence, the length of the uphill cable is $k = \sqrt{13{,}690.50} \approx 117.01$ feet.   ■

PROOF OF THE LAW OF COSINES

Given triangle ABC, position it on a coordinate plane so that angle A is in standard position with initial side c and terminal side b. Depending on the size of angle A, there are two possibilities, as shown in Figure 8–47.

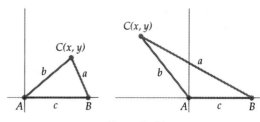

Figure 8–47

The coordinates of B are $(c, 0)$. Let (x, y) be the coordinates of C. Now C is a point on the terminal side of angle A, and the distance from C to the origin A is obviously b. Therefore, according to the point-in-the-plane description of sine and cosine, we have

$$\frac{x}{b} = \cos A \qquad \text{or, equivalently,} \qquad x = b \cos A,$$

$$\frac{y}{b} = \sin A \qquad \text{or, equivalently,} \qquad y = b \sin A.$$

Using the distance formula on the coordinates of B and C, we have

$$a = \text{distance from } C \text{ to } B$$
$$= \sqrt{(x - c)^2 + (y - 0)^2} = \sqrt{(b \cos A - c)^2 + (b \sin A - 0)^2}.$$

Squaring both sides of this last equation and simplifying, using the Pythagorean identity, yields

$$a^2 = (b \cos A - c)^2 + (b \sin A)^2$$
$$a^2 = b^2 \cos^2 A - 2bc \cos A + c^2 + b^2 \sin^2 A$$
$$a^2 = b^2(\sin^2 A + \cos^2 A) + c^2 - 2bc \cos A$$
$$a^2 = b^2 + c^2 - 2bc \cos A.$$

This proves the first equation in the Law of Cosines. Similar arguments beginning with angle B or C in standard position prove the other two equations.

EXERCISES 8.3

Directions: Standard notation for triangle ABC is used throughout. Use a calculator and round off your answers to one decimal place at the end of the computation.

In Exercises 1–16, solve the triangle ABC under the given conditions.

1. $A = 40°, b = 10, c = 7$

2. $B = 40°, a = 12, c = 20$

3. $C = 118°, a = 6, b = 12$

4. $C = 52.5°, a = 6.5, b = 9$

5. $A = 140°, b = 12, c = 14$

6. $B = 25.4°, a = 6.8, c = 10.5$

7. $C = 78.6°, a = 12.1, b = 20.3$

8. $A = 118.2°, b = 16.5, c = 10.7$

9. $a = 7, b = 3, c = 5$

10. $a = 8, b = 5, c = 10$

11. $a = 16, b = 30, c = 32$

12. $a = 5.3, b = 7.2, c = 10$

13. $a = 7.2, b = 6.5, c = 11$

14. $a = 6.8, b = 12.4, c = 15.1$

15. $a = 12, b = 16.5, c = 20.6$

16. $a = 5.7, b = 20.4, c = 16.8$

17. Find the angles of the triangle whose vertices are $(0, 0)$, $(5, -2)$, $(1, -4)$.

18. Find the angles of the triangle whose vertices are $(-3, 4)$, $(6, 1)$, $(2, -1)$.

19. In Example 4, suppose that the angle between the two tracks is $112°$ and that the average speeds are 90 kilometers per

hour for the first train and 55 kilometers per hour for the second train. How far apart are the trains after two hours and 45 minutes?

20. Suppose that the boat in Example 5 goes 25 miles due east and then changes course 56° northward. After traveling 50 miles on this course, how far is the boat from Chicago?

21. The sculptor builds a smaller version of the sculpture in Example 6, in which the beams are six feet and nine feet long, respectively, and the cable is 10.4 feet long. If the six-foot beam makes an angle of 40° with the ground, what angle does the nine-foot beam make with the ground?

22. Suppose that the tower in Example 7 is 175 feet high and that the cable on the downhill side is 120 feet from the base of the tower. How long is that cable?

23. The pitcher's mound on a standard baseball diamond (which is actually a square) is 60.5 feet from home plate (see the figure). How far is the pitcher's mound from first base?

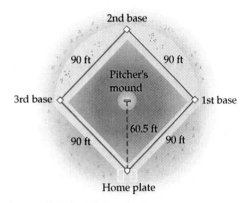

24. At Wrigley Field in Chicago, the straight-line distance from home plate over second base to the center field wall is 400 feet. How far is it from first base to the same point at the center field wall? [*Hint:* Adapt and extend the figure from Exercise 23.]

25. A stake is located 10.8 feet from the end of a closed gate that is 8 feet long. The gate swings open, and its end hits the stake. Through what angle did the gate swing?

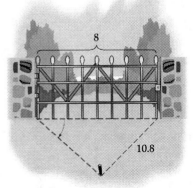

26. The distance from Chicago to St. Louis is 440 kilometers, that from St. Louis to Atlanta 795 kilometers, and that from Atlanta to Chicago 950 kilometers. What are the angles in the triangle with these three cities as vertices?

27. A satellite is placed in an orbit such that the satellite remains stationary 24,000 miles over a fixed point on the surface of the earth. The angle *CES*, where *C* is Cape Canaveral, *E* is the center of the earth, and *S* is the satellite, measures 60°. Assuming that the radius of the earth is 3960 miles, how far is the satellite from Cape Canaveral?

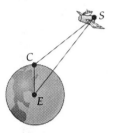

28. One plane flies west from Cleveland at 350 mph. A second plane leaves Cleveland at the same time and flies southeast at 200 mph. How far apart are the planes after 1 hour and 36 minutes?

29. A weight is hung by two cables from a beam. What angles do the cables make with the beam?

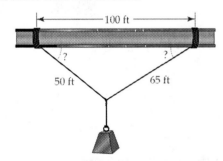

30. Two ships leave port, one traveling in a straight course at 22 mph and the other traveling a straight course at 31 mph. Their courses diverge by 38°. How far apart are they after 3 hours?

31. A boat runs in a straight line for 3 kilometers, then makes a 45° turn and goes for another 6 kilometers (see the figure). How far is the boat from its starting point?

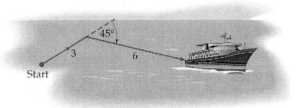

32. A plane flies in a straight line at 400 mph for 1 hour and 12 minutes. It makes a 15° turn and flies at 375 mph for 2 hours and 27 minutes. How far is it from its starting point?

33. A surveyor wants to measure the width *CD* of a sinkhole. So he places a stake *B* and determines the measurements shown in the figure. How wide is the sinkhole?

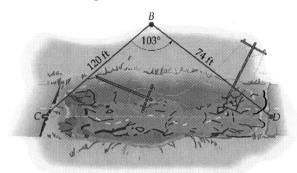

34. A straight tunnel is to be dug through a hill. Two people stand on opposite sides of the hill where the tunnel entrances are to be located. Both can see a stake located 530 meters from the first person and 755 meters from the second. The angle determined by the two people and the stake (vertex) is 77°. How long must the tunnel be?

35. A 400-foot-high tower stands on level ground, anchored by two cables on the west side. The end of the cable closest to the tower makes an angle of 70° with the horizontal. The two cable ends are 100 feet apart, as shown in the figure. How long are the cables?

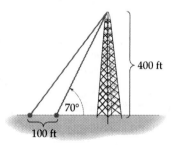

36. One diagonal of a parallelogram is 6 centimeters long, and the other is 13 centimeters long. They form an angle of 42° with each other. How long are the sides of the parallelogram? [*Hint:* The diagonals of a parallelogram bisect each other.]

37. A ship is traveling at 18 mph from Corsica to Barcelona, a distance of 350 miles. To avoid bad weather, the ship leaves Corsica on a route 22° south of the direct route (see the figure). After 7 hours, the bad weather has been bypassed. Through what angle should the ship now turn to head directly to Barcelona?

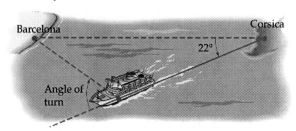

38. A plane leaves South Bend for Buffalo, 400 miles away, intending to fly a straight course in the direction 70° (aerial navigation is explained in Exercise 41 of Section 8.2). After flying 180 miles, the pilot realizes that an error has been made and that he has actually been flying in the direction 55°.

(a) At that time, how far is the plane from Buffalo?
(b) In what direction should the plane now go to reach Buffalo?

39. Assume that the earth is a sphere of radius 3960 miles. A satellite travels in a circular orbit around the earth, 900 miles above the equator, making one full orbit every 6 hours. If it passes directly over a tracking station at 2 P.M., what is the distance from the satellite to the tracking station at 2:05 P.M.?

40. A surveyor has determined the distance and angles in the figure. He wants you to find the straight-line distance from *A* to *B*. Do so.

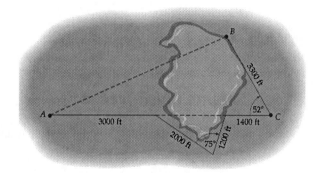

41. A parallelogram has diagonals of lengths 12 and 15 inches that intersect at an angle of 63.7°. How long are the sides of the parallelogram? [See the hint for Exercise 36.]

42. Two planes at the same altitude approach an airport. One plane is 16 miles from the control tower and the other is 22 miles from the tower. The angle determined by the planes and the tower, with the tower as vertex, is 11°. How far apart are the planes?

43. Assuming that the circles in the figure are mutually tangent, find the lengths of the sides and the measures of the angles in triangle *ABC*.

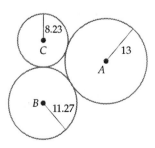

44. Assuming that the circles in the figure are mutually tangent, find the lengths of the sides and the measures of the angles in triangle *ABC*.

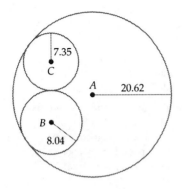

THINKERS

45. A rope is attached at points *A* and *B* and taut around a pulley whose center is at *C*, as shown in the figure (in which *AC*

has length 8 and *BC* length 7). The rope lies on the pulley from *D* to *E* and the radius of the pulley is 1 meter. How long is the rope?

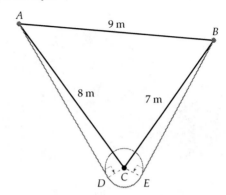

46. Use the Law of Cosines to prove that the sum of the squares of the lengths of the two diagonals of a parallelogram equals the sum of the squares of the lengths of the four sides.

8.4 The Law of Sines

Section Objectives
■ Use the Law of Sines to solve oblique triangles.
■ Use the Law of Sines to solve applied problems.

To solve oblique triangles in cases in which the Law of Cosines cannot be used, we need this fact.

Law of Sines

In any triangle *ABC* (in standard notation),

$$\frac{\sin A}{a} = \frac{\sin B}{b} = \frac{\sin C}{c}.*$$

Proof Position triangle *ABC* on a coordinate plane so that angle *C* is in standard position, with initial side *b* and terminal side *a*, as shown in Figure 8–48.

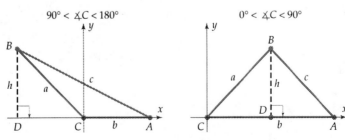

Figure 8–48

*An equality of the form $u = v = w$ is shorthand for the statement $u = v$ and $v = w$ and $w = u$.

In each case, we can compute sin C by using the point B on the terminal side of angle C. The second coordinate of B is h, and the distance from B to the origin is a. Therefore, by the point-in-the-plane description of sine,

$$\sin C = \frac{h}{a} \qquad \text{or, equivalently,} \qquad h = a \sin C.$$

In each case, right triangle ADB shows that

$$\sin A = \frac{\text{opposite}}{\text{hypotenuse}} = \frac{h}{c} \qquad \text{or, equivalently,} \qquad h = c \sin A.$$

Combining this with the fact that $h = a \sin C$, we have

$$c \sin A = a \sin C.$$

Dividing both sides of the last equation by ac yields

$$\frac{\sin A}{a} = \frac{\sin C}{c}.$$

This proves one equation in the Law of Sines. Similar arguments beginning with angles A or B in standard position prove the other equations. ■

The Law of Sines can be used to solve triangles in these cases:

1. Two angles and one side are known (AAS).

2. Two sides and the angle opposite one of them are known (SSA).

EXAMPLE 1

AAS If $B = 20°$, $C = 31°$, and $b = 210$ in Figure 8–49, find the other angles and sides.

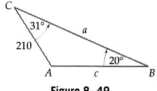

Figure 8–49

SOLUTION   Since the sum of the angles of a triangle is $180°$,

$$A = 180° - (20° + 31°) = 180° - 51° = 129°.$$

To find side c, we observe that we know three of the four quantities in one of the equations given by the Law of Sines.

$$\frac{\sin B}{b} = \frac{\sin C}{c}$$

Substitute known quantities: $\dfrac{\sin 20°}{210} = \dfrac{\sin 31°}{c}$

Multiply both sides by 210c: $c \sin 20° = 210 \sin 31°$

Divide both sides by sin 20°: $c = \dfrac{210 \sin 31°}{\sin 20°} \approx 316.2.$

Side a is found similarly. Beginning with an equation of the Law of Sines involving a and three known quantities, we have:

$$\frac{\sin B}{b} = \frac{\sin A}{a}$$

Substitute known quantities: $\dfrac{\sin 20°}{210} = \dfrac{\sin 129°}{a}$

Multiply both sides by 210a: $a \sin 20° = 210 \sin 129°$

Divide both sides by sin 20°: $a = \dfrac{210 \sin 129°}{\sin 20°} \approx 477.2.$ ■

THE AMBIGUOUS CASE (SSA)

In the AAS case, there is exactly one triangle that satisfies the given data.* But when two sides of a triangle and the angle opposite one of them are known (SSA), there may be one, two, or no triangles that satisfy the given data. Figure 8–50 shows some of the possibilities when sides a and b and angle A are given.

No Solution	*One Solution*	*Two Solutions*
(side a is too short)		

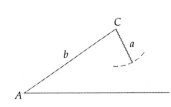
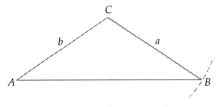
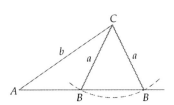

Figure 8–50

Determining the situation geometrically may require careful measurement and drawing. So it will be easier to use an analytic approach for solving SSA triangles, as illustrated in the next four examples.

EXAMPLE 2

SSA   Solve the triangle ABC when $A = 65°$, $a = 6$, and $b = 7$.

SOLUTION   To find angle B, we use an equation from the Law of Sines that involves B and three known quantities.

$$\frac{\sin B}{b} = \frac{\sin A}{a}$$

Substitute given values: $\dfrac{\sin B}{7} = \dfrac{\sin 65°}{6}$

Multiply both sides by $6 \cdot 7$: $6 \sin B = 7 \sin 65°$

Divide both sides by 6: $\sin B = \dfrac{7 \sin 65°}{6} \approx 1.06$

There is no angle B whose sine is greater than 1. Therefore, there is no triangle satisfying the given data.   ∎

---

*Once you know two angles, you know all three (their sum must be $180°$). Hence, you know two angles and the included side. Any two triangles satisfying these conditions will be congruent by the ASA Theorem of plane geometry.

When there is no solution for an SSA problem, that fact will become apparent as it did in Example 2, with an impossible value for sine. In other cases, you should use the following identity to determine whether there are one or two solutions, as illustrated in Examples 3 and 4.*

Supplementary Angle Identity

If $0° \le \theta \le 90°$, then

$$\sin \theta = \sin(180° - \theta).$$

EXAMPLE 3

SSA   Solve triangle ABC when $B = 50°$, $b = 12$ and $c = 11$.

SOLUTION   A rough picture of the situation is in Figure 8–51. We must find angles A and C and side a. We begin with an equation from the Law of Sines that involves the three known quantities.

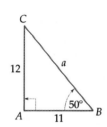

Figure 8–51

$$\frac{\sin C}{c} = \frac{\sin B}{b}$$

Substitute given values: $\dfrac{\sin C}{11} = \dfrac{\sin 50°}{12}$

Multiply both sides by 11: $\sin C = \dfrac{11 \sin 50°}{12} \approx .7022$

A calculator shows that one possibility for C is $\sin^{-1}(.7022) \approx 44.6°$. According to the supplementary angle identity,

$$\sin(180° - 44.6°) = \sin 44.6° = .7022.$$

So another possibility is $C = 180° - 44.6° = 135.4°$. If $C = 135.4°$, however, then $B + C = 50° + 135.4° = 185.4°$, which is impossible in a triangle. So the only solution here is $C = 44.6°$. Consequently,

$$A = 180° - B - C = 180° - 50° - 44.6° = 85.4°.$$

Finally, we use the Law of Sines to find a.

$$\frac{\sin B}{b} = \frac{\sin A}{a}$$

Substitute known values: $\dfrac{\sin 50°}{12} = \dfrac{\sin 85.4°}{a}$

Multiply both sides by $12a$: $a \sin 50° = 12 \sin 85.4°$

Divide both sides by $\sin 50°$: $a = \dfrac{12 \sin 85.4°}{\sin 50°} \approx 15.6$ ∎

---

*The identity was proved for all angles in Example 2 of Section 7.2. An alternate proof that does not depend on Chapter 7 is in Exercise 50.

EXAMPLE 4

SSA   Solve triangle ABC when $a = 7.5$, $b = 12$, and $A = 35°$.

SOLUTION   The Law of Sines shows that

$$\frac{\sin B}{b} = \frac{\sin A}{a}$$

Substitute given values: $$\frac{\sin B}{12} = \frac{\sin 35°}{7.5}$$

Multiply both sides by 12: $$\sin B = \frac{12 \sin 35°}{7.5} \approx .9177$$

The SIN^{-1} key shows that $66.6°$ is a solution of $\sin B = .9177$. Therefore, $180° - 66.6° = 113.4°$ is also a solution of $\sin B = .9177$ by the supplementary angle identity. In each case the sum of angles A and B is less than $180°$:

Case 1. $A + B = 35° + 66.6° = 101.6°$

Case 2. $A + B = 35° + 113.4° = 148.4°$.

So there are two triangles ABC satisfying the given data, as shown in Figure 8–52.

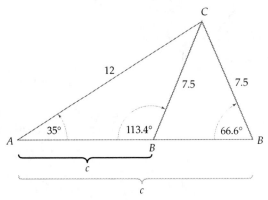

Figure 8–52

Case 1. $A = 35°$ and $B = 66.6°$. Then

$$C = 180° - A - B = 180° - 35° - 66.6° = 78.4°.$$

By the Law of Sines,

$$\frac{\sin A}{a} = \frac{\sin C}{c}$$

Substitute known values: $$\frac{\sin 35°}{7.5} = \frac{\sin 78.4°}{c}$$

Multiply both sides by 7.5c: $c \sin 35° = 7.5 \sin 78.4°$

Divide both sides by $\sin 35°$: $$c = \frac{7.5 \sin 78.4°}{\sin 35°} \approx 12.8.$$

Case 2. $A = 35°$ and $B = 113.4°$. Then

$$C = 180° - A - B = 180° - 35° - 113.4° = 31.6°.$$

By the Law of Sines,

$$\frac{\sin A}{a} = \frac{\sin C}{c}$$

Substitute known values: $$\frac{\sin 35°}{7.5} = \frac{\sin 31.6°}{c}$$

Multiply both sides by 7.5c: $$c \sin 35° = 7.5 \sin 78.4°$$

Divide both sides by $\sin 35°$: $$c = \frac{7.5 \sin 31.6°}{\sin 35°} \approx 6.9.$$ ■

EXAMPLE 5

SSA   Solve triangle ABC when $b = 13$, $c = 15$, and $B = 60°$.

SOLUTION   Looking at the rough sketch in Figure 8–53 and using the Law of Sines, we have

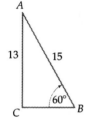

Figure 8–53

$$\frac{\sin C}{c} = \frac{\sin B}{b}$$

Substitute given values: $$\frac{\sin C}{15} = \frac{\sin 60°}{13}$$

Multiply both sides by 15: $$\sin C = \frac{15 \sin 60°}{13} \approx .99926$$

One solution of $\sin C = .99926$ is $C = \sin^{-1}(.99926) \approx 87.8°$. A second solution is $C \approx 180° - 87.8° = 92.2°$. In each case the sum of angles B and C is less than 180°, as you can easily verify. Consequently, there are two possible triangles.
Case 1. $B = 60°$ and $C = 87.8°$. Then

$$A = 180° - B - C = 180° - 60° - 87.8° = 32.2°.$$

By the Law of Sines

$$\frac{\sin B}{b} = \frac{\sin A}{a}$$

Substitute given values: $$\frac{\sin 60°}{13} = \frac{\sin 32.2°}{a}$$

Multiply both sides by 13a: $$a \sin 60° = 13 \sin 32.2°$$

Divide both sides by $\sin 60°$: $$a = \frac{13 \sin 32.2°}{\sin 60°} \approx 8.0$$

Case 2. $B = 60°$ and $C = 92.2°$. Then

$$A = 180° - B - C = 180° - 60° - 92.2° = 27.8°.$$

Finding side a is the same as in *Case 1,* with 32.2° replaced by 27.8°:

$$a = \frac{13 \sin 27.8°}{\sin 60°} \approx 7.0.$$ ■

NOTE

If you know one angle and all three sides of a triangle, you may use either the Law of Cosines or the Law of Sines to find another angle. Using the Law of Cosines is straightforward, but using the Law of Sines can lead to extra work if you are not careful. If you do use the Law of Sines, you should first find the sine of the angle opposite one of the two shorter sides of the triangle. Then the SIN^{-1} key will produce the correct angle and the supplementary angle identity will not be needed. If the Law of Sines is used to find the angle opposite the longest side, however, you must test both the angle given by the SIN^{-1} key and the angle obtained from it by the supplementary angle identity to see which one is consistent with the known facts. Failure to do check both possibilities can result in error (Exercise 51).

 APPLICATIONS

EXAMPLE 6

An airplane A takes off from carrier B and flies in a straight line for 12 kilometers. At that instant, an observer on destroyer C, located 5 kilometers from the carrier, notes that the angle determined by the carrier, the destroyer (vertex), and the plane is 37°. How far is the plane from the destroyer?

SOLUTION   The given data provide Figure 8–54.

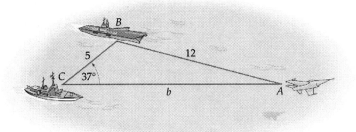

Figure 8–54

We must find side b. To do this, we first use the Law of Sines to find angle A.

$$\frac{\sin A}{a} = \frac{\sin C}{c}$$

Substitute known values: $$\frac{\sin A}{5} = \frac{\sin 37°}{12}$$

Multiply both sides by 5: $$\sin A = \frac{5 \sin 37°}{12} \approx .2508$$

The SIN^{-1} key on a calculator shows that 14.5° is an angle whose sine is .2508. The supplementary angle identity shows that $180° - 14.5° = 165.5°$ is also an angle with sine .2508. But if $A = 165.5°$ and $C = 37°$, the sum of angles A, B, C would be greater than 180°. Since this is impossible, $A = 14.5°$ is the only solution here. Therefore,

$$B = 180° - (37° + 14.5°) = 180° - 51.5° = 128.5°.$$

Using the Law of Sines again, we have

$$\frac{\sin C}{c} = \frac{\sin B}{b}$$

Substitute known values: $\quad\dfrac{\sin 37°}{12} = \dfrac{\sin 128.5°}{b}$

Multiply both sides by $12b$: $\quad b \sin 37° = 12 \sin 128.5°$

Divide both sides by $\sin 37°$: $\quad b = \dfrac{12 \sin 128.5°}{\sin 37°} \approx 15.6.$

Thus, the plane is approximately 15.6 kilometers from the destroyer. ∎

EXAMPLE 7

A plane flying in a straight line passes directly over point A on the ground and later directly over point B, which is 3 miles from A. A few minutes after the plane passes over B, the angle of elevation from A to the plane is 43° and the angle of elevation from B to the plane is 67°. How high is the plane at that moment?

SOLUTION If C represents the plane, then the situation is represented in Figure 8–55. We must find the length of h.

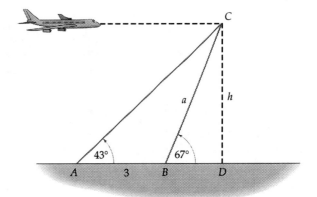

Figure 8–55

Note that angle ABC measures $180° - 67° = 113°$, and hence,

$$\angle BCA = 180° - (43° + 113°) = 24°.$$

We use the Law of Sines to find side a of triangle ABC.

$$\frac{\sin 24°}{3} = \frac{\sin 43°}{a}$$

Multiply both sides by $3a$: $a \sin 24° = 3 \sin 43°$

Divide both sides by $\sin 24°$: $a = \frac{3 \sin 43°}{\sin 24°} \approx 5.03$

Now in the right triangle CBD, we have

$$\sin 67° = \frac{\text{opposite}}{\text{hypotenuse}} = \frac{h}{a} \approx \frac{h}{5.03}.$$

Therefore, $h \approx 5.03 \sin 67° \approx 4.63$ miles.   ■

EXERCISES 8.4

Directions: *Standard notation for triangle ABC is used throughout. Use a calculator and round off your answers to one decimal place at the end of the computation.*

In Exercises 1–8, solve triangle ABC under the given conditions.

1. $A = 44°, B = 22°, a = 6$
2. $B = 33°, C = 46°, b = 4$
3. $A = 110°, C = 40°, a = 12$
4. $A = 105°, B = 27°, b = 10$
5. $B = 42°, C = 52°, b = 6$
6. $A = 67°, C = 28°, a = 9$
7. $A = 102.3°, B = 36.2°, a = 16$
8. $B = 93.5°, C = 48.5°, b = 7$

In Exercises 9–32, solve the triangle. The Law of Cosines may be needed in Exercises 19–32.

9. $b = 12, c = 20, B = 70°$
10. $b = 30, c = 50, C = 60°$
11. $a = 15, b = 12, B = 20°$
12. $b = 12.5, c = 20.1, B = 37.3°$
13. $a = 5, c = 12, A = 102°$
14. $a = 9, b = 14, B = 95°$
15. $b = 12, c = 10, C = 56°$
16. $a = 12.4, c = 6.2, A = 72°$
17. $A = 41°, B = 6.7°, a = 5$
18. $a = 30, b = 40, A = 30°$
19. $b = 4, c = 10, A = 75°$
20. $a = 50, c = 80, C = 45°$

21. $a = 6, b = 12, c = 16$
22. $B = 20.67°, C = 34°, b = 185$
23. $a = 16.5, b = 18.2, C = 47°$
24. $a = 21, c = 15.8, B = 71°$
25. $b = 17.2, c = 12.4, B = 62.5°$
26. $b = 24.1, c = 10.5, C = 26.3°$
27. $a = 10.1, b = 18.2, A = 50.7°$
28. $b = 14.6, c = 7.8, B = 40.4°$
29. $b = 12.2, c = 20, A = 65°$
30. $a = 44, c = 84, C = 42.2°$
31. $A = 19°, B = 35°, a = 110$
32. $b = 15.4, c = 19.3, A = 42°$

33. A surveyor marks points A and B 200 meters apart on one bank of a river. She sights a point C on the opposite bank and determines the angles shown in the figure. What is the distance from A to C?

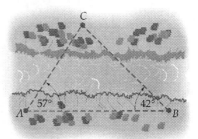

34. A forest fire is spotted from two fire towers. The triangle determined by the two towers and the fire has angles of 28° and 37° at the tower vertices. If the towers are 3000 meters apart, which one is closer to the fire?

35. A visitor to the Leaning Tower of Pisa observed that the tower's shadow was 40 meters long and that the angle of elevation from the tip of the shadow to the top of the tower was 57°. The tower is now 54 meters tall (measured from the ground to the top along the center line of the tower). Approximate the angle α that the center line of the tower makes with the vertical.

36. A pole tilts at an angle 9° from the vertical, away from the sun, and casts a shadow 24 feet long. The angle of elevation from the end of the pole's shadow to the top of the pole is 53°. How long is the pole?

37. A side view of a bus shelter is shown in the figure. The brace d makes an angle of 37.25° with the back and an angle of 34.85° with the top of the shelter. How long is this brace?

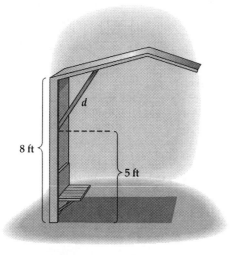

38. A straight path makes an angle of 6° with the horizontal. A statue at the higher end of the path casts a 6.5-meter-long shadow straight down the path. The angle of elevation from

the end of the shadow to the top of the statue is 32°. How tall is the statue?

39. A vertical statue 6.3 meters high stands on top of a hill. At a point on the side of the hill 35 meters from the statue's base, the angle between the hillside and a line from the top of the statue is 10°. What angle does the side of the hill make with the horizontal?

40. A fence post is located 50 feet from one corner of a building and 40 feet from the adjacent corner. Fences are put up between the post and the building corners to form a triangular garden area. The 40-foot fence makes a 58° angle with the building. How long is the building wall?

41. Two straight roads meet at an angle of 40° in Harville, one leading to Eastview and the other to Wellston. Eastview is 18 kilometers from Harville and 20 kilometers from Wellston. What is the distance from Harville to Wellston?

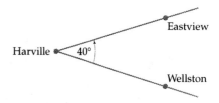

42. Each of two observers 400 feet apart measures the angle of elevation to the top of a tree that sits on the straight line between them. These angles are 51° and 65°, respectively. How tall is the tree? How far is the base of its trunk from each observer?

43. A string of lights is to be placed over one end of a pond (from A to B in the figure). If angle A measures 49°, angle B measures 128°, and BC is 144 meters long, what is the minimum possible length for the string of lights?

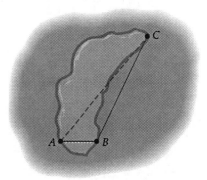

44. A triangular piece of land has two sides that are 80 feet and 64 feet long, respectively. The 80-foot side makes an angle of 28° with the third side. An advertising firm wants to know whether a 30-foot long sign can be placed along the third side. What would you tell them?

45. From the top of the 800-foot-tall Cartalk Tower, Tom sees a plane; the angle of elevation is 67°. At the same instant, Ray, who is on the ground, 1 mile from the building, notes that his angle of elevation to the plane is 81° and that his angle of elevation to the top of Cartalk Tower is 8.6°. Assuming that Tom and Ray and the airplane are in a plane perpendicular to the ground, how high is the airplane?

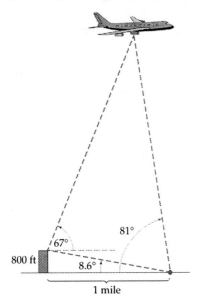

800 ft
67°
81°
8.6°
1 mile

46. A plane flies in a direction of 105° from airport A. After a time, it turns and proceeds in a direction of 267°. Finally, it lands at airport B, 120 miles directly south of airport A. How far has the plane traveled? [*Note:* Aerial navigation directions are explained in Exercise 41 of Section 8.2.]

47. Charlie is afraid of water; he can't swim and refuses to get in a boat. However, he must measure the width of a river for his geography class. He has a long tape measure but no way to measure angles. While pondering what to do, he paces along the side of the river using the five paths joining points A, B, C, and D. If he can't determine the width of the river, he will flunk the course.

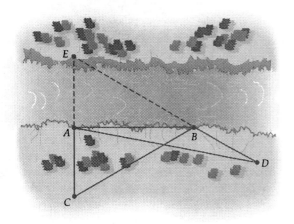

(a) Save Charlie from disaster by explaining how he can determine the width AE simply by measuring the lengths AB, AC, AD, BC, and BD and using trigonometry.
(b) Charlie determines that $AB = 75$ feet, $AC = 25$ feet, $AD = 90$ feet, $BC = 80$ feet, and $BD = 22$ feet. How wide is the river between A and E?

48. A plane flies in a direction of 85° from Chicago. It then turns and flies in the direction of 200° for 150 miles. It is then 195 miles from its starting point. How far did the plane fly in the direction of 85°? (See the note in Exercise 46.)

49. A hinged crane makes an angle of 50° with the ground. A malfunction causes the lock on the hinge to fail and the top part of the crane swings down. How far from the base of the crane does the top hit the ground?

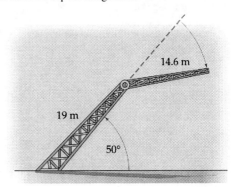

14.6 m

19 m

50°

50. When $0° \le \theta \le 90°$, the figure and parts (a)–(d) below provide a proof of the supplementary angle identity:
$$\sin \theta = \sin(180° - \theta).$$

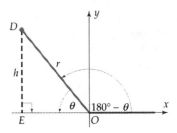

(a) What is the second coordinate of D?
(b) Use the point-in-the-plane description to find $\sin(180° - \theta)$.
(c) Use right triangle DEO to find $\sin \theta$.
(d) What do you conclude from parts (b) and (c)?

51. Given triangle ABC, with $B = 60°$, $a = 7$, and $c = 15$, solve the triangle as follows.

(a) Show that $b = 13$. [*Hint:* Example 1 of Section 8.3.]
(b) Use the Law of Sines to find angle C.
(c) Use the fact that the sum of the angles is 180° to find angle A.

Answers

Chapter 1

Section 1.1, page 13

1.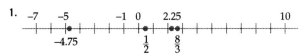

3. Positive **5.** Positive **7.** Negative

9. $\dfrac{2040}{523}, \dfrac{189}{37}, \sqrt{27}, \dfrac{4587}{691}, 6.735, \sqrt{47}$

11. $-4 > -8$ **13.** $\pi < 100$ **15.** $z \geq 4$

17. $d \leq 7$ **19.** $z \geq -17$ **21.** $5 > -3$

23. $>$ **25.** 3 **27.** 5

29. 0 **31.** $b + c = a$

33. a lies to the right of b. **35.** $a < b$

37.

39.

41.

43. $[5, 10]$ **45.** $(-3, 14)$ **47.** $[-9, \infty)$

49. 6.506×10^9 **51.** $5.91 \cdot 10^{12}$ **53.** $2 \cdot 10^{-9}$ m

55. 150,000,000,000 m

57. .00000000000000000016726 kg

59. (a) 8.365×10^{12}; 2.984×10^8 (b) \$28,032.84

61. 4 **63.** 6/5 **65.** 2

67. u^2 **69.** 11 **71.** 0

73. 169 **75.** $\pi - \sqrt{2}$ **77.** π

79. $<$ **81.** $>$ **83.** $<$

85. 7 **87.** 14.5 **89.** $\pi - 3$

91. $\sqrt{3} - \sqrt{2}$ **93.** $\dfrac{4 \cdot \pi \cdot \sqrt{805}}{161} \approx 2.21$

95. $|x - 143| \leq 21$; $|x - 163| \leq 26$

97. 15 **99.** 30 **101.** t^2

103. $b - 3$ **105.** $-(c - d) = d - c$

107. 0

109. $|(c - d)^2| = (c - d)^2 = c^2 - 2cd + d^2$

111. $|x - 5| < 4$ **113.** $|x + 4| \leq 17$

115. $|c| < |b|$

117. The distance from x to 3 is less than 2 units.

119. The distance from x to -7 is at most 3 units.

121. (a) iii (b) i (c) ii (d) v (e) iv

123. $x = 1$ or -1 **125.** $x = 1$ or 3

127. $x = -\pi + 4$ or $-\pi - 4$ **129.** $-7 < x < 7$

131. $3 < x < 7$ **133.** $x \leq -5$ or $x \geq 1$

135. Since $|a| \geq 0$, $|b| \geq 0$, and $|c| \geq 0$, the sum $|a| + |b| + |c|$ is positive only when one or more of $|a|, |b|, |c|$ is positive. But $|a|$ is positive only when $a \neq 0$; similarly for b, c.

Special Topics 1.1.A, page 18

1. $.7777 \cdots$ **3.** $.8181 \cdots$

5. $3.142857142857 \cdots$ **7.** $\dfrac{37}{99}$

9. $\dfrac{758,679}{9900} = \dfrac{252,893}{3300}$ **11.** $\dfrac{5}{37}$

13. $\dfrac{517,896}{9900} = \dfrac{14,386}{275}$ **15.** No

17. Yes **19.** No **21.** Yes

23. If $d = .74999 \cdots$, then $1000d - 100d = (749.999 \cdots) - (74.999 \cdots) = 675$. Hence $900d = 675$ so that $d = \dfrac{675}{900} = \dfrac{3}{4}$. Also $.75000 \cdots = .75 = \dfrac{75}{100} = \dfrac{3}{4}$.

25. .0588235294117647058823

27. $\dfrac{1}{29} = .0344827586206896551724137931034\overline{4} \cdots$

29. $\dfrac{283}{47} =$

6.0212765957446808510638297872340425531914893617021\overline{2} \cdots

31. All of these numbers are *approximations* of $1/17$, but *not* equal to $1/17$. If you subtract $1/17$ from any one of them, the answer is not 0.

Section 1.2, page 25

1. $1000k^{13/4}$ **3.** $c^{42/5} \cdot d^{10/3}$ **5.** $\dfrac{1}{3y^{2/3}}$

7. $\dfrac{a^{1/2}}{49b^{5/2}}$ **9.** a^x **11.** $x^{7/6} - x^{11/6}$

13. $x - y$ **15.** $x + y - (x + y)^{3/2}$

17. $(x^{1/3} + 3)(x^{1/3} - 2)$ **19.** $(x^{1/2} + 3)(x^{1/2} + 1)$

21. $(x^{2/5} + 9)(x^{1/5} + 3)(x^{1/5} - 3)$

23. $x^{-1/2}$

25. $a(a + b)^{1/2}$

27. $4t^{27/10}$

29. $4\sqrt{5}$

31. $6\sqrt{2}$

33. $\dfrac{-2 + \sqrt{11}}{5}$

35. $-\sqrt{2}$

37. $15\sqrt{5}$

39. $\dfrac{4a^4}{|b|}$

41. $\dfrac{|d^5|}{2\sqrt{c}}$

43. $\dfrac{a^2\sqrt[3]{b^2}}{c}$

45. $\dfrac{3\sqrt{2}}{4}$

47. $\dfrac{3\sqrt{3} - 3}{4}$

49. $\dfrac{2\sqrt{x} - 4}{x - 4}$

51. $5\sqrt[3]{4}$

53. $\dfrac{\sqrt[3]{9} - \sqrt[3]{3} + 1}{4}$

55. $\dfrac{\sqrt[3]{2} + 1}{3}$

57. $\dfrac{1}{\sqrt{x + h + 1} + \sqrt{x + 1}}$

59. $\dfrac{2x + h}{\sqrt{(x + h)^2 + 1} + \sqrt{x^2 + 1}}$

61. About 35,863,131 mi

63. About 886,781,537 mi

65. About 5,312,985

67. About 20,003,970

69. (a) Any even power of a real number is never negative.
(b) $\sqrt[3]{-8} = -2$, but $\sqrt[6]{(-8)^2} = 2$

71. (a) Since its graph passes the horizontal test, f is one-to-one and hence has an inverse.

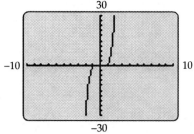

(b) $(g \circ f)(x) = g(f(x)) = (f(x))^{1/5} = (x^5)^{1/5} = x$ and $(f \circ g)(x) = f(g(x)) = (g(x))^5 = (x^{1/5})^5 = x$
(c) Since its graph does not pass the horizontal test, f is not one-to-one and hence has no inverse.

73. The graph of g is the graph of $f(x) = \sqrt{x}$ shifted horizontally 3 units to the left.

75. The graph of k is the graph of $f(x) = \sqrt{x}$ shifted horizontally 4 units to the left and vertically 4 units downward.

77. (a)

L	C	$Q = L^{1/4}C^{3/4}$
10	7	7.65
20	14	15.31
30	21	22.96
40	28	30.61
60	42	45.92

(b) If both labor and capital are doubled, output is doubled. If both are tripled, output is tripled.

79. (a)

L	C	$Q = L^{1/2}C^{3/4}$
10	7	13.61
20	14	32.37
30	21	53.73
40	28	76.98
60	42	127.79

(b) If both labor and capital are doubled, output is multiplied by $2^{5/4}$. If both are tripled, output is multiplied by $3^{5/4}$.

Section 1.3, page 32

1. $8 + 2i$

3. $-2 - 10i$

5. $-1/2 - 2i$

7. $\dfrac{\sqrt{2} - \sqrt{3}}{2} + 2i$

9. $1 + 13i$

11. $-30i$

13. $-21 - 20i$

15. 4

17. $-i$

19. i

21. i

23. $\dfrac{3 - 2i}{13}$

25. $-\dfrac{4}{3}i$

27. $\dfrac{12}{41} - \dfrac{15}{41}i$

29. $-\dfrac{5}{41} - \dfrac{4}{41}i$

31. $\dfrac{10}{17} - \dfrac{11}{17}i$

33. $\dfrac{7}{10} + \dfrac{11}{10}i$

35. $-\dfrac{113}{170} + \dfrac{41}{170}i$

37. $6i$

39. $\sqrt{14}i$

41. $-4i$

43. $11i$

45. $(\sqrt{15} - 3\sqrt{2})i$

47. $2/3$

49. $-41 - i$

51. $(2 + 5\sqrt{2}) + (\sqrt{5} - 2\sqrt{10})i$

53. $\dfrac{1}{6} - \dfrac{1}{6}i\sqrt{5}$

55. $x = 2, y = -2$

57. $x = -3/4, y = 3/2$

59. $\dfrac{1}{3} + \dfrac{\sqrt{14}}{3}i, \dfrac{1}{3} - \dfrac{\sqrt{14}}{3}i$

61. $-2 + 0i, -3 + 0i$

63. $\dfrac{1}{4} + \dfrac{\sqrt{31}}{4}i, \dfrac{1}{4} - \dfrac{\sqrt{31}}{4}i$

65. $-42 - 2.5i, -42 + 2.5i$

67. $2 + 0i, -1 + \sqrt{3}i, -1 - \sqrt{3}i$

69. $1 + 0i, -1 + 0i, 0 + i, 0 - i$

71. -1

73. (a) (i) 5   (ii) 25   (iii) 8
(iv) 8   (v) 8
(b) mod$(5 + 12i)$

75. $\overline{zw} = \overline{(a + bi)(c + di)}$
$= \overline{(ac - bd) + (bc + ad)i}$
$= (ac - bd) - (bc + ad)i$
$\overline{z} \cdot \overline{w} = \overline{(a + bi)} \cdot \overline{(c + di)}$
$= (a - bi)(c + di)$
$= (ac - bd) - (bc + ad)i$
Thus $\overline{zw} = \overline{z} \cdot \overline{w}$

77. $\overline{\overline{z}} = \overline{\overline{a + bi}} = \overline{a - bi} = a + bi = z$

79. (a) $\dfrac{z + \overline{z}}{2} = \dfrac{(a + bi) + (a - bi)}{2} = \dfrac{2a}{a} = a$

(b) $\dfrac{z - \overline{z}}{2i} = \dfrac{(a + bi) - (a - bi)}{2i} = \dfrac{2bi}{2i} = b$

81. (a) (i) $(a, b) + (c, d) = (a + c, b + d) = (c + a, d + b)$
$= (c, d) + (a, b)$
(ii) $[(a, b) + (c, d)] + (e, f) = (a + c, d + d) + (e, f)$
$= ((a + c)) + e, (b + d) + f)$
$= (a + (c + e), b + (d + f))$
$= (a, b) + [(c, d) + (e, f)]$
(iii) $(a, b) + (0, 0) = (a + 0, b + 0) = (a, b)$
(iv) $(a, b) + (-a, -b) = (a + (-a), b + (-b)) = (0, 0)$

(b) (i) $(a, b)(c, d) = (ac - bd, bc, + ad)$
$= (ca - db, cb + da) = (c, d)(a, b)$
(ii) $[(a, b)(c, d)](e, f) = (ac - bd, bc + ad)(e, f)$
$= (ace - adf - bcf - bde,$
$acf + ade + bce - bdf)$
$= (a, b)(ce - df, cf + de)$
$= (a, b)[(c, d)(e, f)]$
(iii) $(a, b)(1, 0) = (a \cdot 1 - b \cdot 0, a \cdot 0 + b \cdot 1) = (a, b)$
(iv) $(a, b)(0, 0) = (a \cdot 0 - b \cdot 0, a \cdot 0 + b \cdot 0) = (0, 0)$

(c) (i) $(a, 0) + (c, 0) = (a + c, 0 + 0) = (a + c, 0)$
(ii) $(a, 0)(c, 0) = (a \cdot c - 0 \cdot 0, a \cdot 0 + c \cdot 0) = (ac, 0)$

(d) (i) $(0, 1)(0, 1) = (0 \cdot 0 - 1 \cdot 1, 0 \cdot 1 + 0 \cdot 1) = (-1, 0)$
(ii) $(b, 0)(0, 1) = (b \cdot 0 - 0 \cdot 1, b \cdot 1 + 0 \cdot 0) = (0, b)$
(iii) $(a, 0) + (b, 0)(0, 1) = (a, 0) + (0, b) = (a + 0, 0 + b)$
$= (a, b)$

Section 1.4, page 43

1. $A(-3, 3)$; $B(-1.5, 3)$; $C(-2.5, 0)$; $D(-1.5, -3)$; $E(0, 2)$;
$F(0, 0)$; $G(2, 0)$; $H(3, 1)$; $I(3, -1)$

3. $(-6, 3)$ **5.** $(4, 2)$

7.
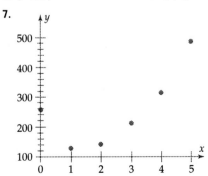

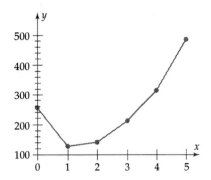

9. (a) Quadrant IV   (b) Quadrants III or IV

11. (a)
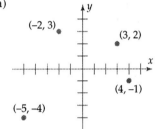

(b)
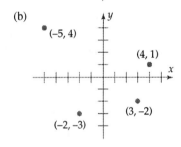

(c) They are mirror images of each other, with the x-axis being the mirror. In other words, they lie on the same vertical line, on opposite sides of the x-axis, the same distance from the axis.

13. $13; \left(\dfrac{-1}{2}, -1\right)$ **15.** $\sqrt{10}; \left(\dfrac{-3}{2}, \dfrac{7}{2}\right)$

17. $\sqrt{6 - 2\sqrt{6}} \approx 1.05; \dfrac{\sqrt{2} + \sqrt{3}}{2}, \dfrac{3}{2}$

19. $\sqrt{2} \cdot |a - b|; \left(\dfrac{a + b}{2}, \dfrac{a + b}{2}\right)$

21. $(-3.5, 4.6)$ **23.** $13 + 2\sqrt{2} + \sqrt{13}$

25. 15 square units

27. Hypotenuse from $(1, 1)$ to $(2, -2)$ has length $\sqrt{10}$; other sides have lengths $\sqrt{2}$ and $\sqrt{8}$. Since $(\sqrt{2})^2 + (\sqrt{8})^2 = (\sqrt{10})^2$, this is a right triangle.

29. The distances are $(1, 4)$ to $(5, 2)$: $\sqrt{20}$; $(5, 2)$ to $(3, -2)$: $\sqrt{20}$; $(3, -2)$ to $(1, 4)$: $\sqrt{40}$. But $(\sqrt{20})^2 + (\sqrt{20})^2 = 40 = (\sqrt{40})^2$, so the triangle is a right triangle with hypotenuse $\sqrt{40}$.

31. (a) About 45 yd

(b) $\left(34\frac{1}{6}, 27\frac{1}{2}\right)$

33. (a)

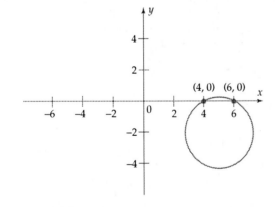

(b) $(2009, .85)$

(c) If linear growth is assumed, the midpoint suggests that there will be 850 million passengers in 2009.

35. No   **37.** Yes   **39.** No

41. $x = 1, 5; y = -5$

43. $x = 5, -1; y = \sqrt{5}, -\sqrt{5}$

45. $x = 0, -10; y = 0, 8$

47. (a) Approximately 7.3 million.
(b) Approximately 2007; Approximately 7.8 million.
(c) 2000–2003, 2011–.

49. (a) Under 56;   (b) Age 56;
(c) Retiring at age 60: about \$30,000; retiring at age 65: About \$35,000.

51. B   **53.** C

55. $(x + 3)^2 + (y - 4)^2 = 4$

57. $x^2 + y^2 = 3$

59. $(x - 5)^2 + (y + 2)^2 = 5$

61. $(x + 1)^2 + (y - 3)^2 = 9$

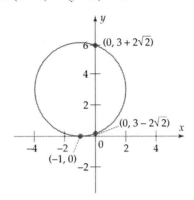

63. Center: $(-4, 3)$; radius: $2\sqrt{10}$

65. Center: $(-3, 2)$; radius: $2\sqrt{7}$

67. Center: $\left(-\dfrac{25}{2}, -5\right)$; radius: $\dfrac{\sqrt{677}}{2}$

69. (a) On   (b) Outside   (c) Inside
(d) Outside   (e) On

71. $(x - 3)^2 + (y - 3)^2 = 18$

73. $(x - 1)^2 + (y - 2)^2 = 8$

75. $(x + 5)^2 + (y - 4)^2 = 16$

77. $x^2 + y^2 - 4x - 2y = 0$

79. $(-3, -4)$ and $(2, 1)$

81. Assume $k > d$. The other two vertices of one possible square are $(c + k - d, d)$, $(c + k - d, k)$; those of another square are $(c - (k - d), d)$, $(c - (k - d), k)$; those of a third square are $\left(c + \dfrac{k - d}{2}, \dfrac{k + d}{2}\right)$, $\left(c - \dfrac{k - d}{2}, \dfrac{k + d}{2}\right)$.

83. $(0, 0)$, $(6, 0)$

85. $(3, -5 + \sqrt{11})$, $(3, -5 - \sqrt{11})$

87. $x = 6$

89. M has coordinates $(s/2, r/2)$ by the midpoint formula. Hence the distance from M to $(0, 0)$ is

$$\sqrt{\left(\frac{s}{2} - 0\right)^2 + \left(\frac{r}{2} - 0\right)^2} = \sqrt{\frac{s^2}{4} + \frac{r^2}{4}},$$

and the distance from M to $(0, r)$ is the same:

$$\sqrt{\left(\frac{s}{2} - 0\right)^2 + \left(\frac{r}{2} - r\right)^2} = \sqrt{\left(\frac{s}{2}\right)^2 + \left(-\frac{r}{2}\right)^2}$$

$$= \sqrt{\frac{s^2}{4} + \frac{r^2}{4}}$$

as is the distance from M to $(s, 0)$:

$$\sqrt{\left(\frac{s}{2} - s\right)^2 + \left(\frac{r}{2} - 0\right)^2} = \sqrt{\left(-\frac{s}{2}\right)^2 + \left(\frac{r}{s}\right)^2}$$

$$= \sqrt{\frac{s^2}{4} + \frac{r^2}{4}}.$$

91. Place one vertex of the rectangle at the origin, with one side on the positive x-axis and another on the positive y-axis. Let $(a, 0)$ be the coordinates of the vertex on the x-axis and $(0, b)$ the coordinates of the vertex on the y-axis. Then the fourth vertex has coordinates (a, b) (draw a picture!). One diagonal has endpoints $(0, b)$ and $(a, 0)$, so that its length is $\sqrt{(0 - a)^2 + (b - 0)^2} = \sqrt{a^2 + b^2}$. The other diagonal has endpoints $(0, 0)$ and (a, b) and hence has the same length: $\sqrt{(0 - a)^2 + (0 - b)^2} = \sqrt{a^2 + b^2}$.

93. The circle $(x - k)^2 + y^2 = k^2$ has center $(k, 0)$ and radius $|k|$ (the distance from $(k, 0)$ to $(0, 0)$). So the family consists of every circle that is tangent to the y-axis *and* has center on the x-axis.

95. The points are on opposite sides of the origin because one first coordinate is positive and one is negative. They are equidistant from the origin because the midpoint on the line segment joining them is

$$\left(\frac{c + (-c)}{2}, \frac{d + (-d)}{2} \right) = (0, 0).$$

Section 1.5, page 59

1. (a) C (b) B (c) B (d) D

3. $\dfrac{5}{2}$ **5.** 4 **7.** $t = 22$ **9.** $t = \dfrac{12}{5}$

11.

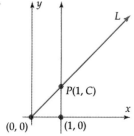

Slope of $L = \dfrac{C - 0}{1 - 0} = C$

13. (d) **15.** (a)

17. $y = 4x + 5$ **19.** $y = -2.3x + 1.5$

21. $y = -\dfrac{2}{3}x + 2$ **23.** $y = \dfrac{3}{4}x - 3$

25. Slope 2; y-intercept 5

27. Slope $\dfrac{-3}{7}$; y-intercept $\dfrac{-11}{7}$

29. $y = x + 3$ **31.** $y = -x + 8$

33. $y = -x - 5$ **35.** $y = \dfrac{-12}{5}x + \dfrac{87}{25}$

37.

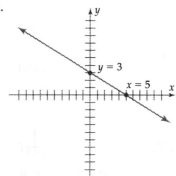

39.

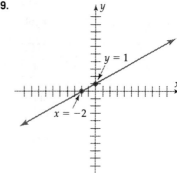

41.

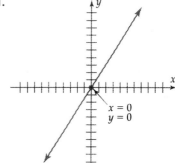

43. Perpendicular **45.** Parallel

47. Parallel **49.** Perpendicular

51. Yes **53.** $y = -\dfrac{1}{2}x + 6$

55. $y = \dfrac{-1}{5}x + \dfrac{13}{5}$ **57.** $y = 3x + 7$

59. $y = \dfrac{3}{2}x$ **61.** $y = x - 5$

63. $y = -x + 2$ **65.** $k = \dfrac{-11}{3}$

67. $y = \dfrac{-3}{4}x + \dfrac{25}{4}$ **69.** $y = \dfrac{-x}{2} + 6$

71. Both have slope $\dfrac{-A}{B}$.

73. (a) $(0, 60), (5, 66)$ (b) $y = 1.2x + 60$
(c) $64{,}800{,}000$ (d) 2010

75. (a) $y = .03x$ (b) About 158.33 ft

77. (a) $y = \dfrac{-1}{550}x + 212$

(b) $211°$ (c) $209.6°$ (d) $206.3°$ (e) $199.5°$

79. (a) $y = .23x + 3.2$ (b) $7{,}800{,}000$ (c) 2020

81. (a) $y = \dfrac{2.75x + 26{,}000}{x}$ (b) $104{,}000$

83. (a) $r = 1.4x$ (b) $24{,}167$ items

85. (a) $y = 60 - 2x$ (b) $y = 80 - 2x$ (c) $y = 160 - 4x$

87. (a) $F = \dfrac{9}{5}C + 32$ (b) $C = \dfrac{5}{9}(F - 32)$ (c) $-40°$

89. (a) 12.5 gpm; 8.33 gpm; 25 gpm.   (b) $y = -10x + 75$

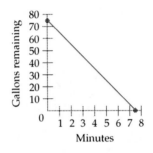

91. (a) $y = -1360x + 15{,}350$ (b) \$1360 per year
(c) \$7190

93. Let $y = mx + b$ and $y = mx + c$ be equations of lines with same slope m, and $b \neq c$. Suppose (x_1, y_1) is an arbitrary point lying on both lines. Then, $y_1 = mx_1 + b$ and $y_1 = mx_1 + c$. So, $mx_1 + b = mx_1 + c$ and, $b = c$, a contradiction. Thus, the lines share no point in common so must be parallel.

95.

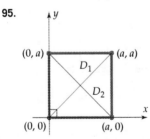

Equation of D_1: $y = x$, with slope 1
Equation of D_2: $y = -x + a$, with slope -1
(slope D_1)(slope D_2) $= (1)(-1) = -1$

Section 1.6, page 73

1. $P: \left(2, \dfrac{\pi}{4}\right)$, $Q: \left(3, \dfrac{2\pi}{3}\right)$, $R: (5, \pi)$, $S: \left(7, \dfrac{7\pi}{6}\right)$, $T: \left(4, \dfrac{3\pi}{2}\right)$,
$U: \left(6, -\dfrac{\pi}{3}\right)$, $V: (7, 0)$

3.

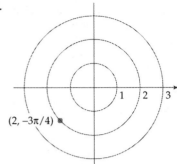

$(2, -3\pi/4)$

5.

$(-3, -5\pi/3)$

Many answers are possible in Exercises 7–12 in addition to those given here.

7. $\left(3, \dfrac{7\pi}{3}\right), \left(3, -\dfrac{5\pi}{3}\right), \left(-3, \dfrac{4\pi}{3}\right), \left(-3, -\dfrac{2\pi}{3}\right)$

9. $\left(2, \dfrac{4\pi}{3}\right), \left(2, -\dfrac{8\pi}{3}\right), \left(-2, \dfrac{\pi}{3}\right), \left(-2, -\dfrac{5\pi}{3}\right)$

11. $\left(\sqrt{3}, \dfrac{11\pi}{4}\right), \left(\sqrt{3}, -\dfrac{5\pi}{4}\right), \left(-\sqrt{3}, \dfrac{7\pi}{4}\right), \left(-\sqrt{3}, -\dfrac{\pi}{4}\right)$

13. $\left(\dfrac{3}{2}, \dfrac{3\sqrt{3}}{2}\right)$ **15.** $\left(\dfrac{\sqrt{3}}{2}, -\dfrac{1}{2}\right)$

17. $(.4255, -1.438)$ **19.** $(-3.604, 1.736)$

21. $\left(6, -\dfrac{\pi}{6}\right)$ **23.** $\left(\sqrt{2}, \dfrac{\pi}{4}\right)$

25. $\left(6, \dfrac{\pi}{3}\right)$ **27.** $(2\sqrt{5}, 1.107)$

29. $(5.59, 2.6679)$ **31.** $\left(2, \dfrac{3\pi}{2}\right)$

33. $(4.47, 2.0344)$ **35.** $r = 5$

37. $r = 12 \sec \theta$ **39.** $r = \dfrac{1}{\sin \theta - 2 \cos \theta}$

41. $x^2 + y^2 = 9$ **43.** $y = \dfrac{x}{\sqrt{3}}$

45. $x = 1$ **47.** $x^3 + xy^2 = y$

49. $x^2 + y^2 = 2y$ **51.** $x^2 = 16 - 8y$

53.

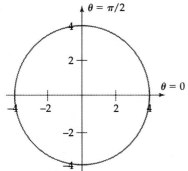

55.

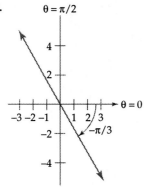

57.

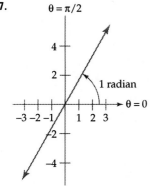

59.

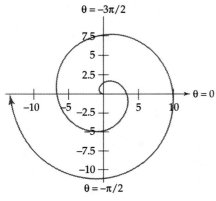

61.

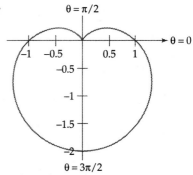

63.

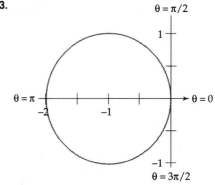

65.

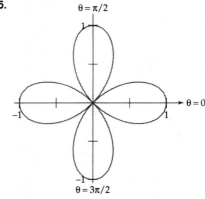

67.

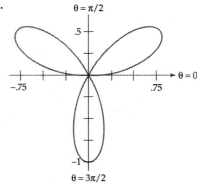

69.

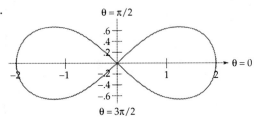

71.

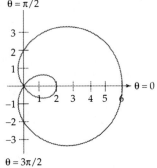

73.

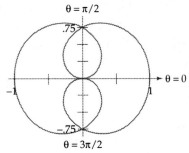

75.

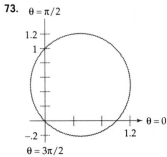

77.

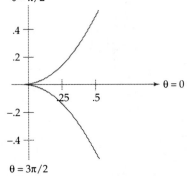

79.

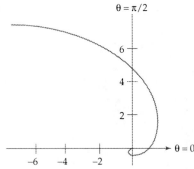

81.

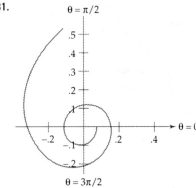

83. (a)

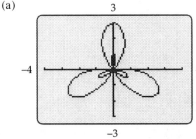

(b)

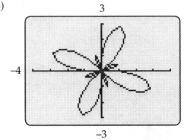

(c)

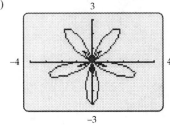

85. $r = a \sin \theta + b \cos \theta$

$r^2 = ar \sin \theta + br \cos \theta$

$x^2 + y^2 = ay + bx$

$x^2 - bx + \dfrac{b^2}{4} + y^2 - ay + \dfrac{a^2}{4} = \dfrac{a^2 + b^2}{4}$

$\left(x - \dfrac{b}{2}\right)^2 + \left(y - \dfrac{a}{2}\right)^2 = \dfrac{a^2 + b^2}{4}$

This is the equation of a circle.

87. The distance from (r, θ) to (s, β) is given by the Law of Cosines.

$$d^2 = r^2 + s^2 - 2rs \cos(\theta - \beta)$$

$$d = \sqrt{r^2 + s^2 - 2rs \cos(\theta - \beta)}$$

Chapter 2

Section 2.1, page 82

1. This is a function because, for every input there is a unique output.

3. This could not be a table of values of a function, because two output values are associated with the input -5.

5. 6   **7.** -2 **9.** -17

11. This defines y as a function of x.

13. This defines x as a function of y.

15. This defines both y as a function of x and x as a function of y.

17. Neither

19.

X	Y₁
-2	-2
-1.5	-3.25
-1	-4
-.5	-4.25
0	-4
.5	-3.25
1	-2

X=-2

X	Y₁
1.5	-.25
2	2
2.5	4.75
3	8
3.5	11.75
4	16
4.5	20.75

X=4.5

21.

X	Y₂
-8	59
-6	31
-4	11
-2	1
0	5
2	1
4	11

X=-8

X	Y₂
6	31
8	59
10	95
12	139
14	191
16	251
18	319

X=12

23. $8.40, $31.69, $693.75, $521.25, $262.50, $2150.17

25. A function may assign the same output to many different input.

27. Postage is a function of weight, but weight is not a function of postage; for example, all letters less than one ounce use the same postage amount.

29. This could not be the rule of a function, since, for example, it would assign two numbers (2 and -2) to the input 4.

31. (a) Jan. 2000, 8½%. Jan. 2001, 9½%. Mid-2005, 6%.
(b) After Jan. 2002 until Dec. 2004.
(c) The prime rate is a function of time, but time is not a function of the prime rate.

33. (a) $A = x^2$ (b) $A = \dfrac{d^2}{2}$

35. $S = 10\pi r^2$ **37.** $C = 125x + 26{,}000$

39. (a) $y = 2.3107x + 20.0821$ (b) $40.9 million

41. Output for -2 is -2. The output for -1 is 0. The output for 0 is approximately 1¼ and the output for 1 is approximately 2¾.

43. Output for -2 is -1. The output for 0 is 3. The output for 1 is 2.

The output for 2.5 is -1.

The output for -1.5 is 0.

45. Output for -2 is 1. The output for -1 is -2.9. The output for 0 is -1. The output for ½ is 1. The output for 1 is 1½.

47. (a) $x > 0$
(b) $-1 \le y \le 1$ where $y = \cos(\ln x)$

49. (a) For a nonnegative number, the part of the number to the left of the decimal point (the integer part) is the closest integer to the left of the number on the number line.
(b) the negative integers.
(c) negative numbers that are not integers.

51. (a)

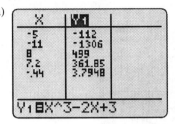

(b) $10^3 - 2(10) + 3 = 983$

Section 2.2, page 92

1. (a) $-.8$ (b) $-.75$ (c) $-.4$ (d) $-.125$ (e) 0

3. $\sqrt{3} + 1$ **5.** $\sqrt{\sqrt{2} + 3} - \sqrt{2} + 1$

7. 4   **9.** 17.75

11. $\pi^2 + 2\pi + 3 + \dfrac{1}{\pi + 1}$ **13.** $(a + k)^2 + \dfrac{1}{a + k} + 2$

15. $x^2 - \dfrac{1}{x} + 2$ **17.** $x^2 - 6x + 11 + \dfrac{1}{x - 3}$

19. $s^2 + 2s$ **21.** $t^2 - 1$

23. $\sqrt{11} - 7$ **25.** 1

27. 3   **29.** $1 - 2x - h$

31. $\dfrac{1}{\sqrt{x + h} + \sqrt{x}}$ **33.** $2x + h$

35. (a) $f(a) = a^2, f(b) = b^2, f(a + b) = (a + b)^2 = a^2 + 2ab + b^2$, so $(a + b)^2 \neq a^2 + b^2$, that is, $f(a + b) \neq f(a) + f(b)$
(b) $f(a) = 3a, f(b) = 3b, f(a + b) = 3(a + b) = 3a + 3b = f(a) + f(b)$.
(c) $f(a) = 5, f(b) = 5, f(a + b) = 5, f(a + b) \neq f(a) + f(b)$

37. $c = -2$

39. (a) $-3 \leq x \leq 4$ (b) $-2 \leq y \leq 3$ (c) -2
(d) $1/2$ (e) 1   (f) -1

41. $|x|$

43. (a) $x \leq 20$ (b) 3   (c) -1 (d) 1   (e) 2

45. all real numbers   **47.** all real numbers

49. $x \geq 0$ **51.** all real numbers except 0

53. all real numbers

55. all real numbers except 3 and -2

57. $6 \leq x \leq 12$

59. Many examples including $f(x) = x^2$ and $g(x) = x^4$.

61. Many examples including $g(x) = x^3$.

63. $3/2, -4$ **65.** $\dfrac{-3 \pm \sqrt{21}}{2}$

67. $f(x) = 8 - 3x^2$ **69.** $P(x) = .7x - 1800$

71. (a) $38 + .72y$
(b) $2 + .72x$

73. $d = \begin{cases} 55t & 0 \leq t \leq 2 \\ 20 + 45t & t > 2 \end{cases}$

75. (a) $y = 108 - 4x$
(b) $V = x^2(108 - 4x) = 108x^2 - 4x^3$

77. $C = 2t^2 + \dfrac{20}{t}$

79. (a) $f(x) = 18.3x + 244.4$
(b) $g(8) = 391, g(11) = 446$. These are not that accurate, but in the right ballpark
(c) $g(10) = 427$
(d) $g(21) = 629$

Section 2.3, page 105

1. Yes, $f(3) = 0$ **3.** No

5.

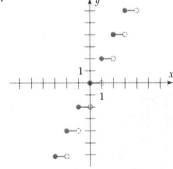

7.

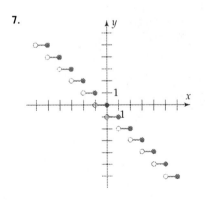

9.

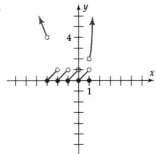

11. The graph fails the vertical line test; hence, it cannot be the graph of a function. For example, $x = 3$ corresponds to both 5 and 9.

13. $[-3, 5]$ **15.** $[-3, 3)$ **17.** 3.5

19. 4.5   **21.** 1 and 5

23. (a) $h(x) = \begin{cases} \dfrac{x}{2} - 2 & x \geq 0 \\ -\dfrac{x}{2} - 2 & x < 0 \end{cases}$

(b)

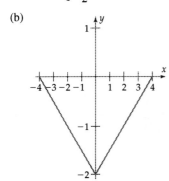

25. If $0 \leq x \leq 2$, then $x - 2 \leq 0$. So by the definition of absolute value, $|x - 2| = -(x - 2) = -x + 2$. Also, since $x \geq 0$, $|x| = x$. Hence, $f(x) = |x| + |x - 2| = x - x + 2 = 2$ for all x between 0 and 2.

27. Maxima at $(\pm 4, 0)$, minimum at $(0, -4)$

29. Maximum at $(-1, 3)$, minimum at $(1, -1)$

31. None

33. Decreasing when $x < -5.8$ and $x > .46$, increasing when $-5.8 < x < .46$

35. Only decreasing in $(-\infty, 0) \cup (0, \infty)$

37. (a) $2x + 2z = 100$
(b) $A(x) = x(50 - x)$
(c)

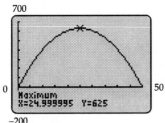

$x = 25$ inches, $z = 25$ inches

39. (a) $S = 2x^2 + 4xh$
(b) $x^2h = 867$
(c) $S = 2x^2 + \dfrac{3468}{x}$
(d)

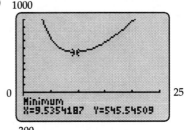

$x = 9.5354$ inches, $h = 9.5354$ inches

41. (a) (iv)   (b) (i)   (c) (v)   (d) (iii)   (e) (ii)

43.

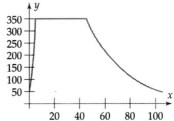

Domain is $x \geq 0$, range is $50 \leq y \leq 350$.

45.

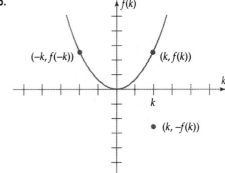

47. (a) 9%, 16%, 8%
(b) Lowest: 2003. Highest: 1990
(c) 1980–1983; steepness of curve

49. (a) False
(b) False
(c) False

51.

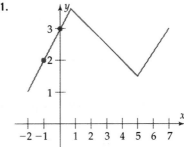

53. (a)

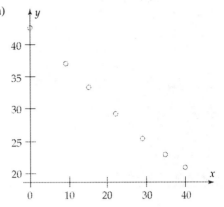

(b) $y = -.545x + 41.8$ (c) $27.7\%, 15.7\%$ (d) 2014
(e) It will disappear completely in 2042 according to this model.

55.

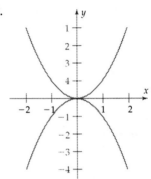

57. (a) $(-\infty, 4]$ (b) $[2, \infty)$
(c)

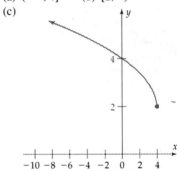

59. After 15 minutes she took a break then picked up her pace for 10 minutes. After 30 minutes she jogged back home at a constant rate for a total jog of 55 minutes.

Section 2.4, page 112

1. $-6 \le x \le 44, 0 \le y \le 16$
3. $-2 \le x \le 32, -60 \le y \le 60$
5. $-16 \le x \le 2, -60 \le y \le 60$
7. $-50 \le x \le 50, -7 \le y \le 3, -7 \le t \le 3$ (answers will vary)
9. $-8 \le x \le 5, -5 \le y \le 5, -5 \le t \le 5$ (answers will vary)
11. $-10 \le x \le -7, 0 \le y \le 2, 0 \le t \le 2$ (answers will vary)

13.

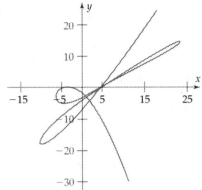

It crosses itself 6 times

Section 2.5, page 120

1. H   **3.** F   **5.** K   **7.** C
9.

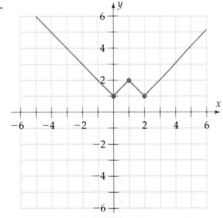

11.

t	$f(t)$	$g(t) = f(t) - 3$	$h(t) = 4f(-t)$	$i(t) = f(t - 1) - 2$
-2	3	0	20	Not possible
-1	6	3	0	1
0	8	5	32	4
1	0	-3	24	6
2	5	2	12	-2

13.

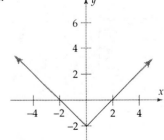

15.

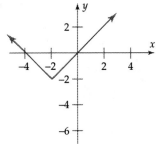

17. $-15 \le x \le 15$ and $-12 \le y \le 10$

19. $-5 \le x \le 7$ and $-10 \le y \le 10$

21.

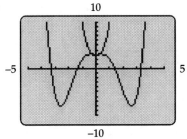

23. Shift 2 units to the left then 5 units up.

25. Reflect across the x-axis, then stretch vertically by a factor of 2, and then shift 10 units up.

27. $g(x) = -x^2 + x + 2$ **29.** $f(x) = -\frac{1}{2}\sqrt{-(x + 3)}$

31. (a) $g(x) = x^2 - 2x + 6$
  (b) difference quotient for f: $2x + h$; difference quotient for g: $2x + h - 2$
  (c) $2x + h - 2 = 2(x - 1) + h = d(x - 1)$

33.

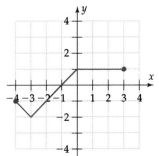

35.

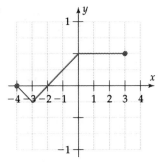

37.

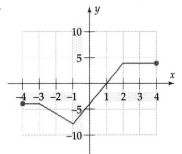

39.

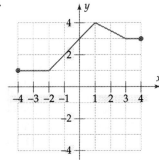

41.

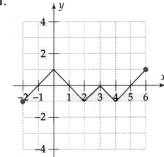

43.

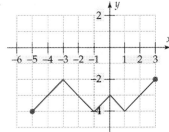

45.

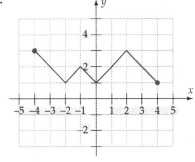

47. (a) The graph shifts 35 units up.
(b) The graph stretches in the y-direction.

49.

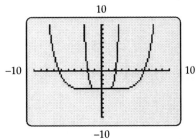

51. The graph of $f(cx)$, with $c > 1$, is the graph of $f(x)$ contracted toward the y-axis by a factor of c.

53.

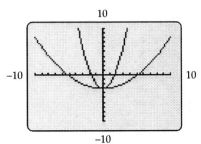

55.

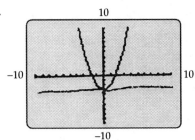

57.

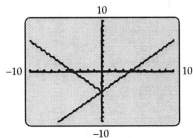

59.

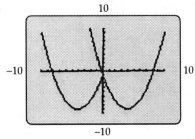

61. For $x > 0$, $f(x)$ and $g(x)$ are the same. For $x < 0$, $g(x) = f(-x)$.

63.

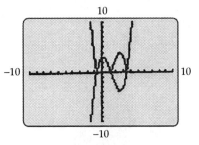

65.

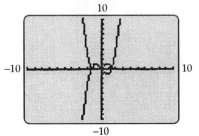

67. (a)

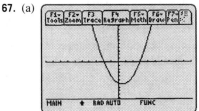

$h(x)$ will look just like $f(x)$, shifted 1000 units to the right

(b) $990 < x < 1010$, $-10 < y < 10$

(c) The problem is difficult because we have to include x values that are 1000 units apart, which makes seeing any details of the graphs impossible.

(d) $g(x)$ should look like $f(x)$, only stretched by a factor of 1000

(e) $-10 < x < 10$, $-10000 < y < 10000$. While we can display both f and g, any window that shows g in detail will not show f in detail.

Section 2.6, page 131

1. $x^3 - 3x + 2$; $-x^3 - 3x + 2$; $x^3 + 3x - 2$

3. $x^2 + 2x - 5 + \dfrac{1}{x}$; $\dfrac{1}{x} - x^2 - 2x + 5$; $x^2 + 2x - 5 - \dfrac{1}{x}$

5. $-3x^4 + 2x^3$; $\dfrac{-3x + 2}{x^3}$; $\dfrac{x^3}{-3x + 2}$

7. $x^2 - 25$, $\dfrac{x + 5}{x - 5}$, $\dfrac{x - 5}{x + 5}$

9. All real numbers except 0; all real numbers except 0

11. $-4/3 \le x \le 2$; $-4/3 < x \le 2$

13. 0

15. 30

17. 49; 1; −8

19. −3; −3; 0

21. $-3x^3 + 2$, all real numbers; $(-3x + 2)^3$, all real numbers

23. $\dfrac{1}{2x^2 - 1}$, all real numbers except $\dfrac{\pm\sqrt{2}}{2}$; $\dfrac{-4x^2 - 4x}{4x^2 + 4x + 1}$, all real numbers except $-1/2$

25. x^6; x^9

27. $\dfrac{1}{x^2}$; x

29. $(f \circ g)(x) = f(g(x)) = 9g(x) + 8 = 9\left(\dfrac{x - 8}{9}\right) + 8 =$

$x - 8 + 8 = x$; $(g \circ f)(x) = g(f(x)) = \dfrac{f(x) - 8}{9} =$

$\dfrac{9x + 8 - 8}{9} = \dfrac{9x}{9} = x$

31. $(f \circ g)(x) = f(g(x)) = \sqrt[3]{g(x)} + 2 = \sqrt[3]{(x - 2)^3} + 2 =$

$x - 2 + 2 = x$; $(g \circ f)(x) = g(f(x)) = (f(x) - 2)^3 =$

$(\sqrt[3]{x} + 2 - 2)^3 = (\sqrt[3]{x})^3 = x$

33.

x	$f(x)$	$g(x) = f(f(x))$
−4	−3	−1
−3	−1	1/2
−2	0	1
−1	1/2	5/4
0	1	3/2
1	3/2	2
2	1	3/2
3	−2	0
4	−2	0

35.

x	$(g \circ f)(x)$
1	4
2	2
3	5
4	4
5	4

37.

x	$(f \circ f)(x)$
1	1
2	3
3	3
4	5
5	1

There may be correct answers to Exercises 39–44, other than those given here.

39. Let $g(x) = x^2 + 2$ and $h(t) = \sqrt[3]{t}$. Then $(h \circ g)(x) = h(g(x)) = \sqrt[3]{g(x)} = \sqrt[3]{x^2 + 2}$.

41. Let $g(x) = 7x^3 - 10x + 17$ and $f(t) = t^7$. Then $(f \circ g)(x) = f(g(x)) = (7x^3 - 10x + 17)^7$.

43. Let $h(x) = x^2 + 2x$
$k(t) = t + 1$

45. Domain of $f \circ g : x \geq 0$ Domain of $g \circ f : x \geq 0$

47. Domain of $f \circ g : x \geq -2$ Domain of $g \circ f : x \geq -10$

49. (a) $2x^6 + 5x^2 - 1$
(b) $4x^6 + 20x^4 - 4x^3 + 25x^2 - 10x + 1$
(c) The answers are not the same. We conclude $f(x^2) \neq (f(x))^2$ in general.

51.

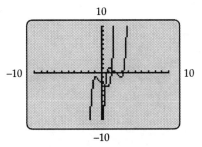

Functions are not the same.

53. $x^2 + 6x + 10$; $2x + h + 6$

55. $\dfrac{2}{x}$; $\dfrac{-2}{x(x + h)}$

57. (a) about 1.22×10^{-4} square inches, about 2.5×10^{-6} square inches, about 1.36×10^{-7} square inches
(b) no, no, over a certain time period

59. (a) $A = \dfrac{\pi}{4}d^2 = \dfrac{\pi}{4}\left(6 - \dfrac{50}{t^2 + 10}\right)^2$
(b) about .7854 square inches, about 22.265 square inches
(c) about 11.4 weeks

61. $V(t) = \dfrac{256\pi t^3}{3}$, about 17,157 cm³

63. $s(t) = \dfrac{10t}{3}$

65. $f(x) = |x|$

67. (a) As the composition is applied you will stabilize at $-.1708$
(b) yes.
(c) Now we wind up oscillating between $-.8873$ and $-.1127$ (starting at either 0 or 1)
(d) We wind up cycling between four numbers this time.

Section 2.7, page 143

1. (a) 14 ft per sec
(b) 54 ft per sec
(c) 112 ft per sec
(d) 93.3 ft per sec

3. (a) 9954.5 million subscribers/year
(b) 19218.6 million subscribers/year

5. (a) Decreasing at 291,000 per year
(b) Increasing at 541,800 per year
(c) Increasing at 353,500 per year
(d) Increasing at 179,778 per year
(e) Fastest from 1985 to 1995, slowest from 2005 to 2014

7. (a) 29.18   (b) 51.8
(c) 24.08   (d) 33.5
(e) 1999 to 2001

9. (a) $5000 per page
   (b) $1875 per page
   (c) $625 per page
   (d) $1750 per page
   (e) No, no, no

11. 4   13. -7 15. .371

17. .417   19. 7   21. $2x + 3 + h$

23. $3x^2 + 3xh + h^2$

25. $-\dfrac{5}{p(p + h)}$

27. (a) 49.2
    (b) 48.1
    (c) 48
    (d) 48

29. Decreasing at $-\dfrac{1}{500}$.

31. (a) They started at the same profit and ended at the same profit.
    (b) Dec 2008

33. (a) 10
    (b) -15
    (c) 5

35. (a) $y = 13.58x + 184.95$
    (b) 13.58
    (c) 12.8, 16.8. They are similar.
    (d) 2010

Section 2.8, page 155

1. No   3. Yes   5. Yes

7. Yes   9. $f^{-1}(x) = -x$ 11. $f^{-1}(x) = \dfrac{x + 4}{5}$

13. $f^{-1}(x) = \sqrt[3]{\dfrac{-x + 5}{2}}$ 15. $f^{-1}(x) = \dfrac{x^2 + 7}{4}$

17. $f^{-1}(x) = \dfrac{1}{x}$ 19. $f^{-1}(x) = \dfrac{1 - x}{2x}$

21. $f^{-1}(x) = \sqrt[3]{\dfrac{-5x - 1}{x - 1}}$

23. $f(g(x)) = x$ and $g(f(x)) = x$

25. $f(g(x)) = x$ and $g(f(x)) = x$

27. $f(g(x)) = x$ and $g(f(x)) = x$

29. $f(f(x)) = x$

31. (a) 48
    (b) 2
    (c) 5
    (d) 12
    (e) Not enough information
    (f) Not enough information
    (g) Not enough information

33.

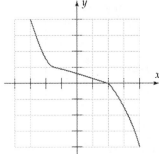

35.

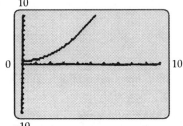

37.

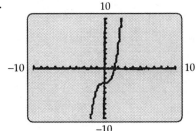

39.

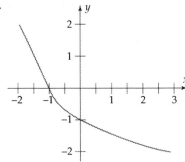

41. $x \geq 0$ 43. $x \geq 0$

45. (a) $f^{-1}(x) = \dfrac{x - 2}{3}$

    (b) $f^{-1}(1) = \dfrac{-1}{3}, \dfrac{1}{f(1)} = 1/5$, therefore not equal

47. $g(x) = \dfrac{x - b}{m}$

49. (a) -1
    (b) 1
    (c) since the slopes are negative reciprocal of each other, the lines are perpendicular to each other as well as symmetric with respect to the $y = x$ axis.

51. $f(g(x)) = x$ and $g(f(x)) = x$

53. True. Rotating the graph of an increasing function over $y = x$ gives an increasing function.

Section 2.9, page 163

1. This is a polynomial with leading coefficient 1, constant term 1, and degree 3.

3. This is a polynomial with leading coefficient 1, constant term -1, and degree 3.

5. This is a polynomial with leading coefficient 1, constant term -3, and degree 2.

7. This is not a polynomial.

9. This is not a polynomial.

11. Quotient: $3x^3 - 3x^2 + 11x - 17$; remainder: 18

13. Quotient: $x^2 + 2x - 6$; remainder: $-7x + 7$

15. Quotient: $x^2 + 2x + 3$; remainder: 0

17. Quotient: $5x^2 + 5x + 5$; remainder: 0

19. No   **21.** Yes

23. $x = \{2, -5\}$ **25.** $x = \{2\sqrt{2}, -1\}$

27. $x = \{-3, 0\}$ **29.** The remainder is 2.

31. The remainder is 31.4375. **33.** The remainder is -36.

35. The remainder is 183,424.

37. The remainder is $5{,}935{,}832\pi$.

39. No   **41.** No

43. Yes   **45.** Yes

47. $(x + 4)(2x - 7)(3x - 5)$

49. $(x - 3)(x + 3)(2x + 1)^2$

51. $f(x) = x^5 - 3x^4 - 5x^3 + 15x^2 + 4x - 12$

53. $f(x) = x^5 - 5x^4 + 5x^3 + 5x^2 - 6x$

55. $f(x) = x^3 - 4x^2 - 25x + 28$

57. $f(x) = (x - 1)(x + 1)$

59. $f(x) = (x - 1)^2(x - 2)^2(x - \pi)^2$

61. $f(x) = .25(x - 8)(x - 5)x$

63. $k = -9$ **65.** $k = 1$

67. If $x - c$ were a factor, by the Factor Theorem, c would be a root. Then $c^4 + c^2 + 1 = 0$. This equation has discriminant given by $1^2 - 4(1)(1) = -3$, hence it has no real roots. Thus $x - c$ cannot be a factor for any real c.

69. (a) $(x + 2)$ is not a factor of $x^3 - 2^3$.
(b) $(-c)^n + c^n = -c^n + c^n = 0$.

71. $k = 5$

73. $-3, 2 - 4\sqrt{5}, 2 + 4\sqrt{5}$

Section 2.10, page 173

1. Yes   **3.** No   **5.** No

7. This could be the graph of a polynomial function of degree at least 3 or 5.

9. Not the graph of a polynomial function.

11. This could be the graph of a polynomial function of degree at least 5.

13. In a very large window like $-50 \le x \le 50$, $-100{,}000 \le y \le 1{,}000{,}000$ the graph looks like the graph of $y = x^4$.

15. Roots $-2, 1, 3$; each has (odd) multiplicity 1.

17. Root -2 has multiplicity 1, root -1 has multiplicity 1, and root 2 has (even) multiplicity 2 (or possibly higher).

19. (e)   **21.** (f)   **23.** (c)

25. Since this is a polynomial function of degree 3, the complete graph must have another x-intercept.

27. Since this is a polynomial function of degree 4 with positive leading coefficient, both of the ends should point up; here they are pointing down.

29. $-5 \le x \le 5$, $-50 \le y \le 30$

31. $-6 \le x \le 6$, $-60 \le y \le 320$

33. $-3 \le x \le 4$, $-35 \le y \le 20$

35. $-33 \le x \le -2$, $-50{,}000 \le y \le 260{,}000$ then $-2 \le x \le 3$, $-20 \le y \le 30$

37. (a) The graph of a cubic polynomial can have no more than two local extrema. If only one, the ends would go in the same direction. Hence it can have two or none.
(b) When the end behavior and the number of extrema are both accounted for, these four shapes are the only possible ones.

39. (a) The ends go in opposite directions, so the degree is odd.
(b) Since if x is large and positive, so is $f(x)$, the leading coefficient is positive.
(c) Root -2 has multiplicity 1, root 0 has multiplicity at least 2, root 4 has multiplicity 1, root 6 has multiplicity 1.
(d) Adding the multiplicities from **c**, the polynomial must have degree at least 5.

41.

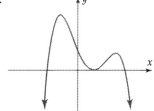

43. x intercepts: $1, 1 \pm \sqrt{3}$;
local max: $(2, 2)$;
local min: $(0, -2)$

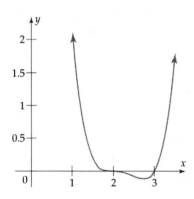

45. x intercepts: $2, 3$;

local min: $\left(\dfrac{11}{4}, -\dfrac{27}{256}\right)$

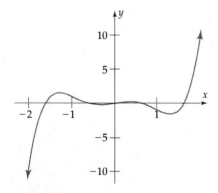

47. x intercepts: $\dfrac{\pm 1 \pm \sqrt{5}}{2}$, 0; local max: $(-1.30, 1.58)$
$(.345, .227)$; local min: $(-.345, -.227)(1.30, -1.58)$

49. (a)

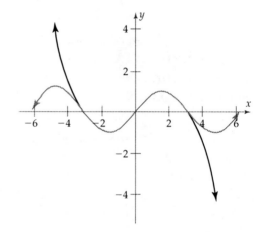

(b) 4950, 3750. The rate of increase is decreasing.
(c) After this point, you get less and less benefits for a unit of expenditure.

51. 6 additional trees per acre

53. $r = 3.046, h = 12.18$

55. It is a good approximation for $-3 < x < 3$.

57. It is a good approximation for $-3 < x < 2.25$.

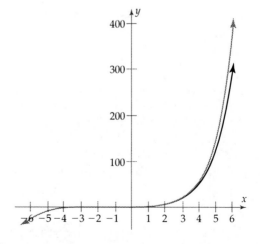

59. (a)

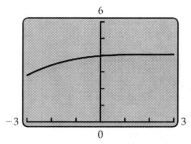

If the graph had the horizontal portion appearing in the window, then the equation $g(x) = 4$ would have infinitely many solutions, which is impossible, since a polynomial equation of degree 3 can have at most three solutions.

(b) $1 \le x \le 3$ and $3.99 \le y \le 4.01$

(c) If the graph of a polynomial of degree n had a horizontal portion appearing in the window, it would be a portion also of the line $y = k$. Then the equation $f(x) = k$ would have infinitely many solutions, which is impossible, since a polynomial equation of degree n can have at most n solutions.

61. (a)

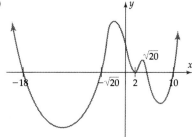

(b)

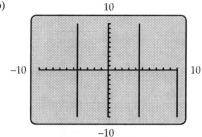

(c)

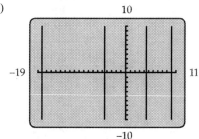

(d) Different windows would be needed for different portions of the graph. $-20 \le x \le -3$ and $-5 \times 10^6 \le y \le 10^6$; then $-3 \le x \le 2$ and $-5000 \le y \le 60{,}000$; then $1 \le x \le 5$ and $-5000 \le y \le 5000$; finally $5 \le x \le 11$ and $-100{,}000 \le y \le 100{,}000$.

Chapter 3

Section 3.1, page 193

1. $\left(-\infty, \dfrac{4}{3}\right) \cup \left(\dfrac{4}{3}, \infty\right)$ i.e. $x \ne \dfrac{4}{3}$ **3.** All real numbers

5. $(-\infty, -3) \cup (-3, -1) \cup (-1, 3) \cup (3, \infty)$

7. $f(x) = \dfrac{2x^2}{x^2 - 9}$

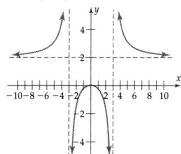

9. $f(x) = \dfrac{-x^4 + 36}{(x + 3)(x - 1)(x + 1)(x - 3)} = \dfrac{-x^4 + 36}{x^4 - 10x^2 + 9}$

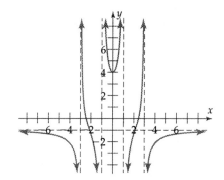

11. F   **13.** A

15. Vertical asymptotes at $x = 0$ and $x = 1$

17. Vertical asymptotes at $x = \dfrac{-7 \pm \sqrt{41}}{2}$

19. Horizontal asymptote: $y = 0$. All viewing windows will work.

21. Horizontal asymptote: none

23. Horizontal asymptote: $y = \dfrac{2}{3}$. $-25 < x < 25$, $-5 < y < 5$

25. Vertical asymptote: $x = 2$
Horizontal asymptote: $y = 0$
y-intercept: $-\dfrac{1}{2}$

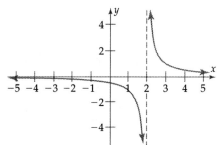

27. Vertical asymptote: $x = -1$
Horizontal asymptote: $y = 2$
y-intercept: 0

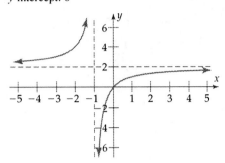

29. Vertical asymptotes: $x = 2, x = 3$
Horizontal asymptote: $y = 0$
Hole: $\left(0, \dfrac{1}{6}\right)$
y-intercept: none

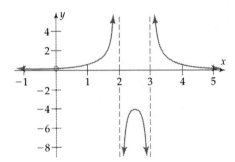

31. Horizontal asymptote: $y = 0$
y-intercept: 2

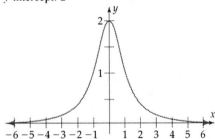

33. Vertical asymptotes: $x = -5, x = 1$
Horizontal asymptotes: $y = 0$
y-intercept: $-\dfrac{1}{5}$

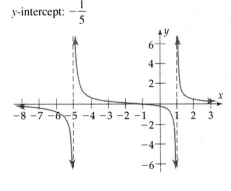

35. Vertical asymptotes: $x = 2, x = -1$
Horizontal asymptotes: $y = 2$
Holes: $\left(-2, \dfrac{9}{4}\right)$
y-intercept: $\dfrac{1}{2}$

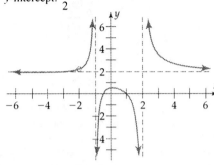

37. Three windows are needed: $-5 \le x \le 4.4$ and $-8 \le y \le 4$; then $-2 \le x \le 2$ and $-.5 \le y \le 5$; finally, $-15 \le x \le -3$ and $-.07 \le y \le .02$

39. $-9.4 \le x \le 9.4$ and $-4 \le y \le 4$

41. $-5 < x < 15, -2 < y < 2$

43. $\dfrac{-1}{x(x + h)}$

45. $-\dfrac{3}{(x - 2)(x + h - 2)}$

47. $-3\left(\dfrac{2x + h}{x^2(x + h)^2}\right)$

49. (a) $-1/4$ (b) $-1/9$ (c) They are identical.

51. (a) $g(x) = \dfrac{x - 1}{x - 2}$ (b) $g(x) = \dfrac{x - 1}{-x - 2}$

(c)

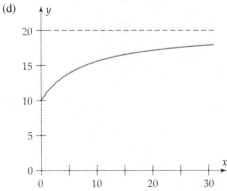

53. 8.4343 in. by 8.4343 in. by 14.057 in.

55. (a) 10
(b) 17
(c) Number of figures $= \dfrac{20 + 5t}{2 + .25t}$
(d)

(e) He will be able to buy 18 in the year 2012. He will never be able to buy 21.

57. (a) $x + \dfrac{400}{x}$

(b) $30 - 10\sqrt{5} < x < 30 + 10\sqrt{5}$ or $(7.6 < x < 52.4)$

(c) $20, 20 \times 10$

59. (a) $h_1 = h - 2$

(b) $h_1 = 150/\pi r^2 - 2$

(c) $\pi(r - 1)^2 (150/\pi r^2 - 2)$

(d) Otherwise $(r - 1)$ would be negative.

(c) $r = 2.879, h = 5.759$

61. (a) 9.801 m/s^2

(b)

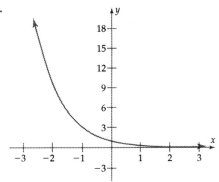

(c) No

Section 3.2, page 205

1.

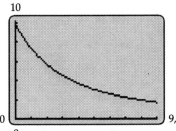

3.

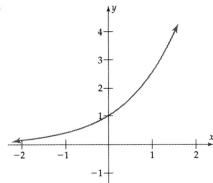

5.

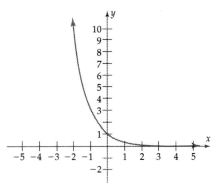

7.

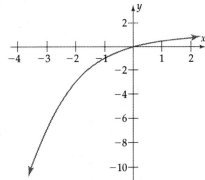

9.

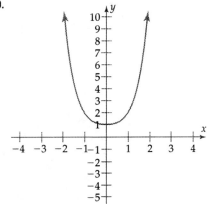

11. Shift vertically 5 units down.

13. Stretch away from the x-axis by a factor of 3.

15. Shift horizontally 2 units left, then shift vertically 5 units down.

17. Line A: $j(x)$
Line B: $g(x)$
Line C: $h(x)$
Line D: $f(x)$

19. Neither   **21.** Even   **23.** Even

25. 90   **27.** $-\dfrac{4}{27}$

29. $1000(2^{1.001} - 2) = 1.387$

31. $1000(e^{1.001} - e) = 2.720$

33. $\dfrac{10^{x+h} - 10^x}{h}$ **35.** $\dfrac{2^{x+h} + 2^{-x-h} - 2^x - 2^{-x}}{h}$

37. $-4 \le x \le 4, \ -1 \le y \le 10$

39. $-4 \le x \le 4, \ -1 \le y \le 10$

41. $-10 \le x \le 10, \ -10 \le y \le 10$

43. $-5 \le x \le 10, \ -1 \le y \le 6$

45. The negative x-axis is an asymptote; $(-1.443, -.531)$ is a local minimum.

47. No asymptote; $(0, 1)$ is a local minimum.

49. The x-axis is an asymptote; $(0, 1)$ is a local maximum.

51. (a) 100   (b) 569; 3242   (c) 13 weeks
(d) No, at some point there will not be enough space for the fruit flies and the rate the fly population grows will decrease.

53. (a) $k = 15$ (b) About 12.13 psi
(c) About .0167 psi

55. (a) About 74.1 years, about 76.3 years   (b) 1930

57. (a) 10 beavers, 149 beavers
(b) After about 9.5 years

59. (a)

Time (hours)	Number of Cells
0	1
.25	2
.5	4
.75	8
1	16

(b) $C(t) = 2^{4t}$

61. (a) $f(x) = 6(3^x)$ or $f(x) = 18(3^{x-1})$
(b) 3   (c) No; yes

63. (a)

Folds	0	1	2	3	4
Thickness	.002	.004	.008	.016	.032

(b) $f(x) = .002(2^x)$ (c) 2097.15 in. = 174.76 ft
(d) 43

65. (a) $f(x) = 1200(1.04)^x$ (b) 1349.84; 1503.57
(c) After approximately 11 years and 1 month

67. (a) $100.4(1.014)^x$ (b) 115.3 million   (c) 2016

69. (a) $32.44e^{.02216x}$
(b) 40.49 million; 56.45 million   (c) 2024

71. About 256; about 654

73. (a) $f(x) = .75^x$ (b) About 8 ft

75. (a) $M(x) = 5(0.5^{x/5730})$ (b) 3.08 g; 1.90 g
(c) After about 13,305 years

77. $f(x) = a^x$ for any nonnegative constant a.

79. (a) The graph of f is the mirror image of the graph of g
(b) $k(x) = f(x)$; see part (a).

81. (a) Not entirely   (b) $f_8(x)$
(c) Not at the right side; $f_{12}(x)$

Section 3.3, page 217

1. 4   **3.** -2.5

5. $10^3 = 1000$ **7.** $10^{2.88} = 750$

9. $e^{1.0986} = 3$ **11.** $e^{-4.6052} = .01$

13. $e^{z+w} = x^2 + 2y$ **15.** $\log .01 = -2$

17. $\log 3 = .4771$ **19.** $\ln 25.79 = 3.25$

21. $\ln 5.5527 = 12/7$ **23.** $\ln w = 2/r$

25. $\sqrt{43}$ **27.** 15   **29.** .5

31. 931   **33.** $x + y$ **35.** x^2

37. $f(x) = 4e^{3.2189x}$ **39.** $g(x) = -16e^{3.4177x}$

41. $\left(\dfrac{1}{e^3}\right)^x = .0498^x$ **43.** $x > -1$

45. $x < 0$

47. (a) for all $x > 0$.
(b) According to the fourth property of logarithms, $e^{\ln x} = x$ for every $x > 0$.

49. They are the same for $x > 0$. If $x < 0$, $g(x)$ does not exist, while $f(x)$ is symmetric with respect to the y-axis.

51. Stretch vertically by a factor of 2 away from the x-axis.

53. Shift horizontally 4 units to the right.

55. Shift horizontally 3 units to the left, then shift vertically 4 units down.

57.

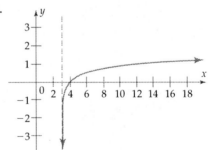

59.

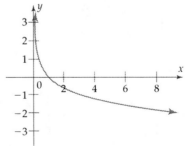

61. $0 \le x \le 20$ and $-10 \le y \le 10$; then $0 \le x \le 2$ and $-20 \le y \le 20$

63. $-10 \le x \le 10$ and $-3 \le y \le 3$

65. $0 \le x \le 20$ and $-6 \le x \le 3$

67. $-10 \le x \le 10$ and $-10 \le y \le 10$

69. .5493   **71.** $-.2386$

73. (a) $\dfrac{\ln(2 + h) - \ln(2)}{h}$

(b) .49875415; .499875042; .499987501; .49999875

(c) .24968802; .249968755; .249996875; .24999970

(d) Answers will vary

(e) About 2.5

75. $(f \circ g)(x) = \dfrac{1}{1 + e^{-\ln(x/1-x)}} = \dfrac{1}{1 + \dfrac{1}{e^{\ln(x/1-x)}}}$

$$= \dfrac{1}{1 + \dfrac{1}{\dfrac{x}{1-x}}} = \dfrac{1}{1 + \dfrac{1-x}{x}} = \dfrac{1}{\dfrac{1}{x}} = x;$$

$(g \circ f)(x) = \ln\left(\dfrac{\dfrac{1}{1 + e^{-x}}}{1 - \dfrac{1}{1 + e^{-x}}}\right) = \ln\left(\dfrac{\dfrac{1}{1 + e^{-x}}}{\dfrac{e^{-x}}{1 + e^{-x}}}\right)$

$= \ln\left(\dfrac{1}{e^{-x}}\right) = \ln(e^x) = x$

77. $A = -9, B = 10$

79. About 4392 meters

81. (a) 26.55 billion pounds, 27.72 billion pounds

(b) 2022

83. (a) About 9.9 days

(b) 6986 people

85. (a) No ads: about 120 bikes; $1000: about 299 bikes; $10,000: about 513 bikes.

(b) $1000: yes, $10,000: no.

(c) $1000: yes, $10,000: yes.

87. $n = 30$ gives an approximation with a maximum error of .00001 when $-.7 \le x \le .7$.

89. (a) Answers will vary.

(b) (28.087, 29.087)

(c) 2529

Section 3.4, page 224

1. $\ln(x^2 y^3)$ **3.** $\log(x - 3)$ **5.** $\ln(x^{-7})$

7. $\ln(e - 1)^3$ **9.** $\log(20xy)$ **11.** $2u + 5v$

13. $\dfrac{1}{2}u + 2v$ **15.** $\dfrac{2}{3}u + \dfrac{1}{6}v$

17. False; the right side is not defined when $x < 0$, but the left side is.

19. True by the Power Law

21. False; the graph of the left side differs from the graph of the right side.

23. False

25. $a = 10, b = 10$, among many examples

27. Since $v = e^{\ln v}$ and $w = e^{\ln w}$, we have $\dfrac{v}{w} = \dfrac{e^{\ln v}}{e^{\ln w}} = e^{\ln v - \ln w}$ by the division property of exponents. So raising e to the exponent $(\ln v - \ln w)$ produces $\dfrac{v}{w}$. But the exponent to which e must be raised to produce $\dfrac{v}{w}$ is, by definition, $\ln\dfrac{v}{w}$. Therefore, $\ln\dfrac{v}{w} = \ln v - \ln w$.

29. 4.7   **31.** 3.176

33. 40   **35.** 100

37. I must be squared.

39. Following the hint: $10^{\log c} = c$ because $\log c$ is the exponent to which 10 must be raised to produce c. Taking the natural logarithm of both sides produces $\ln(10^{\log c}) = \ln(c)$, but $\ln(10^{\log c}) = \log c \cdot \ln 10$ by the power law for logarithms. Thus, $\log c \cdot \ln 10 = \ln c$, and dividing both sides of this equation by $\ln 10$ produces the desired result.

41. If c is a positive number, then c can be written in scientific notation as $c = b \times 10^k$, where $1 \le b < 10$ and k is an integer. Then $\log c = \log(b \times 10^k) = \log b + \log(10^k) = \log b + k$.

43. (a)

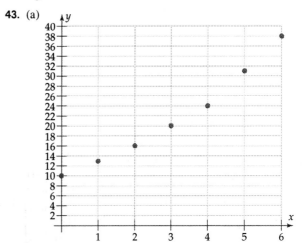

Wayland. It appears to be exponential.

(b)

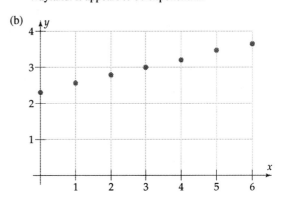

(c) Wayland. It now appears linear in part b.

Section 3.5, page 233

1. -1 **3.** 0 **5.** 0

7. 0 **9.** 0

11. $\sin t = 1/\sqrt{5},\ \cos t = -2/\sqrt{5},\ \tan t = -1/2$

13. $\sin t = -4/5,\ \cos t = -3/5,\ \tan t = 4/3$

15. $\sqrt{3}/2,\ 1/2,\ \sqrt{3}$ **17.** $-\sqrt{2}/2,\ \sqrt{2}/2,\ -1$

19. $\sqrt{2}/2,\ -\sqrt{2}/2,\ -1$ **21.** $1/2,\ -\sqrt{3}/2,\ \dfrac{-\sqrt{3}}{3}$

23. $\sin\left(-\dfrac{23\pi}{6}\right) = \dfrac{1}{2},\ \cos\left(-\dfrac{23\pi}{6}\right) = \dfrac{\sqrt{3}}{2},\ \tan\left(-\dfrac{23\pi}{6}\right) = \dfrac{\sqrt{3}}{3}$

25. $\sin\left(-\dfrac{19\pi}{3}\right) = -\dfrac{\sqrt{3}}{2},\ \cos\left(-\dfrac{19\pi}{3}\right) = \dfrac{1}{2},\ \tan\left(-\dfrac{19\pi}{3}\right) = -\sqrt{3}$

27. $\sin\left(-\dfrac{15\pi}{4}\right) = \dfrac{\sqrt{2}}{2},\ \cos\left(-\dfrac{15\pi}{4}\right) = \dfrac{\sqrt{2}}{2},\ \tan\left(-\dfrac{15\pi}{4}\right) = 1$

29. $\sin\left(-\dfrac{17\pi}{2}\right) = -1,\ \cos\left(-\dfrac{17\pi}{2}\right) = 0,$

$\tan\left(-\dfrac{17\pi}{2}\right)$ is not defined

31. $-\sqrt{3}/2$ **33.** $-\sqrt{2}/2$ **35.** $\dfrac{\sqrt{2}}{4}(1 - \sqrt{3})$

37. $\sin t = 5/\sqrt{34};\ \cos t = 3/\sqrt{34};\ \tan t = 5/3$

39. $\sin t = -5/\sqrt{41};\ \cos t = -4/\sqrt{41};\ \tan t = 5/4$

41. $\sin t = -8/\sqrt{67};\ \cos t = \sqrt{3/67};\ \tan t = -8/\sqrt{3}$

43. (a) 467 mph   (b) 1458 mph

45. (a)

Date	Jan 1	Mar 1	May 1
Average Temperature	31.7	43.8	68.3

Date	July 1	Sept 1	Nov 1
Average Temperature	80.9	69.0	44.5

(b)

Date	June 1	June 4	June 7	June 10
Average Temperature	77.4	78.0	78.6	79.1

Date	June 13	June 16	June 19	June 22
Average Temperature	79.6	80.0	80.3	80.5

Date	June 25	June 28
Average Temperature	80.7	80.8

47. $-2/\pi$ **49.** $\dfrac{-\sqrt{3} - 1}{7\pi}$

51. $\dfrac{2\sqrt{2}}{3\pi}$ **53.** $\dfrac{4\sqrt{3}}{\pi}$

55. (a) $-.420686;\ -.416601;\ -.416192;\ -.416151$
(b) $\cos 2 \approx -.416147$

57. $\sin t = -2/\sqrt{5};\ \cos t = 1/\sqrt{5};\ \tan t = -2$

59. $\sin t = -5/\sqrt{34},\ \cos t = 3/\sqrt{34},\ \tan t = -5/3$

61. $\sin t = 1/\sqrt{5},\ \cos t = -2/\sqrt{5},\ \tan t = -1/2$

63. Quadrant I: $\sin t(+),\ \cos t(+),\ \tan t(+)$;
Quadrant II: $\sin t(+),\ \cos t(-),\ \tan t(-)$;
Quadrant III: $\sin t(-),\ \cos t(-),\ \tan t(+)$;
Quadrant IV: $\sin t(-),\ \cos t(+),\ \tan t(-)$

65. Positive since $0 < 1 < \pi/2$

67. Negative since $\pi/2 < 3 < \pi$

69. Positive since $0 < 1.5 < \pi/2$

71. $t = \dfrac{\pi}{2} + 2\pi n,\ n$ any integer   **73.** $t = \pi n,\ n$ any integer

75. $t = \dfrac{\pi}{2} + \pi n,\ n$ any integer

77. $\sin(\cos 0) = \sin 1$, while $\cos(\sin 0) = \cos 0 = 1$. Since $\sin 1 < 1$ (draw a picture!), $\cos(\sin 0)$ is larger than $\sin(\cos 0)$.

79. (a) Each horse moves through an angle of 2π radians in 1 min. The angle between horses A and B is $\pi/4$ radians ($= \frac{1}{8}$ of 2π radians). It takes $\frac{1}{8}$ min for each horse to move through an angle of $\pi/4$ radians. Thus the position occupied by B at time t will be occupied by A $\frac{1}{8}$ min later, that is, at time $t + \frac{1}{8}$. Therefore, $B(t) = A\left(t + \frac{1}{8}\right)$.
(b) $C(t) = A\left(t + \frac{1}{3}\right)$.
(c) $E(t) = D\left(t + \frac{1}{8}\right);\ F(t) = D\left(t + \frac{1}{3}\right)$.
(d) The triangles in Figure S are similar, so that $\dfrac{5}{1} = \dfrac{D(t)}{A(t)}$. Therefore, $D(t) = 5A(t)$.
(e) $E(t) = 5B(t) = 5A\left(t + \frac{1}{8}\right);\ F(t) = 5C(t) = 5A\left(t + \frac{1}{3}\right)$.
(f) Since horse A travels through an angle of 2π radians each minute and its starting angle is 0 radians, then at the end of t min horse A will be on the terminal side of an angle of $2\pi t$ radians, at the point where it intersects the unit circle. $A(t)$ is the second coordinate of this point; hence, $A(t) = \sin(2\pi t)$.
(g) $B(t) = A\left(t + \frac{1}{8}\right) = \sin\left[2\pi\left(t + \frac{1}{8}\right)\right] = \sin(2\pi t + \pi/4);\ C(t) = \sin(2\pi t + 2\pi/3)$
(h) $D(t) = 5\sin(2\pi t);\ E(t) = 5\sin(2\pi t + \pi/4);$
$f(t) = 5\sin(2\pi t + 2\pi/3)$

Chapter 4

Section 4.1, page 249

1. $x = 8$

3. $x = \dfrac{-5}{6}$

5. $y = -32$

7. $y = \dfrac{x + 5}{3}$

9. $b = \dfrac{2A - hc}{h}$ $(h \neq 0)$

11. $h = \dfrac{4V}{\pi d^2}$ $(d \neq 0)$

13. $x = 3$ or 5

15. $x = -2$ or 7

17. $y = \dfrac{1}{2}$ or -3

19. $t = -2$ or $\dfrac{-1}{4}$

21. $u = 2$ or $\dfrac{-2}{3}$

23. $x = 1 \pm \sqrt{13}$

25. $x = \dfrac{1 + \sqrt{5}}{2}$ or $\dfrac{1 - \sqrt{5}}{2}$

27. 2

29. 2

31. 1

33. $x = 2 \pm \sqrt{3}$

35. $x = -3 \pm \sqrt{2}$

37. No real solutions

39. $x = \dfrac{-1}{2} \pm \sqrt{2}$

41. $x = \dfrac{-1 \pm \sqrt{2}}{2}$

43. $x = -3$ or -6

45. $x = \dfrac{-1 \pm \sqrt{2}}{2}$

47. $x = \dfrac{-3}{2}$ or 5

49. No real solutions

51. No real solutions

53. $x \approx 1.824$ or 0.470

55. $x = 13.79$

57. $y = \pm 1$ or $\pm\sqrt{6}$

59. $x = \pm\sqrt{7}$

61. $y = \pm 2$ or $\dfrac{\pm 1}{\sqrt{2}}$

63. $x = \pm\dfrac{\sqrt{5}}{5}$

65. No real solution

67. 1

69. $x = \dfrac{2}{5}$

71. $x = \dfrac{-5 \pm \sqrt{57}}{8}$

73. $x = \dfrac{3}{4}$ or -2

75. 2011

77. 2006

79. 1500

81. About 6.32 sec

83. (a) About 4.38 sec   (b) 50 sec

85. (a) $670.5 \dfrac{\text{lb}}{\text{ft}^2}$ (b) 14,400 ft

87. 1960

89. (a) 2003   (b) 2007   (c) mid-2010

91. (a) About 32 and 62   (b) About 17 and 77

93. (a) 73.53%   (b) 84.75%   (c) 91.74%

95. $k = 10$ or -10

97. $k = 16$

99. Yes

101. No

103. $k = 4$

105. (a) $x = \dfrac{-5 \pm \sqrt{17}}{2}$

(b) Answers vary

(c) $x \approx -.3068$ or $.6959$ or -1.1183 or 1.3959

Section 4.1.A, page 253

1. $x = 3$ or -6

3. $x = \dfrac{3}{2}$

5. $x = 2$

7. $x = \dfrac{3}{2}$

9. $x = -5, -3, -1, 1$

11. $x = \dfrac{5 \pm \sqrt{33}}{2}, 1, 4$

13. Upper control limit: 0.0497;
Lower control limit: -0.0097

Section 4.1.B, page 257

1. A varies directly as the square of r; the constant of variation is π.

3. A varies jointly as l and w; the constant of variation is 1.

5. V varies jointly as the square of r and h; the constant of variation is $\dfrac{\pi}{3}$.

7. $a = \dfrac{k}{b}$

9. $z = kxyw$

11. $d = k\sqrt{h}$

13. $v = ku; k = 4$

15. $v = k/u; k = 16$

17. $t = krs; k = 4$

19. $w = kxy^2; k = 2$

21. $T = kpv^3/u^2; k = 16$

23. $r = 4$

25. $b = \dfrac{9}{4}$

27. $u = 50$

29. $r = 3$

31. \$1521.00

33. 12 lb

35. 80 kg/cm^2

37. 400 ft

39. 30 in.

41. 3750 kg

43. (a) 2400 lb   (b) No more than 4 ft

Section 4.2, page 264

1. $x = -1, 1, 3$

3. $x = -2, 1, 4$

5. $x = -\dfrac{2}{3}, \dfrac{-1}{2}, 3$

7. $x = -2, 0, \dfrac{1}{2}, 3$

9. $x = -3, 2$

11. $x = -1, \dfrac{3}{2}, 2$

13. $x = -5, 2, 3$

15. $x = 1$

17. $(x - 1)(2x^2 + 3)$

19. $x^3(x - 4)(x^2 + 3)$

21. $(x - 2)^3(x^2 - 7)$

23. Lower bound: -5; upper bound: 2

25. Lower bound: -1; no upper bound less than 3

27. Lower bound: -8; upper bound 4

29. $x = \left\{-2, \dfrac{-1}{2}, 3\right\}$

31. $x = \left\{-\dfrac{1}{3}, \dfrac{1}{2}, 2\right\}$

33. $x = \left\{2, \dfrac{\sqrt{37} - 5}{2}, \dfrac{-(\sqrt{37} + 5)}{2}\right\}$

35. $x = \left\{\dfrac{1}{2}, -\sqrt{3}, -\sqrt{2}, \sqrt{3}, -\sqrt{2}\right\}$

37. $x = \{-1, 4, \sqrt{3}, -\sqrt{3}\}$

39. $x = 50$, $x = -2.24698$, $x = -0.5549581$, $x = 0.80193774$

41. (a) The only *possible* rational roots of $x^2 - 2$ are $1, -1, 2, -2$. None of those numbers are roots of the polynomial, so the square root of two is irrational.
(b) The only *possible* rational roots of $x^2 - 3$ are $1, -1, 3, -3$. None of those numbers are roots of the polynomial, so the square root of three is irrational.
(c) The only *possible* rational roots of $x^2 - 4$ are $1, -1, 2, -2, 4, -4$. We try them all and find that 2 and -2 both are roots of the polynomial.

43. (a) 5.78 per 100,000 and 5.62 per 100,000
(b) Middle of 1997
(c) 1995
(d) 2004
(e) 2002–2004

45. The sides should be 2 inches.

47. (a) 6 degrees per day, 6.6435 degrees per day
(b) $t = 2.033$ and $t = 10.7069$ (days)
(c) $t = 5.0768$ and $t = 9.6126$
(d) $t = 4$

49. (a) The carrying capacity is an upper bound on the population of bunnies, while the threshold population is a lower bound.
(b) The population is increasing
(c) It is decreasing
(d) It is decreasing
(e) $kx(x - T)(C - x)$
(f) $x = T, x = C, x = 0$

Section 4.3, page 271

1. $x = 7$ **3.** $x = -\dfrac{9}{4}$ **5.** $x = -2$

7. $x = \pm 3$ **9.** $x = -1$ or 2 **11.** $x = 9$

13. $x = \dfrac{1}{2}$ **15.** $x = \dfrac{1}{2}$ or $x = -4$

17. $x \approx \pm .73$

19. $x \approx -1.17$ or $x \approx 2.59$ or $x = -1$

21. $x = -5$ or $x = 3$ **23.** $x = 6$

25. $x = 3$ or 7 **27.** $r = 4.658$

29. $r \approx 8.019$ **31.** $b = \dfrac{a}{\sqrt{A^2 - 1}}$

33. $x = \sqrt{1 - \dfrac{1}{y^2}}$ **35.** No solution

37. $x = 36$ **39.** $x = -1$ or -8

41. $x = 16$ **43.** $x \approx 105.236$

45. $x \approx -.283$

47. (a) 11.47 ft or 29.91 ft   (b) 21 ft

49. Approx. 6.205 mi

51. (a) 1600 feet   (b) 9.52 seconds

Section 4.4, page 281

1. $(-\infty, 3/2)$ **3.** $(-2, \infty)$

5. $(-\infty, -8/5]$ **7.** $(1, \infty)$

9. $(2, 4)$ **11.** $[-3, 5/2)$

13. $(-4/45, \infty)$ **15.** $[-7/17, \infty)$

17. $[-1, 1/8)$ **19.** $[5, \infty)$

21. $x < \dfrac{b + c}{a}$ **23.** $c < x < a + c$

25. $1 \le x \le 3$

27. $x \le \dfrac{1 - \sqrt{33}}{2}$ or $x \ge \dfrac{1 + \sqrt{33}}{2}$

29. $-1 \le x \le 0$ or $x \ge 1$

31. $-1 < x < 1$ and $x < -3$

33. $-2 < x < -1$ or $1 < x < 2$

35. $.5 < x < .84$ **37.** $x < -1/3$ or $x > 2$

39. $x > 1$ **41.** $-3 < x < 1$ or $x \ge 5$

43. $-\sqrt{7} < x < \sqrt{7}$ or $x > 5.34$

45. $x < -3$ or $1/2 < x < 5$ **47.** $x \le 0$ or $x \ge 1$

49. $x > -1.43$ **51.** $x \le -3.79$ or $x \ge .79$

53. Approximately 8.608 cents per kwh

55. More than $37,500

57. (a) They would have to talk more than 6 months.
(b) They are saving between 42 and 60 dollars per month, not counting the up-front fees to switch.

59. $1 < x < 19$ and $y = 20 - x$

61. $10 < x < 35$ **63.** $1 \le t \le 4$ **65.** $2 < t < 2.25$

67. (a) $x^2 < x$ when $0 < x < 1$ and $x^2 > x$ when $x < 0$ or $x > 1$.
(b) If c is nonzero and $|c| < 1$, then either $0 < c < 1$ or $-1 < c < 0$ (which is equivalent to $1 > -c > 0$). If $0 < c < 1$, then $|c| = c$ and c is a solution of $x^2 < x$ by part (a), so that $c^2 < c = |c|$. If $1 > -c > 0$, then $|c| = -c$, which is a solution of $x^2 < x$ by part (a), so that $c^2 = (-c)^2 < (-c) = |c|$.
(c) If $|c| > 1$, then either $c < -1$ or $c > 1$. In either case, c is a solution of $x^2 > x$ by part (a).

69. No solutions

71. $(-\infty, \infty)$, all real numbers are solutions.

73. $x = -2, x = 3$ **75.** No solutions

77. $x = \dfrac{5}{2}$

Section 4.5, page 286

1. $-4/3 \le x \le 0$ **3.** $7/6 < x < 11/6$

5. $x \le -11/20$ or $x \ge -1/4$

7. $x < -53/40$ or $x > -43/40$

9. $x \le -7/2$ or $x \ge -5/4$ **11.** $-1/7 < x < 3$

13. $-\sqrt{3} < x < -1$ or $1 < x < \sqrt{3}$

15. $x < -\sqrt{6}$ or $x > \sqrt{6}$

17. $x \le -2$ or $-1 \le x \le 0$ or $x \ge 1$

19. $-1.43 < x < 1.24$ **21.** $x < -.89$ or $x > 1.56$

23. $x \le 2$ or $x \ge 14/3$

25. $-1.13 < x < 1.35$ or $1.35 < x < 1.67$

27. $(-\infty, \infty)$, all real numbers are solutions.

29. $x = 1, x = 2$

31. If $|x - 3| < E/5$, then multiplying both sides by 5 shows that $5|x - 3| < E$. But
$$5|x - 3| = |5| \cdot |x - 3| = |5(x - 3)|$$
$$= |5x - 15| = |(5x - 4) - 11|. \text{ Thus,}$$
$$|(5x - 4) - 11| < E.$$

33. (a) $2.999 < x < 3.001$
(b) $|\delta - l| < .001$ where δ is the desired length, and l is the length of the manufactured rod.

Section 4.6, page 292

1. (a) $1469.33
(b) $1485.95
(c) $1489.85
(d) $1491.37

3. 633.39   **5.** 674.17   **7.** 819.32

9. 686.84   **11.** $3325.29   **13.** $3359.59

15. (a) 7095.36   (b) No

17. Fund C **19.** $385.18   **21.** $1,162,003.14

23. About 5%   **25.** About 5.92%

27. (a) 9 years   (b) 9 years   (c) 9 years
(d) Investment amount and doubling time are independent.

29. 9.9 years

31. (a) 907.50
(b) CD, since the CD earns 918.06
(c) 971.27; you would make more money this way.

Section 4.7, page 300

1. $x = 4$ **3.** $x = 1/9$ **5.** $x = \dfrac{1}{2}$ or -3

7. $x = -2$ or $-1/2$ **9.** $x = \ln 5/\ln 3 \approx 1.465$

11. $x = \ln 3/\ln 1.5 \approx 2.7095$

13. $x = \dfrac{\ln 3 - 5\ln 5}{\ln 5 + 2\ln 3} \approx -1.825$

15. $x = \dfrac{\ln 2 - \ln 3}{3\ln 2 + \ln 3} \approx -.1276$

17. $x = (\ln 5)/2 \approx .805$

19. $x = (-\ln 3.5)/1.4 \approx -.895$

21. $x = 2\ln(5/2.1)/\ln 3 \approx 1.579$

23. $x = 0$ or 1

25. $x = \ln 2 \approx .693$ or $x = \ln 3 \approx 1.099$

27. $x = \ln 3 \approx 1.099$

29. $x = \ln 2/\ln 4 = 1/2$ or $x = \ln 3/\ln 4 \approx .792$

31. $x = \ln(t + \sqrt{t^2 + 1})$

33. (a) If $\ln u = \ln v$, then $u = e^{\ln u} = e^{\ln v} = v$.
(b) No, if u and v are negative then $\ln u$ and $\ln v$ are undefined.

35. $x = 9$ **37.** $x = 5$ **39.** $x = 6$ **41.** $x = 3$

43. $x = \dfrac{-5 + \sqrt{37}}{2}$ **45.** $x = 9/(e - 1)$

47. $x = 5$ **49.** $x = \pm\sqrt{10001}$

51. $x = \sqrt{\dfrac{e + 1}{e - 1}}$ **53.** .444 billion years

55. 14.95 days   **57.** Approximately 3.8132 days

59. About 3689 years old   **61.** About 2534 years ago

63. About 6.99%

65. (a) About 22.5 years   (b) About 22.1 years

67. $3197.05   **69.** 79.36 years

71. (a) .0146   (b) 2024

73. (a) $k \approx 21.459$ (b) $t \approx .182$

75. (a) 20 at the beginning and 2500 3 hours later
(b) $\dfrac{\ln 2}{\ln 5} \approx .43$

77. (a) 200 people; 2795 people
(b) After 6 weeks

79. (a) 16 years from this year
(b) 24 years from this year

81. (a) $c = \dfrac{250}{3}; k = -\left(\dfrac{1}{4}\right)\ln\left(\dfrac{2}{5}\right)$ (b) 12.43 weeks

Section 4.8, page 311

1. 3   **3.** 3   **5.** 2

7. $x = -2.42645$ **9.** -1.4526 **11.** -1.4751

13. 1.1921235   **15.** -1.379414 **17.** 1.3289

19. -2.1149 **21.** $x = 2.1017$ **23.** $x = -1.7521$

25. $x = .9505$ **27.** $x = 0$ or 2.2074

29. $x = 2.3901454$

31. $x = -.6513878188$ or 1.151387819

33. $x = 7.033393042$ **35.** $x = 2/3$

37. $x = 1/12$ **39.** $x = \sqrt{3}$

41. $x = 1.4528$ or -112.00 **43.** 3.00242

45. 1.7388   **47.** 2009

49. (a) late 2003
(b) mid 2010

51. about 96 ft   **53.** late 2012

Chapter 5

Section 5.1, page 323

1. The values are a solution.

3. The values are a solution.

5. The values are not a solution.

7. $x = 6/5, y = 8/5$ 9. $x = 2/7, y = -11/7$

11. $r = 5/2, s = -5/2$ 13. $x = \frac{3}{2}c, y = d - \frac{1}{2}c$

15. $x = 28, y = 22$ 17. $x = 2, y = -1$

19. Inconsistent

21. $x = b, y = \frac{4b - 2}{5}$, where b is any real number.

23. $x = -6, y = 2$ 25. $x = 13.2, y = 3.6$

27. $x = 7/11, y = -7$ 29. $x = 1, y = 1/2$

31. (a) Solve each equation for y, and observe that a positive slope represents an increasing population; a negative slope represents a decreasing population.
    (b) 1988

33. 2115

35. $x = \frac{rd - sb}{ad - bc}, y = \frac{as - rc}{ad - bc}$

37. Since the two lines have slopes $-\frac{1}{2}$ and 2, they are perpendicular and intersect at one point, regardless of c. Therefore, there is exactly one solution for the system. Alternatively, solve the system to find that the only solution is $x = \frac{3c + 8}{15}, y = \frac{6c - 4}{15}$.

39. $c = -3, d = 1/2$

41. Equilibrium quantity is 20,000; equilibrium price is $17.

43. Equilibrium quantity is 4000; equilibrium price is $180.

45. 145 adults; 55 children

47. Boat: 18 mph; current: 2 mph

49. $1\frac{1}{2}$ lb cashews and $4\frac{1}{2}$ lb peanuts

51. 24 grams of 50% alloy; 16 grams of 75% alloy

53. (a) Electric: $y = 2000 + 960x$, solar: $y = 14,000 + 114x$
    (b) Electric: $6800, solar: $14,570
    (c) The costs will be the same when $x = 14.2$. Electric heating will be cheaper before that, solar afterwards.

55. (a) $R = 250,500x$
    (b) $C = 1,295,000 + 206,500x$
    (c) $P = R - C = 44,000x - 1,295,000$
    (d) $R = 109,000x, C = 440,000 + 82,000x$,
        $P = R - C = 27,000x - 440,000$
    (e) 50.3 weeks, $918,000
    (f) It would be better to open off Broadway if a run of 50 weeks or less is expected.

57. (a) $R = 60x$
    (b) 400 hedge trimmers

59. Since the break-even point is above the maximum number that can be sold, the product should not be produced.

61. $14,450 at 9%, $6,450 at 11%

63. (a) $y = .373x + 27.02$
    (b) $y = .624x + 23.65$ (c) 2003

65. 80 bowls and 120 plates

Section 5.2, page 332

1. $x = 3, y = 9$ or $x = -1, y = 1$

3. $x = \frac{-1 + \sqrt{41}}{4}, y = \frac{21 - \sqrt{41}}{8}$ or $x = \frac{-1 - \sqrt{41}}{4}, y = \frac{21 + \sqrt{41}}{8}$

5. $x = 7, y = 3$ or $x = 3, y = 7$

7. $x = 0, y = -3$ or $x = 8, y = 1$

9. $x = 2, y = 0$ or $x = 4, y = 2$

11. $x = 4, y = 3$ or $x = -4, y = 3$ or $x = \sqrt{21}, y = -2$ or $x = -\sqrt{21}, y = -2$

13. $x = -1.6237, y = -8.1891$ or $x = 1.3163, y = 1.0826$ or $x = 2.8073, y = 2.4814$

15. $x = -1.9493, y = .4412$ or $x = .3634, y = .9578$ or $x = 1.4184, y = .5986$

17. $x = -.9519, y = -.8145$

19. No solutions

21. $x = 2 + \sqrt{5}, y = -1 + \sqrt{5}$ or $x = 2 - \sqrt{5}, y = -1 - \sqrt{5}$

23. $x = -4.8093, y = 19.3201$ or $x = -3.1434, y = 7.7374$ or $x = 2.1407, y = 7.7230$ or $x = 2.8120, y = 11.7195$

25. $x = -3.8371, y = -2.2596$ or $x = -.9324, y = -7.7796$

27. $x = -1.4873, y = .0480$ or $x = -.0480, y = 1.4873$ or $x = .0480, y = -1.4873$ or $x = 1.4873, y = -.0480$

29. The intersection point nearest the origin is $(2.4, 3.2)$.

31. Two possible boxes: One is 2 by 2 by 4 meters and the other is approximately 3.1231 by 3.1231 by 1.6404 meters.

33. -13 and -4 35. 30 and 4.25; 4.25 and 30

37. 16 and -14 39. 16.5 feet by 10 feet

41. 32.1 cm and 14.0 cm

Section 5.3, page 345

1. $\begin{pmatrix} 2 & -3 & 4 & 1 \\ 1 & 2 & -6 & 0 \\ 3 & -7 & 4 & -3 \end{pmatrix}$ 3. $\begin{pmatrix} 2 & -\frac{5}{2} & \frac{2}{3} & 0 \\ 1 & -\frac{1}{4} & 4 & 0 \\ 0 & -3 & \frac{1}{2} & 0 \end{pmatrix}$

5. $3x - 5y = 4$
   $9x + 7y = 2$

7. $x + z = 1$
$ x - y + 4z - 2w = 3$
$ 4x + 2y + 5z = 2$

9. $x = 3/2, y = 5, z = -2, w = 0$

11. $x = 3 - 2t, y = 5 - 3t, z = 2, w = t$, where t is any real number.

13. $y = 3/2, x = 3/2, z = -3/2$

15. $z = t, y = -1 + \frac{1}{3}t, x = 2 - \frac{4}{3}t$, where t is any real number.

17. $x = -14, y = -6, z = 2$

19. $x = 100, y = 50, z = 50$

21. $z = t, y = -2t + 1/2, x = t$, where t is any real number.

23. $x = 2, y = 3$

25. No solution

27. $z = t, y = t - 1, x = -t + 2$, where t is any real number.

29. $x = y = z = 0$

31. $x = -1, y = 1, z = -3, w = -2$

33. $x = 7/31, y = 6/31, z = 1/31, w = 29/31$

35. $x = 1/2, y = 1/3, z = -1/4$

37. $x = 3/5, y = 1/5$ \qquad **39.** $x = -1, y = 2$

41. $A = 1, B = 3$

43. $A = -3/25, B = 3/25, C = 7/5$

45. $A = 2, B = 3, C = -1$

47. $3000 from friend, $6000 from the bank, $1000 from the insurance company

49. $15,000 in the mutual fund, $30,000 in bonds, $25,000 in the fast-food franchise

51. 6 cups of Progresso, 9 cups of Healthy Choice, 2 cups of Campbell's. The serving size is 1.7 cups.

53. Three possible solutions: 18 bedroom models, 13 living room models, 0 whole-house models, or 16 bedroom models, 8 living room models, 2 whole-house models, or 14 bedroom models, 3 living room models, 4 whole-house models

55. (a) X-ray 1: $a + b$. X-ray 2: $a + c$.
(b) $a = .405, b = .345, c = .195$
(c) A is bone, B is tumorous, C is healthy.

57. 2000 chairs, 1600 chests, and 2500 tables.

59. (a) $x + t = 1000$
$ x + y = 1100$
$ y + z = 700$
$ t + z = 600$
(b) $z = 600 - t, y = 100 + t, x = 1000 - t$
(c) The smallest number of cars leaving A on 4th Avenue is 0; the largest is 600. The smallest number of cars leaving A on Euclid is 400; the largest is 1000. The smallest number of cars leaving C on 5th Avenue is 100; the largest is 700. The smallest number of cars leaving C on Chester is 0; the largest is 600.

Chapter 6

Section 6.1, page 356

1. $2\pi/9$ \qquad **3.** $\pi/9$ \qquad **5.** $\pi/18$

7. About $\dfrac{\pi}{3}$ \qquad **9.** About $\dfrac{-3\pi}{4}$

11. $\dfrac{9\pi}{4}, \dfrac{17\pi}{4}, \dfrac{-7\pi}{4}, \dfrac{-15\pi}{4}$

13. $\dfrac{11\pi}{6}, \dfrac{23\pi}{6}, \dfrac{-13\pi}{6}, \dfrac{-25\pi}{6}$

15. No \qquad **17.** Yes \qquad **19.** $5\pi/3$

21. $3\pi/4$ \qquad **23.** $3\pi/5$ \qquad **25.** $7 - 2\pi$

27. $\pi/30$ \qquad **29.** $-\pi/15$ \qquad **31.** $5\pi/12$

33. $3\pi/4$ \qquad **35.** $-5\pi/4$ \qquad **37.** $31\pi/6$

39. $36°$ \qquad **41.** $-18°$ \qquad **43.** $135°$

45. $4°$ \qquad **47.** $-75°$ \qquad **49.** $972°$

51. $4\pi/3$ \qquad **53.** $7\pi/6$ \qquad **55.** $41\pi/6$

57. 7π \qquad **59.** 4π \qquad **61.** 42.5π

63. $2\pi k$

Section 6.2, page 364

1. $(fg)(t) = 3\sin^2 t + 6\sin t \cos t$

3. $3\sin^3 t + 3\sin^2 t \tan t$ \qquad **5.** $(\cos t - 2)(\cos t + 2)$

7. $(\sin t - \cos t)(\sin t + \cos t)$

9. $(\tan t + 3)^2$ \qquad **11.** $(3\sin t + 1)(2\sin t - 1)$

13. $(\cos^2 t + 5)(\cos t + 1)(\cos t - 1)$

15. $(f \circ g)(t) = \cos(2t + 4), (g \circ f)(t) = 2\cos t + 4$

17. $(f \circ g)(t) = \tan(t^2 + 2), (g \circ f)(t) = \tan^2(t + 3) - 1$

19. Yes \qquad **21.** No \qquad **23.** No

25. $\sin t = -\sqrt{3}/2$ \qquad **27.** $\sin t = \sqrt{3}/2$

29. $-3/5$ \qquad **31.** $-3/5$ \qquad **33.** $3/4$

35. $-3/4$ \qquad **37.** $-\sqrt{21}/5$ \qquad **39.** $-2/5$

41. $-\sqrt{21}/5$ \qquad **43.** $\dfrac{\sqrt{2 + \sqrt{2}}}{2}$ \qquad **45.** $\dfrac{\sqrt{2 - \sqrt{2}}}{2}$

47. $\sin^2 t - \cos^2 t$ \qquad **49.** $\sin t$

51. $|\sin t \cos t| \sqrt{\sin t}$ \qquad **53.** $1/4$

55. $\cos t + 2$ \qquad **57.** $\cos t$

514   ANSWERS

59. (a) $Y_2 = f(t) = 22.7 \sin(.52x - 2.18) + 49.6$ and $Y_3 = f(x + 12.083) = 22.7 \sin(.52(x + 12.083) - 2.18)$

X	Y2
1	26.99
2	28.974
3	36.411
4	47.334
5	58.056
6	67.932
7	72.161

Y2=22.7sin(.52X...

X	Y2
8	70.426
9	63.185
10	52.353
11	40.794
12	31.562
13	27.099
14	28.584

Y2=22.7sin(.52X...

X	Y3
1	26.99
2	28.974
3	36.411
4	47.334
5	58.056
6	67.932
7	72.161

Y3=Y2(X+12.083)

X	Y3
8	70.426
9	63.185
10	52.353
11	40.794
12	31.562
13	27.099
14	28.584

Y3=Y2(X+12.083)

(b) Yes; the period is 12.083, which is a reasonable approximation of the expected period of 12 months.

61. (a) 0; about 76.5%; about 51.3%

(b) $Y_4 = g(t) = .5\left(1 - \cos\dfrac{2\pi t}{29.5}\right)$ and $Y_5 = g(t + 29.5)$

$$= .5\left(1 - \cos\dfrac{2\pi(t + 29.5)}{29.5}\right)$$

X	Y4	Y5
0	0	0
1	.0113	.0113
2	.04468	.04468
3	.09864	.09864
4	.17074	.17074
5	.25772	.25772
6	.35565	.35565

Y4=.5(1-cos(2πX...

X	Y4	Y5
7	.46011	.46011
8	.56636	.56636
9	.66962	.66962
10	.76521	.76521
11	.84882	.84882
12	.91666	.91666
13	.96567	.96567

Y5=Y4(X+29.5)

X	Y4	Y5
14	.99363	.99363
15	.99929	.99929
16	.98238	.98238
17	.94368	.94368
18	.88492	.88492
19	.80876	.80876
20	.71865	.71865

Y4=.5(1-cos(2πX...

X	Y4	Y5
21	.61866	.61866
22	.51331	.51331
23	.40736	.40736
24	.30559	.30559
25	.21261	.21261
26	.13261	.13261
27	.06922	.06922

Y5=Y4(X+29.5)

X	Y4	Y5
28	.0253	.0253
29	.00283	.00283
30	.00283	.00283
31	.0253	.0253
32	.06922	.06922
33	.13261	.13261
34	.21261	.21261

Y4=.5(1-cos(2πX...

(c) Late on day 14 ($t = 14.75$)

63. $f(t + k) = \cos 3\left(t + \dfrac{2\pi}{3}\right) = \cos(3t + 2\pi) = \cos 3t = f(t)$

65. $f(t + 2) = \sin(\pi(t + 2)) = \sin(\pi t + 2\pi) = \sin(\pi t) = f(t)$

67. $f\left(t + \dfrac{\pi}{2}\right) = \tan 2\left(t + \dfrac{\pi}{2}\right) = \tan(2t + \pi) = \tan(2t) = f(t)$

69. (a) There is no such number k.

(b) If we substitute $t = 0$ in $\cos(t + k) = \cos t$, we get $\cos k = \cos 0 = 1$.

(c) If there were such a number k, then by part (b), $\cos k = 1$, which is impossible by part (a). Therefore, there is no such number k, and the period is 2π.

Section 6.3, page 374

1. $t = \ldots, -2\pi, -\pi, 0, \pi, 2\pi, \ldots$; or $t = \pi k$, where k is any integer

3. $t = \ldots, -7\pi/2, -3\pi/2, \pi/2, 5\pi/2, 9\pi/2, \ldots$; or $t = \pi/2 + 2\pi k$, where k is any integer

5. $t = \ldots, -3\pi, -\pi, \pi, 3\pi, \ldots$; or $t = \pi + 2k\pi$, where k is any integer

7. 11   **9.** 1.4

11. Shift the graph of f vertically 3 units upward.

13. Reflect the graph of f in the horizontal axis.

15. Shift the graph of f vertically 5 units upward.

17. Stretch the graph of f away from the horizontal axis by a factor of 3.

19. Stretch the graph of f away from the horizontal axis by a factor of 3, then shift the resulting graph vertically 2 units upward.

21. Shift the graph of f horizontally 2 units to the right.

23. D   **25.** B   **27.** F   **29.** G

31. 2 solutions   **33.** 2 solutions

35. 2 solutions   **37.** 2 solutions

39. Possibly an identity   **41.** Possibly an identity

43. Possibly an identity   **45.** Not an identity

47. Possibly an identity   **49.** Not an identity

51. No   **53.** Yes; period 2π

55. Yes; period 2π **57.** No

59. No

61. (a) Yes if proper value of k is used; no

(b) $0, 2\pi, 4\pi, 6\pi$, etc. So why do the graphs look identical?

63. (a) 80

(b) 14 or 15 on 96-pixel-wide screens; up to 40–50 on wider screens; quite different from part (a). Explain what's going on. [*Hint:* How many points have to be plotted in order to get even a rough approximation of one full wave? How many points is the calculator plotting for the entire graph?]

65. (a) $-\pi \le t \le \pi$

(b) $n = 15$; $f_{15}(2)$ and $g(2)$ are identical in the first nine decimal places and differ in the tenth, a very good approximation.

67. $r(t)/s(t)$, where $r(t) = f_{15}(t)$ in Exercise 65 and $s(t) = f_{16}(t)$ in Exercise 66.

69. The y-coordinate of the new point is the same as the x-coordinate of the point on the unit circle. To explain what's going on, look at the definition of the cosine function.

Section 6.4, page 386

1. Amplitude: 3, period: π, phase shift: $\dfrac{\pi}{2}$

3. Amplitude: 5, period: $\dfrac{2\pi}{5}$, phase shift: $\dfrac{-1}{25}$

5. Amplitude: 1, period: 1, phase shift: 0

7. Amplitude: 6, period: $\dfrac{2}{3}$, phase shift: $\dfrac{-1}{3\pi}$

9. $f(t) = 3 \sin\left(8t - \dfrac{8\pi}{5}\right)$ **11.** $f(t) = \dfrac{3}{4} \sin(\pi t)$

13. $f(t) = 7 \sin\left(\dfrac{6\pi}{5}t + \dfrac{3\pi^2}{5}\right)$

15. $f(t) = 2 \sin 4t$

17. $f(t) = 1.5 \cos \dfrac{t}{2}$

19. (a) $\pi/100$
(b) The graph makes 200 complete waves between 0 and 2π.
(c) $0 \le x \le \pi/25$; $-2 \le y \le 2$

21. (a) $\dfrac{2\pi}{900}$
(b) The graph makes 900 complete waves between 0 and 2π.
(c) $0 \le x \le \dfrac{2\pi}{225}$; $-2 \le y \le 2$

23. (a) $f(t) = -12 \sin\left(10t + \dfrac{\pi}{2}\right)$
(b) $g(t) = -12 \cos 10t$

25. (a) $f(t) = -\sin 2t$
(b) $g(t) = -\cos\left(2t - \dfrac{\pi}{2}\right)$

27.

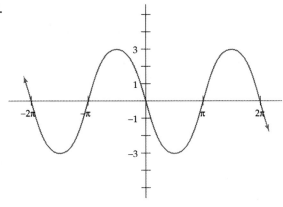

29.

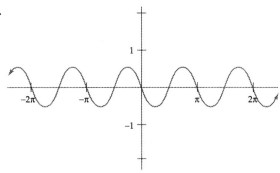

31.

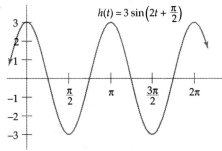

$h(t) = 3 \sin\left(2t + \dfrac{\pi}{2}\right)$

33. Local maximum at $t = 5\pi/6 \approx 2.6180$; local minimum at $t = 11\pi/6 \approx 5.7596$

35. Local maxima at $t = \pi/6 \approx .5236$, $t = 5\pi/6 \approx 2.6180$, $t = 3\pi/2 \approx 4.7124$; local minima at $t = \pi/2 \approx 1.5708$, $t = 7\pi/6 \approx 3.6652$, $t = 11\pi/6 \approx 5.7596$

37. $A \approx 3.606$; $b = 1$; $c \approx .5880$

39. $A \approx 3.8332$; $b = 4$; $c \approx 1.4572$

41. The waves do not have the same amplitude.

43. (a) The person's blood pressure is 134/92.
(b) The pulse rate is 75.

45. (a) Maximum is 79.5 cubic inches; minimum is 30.5 cubic inches.
(b) every 4 seconds
(c) 15

47. Period: $\dfrac{1}{980,000}$ seconds; frequency: 980,000

49. $f(t) = 125 \sin(\pi t/5)$

51. $f(t) = \cos 20\pi t + \sqrt{16 - \sin^2(20\pi t)}$

53. $h(t) = 6 \sin(\pi t/2)$

55. $h(t) = 6 \cos(\pi t/2)$

57. $d(t) = 10 \sin(\pi t/2)$

59. (a) At least four (starting point, high point, low point, ending point)
(b) 301
(c) Every calculator is different; the TI-84+ plots 95 points; others plot as many as 239.
(d) Obviously, 239 points (or fewer) are not enough when the absolute minimum is 301.

61. (a)
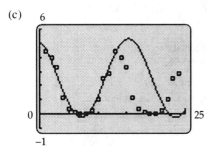

(b) The data appears to be approximately periodic. An appropriate model is $f(t) = 1.1371 \sin(.6352t - .6366) + 7.4960$.

(c) No; the model is only a fair approximation of the data and, in any case, unemployment is hard to predict.

(d) $g(x) = 24.85 \sin(.52x + (-2.15)) + 48.95$

(e) 12.05 months, yes it fits better.

63. (a) $f(t) = 2.77 \cdot \sin(.39x + 1.91) + 2.52$

(b) $f(x)$ has period ≈ 16.1. One would expect a period of 12.

(c)

6

0 ———————————— 25

−1

(d) $g(x) = 2.17 \sin(.51x + 1.04) + 1.71$

(e) $g(x)$ has period ≈ 12.3, and it seems to fit better than $f(x)$.

65. (a) $k = 9.8/\pi^2$

(b) When k is replaced by $(k + .01\%$ of $k)$, the value of ω changes and the period of the pendulum becomes approximately 2.000099998 sec, meaning that the clock loses .000099998 sec every 2 sec, for a total of approximately 397.43 sec (6.62 min) during the three months.

Section 6.5, page 396

1. Fourth quadrant   **3.** Second quadrant

5. Fourth quadrant

7. $\sin t = 4/5$, $\cos t = 3/5$, $\tan t = 4/3$, $\cot t = 3/4$, $\sec t = 5/3$, $\csc t = 5/4$

9. $\sin t = 12/13$, $\cos t = -5/13$, $\tan t = -12/5$, $\cot t = -5/12$, $\sec t = -13/5$, $\csc t = 13/12$

11. $\sin t = 5/\sqrt{26}$, $\cos t = -1/\sqrt{26}$, $\tan t = -5$, $\cot t = -1/5$, $\sec t = -\sqrt{26}$, $\csc t = \sqrt{26}/5$

13. $\sin t = \sqrt{3}/\sqrt{5}$, $\cos t = \sqrt{2}/\sqrt{5}$, $\tan t = \sqrt{3}/\sqrt{2}$, $\cot t = \sqrt{2}/\sqrt{3}$, $\sec t = \sqrt{5}/\sqrt{2}$, $\csc t = \sqrt{5}/\sqrt{3}$

15. $\sin t = \dfrac{3}{\sqrt{12 + 2\sqrt{2}}}$, $\cos t = \dfrac{1 + \sqrt{2}}{\sqrt{12 + 2\sqrt{2}}}$, $\tan t = \dfrac{3}{1 + \sqrt{2}}$, $\cot t = \dfrac{1 + \sqrt{2}}{3}$, $\sec t = \dfrac{\sqrt{12 + 2\sqrt{2}}}{1 + \sqrt{2}}$, $\csc t = \dfrac{\sqrt{12 + 2\sqrt{2}}}{3}$

17. About 154.74 ft

19. (a) $0 \le x \le 150$ and $-5 \le y \le 20$
(b) About 15.16 ft   (c) About 143 ft

21. $\sin\left(\dfrac{4\pi}{3}\right) = -\dfrac{\sqrt{3}}{2}$, $\cos\left(\dfrac{4\pi}{3}\right) = -\dfrac{1}{2}$, $\tan\left(\dfrac{4\pi}{3}\right) = \sqrt{3}$, $\cot\left(\dfrac{4\pi}{3}\right) = \dfrac{1}{\sqrt{3}}$, $\sec\left(\dfrac{4\pi}{3}\right) = -2$, $\csc\left(\dfrac{4\pi}{3}\right) = \dfrac{-2}{\sqrt{3}}$

23. $\sin\left(\dfrac{7\pi}{4}\right) = -\dfrac{\sqrt{2}}{2}$, $\cos\left(\dfrac{7\pi}{4}\right) = \dfrac{\sqrt{2}}{2}$, $\tan\left(\dfrac{7\pi}{4}\right) = -1$, $\cot\left(\dfrac{7\pi}{4}\right) = -1$, $\sec\left(\dfrac{7\pi}{4}\right) = \sqrt{2}$, $\csc\left(\dfrac{7\pi}{4}\right) = -\sqrt{2}$

25. $\sin\left(\dfrac{-11\pi}{4}\right) = -\dfrac{\sqrt{2}}{2}$, $\cos\left(\dfrac{-11\pi}{4}\right) = \dfrac{-\sqrt{2}}{2}$, $\tan\left(\dfrac{-11\pi}{4}\right) = 1$, $\cot\left(\dfrac{-11\pi}{4}\right) = 1$, $\sec\left(\dfrac{-11\pi}{4}\right) = -\sqrt{2}$, $\csc\left(\dfrac{-11\pi}{4}\right) = -\sqrt{2}$

27. -3.8287

29. (a) 5.6511; 5.7618; 5.7731; 5.7743 (b) $(\sec 2)^2$

31. $\cos t + \sin t$ **33.** $1 - 2\sec t + \sec^2 t$

35. $\cot^3 t - \tan^3 t$ **37.** $\csc t(\sec t - \csc t)$

39. $(-1)(\tan^2 t + \sec^2 t)$

41. $(\cos^2 t + 1 + \sec^2 t)(\cos t - \sec t)$

43. $\cot t$ **45.** $\dfrac{2\tan t + 1}{3\sin t + 1}$

47. $4 - \tan t$

49. $\tan t = \dfrac{\sin t}{\cos t} = \dfrac{1}{\cos t / \sin t} = \dfrac{1}{\cot t}$

51. $1 + \cot^2 t = 1 + \dfrac{\cos^2 t}{\sin^2 t} = \dfrac{\sin^2 t + \cos^2 t}{\sin^2 t} = \dfrac{1}{\sin^2 t} = \csc^2 t$

53. $\sec(-t) = \dfrac{1}{\cos(-t)} = \dfrac{1}{\cos t} = \sec t$

55. $\sin t = \dfrac{\sqrt{3}}{2}$, $\cos t = -\dfrac{1}{2}$, $\tan t = -\sqrt{3}$, $\csc t = \dfrac{2\sqrt{3}}{3}$, $\sec t = -2$, $\cot t = -\dfrac{\sqrt{3}}{3}$

57. $\sin t = 1$, $\cos t = 0$, $\tan t$ is undefined, $\cot t = 0$, $\sec t$ is undefined, $\csc t = 1$

59. $\sin t = \dfrac{12}{13}$, $\cos t = -\dfrac{5}{13}$, $\tan t = -\dfrac{12}{5}$, $\cot t = -\dfrac{5}{12}$, $\sec t = -\dfrac{13}{5}$, $\csc t = \dfrac{13}{12}$

61. Possibly an identity   **63.** Not an identity

65. Look at the graph of $y = \sec t$ in Figure 6–84 on page 501. If you draw in the line $y = t$, it will pass through $(-\pi/2, -\pi/2)$ and $(\pi/2, \pi/2)$, and obviously will not intersect the graph of $y = \sec t$ when $-\pi/2 \le t \le \pi/2$. But it will intersect each part of the graph that lies above the horizontal axis, to the right of $t = \pi/2$; it will also intersect those parts that lie below the horizontal axis, to the left of $-\pi/2$. The first coordinate of each of these infinitely many intersection points will be a solution of $\sec t = t$.

67. (a) $\dfrac{\cos\theta\sin\theta}{2}$ (b) $\dfrac{\tan\theta}{2}$ (c) $\dfrac{\theta}{2}$

Chapter 7

Section 7.1, page 407

1. $\dfrac{\sqrt{2}+\sqrt{6}}{4}$ **3.** $\dfrac{\sqrt{2}+\sqrt{6}}{4}$ **5.** $2-\sqrt{3}$

7. $-2-\sqrt{3}$ **9.** $\dfrac{-\sqrt{2}-\sqrt{6}}{4}$ **11.** $\dfrac{\sqrt{6}+\sqrt{2}}{4}$

13. $\cos x$ **15.** $-\sin x$ **17.** $\dfrac{-1}{\cos x}$

19. $-\sin 2$ **21.** $\cos x$ **23.** $-2\sin x \sin y$

25. $\dfrac{4+\sqrt{2}}{6}$ **27.** $\dfrac{-\sqrt{3}+2\sqrt{6}}{10}$ **29.** $\dfrac{4+3\sqrt{3}}{10}$

31. $\dfrac{4-3\sqrt{3}}{10}$

33. From the figure, $\sin t = \dfrac{4}{5}$ and $\cos t = \dfrac{3}{5}$. So,

$5\sin(x+t) = 5(\sin x \cos t + \cos x \sin t) =$

$\sin x \cdot 5\cos t + \cos x \cdot 5\sin t = \sin x \cdot 5\left(\dfrac{3}{5}\right) +$

$\cos x \cdot 5\left(\dfrac{4}{5}\right) = 3\sin x + 4\cos x$

35. $\dfrac{f(x+h)-f(x)}{h} = \dfrac{\cos(x+h)-\cos x}{h}$

$= \dfrac{\cos x \cos h - \sin x \sin h - \cos x}{h}$

$= \dfrac{\cos x(\cos h - 1) - \sin x \sin h}{h}$

$= \cos x\left(\dfrac{\cos h - 1}{h}\right) - \sin x\dfrac{\sin h}{h}$

37. $\sin(x+y) = \sin(x-(-y)) = \sin x \cos(-y)$
$-\cos x \sin(-y) = \sin x \cos y - \cos x(-\sin y)$
$= \sin x \cos y + \cos x \sin y$

39. $\dfrac{\cos(x-y)}{\cos x \cos y} = \dfrac{\cos x \cos y + \sin x \sin y}{\cos x \cos y}$

$= \dfrac{\cos x \cos y}{\cos x \cos y} + \dfrac{\sin x \sin y}{\cos x \cos y} = 1 + \tan x \tan y$

41. $\dfrac{\sin(x-y)}{\sin x \sin y} = \dfrac{\sin x \cos y - \cos x \sin y}{\sin x \sin y}$

$= \dfrac{\sin x \cos y}{\sin x \sin y} - \dfrac{\cos x \sin y}{\sin x \sin y} = \cot y - \cot x$

43. $\dfrac{\sin(x+y)}{\sin x \cos y} = \dfrac{\sin x \cos y + \cos x \sin y}{\sin x \cos y}$

$= \dfrac{\sin x \cos y}{\sin x \cos y} + \dfrac{\cos x \sin y}{\sin x \cos y} = 1 + \cot x \tan y$

45. $\sin(x+y) = -44/125$; $\tan(x+y) = 44/117$; $x+y$ lies in quadrant III.

47. $\cos(x+y) = -\dfrac{56}{65}$; $\tan(x+y) = \dfrac{33}{56}$; $x+y$ lies in quadrant III.

49. $\sin u \cos v \cos w + \cos u \sin v \cos w +$
$\cos u \cos v \sin w - \sin u \sin v \sin w$

51. If $x+y = \dfrac{\pi}{2}$, then $y = \dfrac{\pi}{2} - x$ and $\sin y = \sin\left(\dfrac{\pi}{2} - x\right)$
$= \cos x$. Thus, $\sin^2 x + \sin^2 y = \sin^2 x + \cos^2 x = 1$.

53. $\sin(x-\pi) = \sin x \cos\pi - \cos x \sin\pi = \sin x(-1) -$
$\cos x(0) = -\sin x$

55. $\cos(\pi - x) = \cos\pi \cos x + \sin\pi \sin x = (-1)\cos x +$
$(0)\sin x = -\cos x$

57. $\sin(x+\pi) = \sin x \cos\pi + \cos x \sin\pi = \sin x \cdot (-1) +$
$\cos x \cdot (0) = -\sin x$

59. $\tan(x+\pi) = \dfrac{\tan x + \tan\pi}{1 - \tan x \tan\pi} = \dfrac{\tan x + 0}{1 - \tan x \cdot 0} = \tan x$

61. $\dfrac{1}{2}[\cos(x-y) - \cos(x+y)]$

$= \dfrac{1}{2}[\cos x \cos y + \sin x \sin y - (\cos x \cos y - \sin x \sin y)]$

$= \dfrac{1}{2} \cdot 2\sin x \sin y = \sin x \sin y$

63. $\cos(x+y)\cos(x-y)$
$= (\cos x \cos y - \sin x \sin y)(\cos x \cos y + \sin x \sin y)$
$= \cos^2 x \cos^2 y - \sin^2 x \sin^2 y$

65. $\dfrac{\cos(x-y)}{\sin x \cos y} = \dfrac{\cos x \cos y + \sin x \sin y}{\sin x \cos y} = \dfrac{\cos x}{\sin x} + \dfrac{\sin y}{\cos y}$

$= \cot x + \tan y$

67. This is not an identity.

69. $\dfrac{\sin(x+y)}{\sin(x-y)}$

$= \dfrac{\sin x \cos y + \cos x \sin y}{\sin x \cos y - \cos x \sin y} \cdot \dfrac{1/\cos x \cos y}{1/\cos x \cos y}$

$= \dfrac{\dfrac{\sin x}{\cos x} + \dfrac{\sin y}{\cos y}}{\dfrac{\sin x}{\cos x} - \dfrac{\sin y}{\cos y}} = \dfrac{\tan x + \tan y}{\tan x - \tan y}$

71. Not an identity   **73.** Not an identity

Section 7.2, page 416

1. $\sin 2x = \dfrac{120}{169}$, $\cos 2x = \dfrac{119}{169}$, $\tan 2x = \dfrac{120}{119}$

3. $\sin 2x = \dfrac{24}{25}$, $\cos 2x = -\dfrac{7}{25}$, $\tan 2x = -\dfrac{24}{7}$

5. $\sin 2x = \dfrac{24}{25}$, $\cos 2x = \dfrac{7}{25}$, $\tan 2x = \dfrac{24}{7}$

7. $\sin 2x = \dfrac{\sqrt{15}}{8}$, $\cos 2x = 7/8$, $\tan 2x = \dfrac{\sqrt{15}}{7}$

9. (a) Length $= 2x$, height $= y$, area $= 2xy$
   (b) $x = 3\cos t$, $y = 3\sin t$
   (c) $A = 2xy$
   $A = 2(3\cos t)(3\sin t)$
   $A = 9(2\sin t \cos t)$
   $A = 9\sin 2t$

11. $\dfrac{\sqrt{2+\sqrt{2}}}{2}$ **13.** $\dfrac{\sqrt{2+\sqrt{2}}}{2}$ **15.** $2 - \sqrt{3}$

17. $\dfrac{\sqrt{2+\sqrt{3}}}{2}$ **19.** $\dfrac{\sqrt{2-\sqrt{2}}}{2}$ **21.** $1 - \sqrt{2}$

23. $\dfrac{\sqrt{2+\sqrt{2+\sqrt{2}}}}{2}$ **25.** $\dfrac{\sqrt{2-\sqrt{2+\sqrt{3}}}}{2}$

27. $\sin\dfrac{x}{2} = \dfrac{\sqrt{30}}{10}$, $\cos\dfrac{x}{2} = \dfrac{\sqrt{70}}{10}$, $\tan\dfrac{x}{2} = \sqrt{\dfrac{3}{7}}$

29. $\sin\dfrac{x}{2} = \dfrac{1}{\sqrt{10}}$, $\cos\dfrac{x}{2} = -\dfrac{3}{\sqrt{10}}$, $\tan\dfrac{x}{2} = -\dfrac{1}{3}$

31. $\sin\dfrac{x}{2} = \dfrac{\sqrt{50+20\sqrt{5}}}{10}$, $\cos\dfrac{x}{2} = -\dfrac{\sqrt{50-20\sqrt{5}}}{10}$,
   $\tan\dfrac{x}{2} = -(\sqrt{5} + 2)$

33. $\dfrac{1}{2}\sin 10x - \dfrac{1}{2}\sin 2x$ **35.** $\dfrac{1}{2}\cos 6x + \dfrac{1}{2}\cos 2x$

37. $\dfrac{1}{2}\cos 20x - \dfrac{1}{2}\cos 14x$ **39.** $2\sin 4x \cos x$

41. $2\cos 7x \sin 2x$

43. $2\cos\left(\dfrac{7x}{2}\right)\cos\left(\dfrac{-3x}{2}\right) = 2\cos\left(\dfrac{7x}{2}\right)\cos\left(\dfrac{3x}{2}\right)$

45. .96   **47.** .28

49. .316   **51.** $4\cos^3 x - 3\cos x$

53. $\cos x$ **55.** $\sin 4y$ **57.** 1

59. Use the fourth product to sum identity with $\dfrac{1}{2}(x + y)$ in place of x and $\dfrac{1}{2}(x - y)$ in place of y.
$$2\cos\left[\dfrac{1}{2}(x+y)\right]\sin\left[\dfrac{1}{2}(x-y)\right]$$
$$= 2 \cdot \dfrac{1}{2}\left[\sin\left(\dfrac{1}{2}(x+y) + \dfrac{1}{2}(x-y)\right)\right.$$
$$\left. - \sin\left(\dfrac{1}{2}(x+y) - \dfrac{1}{2}(x-y)\right)\right] = \sin x - \sin y$$

61. Use the second product to sum identity with $\dfrac{1}{2}(x + y)$ in place of x and $\dfrac{1}{2}(x - y)$ in place of y.
$$-2\sin\left[\dfrac{1}{2}(x+y)\right]\sin\left[\dfrac{1}{2}(x-y)\right]$$
$$= -2 \cdot \dfrac{1}{2}\left[\cos\left(\dfrac{1}{2}(x+y) - \dfrac{1}{2}(x-y)\right)\right.$$
$$\left. - \cos\left(\dfrac{1}{2}(x+y) + \dfrac{1}{2}(x-y)\right)\right] = -(\cos y - \cos x)$$
$$= \cos x - \cos y$$

63. $\sin 16x = \sin 2(8x) = 2\sin 8x \cos 8x$

65. $\cos^4 x - \sin^4 x = (\cos^2 x + \sin^2 x)(\cos^2 x - \sin^2 x)$
   $= 1(\cos^2 x - \sin^2 x) = \cos 2x$

67. This is not an identity.

69. $\dfrac{1 + \cos 2x}{\sin 2x} = \dfrac{1 + 2\cos^2 x - 1}{2\sin x \cos x} = \dfrac{2\cos x \cos x}{2\sin x \cos x} = $
   $\dfrac{\cos x}{\sin x} = \cot x$

71. $\sin 3x = \sin(2x + x) = \sin 2x \cos x + \cos 2x \sin x$
   $= 2\sin x \cos x \cos x + (1 - 2\sin^2 x)\sin x = 2\sin x \cos^2 x$
   $+ \sin x - 2\sin^3 x = 2\sin x(1 - \sin^2 x) + \sin x - 2\sin^3 x$
   $= \sin x(2 - 2\sin^2 x + 1 - 2\sin^2 x) = \sin x(3 - 4\sin^2 x)$

73. This is not an identity.

75. $\csc^2\left(\dfrac{x}{2}\right) = \dfrac{1}{\sin^2\left(\dfrac{x}{2}\right)} = \dfrac{1}{\left(\pm\sqrt{\dfrac{1 - \cos x}{2}}\right)^2}$
$$= \dfrac{1}{\dfrac{1 - \cos x}{2}} = \dfrac{2}{1 - \cos x}$$

77. $\dfrac{\sin 5x - \sin 3x}{2\cos 4x} = \sin x$ *Proof:* $\dfrac{\sin 5x - \sin 3x}{2\cos 4x} =$
$$\dfrac{2\cos\left(\dfrac{8x}{2}\right)\sin\left(\dfrac{2x}{2}\right)}{2\cos 4x} = \dfrac{2\cos 4x \sin x}{2\cos 4x} = \sin x.$$

79. $\dfrac{\cos x + \cos 3x}{2\cos 2x} = \cos x$ *Proof:* $\dfrac{\cos x + \cos 3x}{2\cos 2x} =$
$$\dfrac{2\cos 2x \cos(-x)}{2\cos 2x} = \cos(-x) = \cos x$$

81. $\dfrac{\sin 3x - \sin x}{\cos x + \cos 3x} = \tan x$ *Proof:* $\dfrac{\sin 3x - \sin x}{\cos x + \cos 3x} =$
$$\dfrac{2\cos(2x)\sin x}{2\cos(2x)\cos(-x)} = \dfrac{\sin x}{\cos(-x)} = \dfrac{\sin x}{\cos x} = \tan x$$

83. $\dfrac{\sin x - \sin 3x}{\cos x + \cos 3x} = \dfrac{2\cos\left(\dfrac{x+3x}{2}\right)\sin\left(\dfrac{x-3x}{2}\right)}{2\cos\left(\dfrac{x+3x}{2}\right)\cos\left(\dfrac{x-3x}{2}\right)}$
$$= \dfrac{\sin(-x)}{\cos(-x)} = \dfrac{-\sin x}{\cos x} = -\tan x$$

85. $\dfrac{\sin 4x + \sin 6x}{\cos 4x - \cos 6x} = \dfrac{2 \sin 5x \cos x}{2 \sin 5x \sin x} = \dfrac{\cos x}{\sin x} = \cot x$

87. $\dfrac{\sin x + \sin y}{\cos x - \cos y} = \dfrac{2 \sin\left(\dfrac{x+y}{2}\right)\cos\left(\dfrac{x-y}{2}\right)}{-2 \sin\left(\dfrac{x+y}{2}\right)\sin\left(\dfrac{x-y}{2}\right)}$

$= \dfrac{-\cos\left(\dfrac{x-y}{2}\right)}{\sin\left(\dfrac{x-y}{2}\right)} = -\cot\left(\dfrac{x-y}{2}\right)$

89. (a) Use Strategy 6: Prove that $(1 - \cos x)(1 + \cos x) = \sin x \sin x$.

$(1 - \cos x)(1 + \cos x) = 1 - \cos^2 x = \sin^2 x = \sin x \sin x$

Therefore $\dfrac{1 - \cos x}{\sin x} = \dfrac{\sin x}{1 + \cos x}$

(b) On page 539, we proved that $\tan\left(\dfrac{x}{2}\right) = \dfrac{1 - \cos x}{\sin x}$.

Hence, by part (a) $\tan\left(\dfrac{x}{2}\right) = \dfrac{1 - \cos x}{\sin x} = \dfrac{\sin x}{1 + \cos x}$.

91. $\dfrac{\sqrt{2 + \sqrt{2 + \sqrt{2 + \sqrt{2}}}}}{2}$

Section 7.3, page 427

1. $\pi/2$ **3.** $-\pi/4$ **5.** 0

7. $\pi/6$ **9.** $-\pi/4$ **11.** $-\pi/3$

13. $2\pi/3$ **15.** $.3576$ **17.** -1.2728

19. $.7168$ **21.** $-.8584$ **23.** 2.2168

25. $\cos u = 1/2; \tan u = -\sqrt{3}$

27. $\pi/2$ **29.** $5\pi/6$ **31.** $-\pi/3$

33. $\pi/3$ **35.** $\pi/6$ **37.** $4/5$

39. $4/5$ **41.** 2.4 **43.** $\sqrt{22}/5$

45. $2/\sqrt{13}$ **47.** $1/\sqrt{21}$

49. $\cos(\sin^{-1} v) = \sqrt{1 - v^2} \quad (-1 \le v \le 1)$

51. $\tan(\sin^{-1} v) = \dfrac{v}{\sqrt{1 - v^2}} \quad (-1 < v < 1)$

53. $\cos(\tan^{-1} v) = \dfrac{1}{\sqrt{1 + v^2}}$

55. $\sin(2 \cos^{-1} v) = 2v\sqrt{1 - v^2} \quad (-1 \le v \le 1)$

57. $\tan(\cos^{-1} v) = \tan\left(\dfrac{\pi}{2} - \sin^{-1} v\right) = \cot(\sin^{-1} v)$

59.

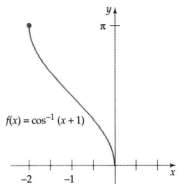

$f(x) = \cos^{-1}(x + 1)$

61.

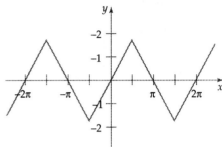

63. (a) $t = \dfrac{1}{2\pi f}\sin^{-1}\left(\dfrac{V}{V_{\max}}\right) + \dfrac{n}{f} \quad (n = 0, \pm 1, \pm 2, \ldots)$

(b) $t = 5.8219 \times 10^{-4}$ sec

65. (a) $\theta = \sin^{-1}(40/x)$

(b) $\theta = .16$ radians or $9.2°$

67. (a) $t = \tan^{-1}\left(\dfrac{h}{4}\right)$

(b) $t \approx .0624$ radians; $t \approx .2450$ radians; $t \approx .4636$ radians

(c) about 1.6912 mi

69. (a) $t = \tan^{-1}\left(\dfrac{30}{x}\right) - \tan^{-1}\left(\dfrac{6}{x}\right)$ (b) about 13.4 ft

71. (a) $\theta = \tan^{-1}\left(\dfrac{25}{x}\right) - \tan^{-1}\left(\dfrac{10}{x}\right)$ (b) 15.8 ft

73. No horizontal line intersects the graph of $f(x) = \csc x$ more than once when $-\pi/2 \le x \le \pi/2$ (see Figure 6–85). Hence, the restricted cosecant function has an inverse function, as explained in Section 3.7.

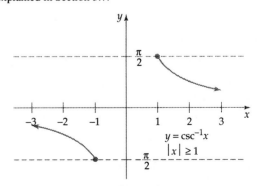

$y = \csc^{-1} x$
$|x| \ge 1$

75. Let $\cos u = w$ with $0 \le u \le \pi$. Then $u = \cos^{-1} w$ and $\cos^{-1}(\cos u) = \cos^{-1} w = u$. Let $u = \cos^{-1} v$. Then $\cos u = v$ and $\cos(\cos^{-1} v) = \cos u = v$.

77. Let $u = \sin^{-1}(-x)$. Then

$$-x = \sin u \quad (-\pi/2 \le -u \le \pi/2)$$
$$x = -\sin u$$
$$x = \sin(-u)$$
$$\sin^{-1} x = -u \quad (-\pi/2 \le -u \le \pi/2)$$
$$\sin^{-1} x = -\sin^{-1}(-x)$$
$$\sin^{-1}(-x) = -\sin^{-1} x$$

79. Let $u = \cos^{-1}(-x)$. Then $-x = \cos u$. Note that $0 \le u \le \pi$; hence, $-\pi \le -u \le 0$, which implies that $0 \le \pi - u \le \pi$. Hence,

$$x = -\cos u$$
$$x = \cos(\pi - u) \quad \text{(from the stated identity)}$$
$$\pi - u = \cos^{-1} x$$
$$u = \pi - \cos^{-1} x$$
$$\cos^{-1}(-x) = \pi - \cos^{-1} x$$

81. Let $u = \cot x$. Then

$$\tan(\pi/2 - x) = \cot x = u \quad (0 < u < \pi,$$
$$\text{hence, } -\pi/2 < \pi/2 - x < \pi/2)$$

$$\pi/2 - x = \tan^{-1}(u) = \tan^{-1}(\cot x)$$

83. Let $u = \sin^{-1} x$. Then $\sin u = x$, $(-\pi/2 < u < \pi/2)$

$$\tan u = \frac{\sin u}{\cos u} = \frac{\sin u}{\sqrt{1 - \sin^2 u}} = \frac{x}{\sqrt{1 - x^2}}$$

(positive square root, since u lies in quadrant I or IV)

$$u = \tan^{-1}\left(\frac{x}{\sqrt{1 - x^2}}\right)$$

$$\sin^{-1} x = \tan^{-1}\left(\frac{x}{\sqrt{1 - x^2}}\right)$$

85. The statement is false. For example, let $x = 1/2$.

$$\tan^{-1}\left(\frac{1}{2}\right) \approx .4636, \text{ but } \frac{\sin^{-1}(1/2)}{\cos^{-1}(1/2)} = \frac{\pi/6}{\pi/3} = \frac{1}{2}$$

Section 7.4, page 438

In the answers for this section $k = 0, \pm 1, \pm 2, \pm 3, \ldots$

1. $x = .4836 + 2k\pi$ or $2.6580 + 2k\pi$

3. $x = 2.1700 + 2k\pi$ or $-2.1700 + 2k\pi$

5. $x = -.3402 + k\pi$ **7.** $x = .4101 + k\pi$

9. $x = \pm 2.2459 + 2k\pi$ **11.** $x = .1193$ or 3.0223

13. $x = 1.3258$ or 4.4674

15. $x = \dfrac{\pi}{3} + 2k\pi$ or $\dfrac{2\pi}{3} + 2k\pi$

17. $x = -\dfrac{\pi}{3} + k\pi$

19. $x = 5\pi/6 + 2k\pi$ or $-5\pi/6 + 2k\pi$

21. $x = -\dfrac{\pi}{6} + 2k\pi$ or $\dfrac{7\pi}{6} + 2k\pi$

23. $x = \dfrac{\pi}{6} + 2k\pi$ or $\dfrac{5\pi}{6} + 2k\pi$

25. $\theta = 82.8°$ or $262.8°$ **27.** $\theta = 114.8°$ or $245.2°$

29. $\theta = 210°, 270°, 330°$ **31.** $\theta = 60°, 120°, 240°, 300°$

33. $\theta = 120°, 240°$ **35.** $\alpha = 65.4°$

37. $\alpha = 30°$ **39.** $\theta = 27.6°$

41. $\theta = 14.2°$

43. $x = -\dfrac{\pi}{6} + k\pi$ or $\dfrac{2\pi}{3} + k\pi$

45. $x = \pm\dfrac{\pi}{2} + 4k\pi$ **47.** $x = -\dfrac{\pi}{9} + \dfrac{k\pi}{3}$

49. $x = \pm.7381 + \dfrac{2k\pi}{3}$ **51.** $x = 2.2143 + 2k\pi$

53. $t = 1.8546; A = 11.18$ **55.** $t = 1.6961; A = .35$

57. $t = 1.9346, L = 16.47$ **59.** $t = 1.6236, L = 11.61$

61. (a) $A = 2x(2\cos 2x) = 4x\cos 2x$
(b) $x = .3050$ and $x = .5490$

63. $x = 5.9433$ and 3.4814

65. $x = \dfrac{3\pi}{4}, \dfrac{7\pi}{4}, 1.9513, 5.0929$

67. $x = \pi/2, 3\pi/2, \pi/4, 5\pi/4$

69. $x = \pi/2, 3\pi/2, \pi/6, 5\pi/6$

71. $x = .8481, 2.2935, 1.7682, 4.9098$

73. $x = .8213, 2.3203.$

75. $x = 1.2059, 4.3475, .3649,$ and 3.5065

77. $x = 1.0591, 4.2007, 2.8679,$ and 6.0095

79. No solution

81. $x = \pi/2, 3\pi/2, 7\pi/6, 11\pi/6$

83. $x = \pi/6, 5\pi/6$

85. $x = 7\pi/6, 11\pi/6, \pi/2$

87. $x = 0, \pi/3, 5\pi/3$

89. $x = .5275 + k\pi$ or $x = 1.6868 + k\pi$

91. $x = .4959, 1.2538, 1.5708, 1.8877, 2.6457,$ or $4.7124.$ Since the function is periodic with period 2π, all solutions are given by each of these six roots plus $2k\pi$.

93. $x = .1671, 1.8256, 2.8867,$ or $4.5453.$ Since the function is periodic with period 2π, all solutions are given by each of these four roots plus $2k\pi$.

95. $x = 1.2161 + 2k\pi$ or $x = 5.0671 + 2k\pi$

97. $x = 2.4620 + 2k\pi$ or $x = 3.8212 + 2k\pi$

99. $x = .5166 + 2k\pi$ or $x = 5.6766 + 2k\pi$

101. (a) days 60 and 282 (March 2 and October 10)
(b) day 171 (June 21)

103. $\theta = .5475$ or 1.0233 **105.** $13.25°$ or $76.75°$

107. The basic equations $\sin x = c$ and $\cos x = c$ have no solutions if $c > 1$ or $c < -1$.

109. The solutions $x = 0$ and $x = \pi$ are missed due to dividing by $\sin x$ (which is 0 when $x = 0$ or π).

Chapter 8

Section 8.1, page 450

	sin	cos	tan	csc	sec	cot
1.	$\dfrac{3\sqrt{13}}{13}$	$\dfrac{2\sqrt{13}}{13}$	$\dfrac{3}{2}$	$\dfrac{\sqrt{13}}{3}$	$\dfrac{\sqrt{13}}{2}$	$\dfrac{2}{3}$
3.	$\dfrac{7}{\sqrt{58}}$	$\dfrac{-3}{\sqrt{58}}$	$\dfrac{-7}{3}$	$\dfrac{\sqrt{58}}{7}$	$\dfrac{-\sqrt{58}}{3}$	$\dfrac{-3}{7}$
5.	$\dfrac{-\sqrt{22}}{11}$	$\dfrac{-3\sqrt{11}}{11}$	$\dfrac{\sqrt{2}}{3}$	$\dfrac{-\sqrt{22}}{2}$	$\dfrac{-\sqrt{11}}{3}$	$\dfrac{3\sqrt{2}}{2}$

7. $\sin \theta = \dfrac{\sqrt{2}}{\sqrt{11}}$

$\cos \theta = \dfrac{3}{\sqrt{11}}$

$\tan \theta = \dfrac{\sqrt{2}}{3}$

9. $\sin \theta = \dfrac{\sqrt{3}}{\sqrt{7}}$

$\cos \theta = \dfrac{2}{\sqrt{7}}$

$\tan \theta = \dfrac{\sqrt{3}}{2}$

11. $\sin \theta = \dfrac{h}{m}$

$\cos \theta = \dfrac{d}{m}$

$\tan \theta = \dfrac{h}{d}$

13. $c = 36$

15. $c = 36$

17. $c = 8.4$

19. $h = 25\sqrt{2}/2$ **21.** $h = 300$ **23.** $h = 50\sqrt{3}$

25. $c = 4\sqrt{3}/3$ **27.** $a = 10\sqrt{3}/3$

29. $\angle A = 50°, a = 7.7, c = 6.4$

31. $\angle C = 76°, b = 66.1, c = 64.2$

33. $\angle C = 25°, a = 10.7, b = 11.8$

35. $\angle C = 18°, a = 3.3, c = 1.1$

37. $\theta \approx 48.6°$ **39.** $\theta \approx 48.2°$

41. $\angle A = 28.1°, \angle C = 61.9°$

43. $\angle A = 44.4°, \angle C = 45.6°$

45. $\angle A = 48.2°, \angle C = 41.8°$

47. $\angle A = 60.8°, \angle C = 29.2°$

49. (a) $A = \dfrac{1}{2}ah$ (b) $\sin \theta = \dfrac{h}{b}$
(c) $h = b \sin \theta$ follows immediately from (b).
(d) $A = \dfrac{1}{2}ah = \dfrac{1}{2}ab \sin \theta$

51. $A = 29.6$ **53.** $A = 220$

55. (a) $\sin \theta = a/c = \cos \alpha$
(b) Since $\theta + \alpha + 90° = 180°$, $\theta + \alpha = 90°$.
(c) Since $\theta + \alpha = 90°$, $\alpha = 90° - \theta$; thus, $\sin \theta = \cos \alpha = \cos(90° - \theta)$

Section 8.2, page 461

1. $\angle A = 74°, c = 29.0, a = 27.9$

3. $\angle A = 36.9°, \angle B = 53.1°$

5. $w = 100.7$ ft   **7.** About $68°$ **9.** 23.0 m

11. About 15.3 ft   **13.** 276.3 ft

15. About 3402.8 ft   **17.** 85.9 ft

19. 27.5 ft. It is not safe for him to jump.

21. No   **23.** 8598.3 ft (1.6 mi)

25. $30°$ **27.** 351.1 m   **29.** 1.53 mi

31. 25.4 m   **33.** 3.52 m   **35.** 52.5 mph

37. 18.67 ft, $\theta \approx 53.13°$

39. 205.7 ft   **41.** 173.2 mi

43. (a) 56.7 ft   (b) 9.7 ft

45. (a) Area $= 200 \sin t \cos t$
(b) $t = 45°$; approximately 14.14 by 7.07 ft

47. 449.1 ft

Section 8.3, page 471

1. $a = 6.5; B = 95.9°; C = 44.1°$

3. $c = 15.7; A = 19.7°; B = 42.3°$

5. $a = 24.4; B = 18.4°; C = 21.6°$

7. $c = 21.5; A = 33.5°; B = 67.9°$

9. $A = 120°; B = 21.8°; C = 38.2°$

11. $A = 29.7°; B = 68.2°; C = 82.1°$

13. $A = 38.8°; B = 34.5°; C = 106.7°$

15. $A = 35.6°; B = 53.2°; C = 91.2°$

17. $A = 77.5°; B = 48.4°; C = 54.1°$

19. 334.9 km   **21.** $54.7°$ **23.** 63.7 ft

25. $84.9°$ **27.** $26,205$ mi

29. For the left-hand cable, $A = 34.2°$; for the right-hand cable, $B = 25.6°$

31. 8.4 km   **33.** 154.5 ft

35. 425.7 ft; 469.4 ft   **37.** $33.44°$

39. 978.7 mi   **41.** 7.2 in. and 11.5 in.

43. $a = 19.5; b = 21.23; c = 24.27$.
$A = 50.2°; B = 56.8°; C = 73.0°$.

45. 16.99 m

Section 8.4, page 482

1. $C = 114°, b = 3.2, c = 7.9$

3. $B = 30°, b = 6.4, c = 8.2$

5. $A = 86°, a = 8.9, c = 7.1$

7. $C = 41.5°, b = 9.7, c = 10.9$

9. No solution.

11. Case 1: $A = 154.7°, C = 5.3°, c = 3.3$
    Case 2: $A = 25.3°, C = 134.7°, c = 24.9$

13. No solution.

15. Case 1: $B = 95.8°, A = 28.2°, a = 5.7$
    Case 2: $B = 84.2°, A = 39.8°, a = 7.7$

17. $b = .84, c = 5.6, C = 132.3°$

19. $a = 9.8, B = 23.3°; C = 81.7°$

21. $A = 18.6°, B = 39.6°, C = 121.8°$

23. $c = 13.9, A = 60.1°, B = 72.9°$

25. $A = 77.7°, C = 39.8°, a = 18.9$

27. No solution.

29. $a = 18.5, B = 36.7°, C = 78.3°$

31. $C = 126°, b = 193.8, c = 273.3$

33. 135.5 m   35. $\alpha = 5.4°$ 37. 5.0 ft

39. 5.3°   41. 30.1 km   43. 9.99 m

45. About 9642 ft

47. (a) Solve triangle ABC to find $\angle BAC$, the angle at A.
    $180° - \angle BAC = \angle EAB$: Solve triangle ABD to find
    $\angle ABD$, the angle at B. $180° - \angle ABD = \angle EBA$. Now
    solve triangle EAB using the two angles and included
    side to find EA.
    (b) About 94 ft

49. 13.36 m

51. (a) See Example 1 of Section 8.3.
    (b) 92.2°
    (c) 27.8°
    If you did not get the correct answer in part (b), look at
    Example 5 and the Note following it.